MR. JUSTICE MURPHY

Justice Frank Murphy, 1949. Time-Life, Inc.

Mr. Justice Murphy

A POLITICAL BIOGRAPHY

BY J. WOODFORD HOWARD, JR.

PRINCETON, NEW JERSEY

PRINCETON UNIVERSITY PRESS

1968

TO MY MOTHER AND FATHER

PREFACE

SINCE his death in 1949, Frank Murphy has occupied a discrete and somewhat paradoxical place in American political history. In his prime, Murphy was one of Franklin D. Roosevelt's most influential and colorful lieutenants. During a decade of service on the United States Supreme Court he also emerged as a prototype of the modern libertarian judge. Many crusades he championed as a politician have since become accepted government practice; many a lonely dissent has since become law. Yet Murphy's political career has been virtually forgotten and lawyers remember him mainly as a symbol of militant partisanship in politics and law. While still a hero of a liberal minority who revere the Supreme Court as much for its literature as for its law, Mr. Justice Murphy, in dominant professional opinion, has become one of those rare jurists whose service on the nation's highest bench lowered rather than elevated his public stature.

My purpose in writing this book is not to debate Murphy's place in history nor to defend his substantive choices in continuing controversies over public policy. My aim is to examine his public career as it relates to the development of political leadership in the United States and to the role of the judiciary in the American system of government. Accordingly, the first part of the book analyzes his meteoric climb from a criminal judge and mayor of depression-torn Detroit to Governor General and High Commissioner of the Philippine Islands, from Governor of Michigan and Attorney General of the United States to Associate Justice of the United States Supreme Court. The central theme of Part I is the interplay of personality and office in his political growth. The second part is devoted to his development and contributions as a Supreme Court Justice. After analysis of his assimilation into the judiciary, the theme resumes of interplay among personality, values, and institution as elements of judicial choice. The concluding chapter enlarges the perspective to Murphy as a symbol in larger controversies concerning law and discretion in the judicial process and to his place in the American reform tradition.

Certain risks are inherent in using traditional biographical methods for these purposes. Political biography risks emphasizing office over the man, the man over his milieu, and his rhetoric over concrete results. It also risks imposing external order on untidy events. Because personality and rhetoric were essential tools in Murphy's political armory, I have decided to use his words as much as possible in order to flesh out the character and to leave the reader room for personal judgment.

Because Murphy's career touched so many aspects of policy, I have also attempted to present the evidence in forms usable to other scholars without sacrificing narrative. But these decisions require emphasis on public career rather than on personal life, and the reader has a right to question whether the balances have been kept.

In addition, a biography of Murphy raises special problems of sources. Frank Murphy was an egocentric with an eye to history and an office-holder blessed with a faithful staff that kept voluminous records— good, bad, and indifferent. He was also an inveterate note-taker who, at the same time, committed to paper little that was sensitive about his own decisions or perceptions. Hence a Murphy biographer has to face more than the usual gluts and gaps; he faces letters and notes which he suspects were really written for the biographer! He faces intriguing notes and scraps about other public figures which he knows were hurriedly prepared, one-sided, and apt to contain factual and perceptual errors. I have opted to use these materials, even at the risk of employing everyday language and of making mistakes, because of the richness of the sources and the light they shed on decision-making processes. But the reader should be cautioned to keep in mind the hazards of the method, even while it represents a step toward truth.

Use of these source materials, especially intra-Court memoranda and Justice Murphy's notes of secret judicial conferences, raises a final question about the propriety, as distinct from the reliability, of penetrating behind the great velvet curtains of the Supreme Court with private judicial papers. Some lawyers believe the public has no legitimate interest in judicial decisions beyond published opinions. Personally, I believe the public in a democracy has a right to know how its judges decide cases, and I share the view expressed by Charles Evans Hughes and others that knowledge of how courts operate would vindicate popular respect for the judiciary. In my opinion, no impropriety exists in using private papers so long as a writer does not invade the *current* privacy of the Court as a decisional agency or the privacy of its functioning members. On the other hand, to deny that premature disclosure of working exchanges can disturb the decisional system underestimates special needs of the judiciary and claims too much for contemporary history. Consequently, I have attempted to follow a middle course that will illuminate my subject without embarrassing individuals or the Court. Thus I have not quoted from the papers of any Justice without permission. I have quoted conference notes only in support of matters already known or fairly inferable, and not when I thought that quotation might be misconstrued as an effort to discredit a Justice. I have left some items to the future, when the dangers have passed, while leaving other remarks unattributed—enough, I trust, to keep identities obscure. I have identified no clerk until he left the Court, and I have shied away from extensive treatment of any Justice still on the bench, though the cost is to present Justices Black and Douglas as relatively wooden characters.

Doubtless there will be earnest partisans and defenders of the Court who will still take offense. Equally earnest sleuths will object to dependence on my scholarly judgments about withholding information. For the Murphy papers do shake some sacred categories in the contemporary dialogue over the judicial function, and when meshed with other sources they probably will shake some more. My only answer is that I have no wish to make a tough job tougher. Nor do I wish to diminish the scant supply of hard data by tempting judges to destroy their records. No one can plow through the extensive papers left by a Harlan Fiske Stone or a Frank Murphy without renewed respect for the integrity, dedication, and wit of the human beings on the Court —or of the need to relieve them from additional pressures.

With these reservations made, I hope that this book will contribute to an understanding of American politics and the judicial process without doing violence to the utility which inheres in the venerable tool of judicial biography.

Any book depends heavily on the minds and ears of others. The many colleagues and friends who lent both have my lasting thanks. In particular, I would like to thank Professor Alpheus T. Mason for his sustained encouragement and wise counsel; Eugene Gressman and Eleanor Bumgardner Wright for their help in getting the project started; and the busy men and women who answered questions and submitted to off-the-record interviews—Thurman Arnold, Roger Baldwin, James V. Bennett, Benjamin V. Cohen, Edward S. Corwin, Charles J. Hedetniemi, Sr., Alexander Holtzoff, J. Weldon Jones, Edward G. Kemp, Norman M. Littell, S.L.A. Marshall, Matthew F. McGuire, Irene Murphy, and Lee Pressman.

I also learned much from the criticisms of Mrs. Eugene P. Chase, James E. Clayton, John P. Frank, Eugene Gressman, J. Weldon Jones, Edward G. Kemp, Allan Kornberg, and Rocco J. Tresolini, all of whom read parts of the manuscript during various stages of preparation. I am indebted to several gifted students for aid in documentation— Cornelius Bushoven, Robert E. Detweiler, Thomas and Eleanor Flanagan, Martha Berry Fletcher, and J. P. Jones—and to Mrs. Pauline Anglin and Mrs. Mary Ellen Earp for typing the manuscript. My work was lightened by the cooperative staffs of the Burton Historical Collection of the Detroit Public Library, the Franklin D. Roosevelt Library, the Harry S Truman Library, the Manuscript Division of the Library of Congress, and especially the Michigan Historical Collections of the University of Michigan. The Tamiment Institute, publisher of *Labor History*, as well as the *Journal of Politics, Pacific Historical Review*, and *Vanderbilt Law Review*, permitted me to reprint portions of journal articles about Frank Murphy. Quotations from the *New York Times* are copyrighted by The New York Times Company and reprinted by permission. The Lafayette College Research Fund, the Duke University Research Council, and the Ford Grant for Research in Public Affairs helped sustain research costs. And my family endured.

Responsibility for the final product, of course, is mine.

June 1968   J.W.H.

CONTENTS

PART I

CHAPTER 1

THE GOOD OLD PATRIOTIC

FERVOR, 1890-1919

THE lives of politicians in the United States are often adorned to suit the public taste. The early years of Frank Murphy, following custom, have been embellished with political romance. Some observers have attempted to squeeze him into the log-cabin tradition; others have portrayed him as a transplanted Irish patriot, rebelling against social wrong. Murphy himself did little to dispel the romantic gloss—even the white lies which reduced his age—so that a storybook quality still clings to his early life.[1] Actually, his upbringing suggests anything but youth stung to protest. The most impressive features of his formative years, after what has been said and written, are their commonplace character and routine respectability.

Frank Murphy was born on April 13, 1890—and christened Francis William—in a spare frame building in the village of Sand Beach, Michigan.[2] His parents, John F. and Mary Brennan Murphy, who originally came from Guelph, Ontario and Whitehall, New York, were relatively recent settlers in the "Thumb" district of Michigan. Their struggle to establish themselves, like the northern winter, was hard. But the Murphys had risen to moderate prosperity by the time Frank, the third of four children, was old enough to comprehend the difference. Harbor Beach, as the town was renamed, was a small farm community on the Michigan shore of Lake Huron; and by its standards the family lived in moderate comfort. Murphy's father was a country lawyer. Despite financial problems that seemed endless, he was able to educate his children beyond average expectations and to participate as he liked in public affairs. If he thereby denied his son the glamor of humble origins, he provided him with credentials no less valuable for a life in politics. Frank Murphy came from small-town, middle-class, and politically alert America. In class and in values, he was indistinguishable from thousands of his generation.

The principal differences were that he also was of Irish ancestry, a Roman Catholic, and a Murphy. Physically and temperamentally Murphy was richly endowed with characteristics commonly associated with the Irish. A person of medium build and sensitive features, he had the inevitable freckles and the wiry red hair, the passionate streak and the eloquence, often found among "children of the Rosaleen." He also had a revolutionary heritage. His great-grandfather was hanged by the British for rebellion in Ireland, his paternal grandparents were "forty-eighters" from County Mayo, and his own father was jailed as a youth in Canada for participating in Fenian disturbances.[3] Family traditions of rebellion may have impressed the boy Frank. Versed in the history of the resistance, he himself made contact with the Fenian movement as a student in Dublin, and was fond of recalling his heritage to Filipino nationalists. His revolutionary lineage, which contributed to his suspicion of the British and reinforced his ardent belief in the Wilsonian principle of self-determination, lent color to his unmistakably Gaelic personality and made radicalism respectable. Beyond that, nonetheless, the tie was more family folklore and good press copy than the cause of political activism.[4]

So, too, was the myth that Murphy's militancy derived from a narrowly averted maternal ambition that he become a priest. That Mary Murphy and Catholicism were two of the deepest influences on his life is beyond dispute. The Murphys, however, were too anticlerical in practice to have pushed him toward the priesthood. The father, enamored of Jefferson and his teachings, was skeptical about the verities of priests; the Murphy women, with little thought of religious conflict, regularly provided musical accompaniment to Protestant church services in Harbor Beach; and none of the children attended parochial schools. The Murphys, in common parlance, thought of themselves as "good Catholics" because they took their religion seriously, but sectarian barriers fell before the practicalities of life in a small midwestern town. Substantively, the family also shared a dominant secular ideology which borrowed heavily from the Enlightenment, American nationalism, and the Social Gospel. Whether their ideology was labeled "liberalism" or the "American dream," they were living proof that Catholicism as well as Calvinism did not escape the pluralistic influences of the American environment. Nor did the Murphys pretend otherwise. Describing himself as "something of a humanist," the Justice in later years did not hesitate to serve as godfather to non-Catholic children. When he was reprimanded by a Washington cleric for participating in forbidden rites he responded, with Irish deviltry showing, by obtaining for the children special blessings from the Pope.[5]

Murphy was molded in his religious attitudes, as in most others, more by his family than by any other influence; and he remained unusually responsive to familial ties for the rest of his life. To fathom their full reach on his personality and political style, indeed, would tax psychoanalysis. So profound were the interactions of Murphy and his im-

mediate family that it is difficult to avoid associating them with stereo-
typed versions of the Irish clan. Even discounting a common theatricality, their family story was not far removed from the Gaelic agonies of
Eugene O'Neill.

From his father, Murphy inherited his eloquence, his bushy eyebrows,
his Anglophobia, and a strong sense of political direction. A rugged
man of rebellious temperament, John F. Murphy was an earthy humanist and the town radical. He was a Bryan Democrat in Republican
territory, a man who prized independence, and a Populist with an aversion to banks, insurance companies, and most large organizations. John
Murphy also was a perennial candidate for the office of county prosecutor and a staunch supporter of the Democratic party. During the Cleveland administration he was elected prosecuting attorney of Huron
County; and after the Democratic victory of 1914 he was rewarded
with the postmastership of the town.[6] But because he was a robust
drinker during his children's early years, Murphy's father was little
appreciated by them until they matured. During their youth he figured
mainly as a pugnacious counterpoise to the mother who in many ways
was his opposite and who, more than any single person, shaped Frank
Murphy's character.

Mary Murphy was a deeply religious woman of self-effacing kindness
and gentle tolerance. Dark-haired and blue-eyed, she was not a large
woman physically; but in the subtle ways of matriarchs everywhere,
she dominated the values and training of her children, who idealized
her in turn. Her influence, while pervasive among them all, affected
Frank especially. From his mother, Murphy inherited an abiding attachment to the Roman Catholic church and its moral universe. She
also implanted in him a sense of personal destiny and an ethical code
he never lost. Great moral champions like Lincoln, rather than his
father, were the models which she presented for emulation. In guiding
his religious education, she instilled in him the ideals that man is his
brother's keeper, that salvation lies in good works, and that, in Murphy's words, the "most precious virtue of all is the desire to serve mankind."[7] Christian idealism and a belief that life was a moral mission
became vibrant articles of his faith at an early age.

These standards, though avowedly idealistic, were by no means
unique to the Murphys. Vestiges of Victorian uplift were at work on
the entire generation. Young men at the turn of the century, regardless
of religion, were trained to an "ideal of service."[8] Schoolboys and elders
alike echoed the fervent nationalism which the Murphys, as newcomers,
felt to the full. During the two decades in which Frank Murphy grew

to manhood, the United States attained great power status, yet blanketed the facts of physical power in the transcendentalist idiom of the "American mission." Idealism and sentimental innocence probably reached their peak. In an era when men were unashamed of "noble" ideals, more sophistication than most Americans had or cared to have was necessary to ponder whether their values and experience were universally valid. Certainly this was so of the Murphys. America's experiment in liberty, as Lincoln had preached, had meaning for "all men, in all lands, everywhere."[9] And in that gospel they gloried. Of all his contemporaries who reached positions of authority, perhaps only immigrant Felix Frankfurter rivaled Murphy in emotional commitment to the uniqueness of the "American experiment." God, as Herman Melville said, made Americans a "chosen people."[10]

Catholicism and fervent patriotism might well have produced opposite political tendencies had they not been accompanied by two other influences that loosened Murphy's attachment to the status quo—Progressivism and the catalyst of personality. The Progressive movement, despite its nativist and isolationist yearnings, was of fundamental significance because its emphasis on social justice and on humanizing the industrial system furnished political idealism with concrete goals. More important, it provided a focus for the projection of religious ideals on political objects. Progressivism, in this sense, served the same function for the Murphys that the Christian Democracy movement accomplished for Catholic liberals in Europe. Their humanism and nationalism were fused into religious underpinnings from the start. If moral superiority was implicit in their belief system, the counterpart for them was rejection of the Spencerian orthodoxies of the day. Frank Murphy was reared in an egalitarian tradition; he was also reared to assume that all individuals, especially the strong, are responsible for alleviating the human condition. "I do not advocate paternalism," he often declared, but "we must never forget the obligation of the strong toward the weak. The first and fundamental tenet of civilized society is joint responsibility for the common welfare."[11]

Activating his social conscience was the personality. Frank Murphy was a born activist. Action, in part, was merely the expression of Christian idealism and the Social Gospel, the belief that the "acid test" of faith was daily practice. The moral man, in Murphy's view, could not "remain silent in the face of wrong."[12] The moral man was duty-bound to fight "militantly for justice" in all aspects of life, or else be spiritually lost. All his life Murphy espoused social action as religious dictate and the watchword of his personal philosophy. The good life was "crowned by action."[13] Yet Christian witness dovetailed with elements deep within his psyche. Passionate by temperament and quickly sympathetic, Murphy probably turned to politics because it provided a wider outlet for his manifold energies than priesthood or profession. Eager for attention, and talented as a showman, he found his forte in crusades and evangelism. Furthermore, his very emotional makeup depended heavily on an ethic of action. The grace of God, if not mother love itself, was redeemed only by superior attainment. The cardinal evil of the well-endowed was to waste their gifts. Talented men must "serve"; talented men were judged by higher standards; and if they could do no more in face of evil, talented men at least could sound off. Silence was immoral.

It was assumed that Murphy was gifted. "Mother always pushed Frank," his brother George once remarked. "She was so sure that he was going to go far."[14] Though it is doubtful that his mother envisaged any particular career for him, she was convinced that he had the makings of a moral giant. Murphy spent the rest of his life trying to live up to his mother's lofty standards. And when she died in 1924, leaving him to die, as he said, "ten thousand deaths," his sister Marguerite filled the void with the same conviction that "you are not like the others Frankie, you are so much better."[15] Whether right or wrong, Murphy was fired from the beginning with an intense ambition and a reward system that called for humanitarian works. Through maternal influence he began to conceive of the good life—not as material success, not even as "social priesthood," which journalists of the 1930s would popularize—but as a moral mission dedicated to human betterment. However vague the goal, Murphy would be forever inspired and frustrated by the impossible standards imposed during his youth.[16]

Murphy's mother also taught him the virtues of ascetic self-discipline. It was she who gave him the Bible which, with great public flourish, he read daily and with which, his hand at an appropriate passage, he took his respective oaths of office. Of this tattered and beloved Bible, Murphy once said: "When I was in high school, my mother gave me this copy, telling me she wished me to read it. I have done so every day since. . . . I find in it not only much wisdom and beauty, much solid food for the soul and poetry, but that discipline which is a necessity of human nature. In the Old Testament, especially, one finds a powerful aid to this self-discipline."[17] To the traditional mother's plea that he forego alcohol and tobacco until manhood, Murphy went further; he rejected them forever. Wine and tobacco impaired one's efficiency; and from his adolescence he had resolved to "succeed," if only to fulfill his mother's faith and love. The result was a strange duality of character that left observers perplexed. Flamboyant in rhetoric, yet austere in personal habits; intensely idealistic and dedicated, yet gregarious and pragmatic in power, he appeared to be an unresolved character of incredible mix. Murphy, as one girlfriend noted in 1919, had "a most peerless way of talking like a saint and then slipping over goodness knows what."[18]

Duality, in fact, did not encase the total personality. Tempting as it is to categorize him as a composite of his parents, or as a clinical case of mother domination, part of the essential Murphy keeps slipping out. Maternal influences, to be sure, were so strong that one prominent psychiatrist who examined him in mid-career diagnosed Murphy as having as pronounced an Oedipus complex as any patient in his experience. Yet maternal influences were in part conflicting and not without competition. Murphy did not grow up in dreary dedication, nor were his youthful goals any more precise than the "success" and the "service" on which the whole generation fed. Neither was masculinity eschewed in his rearing. While Murphy and his brothers, Harold and George, learned to place women on pedestals, that was hardly an uncommon norm in Edwardian times, particularly among the Irish. An ethnic interpretation is incomplete, on the other hand, because there were not enough Irish descendants in Michigan to form an identifiable grouping and because Harbor Beach, an environment he recalled as an idyllic boy's world, broke the common urban mold. However urbanized his subsequent political orientation, Murphy developed in an atmosphere of robust humor and physical competition of a small midwestern town, which offset both family stresses and a ghetto mentality. All his life, he felt attuned to the problems of plain people, enjoyed earthy jokes, and took fierce pride in physical fitness. Though an indifferent choirboy in his own estimation, Murphy as a youngster was a scrappy competitor on the local football, baseball, and track teams. Though an insomniac as an adult, and a bit of a hypochondriac, he became a skilled horseman who always held "sissies" and the "flabby" in some contempt. Sheer physical stamina, he boasted privately, was his trump card against the weary negotiators of the 1937 sit-down strikes. And for all his later eminence, or the pomp of office he so thoroughly enjoyed, he never quite outgrew his Harbor Beach origins. The same environment that led him to drop the name "Francis William" for plain "Frank" also made him prize the acquaintance of famous athletes like Gene Tunney and Frank "Lefty" O'Doul in the same breath with the socialites, statesmen, and stars of stage and screen who later filled his social life. In his infatuation with celebrities, no less than in his love of sports, a quality of small-town boyishness was irrepressible.

Small-town and middle-class roots, rather than urban and working-class origins, were key differences that distinguished Murphy from the typical Irish politicians of his generation. The differences were important because they helped to shape his romantic and optimistic world view and his rhetorical style. They also gave him the advantage of entering politics from the middle-class and on terms with his own personality. Rather than a spokesman of an aspirant ethnic interest linked to an urban machine, he entered politics as an independent gladiator who championed the cause of urban minorities in the idiom of older, agrarian ideals. Such an idiom satisfied middle-class values and a romantic self-image. But otherwise, there is no denying the parallel to romanticized accounts of Irish families in America or the impact of his own family on him.[19] Melodramatic, and seldom embarrassed by sentimentality or exaggeration even as they radiated irresistible charm, the Murphys were admittedly a "collection of odd-balls." Besides a rebellious immigrant father and a mystical mother, he was surrounded by an adoring sister and two hearty brothers who idealized their women, married late, and gave him unquestioning loyalty. Even their frame Victorian house with its wide porches they called "Tara's Hall."

A backdrop of reality stood behind the romantic facade. There were vanities, which led his sister to trim three years from her age and the others to follow suit so as to make Frank appear even more "brilliant" in public. There were constant demands for the anointed one's attentions and help, which caused him lifelong financial drain and emotional pain. For a champion of governmental purity, Murphy had a curious blindspot about carrying family members in his entourage at public expense. He seemed to assume the money was well spent for the psychic support of a public servant whose integrity was beyond challenge. "I need them and they need me," was his way of expressing his own powerful and enduring attachments.[20] Murphy never married, though he was engaged to Joan Cuddihy, of the *Literary Digest* family, when he died. Not until late in life were the chains of familial obligation broken sufficiently for him to be emotionally independent. His career and family, to the many women who chased him, seemed all-consuming. "A remarkable Judge no doubt, but as a beau—oh NO!" one of them bitterly complained in 1923. "You only care for yourself and your mother."[21] For by the time Murphy went to college he was the main hope of an ambitious and sentimental clan, and his own complex character was well set. Fervent and intense, but lusty in taste and humor; ambitious and articulate, but gifted with instincts of saying what people liked to hear, he was a born actor and a cache of contradictions. Yet no one questioned, when he was graduated from Harbor Beach High School with an oration "On Character," that he was "one of the brightest students the school has ever had" and a young man with a beckoning future.[22] Personality, not brain or brawn, already had made its impress. Only the vineyard of his labor, as an Irishman might say, seemed left to his fates.

II

In 1908, Murphy entered the University of Michigan, like his father before him, to study law. An attack of diphtheria forced him to withdraw for a time, and prevented his taking the A.B. degree—or so his family explained. But he was not a brilliant student anyway. Neither did he fall under the spell of any particular teacher. As an undergraduate, though he impressed instructors such as his future aide, Joseph R. Hayden, as intelligent enough, he seemed more interested in extracurricular activities than in intellectual pursuits.[23] During summers he worked at a local starch factory, whose eleven-hour day at 17½ cents an hour he dubbed "labor slavery." Financially Murphy managed to lead the life of an active collegian.[24] He became agitated over the snobbery of the fraternity system—yet joined Sigma Chi. He worked hard at sports, yet never rose above the football scrubs. He was widely known on campus—if only as the audacious undergraduate who cautioned a chastising dean that he was speaking to a future president of the United States! Yet notoriety did not come from campus politics or organizational leadership. Personal charm and oratory, the things which came naturally, were where he excelled. On the strength of these, he made a host of friends from across the state and was chosen as a member of the senior honor society, Michigamua, under the sobriquet "Wild Mustard Murphy."

One friendship is worthy of particular note. At Ann Arbor Murphy became the friend of Edward Gearing Kemp, Phi Beta Kappa, an editor of the *Michigan Daily* and the *Law Review*, and onetime secretary of Chase S. Osborn, the flamboyant Progressive governor of Michigan. In contrast to Murphy, Kemp was old-stock Protestant, conservative, and, by common consensus, the possessor of "the greater intellect."[25] Oppositeness very likely made the bonds of a lasting friendship; for Kemp and Murphy served in the army together, became law partners, and in time Kemp subordinated his own ambitions to become Murphy's chief adviser, most trusted confidant, and intellectual foil. Murphy doubtless would have secured Kemp's appointment as a federal judge, for which he thought him well-suited, had he not become the indispensable aide. A mutual friend probably caught the essence of the relationship when he observed to Kemp that, while men like Murphy and Paul V. McNutt were "born to lead and act, the chromosomes had something else in mind for us. We do well to recognize it."[26] Despite considerable charm and talent of his own, Kemp seemed content playing the role of an alter ego whose main function in life was keeping his impetuous friend out of trouble. Even when Murphy became a Supreme Court Justice and Kemp general counsel of the Budget Bureau, that relationship did not cease.

Murphy's college career was a fortunate convergence of temperament and the times. The teens was perhaps the golden age of alma mater sentiment in the United States. Athletics were institutionalized, social fraternities flourished, and college sentimentality reached its peak. Murphy articulated these values exuberantly. Grimly proud of his own hazing as a freshman, he was especially active as an evangelist of school spirit. "It is a sad fact, but true," he declared at a class rally in 1914, "that the student body has less reverence for university traditions now than it had four years ago. This should not be. A man without love for his Alma Mater is a man without a country." Small wonder that even after graduation, the "boy orator" was in demand for campus pep rallies. A Murphy speech, as the *Michigan Daily* commented, was a "Verbal Tornado."[27]

Not all of his student days were spent in histrionics and frolic, however. In law school, which he entered on probationary status in 1911, a poor first year had a sobering effect sufficient to produce a near-B average in his second year and the summer session that followed. After a third year with a C average, plus some faculty adjustment of a freshman mark, Murphy was graduated with his class in June 1914. His undistinguished academic record, while no handicap to professional advance, has spawned a popular legend that the only graduate of Michigan Law School to reach the Supreme Court was the dunce of his class. A more accurate description is that he was an average student whose performance was erratic because his interests were dispersed. His very grades were symptomatic of the differences of outlook that would develop between Murphy and elite members of the American bar. His strongest subjects were those with lowest professional prestige —equitable remedies, domestic relations, and criminal law; his weakest subjects came from the core of professional concentration—property, trial practice, and especially mortgages, the only subject he actually failed.[28]

Symptomatic also were his future relations with the Michigan Law School. Despite a fierce loyalty to Michigan as a midwestern Harvard, and his insistence on using Michigan graduates as his clerks, Murphy always seemed something of an embarrassment to his alma mater. His overtures to members of the law faculty, with one or two exceptions, seldom yielded more than formal responses. Law students soon learned that the embarrassed silence with which his opinions were greeted by their teachers could be safely turned into ridicule. A distant relationship between a Justice and his law school is unusual, given the ways of deans; but it is understandable when it is recalled that Murphy was not a leader of his class, showed little intellectual interest in law as a discipline, and bore no marked imprint from the school itself, as Felix Frankfurter so often acknowledged from Harvard. The fact is, one of the nation's best law schools failed in the professional socialization of Frank Murphy as a lawyer. Contrasting receptions given to Murphy as an alumnus by Michigan's political science and law faculties were a clear barometer of this primary fact: from his student days on, Law was not his mistress.

Politics, even then, was a powerful distraction. Murphy came of age during a period of enormous reformist ferment. As the word "democracy" came into lasting vogue he did not escape the manifold changes taking place on the American intellectual scene. The steady assault of scholars, churchmen, and publicists had effectively broken the mighty grip of Social Darwinism on the American mind. While Charles A. Beard was returning the Founding Fathers to the ranks of the mortal with his *An Economic Interpretation of the Constitution*, John Dewey was expounding pragmatism as the test of political action. While Benjamin N. Cardozo and Roscoe Pound were legitimizing the concept of "social needs" in law, the state of Wisconsin was becoming a virtual laboratory of social experiment. Churches generally were moving in the direction of "social service." At the same time that Father John A. Ryan stirred Catholic circles by demanding concern for the temporal as well as the transcendental needs of the flock, Protestantism was going humanistic. Implicitly, many congregations were replacing doctrines of original depravity with de facto faith in the potential of man. In the minds of many, God's grace was supplanted by human goodness. If this shift constituted the sin of pride, they were untroubled. Having conquered a continent to create an organism of material plenty, Americans seemed justified in the optimistic faith, which Murphy shared, that every "human problem is soluble."[29] The New World had come of age; despite its imperfections, men looked to the future with hope.

The gospel of progress was more popular than ever. Rather than deflate it, reformers were turning Darwinism to their own ends. Progress might be inevitable, but experience showed that it depended on cooperation as much as conflict. Human conduct could comport with Christian charity without mutilating the species. At least some of the abuses which had arisen in the early stages of industrial growth could be remedied. And after a binge of muckraking, who could doubt that abuses flourished? A "quickening sense of the inequities, injustices, and fundamental wrongs" of American society, as William Allen White noted, had driven thousands of young people to the banners of reform during the 1890s. The protest William Jennings Bryan and Theodore Roosevelt championed during that decade and the next aroused even more thousands to support Woodrow Wilson's "New Freedom" in the teens. Just as Murphy reached manhood, a new era of "social reconstruction" was at hand.[30]

The reconstruction Progressive reformers charted for themselves was of Herculean proportions, but American liberal thought has been riding on it ever since. However complex their origins, the basic impetus of Progressives was to restore "sane individualism," as Murphy later called it, to mass industrial society.[31] However contradictory their nostrums, the basic goal was to expunge the obstacles to free individual development from American life. Politically, the people could revive popular rule by primaries, popular election of senators, and the devices of initiative, referendum, and recall. Politics could be cleansed of bosses by the secret ballot, by overthrowing the convention system, and by elevating the tone of political behavior with female suffrage. The economic foundations of the American freeman could be restored, as Louis Brandeis argued, by reviving competition, destroying "bigness," and establishing "industrial democracy." And if that were done, the credo of equal opportunity at last would be implemented, the ancient ideals of the Republic would be reconciled with the industrial system, and American democracy would achieve the modern quest— "social justice."[32]

All this was the meaning of the New Freedom, and to it all Frank Murphy thrilled. Woodrow Wilson was his idol. Predisposed by his father's Populism to the Democratic party, he found himself at home among a host of zealots who shared his ideal of service. Everywhere do-gooders were coming out of hiding, and Murphy was not one to miss a fight. Even as a student he put his rhetoric to use in the 1912 campaign by making stump speeches in the hinterlands for the Democrats, whose handbills advertised him as the "Hon. Frank Murphy of New York" to disguise his student identity.[33] Murphy was becoming fascinated with politics.

Whether his interest would blossom into permanent commitment, however, depended on opportunities not available at home. After admission to the bar in 1914, he went to Detroit, where he became a clerk in the law firm of Monaghan & Monaghan at five dollars a week. He gained useful trial experience during his early years of practice, especially in criminal law, but his activities ranged beyond the practice of law. To supplement his income Murphy taught English at night to Hungarian immigrants. This experience provided invaluable lessons about ethnic minorities, whose needs and aspirations Progressives frequently ignored. Not least was the strategic role played by the clergy in activating them politically. Murphy also made friends rapidly in the city and cultivated politicians. In Judge William F. Connolly, he found a mentor who introduced him to the practical political world. The young lawyer used to gather by the hour with Connolly and other members of "the courthouse crowd" at the old Addison Hotel to talk politics. Quietly, Murphy sat at their feet and learned.[34] But at this point, the First World War intervened and Murphy had to delay entering the political arena.

World War I had a profound emotional impact on Murphy. The American entry stimulated both idealistic and ascetic sides of his character into an unforgettable experience. Later, some colleagues wondered whether he ever recovered from it, because as a civil administrator Murphy had impulses for disciplined operations which irritated officials unaccustomed to limitations on personal telephone calls or to punctuality. But whether a martinet or a purist, Murphy would not have denied the war's effect. "Love of country and a desire to serve bring out the best there is in a man," he declared in 1918. The conflict for him was "the greatest adventure the world has ever known." It was a "time to serve."[35]

Shortly after the outbreak of hostilities in 1917, he entered officer candidate school at Ft. Sheridan, Illinois, where he was commissioned a first lieutenant in the infantry. After additional training in trench warfare at Cambridge, Massachusetts, he spent the next few months in frustration as an instructor with the 340th Infantry at Camp Custer while longing for the front. On the side, he helped to prosecute "a pair of crooks" for defrauding the government in the spring of 1918, and turned down overtures from Huron County to make a bid for the Democratic nomination to Congress. His clear preference was the army, where he thought "real men" should be; yet he could not resist preaching. When he heard of racial discord among civilians, he sounded off: "I for one am an Irish-American who never again wants to be called Irish-American, but American. Nationalities among us have been obliterated. Religions have been merged. . . . We have only one division among all of us now, the division of courage." What America needed was "the good old patriotic fervor."[36]

Full of the fervor himself, Murphy made florid morale-building speeches whenever he could; and the response was usually in kind. "This brilliant, noble young man, who is so loyal to the Stars and Stripes," was a "hero" of the hometown weekly.[37] But for himself the test was France. In July 1918, Murphy finally was sent overseas with the AEF and was soon promoted to captain in the 39th Infantry. Armistice came, however, before he could participate in combat. During the next year his company occupied Honningen, Germany, near the Rhine, where he reported that he was "very happy," and where he was recommended for another promotion as reward for "marked ability in administration and discipline."[38] He also took advantage of a brief army fellowship during the armistice to study law at Lincoln's Inn and at Trinity College, Dublin; and he managed time for a Paris fling. But by mid-1919 he was ready to return to the United States, rather disgusted with war, suspicious of European intrigue, and hopeful for the peace his idol was negotiating in Paris. For all his disappointment over having missed the fight, the conflict nonetheless gave him a practical political asset which he soon capitalized with great effect: he was an overseas veteran of the "Great War."

On his return from Europe at the age of 29, Murphy possessed no bold designs for political action. He yearned to enter politics, but in Michigan the prospects were bleak for an Irish Catholic Democrat. What then appeared as handicaps, he later insisted, "alone have pulled me thus far."[39] Yet the fact remained that he had several strikes against him and little to offer except eloquence, a solid education, and sheer personal magnetism. None of these qualities at the time was exceptional. Neither were his principles. His imagination was fired, not by the social criticism of Veblen, Mencken, or Bourne, but by the very conventional precepts they warred against. However sentimental and innocent, Murphy was no rebel. His faith was a composite of the religious idealism and patriotic fervor which were part and parcel of orthodox creed.

The distinctive thing about Murphy, and the key to understanding, was not what he thought, but how seriously he took what people were supposed to think. Murphy had fervor. Every interest, high or low, was translated into a moral quest. And every cause was defended in the rhetorical idiom of a revivalist preacher. Even as his generation became "lost" in fashionable disillusionment, the fires of his youthful idealism were never really banked. Revering Christian ideals and Progressive political wisdom, he had sincere humanitarian impulses that were all bound up with compulsive needs for esteem and approval. Somehow, without patrician pretense in a small midwestern town, he acquired a romantic flair and a drive to leave an imprint on history. Other contemporaries had that quality—Roosevelt, Hitler, de Gaulle. A sense of destiny in a politician is not free from danger. Yet Murphy's idea was tempered by a sense of humor and by a conscience that was a counterpart of the goal. His was an exalted ambition to excel in the public service according to the precepts of the American dream. Service to humanity, he no doubt believed, offered "the highest honor and the noblest distinction that man can attain."[40] Coveting both, he fixed that dedication onto government in the nation's most highly industrialized city.

CHAPTER 2

DEW AND SUNSHINE,

1919-1931

DETROIT after the First World War was what Los Angeles became after the second—a symbol of American productive power and urban growth. The development of mass production in the automobile industry, plus the wartime boom, transformed the city from a quiet lake port to the hub of an industrial empire in less than two decades. Between 1900 and 1925 Detroit's population jumped from 285,000 to nearly 1.5 million, making the city the fourth largest and fastest growing metropolitan area in the country. A third of its population were factory workers; over 200 thousand were employed in automobile factories alone. The late 1920s merely accelerated the trends. Detroit was not only the target of a great labor migration but the seeming epitome of the "New Era," the vaunted promise of business ideology to produce a technological revolution and prosperity for all.[1]

Several sources of tension nevertheless lurked beneath the boom. Labor unrest, for one thing, existed alongside general prosperity. Despite high hourly wage rates, employment in the auto industry was seasonal and annual incomes relatively low. Large-scale unemployment, after the recession of 1921 and the layoffs during Ford's Model A changeover in 1927-28, was not unusual in Detroit. With a few notable exceptions, moreover, hiring practices and working conditions were poorly calculated to promote job security. Mass production may have brought the automobile to the average consumer, but in labor circles the achievement was attributed less to Henry Ford's production genius than to rapid turnover of workers and the speed-up along assembly lines. High wage rates, "partnership" propaganda, and paternalistic schemes, all were unable to obscure insecurities, superannuation among workers, and plain indignities that spawned deep discontents. Detroit, as the future soon revealed, lacked the foundations of stable industrial peace.[2]

Boosters advertised the "motor capital" as an unorganized, open shop city, and rightly so. The American Federation of Labor, as late as 1930, had a membership of only 16,000 in the entire state and little talent at organizing unskilled workers. A moribund Auto Workers Union could claim only half that number, and many of them were commonly sus-

pected of Wobblie infection. Detroit was notoriously poor union territory compared to other industrial centers. Auto manufacturers satisfied
their demand for workers by the lure of high wages, which attracted
a constant supply. They successfully resisted unionization not only by
resort to espionage and blacklist tactics but also by taking advantage
of dissension within labor's ranks. Experienced unionists among unskilled auto workers were few. Those that did exist, mainly southern
coal miners and European immigrants, were easily spotted and handicapped by cultural differences. A leadership vacuum resulted, in spite
of New Freedom efforts to support organization. While national labor
leaders squabbled over craft versus industrial unionism as the best means
of organizing the new wave of unskilled workers, local leadership
often passed by default to radicals who were the only disciplined organizers available, a condition which soured management all the more.
Only after the strikes of the thirties and the communist purges of the
forties was it clear how costly the policies toward organizing workers
in mass production industries had been.[3]

Ethnic conflicts aggravated tensions. Detroit in the twenties teemed
with diversity. Less than half its population in 1925 was native-born
white. In addition to heavy "new" immigration among East European
and Mediterranean nationalities, the influx included thousands of southern laborers and Negroes. "Americanization" committees from civic
organizations and nationality groups worked diligently to help assimilate immigrants into community life; considering the magnitude of the
task, it is remarkable that so many were absorbed so soon. Racial and
religious antagonisms were sharp, however, and little was done for
poor whites and Negroes. Neither did the city escape the rise of organized crime, which fed on Prohibition and exploitation of these very
groups, nor the midwestern revival of the Ku Klux Klan. Detroit, to
be sure, averted the wartime race riots of Chicago and East St. Louis;
the local Klan made greater headway against Catholics than against
colored people; and in political power it paled by the side of the organization in Indiana. Yet Klan-related politicians came close to cap-
turing city hall in a riot-charged election in 1924.[4] And while newspaper rivalry probably magnified the seriousness of both crime and the
Klan, the two were symptoms of deeper social problems that made the
city an unruly giant, difficult to govern.

Politically, this was not always so. Only recently, under the leadership
of Mayors John C. Lodge and James Couzens, millionaire ex-partner
of Henry Ford, Detroit had been one of the best governed cities in the
country, regardless of size. Detroit had home rule and a nonpartisan

ballot; it had a municipally owned street railway system and extensive civil service. These, plus freedom from corruption, served as models of Progressive ideals of nonpartisan city government. Municipal indebtedness, it is true, mushroomed after 1918 to meet enormous demands for capital improvements and public service in a city that grew by 50,000 people per year. Like most great metropolitan complexes, the city also was a patchwork of governments. A culture which equated progress with physical growth produced few complaints that public outlays abetted private speculation, overexpansion, and irregular development. But that is what occurred. When the crash came, Detroit had an indebtedness of over 300 million dollars—an increase of seven thousand percent since 1910—and yet one of the lowest tax rates of any major city.[5] One 30-million dollar bond issue had built a suburban water system that went 90 percent unused.[6] Detroit's experience in these respects was not unique; the difference was that its growth was so swift that neither government services nor political concepts ever matched the need. Government itself, in the now familiar process of rapid urbanization, was a victim of growing pains.

The departure of Couzens for the Senate in 1922 signaled the suspension of serious municipal reform. It would be inaccurate to suggest, however, that the Progressives in Detroit or elsewhere were silenced by the "roaring twenties." Instead, they retreated to whatever strongholds they could find, in state governments and above all the cities, to build anew. This retreat, in one sense, was merely part of the endless ebb and flow of political forces along the fragmented political structures of the United States. But, in another sense, the rebuilding of Progressivism and its absorption into the liberalism of the 1930s is a neglected episode in American history. The New Dealers of the thirties did not materialize from nowhere. They came, often articulate and more experienced than credited, from state and municipal governments.[7] During the 1920s a new generation of leaders developed the ideas and alliances of an urban-based coalition that dominates national politics to this day. Frank Murphy's rise in Detroit was an essential part of that story.

II

More than anything else, Detroit fixed Murphy's ambition onto government service. The conditions created by its prodigious growth sharpened both his social consciousness and his political opportunities. In Detroit Murphy made the discovery that public righteousness, vigorously displayed, could be effective politics. He also found an environment congenial to his self-perception as a moral champion independent of party organization and to the accompanying evangelical style. Only in a burgeoning city of open mobility and easy contact could Murphy have risen so fast. Only in a city with a nonpartisan political system could he have united so diverse an assortment of supporters by the single thread of personal allegiance. His rise to national prominence as a liberal was an evolutionary process based partly on luck, partly on hard political work, but mainly on the successful exploitation of personality.

His first foray into public affairs, soon after his return from war, set the pattern with customary splash. While Murphy was overseas, Democratic friends had obtained his appointment as assistant to federal attorney John E. Kinnane of the eastern district of Michigan. One of his first cases was a 30-million dollar war frauds prosecution before Judge Arthur J. Tuttle against a conspiracy of several army officers and civilian brokers to eliminate competitive bidding in surplus ordnance. The nature of the case, coupled with hot denunciations of "blood money" by the prosecutor, turned the trial into a three-month spectacular. After one defendant turned state's evidence, Murphy won convictions of two millionaires and citations for himself from General Pershing and Attorney General Palmer. And locally a legend grew that in his year and a half as federal attorney, he never lost a case.[8]

His tenure as prosecutor was too brief to give the reputation much meaning. He lost the post in 1920 when the Republicans returned to power. But politics already had cast its spell. With little organized support he jumped into the 1920 campaign as the Democratic candidate for Congress in the Republican stronghold of East Detroit and lost to Judge George B. Codd by a four-to-one margin. The defeat did little damage, however, because he succeeded in the main object—attracting notice. Woodbridge N. Ferris, an ex-senator and the Democratic candidate for governor commented on election eve: "You have got brains, you have had splendid training, you are an orator first, last and all of the time. . . . Tomorrow Cox and I and most democrats will be buried out of sight. . . . You are probably just beginning." "I am looking forward to great things."[9]

After the Democratic defeat Murphy earnestly set about building a political base in Detroit. From 1920 to 1923 he engaged in private practice in partnership with Edward G. Kemp. In 1922 he began teaching night classes in criminal law at the Detroit College of Law, a Jesuit institution later affiliated with the University of Detroit. His teaching, which followed a mixture of hornbook and case-method styles, was not particularly distinguished; but Murphy was popular with students, some of whom later became political leaders among Detroit's minority groups and his ardent supporters. He also was received in the bar as a promising trial lawyer. More important, he made solid connections among the clergy and veterans groups. Contrary to popular stereotypes about the making of liberals, Murphy did not spring into politics as a spokesman of labor or of Irish Catholics. Until the elections of 1936, in fact, his principal Detroit allies were the American Legion, Father Charles E. Coughlin, and the local outlet of William Randolph Hearst![10]

While Murphy never ceased talking in the Progressive idiom, it is a critical datum that he bypassed party in building political fences and amassed a personal following from an extraordinary variety of interests and groups. The American Legion, which chose him as local post commander in 1921 before he withdrew, was for many years a source of camaraderie and his first organized support. The *Detroit Times*, a newly acquired voice of the Hearst chain, soon followed suit. In accounting for his rise, it would be difficult to overestimate Murphy's debt to the *Times*. Through friendship with its editors, Joseph A. Mulcahy and Henry A. Montgomery, he not only established friendly relations with many mobile members of the working press; he also grasped the potentialities of mass publicity for a career in which few successfully defy the law of Everett M. Dirksen: "exposure is the business." Press backing made it possible for a newcomer like Murphy to compete in Detroit. An organizational void created by nonpartisan elections was filled in large part by the established dailies, the *Detroit News* and the *Detroit Free Press,* and their allies. The *Times,* struggling for survival in a circulation war, also needed causes. Building up Frank Murphy was one of them. Thus a political lone wolf and the *Times* grew up together, fighting each other's battles and making mutual enemies, as they collected the city's sundry outsiders into an opposition and then a victorious political force. Long after the job was done, Murphy extended the credit due when he remarked, "I consider it the happiest friendship any man in public office ever made with a newspaper and, as Mr. Hearst put it, perhaps the longest one too."[11]

Although friendship with Father Coughlin, powerful radio priest of the Shrine of the Little Flower, did not develop until both men were established, Murphy's ability to make unexpected alliances was a key to his uniquely personal political style. Fancying himself as a political independent in the image of the great Progressive senators, Borah, Norris, and LaFollette, he found an environment that fostered personalized politics. Temperamentally, Murphy would have been handicapped had he been forced to work his way up through a city machine. Neither would he have been comfortable closeted by class. Detroit's nonpartisan, unorganized politics, because it satisfied personal yearnings for attention and tolerated a lone-wolf temperament, suited Frank Murphy well.

In the 1920s, indeed, he cut a dashing figure in Detroit, a fact which the *Times* publicized at every opportunity. In demand as a speaker at the rallies of the lowly no less than at elegant parties at Grosse Pointe, he developed a wide range of personal and professional contacts. Itinerant national figures such as columnist Mark Hellinger and actress Ann Harding, became close friends. He cultivated assiduously liberal leaders who visited Detroit. Just as his clerical connections revealed a monkish tendency, so the romantic, fun-loving side of his character found outlet in a glittering social life. Politically Murphy may have championed the poor, but socially he always gravitated toward the rich. Byron C. Foy, future son-in-law of Walter P. Chrysler, was his Detroit roommate. Through Foy and former university chums, he developed friendships among the Chrysler executives and other members of Detroit's business elite. Acquaintances in the business world also helped him with investments so that money ceased to be a serious constraint. Murphy was always fairly careless about personal finance, but by 1925 he was making stock transfers in five figures, in association with the Foys, besides taking European vacations and giving substantial help to his brothers. Even for Detroit, his climb was swift. Murphy was not only getting ahead but making money; and that, as his sister reported parental approval, "always pleases Papa."[12]

The connections paid off handsomely in Murphy's second bid for office, the race for Recorder's Court in 1923. The court at that time was both a civil court of record and Detroit's highest criminal bench. In 1920 the city criminal courts were consolidated into a single system according to up-to-date concepts. The seven Recorder's Court judges, who drew relatively high salaries of $11,500, had a unified calendar and the assistance of a small but expert staff organized into a probation department and a psychiatric clinic.[13] Hardly was the system established, however, when the court became the center of controversy. Personality clashes, philosophic disagreement over "hard" versus "soft" approaches to criminal justice, and especially the control of the docket by a judicial bloc known as the "Big Four" became daily rations in a larger newspaper battle over issues of crime control. The *Free Press* and the *News* supported the Big Four, but the *Times*, which reflected Hearst's strong views on crime, backed the minority judges, Edward J. Jeffries and John Faust. Together, they induced Murphy to spearhead a campaign to break Big Four dominance.

"I am not a shrinking violet who claims to have heard the call of the people," he confessed on entering the race. But with active Legion backing, he made a vigorous campaign emphasizing his youth, his war record, and the sanctity of judicial independence. The election, by virtue of the *Times*-Murphy crusading, was unusually spirited. Headlines flourished and tempers flared. Accusing the *News* of linking him with the underworld, Murphy retaliated by pledging to bring harmony to the court and to eliminate "the pollution of political pull." In the primary he was eighth among twelve candidates, but he showed impressive vote-getting power in the general elections by topping the field. At thirty-three, Murphy was one of the youngest men ever to win a six-year term on the court.[14]

On the surface, victory had gone to a flashy personality of little substance. Yet beneath the glamor and press agentry, Murphy was undergoing a subtle process of maturation and growth. The world scene, to be sure, he continued to view through culture-bound eyes; the United States he regarded as a "great moral giant," a nation "unmatched for moral leadership" in an otherwise evil world. In keeping with his liberal self-image, he also was agitated by the *causes célèbres* of the day —the Palmer Raids, the Sacco-Vanzetti prosecution, the Scopes trial— and he accepted uncritically the nostrums of civil service, unicameralism, and old-age insurance associated with his Progressive heroes. Concrete social conditions in Detroit, by contrast, carried him deeper than popular nostrums. The immigrants, whose "terrific social and economic problems" appealed to his sympathies, were a notable example of independent probing, despite confidential warnings from other political figures against flirting with Leftists.[15] Murphy's old college friends were struck by the independent drift in his outlook; they were surprised by his widening associations among social workers, ethnic leaders, and religiously oriented social action groups, for example, Reinhold Niebuhr's Fellowship of Reconciliation. No longer was he even being guided by the courthouse crowd; Murphy was finding others from whom to learn. No longer was his language riddled with stock political clichés; the phrase "social and economic forces" was taking on almost spiritual tones. By the mid-twenties he was a thoroughgoing environmentalist in search of a cause.

This attitude was evident on Recorder's Court from the start. After ascending the bench in January 1924, Murphy pledged the full development of the probation department and the psychiatric clinic, which his opponents had sponsored, as "indispensable adjuncts" in the administration of justice. "Courts alone cannot do away with the criminal," he said.[16] Crime was obviously a complex social phenomenon, deeply rooted in the structure of society and in "the human equation." To eradicate it fully was probably hopeless; to attack it in the courts was to start at the wrong end. Still, the quality of justice was intimately related to its administration, and here Murphy concentrated his fire. Within a month he solicited reports concerning the technical adequacy of the staff, the reasons for low probation rates among Negroes, and the means of eliminating loitering in the court. There was "far too much hanging around this building" for his taste and too little judicial supervision of administrative matters like bail. Was private bonding the cause of both?[17]

The answers, which came slowly because of gaps in knowledge, awoke him to the implications of judicial administration for criminal justice and civil liberty. In Detroit over half the suspects arrested by police were never indicted; only seven percent of those indicted were sentenced. Consolidation of criminal courts had reduced the backlog of cases, but over 250 felons awaited trial because of delay or inability to obtain bail. No one knew precisely why Negroes were slighted in probation, but all the signs pointed to race and poverty. So did Murphy's own observations of sentencing practices on Recorder's Court. Early as a judge, he concluded that the quality of criminal justice was marred by serious inequities and indifference. Experience confirmed his campaign assertions that "we have been groping blindly in the past and present, hit or miss, narrow and unscientific methods of dealing with crime."[18] Something had to be done about mass production criminal justice in the city.

In the improvement of criminal justice, Murphy first found a cause and a basis with which to bid for national prominence. From Recorder's Court onward he became an ardent spokesman of "enlightened" reforms—research as "our greatest weapon" in treating crime on "an intelligent and scientific basis rather than by rule of thumb"; public defenders for indigents, a movement then making initial headway in Los Angeles and Connecticut; indeterminate sentences and probation; elimination of judicial patronage; and above all, bringing defendants speedily to trial. Murphy became well read in criminology and eager to apply the best that scholars and social workers had to offer. He developed lifelong interests in penology and in the scientific study of alcoholism, drug addiction, and other causes of crime. He opposed Prohibition "because I am for temperance." He fought capital punishment as being a barbarism all his life. "Only the helpless hang," he declared.[19] And though he failed in an effort to secure the "best man in the country," Winfred Overholser, for the psychiatric clinic, within three years after assuming office Murphy was the acknowledged administrative leader of Recorder's Court. The court in that period established a central bonding bureau, placed probation officers in civil service, and cleared its docket. When he resigned in 1930, Recorder's Court faced the smallest backlog of cases since consolidation a decade before. Average waiting time had been reduced from nearly two months to a week.[20]

Courtroom manner, even more than his administrative interests, gave Murphy a reputation for humanitarianism as a judge. For presenting life in the raw, few institutions rival a criminal court in a large city. Murphy's court became a favorite among reporters and underdogs because the proceedings were colorful and the judge sympathetic. Judge Murphy, as one defendant recalled, was "the first man who ever took my troubles seriously, or showed me any mercy or compassion, or withheld his hand when he could have struck." Reporters compared him to "a bishop hearing confession."[21] Predictably, traditionalists took offense at the unorthodox pleadings sometimes permitted and the occasional unorthodox response. Predictably, also, the judge was a "loner" on the bench. But the results could not be gainsaid. The percentage of defendants sentenced in Recorder's Court actually rose, along with the number on probation and the legal aid deficit, during Murphy's tenure on the bench.[22] A humane approach, he believed, did not necessarily mean sentimentality; it meant prompt trial and "individualization" of each case.

Though his views were advanced, Murphy midway in his first term was firmly established in Detroit as a judge of character and intelligence. At the same time, he was careful to do all the things which elected judges are forced to do, as Raymond Moley complained in a classic study, to catch public notice in nonpartisan electoral systems. Besides his teaching, the judge was a ready participant in church socials, father-son banquets, and in worthy causes regardless how obscure. Murphy at one time even became a board member of a Niebuhr sponsored group, the American League for India's Freedom! Moreover, it was then that he developed habits of personal consideration for a favored few—remembering anniversaries, sending little gifts, writing flattering notes—which became a personal hallmark and a counterweight to what many regarded as an inconsiderate nature.[a] Murphy also served as an arbitrator in wage and contract disputes in which he demonstrated a willingness to consider cost-of-living and productivity factors far ahead of his time. Politics, of course, was involved. Politics was shrewdly played when he loudly declined small arbitration fees from workmen, while pressing quietly for his $7,500 fee in the lengthy Ford-Blair arbitration of 1928.[23] Yet, even when he proceeded politically, Murphy had a way of disarming critics. Two episodes, which gave him an opportunity to crusade before large audiences, had lasting political repercussions.

In 1924, Mayor John W. Smith asked him to conduct a one-man grand jury investigation into alleged scandals in the administration of public works. The task was tricky, the judge remarked, "considering the political crosscurrents and the intense newspaper rivalry I must stay clear of"; but after four months of inquiry, he issued a scathing denunciation of collusive bidding in the street and motor transportation departments. "The situation calls for something more than the punishment of a few betrayers of the public trust," he declared. "It calls for a new spirit, strong and courageous, deep down in the political life of this city. . . ."[24] Although the *Detroit News* dismissed the irregularities as politically inspired "chicken feed," the Murphy report drew national publicity because corruption in Detroit was so unexpected. The city needed "a scrubbing that is long due," commented Arthur H. Vandenberg's *Grand Rapids Herald*. Mulcahy, too, was reportedly "very pleased with the way things are developing." As a champion of clean government, Judge Murphy was making political headway.[25]

A year later he became immersed in the *Sweet* trial, one of the major civil liberties cases of the day. The heart of the *Sweet* case was discrimination in housing. Between 1910 and 1925, Detroit's Negro population had quadrupled without a corresponding increase in housing. When Negroes began spilling over into white districts, they met stiff opposition from neighborhood "improvement associations." Riots and forcible evictions soon followed. By 1925 the situation was so serious that the mayor sounded a public alarm. "A single fatal riot," said he, "would injure this city beyond remedy."[26]

[a] A good example occurred at the outbreak of World War II when, as a harried Attorney General, he found time to write Mrs. Harold L. Ickes, wife of the Secretary of the Interior: "Harold left the war meeting of the Cabinet Monday. I knew that only you and his hopes would tear him from that dramatic session and so I penned in my notes as he walked out head high 'I hope its a boy and a scrapper like his dad.' I also hope he will have the beauty of character of his lovely mother." FM to Mrs. Harold Ickes, Sept. 6, 1939, Box 77.

In September 1925 a fatal riot did occur when Dr. Ossian Sweet, a Negro gynecologist, occupied a house in a predominantly East European section of the city. Despite police protection, a mob gathered for two days. The house was stoned on the second night, the occupants panicked, and someone fired into the crowd, killing one white bystander and wounding another. The case took on national significance when the NAACP hired Clarence Darrow and Arthur Garfield Hays to defend 11 Negroes against charges of murder.

Public feeling was high as the case moved to Recorder's Court. Judge Murphy, whose "Irish" was up, apparently maneuvered to preside. "Every judge on this bench is afraid to touch the case," he reportedly commented. "They think it's dynamite. They don't realize that this is the opportunity of a lifetime to demonstrate sincere liberalism and judicial integrity at a time when liberalism is coming into its own." The *Sweet* case became such a demonstration. NAACP official Walter White, though at first discouraged, expressed gratified surprise at finding "a most extraordinary degree of even-handed justice, an experience which, unfortunately, the Negro defendant could duplicate in few courts of law, North or South." For the judge immediately released Mrs. Sweet on bail; and as Darrow opened argument on "the law of love," he insisted on an atmosphere of calm that made the trial, as David Lilienthal reported in the *Nation*, "probably the fairest ever accorded a Negro in this country."[27]

The first trial of 11 Negroes ended in a hung jury. The state then agreed to separate prosecution of Henry Sweet, a Wilberforce College student who was the only defendant to admit having fired a gun. Though the issues were similar, Darrow made one of his great arguments in a seven-hour closing plea. The case was a "milestone in the progress of the human race," he told the jury. "The hopes and fears of a race are in your keeping." And he won acquittal.[28]

Judge Murphy, as well as the jury, was moved by Darrow's performance. Returning to his chambers, he told a friend: "This is the greatest experience of my life. That was Clarence Darrow at his best. I will never hear anything like it again. He is the most Christlike man I have ever known."[29] The feeling was mutual. The calm of the case lay partly in prosecution strategy not to arouse the great defender, but Darrow gave the credit to the judge. Murphy's instructions regarding circumstantial evidence, on which the state leaned heavily, and his reminders that Michigan required "absolute, unconditional equality" before the law, had set the stage for the defense to do its work. While Murphy regarded his part as merely enforcing legal equality, Darrow insisted to the end that "it was the first time in all my career where a judge really tried to help, and displayed a sympathetic interest in saving poor devils from the extreme forces of the law, rather than otherwise." "When I went to court to arrange for the trial," he wrote in his memoirs, "I found a judge who not only seemed human, but who proved to be the kindliest and most understanding man I ever happened to meet on the bench. . . ."[30]

The empathy between the old man and the young was not hard to fathom. Both shared an environmental outlook toward crime and punishment. Until the conditions creating crime were eradicated, society was sinning as well as being sinned against. Darrow had spent a lifetime articulating this theme, so much so that he bordered on a theory that individuals bear little responsibility for crime. Murphy's most forceful exposition of environmentalism came in a 1927 radio debate with Harry N. Nimmo, editor of the Detroit weekly, *Saturday Night*, over revival of capital punishment in Michigan. In his own fervid style, Murphy echoed Darrow's famed argument against death penalties three years before. Death penalties did not deter crime; instead they set a pernicious example. Death penalties were not applied evenly; instead they worked vengeance on the weak. Death penalties "only muddle the question of law enforcement" with false diagnosis, said Murphy.

The problem of crime is interwoven with social and economic conditions. I suggest that those who yearn for the return of the hangman's noose might direct their thought to the lack of social justice, to the drab social conditions that manufacture fodder for the gibbet. . . . The squalor of the cradle in the unlighted, unheated attic of the city slum is where we must begin our study of crime . . . and those who would solve the problem of crime will do well to seek its causes at their source, and strive to apply the remedy at the beginning rather than at the end of a sordid life story. I have no patience with that lofty assumption of virtue which asserts itself in loud clamor for cruel chastisement of human frailty and yet which never raises a voice above a whisper in protest against the social [and] economic burdens which bear down on human weaknesses to the breaking point. I have no sympathy for crime, but as I sit on the bench of Recorder's Court and witness the drab parade of crushed hopes and broken lives pass by, I cannot help but feel that a God of Justice will not omit from his reckoning the social and economic factors that largely muster this tragic array. . . . Crime thrives . . . because justice is neither swift nor sure in this land of ours. This is the evil to be remedied.[31]

Darrow and Murphy parted company, however, on one vital attitude. The defense attorney saw "nothing whatever today" in the "old call of

speedy and certain justice, which only means speedy and certain vengeance, and a denial of justice." "Nobody knows what is justice, let alone
swift or certain," Darrow snorted in criticizing Murphy's speech. "I
think the lawyers who know little about this subject and care less have
overworked the idea. . . . They have talked themselves hoarse on the
law's delays and technicalities . . . although they were not technicalities,
they were substantial rights." The real problem, in his view, was not
delay, but the reverse—insufficient time to prepare defense before unpopular defendants were rushed into publicity trials. Still, Darrow commended Murphy's speech as "true and brave and human like everything
that you have done," offered his help in getting it published, and appointed him to the advisory committee of the American League to
Abolish Capital Punishment. After all, the two men were trading stock
tips, and one good turn between radicals deserved another.[32]

Because it was a publicity trial the *Sweet* case rebounded to Murphy's
benefit. Nationally, it enhanced his professional standing as a liberal
criminal judge. Soon thereafter he was invited to participate in the
Hearst-sponsored Crime Study Commission, which Murphy followed
up by agitating for continuing research lest the effort "rest on its oars."[33]
Making friends with Sanford Bates, the federal director of prisons, he
also addressed the National Association of Probation Officers in a speech
which the Hearst papers disseminated widely.[34] In 1930 his experiments with sentencing, in which his staff compiled elaborate psychological and sociological case histories for his use in tailoring punishment to individuals, were featured in a glowing *Nation* article that drew
favorable responses from sociologists and forward-looking judges such
as Baltimore's Joseph N. Ulman, who likewise were troubled by the
"hunch system" of sentencing. Except for systematic charts, the innovation was in practice, not concept. The judge, who himself asked
Walter White of the NAACP to see that a copy crossed the desk of
the liberal knight, Felix Frankfurter, now was simply of sufficient interest and influence to spread the word.[35]

The political consequences of the *Sweet* case overpowered the professional. During the trial Murphy established cordial relations with a
nucleus of leaders in the civil liberties movement—White, Darrow, and
Hays of the NAACP, then Roger N. Baldwin and Morris L. Ernst
of the American Civil Liberties Union. Later, he became a board member of the NAACP; and though he sometimes disagreed with the
ACLU, as in the case of their opposition to a Philippines sedition law,
he was unusually sensitive to the organization's viewpoint.[36] The *Sweet*
case also entrenched Murphy locally as a champion of ethnic minori-

ties par excellence. By reelection time in 1929 he had long since crossed
the divide into urban liberalism. As he wrote the editor of Detroit's
Hungarian News, "my interest in the social and economic problems of
the community have naturally led me to an intimacy with the minority
groups, and, while it has not altogether done so, in some measure it
has alienated from me the more conservative groups in the city, so it is
upon my friends in the minority who have their peculiar problems
that I must lean in the main."[37] So doing, Murphy was reelected by
an even larger plurality than in 1923. His strength was general; but
heavy majorities in Ward 21 on the city's northeastern edge furnished
a surprising clue to his appeal in Detroit. Neither working-class, Irish,
nor Negro, Ward 21 was predominantly what he was—young, second
generation Catholic, middle to upper-middle class, and on the make.
A combination of veterans groups and Hearst reporters, of ethnic
minorities and aspirant Catholics, may have seemed weird; but it reflected solid patterns in American urban politics—to wit, the tendency
of ethnic and religious groups to draw their political leaders from second generation and middle-class strata, especially in nonpartisan electoral systems which tend to favor middle-class "personalities" over
party professionals. An early manifestation of larger political trends,
Murphy's reelection brought forth a new standard-bearer for the scat-
tered liberal forces in Detroit. The only question, for him, was whether
the time was ripe for "a new movement of young men who are willing
to discard the old-trading political ways" and to work their "wholesome
influence for the fastest growing city on earth."[38]

III

Even while campaigning for reelection to Recorder's Court Murphy
contemplated running for mayor. His impressive victory in the spring
of 1929 not only focused speculation on him as a possible candidate,
but also whetted his own appetite for the post. Immediately after reelection as judge he began wrestling with the idea of running in the fall
"if the sentiment is good."[39] Opposition from powerful groups, reportedly the *News* and the *Free Press*, persuaded him to stay out of
the race, but in the summer of 1930 the opportunity suddenly recurred.
Mayor Charles W. Bowles, who had been the Klan-supported candidate
in 1924, was recalled. The specific charges against Bowles were many—
mismanagement of the street railway system, political influences in the
police force, collusion in purchasing—and a general belief flourished
that Bowles sought to utilize Detroit's strong mayor system to convert

a nonpartisan government into a personal machine. Together, these issues culminated in one of the country's earliest municipal recalls. The *Detroit News* and *Free Press* were prominent backers of the recall movement; so was Gerald E. Buckley, a radio announcer with a popular following similar to that of Father Coughlin in later years. The recall of Bowles was successful, but on election eve Buckley was assassinated in the lobby of a downtown hotel. After so much controversy—and ten other murders that fortnight—the political scene was in turmoil.[40]

The sudden events presented Murphy with an agonizing choice. On the one hand, the pressures to run for the unexpired term greatly increased. The *Times* hierarchy put on the heat, if only because the recall affair caught them on the wrong side. Frank X. Martel, president of the Detroit Federation of Labor, added fuel to the fire by pledging labor's support. "It is generally recognized that there is but one man in the city of Detroit . . . who can redeem our city," he wrote. Strong sentiment for the judge, as an apparently clean and unattached candidate who could restore public confidence, also was evident from many unsolicited letters he received urging him that it was his "civic duty to run."[41]

To do so, on the other hand, entailed dangerous risks. Both the purpose and the price of nonpartisan systems is weak party organization. Murphy had the *Times* behind him, but his candidacy would come late and in opposition to two ex-mayors and to George Engel, a respected candidate of an already organized recall movement. His candidacy risked reviving the anti-Catholic bigotry of the recent presidential campaign, as clerical friends warned; worse still, it risked splitting the vote sufficiently to reelect Bowles. Defeat in those circumstances might well mean political suicide. To survive Murphy would have to go for broke. And even if he won, his friend Joseph A. Mulcahy wondered from California "if it is worthwhile." Cleaning up the "mess" in Detroit would require the appointment of honest, capable men to head the departments under fire, men willing to make great sacrifices. Elements opposed to him in the past, while they might welcome his candidacy now, would capitalize on any deficiency. "Beware of that gang," Mulcahy cautioned. "You would be drawn and quartered as they have drawn and quartered Bowles."[42]

But Murphy read the signs differently. Quietly he engineered a draft through *Times* and Legion connections, and petitions were circulated in Fisher Body plants. Publicly, before a large gathering at the Ft. Wayne Hotel, he threw down the gauntlet in a speech long remembered in Detroit. "I will not be a self-starter nor will I be a candidate as the pick of any clique, faction or cabal," he declared in a nonpartisan bid. Unless he received a signal of "general public demand for me to lead this fight for good government," he said, "I shall consult my own interests and inclinations and remain on the bench."

I have not made and will not make any promises, trades, deals or combinations. I have not accepted and will not accept any campaign contributions. A mayor chained by pre-election deals or mortgaged by campaign cash is bound to be a sorry incubus on the city.

If the people of Detroit want me for mayor, the law provides a way for them to say so. The theory of the primary law is that the people select their candidates for office. This is my idea of popular government.[43]

Calling for a bold "new deal" in municipal government, Murphy campaigned on a platform of outright reform. "What is the use of misleading the people?" he asked. Detroit was "in ashes," the people were "dead broke," the city was "a political ruin." While conceding his lack of administrative experience, he outlined a program, which Martel had suggested earlier, that was shrewdly attuned to mass concerns. At a minimum, he pledged a new broom and restoration of businesslike administration to Detroit. Specifically, that meant elimination of the street railway deficit to thwart efforts to return mass transit to private enterprise; it also meant debt reduction and completion of civil service reform to eradicate the "spoils system and the politics of the gang."[44] Although a strong mayor was perhaps incompatible with popular notions of businesslike administration, his second field of concentration—public welfare—certainly was. Pledging "to do something for the unemployed," he outlined concrete proposals—unemployment surveys, consolidation of employment services, and increased welfare appropriations—to assist the unfortunate. "We will take care of our sick," he declared. "We will take care of our aged. . . . We will, with all the Master has given us, tackle the problem of unemployment. . . . We are going to fight this fight in a progressive way . . . inspired by the philosophy that we are here to enrich the earth, to lift the weak, to comfort the aged, to aid the jobless." "If we forget this mission, we beggar ourselves." "What this town needs is the dawn of a new day, the dew and sunshine of a new morning."[45]

Thenceforth, "dew and sunshine" became a symbol of Murphy's brand of politics in Detroit. The very shift of opposition strategy from charges of conniving to reelect Bowles to charges of pulling "porkchops down out of the sky," indicates how swiftly he dominated the campaign. Eschewing the radio techniques of his opponent, mainly for lack of money, he took to the stump with flaming rhetoric, stole Bowles' thunder about press domination, and placed the recall movement on the defensive with the welfare issue. Only the people had the right to pick a mayor, he said; for the opposition press to do it was but a "high toned form of 'gang rule.'" All the people should benefit from government, he said; for the administration to ignore unemployment was immoral. With old-fashioned oratory, Murphy blended Progressive ideas about political purity with the new social consciousness of modern liberalism. Equating public service with his own private mission, he claimed for government a role as champion of the underprivileged. The inevitable charges of demagoguery he met with excerpts from Pope Leo's *Rerum Novarum* and other lexicons of applied Christianity. And despite the ridicule of his rhetoric—and the occasional dread—the combination worked magic.

Depression had struck. Every barometer indicated that the hoped-for recovery of 1930 was shortlived. By the month of the election employment had fallen 50 percent below the level of 1929, while personal income and bank deposits registered similar declines. In the wake of the stock market crash a customary pattern was being set: Detroit was hit faster and harder by economic downturn than the rest of the country. Although Murphy offered few specific remedies his recognition of government responsibility inspired confidence. By the mere pledge that no one would go hungry "because of circumstances beyond his control," a new philosophy of government was in the offing. A prelude to the New Deal was taking shape. To the surprise of most, he won by a plurality of 12,000 votes.[46/b]

By gambling heavily, Murphy won "a remarkable personal victory" and, as politicians then noted, "the opportunity of a lifetime" to build beyond.[47] Fully aware of the potentialities he wasted little time. Even while his election was being contested by Bowles, he announced the formation of the Mayor's Committee Against Unemployment, a nonpartisan group of industrial, labor, and civic leaders to formulate plans for reemployment and to supplement the work of government welfare agencies. Then, after the election contest was dropped, he presented to the Common Council, the city's legislative organ, a three-point program to restore "business administration" to the street railways, confidence to the city's 41,000 employees, and aid to its army of idle men.[48]

Executive action was the watchword for the first two problems,

[b] The vote was: Murphy—106,637; Bowles—93,985; Engel—85,650; Smith—21,735. Richard M. Reading to FM, Sept. 19, 1930, Box 10.

which were essentially matters of budget and personnel control. Murphy's first executive order required civil service examinations for vacancies, which had the effect of placing the last open department, street railways, under civil service by 1933.[49] That the order was no idle gesture was apparent when the mayor began to announce his department heads. For police commissioner he chose James K. Watkins, a conservative corporation lawyer; for purchasing and then public works and street railways, he chose Joseph E. Mills, a Republican Packard executive; for corporation counsel, he chose Clarence E. Wilcox, another distinguished lawyer; and so the list went—G. Hall Roosevelt as controller, John F. Ballenger as director of public welfare, and professional workers for lesser posts in the prisons, hospitals, and parks. Because the key appointments were mostly prominent men with business ties, liberals protested. But ideologues missed, as they always would, a central facet of Murphy's style. He was distinctly old-fashioned about budgets, political purity, and civic harmony. Balanced budgets and professional personnel practices, for him, were but logical and necessary corollaries of positive government functions. Moreover he shared Progressive impulses to remove politics from politics. "I am not much of an enthusiast about mere party success," he said. "Too few of us in politics are willing to be defeated" for the sake of progressive reforms. From the beginning he conceived his government as a united, nonpartisan effort in the spirit of the city charter. And by a single stroke, his appointments calmed the opposition, demonstrated his sincerity of purpose, and set what some consider to be a peak of competence in Detroit's civic life.[50]

Detroit, in this respect, revealed Murphy's special strengths and weaknesses in administration. Though he liked to think of himself as an executive, he was a political leader rather than an administrator. Unorganized and temperamental, he disliked keeping routine hours or appointment schedules. City hall in his administration, like the White House under Andrew Jackson, swarmed with people trying to see their friend, the mayor, and disgruntled when they failed. The mayor also disliked anonymity. Much of his time was spent racing about the city, feeling the pulse and being seen, and making dramatic late entrances complete with bodyguards and female entourage. Serious work was reserved for the wee hours, and physical breakdowns were frequent. For someone who regarded himself as a man of action, Murphy was also peculiarly vulnerable to charges that action stopped at rhetoric. He created chronic problems for professional administrators beneath him by announcing bold policies in public, yet avoiding the concrete moves required for their implementation until political balances were carefully weighed. In every office subordinates complained that they would bring a problem to him for decision, only to have Murphy duck the issues with a melodramatic cock of the profile in a myopia of pious preachment. Working for Murphy thus was never easy. He understood the principle of loyalty upward much more than loyalty downward. His dedication usually sufficed for colleagues to forgive his deficiencies, to be sure, and he often ingratiated himself among close subordinates by jokes against himself and by self-criticism. For professional administrators and ruffled citizens, however, the way he ran his office was another indication that Murphy was an odd character—and not quite respectable.

On the other hand, Murphy had one talent that made up for a multitude of administrative sins. He battled hard in every post for "the best men" available for key positions, regardless of patronage. Then he gave them their head, provided backing and political direction—and reaped the glory. Full delegation of power, coupled with a willingness to listen and a contagious dedication, attracted men of ability and ideas to his side. "He put a flag on my back and I marched," was the way one lawyer described the process. The imaginative response to depression in Detroit showed that his mayoralty was no exception. "A new freshness in life," Murphy remarked after the initial appointing was done, "is going into City government, I am sure."[51]

A new freshness, requiring concerted action by private and public agencies, was essential for the innovating part of his program—help for the idle. In 1930, Murphy echoed President Hoover's hope that economic decline was temporary, but he was under no illusions about the ability of municipal government to solve it. "The cure for unemployment is employment," he told the Common Council, a task that was obviously beyond the capacity of Detroit. "But right now," the mayor argued in a plea for immediate action, "the situation is acute, winter is closing in on us, thousands of men have been sleeping in the parks all summer. We must provide them with shelter and, if possible, we must get them jobs." The only good politics was "service to the people," and there was "nothing visionary or socialistic or communistic or anything else" about that.[52]

The first task was to identify the needy. The Mayor's Unemployment Committee sponsored a quick registration drive and the results produced a shock. More than 120,000 persons registered as jobless; 20,000 signified desperate need. Though Detroit had long maintained modern public welfare services (a monthly caseload of 15,000 by 1930) no one was prepared for such numbers.[53] While national leaders preached confidence lest crisis deepen, and extolled private charity lest moral fiber weaken, unemployment in Detroit was already at emergency proportions. The city thus became a testing ground for two competing policies—President Hoover's deeply felt principle that unemployment relief was a private and local affair, and the mayor's equally strong commitment to relief as a public responsibility. The difference between the two was slight at first; it was obscured further by Murphy's emphasis on cooperative efforts by public and private agencies, but the very struggle to meet the responsibility municipally turned Detroit's mayor into one of the earliest champions of federal relief. Filling a leadership vacuum on the issue gave Murphy a moral crusade which he capitalized on to gain national political prominence.

Overwhelmed by numbers, Detroit improvised as best it could. The mayor obtained funds from Common Council for a free municipal employment bureau, municipal lodging houses, and additional welfare. The Unemployment Committee, which was conceived originally to study unemployment conditions and to organize work projects, shifted attention to emergency relief. Organizing itself into subgroups on housing, clothing, employment, and the like, it became the fulcrum of a large volunteer effort that was part public and part private in character. With city funds it ran transient lodges for homeless men in idle factories donated by Studebaker and Fisher. With volunteer help it organized "creative work" projects by staggering shifts, spreading hours, and consolidating neighborhood odd jobs into fulltime work. It established food and clothing distribution centers, set dietary standards for recipients of public relief, and provided tools and seed for "Thrift Gardens" on empty lots, an idea the mayor claimed to have borrowed from George Catlin's stories of Pingree's potato patches in the panic of 1893. For a time Murphy even organized a study group of industrialists, including Walter P. Chrysler and Edsel Ford, to plan against recurrence of mass unemployment. During the first flush of enthusiasm all Detroit seemed busy.[54]

The overlapping functions between the Unemployment Committee and city agencies like the welfare department, which dispensed relief, were a source of public and bureaucratic confusion. The Committee also had the weaknesses of any large-scale enterprise hastily improvised from volunteers. But in the fall of 1930 the nation was watching Detroit's pioneering program with approving interest. No city in America, the *New York Times* observed, has produced "a more systematic or sensible effort . . . to ameliorate the economic condition" of the idle. In

Detroit itself there was even talk that the new mayor, with his capacity for pressing most citizens to the wheel, was something of a political genius. He had restored confidence in honest government and provided leadership just in time. Hopes ran high that something might come from concerted action after all. The *Detroit News* commented: "Altogether, a healthier, more hopeful atmosphere is being created. Detroit looks to the long winter with less dread, with the belief that better times are coming."[55]

Optimism faded when winter came. Detroit's effort, to be sure, had produced impressive results. In addition to direct public relief, the Mayor's Committee by March 1931 had provided clothing to 125,000 people, two million meals, and shelter for 12,000 homeless men, while the municipal employment bureau had located 25,000 jobs, a record which surpassed even the established services of the state. But despite the "spirit of helpfulness" which the mayor observed among all classes, "creative work" obviously was beyond volunteer efforts and the city of Detroit. Employment indices were half the 1929 level; 200 thousand men and women were out of work; unemployment was a national and international crisis. "All we can do," said the mayor, "is in the nature of 'first aid' and temporary relief only."[56]

Even that much was heading for crisis. Relief as a public function was well established in Detroit, so much so that the effort by 1930 was 98 percent in government hands. But because they were rushed, and because they accepted the false optimism of early recovery, welfare administrators made no attempt to reorganize or to reduce standards of relief, which took the form of checks for food, clothing, rent, and fuel. The result was that within three months after Murphy took office, the city's public welfare load rose to 46,000 families at a monthly cost of two million dollars—a tenfold increase in little over a year. Even with a year's residency requirement, and excluding the work of the Mayor's Committee or private charities, the city of Detroit in January 1931 was providing direct relief to 190,000 persons, or roughly 12 percent of its population. And a plateau of 100,000 welfare recipients became a permanent budgetary fixture for the next two years. By whatever measure, Detroit's public relief effort was without parallel in the nation.[57]

Commitment to this policy, in the face of mounting evidence that it would be of long duration, soon overshadowed everything else in Murphy's mayoralty. Other issues, it is true, helped to chill the initial honeymoon. The mayor and his mentor, Judge Connolly, broke over policy and patronage. The mayor's support, and then reversal, of an AFL move to limit the importation of Canadian labor almost cost him the representatives of both sides on the Unemployment Committee. His political conception of strong-mayor leadership, with its attendant salesmanship and publicity, also produced misgivings about his commitment to strictly "business administration." "Is it necessary for our mayor to be hourly in the limelight [and] sunshine of publicity?" the Detroit *Civic Searchlight* asked. "Or is the office of mayor a big, hard job, largely administrative in character?"[58]

Yet these differences were mild compared to the battle brewing over public relief. As the welfare load peaked in the winter of 1931 the very principle of relief as a government function was on the block.

The immediate cause was a fiscal crisis simple enough on the surface but of complex origins. Swelling relief rolls put massive pressure on the budget, but an inherited deficit magnified the strain. The annual 1930-31 relief appropriation of $200,000 was only a fifth of the *monthly* relief cost when Murphy took office, and only a tenth of the monthly cost by winter. The welfare load, in other words, had already wrecked the budget of his predecessor, though a chronic underestimate of snow removal charges was also involved. Spiralling relief costs now meant a deficit of $13 million. Under ordinary circumstances a deficit that size could have been carried without difficulty in a city with property valuations of $3.6 billion; but the deficit coincided with a sudden contraction of credit in national bond markets. Murphy not only inherited a 300-million-dollar debt; a fifth of that debt was short-term credits, contracted in violation of the city charter for lack of retirement provisions, which had to be carried from operating revenues. Detroit, in short, entered the depression with twenty-six cents of every tax dollar earmarked for debt retirement.[59] Fixed obligations for education also were beyond the mayor's control. Reaping the harvest of overexpansion, Detroit had "a serious enough problem" in bond markets, in the opinion of banking experts, without contemplating additional borrowing. Long-term refunding of past debt, not to speak of welfare loans, was out of the question. The only course short of default, according to the Committee on City Finances, a group representing Detroit's principal business organizations, was a program of retrenchment, "more effective budget control," and possibly higher taxes. However tempting it was to dismiss orthodox advice in the name of emergency, Murphy accepted it, as the official responsible for "the City's credit and good name." "The city has reached the limit of the taxpayers ability to pay," he said. The cost of government had to be reduced to lighten their load.[60]

Retrenchment and safeguarding the city's financial integrity, in addition to unemployment relief, thus became fixed commitments of Murphy's regime. Acting on recommendations of financial leaders called in to help, the administration undertook strict budgetary control in the winter of 1931. It created a quarterly allotment system and a permanent budget bureau. It created a 10 percent forced reserve and forbade appropriation transfers. And it created "Economy and Efficiency" committees in all departments to trim additional fat and passed a budget that covered past deficits and operating costs for the coming year. But the effort was soon undone. Tax delinquencies of $13.5 million—almost 20 percent of the tax budget—undermined all that was planned.[61] Tax delinquencies, because they had the same effect every year, thus became the *bête noire* of budget planners in Detroit. Tax delinquencies, along with interest payments and welfare costs, formed a triad of intolerable strain.

Because of their size and novelty, relief costs loomed in the public mind as the prime cause of fiscal trouble. Of the three, however, relief was the least difficult to manage. For interest charges were double in amount and delinquencies were unpredictable. Though he was appalled that a city so rich as Detroit was incapable of spending its money "where it ought to be spent—in the relief of victims of unemployment," Murphy could not escape feeling trapped in a budgetary "riddle" not of his own making.[62] Between debt charges, relief costs, and now tax delinquencies, the budget was caught in a vicious squeeze. The only solution lay in long-term refunding at cheaper rates and tax reduction to stabilize income.

But how? The more tax collections fell, the more Detroit had to borrow; the more it borrowed, the less would be left for regular expenses; and unless it lived within income, refunding was impossible. Tax increases were out of the question. "So much utter wretchedness" existed in Detroit, the mayor noted, "so many home owners are having their life savings and property slip away," that property taxes had to be reduced, not lifted.[63] Economy in government, though essential, also had limits. Emergency retrenchment required to offset tax delinquencies was accomplished in 1931 by releasing five thousand employees and by halving welfare costs, through a reduction of relief, to food and emergency shelter only. These cuts left a budget 90 percent in wage items; and as a "pro-public" man, the mayor feared that the example set by government payroll cuts would produce chaotic lowering of standards everywhere, thus leaving "the struggle of years abandoned in a moment of panic. . . ." Because falling revenues, not relief costs, were the heart of the matter, Murphy concluded early that the time was "rapidly approaching when our large cities face financial ruin unless they are relieved."[64] Even if welfare were eliminated from the tax budget altogether, the riddle would remain.

There was no escaping the fact that depression threw Detroit into fiscal crisis brought on by a "reckless and extravagant past."[65] The only course was to ride out the storm, pending a recovery that permitted cheaper credit and stable revenues. Meantime, the city confronted a stark reality: unless government provided emergency relief, the minimum needs of thousands of people would not be met. Municipal government would have to shoulder that burden too. Any other choice, said the mayor, was "stupid and unthinkable."[66]

That Detroit's relief program was a dole, and no more, Murphy was the first to admit. While he took obvious pride in it, he outlined the program before Senator Norris's Conference of Progressives in 1931 as merely unemployment insurance, "handled in a shabby and unfortunate way." He regarded Detroit's experience as proof of Keynesian analysis and of the need for a permanent cushion of social security. "The key to the question, if there is one key to unlock its mystery," he declared, "is in the redistribution of the purchasing power of the people."[67] But while Murphy advocated unemployment insurance as a permanent goal, it was becoming increasingly difficult to maintain even Detroit's traditional policies of stopgap relief. The pressure of the first fiscal crisis in 1931 erupted into a frontal assault on the dole.

Prominent members of the Board of Commerce denounced the welfare program as "paternalism" inspired by Moscow and its recipients as "midwestern derelicts" and "parasites." The administration was accused of extravagance, of attracting the paupers of the land to share in Detroit's largess, and of all those evils attributed to unemployment relief, then and now. The Fisher Lodges for single men, which touched ideological nerves about self-reliance, drew special fire. Even though the police commissioner argued that "it would be not only a humane thing but also a wise thing to get these men off the streets in some way or other," a constant crusade and occasional vetoes of council cuts were necessary to keep them going.[68] The mayor's policy of designating areas such as Grand Circus Park for free public assembly also added heat. Murphy might defend the policy of free discussion as "obedience to fundamental law" with least public inconvenience, and as "the best antiseptic for what we may consider to be poisonous ideas"; but police-protected communist rallies in public parks and before city hall seemed to verify conservative suspicions that the mayor was a dangerous radical. To citizens who endured the agitation—or who shared his fear that "extremism" was on the rise—the plaudits of eastern libertarians were irrelevant.[69] And the mayor's relations with veterans groups underwent strain.

At the extremes, the controversy was merely highly vocal expression of standard right-wing viewpoints, aggravated by yearnings for ready answers to Detroit's baffling problems. Yet even liberals mounted an attack. The drum-beating over the volunteer character of the relief program, it was said, obscured the waste, the administrative inadequacies, and the shortage of trained professionals in the welfare system. Charges of waste in the department of public welfare became so widespread that, fearing a loss of public confidence, the mayor appointed a committee headed by Reverend Edward H. Pence to investigate. Though the committee found little evidence of fraud, its report confirmed professional criticism of serious organizational errors. The Unemployment Committee's mass registration campaign, while undertaken in the interest of speed, had been launched without plan or even analysis of whether the welfare department was prepared to administer a tenfold increase. The "usual excellent" standards of the department had deteriorated as a result; a necessary condition of laxity had permitted "malingerers" onto the relief rolls; jurisdictional conflicts flourished among welfare agencies, and social workers were demoralized by overwork. A social worker in Detroit tended to as many families as the average laundryman. "So far then," commented Irene Murphy, the mayor's sister-in-law and a welfare supervisor in her own right, "we have been inadequate and stand justly accused." "Something different must be planned before next winter."[70]

Discriminating criticism of welfare policy, however, was soon smothered under ideological thunder from both sides. Officials in city hall were less inclined to admit their impulsiveness than to point to other sources of their difficulties—tax delinquencies and unequal distribution of the welfare load. "The cause of the city's present financial plight," ran John J. Gorman's version of the refrain, "can be summed up in two words—UNPAID TAXES."[71] That problem also was aggravated by Detroit's metropolitan configuration. Relief costs were borne almost exclusively by city property taxes. Several of the area's largest employers, on the other hand, were located outside city limits and neither paid taxes to the city nor contributed to its charities nor assisted their own unemployed workers. Though some manufacturers in Detroit had exemplary private relief programs, Murphy found it difficult not to hold the outsiders responsible for having attracted thousands of workers to Detroit and then dumping them onto city relief rolls when the going was rough. One sample survey estimated that 40 percent of those receiving city welfare came from this source.[72]

"That's the unfair part of it," the mayor complained bitterly. The city's 300,000 taxpayers were saddled with a metropolitan load. "I believe that the unemployed and the needy should be cared for decently by the government," he told a friend. "I also believe that the load should be more equitably distributed" among private employers and state and federal agencies. "In the absence of the rest of them doing their duty," he insisted nevertheless, "we are not going to fail in ours. While we are doing everything we can, we will agitate to bring the others to do their share." Responding to criticism with counterattack, the mayor announced publicly that "municipal government cannot continue indefinitely under the staggering load." "Cooperation from the State and county and from the employers of labor themselves must be sought."[73] The limits of property taxation were reached. Murphy's agitating began accordingly.

The trouble was that responses were painfully slow. The fairest way to equalize, Murphy believed, was direct federal relief based on the progressive income tax. Yet the federal government was in "social retreat." Equalization on a metropolitan basis was a possibility; and Detroit's majority representation on Wayne County's board of supervisors —when the mayor could muster sufficient attendance—did enable the city to shift some of the load. Yet a metropolitan solution was inherently limited by governmental diffusion, state ceilings on borrowing, and the simple fact that Detroit taxpayers paid 80 percent of county taxes anyway.[74] The state ultimately responded by approving the city's application for RFC welfare loans when they became available in 1932, and by raising a 12-million-dollar welfare fund from sales taxes which Detroit shared in 1933. Yet even then, Michigan and Ohio were the only states to require repayment of RFC welfare loans on the theory that state government bore no responsibility for relief—a theory Murphy condemned as "all wrong." And in the peak period of 1931 the city's appeals to Lansing were met by silence, even though Detroit paid half of the state's taxes, too.[75]

In 1931 the mayor's agitation thus centered on private manufacturers, especially Henry Ford. Having only one major factory in Detroit, Ford paid little in property taxes and did not contribute to the community fund, in contrast to his son, Edsel, who contributed $130,000 and served on the city Fine Arts Commission. Ford's depression nostrum of high wages and mass rehiring, though announced with great fanfare, received a sour reaction in city hall. Relief officials feared that it would undermine the seniority status of older workers, thereby enlarging Detroit's welfare rolls.[76] In July, just as the administration was forced by tax delinquencies into emergency budget review—and just as a clerk was caught embezzling welfare funds—the sniping erupted into open battle. The city relief administrator released a report charging that the largest single industry in the metropolitan area, the Ford Motor Company, was responsible for 14 percent or the largest number of workers on Detroit's rolls; and company officials responded with a biting assault on not only the administration, but the very function of public relief. Charging that roughly a third of the names released had never worked at Ford at all, they said: "The principal charity needed in Detroit last winter was jobs. It takes no great administrative genius to scatter as much as $2,000,000 a month, but it does require ability to get something in return. The municipal government of Detroit provided all sorts of opportunities to pauperize the people but no opportunity to maintain their self-respect."[77]

The mayor investigated the relief list in turn and found only 31 cases of fraud, a "trivial" number, in his view, "compared with the general picture of good accomplished." But the issue was no less basic to him. "All this criticism of our welfare policy," he declared, "emanates from sources opposed to the principle of government support of the indigent. We have a battle on our hands and we are going to fight it."[78] "These people are victims of economic conditions, beyond their control and beyond their power of analysis. The city of Detroit must stand between them and starvation. It is a duty that we cannot sidestep."[79]

Murphy took the issue to the polls in the fall elections of 1931, and won reelection by a landslide.[c] However conservatives might damn the "welfare vote," the open antagonism of the Ford organization probably helped rather than hurt the mayor, whose strength was now overwhelming in the working-class and ethnic wards of Detroit. Close cooperation with religious social-action groups, especially with Father Coughlin's growing organization, also strengthened Catholic support. The time had not yet come when liberals found it necessary to distinguish egalitarian and libertarian segments of their movement. God's charity, as Coughlin called it, was an issue around which Hearst, Coughlin, and Murphy could readily unite. The election itself demonstrated that the paramount issue was relief. On the strength of it, Mur-

[c] Murphy polled a majority in the October primary; his plurality in November was over 80,000 votes. See primary data, Box 10, Murphy Papers. *Detroit Free Press*, April 22, 1933.

phy developed close personal ties with the Dearborn priest; and both in public and in private he praised Coughlin's "grand" voice, "spirit and interest in our problems."[80] The results were not only mutually beneficial arrangements for the administration of Detroit relief, but mutually beneficial political influence.

By taking the offensive on the relief issue, Murphy thus emerged with his policies vindicated and his national prestige as a liberal greatly enhanced. Congratulatory messages from liberals Gifford Pinchot, Newton D. Baker, and Robert M. LaFollette left little doubt of the implications. "Never in my short memory," wrote Arthur H. Vandenberg, Jr., "has a man in public life so completely captured the imagination and intelligence of the voting public."[81] Detroit's Irish Catholic mayor, by forming a successful urban coalition and by winning a decisive victory for the principle of public relief, had penetrated the national political consciousness.

CHAPTER 3

THE CITY IS STRAPPED,

1931-1933

THE winter of 1931-32 lent force to the *New York Times'* observation that the lucky candidates for mayor in Detroit "will probably be the nine who fail."[1] Once voters reaffirmed the principle of public relief, the battle shifted to a protracted financial struggle. Actually two issues were merged—government aid to the needy and a larger problem of municipal finance. Because unemployment relief often was treated in public debates as the sole source of strain, the ideological content of the relief question obscured the complex nature of the latter. But the very struggle to maintain regular municipal services as well as relief brought Murphy into a position of leadership on municipal fiscal policy in general. In taking that lead, however, he was compelled less by theory than by one simple dictate: finding money for the city of Detroit.

The Murphy administration had weathered the first budget crisis of 1931 by orthodox measures of severe retrenchment and private borrowing. "A disposition to attack the problem earnestly," which was a banker's euphemism for the willingness of officials to cut another 11 percent from a budget already $24 million below budget requests, enabled the city to obtain short-term credits up to $20 million from a syndicate of Detroit and New York banks.[2] The credits—granted on the conditions that the mayor and the Common Council pledge to live within their income and on quarterly review of the pledge by a Citizens Finance Committee headed by banker Ralph Stone—covered past deficits and regular services for the coming year. But it did not cover an anticipated 7.5-million-dollar relief expenditure, which the administration hoped to meet with federal aid. And while spending agencies made "a splendid showing" by remaining within their fall quarterly allotments, a rise in tax delinquencies pulled the rug from underneath the budget again. No sooner was one storm weathered than a worse one ensued.[3]

The mayor already had been warned in the summer of 1931 that "drastic steps," in the form of holidays on special assessments and public improvements, would be necessary to satisfy the watchdog committee and to avert default. Even more drastic steps were ahead. Murphy's hopes for federal unemployment relief were quashed when President

Hoover refused to call a special session of Congress to consider emergency aid to the states. Senator Couzens, adapting himself to the President's social theories and to the fact that the regular session of Congress would come too late for the winter's relief, then offered Detroit a million dollars if it could be matched locally with nine.[4] That hope also faded. "Frankly," as Alvan Macauley, the sympathetic president of Packard Motors expressed the consensus, "I do not believe that in addition to the community fund, nine millions additional can be collected out of this community in these times when even the wealthy, or heretofore wealthy, are full of anxiety as to their future financial status." Despite the mayor's appeals that "the distressing facts before me" created an "imperative duty" to raise supplementary welfare funds, and despite the services of Clarence Darrow and Fritz Kreisler at fund-raising drives, Macauley was right. Several leading citizens declined even to serve on the Emergency Relief Committee. One lady expressed confidence in the mayor's ability to "work something out of it all." But in the end, only $651,000 was raised.[5] The limits of private charity also had been reached.

The triad of welfare costs, interest charges, and tax delinquencies, spiralled relentlessly on. At first the mayor hesitated to acknowledge it. Murphy was proud that Detroit had weathered the 1931 crisis with both its welfare system and its credit intact; he was proud also of the "favorable light" its financial performance was receiving in business quarters, as evidenced both by the advance of Detroit bonds on the market and by personal expressions of confidence in him. While Chicago and Philadelphia fell into arrears, he boasted, "Detroit stands erect." Although he supported all efforts to stimulate federal unemployment relief, Murphy, if only to impress on his own department heads the need of economizing in early 1932, expressed his opposition during the Senate debate over RFC municipal loans to "any legislation that would relieve municipal governments from recourse to uncompromising economy" and, as he said privately, "until our hands were clean of every waste."[6] Senator Vandenberg thought this a "sturdy statement of a sound view," as the Senate defeated the Copeland amendment for municipal loans; but as Murphy's proud words were uttered, Detroit's financial position slipped again. While relief costs mounted, tax collections fell; while bankers urged further retrenchment, the mayor and council began to resist with the very "futile grumbling and financial acrobatics" they had condemned only a few months earlier.[7] Before the year was out, Murphy himself was the leading advocate of RFC help.

The situation in 1932 was grim. Even though Detroit's population had dropped by 200,000, department after department protested anticipated budget cuts as below the bone. While the department of public works warned that the holiday on improvements was accumulating severe maintenance costs for the future, public health authorities reported "alarming symptoms" of preventable disease and undernourishment among children. "We feel," they said, "that a minimum of service compatible with the interests of public health has now been reached. . . ."[8] While assessed property valuations dropped a billion dollars below the 1930 figure, the Detroit Citizens League asserted that "property cannot stand further taxation."[9] While private bank deposits fell to half their 1928 level, Ralph Stone passed on confidential reports from out-of-town markets that Detroit was expected to default, a rumor the mayor quickly scotched by pulling newspaper strings.[10] While communist agitation increased, the police force became embroiled in both the "Hunger March" massacre at Dearborn and the Briggs strike riots. After exonerating the police of fault, the mayor met the protests of the ACLU with no little impatience. "There has been so much abuse of the free speech policy of the City recently by the Communists," he told Roger Baldwin, that "our problem now is not one of educating the conservatives to the necessity of free speech and assemblage, demonstrations and the like, but to gain or compel, in some manner, the cooperation of small minority groups who do not share our views on these questions."[11]

While Murphy launched crusades to reduce utility rates and the price of milk, only the gas company cooperated and one utility refused even to talk, conduct which he condemned as "an example of utter selfishness I will not soon forget."[12] While the bankers, who had their own problems, held onto the interest rate and the maxim of no credit to customers who lived beyond income, thousands of letters and job seekers poured into the mayor's office, beseeching aid. Even for political friends, the mayor's secretary, Norman H. Hill, found himself unable "to dig up a single job." Through it all, the mayor somehow managed to attend the charity shows and Legion conventions, the ribbon-cuttings and the games of the Detroit Tigers, functions which any American mayor must attend to keep his job—and this one happened to enjoy. "I often wonder how a human being can live through the position you hold in such times as these," an occasional citizen would write; but for the most part the communications were demands, sometimes civil sometimes not, from people in desperate need. Murphy was "sick at heart" at the sight of the suffering; being mayor of Detroit, he confessed, was a "very thankless and difficult task."[13]

Buffeted from all sides, his nerves snapped. The crisis of 1932 erupted into a battle with the banks. "Real men can take the worst life has to offer," he told the Common Council at the first of the year, "but no man can see children's bread lines and not return to first principles— principles of simple social justice." Detroit, he had vowed, would play straight and not default. "But I assure you," he warned, "that as the selfish promotions of past years have foisted upon this Commonwealth, under the name of government, tremendous obligations of a private nature, I am more disposed to hear the present cry for elemental social justice even above the loud demand for the traditional sanctity of contract."[14] When budget preparations began in February, the warnings became pointed. The mayor refused to pledge retrenchment at a cost of further dismissals and shortening the school year. Was it not time for banks to lower interest rates and to emphasize "men: not money"? At that, the bankers snapped, too. Ralph Stone, head of the Citizens Finance Committee, declared: "The men who have been running the city have been keeping one eye on the ballot box and the other on the pay check, and it is impossible to do that and at the same time solve a gigantic financial problem. The present situation could have been avoided had a proper economy plan been adopted a year ago."[15]

To the Stone group, a proper economy plan meant either the Board of Commerce proposal for a 40-percent reduction in costs or at least a refunding scheme then in planning stage which was based on pay-as-you-go finance. Though the Citizens Committee insisted that methods of retrenchment were the mayor's responsibility, either plan meant deep inroads in the lives of public employees and in welfare. Only after his back was against the wall with no money for payrolls was Murphy willing to pledge the necessary cuts. But in May, when the council refused to approve the dismissals and the mayor proposed federal loans for municipal finance, the squabbling resumed. Threats of repudiation and resort to scrip were heard on the Common Council. Murphy lashed out by stating publicly that Detroit bankers, "who, as a class are without semblance of social responsibility," were out to "starve the poor." Stone responded in kind. He was "dumfounded" by threats to repudiate "solemn pledges" which he personally had endorsed, and was convinced that the mayor sought to divert attention from his own fiscal failures. "Politics is destroying the City's credit," he said. "Politics is making impossible relief to taxpayers next year."[16] Then to the Common Council he denounced the mayor's proposals for federal aid to municipalities as needless and "humiliating," and called for private rehabilitation of city finances. Stone said further:

It probably means much less police and fire protection, school service, recreation and all the rest of the multitude of the services performed by the City. We believe the people are willing to submit to all this in order to put the financial affairs of the City on a sound basis. . . .

As has been recently well said: "The seductive fallacy of Federal aid seems to dull the senses and lull to sleep the pride in local self-government and the joy of independence which characterized our forefathers."[17]

"Isn't he somewhat tardy in that conclusion?" Murphy tartly replied. Banks had been the first among Michigan's 175 corporations to receive RFC help. The real question was not federal aid, but who got it. Congress's failure to include municipalities in the RFC already had provoked Mayor Daniel W. Hoan of Milwaukee to query Senator Borah: "Why, in the name of God, must the banks have all the concessions?"[18] The Populism of Murphy's past, and the problems of the present, now prompted a similar outcry from him. Condemning the application of "business ruthlessness to the trusteeship of the public service," Murphy declared in a statement to "my people":

Mr. Stone doesn't know the problems of the City. . . . He does not know that prisoners in our penal institutions receive fare better than all of our welfare cases at present; that thousands of our school children are without nutritious food and without health protection, and that the morale of policemen and firemen and school teachers, charged with the grave ministry of public service, is rapidly weakening. I wonder if he knows of the weekly struggle between Communists and welfare workers for control of the City's welfare problems. . . .

In case the bankers don't know it, they had better learn without delay that we are fast approaching a crisis and thousands in our community and throughout the State are now reduced to wretchedness and misery; and that a great cooperative plan on the part of Federal, State and municipal governments is the sensible way to prepare for it.[19]

Politics were being played. Basic choices of public policy, in addition to the votes of teachers and city employees, were at stake. The "evil" in Stone's statement, Murphy thought, was that it misled the people about the economy measures already taken. If the bankers did not understand the essentials of political as well as economic survival, however, no one could dispute their sums. The budget passed for fiscal 1932-33 would produce an $18-million deficit; that could only mean, Stone warned, "a default on payrolls."[20] Even worse, the mayor's own controller echoed Stone's charges that adverse publicity had destroyed the carefully tended advance in Detroit's credit position. Now the work had to be redone. The only salvation for Detroit was a refunding plan backed by "a united front," the burial of private prejudices, and a mayor who held his tongue.[21]

For Murphy there was no real choice. Doggedly, he stuck to the charted course. He refused to consider abolition of relief. "If the Federal Government does not play a part," he asserted, "we cannot permit these people to starve." Default, on the other hand, would be catastrophic. "Every government, no matter its humanitarian and social ideals," he conceded, "must be sound in its fiscal phase, must keep its credit good, otherwise it simply crumbles." The only alternative was "extraordinary economies."[22]

In the spring of 1932 the city of Detroit discharged another 5,000 employees, made another 10 percent wage cut, and resorted to payless days and the shortening of school. Still it was not enough. By summer tax delinquencies of 25 percent produced a $3.5-million deficit. To avert default city workers were forced into a five-day week and postponement of pay. Relief was reduced to survival rations of food, in face of warnings from welfare commissioners that "only chaos and violence can result."[23] The Fisher Lodges, despite similar pleas, were closed. A promising wage-work program for welfare clients was abruptly cancelled; and as grocers began to refuse further welfare credits, the city laid plans for last-resort universal cafeterias. While the mayor appealed for private contributions to charity, Detroit ceased to lead the nation in the share of the relief burden borne by government.[24] Only the belief that they were indispensable safety valves for a depressed populace prevented the closing of public parks. The margin was so close that the question of keeping the museum open hinged on the payroll of a few janitors. The museum's celebrated curators had long since been released. And now 1,200 ex-public employees were on relief. The issue had come to a head. The question was no longer how to finance relief—Detroit in fiscal 1932-33 actually would spend less than a half-million dollars in tax money for relief—the question was how to maintain essential services with solvency; the question was private versus federal rehabilitation of city finance.[25]

Resort to drastic economy measures in the summer of 1932 enabled Detroit to negotiate a five-year refunding plan, based on the sale of tax anticipatory bonds, with its creditors and local industrial interests. That such a plan was possible was a testament both to the retrenchment achieved and to the cooperation which prevailed, despite ideological differences, between city officials and business leaders.[26] But henceforth the effort to rehabilitate city finances became a race between insolvency and local versus federal alternatives. Before the private re-

The Murphy home, Harbor Beach, Michigan. Michigan Historical Collections.

Murphy (center, standing) as quarterback for Harbor Beach High School, 1907.
Michigan Historical Collections.

Judge Frank Murphy. Bachrach *circa* 1924

The new mayor of Detroit, 1930.
Michigan Historical Collections.

Murphy standing by reflecting pool at Malacañan, the historic governor-general's palace in Manila. Michigan Historical Collections.

Politicking at Hyde Park, New York, 1932. l. to r., G. Hall Roosevelt, Gov. Franklin D. Roosevelt, Mayor Murphy.

During Murphy's term as governor of Michigan, union workers overturn a car filled with sheriff's deputies in the "Battle of Running Bulls," Flint, Michigan, January 11, 1937. Associated Press.

Union rally at Cadillac Square, during Chrysler strike, Detroit, March 23, 1937. Wide World.

Murphy is sworn in as an Associate Justice of the U.S. Supreme Court by Justice Stanley Reed in President Roosevelt's office, January 18, 1940. Wide World.

On the stump!

Lt.Col. Murphy, USAR, with "the good old patriotic fervor," tries his hand at operating a machinegun on the range of the Infantry Training School at Fort Benning, Ga., summer 1942. Wide World Photos.

The Supreme Court, 1944 Term. Seated, l. to r.: Stanley Reed, Owen J. Roberts, Harlan F. Stone, Hugo L. Black, Felix Frankfurter. Standing: Robert H. Jackson, William O. Douglas, Frank Murphy, Wiley Rutledge. Harris & Ewing.

The Supreme Court, 1946 Term. Seated, l. to r.: Felix Frankfurter, Hugo L. Black, Fred M. Vinson, Stanley Reed, William O. Douglas. Standing: Wiley Rutledge, Frank Murphy, Robert H. Jackson, Harold H. Burton. Harris & Ewing.

funding scheme could be implemented a series of revolts had to be quelled. The Common Council bucked over earmarking taxes for interest payments, and the war against welfare broke out again. One "citizens' committee" of industrialists damned the city for waste and for failure to require welfare recipients to work. Another group of leading industrialists met at a private luncheon, in Murphy's words, "to straighten me out on my social policies." But apparently the mayor turned the meeting into a rout when he rose, removed his coat as if to fight, and declared: "How dare you spend more money for each luncheon in this room than I need to feed a hungry child for a week!" "I was elected," said Murphy, "not because of their [the industrialists'] views but because I was in opposition to them."[27]

The support of Frederic M. Alger and Alvan Macauley at that meeting Murphy always remembered with special gratitude. Had he lost the confidence of Detroit's industrial elite it would have been impossible to carry on, for in August they all had to close ranks against a taxpayers' strike strong enough to force a referendum calling for tax reductions and a $61-million tax ceiling by charter amendment. Because the ceiling would have destroyed months of fiscal planning by all interested groups and because Murphy suspected that the movement was an underhanded way of "wrecking our government," he fought their "tax muddling plan" without gloves. A glorified town meeting, as Ralph Stone said, was a treacherous way to decide complex issues of city finance.[28] That the movement was defeated by a 3-1 vote confirmed the mayor's salesmanship and his faith in self-government when "the facts are brought lucidly and vigorously before the people."[29] Yet victory at best merely preserved a shaky status quo. By late fall Detroit was at bedrock. The welfare fund was insolvent and the legal borrowing limit was reached. Twenty-one thousand families were receiving only bread and flour, and the only hope for unemployment relief was a RFC loan through the state. Tax delinquencies soared to 36 percent; now 2,500 public employees were on relief.[30] "The problem can no longer be solved by governmental economies," Murphy wrote Theodore Roosevelt, Jr. "That job has been completed in Detroit and is now behind us." For municipal solvency as well as relief, there was "no way out" except emergency federal help.[31]

Murphy's agitation thus turned to federal aid to municipalities as "a second string in the bow."[32] Though the first winter had convinced him that direct federal aid to the unemployed would be necessary to keep cities from going under, it took the financial crisis of 1932 to galvanize him into action on behalf of municipal finance itself. Because

Detroit was a center of public welfare policy, Murphy was consulted frequently by liberals and municipal officials over the country as pressures began to rise for federal aid. Exchanges of ideas and support, including Mayor Hoan's proposals for a national conference of mayors, had already started among the officials of large cities in late 1931.[33] In response to Detroit's budget battle the following spring, Murphy took the initiative by organizing mayors' conferences, first in Michigan and then nationally, to crystallize support behind a three-point scheme of federal aid—a five-billion-dollar "prosperity loan" for public works, direct unemployment relief, and RFC refunding loans to municipalities.[34] "Innate constitutional courage" was required to call "a roomful of mayors together," Mayor James Walker of New York quipped at the first meeting in Detroit in June 1932. The gathering, which was modeled after Senator Norris's Conference of Progressives the year before, was so well rigged by composition and agenda that the doubts of Mayor Bright of Richmond, whether it was time to throw themselves onto national charity, were drowned in the chorus demanding federal aid. Even Father Coughlin's closing prayer echoed the refrain. Said Murphy: "We are here to say . . . that something worse than a cyclone or an earthquake has hit the large American cities—our people are hungry. . . . We cannot sit supinely by and wait for economic laws to operate magically into a solution. It is entirely within the power of enlightened human intelligence to ease and justly distribute the load, thus hastening the work of reconstruction and restoration. . . . This is a crucial moment in the Nation's life. . . . It is not necessary for us to deliberate at length. We have but one objective—help to our people, which only the Federal Government can give adequately."[35]

In June Murphy carried the mayors' memorials, which then emphasized unemployment relief, to President Hoover. Upon rebuff, he started organizing on a stronger basis, with Paul V. Betters of the American Municipal Association and Mayors Hoan and Curley offering solid support. Their emphasis also shifted to refunding. "If the R.F.C. can assist the corporate banks, railroads, and insurance companies," Murphy remarked, "it ought to be available to aid the corporate cities."[36] For by Christmas Detroit was at the end of its rope. Tax delinquencies continued to increase and the city averted default only by tax advances from large manufacturers. Payrolls could not be guaranteed beyond January, and all a welfare client had "to keep body and soul together" was 14 cents a day. The time had come, said Murphy, "when the very existence and integrity of government is at stake." In late December of 1932 the Governor called a special session of the Legislature to pass enabling legislation for the emergency sale of the city's tax bonds. But as this legislation passed quietly, Detroit banks started a national panic, and the country slumped into the darkest economic decline in its history.[37]

To Murphy, the banking panic was "the last straw, the final factor." Unable to draw payroll checks Detroit resorted to scrip, the symbol of financial weakness. The move was just as well, however; only enough cash for February payrolls was on hand. Convinced now that even welfare could not tap the tax budget, the mayor focused pressure on Washington in earnest.[38] In February 1933 he organized the first meeting of the National Conference of Mayors as a permanent interest group representing larger cities. After his election as president of the Conference Murphy made it plain that cities demanded more than unemployment relief. They were asking for RFC refunding loans to prevent municipal collapse. "The quicker Congress realizes the problem the cities of America are facing," he said, "the better."[39]

Bypassing the lame-duck President, the mayors went before the Senate Banking Committee to agitate for future legislation. With Senator Couzens by his side, Murphy put his troubles on the line. "We are trying to keep Detroit from defaulting," he declared. "Detroit has done everything possible to help itself." It had cut the budget 28 million dollars, fired 10,000 employees, made three wage cuts, and drastically cut relief costs. But "the enormous debt charges of the cities and the tax delinquencies, which now reach 40%," the mayor said, "are crushing us. In Detroit the debt charge represents 67 cents out of every tax dollar. The vast burden of destitution is further crushing the citizens. The city is strapped." The state could not help; it faced an "enormous deficit" of its own. "If the Federal Government won't help us, we don't know where we can turn."[40] Private, local, state limits all had been reached. Plainly, crisis was at hand. Fearing the worst, Murphy secretly hired a law firm to prepare federal municipal debt moratorium legislation as a substitute for "the present drifting into default all over the country."[41]

II

Murphy's specific proposals appeared to be lost in the welter of programs launched by Roosevelt's brain trust in the first 100 days, but he had won the fight. The federal government assumed the major burden of unemployment relief; in 1934 Congress enacted a Municipal Debt Adjustment Act based on the proposals and the lobbying of Detroit's legislative team. Though Murphy believed that the final legislation favored creditors unduly, and though the Supreme Court struck down the statute, which was successfully reenacted, his influence thus extended beyond relief to municipal finance.[42] During his second term as mayor, Murphy not only became one of the leading champions of unemployment relief, he also became a friend of Franklin D. Roosevelt, and in that relationship the cause of the cities found a strategically placed friend.

Whether by shrewd design or Irishman's luck, Murphy's appointment of G. Hall Roosevelt as city controller proved a decisive step in his career. Hall Roosevelt was a nephew of Theodore Roosevelt, a brother of Eleanor Roosevelt, and a distant cousin of the man destined for the presidency. Through Hall Roosevelt lasting connections formed between the Irish mayor of Detroit and the patrician governor of New York. While still mayor-elect Murphy inquired through Hall Roosevelt for Governor Roosevelt's advice on relief administration. When Roosevelt's advisers began to build a national organization, Detroit's liberal mayor seemed a natural leader for the Roosevelt forces in Michigan. As Hall Roosevelt explained to Franklin Roosevelt's aide, Louis M. Howe, the Michigan situation hinged on the mayoralty election. "If Murphy gets re-elected he can control the State Convention and the National Committeemen, and will go for Franklin in a big way."[43] The mayor's "tremendous Catholic influence" and his friendship with Father Coughlin, whose support Roosevelt was already courting, boosted Murphy's stock, while he in turn developed a "great admiration" for Roosevelt, his ideas, and his possibilities.[44]

At the mayor's request Governor Roosevelt helped remove the opposition of the Patterson papers in Detroit to Murphy's reelection in 1931. After a landslide victory the mayor's forces busied themselves in support of Roosevelt. "Now that you fellows have won," Louis Howe asked Hall Roosevelt, "isn't it time for us to get busy delegate collecting? We have done absolutely nothing in Michigan waiting for you people to say when to move!"[45] Actually the Roosevelt headquarters misjudged Murphy's organizational strength. By assuming that his prominence in Detroit entitled him to claim state leadership, they failed to perceive the segregation of party regulars and nonpartisan leaders that is typical in states with nonpartisan municipal elections; thus they relied on a political loner in no position to pull party reins. Outstate Democrats, many of whom resembled Republicans in social philosophy, mistrusted the mayor of Detroit. Though Murphy always remained loyal to party when the chips were down the electoral system inevitably weakened party organization in Detroit; and his flirtation with third-party insurgents at the Washington Conference of Progressives, not to mention policy and personality differences, gave state regulars ample cause to resent him as a maverick, "fair weather Democrat." Murphy actually became one of the few politicians from nonpartisan systems ever to achieve state and national leadership; but his relations with the state party organization, at best, were never stronger than ties of necessity and mutual sufferance.[46] In 1931 not even the Detroit faction was fully under his control. A near successful attempt by Judge Connolly and outstate allies to exclude him from the Michigan delegation to the national convention showed just how weak his party position was. Murphy's strength was specialized; he was a leader of urban minorities and a mass evangelist. After the nomination Roosevelt forces leaned more heavily on regular party structures for statewide organization, while leaving Detroit, Coughlin, and evangelism to Murphy.

Murphy, in turn, was under some pressure, both in Michigan and from Al Smith supporters outside, to maintain an uninstructed delegation in the preconvention campaign. But while conceding that Smith was in many ways "the most fit man for President," he was "devotedly" for Roosevelt. "More than any of the others," he told Dudley Field Malone, Roosevelt bore "the plain mark of the Progressive essential to present leadership in the work of modification, restoration and reconstruction the Nation must embrace."[47] In Roosevelt, Murphy always saw a "deeply spiritual" streak and "a natural ruler of men." The effort to block an instructed delegation he dismissed as "simply an effort to thwart the will of the people."[48]

By April 1932 it was an open secret that, despite Judge Connolly's opposition, a combination of Democrats in Detroit and the northern peninsula had the upper hand. Father Coughlin, who had accompanied Murphy and Hall Roosevelt on one of their "social calls" to Hyde Park, was also ready by then "to speak out discreetly" for Roosevelt, while Murphy was inquiring how he could help propagate the news.[49] At the Saginaw party convention in April, the Detroit faction obtained only a first ballot instruction for Governor Roosevelt, but it was assumed by many that the Michigan delegation "would stay by him through thick and thin." "It is going to mean a lot to us," wrote James A. Farley. "We have this fight won, and we must not let it get away from us."[50]

To collect delegates for a nominating convention was one thing; to carry a "rock-ribbed Republican" state was another. Murphy "keeps pounding into me," Hall Roosevelt told FDR, that latent Roosevelt sentiment had to be crystallized at once, or states like Michigan would be lost. "We do not favor waiting for the nomination," he wrote. "There is no time to lose. . . ." Roosevelt clubs, they advised, should be started in the towns and the colleges; state political organizations should be captured and standardized; and above all, Roosevelt should throw aside personalities and go to the people "entirely on principles." The national crisis was "so extreme that humanitarian and economy considerations stand before all else. . . ."[51]

Perhaps the masterful Farley needed no advice from Detroit, but Murphy was convinced that the only way to capture Michigan was "with militant, crusading leadership and if the Party stands for progressive reforms." The only worthwhile election, furthermore, would be one that replaced an administration which had "failed dismally in leadership" with men devoted to "national reconstruction."[52] The implications for state politics also had to be considered. Murphy detected in the fall primaries "a complete turnover in political sentiment" in Detroit and Wayne County, which to him was "a pretty significant thing." The Democratic party was reviving in eastern Michigan after a generation of one-party rule; and he attributed the change to new faces and ideas. His own captaincy of the Detroit faction as well as his future hung in the balance. "A nice vigorous movement of young progressive Democrats will freshen the whole situation," said Murphy. "Nothing but good can come of it."[53/a]

Under the same old banners of political purity and social justice—and also as a passionate "wet"—Murphy sought to provide militant leadership in Michigan. His brother George organized Roosevelt clubs across the state. The mayor politicked among the minorities and municipal officials, and coaxed Catholics into line—a feat which Hall Roosevelt reminded Howe was "one on New York City."[54] After the fall primaries Murphy stumped the state accompanied by William Comstock, the gubernatorial candidate with whom he would soon be sparring over relief, and an entourage of carefully planted, pro-Roosevelt reporters. However much party professionals derided the show, Murphy surprised everyone by tremendous drawing power outstate. At a time when President Hoover was being booed in Detroit, the friend of the unemployed drew the largest political rally in the history of Flint. It was a rugged job; the last few days, as Roosevelt said, were "hectic." But it was superb politics. Democrats captured Michigan's electoral votes for the first time since the GOP was born in 1852.[55]

---

[a] Murphy had his supporters for the vice-presidential nomination in the preconvention campaign, but he denied interest with the remark: "But why bury me in the vice presidency?" FM to Morrison Shafroth, April 8, 1933, Box 11. Also FM to Walter White, Feb. 11, 1932, Box 11, BHC.

Murphy was elated at the outcome. "The beauty of a democracy," he wired Roosevelt, "is that when a great leader arrives the people recognize him as they recognize you. God grant you strength in the huge task ahead." "It has been our inning," he also mused privately; "I am hoping it is something more than a change in the official life of the country and will freshen every phase of social and economic life."[56] As one of the early preconvention supporters, he also was due a rich reward. In the scramble for appointments, Raymond Moley apparently favored him to head the Federal Trade Commission, but Murphy held out for more. "Unfortunately," as Hall Roosevelt informed FDR, "he can hardly abandon his present job without the prospect of real responsibility and has his heart set on the Philippines." It was in character, both for Murphy and the spoils system, that his first interest and only contact with the Philippines prior to the election had been a meeting with the incumbent Governor General, Theodore Roosevelt, Jr., while serving as the host to an American Legion convention in Detroit. The challenge of nation-building in Asia apparently appealed to his romantic imagination. Although Homer S. Cummings had been promised the job, the death of Senator Walsh, who was slated to become Attorney General, settled the matter. Cummings was appointed Attorney General and Murphy was named to the Philippines post, the government's third most lucrative position and one that had been filled in the past by a string of luminaries such as General Leonard Wood, William Howard Taft, and Henry L. Stimson. At 43, Murphy was the youngest of the lot.[57]

Announcement of his appointment in April 1933, though greeted generally as being deserved, left Detroit in midstream. The sudden swing in intraparty balances after his departure was one barometer of how personal had been his leadership. The financial situation, moreover, deteriorated as the city struggled to meet payrolls and to avert collapse. Murphy's last act as mayor, while setting the budget for the coming year, was urgent agitation among New Dealers for a municipal debt moratorium.[58] Eventually Detroit managed to refund its debt, but not before it defaulted one series of water bonds a month after he left.[59] Emergency measures, during the changeover of administrations, did not come in time. Resentment thus rose in Detroit that the mayor was deserting the "Murphy Muddle," though a few expressed belief that his $18,000 Philippines salary was money well spent in getting him out of town.[60] Still, when he left in May, it was apparent that Murphy enjoyed broad popular support. The Detroit Federation of Labor made him an honorary president; and 10,000 people, from Edsel Ford to numerous girl friends and emissaries from Fisher Lodge, gathered at Olympia Gardens to give him a royal sendoff. In bidding them goodbye Murphy confessed that "this isn't exactly the moment of dew and sunshine. . . ." Major problems were ahead for Detroit. The city had to keep "a clean, honest government," one that served humanity "in its every aspect"; and somehow it had to be saved from "economic breakdown."[61] The budget riddle had not been solved.

There is no doubt that Murphy's relief policy aggravated Detroit's financial crisis. In the absence of alternative social security systems the effort to sustain a depressed population by more than twenty million dollars in municipal relief helped to break the bank as it broke new ground. Because its scale was novel and unbearable, and because the recognition of public responsibility was overt, the relief policy created an ideological divide. As the champion of the public principle, Murphy was carried by sheer financial shockwaves along traditional steps of successively higher units of government until he became a leading voice in the cry for the welfare state. The time had come "for a reckoning with this chaotic social and political order," he declared. "We are on the threshold of an era during which we must study and perfect the means by which government may be put once more at the service of humanity. . . . This is no sentimental duty. The rock upon which our government is built is justice—not pity—and these are matters of justice."[62]

Through the politics of reform Murphy jumped into the forefront of Irish politicians who first broke into national prominence in his generation. He also became one of the few Irish Catholics identified with the New Deal's militantly liberal wing. Yet as the smoke cleared from the ideological battle, it is important to distinguish him from stereotypes. In the first place, Murphy's welfare programs were combined with budgetary orthodoxy, clean government impulses, and radical rhetoric. The gap between talk and practice was considerable. Second, while his greatest voting strength came from Catholics and ethnic minorities, his organized allies were not then labor unions, which were weak, but veterans groups, the Hearst press, and the social action elements of churches, *e.g.*, Father Coughlin. Murphy therefore was valuable to the national administration, despite his weak party base in Michigan, precisely because he served as a useful bridge to forces later identified with the Right. Finally, the relief policy was a scapegoat for a much larger fiscal problem. Relief aggravated that problem, of course, by increasing the burden of debt, especially during the frantic initial rush to fill a vacuum of need. But the essential problem, in Murphy's words, was "financing our debt service and keeping pace with the inability of taxpayers to pay their taxes."[63] For this reason, he always vacillated between two poles in assessing his Detroit administration. Was the chief contribution relief or retrenchment? The economy plan, after all, enabled the city to cut operating expenses from $76 to $48 million while tax delinquencies rose from five to 40 percent and the tax base shrank by over one-third. The mayor may have been forced into retrenchment reluctantly; but as controller Chester E. Rightor said, "the record of expenditures requires no defense."[64]

The basic achievement was the blend. Under conditions ripe for explosion and social upheaval, Detroit held onto relief, credit, and confidence in democratic processes when others fell. Mistakes were made, particularly administrative ones, but there is reason behind the belief, which some New Dealers still hold, that Murphy never again matched his performance when depression hit Detroit. For he perceived the issues as the future would, and he approached them with a pragmatism that his rhetoric belied. The municipal government of Detroit, for all its groping, was one of the few islands of sanity in the middle of confusion. That this could have happened in Detroit, of all places, was muted evidence of leadership. So was its quick passage through the convulsion over the principle of public relief. In 1940, when Murphy noted Republican party policymakers embracing the principle of federal responsibility for relief, he observed to Claude G. Bowers: "I could not help thinking back eight years or so to the hectic days in Detroit when that principle was pretty much heresy. But such is progress under the democratic system, and in spite of all the conditions that are still so heart-breaking, how thankful we all should be that in America change comes this way—by peaceful evolution—and not by bayonets and bullets!"[65]

In Detroit Murphy arrived with much unfocused ambition and sentiment to do good. He left it with his political principles sharpened and his political foundations identified, no longer with the agrarian Progressivism which gave them root, but with a new liberalism which expressed urban interests. Championing minorities became his "mission" and government his profession. "Public service is a ministry," he declared—"a life's vocation."[66] The rest was exposition as he went upward and onward with his "destiny" and the New Deal.

CHAPTER 4

A LITTLE NEW DEAL IN THE
ORIENT, 1933-1935

MURPHY became Governor General of the Philippine Islands at a critical turn in their development. A combination of domestic and international conditions produced a
situation so "fraught with grave possibilities for trouble" that his appointment, which came after little consultation and much turnover in
the post, filled some American specialists with foreboding.[1] "I have
known Murphy for years," his former professor, Joseph Ralston Hayden, commented; "it is an outrageous travesty upon every principle of
good government and sound judgment that he should have been sent
out there."[2] The new governor was a "well meaning and delightful fellow," Hayden conceded; he also was close to the President, imbued
with "the most honest (and naïve) intentions of serving his country,"
and had "superb gifts for the great Irish game of politics." The professor even predicted that Murphy would be popular in Manila—but for
the wrong reasons. To govern a possession in the throes of an independence movement and subject to Japanese pressures, Roosevelt was
sending a politician of no great intellect, no knowledge of Asia, and
accompanied by an entourage from Detroit no better prepared than he.
"The whole performance," said Hayden, "is fantastic!"[3]

The misgivings of experts were justifiable. Talented though Murphy
may have appeared, prior experience had not equipped him for the
problems which gripped America's island empire. The Philippine
Islands, despite nationalist propaganda, were not yet a well-integrated
nation. Instead, they were an archipelago of 7,000 islands, mostly un-
inhabited, and stretching 1,000 miles from Formosa to Borneo, that
contained a large diversity of races, languages, and religions, including
a half-million tribal pagans. Three decades of American colonial rule,
despite the millions spent, had made no great dent on Filipino social
structure. Americans merely added another layer onto an indigenous
Malay culture already stamped by centuries of Chinese, Japanese, and
above all Spanish influences. Filipinos made notable advances in health,
education, and political development under American colonialism;
their population doubled between 1900 and 1930, and they had the
highest literacy rate (30 percent) in Southeast Asia. Yet they had little
need of the public relief policies Murphy had championed in Michi-

gan.[4] Theirs was a tropical rather than an industrial economy. Depression had passed them by.

The Philippines, more than anyone cared to admit, were highly underdeveloped. Though the Islands had three times the arable land of Japan, whose size they approximated, vast acreages went uncultivated. The budget and bureaucracy of the central government were smaller than Detroit's.[5] Farming, fishing, and handicraft virtually monopolized the gainful occupations. All but five percent of the 13 million inhabitants lived from tropical agriculture; all but 15 percent were peasants intensively cultivating plots averaging less than four acres per family. Americans had inaugurated a land reform program by the purchase and resale of Spanish church estates and had stimulated agricultural production by free trade policies. But the prime beneficiaries were American businessmen and a native landowning elite. The overwhelming majority of Filipinos were tenants trapped in the *caciquism* and the rural usury endemic to all Asia. Americans also had permitted Filipinos to develop state-owned enterprises such as hotels, banks, railroads, and a development company in lieu of scarce private capital. But Filipino industry was predominantly household handicrafts.[6] Two simple figures tell the tale. In 1934, less than 3 percent of the student population in the first grade finished high school. Per capita income in 1930 was $30 a year.[7] Poverty, not depression, was the basic economic condition. Development, not unemployment, was the central economic concern. The problems of government in Manila were about as close to those in Detroit as Zamboanga to Hamtramck.

Because foreigners had overrun the Islands for centuries, the Philippines were a crossroads of East-West cultural contact. Filipino political and religious practices, as a result, resembled some Latin American patterns. A political system based on personalities and familial ties, plus a deep-seated Catholicism as yet undiluted by anticlericalism, were enduring Hispanic influences which Americans habitually underestimated. The Philippines also manifested classic conditions of southeast Asia. Chinese residents controlled three-fourths of the credit system and merchant trade—and reaped Filipino hostility in the form of poorly enforced exclusion laws and occasional violence. An even more violent minority problem was Filipino conflict with the Moros, the marauding Muslims of Sulu province and the island of Mindanao, who posed serious enough problems of pacification for Americans, not to speak of their fate should colonial protection cease. After the Japanese conquest of Manchuria in 1931, moreover, Filipinos felt threatened by Japan, a problem symbolized by the agricultural settlements in Davao, which provided not only a springboard of imperialist pressure, but also a model of successful tropical colonization that Americans found difficult to match. For United States colonialism was not exempt from a fundamental Western trait: colonial influence was strongest among the upper classes and around the capital. Except for schools and sanitation, American administrators scarcely penetrated the Filipino *barrios* and back-country. The business-minded administrations of the 1920s made no attempt to overhaul the social system that retarded modernization; the opportunity presented in the New Deal period came too late. Americans were preoccupied with depression at home, and Filipino leaders with politics. Independence, if only as a talisman of internal political rivalry, was the burning issue of the hour.[8]

Apart from health and education measures, the chief American legacy was political development. A natural prey of Japan if the United States withdrew, the Philippines boasted the strongest and best led nationalist movement in Southeast Asia. Filipino nationalism, concentrated initially in an elite class, had the advantages of antedating American conquest and of encouragement by American political goals. Ever since President McKinley had knelt to pray for guidance before taking the Islands in 1898, Philippines autonomy had been a fixed national commitment. President Wilson asserted that Americans regarded themselves "as trustees acting not for the advantage of the United States but for the benefit of the people of the Philippine Islands. Every step we take will be taken with a view to the ultimate independence of the Islands. . . ."[9] Strategic and business considerations, it is true, qualified the independence objective in practice—on both sides of the Pacific. The whole history of Philippines independence is one of equivocation and cross-purpose before the strategic and economic realities of the enterprise. Neither side was willing to cut the tie until the Philippines were economically stable and strategically secure. Both sought a special relationship, the precise nature of which eludes them still.[10] Political ideology, nevertheless, strongly influenced both from the start. Filipinos demanded independence even as they feared it; Americans committed themselves to the principle of a self-liquidating empire; and both displayed an almost innocent eagerness about exporting democracy to the Orient.

The objective of political democratization was also qualified in the Filipino environment. The priority of economic development, and the concentration of indigenous leadership among aristocrats, ruled out a serious attack on the land tenure systems and the great social inequalities which impeded democratic growth. Institutional arrangements, furthermore, had to be adjusted to traditional political mores. Early American governors, as Newton D. Baker confessed, had found it necessary "practically to bribe" the Filipino Assembly launched by William Howard Taft.[11] Still, the same condition was not unknown in state legislatures at home. Nor could Filipinos be accused of failure to develop leadership cadres in the freer political climate provided by the Wilson administration. The Jones Act of 1916, following the twin objectives of independence and political democracy, pledged autonomy "as soon as a stable government can be established" and laid the basis for Filipino self-rule. While retaining an American chief executive, who possessed formal powers greater than were normal in the United States, the Act established universal male suffrage, an all-Filipino legislature, and the guidelines for progressive "Filipinization" of the bureaucracy. It is still debatable whether the Harrison and Wood administrations, which symbolized the issue, "Filipinized" too rapidly or too slowly. American administrators seemed perpetually torn between competing objectives of professional proficiency in the bureaus manned by themselves and Filipino political control.[12] It is also debatable whether Filipino political parties developed beyond the one-party factionalism customary in nationalist movements of today. But within a decade after the passage of the Jones Act it was obvious that a younger generation of Filipino leaders was progressing rapidly in political maturation.

Implementation of the Jones Act, on the one hand, provided sufficient confidence in American intentions that leading Filipino nationalists ruled out revolution as a practical or necessary alternative. Their political skill developed so well, on the other hand, that after a breakdown in Filipino cooperation with the Wood administration American governors found it impossible to function without working through their legislative leaders. The secret of successful insular administration, as Henry L. Stimson demonstrated when he set the custom of appointing department heads from the Legislature, was "government by indirection."[13] In that subtle relationship, however, it was not always clear who governed whom. Filipinos were gifted at chipping away the authority of their colonial rulers, both in the classic ways of parliamentary powers of the purse and in the subtle Asian game of "face." All governors general were on guard against it; but erosion continued anyway, mainly because the turnover of chief executives was frequent, because Washington support often failed them in the pinch, and because few wished to risk another impasse. Americans living in Manila generally believed it inconceivable that Filipinos could govern alone, in spite of contrary evidence at their own expense. The British, the

Dutch, and Filipino leaders all worried privately about the impact of American withdrawal on their colonial systems and on the Asian balance of power. But the hold of independence on the public mind was so strong by the 1930s that an indigenous movement to retain United States control was out of the question.[14] The pressures to grant independence in the United States were so strong that it is uncertain whether Americans would have kept control even if asked.

Through a crafty alliance of the noble and the ignoble—Filipino agitation and internal jockeying, American anticolonialism, racism, and farm-bloc pressures—Congress offered the Philippines an independence plan during the close of the Hoover administration. The Hawes-Hare-Cutting Act provided for complete separation after a 10-year transitional period in which the Islands would enjoy Commonwealth status. Under the Commonwealth, Filipinos would control all but their foreign and military affairs, subject to the intervention of the American President, who would be represented in Manila by a resident High Commissioner. Under the Commonwealth, Filipinos also would gradually come under American immigration and import restrictions, ostensibly to prepare them for separation from the United States. Hedging its bet, Congress retained title to military bases and authorized a glorified protectorate in case of financial default. Otherwise, in a decade Filipinos would be set free.

President Hoover, in a penetrating message vetoing the Independence Act, pointed to inescapable dangers in the Commonwealth plan. Besides its threatening strategic implications, the plan left the Philippines economy ill-prepared for the shock of swift separation. Thirty years of free trade had tied the insular economy to the United States as effectively as mercantilism. In the face of world depression and Japanese ambition, could Filipinos sustain their carefully nurtured system of "rising liberty" without continued American help? The alternatives facing an independent Philippines, as the *Louisville Courier-Journal* warned, were not liberty or death, but both.[15]

American political and economic policies had in fact long been contradictory. Although the United States made no attempt to sponsor a social revolution in the Philippines, its trade policy had powerfully stimulated insular economic development. Unlimited free trade after 1909, coupled with high tariffs after 1913, guaranteed Filipinos an open, protected market in the United States. In response, trade between the two countries tripled in two decades, new agricultural export industries rose in the Islands, and a relatively inefficient sugar industry was stimulated to the point that by 1932 sugar accounted for 63 percent of

Philippine exports and a third of the gross national income. Trade with the U.S. composed 87 percent of the insular total; Filipinos enjoyed a favorable American balance sufficient to cover other imbalances and to accrue substantial annual surpluses.[16] Much of the economic development and social progress of the Islands, in other words, derived from a subsidy borne by American consumers. But just as trade policy was viewed in the twenties as nearly "ideal as such things can be made," so in future decades it loomed as an inhibiting paradox. While the United States was preparing Filipinos for political independence its economic policy made their economy as dependent as any colony on earth. While the United States was preparing Filipinos for political democracy, its economic policy intensified rural tenancy and usury, which spawned in turn an agrarian radicalism that harvested the HUK rebellion after World War II. And neither problem has yet been solved.[17]

In the 1930s the effect of trade policy on political independence was considered more important than internal social change. Filipino agricultural products were not merely dependent on a sheltered American market but potentially competitive with domestic crops and Cuban sugar. The independence issue, accordingly, became embroiled in American pressure politics in their rawest form. But the Independence Act of 1933, whether viewed as a cruel bargain or as an effort to reconcile the contradictions once and for all, could not resolve the Philippines question. Application of the tariff provisions of the Act, according to estimates of the American trade adviser in Manila, Evett D. Hester, would destroy 85 percent of total trade, as well as the sugar and new export industries, which in turn would produce a decline of 38 percent in central government revenues and the collapse of most banking institutions and provincial public finance.[18] No government could survive such catastrophic losses. The only alternatives, as Murphy himself informed Washington in December 1933, were either to cushion political independence with special trade relations, which would be difficult politically in view of most-favored-nation clauses and domestic pressures, or to postpone political plans until the Islands were economically weaned.[19] Nevertheless a Democratic Congress was in a warring mood, and powerful economic interests were smarting from depression and what they deemed to be Filipino competition. Pacifists and anticolonialist liberals joined isolationists in urging Filipino self-determination, and army generals urged withdrawal because they thought the Islands indefensible. No one was much interested in Winston S. Churchill's warnings that Commonwealth status itself would disturb a delicate South Asian balance of power. American independence *from* the Philip-

pines was as earnestly sought as independence *for* them. Soon after receiving Hoover's message Congress overrode his veto.[20]

The offer of deferred autonomy provoked sharp discord in the Islands. Independence had been the magic slogan of ambitious politicians
for so long that, even if some took to their beds in fear it might be
forthcoming, independence had become a great tidal movement none
could safely resist. Independence, as used and abused in Filipino discourse, also represented hopes for a taxless millennium as well as fulfillment of ideals fostered, yet frustrated by Americans themselves. But
this was independence with strings. Though the economic provisions
were probably as generous as could be expected, the offer precipitated
a power struggle among the leadership triumvirate of Quezon, Osmeña,
and Roxas, ostensibly over the military and immigration provisions of
the plan, while more radical groups agitated for "immediate, absolute
and complete independence" regardless of apparent risks. No major
faction would have gone to that extreme. Much of the controversy over
the terms of the offer was a smokescreen for Manuel L. Quezon's bid
for control of the Nacionalista party. Filipino opinion was so divided
over the issue, however, that even Manuel Roxas' congratulatory message to the new governor was viewed in the Islands as a veiled attempt
to lure his support of the Hawes plan, which Roxas and Sergio Osmeña
had negotiated. The political situation in Manila was complex and
tense.[21] Frank Murphy was taking office just as fateful decisions were
being made about American Far Eastern policy and Philippine independence.

II

When Murphy sailed into Manila in June 1933—eager, expectant,
and essentially ignorant—he made an instant hit.[22] Since the election of
1932 Filipinos had expressed concern over what the representative of
a professedly liberal administration would bring. President Roosevelt
already had indicated that during the domestic emergency his Philippines policy would be one of "no changes." But liberalism was in the
air, and Murphy arrived with an advance reputation as a reformer of
"broad humanity," whose very appointment Roosevelt had written
Filipinos, gave "ample evidence of my deep interest in your welfare."[23]
Though he described himself as "not a fanatic," the new governor was
a practicing Catholic in a predominantly Catholic country; and it took
the advice of Quezon, whose relations with the church were strained
after he became a Mason, to quash Murphy's idea of making his first
public appearance in the Manila cathedral.[24] If Murphy did not regard

the Philippines as another Ireland he talked as if he did. It mattered little that the revered champion of Filipino freedom, Emilio Aguinaldo, had been jailed for rebellion against American conquerors or that he was having trouble over land deals; Murphy hailed him as a revolutionary hero who "belongs to the world." It mattered little that feeling over independence was running high—that was "not difficult for one of Irish extraction to understand," he said. "I find the whole atmosphere one of comparative peace and gentleness compared with that at home."[25]

Openly idealistic and sentimental, the new governor revealed a temperament that appealed to Filipino hearts. His rhetoric and his "moral tone," his "attention to business and his lack of swagger," impressed them mightily. So did his refusal to follow his predecessor's limitation on social life. Manila was a gay and cosmopolitan capital in the 1930s, and Filipinos put great stock in celebration and *delicadeza*. The fun-loving Murphy fell into line with an extremely active social whirl among members of the diplomatic set and Filipino, American, and Spanish business elites. Not to do so, he maintained, was "unnecessary over-straining in high office." "The Roosevelts are all good stuff," he remarked to a foreign service friend, but "the more you take it simply and as a human being, the less burdensome it grows and the more effective you are. I have never been able to understand why so many men in exalted positions permit themselves to become separated from people and life unless it is born of an unconscious inferiority complex —we politicians never have that particular complex consciously."[26] Malacañan, the historic governor's palace in Manila, began to hum with evening revelry; and local news coverage of a somewhat dazzled Murphy clan in their palace rivaled the glamorous build-up by the *Detroit Times*.

In the Philippines Murphy was fortunate enough to find another environment suited to his personality, one that tolerated the contradictions between public and private life which prevailed throughout his career. Manila actually brought out the worst and best in his character. To begin with, the post encouraged his slipshod administrative practices. Late nights meant late risings as well as erratic office routine —and both habits grew. While Murphy inveighed Filipinos against each evil, Manila also stimulated tendencies toward nepotism and financial carelessness. In order that his sister Marguerite might serve as his hostess, for example, he put her husband, William Teahan, on the payroll; other members of his staff lived in the palace at public expense, even though they were not members of the governor's family. More serious was laxity in his handling of housekeeping appropriations, expense accounts, and discretionary funds. He took such full advantage of government perquisites, including an army-built steeplechase for his riding pleasure, that some considered it abuse.

Murphy appeared as a man of the people, moreover; but in reality he hated the humid climate, which aggravated his sinus problems, travelled relatively little, and left suspicions among servants that he feared to eat Filipino food. Although he worked successfully at setting an egalitarian public example, he hobnobbed with the rich and permitted the privileges of his "pro-consul" role to go to his head. Thereafter, Murphy commonly insisted on receiving the full honors due his post, as well as "franking" of hotel bills for himself and his entourage, much to the embarrassment of the aides who had to arrange details. And yet, despite his love of pomp and the panoply of office, he left a string of tales about broken protocol, social gaucheries, and amorous adventures in Manila which spiced the gossip of several capitals. The Governor General, it was said, would invariably arrive late to official functions and might even arrive at a dinner party in sweaty riding attire. The Governor General, it was said, might fail to show up at his own parties and might not return from after-dinner strolls with a young girl in the garden while aides had to bid the important guests of honor adieu. Diplomats and Filipinos reared according to strict Spanish customs were scandalized by such behavior; even Americans were embarrassed by the rumors to which bachelor leaders are always prone. After all, it hardly fostered better relations when officials kept their daughters away from Malacañan dances for fear of what might happen with the governor during intermission.

Yet Hayden was right. Filipinos liked Murphy and he liked them. A warm and polite people, they tolerated his foibles even as they enjoyed the gossip. Perhaps more than most Americans, they appreciated the difference between a man's private life and his public performance. For Manila also stimulated the best in Frank Murphy—idealism, sympathy, and a contagious skill at exhortation. Because he arrived at the eleventh hour of American rule, there was less opportunity for concrete accomplishments than for explosive mistakes. Exhortation, plus avoidance of trouble, was about all that could be expected. Murphy excelled at preaching. Fascinated with the process of nation-building, and impressed by Filipino responsiveness to "progressive appeals and especially so to anything of a spiritual nature," he perceived that governing the Philippines was going to be "a comparatively easy task."[27] A self-styled Progressive had come to the Islands as a representative of a revived Wilsonian idealism and was playing the part to the hilt.

Murphy's immediate popularity did not rest on showmanship alone, however. Emotionalist rather than analyst, he had an intuitive grasp of Filipino political sensitivity and a graduated personal style that could hardly fail to win positive response. At rhetorical levels, his energetic idealism seemed to instill "new spirit" into old policy.[28] Even before his arrival, he had expressed fondness for Wilson's conception of the American "mission" in the Pacific. "The President has left me a clear field of action," he declared in ports of call. "I come with an open mind." "I am appointed by a liberal administration and whatever part I shall play will be in the interests of the people of the Islands."[29] Describing the Jones Act as a "great charter of human liberty," the governor made it plain from the start that he was an anti-imperialist. His inaugural address and first message to the Legislature, though actually stressing fiscal stability, created favorable impressions because they conveyed, as Manuel Roxas noted, "a new conception of social justice and of the social responsibilities devolving upon government."[30] As the first American governor to speak officially of independence and the social errands of government, Murphy exhibited to Filipinos a personal dedication and a moralistic attitude toward governing that opened doors to Malacañan.[31]

Like Stimson before him, Murphy pledged neutrality in Filipino politics. The decision over Commonwealth status, he announced in his inaugural, was a question solely for "your free determination, without interference and uncontrolled by any force or influence whatsoever." Attempts to "get me mixed up" in local politics, he added later, would be deeply resented.[32] Promises of sympathetic administration and of partisan neutrality reflected more than the demands of the occasion. They also meant more than abstention from policymaking. Murphy clearly sought to transform Filipino agitation over independence into constructive preliminary measures. No sooner had he echoed the taboo against participating in politics than he broke it to plead for a speedy decision on the Commonwealth issue, regardless of result. While no just and enduring settlement of such a question could be made without popular sanction, he lectured, factional bickering was dissipating the united energies needed to prepare for independence. Filipinos had to get down to the business of governing.[33]

Bold as it was, Murphy's plea for unity gave surprisingly little offense. Even though it may have aided Quezon inadvertently, his appeal dampened a divisive debate, and Filipinos took it as a token of an unwillingness to divide-and-rule that "ought to fill us with shame."[34] Apparently the man believed what had been official theory for years: the chief purpose of American administration was to speed the day of independence. Government should establish the economic conditions and the standards of responsibility that would sustain Filipino autonomy. All this had been said many times before, but Murphy conveyed conviction. As he wrote to his superiors in the War Department's Bureau of Insular Affairs, which administered the Islands, "the ability and capacity of the Filipino people to exercise self-government under democratic institutions have been proved and a stable government has been established. It only remains to establish economic conditions and arrangements under which an independent government could thrive."[35] Without discounting the difficulties, he considered his administration's primary objective the strengthening of the economic foundations of independence.

If that meant a little New Deal in the Islands, to Murphy they were one and the same. As one of a new breed of liberals, he could not divorce economics from politics. Nor did he disown the nation's long-term goals of independence and democracy in its own image. Murphy even magnified this dual responsibility by emphasizing the effect of the United States' example on colonialism at large. However hypocritical his generation might regard John Hay's "changeless truth" that "the free can conquer but to save," Murphy looked upon the Philippines as a giant political tutorial.[36] The challenges of America's record as a colonial power evoked in him all the fervor of a born crusader.

But it is important to recognize that Murphy in action was far from a wild American liberal espousing freedom for the natives. While expressing hearty "sympathy with the basic desire of the Filipino people for political independence," he displayed a pragmatism in practice that defied easy labels. For one thing, after a series of War Department briefings and a month's study aboard ship, he was determined to resist attrition of American authority—and for once Filipino leaders were forewarned that Washington would fully support him in that endeavor. Ignorance also bred restraint. "It would be presumptuous for me now, knowing comparatively little of the Philippines situation," he remarked after his appointment, "to express any opinion whatsoever." Besides, Murphy regarded himself as an agent of the policy his government already had set. Although he expressed "grave doubt" privately that Filipino freedom could survive the economic strains of the Independence Act, the policy was for Congress to make and the risk was for Filipinos to take.[37] Whatever their decision, his own job would be much the same. The first objective was to bolster the financial stability of the government and the second was to build mutual confidence for delicate transitions ahead. Only peripherally could there be social reform.

Thus while his public utterance rang with the philosophy of government responsibility for social justice, of making better societies and thereby "better men," Murphy actually began quite cautiously. The only surprises in his first legislative message were proposals for old-age insurance, indeterminate criminal sentences, and female suffrage. The bachelor governor thenceforth became a favorite of Filipino women, as elsewhere. Murphy clearly intended to have "a look around" before attempting fundamental changes. And that very restraint, which befitted both his own unfamiliarity with local conditions and the public preoccupation with the pending Commonwealth decision, was greeted in Manila as evidence of a graduated prudence that recalled the great governors of the past.[38]

Public restraint was matched by caution behind the scenes. In choosing personnel, Murphy atoned for his own inexperience by surrounding himself with experts. He took the advice of General Francis Parker, outgoing chief of the Bureau of Insular Affairs, by retaining the Malacañan staff intact and made appointments only to fill vacancies—Edward G. Kemp for legal adviser, Joseph E. Mills for finance, and Norman H. Hill and Eleanor Bumgardner for personal secretaries. For Vice-Governor General, who also was responsible for public health and education, he successfully supported the appointment of a Republican political scientist, leading Philippines specialist, and personal critic, Joseph R. Hayden.[39]

Murphy was so cautious with Filipinos at first that for once he even had to be reminded to cultivate the press. Wary of political infighting, he also was advised to build personal relations fast. "At present the Cabinet feels shut off from you," an experienced staff member, Louis J. Van Shaick, cautioned him. In the Filipino political system, it would be dangerous to address the Legislature without consulting party leaders or to permit the staff to interpose itself between the chief executive and Filipino cabinet secretaries. Insistence on formal prerogatives, as General Wood had discovered, was no substitute for a "fine accord" among men. With Filipino leaders, as with his first budget, Murphy felt his way. He parlayed inexperience into a fresh look. Filipino distraction over independence gave him time to study and make contacts. And gradually he built relations of goodwill and friendly spirit which he came to regard as "our greatest asset here."[40]

Fortunately a system of factional and personality politics suited Murphy's style. Fortunately, too, he and Quezon, the aristocratic Senate president then emerging as the foremost Filipino leader, got on well. American officials described Quezon as "an impulsive, dynamic man whose actions often have a large element of the emotional and the dramatic in them." Murphy added that Quezon was a proud and "supersensitive" nationalist. Except for an imperious quality which the falsely modest governor lacked, the description fit Murphy like a glove. Both men were jealous of their prerogatives and both understood that their positions as well as their personalities so commanded them to be. Both men were sentimental and affectionate with friends, and both tolerated the other's mercurial temper. Both were astute and magnetic politicians and both were intelligent enough to perceive their mutual ground in anticlerical Catholicism as well as their mutual political needs. Murphy admired Osmeña for his ability and fine character, but he supported Quezon because his support was indispensable. No American could have defeated him on his home ground. Quezon supported Murphy more than expected because of his closeness to Roosevelt and perhaps because it was to Quezon's advantage to inherit strong executive powers.[41] The cordiality that grew became an anchor in Filipino-American relations.

The basis of mutual confidence was visible from the start. Even before his arrival in Manila, Murphy had singled out Quezon for special attention, and Quezon reciprocated with careful advice. In the first meeting of the advisory Council of State, Quezon eased Murphy through the annual school crisis by proposing means to open public schools closed by budgetary shortages. In the second meeting Quezon proposed creation of a labor department from existing agencies, and the governor made the suggestion his own. Murphy in turn chastised the Cabinet for monopolizing meetings with patronage matters at the expense of attention to the "large cardinal questions of legislation, of economy and social justice." Slowly the content did change, if only in deference to his good intentions; gradually a subtle division of labor developed between the two leaders based on personal understanding.[42] In 1934, for example, Murphy accepted Quezon's nominations for the Cabinet according to custom but not until Quezon dropped those implicated in conflicts of interest—which of course was merely an oversight the governor had mentioned to avoid mutual embarrassment, etc.[43]

Sharing formal powers informally was a new experience to Murphy, one that called for considerable tact and patience. Yet he adapted with surprising agility. Within six months American observers in Manila were reporting to Hayden that Murphy was "among the best we have ever had." "The wild Mick has a genius for getting along with people." Since many of Hayden's informants were Protestant clergy, who of all Americans Murphy probably impressed the most, certain reservations were in order. Speaking generally, Murphy was not as popular with Americans in the Islands, who were often conservative and suspicious of New Dealers, as with the Spanish colony and Filipinos. Still, after arriving in Manila, Hayden himself concluded that the new administration was "almost unbelievably successful."[44] Where Stimson had impressed with the clarity of his vision, Murphy, functioning intuitively, operated with unusually sensitive antennae toward the pride of a people habitually treated as politically inferior. Having made "scarcely a misstep," Hayden reported, his former student was "still riding on the crest of the wave" of universal support. More important, he was holding his own in a subtle struggle for control. Murphy, as a colonial governor in a Filipino political environment, was "decidedly making good."[45]

Mass popularity was easy enough to explain. The combined support of Americans and Filipinos took some doing. Besides personality, the primary cause was a program, evolved after close analysis and consultation with Filipino leaders, which calmed American interests and which Murphy sold to Filipinos as necessary preparation for independence. The cornerstone was what he called "progressive economy." His administration was to demonstrate that fiscal stability and social service went hand in hand. If it also was designed to show voters back home that the ex-mayor of Detroit was no spendthrift, the bewildering budget riddle there had convinced him that a sound financial structure was the rock on which permanent social policy is built. To Murphy it was a "great relief" to head a government "unhampered by a crushing debt I had nothing to do with and unburdened by the colossal problem of unemployment"; but with reserves dwindling, and the future uncertain, he told the Council of State, "it is only prudence—sound judgment to err, if we are going to err, on the side of economy."[46] It did not require a Hamilton to perceive that a new nation had few hopes of survival without credit and financial reserves. Sound government finance was indispensable for independence. Retrenchment, accordingly, became Murphy's first priority.

"Fiscal integrity" became a crusade. With stubborn tact and a deft veto Murphy balanced the first budget, and produced a real surprise when it passed in mid-session minus the traditional pork-barrel that Quezon once argued was the *sine qua non* of Filipino politics. With the aid of Joseph E. Mills and insular auditor J. Weldon Jones, he centralized budget operations through executive order by establishing a monthly allotment and revenue report system, a five-percent reserve, and a freeze on programs, positions, and salary increases.[47] The pill was sweetened, to be sure. While Murphy refused to postpone property tax payments in his first real test of will, he always managed to divert sufficient funds to overcome the "recurring educational crisis" of unopened schools. Rather than oppose government businesses, as had General Wood, he sought to give them new life; and the able Mills, who bore this burden, too, taxed his health by returning them to the black. "Utmost economy," even here, was the theme.[48]

The administration was less successful with provincial and municipal budgets, the "critical zone" of insular public finance. It also failed to stabilize the income of public schools. The simple fact was that, even with a third of the budget devoted to education, revenue sources in the Philippines were unequal to demands for free public education through high school. Murphy's administration kept educational expenditures on a plateau during retrenchment, and school attendance rose slightly during his tenure; but his regime was not immune from the chronic pattern of opening schools by ad hoc improvisation.[49] Centralized budget control, nonetheless, as Murphy informed Senator Millard E. Tydings, "justified itself even beyond expectations." A longstanding trend of deficit spending, which his predecessor had begun to arrest, shifted to a small surplus in his first year and a 13-million-peso surplus in the next. Murphy left central government finances in excellent condition. Though he never said so, centralized control also gave him more immediate command of governmental operations than any chief executive had wielded before. Both sides could play the game of informal political leverage. Technical mastery of a centralized budget, a fairly new technique Murphy had learned in Detroit the hard way, gave him a decided advantage over Filipino leaders.[50] Quezon was heard to complain, with some justice, that Americans made him do what their own government failed to do.

Murphy likewise exploited the Governor General's position in the public limelight. When legislators occasionally griped about stinginess or centralization of public finance, he resorted to public scoldings with the maxim, "we are trustees, not proprietors of the public funds." When it became clear that Republican deficit would turn to Democratic surplus, he ordered his lieutenants "to put our best foot forward" by disseminating the news. Part of Norman H. Hill's routine duty was sending Murphy-related press clippings to Michigan newspapers. Should the fiscal achievements of the Murphy administration continue, reporters duly announced, they would "go down as one of the most significant if not spectacular in the Philippines' history."[51] As concrete accomplishments began to accumulate, Filipino press dispatches became almost embarrassing. Murphy, commenting on Filipino expressions of approval which he forwarded to the White House, told Marvin H. McIntyre: "I know it is extravagant and does me more than justice but I am forwarding it only as an indicator of sentiment. . . . [E]verything of this kind pleases me in so far as it leaves the President without worry about the Philippines." And the truth is that this was Roosevelt's standard too.[52/a]

III

A campaign to stabilize public finances was a far cry from popular images of New Dealism. But Murphy was one liberal with a quirk about budgetary orthodoxy. Sound fiscal policy, moreover, was only the start. Once government finances were stabilized in the first year, he unfolded a program of social services that in aggregate proclaimed his intention to leave a second major legacy to the Commonwealth—government responsibility for social welfare. "Human relationships must be given first place in our plans for the future," he told the Legislature in 1934. "We must build here a social, economic and political structure that will endure because it serves the fundamental human needs of the people as well as their material interests." For "good government" he ardently believed, was a "union of both head and heart"; it resulted only when "the desire for it becomes a passion and the demand for it a crusade."[53]

Passion was necessary perhaps because any attempts at social engineering faced massive obstacles. Fundamental American policy that insular government be self-sustaining, Murphy's own retrenchment priority, a political system unresponsive to agrarian masses, and a natural hiatus in new programming before impending constitutional change—all aggravated customary Asian lethargy toward social problems. Before needs of tremendous scope and what they regarded as a national psychology of inertia and indifference, experienced American officials felt deeply frustrated and helpless. The Governor General, they felt, grossly underestimated the force of the social customs he bucked. And some familiar with the finances of the question regarded his efforts as mainly

[a] The contrast with the federal budget did not go unnoticed in Washington. For the barbs of newsmen and the President's praise, see Roosevelt Library: President's Personal File: Press Conferences, V (March 1, 1935), 141-42. Also, *Washington Post*, March 15, 1935.

propaganda for home consumption. "If he is to live as a realist and not as a romanticist," Hayden observed at the outset, Murphy would have to realize that Filipino rather than American traditions would ultimately prevail.[54] But the very character of those traditions—the *pariente* system of clan charity and village nepotism, the dearth of governmental activities aimed at the poor—plainly discomfited him. As he spoke and toured the Islands Murphy insisted on committing the Commonwealth to public welfare services that would be the "most progressive in the Orient."[55] It was then that press agents began to speak of a little New Deal in the Philippines.

The program spanned a broad spectrum of Filipino life. Murphy's interest in legal reforms transformed the Philippines into a virtual laboratory to test his pet theories for "improving, modernizing and humanizing" the machinery of justice. Under his guidance Filipinos established juvenile courts, indeterminate sentences, and adult probation. The governor created a nonpartisan judicial council to recommend personnel and to watch over standards.[56] He sponsored studies to find means of accommodating Mohammedan and national law, and caused a stir by commuting all death penalties. He even managed to install a public defender system.[57]

Innovations in the legal system were combined with imaginative social experiments, ranging from "thrift gardens" and agricultural colonization in rural areas to pilot projects of slum clearance and urban resettlement in Manila. The government established a labor department and an eight-hour day for hazardous occupations. It jolted the city of Manila into completing a long-delayed water filtration system, building play-grounds in the slums, and improving conditions in the city sanatorium, which were considered "disgraceful."[58] It doubled the capacity of the insular psychopath hospital—which Murphy described in a staff meeting as a "medieval madhouse"—built the Islands' first facility for mentally afflicted children, and surveyed prison and leper colonies with a view to abolishing an "age old Spanish penology system," as the governor called it, and rationalizing leper segregation.[59]

Though welfare appropriations doubled, the quantity of work accomplished was pitifully small—and, to specialists, a distressing contrast with the governor's oratory. Concepts of foreign aid and directed social change in underdeveloped countries were over a decade away. Filipinos alone were unable to finance a social service system of insular scale, not to mention the critical need—an all-out war against rural poverty. American efforts in that direction, even had they been forthcoming, doubtless would have faltered before elitist control of the Legislature.

Within the limits imposed, however, what was done was impressive for the way in which it was done. The government program was carefully grafted onto existing operations to maximize the effect of scarce resources. It was a well-engineered piece of "government by indirection" and an effective union of political salesmanship with expertise.

Since they illustrate the mode of operation, two areas of concentration merit closer attention. The Moro problem, which was extremely complex because inner-Moro diversity and exploitation existed within a larger cultural-religious conflict, was, in Hayden's words, a "pretty sick baby" when he took office.[60] Killings and raids between the Moros and the Philippines Constabulary were on the rise; the 1920 jurisdictional agreement between the central government and the Sultan of Sulu was breaking down; and conflicts were rampant among government personnel on the scene. No one presumed to have a quick solution to achieve the ultimate goal of political unification without destroying the distinctive Moro religion and culture. But Murphy had been so impressed by Hayden's pleas in Detroit for an accommodation that would "stand the scrutiny of history" that he sought him for the vice-governorship and resisted requests for action until Hayden arrived. Then he gave the specialist a free hand. After Hayden formulated detailed plans for a "new deal in Moroland," Murphy backed them to the hilt, sold them to responsible Filipino officials who thus far had been bypassed, then mounted a public relations campaign in their support.[61]

To do so raised delicate issues. The plan, which concentrated power in the provincial governors, was formulated by an American having no official connection with the responsible Bureau of Non-Christian Affairs; it reversed past policies of power dispersal at the expense of Manila bureaucracies; and it reinstated as Governor of Sulu the controversial James R. Fugate, a Kentucky mountaineer whose methods of quiet conciliation, for all their unorthodoxy, reduced the clashes with Filipino police, stopped most cattle stealing, and transformed the area of Jolo in a few months from a place of terror to a region of relative security. Because the plan was at the expense of vested economic and bureaucratic interests, in other words, it required political sacrifices and risked a political struggle which Hayden had predicted no governor general would deem worthwhile.[62] But after watching the smooth sailing of the package in Cabinet meetings, and after finding his own office being transformed from an educational sinecure to second in command, Hayden ate his words about his former student. Scholar and politician, indeed, were effecting an ideal relationship in their posts. Hayden reacted with the exuberance of academics who brush against power. Murphy, he informed colleagues at home, was "thoroughly sound"—"in every way a big man." No governor, he told them, had made fewer enemies for better reasons, and none had more carefully upheld the dignity and authority of the United States. No politician in his experience was quicker to grasp the heart of a problem; no political scientist had thought more deeply or devotedly about government; and few men rivaled his political acumen, strength of character, and capacity for work. "From all of this . . . ," Hayden told his Michigan colleague, Jesse S. Reeves, "you must feel that I have 'gone Murphy.' I have!"[63] Close association with the governor, he observed later, gave him "a clearer and higher conception of public service—and of life." Sophisticated realist though he was, Hayden then believed that "Wild Mustard" Murphy was a misunderstood prophet worthy of the White House.[64]

Another example was the public health program whose guiding spirit was the army expert on tropical preventative medicine, Major George C. Dunham. When Murphy arrived in the Philippines, the public health service, as Dunham noted, was at "a very critical stage." Long priorities given to environmental sanitation and epidemic disease had eliminated ancient scourges. But Philippines health standards, though high for Southeast Asia, lagged a generation behind the West. The tuberculosis rate was triple that of the United States, and the infant mortality rate was double; an estimated 85 percent of the rural population had parasites and intestinal diseases; beri beri claimed an annual toll of 15,000 lives, which was merely one mark of widespread malnutrition. In 1933, as a result of recent studies and of reorganization in the Bureau of Public Welfare, the stage was set for the first time to reach poor families in the slums and outlying *barrios*.[65]

To Dunham, families were the crucial target. Beyond modest appropriations to the private Associated Charities and coordination of their work, American policy-makers had done little to replace the Spanish system of subsidized church welfare activities, which had been destroyed for the sake of higher secular policy. Public health authorities still stressed environmental sanitation and health education in the schools. The result, for all the improvements made, was that public health activity reached an insufficient proportion of the poor. Social services were concentrated in Manila, though the greater need was outside; and even in Manila social work was left mainly to private charities. Thousands therefore suffered and hundreds perished for want of elementary information and techniques well within the government's reach.[66]

The new Governor General, while appointing unemployment and rural improvement study committees soon after his arrival, did not appreciate the differences between American and Filipino social problems at first. But the reports of his own committees supported Dunham's theme. There was little unemployment in the Islands; the real enemies were low family income produced by rural tenancy and the loss of breadwinners in the cities. There was little hunger in the Islands; the real enemies were malnutrition and disease caused by ignorance and the lack of tools for self-help.[67] Neither was there a shortage of techniques to improve conditions in the Islands; the real enemies were attitudes of government inertia, upper-class laissez faire, and mass fatalism toward poverty. Propaganda in the public schools was not enough to change those attitudes. Only by reaching underprivileged families directly in the slums and the provinces could the ignorance and lethargy be overcome. So far, families had hardly been touched.[68]

Easily convinced, the governor embraced Dunham's expert proposals, sold most of them to Filipino leaders, and then prodded Dunham for action in areas like housing and relief organization which Murphy knew best. The immediate results were striking. The administration's public health activities not only gave the efforts of his predecessors a "tremendous forward surge," they set new directions.[69] For example the public health nursing service, begun in 1921, was enlarged and extended to the provinces—with "much greater success," Dunham reported, "than I had dared hope." Puerile-culture centers for maternal health, which had begun under private auspices, were subsidized and extended to provincial towns. "Health-social" centers, which were designed as integrated centers for social work, health, and recreational activities among slum families, were started in Manila and the major provincial cities. For the first time the Philippines government assumed responsibility for disaster relief from the Red Cross, and made token appropriations for unemployment relief as a symbol of public responsibility. The first slum clearance project in the Islands reached fruition; and in collaboration with the Rockefeller Foundation, half of an estimated million family latrines needed for minimal rural sanitation were built in a two-year span. Government responsibility for social welfare, a distinctly Western concept, was beginning to show results.[70]

Time and financial limits required that most projects be designed as models to set standards and to spark local initiative. Not many of them survived. The bill to extend public welfare organization to the provinces failed to pass the Legislature, which was a major blow.[71] The most ambitious plan of all—to use the proceeds from Agricultural Adjustment Act processing taxes for rural health and rehabilitation—which was evolved with the aid of Rockefeller Foundation experts and the sugar administrator, Thurman Arnold, floundered in conflicts among sugar producers, health authorities, and the U.S. Department of Agriculture before the Supreme Court delivered the coup de grâce. A desire to maximize immediate effects also reinforced the basic decision not to upset the land tenure system which was the root of agrarian troubles. World War II also wrecked the solid beginnings before they took hold. By postwar standards the results were so meager as to leave an impression that the 1930s was a period of stagnation and wasted opportunity.[72]

Murphy's little New Deal in the Philippines was indeed little. Within their limited means, however, the last-minute efforts of government social planners were important because progress in fact was made, because Filipino leaders including Quezon embraced the principle of public responsibility for social justice, at least for propaganda purposes, and because pilot projects demonstrated that something could be done to correct centuries of social neglect. For Dunham, the decisive catalyst was the Governor General's political leadership. The Murphy administration, he observed, brought "a new epoch in the public health and social progress of the Filipino people."[73] However meager in scope, the measures taken were the first concerted attempts to reach the Filipino underprivileged by use of government planning. It is also interesting that the principal instrument of American social engineering in the Philippines was the U.S. Army.

A fervor emanated from Malacañan which seemed to make the Murphy program more extensive than it was. No little part of his role, to the Governor General, was public education; and he supported his projects with a flamboyant personal crusade to uplift the individual Filipino's "spirit of social service," standards of integrity, and democratic restraint. A Murphy speech on these themes became half-sermon and half-lecture on elementary civics. A Murphy tour was half-inspection and half-"evangelistic campaign."[74] A Murphy brand of politics came to full flower in the Philippines: government was a ministry.

The governor challenged the national lottery as "a menace to our economic health and national character"—and lost. He sponsored an anti-usury drive. But for all Murphy's "pro-public" sympathies, even he balked at Hayden's suggestion of government-owned pawnshops as in Java.[75] He opened the palace to all comers, harangued the Constabulary about third-degree methods, and issued executive orders protecting free speech and assembly as a matter of right. The way to control volatile political gatherings, he wrote, was "to augment police protection rather than resort to the easy and (for officials) more convenient substitute of limiting and circumscribing the exercise of the fundamental rights."[76] Despite the sensitivity of the church-state issue, he upheld the secular principles of the Jones Act and supported the break-up of friar estates as sound policy. Murphy advised the Archbishop of the Philippines to invest church money abroad, rather than in local enterprises, to avoid identification with landlordism. He even backed a divorce law for the Moros. Still, he passed the buck when he could and used personal suasion to pacify clergymen offended by American secularism. His rather distant relations with the Archbishop notwithstanding, Murphy was a master at building clerical alliances, even when they embroiled him in clashes between strong-willed Catholic and Protestant missionaries.[77]

If his lectures on good government sounded banal to sophisticates, few doubted the governor was in earnest. "We seek to establish mass confidence and faith in the government," he asserted. "This is most important. Unless the people believe in the integrity of their government, they will not be loyal to that government."[78] That Murphy sought their personal confidence was obvious in his evangelistic techniques. That he found empathy was manifest in Filipino responses to his personality and his shrewd linkage of policy to preparation for independence. Filipinos considered Murphy not only an "honest, conscientious and competent executive," but among Americans their "best advocate" and "truest friend."[79] Within the limits of law and sound discretion, he plainly regarded himself as a sympathetic champion of another set of underdogs, a fact which they quickly perceived. "I was so anxious to do them justice," he told J. Weldon Jones in a characteristic lecture on American obligations. "As Governor General I conceived it to be my duty . . . to lean backwards in favor of obtaining for our friends in the Philippines their full day in court. We must not forget for a moment our trusteeship and I believe it to be only fair to bear in mind in negotiating every transaction between us, trivial or important, that on one side is our well-established nation with its vast power, resources and able representation and that on the other side there is a people just struggling to its feet. This viewpoint does justice not alone to our charges, in a sense, but also justly interprets the best traditions and ideals of our own country which was never conceived to be just a national organization for shrewd trading."[80]

"What a noble spirit!" Filipinos exclaimed. Here was the obverse of colonial exploitation, a foreign ruler whose major fault even they conceded to be "excessive sympathy" for them.[81] Similar criticism had greeted the beloved Francis B. Harrison in the Wilson era; but far from lapsing into financial weakness, the Murphy administration was credited with fiscal stabilization and social reforms that resembled the technocratic work of General Wood. At the same time, American authority was guarded with a dexterity that recalled Henry L. Stimson, except that Murphy could say "no" gracefully, as Quezon told the Secretary of War, while Stimson "always did it offensively."[82] In short, to Filipinos Murphy more than "merely governed"; he became a "source of inspiration." When Quezon declared that "the best governor we have had so far" was their choice for the first High Commissioner to the Commonwealth, the echo of approval made one conclusion inescapable: as a public personality Frank Murphy "won the Filipino people, body and soul."[83]

CHAPTER 5

A MONUMENT TO THE PRESIDENT,

1934-1936

MURPHY's performance as Governor General had instantaneous political effects. In Washington rumors rose that he would replace Homer S. Cummings in the Cabinet or oppose the Republican presidential aspirant, Arthur H. Vandenberg, for the Senate. The first possibility Murphy dismissed as "all hooey," but the second had some substance. After a long season out of power, the Michigan Democratic party was still "woefully weak," he told James A. Farley.[1] Detroit liberals and the faction headed by Governor William Comstock also had broken into an ugly patronage squabble. After the state patronage chief was implicated in scandal, importunings too strong to ignore confronted Murphy, especially from Detroit candidates, that he lead the state ticket in 1934, lest they all meet defeat. "The party needs you," as Giles Kavanagh relayed the changing tune, "much more than you need the party here."[2]

For all his professed desire to remain neutral in Michigan politics while Governor General, Murphy had kept his finger in the pie. He had backed "honest liberals" Arthur J. Lacy and George Bushnell as contact men for federal patronage before departing to Manila. Even though he disliked patronage fights—"I duck when I can"—he was unable to avoid involvement.[3] National party leaders frequently solicited his views about intraparty disputes, and he bore prime responsibility, along with Farley and Joseph P. Kennedy, for keeping Father Coughlin in line. Coughlin had never identified himself with Democrats as such, but New Dealers considered his radio broadcasts and Union for Social Justice vital sources of mass support. By 1934, Coughlin's allegiance to Roosevelt was showing signs of wear. Murphy corresponded regularly with the priest and his aides, Louis B. Ward and Arthur D. Maguire, and once even telephoned him from Manila (a big event in those days) in order to keep the fences mended. Coughlin, whose responses were increasingly vitriolic about the New Deal policy of aiding banks and Roosevelt's rejection of his inflationary doctrines, gave positive assurances of loyalty through 1934.[4] Still it was difficult to maintain from afar, and the honeymoon clearly was over. New Dealers could not expect support from both bigness-oriented reformers and populistic champions of social justice—the Longs, the Townsends, and the Coughlins—without deft maneuvering. Reluctantly the Governor General permitted Detroit Congressmen to explore with Farley and Roosevelt the possibility of drafting him for the 1934 Senate race.[5]

Murphy's political fortunes were rising in Michigan. The problems he had faced as mayor were better understood; his identification with Roosevelt and his well-publicized performance in the Philippines created favorable popular opinion. Polls and private soundings of his own produced a consensus that he was the only Democrat who could unite the party and defeat Vandenberg in an off-year election.[6] Equally plain, however, was Murphy's preference, which he stated to Roosevelt, "to complete my work unless you desire otherwise." "The orderly completion of our stewardship and careful preparation of the new government," he told the President, "as well as our policies of goodwill, fiscal integrity and social progress require an uninterrupted effort if possible."[7] It was common knowledge that American-Filipino relations had suffered from frequent changes of chief executives—the Commonwealth transition period was no time for another. "We are trustees as I see it," Murphy explained to Michigan friends more informally.[8] "There is a decidedly complicated situation to adjust and the Filipinos need an understanding and sympathetic friend and guide. This is the role I am cast for just now and I must play it. . . . I would feel like a deserter quitting in a crisis if I resigned, except, of course, on one condition. If the President so orders it. I'm a good soldier, and will go. But not otherwise."[9]

Roosevelt, while expressing a wish that Murphy "could be in both places at the same time," refused to intervene in a state contest. The Governor General thus remained in Manila. A relieved Senator Vandenberg, with whom he enjoyed friendly personal relations, observed to Murphy:

It would have been very unfortunate if your tenure had been interrupted at this critical moment in Philippine history. Everybody agrees you would have been by far the strongest Democratic nominee for the Senate against me— and perhaps I cannot entirely disassociate self-interest from these comments. Nevertheless I do have the conviction that you have followed the course of duty in clinging to your Philippine adventure. If the Philippine independence movement succeeds, you can build yourself a monument in the Far East which will be infinitely greater and more lasting than any of us can hope to build through mere service in the Senate.[10/a]

---

[a] Years later, Murphy vainly claimed that "even the President sent me a cable to Manila importuning me to run for Senator at that time. I did not believe it was consonant with our relations with the people in the Philippine Islands. The Governor-

The personal confidence Murphy enjoyed in the Philippines proved to be of no trifling importance for the smooth transition to the Commonwealth. In 1933-34 the independence drive took another unexpected turn. At Quezon's instigation, the Philippines Legislature had rejected the Hawes plan as "unworkable," repudiated the Osmeña-Roxas leadership, and dispatched a new mission under Quezon to negotiate another Independence Act. Preoccupied with domestic emergency, the Roosevelt administration resisted pressures to sponsor trade and immigration revisions, and in spite of an intensive Filipino publicity campaign through Roy Howard's newspaper chain, Quezon faced up to the fact that fundamental changes were politically unfeasible.[11] Because a special mission to Washington was unnecessary to make that discovery, the objectives of the Filipino leader were suspect. To insiders, Quezon appeared to be either of two minds or playing a double game. While pressing the independence theme for party control and public consumption, he was privately advancing the alternative of dominion status to reconcile Filipino self-determination with economic and military vulnerability. While admitting to Senator Hawes that, from the American viewpoint, the only change sought was elimination of army bases, Quezon even then was working on a defense plan with his close American friend, army chief of staff Gen. Douglas A. MacArthur, who almost alone among army strategists believed the Islands could be defended, a belief premised on American reinforcements. Did Filipinos want independence or not?[12/b]

General should not just be a political football so I wired the President to that effect. At that time the New Deal was on the rise. I had been Mayor of Detroit. I had been greatly publicized. I have no doubt that I could have beaten Vandenberg by 250,000 votes. Frank Picard, who was practically unknown, only lost to Vandenberg by eight thousand votes. So you can see what the former Mayor of Detroit and Governor-General would have polled." FM to George Murphy, April 30, 1947, Box 122.

[b] Quezon swung back and forth between alternatives throughout the 1930s, and used the strategy of veiled threats in order to win commitments from the United States. One unsigned letter to Murphy in 1936 regarding Japanese penetration of Davao was typical of his efforts to obtain American reassurances. There he took the position that the United States was the only great power which could be trusted to share in economic development of the Islands. Should Americans withdraw after independence, Filipinos would have no choice but economic cooperation with Japan, while preserving as much of their vital interests as diplomacy would allow. The choice was odious, of course, but the Philippines could not go it alone. A Japanese sphere of influence was preferable to a Japanese invasion. While recognizing that no administration could bind future Congresses, Quezon recommended a trade relations act or occupation of a naval reservation as a signal of American intentions. President of the Philippines to FM, May 5, 1936, Box 35.

American intentions, for that matter, were no freer from ambiguity. A strange congressional alliance of isolationists, pacifists, anti-imperialists, and economizers produced overwhelming sentiment for a clean, if not an accelerated break. The executive branch, on the other hand, equivocated before the economic implications and a prolonged interagency conflict over Asian strategy. The Quezon mission and Japanese declarations about nonrenewal of the Washington naval treaties, which had frozen the fortification of Pacific possessions, touched off a lingering conflict over American military commitments in the Philippines. The gist of the argument was that the navy wanted to keep its bases after independence; the army favored withdrawal because the Islands were thought indefensible and American presence an invitation to Japanese attack. The army-navy dispute was eventually compromised in war plan Orange, which coupled defense of key Philippines bases with reinforcements from Hawaii in the event of Japanese invasion. The two services ultimately reversed their positions, however, and the State Department seemed to have greater interest in trade policy than in issues of appeasement or defense. To put it mildly, coordination among the three principal agencies was poor. Facing a determined Congress and a divided bureaucracy, the White House resisted a showdown over Philippines policy as long as it could. The wily Quezon perhaps could be pardoned for hoping that more was to be gained from a benevolent but indecisive American government.[13]

After a series of quiet compromises, Congress enacted a new independence statute, the Tydings-McDuffie Act of 1934, which provided that army bases would revert to the Philippines after independence but which postponed the naval base and tariff issues to future negotiations. Whether the amendments materially altered the original plan, "only a Solomon could decide."[14] Whether the new Act was "just as bad as the old one from the standpoint of both parties," as Theodore Roosevelt, Jr. thought, the essentials of the Commonwealth plan remained unchanged.[15] President Roosevelt overcame Filipino misgivings by pledging to iron out "imperfections and inequalities" in the future.[16] His assurances, in effect, gave promise of those special relations to cushion political separation which President Hoover, fearing Japan, Congress, and responsibility without control, had refused to give. What Quezon may have lost in formal concessions, he gained in personal power and informal commitments. Quickly he obtained a special session of the Legislature to approve the T–M Act, a move Murphy supported. The governor called a convention to draft a constitution for the

Philippines, which by the terms of the Act would require approval of the President of the United States and the Filipino people in plebiscite.

Throughout the hauling and tugging over Commonwealth arrangements, Murphy conceived of his role as an honest broker between contending factions in the Islands and between Filipinos and the United States. Compared to a few members of Congress or to Quezon, whose knowledge of congressional politics vis-à-vis the Philippines was infinitely superior, Murphy played a subordinate part in the development of public policy. By virtue of his office and his ties with Roosevelt, he was in a position to influence but never to control basic choices. As one of many actors in a vast decision-making network, he could support and occasionally block the initiatives of others. But in the main, he viewed his job as primarily administrative and took for granted that his role was to implement the policy guidelines set by others.

Such a role not only produced a sharp contrast between private and official utterance, but called for considerable diplomacy on the part of a governor general who had serious doubts about the Commonwealth scheme. It also meant that his influence increased by increments as policy unfolded in practice. As a newcomer, Murphy had little opportunity to influence the infighting over the Hawes plan or passage of the Tydings-McDuffie Act. During the Filipino debate over the first Independence Act, he attempted to moderate factional disputes while remaining "scrupulously neutral." Although his plea for quick decision appeared to favor Quezon, Murphy actually tried to discourage new approaches to Congress and to encourage the two factions to conduct a plebiscite over the Hawes plan as a means of burying the hatchet. When that effort failed in a last-minute dispute over framing the question, he interpreted the Legislature's decision as a bona fide refusal to accept independence under suicidal conditions. He then urged Washington officials, "realistically and with mutual confidence," to cooperate with the Quezon mission in modifying "economic policy along lines that would tend rationally toward economic independence"—even if the price was postponement of political plans. Economic preparation, he argued, had to come first.[17]

Even though Congress rejected the advice Murphy defended the second Independence Act as evidence that a colonial power had "kept faith" with a dependent people—and he meant it, too.[18] Yet the more he was drawn into implementing the Tydings-McDuffie Act the more his idealism was tempered by the realities of the situation. Personally his views were a hybrid of the diplomat's emphasis on economic adjust-

ments and of the pacifist-anticolonialist preference for disentanglement
from the Orient and appeasement of Japan. He agreed with that part of
Quezon which advanced dominion status, or at least a longer probationary period, as the ideal solution.[19] He took as given the administration's policy of maintaining the status quo in Pacific armaments in order not to provoke Japan or Congress—it was difficult to say which
was feared most. He also accepted the administration's reading (which
General MacArthur never did) that massive defense appropriations, no
matter how desirable, were impossible to obtain from a neutralist-domi-
nated Congress. Murphy had no reason to dispute the orthodox army
position, which his friend Gen. Frank Parker often expressed, that
except for Corregidor, the Philippines were a military liability and a
provocation to Japan. Like Quezon he dismissed dependence on treaties and the neutralization proviso of the T–M Act as politically naïve.
Considering the fanatical movements within Japan, Murphy had no
doubt—and he told the President so in 1935—that the Japanese would
absorb the Philippines militarily when they could and economically
when they chose should Americans cut the knot.[20] Thus, while favoring
"economic partnership" with Filipinos after independence, he reluctantly came to the isolationist position that the only solution to America's
imperial dilemma was extrication from the western Pacific. "In a nutshell," he wrote former Governor W. Cameron Forbes, "I am firmly
of the belief that we should be entirely out of the Philippines, after
the expiration of the Commonwealth, or strongly in, and not in an
equivocal or secondary position. The maintenance of naval and military bases out here seems to me to invite trouble."[21] If the Islands were
impossible to defend without massive fortifications, which Congress
could not be expected to support, the only alternative was withdrawal
to the Hawaiian-Alaskan perimeter. Commitment without power was
folly.

Just as he viewed the dilemma as the product of "inexorable forces,"
however, so Murphy concluded that it was too late to consider ideal
solutions. Both sides were too deeply committed to independence.
Whether Filipinos could sustain statehood after the Commonwealth
therefore depended on high strategic policy beyond his office and on
down-to-earth trade relations that would gradually adjust the Filipino
economy to separation. Such problems, in his view, could not be solved
in one magic decade, nor by reference to a vague moral responsibility
on the part of the United States. Murphy was a sentimentalist with "a
deep feeling myself" for the ethical obligation of seeing independence
through, for reasons which he listed: "our conquest, their insularity,

state of development compared with our own and the manner in which we have undertaken to set up an independent nation out of a people we have somewhat selfishly made dependent on us." But he was not so sentimental as to perceive no limits to moral responsibility or to excuse a "sloppy approach" to international commitments which required "careful preparation and exact facts."[22] "More and more," he told Kemp in 1935, "I incline to the idea of self-reliance and the Filipino meeting his own problem." "It is unwise and futile to depend on the beneficence of any other country or countries. . . . The endurance and character of the Commonwealth rest squarely on the shoulders of the Filipino; he alone can bring solution to the problems which beset us." Initiatives to defer independence, he concluded, would have to come from them. And for the same reasons he swallowed misgivings about the Commonwealth and did his best to make it work. Emphasizing the positive —that Filipino self-determination would be "a good will asset" for the United States among colonial peoples over the world—Murphy declared: "I am for it with whatever might is mine."[23]

The governor's opportunities for brokerage increased during installation of the Commonwealth. While he resisted the effort to shorten the transitional period, he supported Quezon in speedy implementation of the Tydings-McDuffie Act. Because the constitution was designed for statehood as well as for the Commonwealth, he also maintained an official hands-off policy; to dramatize its Filipino character, he even refused invitations to participate in the convention, whether as president or as "honored guest."[24] Murphy liked to think that he influenced the constitution, nonetheless. He may have a little. Convention members consulted the governor and his staff informally. The convention also chose a unicameral legislature, which he favored, while Quezon, who preferred bicameralism, was absent from the country.[25] Through Murphy, moreover, the convention president, Claro M. Recto, received informal assurances that the most controversial parts of the instrument —unicameralism, indirect elections, nationalization power, and foreign ownership restrictions—would be acceptable to the United States.[26] But it is difficult to conclude that Murphy's personal stamp on the constitution was as great as Filipino lawyers, for example, Recto, or other Americans whose expertise was greater.

Privately Murphy considered several clauses, especially those granting extraordinary presidential powers and involving the judiciary in personnel matters, of "very debatable wisdom." But he saw little incompatibility with the Tydings-McDuffie Act and recommended approval of the instrument. By this time he had become realist enough not to contest Hayden's proposition that what was essentially a "set-up" for "irresponsible autocracy" by the Filipino President and House Speaker was "the *natural* system for the people of these Islands in their present stage of political development." All things considered, Murphy believed that Filipinos had produced an "able, progressive document" and one which, as Hayden added, was "in harmony with the instincts, traditions and past practices of the Filipino people."[27]

In public no one would have suspected that the governor had a doubt. Once it was drafted he became an ardent advocate of the Philippines constitution. Unicameralism, even if Quezon called it an accident, and affirmation of the principle of government responsibility for social justice, were sufficient for him to label the instrument a "splendid document," if not the "best on earth."[28] At each step toward commonwealth, in fact, he perceived his function as political salesmanship. In Manila he had considered it his duty to "interpret the American spirit to the people of this country."[29] Now the time had come to interpret on the other side. Stepping into politics to endorse the Quezon-Osmeña coalition in the interest of national unity, Murphy exuded optimism in Manila, Tokyo, and Washington—while tooting his own horn. The Philippines "are ripe for Commonwealth," he declared. "I doubt if any nation ever started out under as favorable circumstances as the Commonwealth government will enjoy." The "almost unique performance" of a balanced budget, the judicial council "which is absolutely free from politics," and "the most modern and efficient" social services in the Orient, all gave ample proof, he said, that "the government and the people of the Philippines are well prepared for the Commonwealth, which will be a success."[30] Since the Islands were beginning to feel the pinch of agricultural decline, however, the crux of the matter lay in what Murphy left unsaid: the future of American commitments in the Philippines and Filipino export trade. Hoping to expedite settlement of these questions *before* losing control of the government, he set out for home at Roosevelt's call for a thorough airing of the Philippines question, which in truth was a bundle of questions.

Seldom has any colonial governor been accorded a send-off to match the one Filipinos gave Murphy on his departure in January 1935. As thousands cheered his leave-taking, it was obvious he was their logical choice for High Commissioner. Judging by official reactions in Washington, his nomination also was a foregone conclusion. The President threw an elaborate party at the White House in Murphy's honor. His agenda and social schedule resembled those of a visiting potentate.[31] And while it was apparently decided at these meetings that his appointment as High Commissioner would be brief and that General MacArthur would be his probable successor, Murphy's visit occasioned the first coordinated policy review in several years.

Murphy won quick presidential approval of the Philippines constitution and Roosevelt's praise for having done "a remarkable thing in running his office without worry or care to the White House."[32] But despite his warning to Congress and the public that "our job is to befriend the commonwealth," he failed to achieve preferential treatment for Philippines trade. Fearing that Congress would "either do nothing or else act adversely on any such request," Murphy concurred in the administration judgment that it was impracticable to seek amendments to the Independence Act. Filipinos would have to settle for assurances of future joint trade conferences, pending a change in congressional attitudes.[33] Though Murphy pressed to expedite these negotiations the intricate preparations required to dovetail U.S.–Philippines tariffs with the overall reciprocal trade program inevitably meant delay. The government did establish an interdepartmental committee to plan and coordinate Philippines policy, the State Department created a special Philippines section in the Far Eastern Division to guide the effort, and immediate tax benefits were channeled to declining agricultural interests in the Islands.[34] Troublesome side issues concerning aviation franchises and a gentleman's agreement with Japan to limit textile exports also were settled.[35] Murphy defended the High Commission's budget in congressional hearings and laid the groundwork for the capital's sympathetic reception of another Quezon mission. Probably most important, he secured President Roosevelt's specific pledge to hold a trade conference, plus an informal understanding between Roosevelt and Quezon that "everything should be done correctly as soon as possible"—and did little about pending plans for defense.[36] Politician rather than strategist, Murphy laid stress on economic policy.

However short of their goal, Filipinos accepted these arrangements with good grace. So buoyant had they become over independence that on returning to Manila in the summer of 1935 both Murphy and Quezon were welcomed, contrary to orders, as national heroes. In the enthusiasm over prospective Commonwealth the governor was credited with having written "a new chapter in Philippine-American relations."[37] His policies in the Islands, it was felt, had quieted internal political discord and stabilized insular administration; now his understanding intercession between the two governments had restored "an era of good feeling" which made Commonwealth possible. "We have a lot to thank Governor General Murphy for," commented the *Philippines Herald* on his birthday. "May God bless him."[38]

Back in Malacañan, Murphy accelerated the transfer of executive power. National elections were called in September and the inauguration was set for November. More than formalities were involved. As Filipino leaders concentrated on building a national political organization ready to assume power, Murphy entered a race against time to complete his program before surrendering control. As depression began to be felt in Philippines agriculture, widespread discontent was becoming evident in the provinces. Partisans of Aguinaldo and Sakdalista radicals openly advocated revolt to prevent entrenchment of the ruling elite.[39] While Murphy and Quezon were in Washington a momentarily bloody uprising of Sakdalistas in provinces around Manila seriously embarrassed confidence in Filipino self-government, as well as the governor's own reports that conditions there were "peaceful and orderly." Well timed to block the plebiscite over the constitution, the abortive revolt was triggered as much by a demagogic appeal that Commonwealth represented defeat for independence as by the agrarian exploitation on which the movement fed.[40] Murphy dismissed the uprising, initially, as a "purely local, factional political outbreak," which a blundering Constabulary had made unnecessarily bloody, but which gave little "evidence of general unrest of an economic nature reflecting on the United States."[41] To avoid making a martyr of Sakdal leader Benigno Ramos, who impressed both Hayden and Joseph C. Grew as part "crack-pot" and part "political racketeer," Murphy also refused Quezon's demand to brand Ramos or the Sakdal party as outlaws. The peaceful plebiscite and the overwhelming Filipino acceptance of the constitution lent some currency to a strictly political interpretation of the revolt. On his return, however, the lesson began to penetrate that the uprising was an expression of deep agrarian unrest which reflected very much upon the United States. Realism thus replaced romanticism too late, but Murphy thereafter refused to dismiss the rebellion in Luzon as simply a communist power grab. Concluding that economic policy and trade relations should be settled post haste, he wrote to Assistant Secretary of State, Francis B. Sayre, "We may easily delude ourselves should we fail to look below the surface. There is an unusual degree of unrest in the Philippines having its roots in economic and social conditions and its immediate expression is in an undercurrent of political opposition. It seems prudent in the interests of both countries to lay our plans and to execute them as soon as possible, particularly while the general attitude is favorable."[42]

The Filipino Cabinet responded to the outbreak by pressing for faster break-up of friar estates, a policy which the Catholic governor welcomed as "timely and productive of highly desirable social benefits."[43] But Americans had lost control of the Legislature too long ago to contemplate fundamental social reforms. About all Murphy could do now was to invigorate regular programs. That meant energetic tax collections and retrenchment to meet lagging revenues under a slogan of "spend no money and save some money."[44] Retrenchment also meant vetoing some of Murphy's own projects; the combination resulted in a tug-of-war with the Legislature during the closing weeks of his administration. With Murphy's reluctant approval, Filipino women were temporarily denied the vote and public works were included in the budget.[45] While he labored "to keep alive" the trade conference planning Filipino leaders effectively postponed active policy-making until government was in their hands. The consequent restrictions were frustrating; "the chief task of the Americans," Hayden complained, "seems to be that of liquidation, not of construction."[46] The time required to plan for trade conferences was no less irritating to Murphy. We must build here, he said, "a sound economy that will make it possible for the commonwealth government to survive."[47]

Tension began to mount when the aging Aguinaldo threatened mass demonstrations—and intelligence agents reported rumors of assassination plans—to obstruct installation of Quezon's new government, which Aguinaldo claimed was elected by fraud. Putting great stock in the symbols of government, Murphy moved swiftly. Officially he insisted on exhausting regular legal remedies for contested elections. Through cajolery and threats of arrest in private conversations he persuaded Aguinaldo that nothing would be allowed to mar the impression that Filipinos were capable of orderly political change, especially when Vice-President Garner, Secretary of War Dern, and numerous Congressmen would come to Manila with their wives to bless the event.[48]

All was jubilant fanfare when the Commonwealth was inaugurated without incident on November 15, 1935. In the final hours of his government, the outgoing governor announced that the new regime would inherit a surplus of 72 million pesos, that he would decline a gratuity voted by the Legislature, and that he had freed most of the Sakdalista prisoners as "an example of tolerance where differences of opinion are concerned."[49] Once again the praise of his "Job Well Done" was fulsome. He also made useful political contacts as host to a great American junket. Yet Murphy struck a strangely solemn note in handing over the reins of executive power. This was Commonwealth, not independence. All the "fine hopes and enthusiasm" of the occasion could not shroud the trials which had just begun.[50]

II

Vexing difficulties did lurk beneath the Commonwealth festivities. Apart from obvious economic problems, important political and strategic questions remained unanswered. What was the exact nature of United States authority in the Islands? What were its defense commitments? For Murphy, the most immediate problem was political relations between the two governments in Manila, a problem symbolized by the ambiguities of his own office and a narrow escape from an open clash with President Quezon.

The Commonwealth, an experiment in "controlled autonomy," was something new to American constitutional practice. The United States was attempting to divide sovereignty, but no one knew precisely how. One of the major criticisms of the first Independence Act, expressed alike by President Hoover and Manuel L. Quezon, had been ambiguous division of authority. The Tydings-McDuffie Act was equally inexplicit. Preoccupied with domestic crisis the Roosevelt administration was inclined to proceed pragmatically. The role of the High Commissioner, by consensus, would have to be worked out on the job. Uncertainty resulted throughout the decade.

Nebulous authority became Murphy's toughest problem in the Philippines. The T–M Act, beyond declaring that the High Commissioner was the President's personal representative and requiring Filipino officials to furnish him information on request, did not define the powers or functions of the office. The President was given certain routine functions, such as passport and immigration control, which he delegated to the High Commissioner. In addition to trade and foreign policy powers reserved by the Act, the President was also empowered to intervene in specified cases of incompetency or financial default. Americans in the Islands would look to the Commissioner to protect their interests, and his links to the White House made it potentially a strong post.[51] Presidential intervention, nevertheless, would be a tacit admission of failure for the premise that Filipinos were capable of self-rule. As Quezon argued, it would be "unthinkable" that consultations would break down to the point that the power would have to be used. If only to avert that necessity, the High Commissioner's powers of information implied more than reporting. "How much more," as J. Weldon Jones remarked, was the rub.[52]

The problem provoked a miniature Hamilton-Jefferson controversy even before inauguration of the Commonwealth. As planning started in earnest following the 1934 plebiscite Murphy pressed for an official definition of the High Commissioner's duties. These promptings set off a running debate within the government in which two basic positions emerged. Filipino lawyers had learned their lessons well. On the one hand, Quezon and General MacArthur, who was due to become the Commonwealth military adviser after his retirement as chief of staff, viewed the T–M Act as a grant of independence, qualified only by specifically enumerated exceptions in military and foreign affairs. Consequently, Quezon argued, disputed authority should be construed in favor of the insular government and American supervisory powers should be confined to the reserved presidential sector. Not even the President of the United States could intervene elsewhere, Quezon stated publicly, and he was superior in rank only. The High Commissioner, except as the President might otherwise delegate, was essentially a reporter and ambassador.[53]

"A novel arrangement, indeed, for a sovereign state to deal with its dependency through a diplomatic representative!" retorted Edward G. Kemp afterwards. Quezon's position, to the Governor General and his staff, grossly misconstrued the nature of the Commonwealth. Murphy, like President Hoover, feared that Filipino construction of the Act would leave the United States responsible for, but powerless to control, a "subordinate political entity." Murphy, agreeing with Senator Vandenberg, could not accept a relationship in which Filipinos for 10 dangerous years "should have virtually complete autonomy while we 'hold the bag.'" No matter its gloss, he maintained, the Independence Act for the next decade was essentially a "home-rule statute."[54] While the statute greatly expanded "the participation of the Filipino people in their government," he told the War Department, "it does not greatly broaden the authority of the Commonwealth Government." "The fact is Congress did not make the Philippines independent, politically or otherwise." "The powers reserved by the United States are not specifically enumerated. They are plenary." The United States still possessed sovereign authority over the Islands. The High Commissioner, accordingly, was a kind of "viceroy." His powers implied not merely reporting and diplomatic representation but counsel, surveillance, and supervision in areas affecting the interests of the United States.[55] At his "urgent" request, President Roosevelt issued a public reminder of American supremacy on signing the constitution. But more precise aspects of the problem—the status and functions of the High Commissioner—provoked thorny debate.

It was no great surprise when Roosevelt announced Murphy's appointment as High Commissioner in July 1935. Despite the warmth with which the news was received, however, the ambiguities of the office brought him the most serious controversy of his stay in the Islands. For months before the inauguration of the Commonwealth his agitation over the disputed character of American authority had centered on the nature of his own. Throughout 1934-35 he badgered the War Department for an "authoritative interpretation" of the Tydings-McDuffie Act, either by formal declaration or by informal letter of instructions, such as Newton D. Baker had written to Governor Harrison regarding the Jones Act, to clarify the power and position of American officials. Without clarification, Murphy argued, the thrust for independence would make it "difficult, if not impossible, for [the] High Commissioner to support and maintain in practice the position of preeminence, rank and respect necessary for effective discharge of his responsibilities under the law."[56] To avoid constant friction it was of the "utmost importance" that basic questions of procedure, power, and protocol be settled in advance. Otherwise past experience showed that every relationship would have to be negotiated piecemeal, a process to be avoided at all costs. High Commissioners who asserted their authority would have no choice but to make demeaning concessions or to engage in unseemly rivalry with the Commonwealth President. And either alternative risked the friendly relations which were the object of American policy.[57]

Recognizing the delicacy of the problem, General Creed F. Cox, chief of the Bureau of Insular Affairs, withheld submission of a final draft of instructions to the President until the Murphy-Quezon trip to Washington in the spring of 1935.[58] Though Roosevelt issued the statement of American sovereignty in the Philippines, disagreement whether the instructions should be general in character or as specific as the Governor General desired, blocked their publication at that time. After his return to Manila, Murphy realized he had lost an important round. General Cox informed him that detailed instructions were undesirable in view of his "background of experience," that the Commonwealth President would take precedence in rank, and that the High Commissioner would receive "no further emphasis" in inauguration ceremonies.[59] Without consulting him, Secretary Dern sent Murphy a brief letter, approved by the President, instructing the High Commissioner to observe "the trend of affairs, particularly in all matters affecting the interests of the United States," leaving future questions to his "demonstrated judgment, tact, and sympathetic understanding of the policies and aims of this Government."[60] Murphy, outmaneuvered by General MacArthur and apparently influenced by advisers Hester and Kemp, then protested with a flurry of vigorous cables which ignited bureaucratic fireworks and prompted one War Department subordinate to exclaim—"Hell's apopping!"[61]

While satisfied with administrative procedures, Murphy charged that Dern's conception of the office was "a narrowly restrictive view" of the High Commissioner's authority and status. The Commonwealth was "not equivalent to [a] sovereign state nor High Commissioner to Ambassador," he asserted. Neither was the Commissioner a "mere observer" nor a "mere symbol" of American sovereignty. Instead, he was chief of American personnel in the Islands and had power to command information from all Filipino officials. These powers implied a supervisory role and premier rank. If only to avert the need for direct presidential intervention, the Commissioner should be able to advise and to admonish. Even Quezon admitted as much for the reserved presidential sector.[62] Furthermore, as proposed in a draft of formal instructions, Murphy recommended that the Commissioner should possess functions over and above those specifically assigned by the Act or delegated by the President. Time and distance from the mainland required recognition of his implicit executive prerogative to deal with any situation which might threaten "orderly, stable and just government in the Philippines." Linking the question of American sovereignty to his own power, Murphy declared: "Without premier rank and commensurate authority for its chief representative [the] American position in the Philippines would be untenable."[63]

A viceregal view of the office did not go unchallenged. Having requested full governmental review of the question, Murphy met resistance both polite and blunt. The acting Attorney General, Stanley Reed, suggested that the High Commissioner should be primarily an unobtrusive observer.[64] Acting Secretary of War General Douglas MacArthur charged that the Governor General sought to become "super-President of the Commonwealth." In a memorandum to the White House, MacArthur asserted that Murphy's recommendations "would actually limit, rather than extend, the degree of autonomy now enjoyed by the Filipinos." "The United States is launching a new nation," wrote the general.

It should do nothing to detract from or impede such a magnificent undertaking. . . . The situation is unique. It does not call for an inter-governmental
procedure designed to perpetuate a state and feeling of American authority
in the Islands. Rather it should encourage the maximum assumption of independent action on the part of the Islands' authorities consistent with the
interests of the United States and the plain language of the law. . . . The
War Department knows of no appointive official in any government having
powers as great as those desired by Governor General Murphy. In effect, his
recommendations would make the High Commissioner locally independent
of any agency of government, either the Commonwealth or the United States
Government. If the High Commissioner's powers are to be increased over
those of the Governor General, the query arises: "why should the Tydings-
McDuffie law have been enacted . . . ?"

To MacArthur it was self-evident that the Commonwealth President
should have the same social status as other elected heads of government.
Murphy's proposals were "indefensible administratively" and "thoroughly untenable." Secretary Dern's instructions should stand.⁶⁵

Blocked by MacArthur, Murphy awaited the arrival of Dern, at
Roosevelt's suggestion, before raising the issue anew. But his temper
was roused. "I have made it plain that there will be no interference
with local administration unless it should become necessary for the due
protection of the interests of the United States," he wrote Roosevelt.
"It is my intention, and will be the policy of this office, at all times to
show proper respect for the dignity and authority of the Commonwealth Government. . . . It is my purpose to render whatever assistance
and advice may consistently be given without assuming responsibilities
that should be left exclusively to the local government." MacArthur's
charges, he said, "were wholly without foundation and unwarranted."⁶⁶
Indeed, as Murphy saw the issue, they missed the point. The general's
major premise, that the Act created statehood, was both legally and
politically unsound. While MacArthur probably believed that a crowd
of American politicians were attempting to maintain control, Murphy
in turn could not help suspecting him of being blinded by friendship
with the Quezons, personal self-interest, and misguided liberality.⁶⁷
As a matter of policy, of course, intervention in Filipino affairs should
be held to a minimum. But the question was one of legal right and
paramount American interests. "My recommendations on this subject,"
Murphy noted hastily to his staff, "are based on personal knowledge,
familiarity with peculiar local conditions, political temperaments and
alignments, recent and current manifestations of strong sinister under-
currents of opposition to present political leadership having serious as-

pect," as well as fears of reversion to Spanish authoritarian patterns which they all felt but could not openly state. That the War Department did not recognize these conditions, he believed, could only be explained by ignorance or by politics.[68]

Whatever the cause, Murphy believed that the prestige of American statesmanship was at stake. "Our responsibilities here are definite and grave," he wrote the President and the Secretary of War. "Not alone because of internal conditions but on account of the new status of American official authority in the Islands, a very important and uncertain and delicate period of our tenure lies before us." The United States was still responsible for Filipino conduct in the eyes of the world. A tendency to attach "misleading significance" to the Commonwealth, equating it with nationhood, flourished nonetheless in the Islands, the Vatican, and Spain. Similar misconceptions existed at Geneva, and "indications of widespread misunderstanding" of the nation's remaining responsibilities were evident at home. Given American interests in the Philippines and in the Pacific generally, it was imperative to start off with disputes over authority nipped in the bud. One day American power might have to be used. To wait until the event to acknowledge it, in view of eternal processes of attrition, was dangerous. "Afterwards," Murphy warned Dern, "will be too late."[69]

War Department officials in Washington considered these problems to be "hypothetical." Given Quezon's sensitivity to American political tolerances, the predictions of calamity in the governor's cables were doubtless exaggerated. Murphy himself, after all, had conceded that the High Commissioner's job would have to be "worked out as we go along."[70] Yet no sooner had the American inaugural delegation arrived in Manila than the dispute erupted in embarrassing form. Who would receive first place in public honors, the Filipino chief executive or the American High Commissioner? Publication of an informal army protocol list ranking Quezon above every American, and the decision to accord him a 21-gun salute reserved for chiefs of state, provoked additional protests, and the issue came to a head.[71/c] According to Secretary Dern, every American adviser in Manila except General MacArthur, who had sponsored the decision, regarded the honors policy as a blunder, both diplomatically and politically. While happy to vacate Mala-

---

c The list, though prepared by the Bureau of Insular Affairs after consultation with the Protocol Division of the Department of State, was not authorized; but in the absence of an official one, it was accepted as such in the Islands. F. LeJ. Parker to FM, Oct. 9, 1935; Creed F. Cox to FM, Oct. 10, 1935. The State Department blocked invitations to foreign governments, on the other hand, because the Commonwealth was not a sovereign state. Cable, D.C. McDonald to FM, Sept. 28, 1935, Box 28.

cañan in Quezon's favor, and while willing to trim his sights for a palatial High Commissioner's residence as a tactical matter, Murphy believed that the honors question would set an important symbolic precedent, "irrevocably." Dern, who feared that so late a reversal would do "more harm than good," opposed any change and proposed instead to make a statement about the High Commissioner's status which reflected the MacArthur-Quezon position. Murphy, who denounced Dern's proposal as "politically incorrect and legally erroneous," then asked for the President's personal review.[72]

After "long consideration," Roosevelt settled the status question by according both officials 19 guns and by declaring the High Commissioner to be the senior official.[73] Backed once again by the President, though blocked in his desire for written instructions and a public protocol list, Murphy insisted that the reversal be made public. "I am totally disinterested in the matter of honors, salutes and courtesies for their own sake," he declared. "It is my personal belief that the government should stand on its own merits, offering sound economy and social justice rather than public displays and formal honors. In the present case I am unconcerned over any factor other than really good government. Nevertheless, this entails a clear understanding of the American position in the Philippines, while honesty demands that the Filipino people be allowed no misrepresentation of their exact present status. I am anxious to make their autonomous experiment a success. I believe I have proved I am their friend. Therefore, it is essential that we work out our problems together, free from misunderstanding. . . . America . . . is still sovereign here."[74]

But the damage was done. Roosevelt's reversal on the eve of the inauguration offended Quezon, who angrily threatened to boycott the ceremony. It would have been a serious blow to Murphy's prestige had Quezon refused to attend his own inauguration. The threat frightened the Governor General so thoroughly that subordinates feared he would abandon the fight. Murphy mollified Quezon somewhat by making an unpublicized first call on the Filipino President, a move he later regarded as a mistake. But the incident doubtless colored their personal relations and contributed to Murphy's discomfort as High Commissioner. Even though he won the battle, Murphy felt frustrated by the turn of events. Roosevelt's action, he told Hayden, was "perfect."[75]

The President is now hitting the nail squarely on the head. I regret to state that the War Department has not been very helpful in placing the relationship of the two countries and their representatives on a correct and sound basis. The State Department appears to be seeing straight. . . .

I need not tell you how strongly I believe that the authority of the Commonwealth Government should be respected and enforced. It should be our policy to avoid annoying and harassing intermeddling. . . . It should be done, however, with an intelligent conception of American interests and in a manner that will adequately safeguard them.

While our position is apparently now being straightened out step by step, it is deplorable that it wasn't done in good season for an authoritative interpretation of the Act . . . would have done justice to the best interests of both the Philippines and our country and would have avoided the "near situation" created by the intrigue of political adventurers and those promoting self-interests.

I never want to lose sight for a moment of our great mission to do justice to the Filipino people and their government. Inconsequential questions should not make us purblind to the supreme objective of placing these people on their feet firmly and durably.[76]

Having clarified the status of the Commonwealth, Murphy continued to press for an official declaration of his own duties. Secretary Dern still resisted, however, because he believed that "the broader and more general your instructions are, the more effectively you will be able to carry out your mission as High Commissioner." A code of conduct established by precedents was preferable to specific instructions creating mandatory rules, the Secretary observed; most situations could be worked out better "through the cooperative efforts of the chief representatives of the two governments."[77] For all his own emphasis on personal relations, that was precisely the condition Murphy sought to avoid. "Important and paramount national interests," he told General Cox, "should not be left to [the] uncertainty of future negotiation or local Philippine policy." Thus, even after concluding that no instructions would be forthcoming from Dern, Murphy indicated that unless advised or instructed to the contrary he expected to function with substantially the same authority he had previously requested.[78] Recognized power used gingerly was his concept of wise American administration, and he was convinced that it was working in practice. After a few months in office, Murphy informed the President that recognition of American status had produced "wholesome" effects in the Islands and that Filipino leaders were soliciting the "friendly advice and judgment of this office" even more than he had proposed. "Brother MacArthur's" accusations of the year before, he quipped to Hayden, was "a strawman of mastodonic proportions."[79]

Whether Murphy exaggerated his consultations with Filipino officials is hard to say, but officially he got nowhere with his viceregal concept of the office. Dern, in "a neat job of ducking," replied that the guidelines of the office already had been determined by law and his formal letter of instructions. To go beyond reporting, in effect, would be on Murphy's own responsibility. "By virtue of a strict literal construction," Kemp observed acidly, "the United States has no representative in the Philippines with actual authority in matters of government. A glorified and perfected Harrison policy."[80] Retiring to the summer residence at Baguio, Murphy stated again that "it is the policy of the High Commissioner fully and completely to recognize the rights and responsibilities of the Commonwealth government and its officials. I want the Commonwealth to succeed." "I expect to keep myself in the background." Fearful of Filipino control, Americans in Manila regarded his withdrawal as abdication of responsibility; later High Commissioners were not so restrained.[81] Yet as a symbolic figure in a nebulous role, Murphy was frustrated and restless. American authority, he believed, was still uncertain and American interests excessively dependent on personalities and ad hoc bargaining. Privately he was disturbed that the army had been permitted to make political policy and was convinced, despite his respect for Dern, that the War Department needed some political education. Thus, perhaps, was born his ambition to become Secretary of War.

III

Experience as High Commissioner reinforced Murphy's fears. As he and Quezon began to build the precedents that would regulate relations between the two governments in Manila, a series of incidents kept the issue of the High Commissioner's role very much alive. Routine communication between governments posed no problem because an advance understanding had been reached to continue the established circuits through the High Commissioner and the War Department. Quezon also approved the High Commissioner's general request for departmental reports.[82/d] Protocol continued to be an irritant, however— in Murphy's view because the War Department refused to publish a guide forthrightly for fear of offending Quezon.[83] And in the most sensitive areas of government operations, troublesome questions arose.

Quezon served notice that he questioned whether the Secretary of War had any authority over the Commonwealth government except

---

[d] Quezon also reserved the right to communicate with the federal government, as before, through the Filipino Resident Commissioner in Washington. Quezon to FM, Dec. 1, 1935, Box 30.

to relay messages.[84/e] He also balked at supplying information about the Belo Fund (which funded the presidential staff), as well as the minutes of the central government depository, the Philippines National Bank. One was discretionary and the other private, he argued. Even though the High Commissioner admittedly bore special supervisory responsibility over the condition of Commonwealth finance, Quezon frankly stated his belief that Murphy's staff wanted more information than necessary.[85] While willing to inform him personally about these matters "in view of our very close personal relations," Quezon asserted that he, too, was setting precedents and had reached the limit only "because I am sure that it is in a spirit of helpfulness that you have wanted the information sought."[86]

The exchanges were cordial and frank. Despite Quezon's occasional outbursts over protocol, which supported the High Commissioner's contention that Filipinos attached political significance to the subject, Murphy thought it a "healthy sign" that the Commonwealth President was jealous of his government's power. Nor did he blame him for taking the traditional nationalist course.[87] The fault, he felt, was United States failure to clarify its position in advance—which he blamed on MacArthur's "obstruction."[88] Aggravating the situation, no doubt, was slow adjustment by Americans, including Murphy, to Filipino policy control and a tendency by Filipinos, including Quezon, to continue making political hay by nationalist oratory. Even so, Murphy was careful to express his views privately, and Quezon usually came around in the end. Both required effort, nonetheless, and incidents kept recurring. Confused envoys made their representations to Quezon, who in turn demanded a separate voice in international sugar conferences. Nearly every consulate had trouble with proper routing of communications, some perhaps intentionally. Although most incidents were minor in themselves, they created "their quota of confusion and friction."[89] Especially after hearing of "bad precedents" and pressures on acting High Commissioner J. Weldon Jones during his absence in 1936, Murphy was convinced that sound relations could not be established "merely by the exercise of tact and judgment by the High Commissioner." He told acting Secretary of War, Harry H. Woodring, that without definite instructions "the situation will steadily grow worse." Except in foreign affairs, Filipinos simply refused to acknowledge American authority without a debilitating contest.[90]

e Some members of Murphy's staff entertained parallel views regarding the High Commissioner's office and the Bureau of Insular Affairs, but Murphy never raised the issue.

The gravest cause of concern was the defense of the Philippines. On assuming the reins of power, Quezon left no doubt who was in control of the Commonwealth government. In little over a year he reorganized the bureaucracy, cancelled the friar estates program, fired James R. Fugate as Governor of Sulu, nationalized the police, renewed the sedition law, and rammed an ambitious ten-year program of conscription and national defense through a special session of the Legislature.[91] The defense program, which was unveiled in an atmosphere of sponsorship by the American military advisory mission headed by MacArthur, caught the High Commission off guard.[92] Although Murphy had vetoed a defense bill in 1934 and had questioned the necessity of a military mission in conversations with Roosevelt in 1935, he had not offered vigorous opposition to the mission or to MacArthur's appointment.[93] But in the context of Quezon's proposals to abolish the Interior Department, which would not only centralize government operations further but give him control of election machinery, the defense plan filled the High Commissioner with apprehensions.[94]

To begin with, the military mission created an administrative anomaly. Officially, General MacArthur was commander of the Filipino forces who took his orders from Quezon. But as chief of the military mission, the general also was authorized to communicate directly with the Secretary of War and to command broad assistance from the American military commander in the Philippines. The ways and means of his mission, so his orders read, "are largely left to you."[95] The High Commissioner, regardless of the need for military and political coordination, was simply bypassed. "Thus far," Murphy noted in February 1936, "General MacArthur has not in any way, so far as I can learn from General Kilbourne, sought to invoke or exercise any authority under the order. But the order is there and he knows it and the Commanding General knows it and the present Commanding General will soon be succeeded by General Holbrook, who is an appointee of General Mac-Arthur's."[96] The presence of a former chief of staff with such influence in the American army, not to mention a close friend of Quezon's who already had "opposed and neutralized" Murphy's bid for instructions and whom Roosevelt then wanted as Murphy's replacement, might easily embarrass the High Commissioner should they disagree on matters requiring presidential intervention.[97]

That the two men might disagree was highly probable. Although the general's behavior was scrupulously correct, and the High Commissioner ordered his staff to cooperate fully, MacArthur and Murphy were spokesmen for colliding priorities in the Philippines.[98] They also vied for positions of influence with President Quezon. Resentful of Mac-Arthur's bypass and successful interposition in the instructions fight, and jealous of his longstanding intimacy with Quezon, Murphy was suspicious that the defense plan was a smokescreen to find a job for the retired general and fearful of Quezon's intentions. "Sooner or later a decision must be made by this office," he told Kemp, whether Mac-Arthur's orders should be challenged and the mission placed under the High Commissioner's supervision or else be withdrawn. Common-wealth armed forces, it was true, were subject to call by the United States President, which in one sense made both the Commonwealth President and the general agents of the United States. But to Murphy, MacArthur was identified with Filipino interests and subject to Fili-pino control. Personal disagreements aside, no man could serve two masters.[99]

Even MacArthur expressed discomfort over wearing two hats. Clashing personal and administrative loyalties aggravated the conflict, but the crux of the matter was substantive policy. Murphy was a paci-fist. He was realist enough never to question the objective of defense or the Commonwealth's legal competence to provide for it, though he favored an enlarged Constabulary under American command. But in view of virtually unanimous military advice that the defense plan would be futile even if perfected, he regarded MacArthur's proposals as fraught with danger. Murphy worried about the impact of "militari-zation" on Filipino society and its fragile democracy. He fretted over the increased concentration of executive power and the provocation to Japan. Above all, he was dubious whether Filipinos could sustain mil-itary expenditures estimated at 16 million pesos annually, expenditures which actually consumed 22 percent of the budget in 1936, without destroying their hard-won financial stability and draining off funds for essential educational and social services. Because his military advice was premised on theories of static defense, Murphy, along with most peo-ple, probably misunderstood the strategy of deterrence and the daring mobile-force and guerrilla warfare concepts of MacArthur's plan. In any case, the question whether the Philippines were defensible was for Filipinos to decide. But Murphy understood full well that the Philip-pines defense program had not been coordinated within his own gov-ernment and that its economic and strategic implications were the busi-ness of the United States. The question for him was how to oppose.[100]

No more graphic illustration of the High Commissioner's inherent predicament could have been presented than the military defense pro-gram. The MacArthur plan had been devised under the auspices of the War Department and sold as feasible to Quezon without review by the War Department general staff, the State Department, or the Governor General, and without a counterpart financial plan. Indeed, MacArthur's September 18th orders, which were signed by acting Adjutant General E.T. Conley and the acting Secretary of War, probably were written by MacArthur himself. The Philippines defense program thus reflected the serious divergencies of policy which were permitted to run concurrently with no more overview than who saw the President last. Once the program was unveiled in a special session of the fledgling Commonwealth Legislature, however, the High Commissioner could hardly challenge its wisdom without "appearing officious or risking offense"; nor could he recommend intervention without showing that contractual default would result. While his financial aides thought default would result unless drastic cuts were made in education, no prediction could be made until defense plans became more definite. If default did occur after Murphy had held his tongue, on the other hand, he would be charged with derogation of duty. Either way, as Kemp noted, "we are on the spot."[101]

The problem hardened when, following passage of the Defense Act, MacArthur requested the United States to sell the Philippines several hundred thousand rifles and Roosevelt asked for a combined judgment of the need. Murphy, who thought it "injudicious" to arm Filipinos until political conditions were settled and American supervision assured, decided to "cut right through to the fundamentals" by opposing the arms sale. "To hint that appropriations required by the Act are financially burdensome, without demonstrating our case . . . would be futile," he observed, though he did so anyway.[102] The primary concern now was to safeguard American interests from untoward repercussions. What was the reaction in Japan? Was there no way to determine defense needs "scientifically?"[103] Precise facts were difficult to obtain; and before they were available, the President approved the sale, though at a price which crimped MacArthur's budget. The reported Japanese reaction was surprisingly indifferent. After conferring with MacArthur, even Murphy was persuaded that the number of rifles requested reasonably fit the plan. Nevertheless, though he did not recommend a presidential veto, Murphy felt duty bound to register warnings. While informing General Cox that intervention was "premature" he expressed "grave doubts" about the financial risks and urged postponement of further rifle shipments until greater need arose.[104] Murphy refused to despair about the fate of constitutional democracy in the Philippines, as some Americans already were doing and many more later would do by false analogies to Western dictatorships; but he worried "about the increasing transmission of arms."[105] Defense was one thing and a "worthy undertaking." But defense unreconciled with inevitable economic strains, that upset economic and social priorities at the threshold of a delicate probation period, that might provoke Japan or "might lend itself toward suppression or autocracy in the Philippine Islands or that might in addition jeopardize American civil or military authority," he believed, transcended both military judgments and Commonwealth jurisdiction and impinged directly on vital American interests which it was his duty to uphold.[106]

On returning to Washington in June 1936, Murphy spearheaded a drive to bring Philippines policy to a showdown. After conversations in the White House he joined a bureaucratic phalanx consisting of Assistant Secretary of State Sayre, acting Secretary of War Woodring, General Stanley D. Embick, and army chief of staff General Malin Craig to prepare letters for the President's signature having three objects: new instructions to General MacArthur requiring him to coordinate general policy under the High Commissioner; a "friendly but unequivocal" request to Quezon that he suspend further arms purchases pending high-level American review; and a detailed letter of instructions to the High Commissioner, along with a protocol list. Murphy, as Kemp cautioned, was "treading on delicate ground."[107] A struggle for meaningful office, plus a dash of private vengeance, were joined to intra-army disputes and great issues of state.

A series of events ripened the timing for full-scale review of Philippines policy. Murphy's return from Manila was followed in midsummer by General MacArthur's promotion to Field Marshal of the Commonwealth forces, his announcement that Filipinos could go it alone after a decade of preparation, and the death of Secretary Dern. Requests from Generals MacArthur and Holbrook for "an increase of munitions of all kinds" coincided with British proposals to renew the nonfortification provisions of the disarmament treaties due to expire in December.[108] And into the stew Murphy released a lengthy military establishment report which not only left State Department officials "much concerned," but struck fear among partisans of withdrawal and neutralization such as General Embick. Secretary Hull registered his concern to the President over the munitions sale. Even though General Embick indicated that the United States had no plans to fortify the Philippines, the State Department rejected the British proposal as according Japan advantages without reciprocal concessions.[109] Acting Secretary of War Woodring initiated preparation of draft letters to

MacArthur, Quezon, and the High Commissioner; and Murphy agreed to help bring the issues to Roosevelt's attention for "corrective measures." The armaments situation was becoming critical, the chief of staff noted; only the President could resolve whether the United States should expose itself strategically.[110]

On sober thought, Woodring believed it prudent to recall MacArthur for presentation of his views before making a final decision to curtail the Philippines defense program. After all, as General Craig informed Murphy, the War Department actually knew little about the defense scheme, and it was politically risky to embarrass MacArthur in the middle of a presidential campaign. Though Kemp commended Woodring's caution, Murphy himself saw little reason for delay, especially after hearing of proposals in Manila to solicit private donations for military defense.[111] "Thus far I haven't met an army officer in the Philippines or in Washington who shares his view that the Philippines are defensible," he commented; voluntary contributions to equip the Filipino army were simply "indefensible." "The coils of such a system are obvious," Murphy asserted in an ideological display. "They make for not only privilege in government but military despotism and social unrest among the people who suffer because of the concentration of wealth in the hands of a few. Why shouldn't the U.S. be interested in this evil practice? This question goes right to the fundamental proposition. Has the U.S. an interest in the military plans for defense of the Philippine Islands? Of course, we have and we ought to manifest it intelligently."[112]

The military mission was not recalled, as Murphy hoped; but he was instrumental in blocking arms shipments. Conferences between the President, Hull, Woodring, and Craig in mid-September produced a decision to advise Quezon against making additional arms contracts until the United States government could determine its interests in Philippines defense.[113] In November Roosevelt informed the Cabinet that he contemplated neutralization as a means of regional stabilization in Latin America and the western Pacific, and then he instructed the State Department to produce a workable plan.[114] The department, the British, Ambassador Grew, and at first Quezon, were all cool to the idea, a response Roosevelt dismissed as "defeatism." Murphy's cryptic notes of conversations with Roosevelt suggest that despite earlier skepticism he also urged the neutralization alternative on the President, along with the appointment of the genial Christian and son-in-law of Woodrow Wilson, Francis B. Sayre, as his successor, rather than MacArthur.[115]

In the summer and fall of 1936, in short, Murphy turned the advantage of presence in the United States on his Manila opponents. He helped to thwart American military aid to MacArthur, pressed successfully for a complete (though unpublished) honors list, and achieved a State Department commitment to hold preliminary trade talks in 1937, which ultimately resulted in another postponement of tariffs in 1939.[116] His last official act as High Commissioner was criticism of the draft letters to Quezon, MacArthur, and his successor before submission to Roosevelt. While perhaps insensitive to the genuine military insecurity of the Philippine Islands, Murphy at least helped to obtain what had been shockingly absent before—"thoughtful and coordinated" policy review.[117]

Yet events soon swept all plans aside. The Sino-Japanese War, coming only a few months later, upset everyone's calculations. Quezon, frightened by the failure of Chinese defenses, embraced neutralization and sidetracked MacArthur. Roosevelt, while making no move to fortify the Philippines until prodded by Congress, quietly laid aside neutralization. Against an ominous backdrop of aggression in Asia, Murphy's successor Paul V. McNutt called for "realistic re-examination" of Philippines independence. Against stronger manifestations of authoritarianism in Manila, McNutt's successor, Francis B. Sayre, had serious difficulties with Quezon. General MacArthur continued to press for military preparedness as a deterrent to Japan; pacifists like Murphy continued to thwart it. And Filipinos, caught between conflicting American policies, neither of which was fully tried, reaped the worst of both alternatives—a fiercely destructive rather than a soft invasion which American presence invited but was too weak to repel.[118]

IV

Murphy, a strong believer in diplomatic and economic means of reaching an accommodation with Japan, could do little more than obstruct military alternatives. Not only was he a victim of distance, poor coordination, and a largely ceremonial office, but his effectiveness was much reduced by the demands of domestic politics. To subordinates his repeated assertions that "my job here is not completed yet" had a hollow ring, because Murphy knew all along that his tenure as High Commissioner would be brief and that his own career demanded his return to the United States.[119] No little share of his time at Baguio, indeed, was spent taking stateside soundings and laying political plans. The real questions were when and how he should make his return.

For all his good intentions, Murphy was unable to resist the distractions of Michigan politics. The Democratic ticket had been defeated in the 1934 elections, a fate Murphy attributed to their "poor enthusiasm for good government," but which liberals blamed on him.[120] Factional disputes had become so disruptive in 1935 that Roosevelt froze federal appointments in Michigan until Murphy's return trip, whereupon the President made him temporary czar of state patronage in order to resolve differences.[121] More serious, the breach between Roosevelt and two former allies, Father Coughlin and William Randolph Hearst, had become irreparable. Although Murphy had devoted considerable effort during the 1935 trip to "iron out the bumps" with Coughlin, and thought then that Roosevelt and the priest had "buried the hatchet," Coughlin informed him cordially but candidly in 1936 that he could support neither political party, nor even Murphy himself, unless he ran independently.[122/f] Murphy's maneuverings budged Hearst even less. The Democratic party would face election in Michigan without the support of a single statewide newspaper.[123]

The bleaker the party prospects, the stronger became the pressures on Murphy to return as an active candidate. Polls conducted for the Democratic National Committee in the spring of 1936 suggested that "Frank Murphy must be the candidate" for governor if the party wished to carry the state. Murphy was popular in both the depressed Upper Peninsula and his Detroit stronghold and his publicity efforts paid off in surprising strength among Republican defectors.[124] Using intuitive methods, organization leaders reluctantly concluded that Murphy was the only figure with the mass appeal to unite the party, capture or neutralize Coughlin's supporters sufficiently to carry Michigan, and thus strengthen Roosevelt. The margin was close, and on the surface his candidacy would entail personal sacrifice for party loyalty. But there was glory beyond: victory would put him in a splendid position for a presidential bid in 1940.[125]

The evidence suggests that a prime motive for his temporary appointment as High Commissioner was that Murphy would be needed for the 1936 election. When it was announced in May 1936 that he would return home "in accordance with the wishes of President Roose-

---

f After several visits with Coughlin in the spring of 1935 Murphy wrote "Missy" LeHand: "I am confident he will not be aligned with disaffected elements and that in addition, he will be in support of the President especially if in my absence his case is given the intimate and persistent attention it deserves, as I have reviewed it with capable Joseph Kennedy." FM to Marguerite LeHand, May 12, 1935, RL:OF-400-PI. By fall, however, Coughlin's relations with Roosevelt were severely strained. See letters, Box 30.

velt," the cat was out of the bag. Murphy's talk about prospective trade conferences could not disguise the fact that the High Commissioner, along with other Democrats abroad, was getting a leave of absence to participate in the national campaign. For on January 7, 1936 President Roosevelt had asked him to be a candidate for Governor of Michigan.[126/g]

Neither Filipinos nor Murphy himself were happy about the prospect. "Keep Him Here," cried the friendly *Philippines Herald*. "America's mission in the Philippines is something we always believed to be higher than all the imperatives of party convenience." "A man less disposed to cooperate than Commissioner Murphy would mean nothing short of disaster to us."[127] With hardly less modesty Murphy advanced the same position. His decision to run for governor, which required two months to make, was one of the most painful in his life and one which he resisted by proclaiming a desire to remain in Manila.

While "loath to leave," Murphy was not very happy as High Commissioner; he was unhappier over the prospects of a gubernatorial race. The defection of Al Smith, Hearst, and Coughlin, as well as the assault of business forces against Roosevelt, augured a "titanic struggle" ahead; and he regarded his own chances of victory as slim.[128] Intraparty strife was so deep-rooted in Michigan that he believed "one of two things will have to be done; a firm and decisive leadership will have to be taken by someone capable of effecting solidarity and which will mean that some heads will have to be cracked before the job is done right, the other possibility is a movement along the lines of a crusade for good government in our State that would have a freshness and disinterestedness to it that the old prejudices will slip away in the enthusiasm for the new struggle."[129] Leading that crusade had definite appeal, but Murphy was dubious about support. As he analyzed the situation to Joseph A. Mulcahy,

There has been nothing in common between the organized group of Democrats in Michigan and myself. We do not share the same views about public

g James A. Farley quoted the President as saying on May 1, 1935: "Right now, Frank Murphy is doing a splendid job in handling Coughlin. I'm going to make him High Commissioner to the Philippines and bring him back after a month or two so that he may devote his entire time to the Coughlin situation." *Jim Farley's Story: The Roosevelt Years* (New York: McGraw-Hill, 1948), p. 52. Murphy's notes of conversations with the President in the spring of 1935 suggest the same, as does Roosevelt's plan to have MacArthur to succeed him as High Commissioner. On December 23, 1935 Roosevelt wrote Murphy: "A year from now I hope the many miles that now separate us will be lessened." Two weeks later, he requested Murphy to run for governor. Memo, FDR to Farley, Jan. 7, 1936, RL:OF-400-PI. This letter, however, appears to be lost.

service or the same hopes for party interpretation of what is beating in the heart and stirring in the minds of the average citizen who, articulate or otherwise, prays that his government will be an instrument by which life will be made happier and sweeter.

Wayne County officeholders, as well as others throughout the City; Democratic congressmen, especially from Detroit; and brother Farley, who naturally covets the Michigan electoral vote, are the dramatis personae strutting on the front stage of this little drama. In justice to them, let me state that there is considerable to say in their behalf, particularly if I could be successful. However, I am greatly afraid that at least a number of the local officeholders want me to be a candidate because they would win in Detroit and thereabouts even if I were defeated throughout the State. So far as the electoral vote of the State is concerned, if I could win them for President Roosevelt, I ought to undertake the job without question. As a matter of fact, I would not care if I were defeated in a race with anything of even chance to do the President and his cause some good. That's my duty and there won't be the least hesitation on my part on that score.

However, Michigan is one of the most stubborn Republican States in the Union, and if I am anything of a prognosticator myself, I would say that the chances are much more that my head would roll into a basket than that it will wear a crown if I enter the race.

"Another angle" was the effect on American-Filipino relations. He wished no part of the perennial "evil" of disrupting experienced representation in times of need. "The most problematical and delicate ten years of administration in these Islands are ahead of us," Murphy observed, in what resembled an editorial. "These years will require tact, sympathy and wisdom in handling American interests. There is a possibility, and not too remote, that blunders here might be the source of violence not only in the Philippines but with neighbors." "Is it wise to subordinate this problem of cardinal importance in the Far East to the demands of Michigan politics?"[130] "We must not lightly risk the present stability and cordiality prevailing in the Philippines."[131]

Thus for two months Murphy pondered. Even though he knew that organization could not wait, he refused to give the signal. Even though he knew that he followed "a selfish policy," he nonetheless encouraged friends to " 'make-way-the-road' in case I find myself like one of Michigan's game-fish—swimming upstream in the meandering river of wolverine politics."[132] "Despite belief to the contra," he remarked, "I am not coy about either love or politics and while about the former I have been something of a conspicuous failure in regard to the latter I have managed to do what John Cardinal Manning would describe as 'middling well'. . . . I ought to say right now 'I'm in'—that is my duty to friends and the party and the sort of thing I admire. But I can't and be honest or wise. For I don't know—I only know I hope things will take a turn that will free me from this duty—so as to continue my present matchless job."[133] Grasping at straws, Murphy even encouraged the loyal Frank A. Picard, party sacrifice against Vandenberg in 1934, to make the race. But he also knew that all other considerations were secondary to Roosevelt's success.[134] "Though I prefer to remain at my present post," he wrote Father Coughlin, "I cannot be soft in my loyalty to the President in whom I believe, and who reposed this great trust in me." Hinting for support, he added: "I am confident that when the lines of the fierce fight are drawn you will find yourself unable to throw your great strength on the side of the ruthless pack seeking the President's destruction. He has been, right or wrong, on the people's side. His earnestness in alleviating distress, his policy of action in the face of fear in 1932, which seemed to have left the hearts and the consciences of men in high places atrophied, will loom up higher each day than the defects of the administration which naturally have appeared magnified during the recent period of intense emotions. The President has been a valiant and, I think, great emergency leader.

"If events should so shape themselves that I become a candidate, I will stand foursquare for the President and in case I should be elected Governor of Michigan, I need not tell you that I would undertake the task of an ideal state government."[135/h]

[h] For himself, Murphy asked no more than neutrality. He wrote Coughlin: "We have been friends for many years and have endured and suffered a common opposition. I have taken pride in our friendship and while you have been able to do infinitely more for me than I have been able to reciprocate, I was always proud to take my stand for you in every quarter and, of course, I still am. I do not believe you ought to be drawn into anyone's personal political problem, and I think it is to your best interest not to support or be responsible for me for Governor or for any other high public official in our state. I would understand and approve your desire to remain absolutely silent about my candidacy in case I am catapulted into the Home State Arena. Nevertheless, because of our friendship and struggles together, I would feel unhappy in undertaking this political errand in Michigan in the face of your disapproval and opposition; for none more than myself appreciates your kindness, your rare gifts and the vast good you have done in the years you have been spreading the practical Christian gospel and stirring the people into a new-born zeal for social justice." FM to Charles E. Coughlin, Feb. 27, 1936, Box 34.

That the tone of this letter, which was typical of its genre, was not idle flattery was evident in Murphy's defense of Coughlin among liberals at the time. "Just parenthetically," he wrote to Leo Gabel, "don't underestimate Father Coughlin. He has brains and ability and great sincerity and, while he is not perfect as none of us are, he has done a vast amount of good and will wield much influence in the future. I do not agree with him in everything, but have a great respect for him and personally like him very much." Letter, Oct. 30, 1935. Their relations cooled after the 1936 campaign, however, when Coughlin endorsed Murphy's opponent and the anti-Semitism of Coughlin's movement became more pronounced.

In the end, though still hoping for rescue, Murphy bowed to the inevitable. Offering his services to Roosevelt in any capacity, but hoping for a last-minute reprieve, he reminded the President that "proper consideration should be given to the wisdom of preserving the present satisfactory state of affairs in the Philippines." "The importance of party success and of my contingent service in Michigan, whatever it may be," he said, "should be weighed against this large national interest in the Philippines and the Far East generally." "However, if it is believed that party success in Michigan might be achieved through my candidacy and not otherwise, I should consider it my duty to become a candidate and to take responsibility for the decision." "I attach primary importance to the continuation of your leadership. . . ."[136]

Once in the United States, Murphy acknowledged administration pressures to make the race, and the President gave him a payless leave of absence to do so. Filipinos resented this "riskless resignation," though Quezon in a cordial gesture denied it.[137] But the results of Murphy's divided attentions were soon apparent. Having returned for domestic political reasons, and only incidentally for Philippines policy review, he was able to give only part-time attention to that important enterprise. Filipinos in turn were not long in dismantling some of his favorite innovations as Governor General—unicameralism and probation, for example—which prompted his vain reaction: "It seems that I had more confidence in the Filipinos than they had in themselves. . . ."[138] Had there been an overdose of "Progressivism" in the Islands? Had his opposition to Filipino defense plans given offense?

From hindsight, it is plain that Murphy's regime shares responsibility for fundamental omissions in American administration of the Philippines. New Deal economic policy of agricultural tax benefits and postponed tariffs may have been a short-range boon to the insular economy; but it hardly touched, and may well have aggravated, the long-range problems of land distribution, economic diversification, and dependence on American markets which would determine Filipino democratic progress and economic viability. Murphy's own priorities may have been economic and social in character, and certainly no harm was done by his social engineering projects; but they were miniscule compared to the need, and he was unable to resist the pull of political preoccupations. Neither did he attempt to shake the Roosevelt administration's "precept of inaction" regarding Pacific defense, nor even to challenge its contradictions, until his own position as High Commissioner was threatened.[139] In the delicate process of releasing control of the Philippines without disturbing the peace of Asia, Murphy, like everyone else, was caught in the limitations of his post and in strategic premises that proved to be half-wrong and in the end destructive of the very people he tried to befriend.

On the positive side, nevertheless, Murphy's three years in the Philippines were personally the happiest in his adult life, and the most successful politically.[140] In the first place, for all his romanticism, he emerged as a pragmatic diplomat and tough fighter for personal power and what he perceived as the interests of the United States. One by-product of Murphy's brush with MacArthur was perpetual confusion about the meaning of the terms "liberal" and "conservative" in colonial affairs. Second, for all his personal foibles, he captured Filipino confidence in a period of political insecurity and uncertain commitments. However shortsighted American and Filipino indifference to social questions may now appear, Filipinos valued Murphy's political brokerage precisely because intergovernmental relations, not social development, was their dominant concern. Theories of political development, after all, were thin; the independence policy was beyond recall; and American policymakers were so preoccupied with domestic crises that their highest compliment to Murphy was conducting his office without burdening them. If parts of his program fit current liberal fashions more than Filipino needs, few disputed the contemporary judgment that he left "a record that will be hard to surpass in the annals of dependent peoples" or Carlos P. Romulo's conclusion that Murphy's administration was "the best the Philippines had under the American regime."[141] Personally, Murphy was "among the most thoroughly democratic Governors who ever served in the Philippines."[142] Officially, he did much to stabilize financial and political conditions in the Islands while enlarging the sphere of government planning and social responsibility. And he piloted the orderly transfer of executive power in a delicate situation without diminishing ultimate American responsibility, which was forced into play all too soon. If the results fell short of his goal—not "just an incident nor history, but a monument to the President and his administration"—Murphy came close to his articulated purpose of shepherding the Commonwealth transition under an aura of goodwill.[143]

In the last analysis, the "intangible" of personal confidence may have been Murphy's major legacy in the Philippines. Whatever his reservations about the economic and strategic risks of independence, Murphy was an anti-imperialist colonial governor devoted to "giving these people the best start possible," and they knew it. Filipinos accorded him a position of virtual family trust, a relationship evidenced not merely by their reciprocal blarney and their disappointment when he left, but by his mediation during the Quezon-Osmeña presidential succession dispute in World War II and by the offer of HUK rebel leader Louis M. Taruc in 1946 to negotiate a truce if he were named mediator.[144/1] In the process of building confidence, a force which Filipino wartime loyalties showed was more powerful than treaties and formal commitments, Murphy undoubtedly played a substantial part. Considering his initial inexperience and the chances of mishap, it was an impressive performance which Filipinos credited as a "personification" of the stewardship theory of colonial affairs.[145]

Murphy's adaptation to the Filipino environment, in this sense, was a personal tour de force. While the personal basis of his leadership may explain the impermanency of particular projects, Murphy was never again to win such esteem or gratification in office. Nor was he able to escape unmarked from his Philippines odyssey. Like so many ex-colons, he acquired some less than attractive personal habits and became a self-appointed patron of "our dear Philippines" for the rest of his life. The experience also left an imprint on his thought. As Supreme Court Reports reveal, he never lost the habit of political pedagogy ingrained there.[146] Filipino response to the little New Deal in the Islands likewise strengthened Murphy's conviction in the force of ideals and the power of government-by-example. Murphy left the Islands with a new cultural relativism, in which he perceived American anticolonialist ideals less in terms of exporting Western democracy than of encouraging other cultures to bloom. And the Philippines gave him an appreciation of his country's idealist tradition in international affairs, which came to imbue

[1] For the succession dispute, see Ch. XII. Taruc's offer was received while Murphy was in Manila as the United States representative to the burial of Quezon. Though he offered to see Taruc secretly, the Justice declined to participate as mediator. Louis M. Taruc to FM, Aug. 7 and 13, 1946; Leon Daguis to FM, Aug. 10, 1946, Box 120. Also, *NYT*, July 13, 1946, p. 6. Another indicator of his intimacy with Filipinos was Quezon's disarming note after the 1936 elections: "I want to be frank with you: while I with Aurora and all friends have congratulated you upon your victory and did pray for it, especially Aurora who said a rosary everyday, none of us are really happy that you did win. All of us wanted you to return to the Islands and be the High Commissioner for at least the whole term of my administration. You know our country and our people; your heart—we feel sure—is with us. Your policy was and [is] of helpfulness and you were in a position to secure from the Administration in Washington support for that policy. Now, who will replace you that possesses all these qualifications? I know no one. My fear is that they will appoint some man who will not be sympathetic with our aims and purposes and a lot of trouble will be the result. . . ." Manuel L. Quezon to FM, Nov. 8, 1936, Box 38.

his thought with a companion notion that the United States was "the only hope of civilization."[147/j] Later generations might contest the importance of such matters in colonial politics, but in the creative days of the 1930s, Frank Murphy and the Filipino people established an affair of the heart from which neither fully recovered.

[j] After reading a book on the Philippines, Murphy once commented to J. Weldon Jones: "Omniscience of the writers fascinate me. Next to jurists, I expect they are the most naive of all people. Is it kittens or pups that don't open their eyes until nine days following birth? After three years of having my nose to the grindstone in the Philippines and just as I was departing for home I felt that the scales of the western world were falling off my eyes and for the first time I was getting a glimpse of that part of the Lord's footstool we call the Orient. But a professional observer has so little difficulty seeing it all. . . ." FM to Jones, April 28, 1941, Box 96.

CHAPTER 6

THE PEACEFUL WAY,

1936-1937

MURPHY embarked on a difficult task when he ran for Governor of Michigan in 1936. Drafted largely by presidential managers to bolster Democratic chances in a doubtful state, he had a strong popular base in Detroit. National acceptance of the relief principle and his public stature as an administrator in the Philippines had soothed much of the bitterness over his mayoralty. But he was untried in Michigan at large, and the circumstances of the draft, coupled with his own public resistance to it for a month after his return to the United States, complicated an already fragmented political situation. The election was an uphill fight all the way.[1]

Politics in Michigan were still in a transitory stage, between periods of one-party dominance. The Democrats had not yet forged a cohesive coalition. Rather than consolidate the victory of 1932 the party remained a loose alliance of urban liberals whose main strength was the Detroit congressional delegation, middle-of-the-road party regulars centered in the Highway Department, and old-line "constitutional Democrats" whose conservative outlook bore the marks of years of opposition. The fact that Murphy was without organizational ties had made him Roosevelt's logical choice to effect a patronage settlement in 1935; but even though Murphy made no attempt at that time to supplant the prevailing patronage organization with one of his own, his selection as the state standard bearer in 1936 was bound to aggravate intraparty tensions.[2] The President's intervention strengthened the liberal faction at the expense of the others, it rewarded a Detroit independent, and it came three months after organization regulars had settled on the candidacy of former Lieutenant Governor George W. Welsh. Dissension was open and unhealed at the national convention in Philadelphia, which Murphy attended as a Philippines delegate. White House peacemaking was required before key party leaders acquiesced.[3] In July Murphy announced his candidacy as a means of continuing the New Deal, which he asserted was of "first importance to the people of Michigan and the country at large."[4] Professing equal regard for the President, Welsh refused to withdraw; the Comstock faction, which had been left out of the 1935 patronage settlement, supported him; and most regulars remained neutral. "Jim Farley's candidate" faced a rough primary.[5]

Murphy with good reason developed a case of jitters. Both Welsh and the Republican incumbent, Frank D. Fitzgerald, were popular. Murphy had been away for three eventful years. Though he had insisted to Democratic leaders that he would consent to run only under reformist auspices, it was uncertain how outstate voters would respond to a crusade to make theirs "a great progressive state."[6] Except for labor and minority groups, moreover, his organization was improvised. Also, Roosevelt's first term, plus his intervention in state politics, had alienated powerful former allies. Following orders from Hearst, which a personal appeal failed to alter, the *Detroit Times* denounced Roosevelt's attempt to ride Murphy's coattails in the state as "cheap political maneuvering." One *Times* editor informed Murphy privately, "your dear Christian friend, Reverend Coughlin, is sticking in the knife also." Eventually both the *Times* and Coughlin endorsed his opponents.[7] Lacking newspaper support, Murphy informed his managers, Harry Mead and Howell Van Auken, that "our campaign must be won over the radio." Yet radio campaigning was expensive, and Murphy's resources were limited. It took considerable string-pulling to expedite FCC hearings permitting statewide expansion of the one network which supported him.[8/a] A president might pick a gubernatorial candidate; but as a practical matter, how could he help win a state primary? Murphy, once again, was forced to rely mainly upon his own personal charisma.

Rating Murphy's chances as slim, some observers regarded Roosevelt's Michigan strategy as "stupid." Not only did it jeopardize Murphy, it produced an intraparty battle which in turn destroyed all hope of saving Republican Senator James Couzens from the wrath of his own party for having supported the New Deal. What additional strength could Murphy bring Roosevelt anyway? By being forced to give up a post of high salary and responsibility for a $5,000 governor's seat with a two-year term, the *Detroit News* commented, a "capable" mayor and an "excellent" Governor General was making "an arduous sacrifice for

[a] After the primary, Murphy did receive one $5,000 contribution from Joseph E. Davies, half of which he later returned, and another contribution of $2,500 from the Democratic National Committee. The rest was composed of relatively small donations raised locally. "Donations Received for the Governor's Campaign," Oct. 30, 1937, Box 48. FM to Joseph E. Davies, Dec. 17, 1936, Box 39. FM to Harry Mead, Sep. 22, 1936, Box 37. Murphy's own resources had improved to the point that stock holdings valued at $116,608 yielded dividend income of $5,600 in 1936. But that income, which would be necessary to supplement an inadequate state salary, was obviously insufficient to mount a statewide campaign. For stock holdings, see Hayden, Stone & Co. to FM, Oct. 3, 1936, Box 37. Eleanor Bumgardner to FM, Dec. 31, 1936, Box 39.

his party and its chief. We regret, for his sake, that we are compelled to think it vain."[9/b]

"If he confines his talks to the Brotherhood of Man and the Fatherhood of God, there will be nothing to it," a prominent state Democrat told Farley. Yet Murphy did not confine himself to pieties. As the campaign progressed, it was apparent that he had lost none of his magnetism. Detecting broad support of the New Deal, he emphasized personality and programs rather than party to overcome traditional Republican allegiances. "This must be the strategy of my campaign appeal," he observed to Kemp. "First, my appeal while sound must be a human one; a call to the fresh elements of all crowds, parties and especially those who would join in a movement for a vigorous, upright and new sort of government in Lansing. It must be grounded, of course, on an appeal to the little man."[10] Openly proclaiming his purpose of helping to reelect Roosevelt, Murphy went to the people with a platform of avowed reform. Michigan was going to be to the New Deal what Wisconsin had been to Progressivism—a model state government.

The essence of Murphy's campaign was his standard combination of Progressive nostrums with the social philosophy of the New Deal. Besides "rigid economy" and enactment of the recommendations of the Pollock civil service commission, which all candidates endorsed, he called for unicameralism, a secret primary, workmen's compensation, centralized welfare administration, and swift action to bring the state within the federal social security system to free the aged and the unemployed from "the terror of social and economic insecurity."[11] At earthier levels, he identified himself with Frank A. Picard, who was strong outstate; embraced the teacher tenure proposals of the education lobby, which landed him unwittingly in a hotbed of school politics; and rode the rural electrification issue to fill a void in appeals to Michigan farmers, only 25 percent of whose farms then had electricity.[12] Murphy also made much of suspicions that the Fitzgerald administration had been controlled by former state treasurer Frank D. McKay. While denouncing the "frozen indifference" of reactionaries to the poor, he inveighed against "grafters" and "invisible government." "I will go in there a free man or not at all," he dictated to speechwriter Kemp. "At bottom, this is a fight between progressives and the privi-

[b] Even Roosevelt apparently conceded that Murphy was "too good a man to sacrifice" in the Michigan campaign. Chase S. Osborn to Marguerite LeHand, Nov. 3, 1936, Roosevelt Library: President's Secretary's File—337.

leged classes."[13] Candidate Murphy was taking to the stump in his own inimitable way.

"Listen to Our Frankie," the *Detroit Free Press* said. While Murphy pledged deliverance from invisible government, it was common knowledge that he was Roosevelt's "stooge." While he pledged to make state government "clean and honest, financially sound and socially progressive," it was well known that he had been a "squandering" mayor, "liberal only with other people's money."[14] Republicans also were responding in kind, but, sensitive to criticism far more than he revealed, Murphy was especially nettled by the *Free Press*. "Other professions impose ethical standards on their members," he observed to journalist Frederic S. Marquardt. "Should not its members be subject to the same discipline?" But Michigan was a state in which voters were more ideologically divided than most and 1936 was a fulsome year. The contest became so vituperative that Frank Picard once asked Farley to visit the state "so that people will see that you haven't got horns."[15]

However defensive about being the President's choice, Murphy converted New Deal associations into his long suit. In the primary he concentrated on Republicans and ignored his Democratic opponent. Welsh, who sought to demonstrate equal fealty to Roosevelt, was at a hopeless disadvantage on that score. What at first appeared to be a close primary contest turned into a smashing two-to-one victory for Murphy. The size of Republican primary voting was sobering, but close analysis of the vote indicated substantial GOP defection.[16] September polls still put Roosevelt behind, but optimism prevailed in the Democratic camp, except for the gubernatorial candidate himself, that Murphy had "a good chance to win."[17]

As a campaigner Murphy always ran "scared." Though the polls suggested that he led by a narrow margin, he wrote to Norman H. Hill in October: "The odds have been against me. Father C, the press, the Comstock faction [are] all trying to down me. Only a miracle will save me but my flag will be flying and my guns booming until midnight of the 2nd of November."[18] Catholicism was an undercover issue, but for Murphy no less than his adversaries the booming was over the New Deal—the closer to November the more he hugged it. "This campaign is not for me primarily a quest for public office," he asserted. "But it is of vital interest to Michigan to have a governor sympathetic with the progressive program of social justice and economic democracy sponsored by President Roosevelt and the New Deal." And on that note Farley's candidate was "saved."[19]

Roosevelt and Murphy, in fact, switched coats. In the great popular landslide of 1936 Roosevelt carried Michigan by 317,000 votes—the approximate Republican defection in the primary—while Murphy's majority was only 48,000, roughly the margin predicted by the polls. Intuitively he seems to have correctly gauged his marginal strength by striking a New Deal note in the campaign. Murphy carried only 21 of 83 counties by a total popular vote of 51 percent. Even so, the victory was solid considering the opposition. As the fourth Democratic governor in Michigan history Murphy was accompanied into power by a Democratic lower house and a virtual sweep of the state administration. Liberals were jubilant. "Nothing in yesterday's election rejoices my heart more than your own triumph!" wrote Rabbi Stephen S. Wise. "We, far away, think of you as one of the truly significant figures in the democratic leadership of America."[20] Hearst, too, sought to make amends by inviting Murphy to rest at San Simeon; instead he visited Joseph P. Kennedy's Palm Beach home to escape office-seekers and formulate his plans. "After three years in the tropics, this will be an ordeal," he observed to Hill. "As it grew tough during the campaign I used to close my eyes and say to myself 'Well you have been hit by coconuts and you have to recover.' After a long siege we became hardened so now we are already to furrow the field."[21]

Murphy interpreted the victory as a mandate to effect a "new social and political philosophy" in Michigan. While friendly politicians urged him to build a pro-Murphy organization while the iron was hot, with the exception of Wayne County he left those matters to party professionals with the understanding that the major appointments would be strictly according to merit while the rest would require approval of both county and state party chairmen.[22] That decision, though intended as an overture to party harmony, may have been a fatal error for it left party reins in the hands of his natural antagonists. But in the interim period the governor-elect wanted to rest and concentrate on his program. With Hayden rounding up talent, and university professors William Haber and James K. Pollock supplying ideas, Murphy developed plans for a social security system and an overhaul of state administration.[23] The "immediate and supreme objective of the State's New Deal administration," he announced, when asking Governor Fitzgerald to call a special session, was legislation to bring Michigan within federal social security and employment service systems before the deadline expired. Furthermore, he was going to demonstrate that "state government can be perfectly clean and incorruptible." "We may not have great gifts," he said, "but we can fight for our ideals."[24]

Contrary to expectations, however, a fighting idealism did not entail a series of radical reforms. Unicameralism was low in priority. Social justice oratory was balanced by inaugural assurances that "we intend no harm to those cherished institutions of personal liberty or private property." Murphy's first messages to the Legislature, just as in the Philippines, were filled with "amenities and generalities" on which all men could agree.[25] When translated into action, they boiled down to proposals for social security; centralized budget, relief, and welfare operations; installation of civil service; teacher tenure and elimination of loyalty oaths—and a rather courageous appeal for reapportionment as commanded by the state constitution. It was an important, well-considered, but hardly radical, program, most of which even the *Free Press* commended.[26]

Thus while political seers pondered the national implications of the New Deal landslide, in Michigan Murphy calmed the opposition with another "splendid beginning." The new Governor's plans were "forward looking, sane and practical," the *Grand Rapids Herald* commented. "There is but little of the much feared and oft predicted 'dew and sunshine.'" Significant gains toward recovery had been made recently; his concentration on fiscal and administrative improvements was not likely to rock the boat. For those who noted the gap between rhetoric and reality, Murphy once again appeared "off to a fine, fair start."[27]

II

The trouble was, Murphy had an uncanny ability to take office just as storms were about to erupt. Within a week of his inauguration—and in part because of it—Michigan was beset with the worst governmental crisis in its history—the sit-down strikes of 1937.

Unionist ferment had been brewing for some time in the automobile industry. The American Federation of Labor, capitalizing on federal guarantees of organization and bargaining rights under Section 7(a) of the NIRA, had undertaken to organize auto workers nationally in 1934-35. But the AFL was torn by jurisdictional conflicts and weakened by the devotion of President Roosevelt and the Automobile Labor Board to proportional representation rather than to the unionist goal of exclusive bargaining rights for majorities. The AFL was unable to turn a few local successes into a sustained national drive, and the failure to organize auto workers helped to split the labor movement into warring factions. In 1936 the United Automobile Workers, then a small but militant industrial union on the Left, joined John L. Lewis's miners and other unions in the rubber, steel, and textile industries to form the Committee for Industrial Organization, which eventually became a rival organization dedicated to industry-wide rather than craft jurisdiction as the basis of organizing unskilled workers in mass production industries. Following enactment of the Wagner Act, which represented a shift of policy on the part of the President, and the coming of improved business conditions and of friendly governments in the next year, the occasion was ripe for a campaign to gain recognition. CIO unions had no master plan. Each industrial union was more or less on its own. But the David among them picked the giant, General Motors, as their first target.[28]

The UAW, substituting audacity for numbers, chose the sit-down strike out of weakness. Although it had a few strong locals in Cleveland, Toledo, and South Bend, total national membership in 1935 was probably no greater than 25,000—roughly five percent of the workers in the industry. In Michigan the UAW was even weaker. Statewide membership numbered less than 3,600; competing independents, including auto workers associated with Father Coughlin, were roughly equal in size. Even worse was the general debility that resulted from a long period of corporate hostility and a two-front war with AFL leadership. The Big Three manufacturers—Ford, Chrysler, and General Motors—were virtually union-free. One local in Flint was so bereft of strength that it elected a company spy as its chief. Undaunted by the fact that they represented a small fraction of workers, UAW leaders such as former Baptist preacher Homer Martin and the gifted left-wing organizers, Wyndham Mortimer and Robert Travis, were impatient young workers newly emergent from battle with the AFL hierarchy over jurisdiction and the right to elect their own officers. The union for them was the object of militant fervor. The strike was not just a result but a means of stimulating membership. And the sit-down tactic was their weapon to seize rights which Congress had thrice bestowed in vain. To date, not a single UAW local had won a signed Big Three contract.[29]

The sit-down strike, which had paved the way for Leon Blum's united front in France and spasmodic union victories in the United States, was eminently a minority weapon. By taking possession of a strategic assembly line a small number of disciplined workers could halt production of an interlocking industrial combine. An orthodox walkout with mass picketing, which was beyond UAW capabilities, would not be necessary to paralyze a corporate giant. Nor would traditional strike-breaking techniques be effective against such a bottleneck. The fiercely independent UAW locals apparently had no grand strategy even among themselves—eager unionists sat down prematurely in Atlanta and Kansas City in November and December—but a general understanding existed that the main targets were the Fisher tool and die factories in Cleveland and Flint. These plants were among the few where key manufacturing units and locals strong enough to halt production converged. In preparation for the strike, union organizers Mortimer and Travis had concentrated on rebuilding the decimated Flint locals for almost a year.[30] In mid-December, after his Kansas City local struck over discharge of a worker, UAW president Homer Martin called for a companywide bargaining conference, only to be told by GM executive vice-president William S. Knudsen that collective bargaining must take place locally in each of the company's 69 plants. Specific grievances over piece-rate wages, seniority rights, and grievance procedures were high in union priorities; but the central issue became the union's demand to be exclusive bargaining agents for General Motors employees. Upon Knudsen's rebuff, and in alleged fear that the company would remove vital dies from Fisher Body Plant No. 1, impromptu sit-downers seized control of Fisher Body plants in Cleveland on December 28 and in Flint on the next day. Gradually the tie-up spread throughout the General Motors system and the company went to court in Flint for an injunction against trespass. Two days after Murphy took office a general strike against GM was called; 34,000 workers were idled immediately and by mid-January over 135,000 were affected, reducing production to a trickle. Hardly had Murphy caught his breath from Philippines controversy, a gruelling election campaign, and inaugural revelry than his labor friends greeted him with a full-scale crisis. The long-threatened drive for industrial unionism was at hand.[31]

The situation was extremely complex. The company was not alone in resisting UAW recognition. Both the AFL and the Flint Alliance, a local back-to-work movement strongly suspected of corporate sponsorship, opposed the UAW bid for sole representational rights. Other than martial law and a mediation board for public utilities, there was no state authority to intervene and no formal conciliation machinery in Lansing. The new federal NLRB was the only agency available to decide jurisdictional questions or to compel collective bargaining; but General Motors had joined sister corporations in massive resistance to the Wagner Act pending its doubtful approval by the Supreme Court, and the weak UAW was no more eager for a representational election under new federal procedures than was the company. General Motors, in fact, had secured an injunction against NLRB interference in its St. Louis plant. The Wagner Act had been held unconstitutional by the federal circuit court having jurisdiction over Michigan. Even picketing was illegal under a state supreme court ruling. Unions had met overpowering opposition in the industry for decades—and here was a small minority advocating industrial unionism and a guaranteed annual wage. Neither concept enjoyed wide approval. Though the UAW did not demand a closed shop, the strike would have stirred controversy enough without sit-down tactics.[32]

The sit-down, however, converted the strike into trespass and civil disobedience. Union self-help measures thus provoked a prolonged public controversy that bore striking resemblance, in cause and effect, to the racial "sit-ins" of the 1960s. Conservatives, who regarded the tactic as a patent invasion of property rights, clamored for forcible eviction of the strikers. The crux of the issue, William Randolph Hearst later wrote, was "whether we hold to the American or have adopted the Russian system."[33] Only a few liberals defended the legality of the sit-down as such, but union methods attracted considerable popular sympathy because of corporate tactics and defiance of the Wagner Act. Murphy himself once expressed those sentiments by asserting: "I find the employers largely responsible for having forced this powerful weapon on labor. . . . A great injustice has been committed against the workers by the employers in resisting the right of collective bargaining and it has *forced the workers to use the only effective weapon they could find, the Sit-Down strike.*"[34]

But while Americans added a new inflammation to the class-conscious politics of the period, in Michigan the time for theory quickly vanished. Flint verged on panic as vigilantes grouped and outside "goon squads" assembled in that GM-dominated city. All the elements of industrial war were present: a militant labor organization flouting an injunction and employing a potent strike weapon, a company long hostile to labor unions of any sort, other organizations with conflicting jurisdictional claims, and vigilante groups ready to capitalize on public resentment against a small minority which had interrupted the work of GM's 50,000 local employees after a long period of depression. Industrial unionism was not to be recognized without struggle. Murphy faced "the most critical labor conflict of the nineteen thirties."[35]

As Governor he wasted no time asserting government responsibility. The day after the strike was called Murphy intervened "in the interest of the public." "There is going to be no violence in Flint," he assured the city. "There is going to be peace and order."[36] Despite the absence of state mediation machinery, he had long regarded the existence of a large-scale strike as an indication that "something is wrong," which demanded governmental intervention. His personal sympathies, beyond doubt, were with organized labor. Union forces had been instrumental in his election and he was "not unmindful" of their support.[37] For years, moreover, Murphy had insisted that labor "does not intend to impair any one else's interests—only to secure its own just deserts." He regarded collective bargaining as essential to "the general amelioration of gross inequalities and social injustices" which threatened American democracy.[38] Whether a minority or not, the UAW represented "an outraged sense of justice" rising from depression and employer resistance to organization in Michigan. While the sit-down might not be legal, no labor weapon had even been so regarded when first used.[39] The compelling consideration was peaceful settlement by negotiation. Returning from an all-night strike conference in Detroit to open the state Legislature, Murphy emphasized that as a part of his New Deal mandate for social justice: "We are to secure for wage earners an effective voice in the arrangements that govern their working conditions by upholding the principle and the right to orderly collective bargaining. . . . Industrial warfare belongs to the past. Force and violence are not to be tolerated. We want the rights of labor protected and want business to flourish. The government ought to play a helpful part in adjusting differences and settling controversies. It can do this only in an atmosphere of peace and reason and mutual respect."[40]

The great strike was to demonstrate the efficacy of collective bargaining and the precept that "the peaceful way is the right way."[41] And if Murphy himself stood to profit thereby, it was not the first time he would gain by jumping into a policy vacuum.

The initial hurdle was getting the parties to the conference table. As sit-downs spread to 19 plants in seven states, General Motors refused to negotiate until the factories were cleared. Knudsen informed Martin: "Sit-downs are strikes. Such strikers are clearly trespassers and violators of the law of the land. We cannot have bona fide collective bargaining with sit-down strikers in illegal possession of plants. Collective bargaining cannot be justified if one party, having seized the plant, holds a gun at the other party's head."[42] In the eyes of union supporters, Knudsen was calling the kettle black. The impasse was eased for the Governor and federal mediator James F. Dewey, however, when CIO attorneys publicized the fact that state Judge Edward D. Black, who had issued the injunction, owned $219,000 of General Motors stock. Although the judge failed to understand the furor over his participation in the case, since state law offered little choice but to grant injunctive relief, an embarrassed General Motors allowed the injunction to lapse. The union then agreed to drop exclusive recognition as a prerequisite of bargaining, in return for a company pledge to negotiate on a national basis. But the sticking point was evacuation; the company refused to bargain until the men were dislodged, which the UAW refused to do without guarantees against resumption of production, a condition unacceptable to GM. Thus stalemated, the negotiations collapsed. (Unknown to either party, Murphy quietly transferred his own $100,000-plus holdings of GM stock to his sister who sold it at a substantial profit.) The company then took to the offensive, and battle ensued.[43]

On January 11th, in an effort to force the workers out, General Motors shut off the heat in Fisher Body Plant No. 2, while company police attempted to block the importation of food. Strikers rushed the gates to preserve their lifeline, city police attacked, and the picketline became a battleline, known in union histories as "the Battle of the Running Bulls." Police attacked with tear gas and bullets; the strikers retaliated with fire hoses, flying auto parts, and hysterical, picketing wives. By nightfall 24 persons had been injured, 14 of them by gunshot. "Flint was on the brink of civil war."[44] Rushing to the scene, Murphy called out 1,500 national guardsmen to maintain order. Neither party, said he, "by recourse to force and violence, will be permitted to add public terror to the existing economic demoralization." "A serious riot has occurred." "Without wishing to countenance the unlawful seizure of private property, the State has heretofore refrained from taking strong measures in the hope that amicable settlement might be reached."[45] But now the situation was out of control; the state had to intervene.

For all concerned, the signal that Murphy regarded the seizure as illegal, his orders to maintain the status quo, and his instructions that the troops should remain outside the strike area until called, contained a crucial policy decision. To preserve the peace at that point was to prevent forcible ouster of the strikers by private or local force. Nonviolence, in effect, meant state protection of strikers in their illegal occupancy. Government was tolerating civil disobedience. Denounced in Congress and in the press for doing just that, Murphy also defied traditional policy by ordering public relief funds to be made available to the strikers' families. "I do not intend to have children or the aged suffer, whatever the economic conflict may be," he said. Then, he summoned Knudsen and Martin to confer in his Lansing office "without condition or prejudice."[46] "Whatever else may happen," said Murphy, "there is going to be law and order in Michigan." "The public interest and public safety are paramount."[47]

By capping an explosive situation, and by exerting the primacy of public authority, the Governor emerged as the central figure in the effort to settle the strike. Not unmindful of that fact either, he greeted the conferees with a "pro-public" warning:

I want peace and order preserved. . . . At every opportunity I have counseled temperance and restraint. Each side must understand that the public authority is supreme in Michigan.

By tradition and choice we are loyal to democracy and its institutions. We must settle this in the American way. . . . No one should wish or attempt to place the Governor of the State in the position of suspending the law of the land. This is not right and he is not going to do it.

Whatever may be done, I want your conversations to continue in a spirit of reason and good faith until you have agreed on a basis of negotiations among yourselves. . . .

Since "we are all in a sense trustees," company and union bore a "moral obligation" to negotiate under government auspices.[48]

Once again Murphy was asserting powerful new responsibilities for government. In the midst of a growing national debate over the legalities of his course, which found even so respected a columnist as Mark Sullivan condemning it, Murphy issued a wee-hour announcement that "we have arrived at a peace."[49] After 15 hours of negotiation, a truce was arranged whereby the union would evacuate on condition that General Motors would not resume production during a fortnight of bargaining set to begin January 18th. A collective sigh of relief greeted this "common sense" arrangement. Little had been expected from the conference. The "Lansing Truce," by simply renewing negotiations, rebounded to Murphy's credit as an industrial diplomat. Murphy's "masterstroke of diplomacy," enthusiastic editors proclaimed, made him "the man of the hour . . . bound for higher places, even the White House."[50]

Suddenly, in the middle of the evacuation, the UAW repudiated the truce. Shortly before the scheduled evacuation of the Flint factories, the union learned from a reporter that Knudsen had agreed to bargain with the Flint Alliance and planned to resume production in Detroit. Despite the Alliance's willingness to postpone its claims at the Governor's request, the union regarded the action as a "double cross," renewed the strike, and negotiations were broken off. Again Murphy insisted that strikers would be fed, that troops would preserve the status quo, and that the dispute would not be settled "by force and violence while I am Governor."[51]

"We will pull it together somehow," he remarked on leaving for Roosevelt's second inauguration.[52] But efforts at conciliation in Washington were no more successful. Two days of secret—and separate—conferences between Secretary of Labor Frances Perkins and the two principal antagonists, Alfred P. Sloan and John L. Lewis, produced only deadlock. The General Motors president refused to meet Lewis until the union gave up possession, whereupon the CIO president angrily demanded Roosevelt's aid. Said Lewis:

For six months during the presidential campaign the economic royalists represented by General Motors and the DuPonts contributed their money and used their energy to drive this administration out of power.

The administration asked labor to help repel this attack and labor gave its help. The same economic royalists now have their fangs in labor. The workers of this country expect the administration to help the workers in every legal way, and to support the workers in General Motors plants.[53]

Lewis's demand "sounded pretty raw" even to peppery Harold L. Ickes; and the President himself replied that some strike statements were "not in order."[54] For the sit-downs provoked public antagonism seldom equalled by labor tactics. Lewis's statement provided New Deal critics with ammunition about a "collective bargain of 1936," which allegedly lieutenants Perkins and Murphy were now fulfilling.[55] By this time people all over the country were debating the sit-down in terms of catchphrases like "human rights versus property rights," "property rights and no rights," and the worker's "sacred" property right to his job.[56] Stockholders sympathetic to the unionists conducted their own sit-downs by selling GM stock. Letters flooded the Governor's office branding him everything from "traitor" to "statesman." And Michigan's right-wing Congressman, Clare Hoffman, denounced him for "permitting, if not sanctioning, mob rule."[57] Resentment fanned by Lewis's statement was soon neutralized by Sloan's continued refusal to meet so long as the UAW held "our plants unlawfully." President Roosevelt rebuked him in public, and Secretary Perkins was even less guarded. "The American people do not expect them to sulk in their tents because they feel the sit-down strike is illegal," she said. "There was a time when picketing was considered illegal, and before that strikes of any kind were illegal. The legality of the sit-down strike has yet to be determined."[58]

Although the Secretary's remark stirred another tempest, common sense, as Lewis said, dictated negotiation rather than mutual exhaustion. Legal questions aside, it had been obvious all along that General Motors did not relish a bloody, armed eviction of the strikers. Company officials waited for public animosity to crystallize against what they called "a minority who have seized certain plants and are holding them as ransom to enforce their demands."[59] Officially the company maintained that eviction of the strikers was the responsibility of public authorities. Murphy himself welcomed a legal test of the issue, though he believed it desirable to wait until the controversy had cooled. "When this is settled," he maintained, "it will be because of a free conference by participation of both sides." But after Secretary Perkins announced that Sloan "ran out on me" during her second attempt to renew the talks, there was only one place left for the dispute to go— to Michigan, where tension was rising alarmingly.[60]

Wishing to sustain public confidence, Murphy claimed that the situation was not unmanageable. Confidential GM reports also indicated that contrary to the general impression the well-disciplined strikers inside the plants had no arms, had committed no sabotage, had a high regard for the Governor, and acknowledged his right to order them out.[61] Yet peaceful settlement was greatly jeopardized after collapse of the Washington talks. Positions and opinions had solidified. Flint resembled an armed camp. Returning to the offensive, the company announced its intention of resuming production in order to provide jobs for loyal workers, and the Flint Alliance revived its back-to-work claims. As a precaution, the union made plans to seize another strategic production unit, the engine plant at Chevrolet Plant No. 4, in the event of the union's ouster from Fisher No. 1. To forestall resort to arms, the Governor exacted mutual pledges of nonviolence and again asserted the neutrality of state power: "I want it understood," he declared, "that the militia is in Flint to protect life and property, and to safeguard the citizens of that city, whether strikers or non-strikers. It will not be used to break strikes or to take sides in labor disputes."[62]

The pressures to break the strike were tremendous; still Murphy refused to budge, "even if ten thousand men marched up here and asked me to do it." To reminders that President Cleveland had broken the Pullman strike with federal troops, he answered: "This is not 1894." When one group "sat-down" in his office to demand action, he delivered a lecture: "You ought to be ashamed you are being used in this way. . . . There are agent provocateurs at work on an adroit plan to embarrass me and to compel the use of force." Violence would "complicate a tragic situation"; violence would leave lasting scars on the nation. Asked by the Alliance if he would protect workers who returned to their jobs, he responded: "it is your duty to forbear." "Nothing in the world is going to get the Governor of Michigan off the position of working it out peacefully. All the power of General Motors or the Flint Alliance or Mr. Lewis' organization is insufficient to get the Governor off that path." That was "an awfully poor answer to take back when our streets are not safe," the Alliance representatives replied; but Murphy snapped tartly, "I might say yours was not a very good question."[63] Even governors could be obstinate.

Behind the confident exterior, nevertheless, Murphy was worried and wavering toward summary action. "Kemp," he asked hastily on January 27th: "Why not declare martial law in Flint—Close the streets. Plants. Order people to meet for negotiations." That was "a logical question I have been asking myself," his legal aide replied, though the conservative Kemp could not resist posing the opposite query: "Why not use public authority to *protect* and enforce legal rights. . . ?"[64] Consultations with the state attorney general produced the conclusion that the Governor's options were actually quite narrow. Clearly he could not compel employers to accept unionization or even to negotiate. No legal basis for martial law existed until local authority proved inadequate. Neither was he willing to evict the strikers until peaceful remedies were exhausted. Murphy's aides recommended that he might make political gravy by sponsoring a national meeting, resembling the Mayor's Conference, to organize permanent machinery to reduce such costly private warfare. Otherwise he was powerless to intervene beyond persuasion and marshalling public opinion against the parties to settle. And so far, those efforts had failed.[65]

Private initiatives soon forced his hand. The LaFollette Committee entered the scene with shocking disclosures of industrial espionage on the part of auto manufacturers, including the "bugging" of the room of federal conciliator, Edward F. McGrady. While organizers were being beaten in nearby Saginaw on February 1st, both General Motors and the union broke the status quo. Company lawyers returned to court for a sweeping injunction against interference with corporation property.[66] The strikers, after pickets clogged the streets and Roy Reuther led a decoy action against nearby Chevrolet Plant No. 9, occupied the strategic Plant No. 4. Rioting broke out anew. All day long the Governor kept tense watch over the tinderbox at Flint. The sheriff and the city manager, who was later fired for making unauthorized arms purchases, excitedly urged martial law. Murphy withheld action on the advice of Mayor Harold E. Bradshaw, militia commander Joseph H. Lewis, and even Lawrence P. Fisher himself. "Our policy is to keep out until local authorities [are] unable to handle it," he told state adjutant general John S. Bersey. "I am reluctant to send [the] military in until it is necessary for we must command [the] situation immediately."[67]

By nightfall the judgment began to change. Police reported that the new sit-downers were heavily armed, perhaps even with machine guns, and that a hundred cars with reinforcements were on their way from Ohio. Local police, to be sure, had not even been engaged. Strikers made no trouble so long as they were left alone. But if the law were to be enforced, as Kemp asked the mayor, "what then?" Both sides were poised for battle; only a spark was needed to touch off conflagration. And "if it broke into open fight," the Flint police chief asserted, "we could only handle it by shooting several." Acting on a combined judgment that Flint was a powder keg beyond local control, Murphy ordered a military cordon around the plants, inspection of incoming cars from Ohio, and restriction of food imports to those factories occupied by bona fide strikers. "We can't mix sentiments in this," he told Secretary Perkins. "The opportunity to work the matter out in a free atmosphere is gone."[68]

Though bloodshed was averted in the second Flint riot, the situation remained "very ticklish." Feeling that his "strong views" about nonviolence were being abused, and letting off the steam he could not afford to expose in public, Murphy freely vented his wrath behind the scenes. "We have a very savage crowd on our hands," he remarked of the General Motors negotiating team; and he was scarcely more complimentary about the union. "The military would not have been called out last night if you hadn't put them there," he told CIO organizing director, John Brophy. "The Union put them there no one else." The lot of the peacemaker, he observed bitterly, was "taking abuse from both sides."[69]

The second Flint riot committed government authority beyond recall to a strike settlement. On February 2nd Judge Paul V. Gadola issued an evacuation order with a 24-hour deadline. As the Governor's staff prepared a statement that he had "no honorable alternative" but enforcement of the court order, Secretary Perkins, informing Murphy that John L. Lewis had just seen President Roosevelt and was on his way to Detroit, asked the Governor to arrange a conference between Knudsen, Lewis, and himself in view of the President's belief that a "partial solution" could be found. In response, Knudsen and Lawrence

P. Fisher refused to attend except at the President's request. Murphy, who sensed an attempt to embarrass Roosevelt and a slight to himself, rejected their reply and recommended against making the request. Instead, he proposed that Secretary Perkins attempt to arrange an understanding through CIO leader Sidney Hillman that if the union evacuated, Murphy would prevent production by surrounding the plants. Somehow means had to be found to get the men out without embarrassment. "After 2 p.m. tomorrow afternoon," he warned the Secretary, with an eye to the court orders, "I have got to say that I will be obedient to the law or not."[70]

The vise was closing tight. While Murphy and Perkins were arranging for a meeting at the President's behest, Genossee County sheriff Thomas W. Wolcott served the injunction on the strikers. While the strikers hissed and booed the sheriff as he read, from union headquarters there came this message of defiance in their name:

We have decided to stay in the plant. We have no delusions about the sacrifice which this decision will entail.

We fully expect that if a violent effort is made to oust us many of us will be killed. Unarmed as we are, the introduction of the militia, sheriffs or police with murderous weapons will mean a blood bath of unarmed workers.[71]

By no means certain that the strikers were unarmed, the Governor faced a form of insurrection. Certain only that "I am not a representative for the GM or for the labor group but for the people," Murphy vacillated as pressures mounted and his options decreased. On the one hand, he was willing to shoulder responsibility for a deal with the union to avert disaster. He also was willing to lead negotiations between the parties if the President insisted. On the other hand, he feared presidential sponsorship of the meetings. The court order, he felt, doubtless under prodding from Kemp, altered the dispute fundamentally. The elementary duty of a state chief executive was to enforce the law. While Murphy still held his trump card of martial law, which would relieve him of civil process, what if the conference failed? In the end, a higher responsibility prevailed. "The President wants you to do it," Secretary Perkins reportedly informed him over the telephone. Roosevelt, his fingers burned in past auto negotiations, did not want a conference in Washington, "and isn't going to have one." Come what may, the forces of a showdown were converging on Murphy.[72]

Arranging a meeting "in accordance with the wishes of the President," the Governor hoped against hope that an acceptable basis of recognition and evacuation could be found before the deadline, "so we don't have to resort to extreme measures." While national guardsmen began to lay plans for a siege, as distinct from armed assault, to force the workers out, Murphy assured CIO leaders that "the military will never be used against you. I'd leave office first." And he advised authorities in Flint to refrain from any action that might disturb the progress being made.[73] But after two days of arms-length negotiation, in which the Governor of Michigan and James F. Dewey shunted back and forth between negotiating teams in his brother George's office at Recorder's Court—a place chosen to symbolize public power—stalemate still resulted. Even after the President applied more pressure the parties had yet to meet face to face. By February 5th tension was reaching the breaking point. Company counsel secured writs of arrest against sit-down strikers and UAW leaders in Flint. An estimated 2,000 men now inside the plants prepared to resist; countless union men from across the midwest streamed into the city for a showdown battle. And the sheriff, with national publicity, wired the Governor for assistance in executing the writs. Murphy, irate at GM lawyers and Judge Gadola for rejecting his pleas for delay, conceded that he was in a "pretty touchy spot."[74] In the midst of conferences which showed the first glimmer of progress, he confronted an awful choice—refusal to enforce court orders or certain bloodshed.

Grimly he responded with four steps. He authorized the militia to seal off the plants in order to prevent either mob violence or entry by the sheriff and his deputies. He directed the militia to inform the sheriff to stay his hand pending the outcome of that day's conference. "Sheriff has excuse," Murphy noted, "—we are still in conference." He ordered preparation of a letter to Lewis and Martin informing them of his intention to enforce the court order. "If these men cannot agree," he remarked to Secretary Perkins that evening, "I will declare martial law and guarantee them the right to go to and from work." Finally, after a noontime conversation with the President, who by then was in daily contact, Murphy recommended that Roosevelt urge the parties to accept the "Toledo Agreement," an informal recognition device won by the UAW Toledo local in 1935, along with election and nondiscrimination guarantees, as a basis for a truce which would permit evacuation and the beginning of substantive bargaining. The zero hour for eviction came and quietly passed as the Governor took no steps to enforce the court order—and indeed authorized the reverse—pending the outcome of negotiations. Murphy was sticking to course. "I'm not going down in history as 'Bloody Murphy!'" he declared. "I represent the public interest and the public interest requires peace."[75]

With that, impeachment talk erupted in Republican corners of the state Senate, while Representative Hoffman stirred Congress to debate over "armed, open rebellion against the enforcement of the law" in his home state.[76] And it was rumored that Vice-President Garner, who only two months before had written Murphy that he trusted his intelligence to the limit, exploded in a Cabinet meeting over the administration's toleration of civil disobedience.[77] Seldom had the nation been so aroused over an industrial controversy. Some thought they felt the foundations of the Republic shake, for on the same day that the Governor of Michigan refused to enforce a judicial mandate, Roosevelt's court-packing plan was sent to Congress. What had become of a "government of laws"?

III

By suspending enforcement of a court order, Murphy staked his political future on a negotiated settlement. A month of intensifying rancor greatly aggravated the task. Evacuation would have to come as part of agreement on union recognition. All his public pronouncements about the rule of reason, which struck skeptics as romantic delusion, could not disguise a deterioration in his position as mediator after the court order. General Motors' move to arrest the strikers, which he attributed to company lawyers rather than to Knudsen, Murphy regarded as a serious mistake and a deliberate effort to embarrass him. Union negotiators Lewis, Mortimer, and CIO counsel Lee Pressman he also considered no less truculent. Alternating between moods of sweetness, toughness, and occasionally despair, Murphy told Secretary Perkins: "I am having a bad time with these fellows"—and he was. Even as his policy of negotiation rather than force gave the union critical aid, Lewis seemed unmoved by judicial action and unyielding about exclusive bargaining demands.[78] The central issue of the strike remained unsolved.

Nevertheless, internal evidence supports Murphy's contention that he was not indifferent to the needs of law and order and that he deferred enforcement of the court order over a weekend because "peace was imminent."[79] At noon on Friday, February 5th, shortly after he was informed of the sheriff's request for help, the President telephoned Murphy to express support of a truce formula then in the process of formation. According to Roosevelt's understanding of negotiations at that point, Knudsen had agreed not to give more favorable treatment to other organizations, nor to encourage competitive unions, and was willing to make formal guarantees to Secretary Perkins or to Murphy to that effect. Lewis, late the night before, had dropped insistence on recognition of the UAW as bargaining agent for all GM employees and had proposed the Toledo Agreement as a basis of negotiation. Under the agreement the company officially recognized the union as agent for its own members only, but unofficially agreed not to sponsor a company union or to seek a certifying election. The Toledo Agreement, in other words, was a face-saving device granting de facto recognition to the UAW, and Knudsen had admitted as much.[80] Apparently General Motors was now willing to consider the arrangement for a limited truce period. The unsettled issues were the length of the truce and exclusive recognition—whether GM in the meantime would negotiate with other organizations on a national basis. To Roosevelt the parties were "awfully close together"; their positions were "almost identical." "I feel that you have a real chance to bridge the gap," he told Murphy, "and if you want, but it is entirely up to you, I would be glad to say the same thing to both Knudsen and Lewis." "Can't we get these friends together? Let me know. You are doing a swell job, Frank."[81]

Encouraged by the President, Murphy let the court deadline and the sheriff's request pass without commitment one way or another. During afternoon conversations with Secretary Perkins and dinner sessions with Knudsen and Lewis, he began to hammer out a peace formula based on the Toledo Agreement, to which he added provisions for continued bargaining and eventual elections. He also urged that President Roosevelt insist on acceptance of this truce formula. Even though it would postpone formal recognition Lewis would have de facto bargaining rights and exclusive recognition ultimately. The court order and Roosevelt's backing actually enabled Murphy to get Knudsen and Lewis together for the first time, on February 5th. Despite public agitation and the danger of a violent eruption, he began to feel the first signs of progress.[82]

The difficulty was that the positions of the parties were not identical. The UAW was then too weak to risk elections. A few months difference in the period of sole bargaining rights might make all the difference in its ability to acquire the majority membership required for exclusive recognition under the law. Lewis also insisted on formal acceptance of the exclusive bargaining principle. As the noontime crisis passed on February 5th, Lewis's uncompromising behavior left no doubt that sole bargaining rights were still the nexus of dispute. The entreaties of AFL president William Green to Roosevelt and Murphy not to grant those rights—"you must not yield to force and wrong"—

only served to exacerbate the issue.[83] The parley teetered on the brink of collapse for two days of frenzied weekend bargaining.

As an alternative to the Governor's election formula, the company proposed a Toledo Agreement for a 90-day period. Still Lewis held out for exclusive recognition. Irritated by the lack of union response to company concessions, GM negotiators Donaldson Brown and John Thomas Smith once had to be ordered, as Murphy related it, not to walk out. Murphy greatly respected William S. Knudsen, whom he regarded as an industrial genius who wanted to settle a nasty affair and resume production. He later came to have a like respect for John L. Lewis. But at the time, his patience with the union chief was wearing thin. So was his confidence in the security of his own position. On Monday, February 7th, Murphy informed the President that he intended to make public his determination to "uphold the existing laws of the state." "I also told the President," he informed James Dewey shortly afterwards, "that I would continue the conference and that they would have to work out a solution, but that in the meantime I thought that I ought to make my position plain about the order of the court. He said 'you are absolutely right, you are justified in doing that—go right ahead with it.' I then told the President that when I made myself plain Lewis could decide upon the course he was to take and he said 'they will have to decide what they want to do.' "[84]

Murphy had contemplated making such a statement since February 5th, and Kemp was directed to produce a draft. Whether it was designed as an ultimatum to Lewis or was a means of self-protection while the conferences continued is hard to say. Murphy had talked both ways. On the evening of February 8th negotiations were still deadlocked, and the letter was undelivered. A transcription of a telephone conversation between Murphy and Congressman Andrew Transue reveals the same caution and reluctance to decide that he had always shown in the pinch. Said Murphy:

You know I have tried to close it up every day. I have done my best but I am up against two stone walls. Lewis wants to keep the men in the plants until he gets exclusive bargaining and GM doesn't want to give collective bargaining. I don't think it means a thing to him what we have already done. However, he has been very good in this conference. He has been able, patient, stubborn and unyielding in his position. He ought to know that the position he already has is due to the fact that they have a sympathetic government in Washington and Michigan. It has taken on a new status when a court has [ad]judicated. Of course, the negotiations may close up tonight or tomorrow. Then I think I'll have to take a position about it. It has been the greatest strike in the history of the United States—not a fatality, not a man lost his life. Andy, do you yourself think the feeling is strong in Washington? You can't put those men out by force without killing them. I don't want to do it—I don't think you would want to do it in my place. What is the support in Congress for this sit-down business?

Transue replied, "None whatever." [The] Governor finished by saying, "alright, Andy, I'll do something on it tonight."[85]

Murphy finished his letter that night. He also met Lewis alone in what must have been a memorable meeting. Two men of passionate temperament and oratorical power—the one who spoke and looked like a bulldog, the other who talked gently and looked like a priest; the one ill with grippe and the other physically weary—had what the latter called "a grand talk" in Lewis's hotel room which produced "the first ray of hope." As Murphy recounted the meeting to Edward F. McGrady, "I asked the other men, who don't measure up to him at all, to leave, and I am afraid they haven't told him the truth."[86] General Motors had offered a three-months Toledo Agreement, along with a pledge not to bargain with any other group on general policy without the Governor's sanction. The proposal fell short of formal recognition and certifying elections, both of which Murphy supported. But on behalf of the GM offer, he asserted: "I made a most eloquent appeal every [*sic*] made. He said 'You are the most persuasive man I have ever met in my life.'" And that night Lewis agreed to accept the de facto truce arrangement if extended to six months. The labor leader desired not to make the offer unless assured of its acceptance, but the Governor knew "that we can end this strike on that basis."[87] Murphy, at the price of dropping his election proposal, felt that he had Lewis "straightened out."[88]

Following his meeting with Lewis, he exerted every artifice, including presidential pressure on General Motors, "to crowd it through." "This strike has got to go through tonight," he said, "or we are done."[89] While the truce failed to satisfy advocates of exclusive recognition, the main object was to break the deadlock, the terror, and the economic dislocation. No difference of principle remained between the parties, Murphy believed, and a truce would take the heat off Washington—though he remarked ruefully, "it puts it on my doorstep." "I have got to make statements to protect my position."[90] Two days of tight bargaining, plus presidential pressure on Sloan and the duPonts, were required to win General Motors approval and to hammer out the language. Then, on February 11th, six weeks after the strike began, Murphy announced dramatically to an early morning crowd of newsmen: "An agreement has been reached." "It has been a difficult job but reason has prevailed."[91] A pact was signed in Recorder's Court, recognizing the UAW as bargaining agent for "those employees of the Corporation who are members of the Union," in return for a General Motors pledge not to bargain with any other union for six months without the Governor's approval. In New York Alfred P. Sloan announced a companywide pay increase and workers left the plants singing the union refrain, "Solidarity Forever." The great sit-down strike was over.[92]

What had happened to break the impasse? Had Murphy ordered Lewis out or had the parties, all of them eager to avoid bloodshed, simply recognized the limits of possible concession? The precise truth is elusive. Both Murphy and Lewis made subsequent revelations about their meetings which differ sharply in implication. The Murphy version, disclosed two years later before a Senate subcommittee, left the impression that he turned the trick by issuing a private ultimatum to Lewis. In a formal statement, dated February 8th, but marked "read and accepted, 9:15 p.m. February 9, 1937" on the original, Murphy informed Lewis that since the parties had failed to reach an agreement, the time had come for compliance with the court order. The Governor stressed that his policy had been to exhaust every peaceful remedy, but that continued occupancy of the plants and defiance of public authority "have not at any time been viewed as lawful or right." The statement recognized that the claims or equity of today might become the law of tomorrow but that the judiciary had spoken, and that it was the function of the executive to enforce, not to review, its judgment. "I have no alternative but to perform this duty to the best of my ability," wrote Murphy. After all, he reminded Lewis, "the constitutional authority of the courts must be protected if we are to have orderly government and orderly peaceful society, with security for persons and property and freedom from arbitrary action and coercion. This is as important to workers as it is to employers. It is essential to the preservation of democratic principles."[93] Thus confronted with an ultimatum, so the Murphy version goes, Lewis replied simply: "Governor, you win."[94]

The Lewis version, while not disputing that Murphy threatened force, left the opposite impression. At the fifth annual UAW convention in 1940, Lewis asserted to a roar of applause: "It is a matter of public knowledge now that the Governor of this State read me a formal letter in writing demanding that this action be taken by me, and my reply to the Governor of the State when he read that letter, with the knowledge of the President of the United States—and the approval— was this: 'I do not doubt your ability to call out your soldiers and shoot the members of our union out of those plants, but let me say that when you issue that order I shall leave this conference and I shall enter one of those plants with my own people. And the militia will have the pleasure of shooting me out of the plants with them.' The order was not executed."[95]

That Murphy read Lewis a formal ultimatum with the President's approval is scarcely in doubt. The testimony of the two principals was corroborated by the respected James F. Dewey, who said: "I was present. He read Lewis the ultimatum . . . and did so in a fashion which left no doubt as to his determination."[96] The Governor's notes of February 7th indicate that Roosevelt approved his idea of making the statement. A White House aide also made notes of a telephone message following the Lewis-Murphy meeting of February 8th, in which Murphy reported the breakthrough in negotiations and his intention to issue the statement. This conversation was significant because Murphy, contrary to outside suspicions, had abandoned support of exclusive bargaining rights to which the administration was politically committed. Roosevelt, who in past auto strikes had leaned toward management at critical moments, was under considerable pressure not to do so again. Privately, members of the Governor's staff suspected that Secretary Perkins and McGrady still supported the union's position. In contrast, Murphy saw the truce proposal as the "only chance" for a "just" accommodation of union security and property rights and recommended that "the Boss" insist on it for two reasons. First, both General Motors and the AFL opposed exclusive UAW recognition. Second, to accept union demands would be coercive "after the courts have re-adjudicated the lawful possession of the property." As agent for neither company nor union, the state chief executive had to uphold fundamental rights, "which include personal property rights as well." Nor could he delay a statement to that effect "longer than tonight."[97] A governor had to be in the position of sustaining the law of the land.

There is no question that Murphy had agonized over his obligation to enforce the law throughout the sit-down strike. If he helped to sell Roosevelt on the terms of the truce, however, it is doubtful that his statement caused Lewis's change of heart. For his letter was read a day after the breakthrough, in front of Dewey, and at a time when General Motors, not Lewis, was holding out. Any threats used by

Murphy to help soften up Lewis, in short, must have come verbally and privately on February 8th. His formal ultimatum read on February 9th was most probably a pro forma statement designed for two objects, both of which failed: (1) to win Lewis's approval of GM's 90-day truce offer when the company still balked at a longer period, and (2) to protect himself in public. Both men therefore were right in a sense, except that they referred to different meetings. Lewis did yield to Murphy's importunings about dropping exclusive recognition, but not to any ultimatum about evacuating the plants. The court order was not executed because the corporation, not the union, yielded to administration pressure. The matter would be of small importance except for uncorrected false implications and one omission: after all the care in drafting a statement of his position as chief executive, Murphy as governor never made it public. The General Motors strike passed without a hint of his concern for judicial authority and property rights. The result was an impenetrable label as a labor partisan.

Like the temporizing over the court order itself, no grand decision determined this policy. No occasion ever quite presented itself to offset fear of antagonizing labor or to suit Murphy's dramatic flair. Others knew of the letter to Lewis, and begged its release. In the campaign of 1938, Murphy seemed to grope for the right opportunity to speak. Senator Prentiss M. Brown tried to arrange an appearance before the LaFollette Committee, and Murphy himself authorized journalist Joseph H. Creighton to reveal the story in a *Saturday Evening Post* article.[98] But neither invitation materialized. In a continuing political calculus that must have taken tremendous self-control, Murphy maintained a fateful silence that proved to be the costliest error in his political career.

These implications were not immediately apparent. Aware only that a nightmare was over, the public responded to the General Motors settlement as if to magic. Somehow, the *Atlanta Constitution* commented, "a rare figure in public life . . . worked a miracle." The public tribute of the contestants themselves, though their private views were something else again, seemed to express the common judgment. Greeted with laudatory messages from Newton D. Baker, Felix Frankfurter, and numerous New Deal officials, Murphy was widely acclaimed for his "brilliant and statesmanlike" handling of an ominous controversy. Even those like Garner, who believed that he had temporized dangerously, were having second thoughts. Murphy was now being hailed as a "conservative in the broad sense of the term." Against great pressures, he had held fast to the goal of peaceful negotiation long after most men had given up. Wrote President Roosevelt: "Yours has been a high public service for which I desire to express the thanks of the Nation."[99]

When the terms of the truce were announced, nonetheless, the implications for labor-management relations were far from clear. Charging that the UAW had suffered a stinging defeat by surrendering its demands for exclusive representation, which his organization of course opposed, William Green pointed up the disparity between the union's goals and its winnings. However Martin might retort that Green was the "modern Judas Iscariot of the labor movement," the UAW had achieved much less than its original demands, and Green's reminders widened the AFL-CIO breach. Yet from hindsight, the UAW clearly had won a great victory. For the first time, a Big Three auto producer was forced to bargain and to sign a contract with union representatives on a national scale. Partial recognition and the resulting security gave the UAW minority a foothold and an *élan* for rapid unionization that would be difficult to overestimate. Within six months UAW membership jumped from a fraction so small that it was a closely guarded secret to a claimed total of 520,000—all without the aid of the closed shop.[100] Unlike the history of organization in other basic industries, the first national strike of the UAW was not only free from bloodshed; it was unexpectedly successful. Had a less sympathetic administration been in office, its quick road to power undoubtedly would have been rougher. Murphy's policy of negotiation despite the sit-down, in effect, tipped the scales with government support and delivered on New Deal pledges to the CIO.

Whether the General Motors settlement was also a victory for the collective bargaining process that New Dealers claimed is less certain. However Murphy might laud the truce as an "exaltation of reason over brute force and violence," the government, as Knudsen said, "practically ordered" agreement.[101] The President, by encouraging Murphy and pressuring the parties, also played a greater and probably more neutral role than anyone confessed. The General Motors strike thus was a prelude to those large industrial conflicts which revealed with increasing frequency the limits of private economic warfare and the tendency of public authorities to intervene in the name of collective bargaining. But if these implications were then obscure, one result appeared sure. Murphy had jumped into a vacuum of public responsibility and emerged unscathed. While Roosevelt may have called the plays, Murphy bore the responsibility and reaped the glory. A great personal gamble skyrocketed him into national prominence as a leader for sanity in industrial relations. "Next to President Roosevelt himself," the *El Paso Times* observed, "Governor Frank Murphy of Michigan has become the most talked of public figure in the United States." Asking "who won" the strike, *Time* answered: "The first vehicle to roll off G.M.'s revived assembly line will be a band wagon labeled 'Frank Murphy for President in 1940!' "[102]

In February 1937 the apparent victor of the sit-down strike was Murphy himself.

CHAPTER 7

OH, MICHIGAN!

1937-1938

THE aftermath of the General Motors settlement soon upset contemporary calculations. The sit-down strike became a turning point in American industrial relations. The GM truce not only gave the UAW a base for ultimate organization of the auto industry; it gave the entire CIO organizational drive tremendous forward momentum. The GM truce not only widened the split between CIO unions and the AFL, which soon expelled them, it touched off a militant assertion of trade union power. United States Steel and General Electric quickly signed partial recognition pacts, independent auto unions shifted over to the UAW, and then a wave of recognition strikes swept the United States. Labor, across the country, was on the move.[1]

The General Motors contract, indeed, was like the bursting of a reservoir. John L. Lewis and the CIO became magic symbols of pent-up aspirations throughout mass production industries. Workingmen by the thousands flocked to the union. Sit-downs by the score, though often without the neo-military discipline of the prototype, spread with lightning speed. In shipping, textiles, coffin factories, and five-and-dimes from coast to coast, people were sitting down at their jobs. It is difficult not to suspect, along with William Allen White, that the American imagination had been caught up by another craze; like the sit-ins of the 1960s seemingly everyone with a grievance sat down. Over 4,300 strikes, 477 of them sit-downs, occurred in the first 11 months of 1937, a strike rate double that of 1936 and exceeded only in the peak year of 1917. Nearly two million workers were involved; 28 million man-hours were lost.[2] But the sudden rash of strikes was symptomatic of deep disquiet in the popular mood. Even Justice McReynolds noticed a "strange unrest" stalking the land.[3] Workingmen, buoyed by Roosevelt's 1936 mandate and by CIO successes, agitated as never before for improved status in the American scheme of things. That sit-down strikes constituted civil disobedience was less important than their effectiveness. Militancy, with strong ideological overtones, became the mark of a man's social consciousness.

Sit-down strikes were not always the most significant labor weapon, but the rampage of sit-down strikes provoked great public excitement. In some states strikers were appeased; in others they were forcibly

uprooted. Several governors, notably in states having little mass industry, issued warnings against sit-down tactics. "Those who provoke
bloodshed are entitled to no maudlin sympathy for the injuries they
may sustain," Governor Hoffman of New Jersey declared. The "sit-
down is a symbol of communism, which, I suppose, is all right if you
want communism. I don't." While hardly as brash, Wilbur Cross of
Connecticut and six other governors were no less explicit that sit-downs
were intolerable.[4] As the unionization drive accelerated, however, attention focused again on Michigan, where 18 more sit-downs hit General Motors in Flint before its contract was signed, where a wave of
sit-downs swept through the hotels and stores of traditionally open-shop
Detroit, and where 6,000 workers sat down in the Chrysler, Hudson,
and Reo automobile plants. Governor Murphy cut short a vacation
with the Kennedys at Palm Beach to be available in case the auto negotiations failed.[5] With a grim kind of pleasure many of his former critics
blamed his "evil precedent" as the cause of contagion. Toleration of
the General Motors sit-down had come home to its Michigan roost.[6]

"Oh, Michigan!" the *New York Times* exclaimed: first the banking
panic rose from that turbulent state to engulf the land, and now an
epidemic of strikes. To make matters worse, Michigan's chief executive
appeared to be "a man of peace with a strong prejudice against enforcing the law."[7] Murphy agreed to intervene in Detroit after the
Board of Commerce expressed fear for the city's "international civic
reputation."[8] Actually he found it relatively easy to arrange arbitration
proceedings for hotel and department store disputes, but his attitude
stiffened abruptly as he observed the sit-down fever getting out of hand.
For the first time in Michigan, the Detroit police were ousting strikers
by force. Among them were outside organizers, unemployed floaters,
and a few ex-convicts whom the Governor recognized from his days on
the bench. In the middle of a store, he sounded his approval of the
evictions. "A legitimate strike of labor men in good faith commands
respect and a neutral attitude on the part of government officials," he
said. "The State must not be in a position of a strike-breaker, but a
raid is not a strike. . . ." It was a "modified form of banditry and must
be treated as such."[9] Angrily, when informed of union protests alleging
police brutality, he told reporters: "These raids, irresponsibly conducted
in the name of strikes . . . are over. There will be no more of them."[10]

The crucial problem was the Chrysler strike. Although the General
Motors sit-down was the more important dispute because it broke new
ground, the second wave of automobile strikes in some ways was more
disturbing. The Chrysler Corporation, which had been the locus of

Father Coughlin's influence in the labor movement until local president Richard E. Frankensteen led the union into the UAW, had already recognized proportional representation. Negotiations were in progress over shop rules and seniority rights when the workers sat down. Emboldened by fresh victory, unionists chose the number two producer for a decisive showdown over the closed shop and exclusive bargaining rights. These goals seemed unrealistic, however, and the strike ill-prepared. The impulsiveness and bellicosity of the strikers at Chrysler evidenced a lack of union discipline not present at Flint. While the UAW picketed his court, Judge Allan Campbell issued a broad injunction against the sit-down with the warning: "There can be no compromise between the rule of law and the rule of violent self-help."[11] But UAW leaders were defiant. "We did not order them to sit-down," replied Homer Martin, "and we will not order them to come out." Chrysler also was implacable. In order to save his friend from possible embarrassment, De Soto president Bryon C. Foy warned Murphy in confidence not to call a meeting between Walter P. Chrysler and Lewis because Chrysler refused to confer so long as the UAW disregarded courts.[12] With several thousand workers inside the plants and over 100,000 idled by the automobile stoppage; with 30 other sit-downs taking place in the city and the Teamsters ready to quit in sympathy, Detroit felt imperilled by a general strike. Forcible eviction of all strikers would have required an army.[13]

In mid-March Murphy made a series of moves to control the situation. First, he formed a Law and Order Commission, composed of representatives from management, labor, and the public, to recommend corrective measures and mediate smaller strikes until permanent government machinery could be established.[14] Second, he ordered a team of experts—Kemp, William Haber, and E. Blythe Stason of the Michigan Law School—to prepare labor relations and minimum wage legislation for submission to the Legislature.[15] Then as Secretary Perkins and James F. Dewey began to mediate the Chrysler dispute in cooperation with Murphy's office, he issued a strong policy statement, the same one, in fact, he had contemplated making during the General Motors strike but had withheld. On the merits, he made plain his sympathy for the workers. The underlying sources of unrest, he lectured Michigan, were the "injustices and unhealthy conditions that are inherent in an unregulated competitive system," the failure of "backward employers to recognize properly the right of collective bargaining," and the "unduly harsh working conditions and instances of extremely low wages" in the state.[16] But in context, the primary message was a sermon on labor's own interest in law and order.

Obviously Murphy regarded sit-down strikes as "disorderly and unlawful methods of pursuing lawful and worthy objectives." He even included the bugbear of union incorporation among the range of possible alternatives open for consideration by the Law and Order Commission. No private individual or group, he maintained, should possess "unregulated" power to disrupt the delicate economic mechanism on which the livelihood of all depended.[17] Clearly Murphy was making a bid for leadership in what was fast becoming a national preoccupation —industrial conflict. And just as clearly, his labor policy reflected long-term concerns for "social justice" as balanced by the influence of Edward G. Kemp.

Widely extolled as "sound talk" and "wise policy," Murphy's law and order statements contained plain warnings to labor. UAW officials Martin and Frankensteen responded by boycotting the Detroit commission. Hard experience and many defeats, they replied, demonstrated the futility of committees; employers responded only to force.[18] When Martin defied the court injunction and threatened to call a general strike unless Detroit ceased the "brutal eviction and ruthless clubbing" of strikers, when a wild night of rioting took place among the cab drivers in Chicago's Loop—a tremor of fear spread across the country. Concern existed not merely for Lewis's alleged ambition to become labor czar; men feared a challenge to constitutional government.[19] Similar conflicts had rocked Great Britain in 1925, and Mussolini's rise to power had come on the heels of a crushed sit-down movement. Breaking into a routine Senate debate, the aging California Progressive, Hiram Johnson, rose to "issue a feeble warning." "The most ominous thing in our national life today is the sit-down strike," he said. "It is bad for the Government and in the long run it is worse for labor. If the sit-down strike is carried on with the connivance of the public authorities, then the warning signals are out, and down that road lurks dictatorship."[20]

Industrial disorder momentarily pushed aside the court-packing issue. No senator would defend sit-downs as legal; many denounced them as indefensible and "un-American"; but New Dealers found explanations for them in economic injustice, the lawlessness of management, and the behavior of the Supreme Court. "We will have something more than sit-down strikes in the United States," Senator William Borah warned, if basic grievances were not met; but for Senator Hugo L. Black, who lamented that the only lawful alternative being proposed was the "bayonet and the gun," the immediate problem was judge-made. The Supreme Court, he asserted, stood as an "insuperable, impossible obstacle to the passage of laws, either by the States or the Federal Government," which would ameliorate the underlying unrest or give public officials authority to control industrial strife. Of the Court's decision on the Wagner Act, Senator Sherman Minton added, "apparently there is a sit-down over there."[21]

The sit-down strikes and the Supreme Court issues were inevitably linked. As the Wagner Act case moved to oral argument before the Justices, government attorneys Charles E. Wyzanski and Stanley Reed cited the automobile strikes as evidence that "two colossal forces are standing astride the stream of commerce" with instantaneous national effects.[22] While Homer Martin denounced the Court as "the greatest threat to democracy in the United States, outside of fascism," a bloc of conservative senators attributed mass lawlessness to the example set by those "in high places."[23] While Murphy was being condemned for "cowardice" by right-wingers in the House, Representative Martin Dies introduced a resolution to repudiate the sit-downs and investigate the "communistic" CIO. Curious things were happening. AFL unions suddenly appeared benign—despite their participation in over 100 sit-downs. Ardent states'-righters in the antilynch law debate now demanded Roosevelt's intervention in the strikes under the Civil War Force Acts.[24] And liberals now tolerated the lawlessness they condemned in the south.

Liberals commonly dismissed the outcry, in the manner of the *New Republic*, as veiled opposition to effective trade unionism. Yet there was no doubt that militant union tactics, like the racial disturbances of the 1960s, spawned a backlash of popular disfavor. Pressure for an authoritative administration rebuke of sit-down strikes cut across a broad political spectrum. Two spectacular events, a presidential attack on federal courts and the toleration of mass disobedience, indeed, clipped the Democrats' wings at the peak of their power. "What has happened," Walter Lippmann observed, "is that for the first time in their experience the American people are not sure whether the party in control respects the law and means to enforce it." "The political connection between Mr. Lewis and Mr. Roosevelt is the crux of the matter."[25] Taking official cover behind federalism, the President passed the buck to Michigan, whose governor followed the same policy. Silence, so their critics believed, spoke volumes.

But Murphy seemed either unwilling or unable to enforce his law and order stand when the chips were down. His insistence on the conference method and refusal to intervene until requested by local authorities, manifested a higher priority to the new government responsibility of mediating industrial warfare than to the traditional responsibility of enforcing property rights. Technically he did not refuse to enforce orders of the Wayne circuit court. But forcible eviction was beyond local authority if not the militia itself, and it was assumed that he would exhaust all negotiation efforts first. No formal request for state assistance was ever made or offered. The way out, said Murphy, was "to sit with an honest and law-abiding adversary at a conference table and to place faith in his sincerity and integrity of purpose."[26]

For many, the occasion for such a formula had passed. Tension built up dangerously. Even the normally optimistic President admitted "off the record that the thing doesn't look so good."[27] From within the Chrysler plants came another ultimatum purporting to express the workers' resolve "to protect our rights to our jobs with our lives." More threat than supplication, the unionists reminded Governor Murphy—"we elected you"; the choice between peace and war was "flatly up to you."[28]

While Homer Martin called a mass rally on the outside to demonstrate labor's solidarity, tempers became feverish. Reporters flocked to Detroit to witness what the Catholic journal *America* called "Rebellion in Michigan." Correspondent Arthur Krock was writing that only future historians could judge whether "civil war was averted or social disintegration begun" by the New Deal policy of blessing sit-down strikes as an antidote to the conduct of the high court.[29] Attempting to avoid both, Murphy held his ground. Under severe personal fire, including threats of bodily harm, he declared: "The Governor will not permit himself to be stampeded."[30] For behind the official silence he had resolved to break the impasse by all necessary force.

The Chrysler strike, in this respect, was a paradox. Because of its scale, public agitation was greater than during the General Motors sit-down; but the parties never had much doubt that the patience of public authorities was spent. Hardly had Judge Campbell spoken when federal and state officials made plans to evacuate the plants and to renew negotiations, while the Governor made sure of his ground by ordering a thorough review of martial law as it applied to metropolitan Detroit. By mid-March the Chrysler Corporation had signified to Secretary Perkins that it was willing to continue negotiations under nonproduction guarantees once the plants were evacuated and the question of sole bargaining rights eliminated.[31] Only three alternatives were considered to force those conditions on the union—James F. Dewey's plan that the Governor simultaneously demand compliance with the court order and a conference between Chrysler and Lewis to effectuate it; Kemp's proposal for an ultimatum with a deadline; and martial law as a last resort.

The Dewey proposal had the advantage of securing prompt evacuation while saving the faces of Martin and Murphy with the workers. Lewis would have to do the surrendering. That plan probably would have been followed without more ado if Kemp had not forcefully complained that it pressured a single industrialist who was freely bargaining and compromised the rule of law.[32] Kemp, who expressed increasing alarm over the union's closed-shop demands and his friend's knuckling to "private lawless force," convinced Murphy that only on peril of snowballing disobedience and dire political consequences could he fail to give positive public assurances of his determination to uphold the law and private property rights. Silence—no matter how desirable to avoid provocative talk or to hold the workers' confidence and their votes—was producing a dangerous deterioration of public confidence. Once and for all he had to make plain that obedience to public authority was not negotiable.[33]

Thus persuaded, and after assuring the CIO president against arrest in Michigan, Murphy called a conference between Chrysler and Lewis on March 23rd to explore whether adjustment was possible before he took "extreme and costly measures with possible unfortunate consequences." Informing Lewis that he anticipated a request for assistance from local police, he issued an unmistakable public warning:

While respecting rights of workers and seeking to advance their proper interests by lawful means, state government cannot forsake its responsibility and will employ all necessary and available means in this and similar cases to uphold public authority in this state and protect property rights in the interest of the general public.[34]

The purpose of meeting, in other words, was to decide which method would be used to clear the factories; the question of peace or war, though Murphy set no deadline, was up to Lewis.

"Your message suggests that I confer under duress," the CIO chief replied. "Nevertheless and notwithstanding I agree to be present." Special negotiations offered opportunity for greater concessions, or at least for more tightly controlled bargaining, than those in progress. But Walter Chrysler's response was chilling. The corporation, preferring to bargain locally, refused to negotiate with Lewis about exclusive recognition or evacuation, which it regarded as the responsibility of the government and the union. Said Chrysler: "We will not enter into any trade to get the men out of the plants."[35]

Meeting Lewis with the militia chief beside him as a symbol of public power, Murphy arranged a truce that evening. On condition that Chrysler not resume production during negotiations, Lewis ordered the men to withdraw, which, after some initial balking, occurred the next day without incident. The crafty union leader, facing determined public authority and a strike which anti-Martin forces in the UAW viewed as ill-timed, had little choice but to capitulate.[36]

Aside from public terror, all the Chrysler sit-down achieved was negotiation under state rather than private auspices. Even so, Murphy received considerable praise for his handling of an ominous situation. "In these few months past," wrote poet Carl Sandburg, "some of us feel, you have conducted yourself with the austerity and the spare utterance of a true Chief Magistrate in a democracy." "I know something of the inevitable historic background that has ushered in the C.I.O. Anyhow more power to you. . . ."[37] Despite resumption of collective bargaining between Chrysler and Lewis, however, the debate raged on. Evacuation had occurred. Were the dangerous implications of civil disobedience resolved?

There had been truces before. Viewed against the sit-down epidemic across the country and the belligerency of union leaders, Murphy's optimistic assertion that the "spirit of the eve of Good Friday" prevailed over the Chrysler negotiations seemed starry-eyed.[38] Who, reporters asked him, was going to be crucified this time? Although the Chrysler-Lewis meetings apparently went well, William Green publicly repudiated the sit-down weapon as detrimental to labor's long-term interests. Even Representative John W. McCormack scored Frances Perkins for having implied that the legality of the tactic was in doubt. By attaching a rider condemning sit-downs to the Guffey coal bill, Senator James F. Byrnes threw the Senate into another portentous, chicken-and-egg debate over responsibility for the sit-down contagion. Few senators would add anything significant to what had been said before. In one notable address, Senator Robert A. Wagner explained again that the strikes were inevitable responses of men frustrated in the exercise of their legal rights. That proposition was supported by the fact that resort to sit-downs declined by half in the month after the Supreme Court approved the Wagner Act. But to many senators, causation was less important than symptom. At least Congress could speak out against civil disorder, said North Carolina Senator Josiah W. Bailey. "I want a vote. . . ."[39]

Labor's militancy had become a great partisan issue. A powerful bloc of legislators—Borah, Barkley, Robinson, Brown in the Senate, and Maury Maverick in the House—defended Murphy against the "ranting and roaring" of the Right. A few Farmer-Laborites and Dean Leon Green of the Northwestern University Law School even defended the sit-down as a lawful extension of the right to strike.[40] Yet the great majority of the people, according to a Gallup poll, opposed its legalization. However unpleasant they considered the prospect, those who entertained the thought publicly, as did Harvard Law School dean James M. Landis, subjected themselves to widespread attack.[41] For to a growing number the sit-down strike was "incipient revolution," an "alien" distemper which in conjunction with the attack on the Supreme Court threatened the vitals of government under law. As a fateful coalition of Southern Democrats and Republicans began to emerge on both issues an impressive example of popular fears came to the Senate in a telegram from a group of Boston civic leaders headed by a Harvard president emeritus, A. Lawrence Lowell:

Armed insurrection—defiance of law, order and duly elected authority—is spreading like wildfire. It is rapidly growing beyond control.

What determined action by the Governor of Michigan several weeks ago, or a few words of counsel by the President, would have ended summarily, now challenges the supremacy of government itself.

No question of the right of labor to liberal wages and healthful working conditions is involved. This is universally conceded. The issue is far more vital; it dwarfs any other issue now agitating the public mind; it attacks the very foundation of our political and social structure.

If minority groups can seize premises illegally, hold indefinitely, refuse admittance to owners or managers, resist by violence and threaten with bloodshed all attempts to dislodge them, and intimidate properly constituted authority to the point of impotence, then freedom and liberty are at an end, government becomes a mockery, superseded by anarchy, mob rule and ruthless dictatorship.[42]

"Quit hiding under the beds," scolded the *Detroit Free Press*. That dreaded sign of revolution, the UAW demonstration in Cadillac Square, had been "far more orderly than the celebration of the Detroit Tigers winning the world series—and only about one tenth the size."[43] Rebellion was hardly in sight. For once, Murphy and the *Free Press* agreed. "I feel I am standing alone," he remarked to Norman H. Hill, "but I know I am right about it." The trespass was ended; collective bargaining was underway. Taking time out from the Chrysler conferences,

Murphy hit back at his critics. The General Motors settlement had not encouraged, it had reduced industrial strife. "What if there had been a bloody massacre in Flint?" he asked. Serious fighting there would have "precipitated labor conflict of the greatest magnitude in the entire nation." Certainly the sit-downs were illegal, but that did not justify "plunging people into fratricidal conflict when a controversy can be settled peacefully." Of course, communist agitators were fanning conflict, but were not "infamous spies and detectives" doing the same? "I have been urged to 'shoot the workers out of the factories and thus end sit-down strikes once and for all,'" he told an off-year election audience. If the people wanted that, then "they will have to get another man for Governor of Michigan."[44]

The people had to forbear. For labor relations, as for public relief before, Michigan was "blazing a new trail." State government was attempting to demonstrate: "First, obedience to authority, and to show the wisdom of it. Second, the adjudication of issues amicably and in a spirit of reason in conferences." "While we have had our difficulties here," said Murphy, "the reasons for it are obvious."[45] The sit-downs were a natural aftermath of depression and a long period of unfavorable labor relationships. At bottom, they were "a symptom of a fundamental social disorder" so complex, so rooted in the "human equation," that no solution could be worked by "exact legal justice." Citizens, of course, should obey courts, but it was equally axiomatic that "laws must be just and ample so that great human movements don't start bursting through legal structures which do not meet their needs." "We hear talk that there is a revolution in this country," Murphy observed. "That is sheer and utter nonsense." "These are not bad men. They want to do good." These were honest American workingmen, seeking their rights to a larger share in the richness of American life. And if they were wrong in their methods, "they can be taught and the lesson need not be written in blood."[46]

As if to affirm the possibility, 10 days of substantive bargaining settled the Chrysler dispute. Combining proportional representation with mutual pledges against intimidation, the contract was a UAW setback which assurances against company unionism did not mask. The union not only failed to win exclusive bargaining rights, which was the sole object of the sit-down, but the strike aggravated an internal power struggle and exhausted public tolerance of militant tactics. Local union leaders had made serious miscalculations about Murphy's intentions and the popular temper. The Chrysler dispute thus checked the momentum of sit-down tactics in Michigan. Not long thereafter UAW membership began to decline under the combined impact of internal dissension and economic recession.[47]

Still, the Chrysler accord brought a momentary calm. The Hudson and Reo strikes were settled quickly along parallel lines. The Governor arbitrated several more Detroit sit-downs, as well as the Consumers Power strike at Saginaw. Additional manufacturers—Packard, Studebaker, Briggs, and Murray Body—soon signed recognition contracts. (During an uproarious session the House of Representatives rejected the Dies resoluton to investigate the CIO, and the Senate transformed the Byrnes rider into a general resolution condemning all lawlessness in industrial relations: sit-downs, industrial espionage, and refusal to bargain collectively.[48]) Once again Governor Murphy received laurels for winning "another victory for the rule of reason and the conference method."[49] Observing that the agreement was less significant than the procedure of reaching it, S. L. A. Marshall commented for a group of *Detroit News* reporters: "To some of us, the highly important thing is not that the unions and the car manufacturers have signed on the line but that we see the beginning of something we have long hoped for, an implementing of the democracy in the economic sense toward the end of its political preservation. . . . We wish you, not more power, but the same wise use of it." "I meant every word I said to the Press," wrote Walter P. Chrysler. "You have performed a real public service and you can well be proud of it."[50]

Perhaps there was something to beliefs, which Murphy's press agents fostered, that the nation had lucked on a fresh new leader for enlightened industrial relations. Within three months Murphy had placated without bloodshed or loss of labor's confidence two of the most dangerous strikes of the century. Far away in Shanghai, the *Evening Post & Mercury* noted, "if this sort of thing keeps up, he'll be Presidential timber. In fact, he probably is already." A Gallup poll soon verified the observation. His name also figured prominently in speculation about the President's choice as vacancies appeared in the Cabinet and the Supreme Court.[51] Publicly objecting to overtures of support, Murphy expressed a politician's typical hope that union recognition would bring his state industrial peace and him opportunity to install a model government.[52] During a weekend with Roosevelt in January 1938 he may have declined interest in a seat on the Court before the President offered it. Rumors were strong among other contenders that he held the key to the post.[53] Normally Murphy treated such rumors lightly, but this time he seemed serious. "It is best for the Supreme Court and for myself," he said, "that I am not appointed to that august body."[54] After the Chrysler settlement his thoughts were on politics.

The industrial wars opened intriguing political possibilities and fanned Murphy's presidential ambition. Almost overnight, he had jumped from a reluctant governor and party sacrifice to a national celebrity ideally positioned to ride the labor issue into the White House. Privately he expressed doubts that the country was ready for a Catholic president, and a third-term bid by Roosevelt would moot the question. But first-hand experience as governor of the country's most industrialized state at least entitled him to a national forum. Hiring speechwriter Charles J. Hedetniemi, and engaging a speaker's agent, Murphy took full advantage of opportunities for public exposure—so much so that Lieutenant Governor Leo J. Nowicki created a minor tempest by demanding governor's pay for the 41 days Murphy was out of state. Neither did Murphy spurn the boosters who made initial soundings and organizational efforts in Connecticut and California.[55] Nor did he dampen the old habit of projecting personal ambition into lofty goals. Perceiving opportunities for moral leadership in turmoil, Murphy groped toward a conception of giving constructive direction to labor's new-found political power. "Possibly the ability to do this will be the greatest opportunity for political leadership in this country in our generation," Hayden observed after one late-evening discussion during the GM strike.[56] Certainly Murphy made no deals with the CIO on the subject; his labor connections prior to the strikes, after all, had been concentrated in the AFL. But it was equally certain that when he spoke of Michigan his eye was on higher responsibilities. An admirer from afar, Josephus Daniels, caught the portent when he commented from Mexico: "I pray that wisdom may be vouchsafed you. Who knows but you were sent to the Kingdom for such a time as this."[57]

II

Murphy's labor troubles, in fact, were far from finished. Supreme Court approval of the Wagner Act in mid-April touched off another wave of recognition strikes across the country. The economic impact of the automobile sit-downs, perhaps even fear of revolution, may have weighed heavily among the Justices who pulled the "switch in time" of the *Jones & Laughlin* decision. Had they legitimized the Wagner Act earlier, the difficulties in Michigan, as Murphy suggested, probably would have been reduced.[58] Yet once labor began to assert its newly won rights the resistance of Little Steel and other industries indicated that more was at stake than a radical tactic or a rule of law. The violence that raged in steel and mining towns from Pennsylvania to Illinois only heightened the fact that, while armies were rumbling in Europe and Asia, Americans were engrossed in an internal struggle over the workingman's place in society. Industrial relations had become an acute national problem.

In the hot summer of 1937, the United States underwent a transitory convulsion adjusting from one system of labor-management relations to another. Ironically, the direct costs of the Michigan automobile sitdowns—$200,000 in property damage and $500,000 in state relief costs —were considerably cheaper in life, property, and manhours consumed than the orthodox endurance strikes that followed.[59] From hindsight the strikes of 1937 may support the proposition that the American labor movement has been the most violent nonrevolutionary movement in the world; but the middle-class character of labor's goals could have been doubted then. The sheer instability and economic dislocation of the 1937 disturbances, the militancy of the CIO's communist wing, and the hatred of the closed-shop principle inflamed passions and distorted perspectives. Throughout the spring and summer the front pages of the national press resembled sporting scoreboards as the "Day's Strike Developments" were summarized across the country. American industrial warfare modernized as union and company aircraft indulged in dogfights over the airlifting of supplies to nonunion workers trapped inside Ohio steel mills.[60] Opinions had long since frozen around poles of previous prejudice, but a whole new vocabulary came into highly imprecise use. While UAW organizers Walter Reuther and Richard E. Frankensteen were beaten outside his gates, Henry Ford denounced unions as "the worst things that ever struck this earth." "Fordism is fascism," Homer Martin replied; industrial unionism was no less than "communism" to the adversary.[61] The middle ground grew smaller all the time.

It was difficult to maintain dispassionate judgment after five workers were killed and 90 wounded in the Republic Steel riots at Chicago; the streets of Michigan's capital were overrun with demonstrators; and future Supreme Court Justice Harold H. Burton came close to having his car overturned in Cleveland while being called a "dirty strikebreaker" and a "company rat."[62] While retiring Yale president James Rowland Angell observed "menacing shadows" over American free government, a noted liberal, Anna Rosenberg, tried to allay fears of revolution by counseling the same tolerance of violence around

Michigan barricades that one indulged for "youngsters fighting in the streets."[63] Although the critical conflict passed to other states and a new ogre would be found in Governor Earle of Pennsylvania, Murphy became a prominent symbol of what was taking place. Pilloried in Congress for his "yellow streak" and his "supine surrender" to John L. Lewis and his "Communist cohorts," he was the original "labor governor" for better or worse.[64] Writers like John R. Commons, William Allen White, and John Chamberlain might praise the statesmanship and common sense of his labor policy.[65] The *Nation* and the American Civil Liberties Union might list him among their worthies of the year. But in the popular mind Murphy had opened the dike and thus bore the responsibility for a national crisis. It was a "crying shame," Norman Vincent Peale told a Fifth Avenue congregation, that a weakling like Murphy, rather than a "real man" like Teddy Roosevelt or the governors of Connecticut and New Jersey, held office at the outset. The sit-down strike, beyond doubt, was beginning to boomerang.[66]

Murphy's political survival, not to mention a presidential bid, depended on stabilizing industrial conflict. The decisive battles took place outside Michigan, but the turbulent aftermath of the Wagner Act decision killed his presidential ambitions before they took flight. Public patience with sit-down tactics was exhausted even before the Chrysler settlement. In Pennsylvania 3,000 "minutemen" farmers ousted strikers from the Hershey Chocolate plant. The premier of Ontario warned the UAW that sit-downers would be jailed in his province. Vermont outlawed the tactic and the Michigan Senate passed bills making felonies of sit-downs or bargaining during them.[67] The great steel and rubber strikes, though strictly speaking not sit-downs, fanned popular agitation at the same time that successive flareups in Michigan gave appearance of labor run riot.

The immediate result of union recognition in the auto industry was a rash of wildcat sit-downs which jeopardized both the UAW leadership and their political friends. Thirty sit-downs occurred at General Motors' Michigan factories within three weeks after its contract was signed. In three months the total rose to over 150. Wildcat strikes became so common that once, when a few workers who had finished early sat down to await the whistle, the shift coming on assumed there was a strike and returned home. The episode was an unfortunate joke, Homer Martin explained; wildcat strikers were "just a bunch of nuts."[68] Lack of experience in operating as a recognized union under contract no doubt accounted for much union irresponsibility. Management inexperience with new grievance procedures, for that matter, also contributed to a hangover of mutual hostility. Moreover, the contracts negotiated after recognition truces granted few concessions to the union regarding wages, grievance procedures, and seniority rights. Serious substantive issues remained. A fledgling union at the start of its campaign, the UAW was swamped by organizational difficulties incident to rapid growth and beset by factional dissension that plagued it for the next decade.

But after all due explanations were made, the reckless conduct of an auto workers minority gave believers in trade union responsibility genuine cause for alarm. The tag of irresponsibility not only jeopardized settlement with Little Steel, it vitiated Lewis's claim that a CIO contract was "adequate protection for any employer against sit-downs, lie-downs, or any other kind of strike."[69] Episodes like the continuing Consumers Power cut-offs raised fundamental questions about allegiance to democratic procedure, as Secretary Perkins noted to Murphy, and revealed communist influence in the union.[70] And no small consequence was danger to the very political alliances that had proved so helpful to the unionist cause. Soon the CIO leadership attempted to tighten internal discipline by entreaty, threats, and occasional outbursts by Martin himself that "stool-pigeons" and radicals were aboard. Even Martin was not adverse to radical alliances to save his post. But when and how to control rank-and-file militants became a sore point in an internal struggle for union control.[71]

Murphy shared the view that sit-downs were "getting out of hand"; but cautious about offending labor, he pleaded for "mutual forbearance and patience when either side makes mistakes." Given past distrust, it was understandable that labor leaders were unseasoned and workers impulsive. In charting new labor relationships, the country was on an "unknown sea."[72] Murphy wrote: "What could be more natural—even though regrettable—than that labor, in seeking to make the most of its gains and its new freedom, should make mistakes? We would all prefer these mistakes had never been made, but once labor does err, the sensible and enlightened thing in my estimation is not to shoot workmen down but to lead them on the right path."[73]

As labor flexed its muscles in the summer of 1937, however, he combined conciliatory talk with steadily hardening policy. A significant change in method had been apparent in the Detroit evictions and in his public threats to John L. Lewis. Change also was apparent when he chastened the "supersensitive" minority who took "the bit by the teeth" over every local grievance. In May another sit-down at the troublesome Consumers Power plant in Saginaw brought forth irate comment: "I have ordered both sides to appear at my office. . . . There will be other orders from my office if the strike is not halted immediately."[74] The state would not permit sit-downs or curtailed services in public utilities. Nor could it long tolerate civil disobedience. The whole effort at organization would be jeopardized if labor ran wild.

By giving the appearance of anarchy, one hellish week in June gave the death blow to Murphy's national ambitions. First, a riot among lumberjacks in the north took place after vigilantes ousted sit-downers at Newberry, requiring troops to restore the peace. Two days later, several thousand CIO sympathizers marched on the state capitol at Lansing, declared a "holiday," closed factories and downtown businesses, halted traffic, and invaded public buildings in protest over the midnight arrests of eight pickets, including the wife of the local UAW president. The Governor, who was on his way from Detroit, was informed by state police that they had insufficient numbers to disperse the demonstrators. Speeding to the capitol, Murphy told the disgruntled husband, "don't be silly. . . . You can't do it." But he conciliated the crowd: "It is not necessary for you to use unreasonable and arbitrary measures for you to gain your ends." "There will be no injustice practiced upon you while your Governor can prevent it." "You know you will get your rights."[75] Huddling with demonstration leaders and city officials, he obtained speedy bail for the jailed pickets and the "holiday" was over. But the damage was done. The *Grand Rapids Herald* roared: "Whose Governor" spoke to those outlaws? "Your Governor, the Governor of the Mob. Not the Governor of Michigan."[76]

Stepping off a train at Pittsburgh for commencement exercises at Duquesne, Murphy was jolted next by reports that Flint and the Saginaw Valley had been paralyzed again by Consumers Power workers, who pulled the switches on hearing contract terms reached by the CIO and the parent Consumers Power utility. "They can't do that," he said. "The conduct of labor in this case is as despotic as capital's has ever been." Threatening to fly back to Michigan unless service was restored immediately, Murphy received assurances from Lewis that there had been a "misunderstanding," which was another way of saying that union leaders were having difficulty securing rank-and-file approval of compromise agreements.[77]

Then, while CIO leaders ended the Saginaw blackout, in Monroe a town army headed by Mayor Daniel A. Knaggs, who was "open shop and proud of it," smashed a Republic Steel picket line. The Monroe strike-breaking, which Congressman Hoffman supported by an offer of arms, had been threatening for weeks. Murphy attempted to settle the conflict at the last minute, after receiving information that no one locally was willing to shoulder responsibility for negotiating a peace. But he failed. The CIO was a minority, the mill had been installed through the town's collective solicitation, and the ouster was popular locally. The CIO threatened to retaliate against "the Fascist leaders of Monroe" by a mass tri-state demonstration. Frightened by this threat, the mayor and local Democratic committeemen appealed for a declaration of martial law by the Governor, who refused. After an extended wrangle, he did arrange agreement that the rights of speech and assembly would be protected, albeit by "Sabbath truce," state police protection, and virtual isolation of the union rally in the countryside.

The episode in Monroe revealed an unanticipated result of government intervention in labor disputes: a tendency among private parties to pass responsibility for settlement onto public authority. The Lansing and Monroe incidents also aroused tremendous public indignation. Congressman Hoffman called Murphy a traitor; Senator Vandenberg introduced a resolution in Congress to congratulate Monroe's mayor; and as limited picketing resumed, reports came from North Carolina that one J.W. Lindau had offered to raise two million dollars to prevent the nomination of either Governors Earle or Murphy for the presidency.[78] A militant minority and a sensational press, far more than the highly disciplined General Motors strike, painted a picture of labor anarchy in Michigan. Not merely Murphy's national aspirations, but his very effectiveness as Governor, were floundering on the rocks of uncontrolled union agitation.

Labor militancy and the public response doomed Murphy's pet project to control industrial conflict—the Michigan Labor Relations Act. The proposed legislation, designed ostensibly as a state model, attempted to regulate the entire field of industrial relations by defining the rights of labor, the authority of the courts to enjoin, and the power of the state to intervene in industrial disputes. Although it followed Wagner Act guarantees of the right to bargain and to strike without notice, it empowered the governor to seize public utilities if either party refused to negotiate. It authorized the state to investigate controversies without invitation, to limit "stranger" picketing, and to prohibit blockage of public highways and employment entrances.[79] Homer Martin opposed the bill from the beginning, while conservatives objected to seizure power as incipient socialism.[80] Murphy insisted on most of the restrictive provisions, nevertheless. Legitimate labor tactics, in his view, did not include a right to barricade streets or to threaten physical injury. Doing these things was "not becoming to good citizenship," he admonished in the very words of his February critics. "Every illegal act begets some other illegal act or excess."[81] Entreating labor to discipline itself, he maintained that, once bargaining rights were "guaranteed by government, there isn't any excuse for paralysis of our economic life." Murphy refused to endorse UAW candidates in the 1937 Detroit elections, warned against communist infiltration of the CIO, and openly charged that communists had aggravated the automobile strikes, the Lansing "holiday," and the Consumer Power problem in order to obstruct democratic trade unionism. The "anarchistic" and "Communist methods" of a "wilful and irresponsible" few were discrediting a beneficial movement.[82]

The test of his sentiments was approval of the Michigan Labor Relations Act. By the time it reached his desk in August 1937 it was a compromise-toughened measure. Though the bill did not mention the sit-down strike, the Governor lost his seizure power. After William Green added his opposition to the restrictions on picketing, Murphy vetoed the Act on the ground that it could not succeed without support of the interests "primarily affected by it" and called a special session to reconsider the clause on stranger picketing, along with rural electrification.[83] Suspicions were strong that he was surrendering to unionist pressure under Roosevelt's orders, but he hotly denied it. Lee Kreiselman Jaffe, a columnist who voiced that view in print, received one of those self-righteous Murphy rebukes: "If you had waited to get all the facts—which is asking a lot of a columnist—your views would have been different or at least modified. There wasn't any pressure except that of conscience. . . . It will be difficult for any labor relations undertaking to succeed that has justifiable and endless opposition from either industry or labor. I want reasonable and responsible elements among them to work together. I believe it can be done."[84]

Yet Murphy went down to miserable defeat when the Legislature reconvened. After one fist-fight the Senate blocked the amended bill by a tie vote, repassed the original measure, and adjourned. To conservatives the restrictions on labor were at an irreducible minimum. Still, as the *New York Times* observed, the bill was a "significant straw in the wind." True friends of labor were qualifying the guidelines of the Wagner Act in order to curb what business groups were calling "labor anarchy with a government guarantee. . . ." A "labor governor" had caught the public mood.[85]

The country was plainly fed up with industrial strife. At the same time Murphy's labor relations bill was being debated in Lansing the President broke his long silence on the steel strikes by casting "a plague on both your houses"—only to receive a famous rebuke from John L. Lewis about the behavior one who had supped at labor's table was behooved to follow toward his host.[86] By late 1937 it looked as if Governor Murphy might successfully deflect public attention from labor problems onto his reform program. The state was relatively free from strikes. Auto production perked up temporarily and signs of foreign war and domestic recession convinced even labor leaders that it was time to "rake in sail."[87] As deepening recession in 1938 forced his own priorities onto recovery and relief measures, Murphy added his voice to economic stabilization. Deploring the "division in labor's ranks," he exhorted business and government to end "their unnecessary and stupid feud." "We should all strive with one accord to preserve the advance we have made," he said. "What we need right now is stability in employment and business."[88]

When a wildcat sit-down occurred in a Pontiac plant at Flint to repudiate a recently negotiated agreement barring sit-downs, Governor Murphy was reported to have threatened the UAW with immediate eviction. Although he was quick to deny the reports, the prompt evacuation of the plant indicated that all but spasmodic sit-downs were over.[a] Public opinion and union security, Murphy maintained, had destroyed them. However defensible they may have been in the previous winter, when union recognition was insecure and business conditions were favorable, sit-downs were now discredited and inexcusable.

The proper way to settle grievances [Murphy said] is not to suspend the authority of law by taking possession of a shop or factory. That is not collective bargaining. The proper way and the American way is the way of friendly conference and negotiation in a spirit of reason and good faith. The other way leads to anarchy, and eventually to arbitrary and despotic rule.

The government has shown every consideration for the rights and interests of workers, and . . . will continue to do so. But it also has a duty to see that the laws of the land are observed and governmental authority is maintained. Otherwise democratic rule will not endure and individual liberty will perish in the land of its birth.[89]

Murphy's "right-about-face," as he intended, was favorably noted throughout the country. Had he learned some lessons, too? Resenting any implication that he had reversed position, Murphy answered:

[a] When a third sit-down occurred in the Consumers Power plant in 1938, Murphy declared: "Seizure of property will not be permitted in Michigan." "The workers have no right to imperil the health and safety of the public." *Detroit Times*, April 4-5, 1938. The sit-down ended quickly, but to Secretary Perkins the strike was the most serious example of irresponsibility since she took office. Perkins to FM, April 7, 1938, Box 51.

"conditions have changed since last winter."[90] Recession and advances in union recognition were novel justification, perhaps, for a shift on toleration of sit-down strikes. But it was true nonetheless that they brought Michigan's mighty industrial war of 1937 to a shaky suspension. Ostensibly free to concentrate on his program Murphy now faced the impact of those same forces on his administrative plans and political prospects.

III

"It is a pity," one Murphy aide has since observed, "that a government with such high standards of public service is remembered principally for its role in the labor wars."[91] Considering its handicaps, the Murphy administration was one of the most productive state governments of the decade. Notwithstanding a Republican-controlled Senate and the recession of 1938, which cut state revenues by a third, the state took many forward strides toward the model government which Murphy self-righteously proclaimed. Failure on the Little Wagner Act, welfare reorganization, and minimum wage legislation was offset by fulfillment of major planks of his program—a secret primary, social security legislation, unemployment compensation, and teacher tenure. Public school aid, though cut during the recession, reached record proportions. Michigan also made notable advances in mental care and toward the goal of making its penal and probation systems "second to none."[92] Little noted, but of lasting value, was a thorough revamping of the state budget and accounting system under the guidance of Harold D. Smith, a nonpartisan expert who became Roosevelt's respected Budget Director during World War II.[93] Ambitious plans to overhaul the state constitution and government structure were stillborn.[94] Revision of the tax structure, even though the recession revealed that sales taxes provided a shaky revenue base in a one-industry state, also awaited future administrations, including those of his protégé, G. Mennen Williams.[95] After five governors had failed, however, Murphy scored a triumph with civil service. And while he may not have been the "lion of virtue" of Arthur Krock's label, there was little doubt that he gave the state one of the cleanest administrations in its history.[96] For those who looked to the less spectacular events in Michigan, Murphy's administration belied the hackneyed harangues of the Liberty League that New Deal reformers were necessarily corrupt.

The main impetus of accomplishment was the Governor's stock technique of crusading while attracting men of uncommon abilities into government service. Besides Smith, appointees Charles T. Fisher, Jr., and Alvan Macauley, Jr., for banking commissioners, Carl A. Olson for securities regulation, Hilmer Gellein for prison administration, and a dozen others of like distinction lent a quality to state government seldom matched in Michigan or in any other state for that matter. The links between the Governor's office and idea men at Ann Arbor, who respected his skills at public suasion whatever their skepticism about his intellect, recalled LaFollette's Wisconsin. Civil service reform, a program long in the talking stage, was the most revealing. After decades of debate over the merit system, conditions were ripe for a self-styled moral champion to push it through. Once committed to civil service, Murphy attacked the traditional spoils system with messianic zest. Crusading techniques probably were essential to effectuate a plan so easy to accept in principle yet resist in practice. Crusading also was inevitable in a personal sense, for civil service struck old Progressive chords in Murphy that rang louder the more the labor crisis receded into the background. Following passage of civil service legislation in the otherwise disastrous session of 1937, Murphy refused to let up. He established a government modernization commission under Joseph R. Hayden, Arthur W. Bromage, and John L. Dawson to make proposals for thoroughgoing reform of state government. He also revived the unicameral plank. Soliciting Senator George W. Norris's view of Nebraska's one-year experience with a single-house legislature, he asked: "Has the legislature become less progressive? Has it made for greater responsibility in the legislature with regard to the legislative program and financial management?"[97] However doubtful that Michigan could go the full route of nonpartisan elections, Murphy shared the Senator's goal of businesslike administration of state government. It was time, he said, quoting Carl Schurz, to give the whole spoils system "a finishing blow."[98]

In steering the civil service program through the Legislature Murphy had the advantage of a decade of statewide agitation. To implement the Act, however, required considerable political courage by a party so long out of power. An estimated 15 percent of the state's 17,000 employees were expected to fail civil service examinations. "This prospect is pleasing neither to the Republican extremists nor their counterparts in the Democratic party," Murphy told Claude G. Bowers. "But we know that the law is good and that it is being justly administered by a director of unquestionable ability, and of course we are going to stand by it."[99] When he followed the advice of the American Civil Service Association by luring the California personnel director, William Brownrigg, to head the new system, the *Detroit News* hailed it as a "stroke of genius." Going out of state for the best available professional demonstrated his faith in the stricture that "the spoils system is a corruption of democracy."[100] Indeed, the Governor even asked a volunteer group of "Civil Servants for Murphy" to disband lest it compromise the principle. James K. Pollock, the energetic professor who had long championed the cause, commented: "Superb leadership, indefatigable efforts, and now the fine reward and satisfaction of having given the State a high class civil service commission and the best personnel director in the country—all of these are recorded to your lasting credit. No one could have done more—I have never known anybody in the history of state civil service to do so much—and no one could have done better."[101]

Faith in professional administration of state government had its price, however. Murphy's "one man purity league" almost cost him party support.[102] In spite of his recognition of disarray in the state Democratic party, Murphy neglected party affairs recklessly throughout his administration. It would have expected a great deal, of course, for a Detroit maverick who fancied himself a nonpartisan and who became standard-bearer only on party sufferance, to take effective command of state party machinery. Yet he was extraordinarily indifferent to party as an instrument of political action. Basing leadership on programs and personality, as if Michigan were nonpartisan Detroit, Murphy seemed unable to adapt himself to the organizational demands of state as distinct from city politics.

Intraparty tension was probably unavoidable, given its history. But Murphy was also a governor easily irritated by criticism and one who scorned the demands for patronage and loyalty downward as beneath him. Nor was his administration exempt from those vagaries of personality which strained personal loyalties. He lived spartanly in a Lansing roominghouse, it is true, since the state provided no residence. Yet, if anything, the Murphy mythology increased in Michigan. He broke appointments cavalierly, it was said; his office had a miasmic air. He allegedly ignored small-town bigwigs or else descended on them unannounced with great fanfare and the inevitable entourage of secretaries, servile advisers, and newsmen. He would gaily call for a dancing party after the hustings, and someone else would invariably be left with the check. His obvious preference was dancing with young girls, or speaking engagements outstate, rather than performing those social duties among local politicos which common courtesy and political necessity impose on all elected officials. So much was said that a certain amount must have been true. One New Deal luminary marveled at how he found time to know so many pretty women in New York. A few appreciated that he had his own ways of releasing tension, that playing to the gallery was the opposite face of insecurity. But another loyal partisan, after relating how Murphy forsook every opportunity to dance with the admiring wife of a county chairman who asked only that favor for his support, concluded: "What a trial he was to those of us who believed he was a statesman and wanted him to continue in office for the state of Michigan! He loved humanity in the abstract but avoided most as individuals unless they in some way helped to inflate his vanity."

Democratic resistance to civil service brought such tensions to light. Asserting that maintenance of political fences was a "definitely minor consideration," the Governor even attacked state party chairman Edward J. Fry, who had criticized Brownrigg's aggressive installation of the merit system, as being "steeped in the political dogma of boss rule days."[103] For civil service, Murphy not only manifested feelings of moral superiority that irritated both friend and foe; he publicly characterized the party on which his political life depended as a "Tammany outfit."[104] "I have been too long associated with the affairs of government not to understand and appreciate the importance of party organization and party service to our political system," he replied to shocked Michigan Democrats. But for a political loner with Progressive roots it was elementary that modern life required expanding government, increasing specialization of labor, and therefore professional personnel practices in government. "This truth must be frankly recognized," he said. What was good for Michigan was good for the party, and that was that.[105]

Unlike the LaFollettes of Wisconsin, Murphy made no attempt to build a statewide political base for himself or for liberalism as a movement. Therein lay a serious miscalculation of the limits of personality and platforms in mass democracy. As the Governor expressed desires to professionalize welfare organization, which county supervisors successfully blocked by referendum, countless complaints from Democratic party workers reached Washington that his obsession with "that State Civil Service" was blinding him to "the road where *good government* and *good politics* meet."[106] At one time it was estimated that all but seven county chairmen secretly opposed Murphy's reelection because of his indifference to their patronage needs and voices in policy-making councils they helped to install.[107] "The intelligentsia that has been brought into the Party moves on so elevated a plain," one supporter observed, "that they seem to be guided by the false conviction that doing a good job in public office in itself wins reelection. I have never seen it happen myself without considerable political work on the side."[108] And maverick Murphy, a glory-seeking evangelist surrounded by professors, was making political work all the harder.

To make matters worse, the recession forced the administration to shift school construction and highway appropriations into relief. Powerful interests were alienated, as a result, and deficit spending increased his vulnerability to infighting over budgetary priorities. Murray D. Van Wagoner, a future governor and leader of a strong party nucleus in the Highway Department, publicly challenged Murphy's "elementary" proposition that welfare came first; and for a time Van Wagoner was considered a likely opponent in the 1938 primary. Former Governor William A. Comstock did launch an unsuccessful "stop Murphy" movement prior to the party convention.[109] Farley's intervention was again necessary to secure even surface party harmony for the coming Republican onslaught. As the campaign of 1938 got off to an unusually early start, it was apparent that Frank D. Fitzgerald, his previous opponent, would give Murphy the fight of his life.

Despite intraparty conflicts and the opposition generated by civil service, educational retrenchment, and relief policies, Murphy's reelection prospects appeared favorable at first. As his friends analyzed the situation, he could depend on 500,000 unionist votes; farmers could be had for the asking; a small but vocal Progressive group would support him militantly; Negroes would be with him to the end; and Detroit polls indicated sufficient strength to pull him through.[110] But optimism faded with deepening recession. Deficit relief spending, though actually three million dollars less than the 13-million-dollar deficit of Murphy's successor, renewed familiar charges of "unprecedented profligacy."[111] More dangerous was the impact of economic conditions on political attitudes. Would voters retaliate against the party in power? The business slump, with its consequent distress, Murphy regarded as the largest threat. Recession revived class conflict in Michigan politics and memories of the sit-down strikes. Falling prices and the lack of a definite farm program also left the state administration with little to attract rural voters. So by summer 1938, Murphy was clearly on the defensive.[112]

By far the dominant issue, however, was Murphy's conduct in Michigan's labor wars. Endorsement by the Communist party touched off an extremist dialogue that stretched the issues even beyond the normal extravagancies of a vitriolic campaign. Ironically, the same GOP opponents who had questioned his Catholicism in 1936 now accused Murphy of fellow-travelling. To counter the charge, Murphy stressed his church connections, which renewed the religious crossfire.[113] The Dies Committee, forerunner of the House Un-American Activities Committee, launched its career toward the end of the battle by conducting hearings into the links between communism and the sit-downs in Michigan. That communists had led UAW locals in Flint and had fomented tension, Murphy himself had asserted while attempting to woo militant young "hot-heads" back into the democratic fold. But however much he may have sought to provide noncommunist alternatives as part of his proffered leadership, to the witnesses called by the Dies Committee, Judge Gadola and John M. Barringer, the discharged city manager of Flint, the Governor was responsible for "treason" and the "complete breakdown of civil authority" in Michigan. Neither Murphy, who demanded an immediate hearing, nor the participants in the dispute testified. The sit-down strike and the Lansing holiday had obviously been instigated by communists, said Dies; while "open rebellion" took place under his office window, the Governor had done nothing but appease. The connections were plain.[114]

They were "lurid" and "absurdly false," President Roosevelt rejoined in a special press statement which defied his professed policy against intervention in state politics. Writing his answer so that his language would remain "polite enough," the President assailed the House committee for permitting a "coterie of disgruntled Republican office holders" to attack a "profoundly religious, able and law-abiding Governor" on the threshold of a vital election without hearing his version of the affair. The Dies investigation and Roosevelt's counterattack stirred an ideological storm which opened slowly-healing wounds.[115] "I could not remain silent," Roosevelt said, "when a public servant of Governor Murphy's character and convictions was subjected to such slander and misrepresentation."[116] Even Sheriff Wolcott, charging Judge Gadola with "malicious falsehood," rose to Murphy's defense. "The Governor," he said, "merely suggested that I delay the service of this writ over the week-end, giving the conference in Detroit time to settle the strike in a peaceful way, and as yet I have found no other way that would have been as good as the peaceable way. Everyone should be thankful that we had such a man as Governor Frank Murphy in the Governor's chair in Lansing, and I ask you folks to vote the straight Democratic ticket on November 8." Party loyalty was party loyalty, but Dies rightly boasted of influencing the Michigan election. One of the most heated elections in the state's history became a test of the New Deal.[117]

"Pocket-sized Napoleons," Murphy replied, distorted his labor policy for partisan gain. Eventually he repudiated communist endorsement in response to Catholic warnings that he could hardly expect support from both camps.[118] Attempting to make the issue "progressive versus reactionary government," he struggled against a scarcity of time and resources to complete and publicize his program. With publicity trumpets blaring, he also launched new programs—public housing, milk price regulation, and installment-buying controls—to divert attention from the labor issue.[119] But under pressure, Murphy's reputation as a man of difficult temperament began to soar. Norman Hill's delay in broadcasting departmental performance reports, for example, evoked a stern rebuke. Once friendly newsmen found even mild criticism received with indignant rebuttals or stony silence. At times, it seemed, there was only one honest man in Michigan.[120]

As the campaign progressed it became plain that state programs alone excited few voters. Neglect of organization began to tell, as did the Governor's policy of not receiving contributions from anyone doing business with the state. Though Murphy still had great drawing power as a speaker, recession and the Dies investigation kept him on the defensive. "My friends," he would begin, "I wasn't the author of the sit-down strikes—I inherited them."[121] Then over and over he would explain that his course had prevented bloody civil war and lasting rancor in the state. Over and over he would explain that his role had been to mediate and to lead the wayward—both management and labor—to peaceful collective bargaining. An egocentric sense of martyrdom, to grow as the years passed, became evident in such passing remarks as "I alone was responsible for the peace," an earlier version of which Kemp rightly criticized as being "hardly discreet or correct."[122] Outwardly calm, Murphy sent actor Charles Chaplin a favorite saying: "It's a tough fight, but only the game fish swim upstream."[123] Inwardly, he was alarmed. In a vain attempt to recover *Detroit Times* support he wrote Hearst official A.E. Dale in the style of their earlier alliance:

The hustings are calling and soon I'll be preaching the gospel of decent and progressive government from the center of the State to the fresh and unsalted seas. You know the record. . . . But bigoted wealth represented in certain groups of industry and business fighting shoulder to shoulder with the political spoilsmen in both parties and the predatory gamblers, the slot machine operators and other racketeers will make it pretty tough for me. While the press throughout the State has treated my administration with the utmost fairness in regard to news—I doubt that any Governor has had as good a press—still the front office will direct political opposition against me in the campaign largely for pocket-book reasons—to conform with the wishes of large advertisers.

In addition there will be a large number of honest citizens who will disagree with my labor policies. On this latter, however, every day I live to know with more certainty than the day before that I have been and am right about it today.

There are four hundred and twenty-eight papers in Michigan. I know of only one that will be with me. Conceding all weaknesses, I am not that awful.[124]

Roosevelt, though unwilling to visit Michigan after his disastrous defeats in primary purges elsewhere, offered to help in any way "short of taking an actual part in the campaign."[125] He sent Harold Ickes, James Farley, and other notables to make speeches on Murphy's behalf. Federal relief funds poured into the state. Braintrusters Thomas G. Corcoran and Benjamin V. Cohen were assigned to speechwriting, and the President himself made a national radio address to endorse Governors Lehman of New York and Murphy of Michigan. In order to save a loyal disciple, the administration left "no stone unturned."[126] Never in all the sound and the fury, however, did the candidate reveal the one thing that might have saved him: his behind-the-scenes pressure on union leaders in resolving the General Motors, Chrysler, and Lansing holiday disputes.

When the smoke cleared from around the billboards which reputedly read "Vote Christian, Vote Republican," Murphy emerged the loser by 93,000 votes.[127] Increased strength in the northern peninsula and among Detroit's Negroes did not offset heavy losses in industrial areas, such as Saginaw and Flint, which had suffered labor conflicts. Given the state's Republican tradition and lukewarm Democratic support, defeat by a 3½-percent margin was a very respectable run. In fact, Murphy polled the highest Democratic vote in an off-year election to date, strengthened his support among minority groups, and led the rest of the ticket by a substantial margin. Plainly, no Michigan Democrat was stronger.[128] Nevertheless, despite the effects of recession on incumbents of both parties, the defeat was interpreted across the nation as a stinging rebuke to the New Deal. "It was intended," wrote Arthur Krock, "as a vote for public order, property rights, and equal treatment for all economic classes before the law."[129] Murphy, in the minds of most, was a victim of Roosevelt's CIO embrace.

Denying that his labor policy was dictated by the President, Murphy interpreted defeat in the *Nation* as a "tragic interruption" of "good and progressive government" due to revived conservatism and a swing in the national mood.[130] That recession, court-packing, and labor conflicts all contributed to that swing was undeniable, but Murphy himself, noting that Herbert Lehman was the only governor regardless of party to survive in states hardest hit by unemployment, blamed chiefly the recession. "The American people are weary of the superficial unemployment palliatives," he observed. "The recovery program of last June was, in my opinion, six months too late. . . . When the President swings into action he is a magnificent emergency leader and it is unfortunate that the program was delayed for several months and it is even more unfortunate that a recession was allowed to occur. As a result the farmers and the small town people, hostile because of the labor rampage and prices appreciably affected, simply voted a protest."[131]

Lehman's opposition to the court-packing plan contributed perhaps to his narrow victory, and Murphy probably underestimated his own responsibility for the liberal debacle. In any case, he was unrepentant about the sit-downs. "We go out heads erect, for our government has been honest and just," he told Philip Murray. "We have advanced the wage earner's position and we have made him better understood. That we in authority are misunderstood or have to pay the price of doing Justice is unimportant."[132] While privately he confessed bitterness over the desertion of Democrats and former allies like the *Detroit Times*, he did his best to accept the verdict gracefully. To a Republican friend who expressed condolences, he remarked: "I can and do take it like a good American, as you express it. Those things happen in politics and anyone who isn't prepared for them ought not to be in public life. I've always believed that our American system needs two strong parties. Yours almost disappeared two years ago—it is only natural that the pendulum swung part way back."[133] Defeat was "just the old story of democracy's march—two steps forward, then a step back and we will go forward again."[134]

Liberals regarded his loss as "a national misfortune." "I thought that Michigan would have better sense," Harold Ickes commented, "but I know that your head is unbowed." From ambassadors to academics down to ordinary party workers, men echoed Burton K. Wheeler's sentiment that "it will not be long before the people will realize their mistake, and acclaim you as Michigan's greatest governor."[135] Wrote economist William Haber: "Not in a generation, if ever, have we had a person in the Governor's office who grasped the problems of modern government as thoroughly as you did and who proceeded to the task of dealing with them with such resolute courage and effectiveness. The tragedy lies in what Michigan lost. Two years more would have given us a firm foundation in good government."[136]

Perhaps more than he realized, Murphy had become a symbol of

New Dealism at the crossroads. The election of 1938 revealed a momentous fissure in the national Democratic coalition. The Senate debates on court-packing and militant union tactics had reflected deep middle-class disaffection and a parting of the ways between southern and liberal Democrats. Neither the New Deal nor Murphy himself would ever be quite the same. As a new Republican-southern conservative coalition began to form in Congress under the leadership of newly elected Robert A. Taft, and as administration priorities shifted to international concerns, it was apparent that the New Deal as a domestic reform movement had lost its steam. Frank Murphy had not simply lost an election, he became one of the most controversial men of the day. There was irony in those developments. Murphy had started as a political independent, indeed, as a bridge to forces now on the Right. Now, after a reluctant race as a party sacrifice, he became a hero of the Left and a symbol of what people feared most in the New Deal —disdain for private property and the reign of law. Murphy, in the labor crisis of the 1930s, met his destiny as a militant liberal.

IV

Murphy's labor policy, though more a cluster of impromptu decisions than a grand design, undoubtedly produced his greatest impact on American society. Given the great social pressures behind the sit-down strikes, industrial unionism probably would have triumphed anyway. But the process would have been slower and costlier had a less sympathetic government been in office. Few public officials had more to do with labor's winning power. Few also had more to do with placating a convulsive transition in American industrial relations. Murphy's methods of conciliation had much to do with the sit-downs' ultimate demise.[137] Thus his mark on American life was immense.

At personal levels Murphy came across to liberals as a moral champion of his mind's eye. Whatever the historical judgment, Murphy displayed a strength of conviction and of self-control as governor that surprised even his associates and excited the imagination of thousands. His guesses were on the side of the future; he gave a virtuoso performance of courage as Hemingway defined it: grace under pressure. And his conciliatory utterance bespoke spiritual depths which, to some at least, shed "a new fine light on the fundamentals."[138] Carl Sandburg, then at work on Lincoln's *War Years*, perceived that quality when he observed: "You came to your one great crisis and met it as though you had trained all your life for it. Many you know not of pray for your health and your inner grace and strength—that they may keep. . . . What was impressive to me, and still is, was the care, precision and brevity of your utterance from one crisis to another: you were on the spot much like Lincoln and handled the crises with the same approach."[139]

Yet that was the rub: just as Lincoln's emphasis on Union cut across abolitionist passions, so Murphy's priority of civil peace clashed with prevailing premises of class struggle and group warfare. Because he compromised the rights of property and helped entrench the CIO, it was irrelevant to many for him to plead that "the greatest industrial crisis in history was settled in an atmosphere of justice and reason, without the suppression of a liberty or the loss of a single life."[140] Spokesmen for property never forgave him. Because he compromised law, it was beside the point that neither party in the automobile strikes wanted armed conflict. Sit-downs spawned civil disobedience, and disobedience required force. Murphy had not flinched from that necessity in the Philippines. Why was Michigan different? "All officials," he had asserted, "must be humble before the majesty of the law."[141] How could his conduct be squared with his own past preachment?

Not one to remain silent, Murphy summoned history, natural right, and social analysis to his defense. And his defense made plain that the labor crisis had a profound impact on him, not only in stimulating well-developed messianic tendencies, but in forcing him to ponder problems of industrial relations and political obedience as few contemporary politicians had to do. His penchant for absorbing ideas from intellectuals gave a gloss of up-to-date liberalism to his speeches over the country, but at bottom his approach was pure Murphy. No one described that outlook more forcefully than he did in 1944, when he wrote former Governor Chase S. Osborn:

One time, in the spring of 1937 and during the course of the sit-down strikes, I met you in the lobby of the Book-Cadillac Hotel. I was impoverished of spirit. It seemed that all those who knew me had lost serenity of spirit. Not a single moment did I harbor the thought of encouraging any lawlessness. Quite the contrary, I carefully prepared an order with the assistance of Don Eduardo [Kemp] and Lady [Eleanor Bumgardner] which demanded obedience to the court's decisions. That order, unknown to the public because it was not publicized, helped break the resistance and brought the General Motors' strike to an end.

Anyway during the whole seven months of the sit-down strikes I had ambitions to weather the complicated question by what I conceived to be the American way, and the Christian way. I did not want to do it as Hitler or Mussolini would have done it. Those two would have made short shrift of American workingmen rights. The rule of reason guided me. I wanted it held aloft. It was reason at the conference table I sought and insisted upon. Always in similar situations—although there never had been one of such magnitude—men had reached for the gun. The idea of turning brother against brother, of releasing revolution in our homeland and making monuments of hate of our factories did not appeal to me. I don't blame those who disagreed with me. I understood their viewpoint but they did not understand mine, which was one of reason and Christianity and Americanism.

And so you may guess the encouragement you gave me when in the course of our foregathering in the lobby of the hotel you pointed a finger at me and said, "Remember the investors have their dollars in those factories, those laboring men have their flesh and blood in them. The investors have an investment of money, the workers have invested their lives. Keep that in mind and you will come out alright."[142]

However sentimental the comparisons, to Murphy they were the heart of the matter. The strikes showed that the man gravitated instinctively to underdogs, sublimated inner conflicts in their defense, and once the commitment was made to champion their cause, he was anything but soft. Fired by the dehumanizing effects of industrialism Murphy translated essentially emotional responses into a lexicon of the liberal's faith. Justice to American workers, he believed, demanded three imperatives —nonviolence, a greater voice for workers in the economic arrangements governing their lives, and a redistribution of wealth sufficient to insure their material security. "Violence," he said, "is a disgrace to civilized man . . . ," a pseudo-solution whose futility the Haymarkets and the Ludlows of the past amply demonstrated.[143] "Machine guns are always the last refuge of the undisciplined, impotent official in time of crisis," he asserted self-righteously. "Patience and tolerance invariably demand more courage and self-control than the vain, bloody exhibitions of weakness that go by the name of 'action.'" A condition rather than a theory, the sit-down strikes he regarded as an "incomparable opportunity for enlightened government to show its worth."[144]

Like most students of industrial relations, Murphy advocated the principle of a balance of power between contending private groups as a prerequisite for industrial peace. The nub of the question was, at what point is equilibrium reached? Obviously he believed government should assist workers in achieving parity in the bargaining process. Against a philosophy such as Ford's that workingmen forsook their freedom by joining unions, he countered that "they're lost if they don't."[145] Only collective labor power could match corporate power. The "right-to-work" was an invitation for employers to divide and rule. In effect, Murphy's professed neutrality favored labor by helping unions secure a position of strength. And he admittedly acted with "historical knowledge of labor difficulties since the Civil War," knowledge that "the rules do change" and that the worker's "God-given right to a job at a living wage" had never been so carefully delineated in law as those of the propertied.[146] Whether his outlook was humanitarian or merely utilitarian was insignificant to Murphy, for he heartily believed that unless workers achieved greater personal security and "human dignity," "the threat of dictatorship will continue to plague us."[147]

As always, the onus fell on government to lead the way. Emphasizing the voluntary basis of healthy industrial relations, Murphy rejected compulsory arbitration as illiberal, impractical, and an intolerable burden on the courts. Nevertheless, he envisaged critical roles for government. First, public authority had to set the rules of permissible contest because large-scale strikes in an interdependent industrial economy were "no longer private disputes." Second, government had to defend larger community interests from contending private forces by serving as independent fact-finder, conciliator, and in the case of deadlock, impartial arbitrator at the conference table. As Murphy stated to Hayden, without embellishment of oratory, following the Chrysler agreement:

Prolonged strikes in the past—even the seven months shipping strike of 1936—seem to me to have been unnecessary. The trouble is they were private fights.

It was necessary for me to remind Mr. Chrysler and Mr. Lewis, even during the last days of the negotiations, that their final word did not end the controversy; that there was a third party—the people of the State represented by the Governor to whom due consideration must be shown.

When a couple of mastodons collide, it is difficult for them to become unentangled without the modest help and influence of the Government which, of course, should always speak for all the people. This influence of impartial government along intelligent and enlightened lines alone can make possible friendly conferences conducted in a spirit of reason and justice.

On the other hand, if I had permitted myself to have been influenced by Corporate power, reactionary writers and conservative public opinion, everything would have been a bloody mess by now instead of desirable sanity.[148]

In a deeper sense government was the key to industrial peace. Strikes were only an index of social disruption. Far more serious were uncontrolled business cycles which ravaged workers' income and the entire economy. Just as anti-poverty programs were the government's long-range response to the racial sit-ins of the 1960s, so Murphy saw "more democracy" and the welfare state as the basic answer to social alienation and industrial strife. The task of government was to soften the gnawing insecurities both expressed. "The problem presented by each is soluble," he declared, "and to admit that we can't find a solution is a confession of the impotency of the democratic system. That is a confession we cannot afford to make." While Murphy conceded that politicians placed too much blame on government for depression and took too much credit for recovery, he believed public policy could cushion the effects of economic maladjustments.[149] "We are not caught in the cogs of a relentless machine over which we have no control," he scribbled in a speech note in 1938. "The economic situation, the social order, the world of international relationships are man's own work. We can change things if we will."[150]

Murphy had never regarded rebellion as imminent in Michigan, but increasingly he placed the New Deal in a context of world upheaval. Keenly aware of events in Europe and Asia he admired and corresponded with Claude G. Bowers, a "fundamentalist liberal," serving as ambassador to Chile. Cordell Hull, whose combination of idealism and practicality appealed greatly to Murphy, left a deep impression by characterizing fascists as a band of "international gangsters."[151] Because one "just can't remain silent in the face of evil," Murphy denounced the book-burnings and pogroms in Germany, and took public issue with Father Coughlin's anti-Semitic broadcasts. Those who would erect walls before the free mind in America, he warned Michigan teachers, not only negated democracy but "themselves constitute a real menace to its security."[152]

Security, in sum, was the crisis of the age. History taught, however, that it was attainable only through regulated change. It would be folly, Murphy thought, for lovers of religion and popular government to ignore the lessons of the Bolshevik and Nazi revolutions. Democracy, too, was not immune from similar cataclysms. Unless the conditions that bred insecurity and disaffection were removed, unless democratic principles were extended to American economic life, he asserted, "the days of political democracy are numbered."[153]

The link between economic security and political freedom was hardly a new idea to Murphy, but the pressures he faced added urgency to the policy he advocated. Echoing the UAW cry for a guaranteed annual wage, he ridiculed fears that social security legislation would regiment society or violate that "rhetorical absurdity," the worker's liberty of contract. "In face of real threats to their dearly-won political liberties, [he said] a people cannot be expected to confuse forever the obnoxious thing, *regimentation* of democracy, with the sensible and enlightened thing, its *implementation*. . . . There is no basic conflict between private enterprise and social security promoted by government. The aim of one, in fact, is the preservation of the other."[154] For the rest of his life, Murphy stressed this theme. Economic deterioration was threatening allegiance to democratic forms. The sit-down strikes could not be considered in isolation; they were symptomatic of basic dislocations in the social order. For his part, "to secure the confidence and obedience of many thousands of men under the strain of a conflict of such vast proportions and strong emotions, without causing disaffection and distrust for the institutions of popular government, required methods vastly different from those a sheriff employs in dealing with an ordinary case of trespass."[155] It required a self-assured democratic leader who was willing to define the public interest, to demonstrate that respect for law is earned not so much by the bludgeon as by its wisdom. Rather than weakening the rule of law Murphy stoutly maintained that his course had won it new converts by showing that the peaceful way was not to be despised and that free government did not creak. Forced by events to grapple with age-old problems of political obedience, Murphy took his stand with the advanced legal thinking of his day. As he told the Detroit Holy Name Society at the peak of the Chrysler strike anxiety, using language from his GM statement to John L. Lewis:

Firmly persuaded as I am of the need of directing our legitimate and lawful efforts toward the advancement of those larger interests which are commonly known as "human rights," I cannot divest myself of the conviction that personal liberty will be of little value to our people if the authority and integrity of our institutions are not preserved and property rights not protected.

I wish, however, to leave this word of warning: Blind adherence to a legalistic philosophy which demands only rigid obedience to the letter of the law and which chooses to ignore the spirit of the law as well as the realities of life, will surely lead to the eventual frustration of the democratic ideal of true freedom.[156]

While the sit-down strikes gave him little time to philosophize, Murphy's priority of peace caused him to stumble into one of the great imponderables of democratic government: can a "government of laws" safely entrust to an executive the latitude which John Locke thought necessary to act "according to discretion for the public good, without the prescription of law and sometimes even against it?"[157] Murphy's answer was forthright: "It is important that government sustain its authority. But it must recognize that laws may lag behind the times and behind the needs of the times, and in some circumstances it is incumbent upon government to refrain from a blind and rigorous enforcement of laws and to so order itself, pending the general adjustment of laws to current conditions, that the greatest public good will ensue."[158]

To soften the law's "inflexible rigour" in such circumstances was precisely Locke's concept of executive prerogative. Though unresolved in theory, American history has largely confirmed the power in practice. Jefferson in the Louisiana Purchase and Lincoln in the Civil War both invoked it.[b] Murphy left the governorship firmly persuaded that time would vindicate him, as it had done Jefferson and Lincoln. The political opportunities may have misfired; his program, as elsewhere, may have been too much, too soon; and his scorn of party organization revealed all over again that his good intentions surpassed his abilities to effectuate them.[159] But election defeat, he told Felix Frankfurter, had in no way "altered our conviction that the peaceful settlement of the great strikes was a positive contribution to the serenity of our people in years to come." Some day they would comprehend what William Allen White meant when he said: "Men like Murphy make poor heroes but they also make history that is easier to read."[160]

Framing the event in terms of revolution the world over, Murphy committed himself more than ever to the philosophy of the welfare state and the law of social needs. Inequality and insecurity among the American masses, he believed, were undermining confidence in democratic values. Grave problems of unemployment remained unsolved. In face of dangers to the American system, "musty precedent" and "blind legalism" had to give way to a greater degree of democracy, "in the economic sense toward the end that it will be politically preserved."[161] Out of compassion for the worker and reverence for freedom itself, Murphy affirmed an ancient adage: "We must love justice rather than its form."[162]

[b] "To lose our country by a scrupulous adherence to written law," Jefferson asserted, "would be to lose the law itself, with life, liberty, property, and all those who are enjoying them with us; thus absurdly sacrificing the ends to the means." "The line of discrimination between cases may be difficult; but the good officer is bound to draw it at his own peril, and throw himself on the justice of his country and the rectitude of his motives." *Writings* (Washington: Thomas Jefferson Memorial Assn., 1904), n. 12, pp. 418 and 422.

CHAPTER 8

A NEW BROOM, 1939

IT HAD been assumed that the President would find places for election casualties, but in late December 1938 he surprised the nation and even political intimates by naming the recently defeated Governor of Michigan to be Attorney General of the United States. After November discussion had centered on what offices would be acceptable to both Murphy and the Senate. Neither seemed easy to satisfy. Murphy at first had talked of returning to private practice for a breathing space. The initial proposals made in Washington had little appeal, he said, and "I could use the income."[1] Yet it would have appeared disloyal on the President's part to allow even temporary retirement for a faithful lieutenant whose defeat many attributed to the White House. And while Murphy confessed physical weariness, he also described himself as determined as never before "about action."[2] The difficulty was where to put him.

Roosevelt, near the end of his second term, had personnel problems in his inner circle. Several members of the original brain trust had broken with the New Deal. Others in the Cabinet had lost their usefulness, at least in the eyes of the President's new crop of liberals; and the politics of the 1940 succession were becoming a divisive force. The presidential family, which reflected the broadly diverse viewpoints common to American Cabinets, was splintering into a conservative Farley-Garner wing as against the liberal Hopkins, Jackson, Ickes, and Wallace factions over the issue of party leadership should the President decide not to seek the unprecedented third term. Daniel Roper and Homer S. Cummings had recently resigned from the Commerce and Justice Departments, and there was dissatisfaction with Harry H. Woodring in War. In view of the rising importance of the War Department and of his previous connection with it, Murphy aspired to be Secretary of War; but so did Undersecretary Louis A. Johnson who had Farley's promise of the post. By common understanding, the attorney generalship had been pledged to the able Solicitor General and court-packing advocate, Robert H. Jackson.

To break a logjam of claims Roosevelt devised an intricate scheme. Harry Hopkins, whom he was apparently grooming for 1940, would be appointed Secretary of Commerce to remove some of his radical taint. Woodring would be eased out of War by making him Minister to Canada, Johnson would succeed him provisionally, and Paul V. Mc-

Nutt would be recalled from the Philippines to replace Hopkins in the latest relief reorganization. Then Johnson would be made High Commissioner, after which Murphy would become Secretary of War and Jackson Attorney General. In the meantime, Murphy would succeed Cummings in the Department of Justice. Something had to give, and since there were four New Yorkers in the Cabinet already, Jackson would have to wait until Hopkins could reestablish his Iowa residence and the rest of the plan could take effect. Swallowing sharp disappointment, Jackson accepted the decision and helped to forestall embarrassment for the "interim" Attorney General by sponsoring his speedy admission to the American Bar Association and to Supreme Court practice.[3]

Jackson's friends were chagrined at his "political sacrifice." "It is a damn shame," the departmental press secretary, Gordon Dean, noted in his diary. Though Harold Ickes and Senator Norris considered Murphy deserving, they likewise condemned the President's use of geographical criteria. Definite promises had been made to Jackson, and presidents had a way of changing their minds.[4] Definite political plans were also afoot, and new personalities tended to upset calculations.

Unaware of the provisional intent behind Murphy's selection, the nation's press opened debate over the qualifications of "the man" responsible for "breakdown" of law in Michigan to administer the nation's top law-enforcing agency.[5] What was the President up to? Apparently he was defying the 1938 reaction by elevating two purebred liberals, Hopkins and Murphy, to the Cabinet. To add insult to injury, he nominated Felix Frankfurter to the Supreme Court. The appointments, as Josephus Daniels' *Raleigh News and Observer* remarked, indicated that there would be "no departure from militant liberal policies." Liberals thus rejoiced over Roosevelt's "wise and reassuring move." In contrast to other Cabinet members, the *Nation* commented, "Mr. Murphy belongs in the category of those who want to practice what the President preaches."[6]

Conservatives, by the same token, regarded his appointment as "another insult to right-thinking people."[7] Past failure to uphold the law was strange qualification indeed for an Attorney General. Murphy, as Senator Styles Bridges and Representative Clare Hoffman catalogued his defects, not only had "communistic associations" but had never practiced law before the Supreme Courts of Michigan or the United States, and was not a property owner. Right-wingers in Congress were not taking the appointment lying down.[8]

Resignation was the dominant mood, even so. If Murphy's treatment of the CIO may have been a "trifle lenient," the sit-downs were over. It was easier to recall with the *New York Times* that he was a man of "great abilities," "sincerity and unassailable honesty." "A liberal and aggressive president is selecting a liberal and aggressive attorney general," the *Kansas City Journal* commented. "That's all there is to it."[9] Although token fireworks could be expected in the Senate, few doubted that Roosevelt would get his way. A president, after all, is entitled to choose his own official family. Senate opposition to Murphy was negligible, especially after Senator Henry F. Ashurst, chairman of the Senate Judiciary Committee, appointed a friendly subcommittee and Vice-President Garner, whom Murphy had informed of his Lewis ultimatum immediately upon his appointment, signified his approval.[10] To dispel any doubts, the nominee threw a blockbuster of his own into the Senate melee. Acting on the advice of Nebraska Senator Edward R. Burke, he insisted that public confidence required him to tell the "real story" of the sit-down affair under cross-examination, even though a subcommittee had already approved his appointment. A somewhat puzzled Senator Logan reopened the hearings. And Frank Murphy therein exploded onto the Washington scene with a remarkable piece of political showmanship.[11]

In a word, he told the Senators that he had broken the General Motors strike by a private ultimatum to John L. Lewis. Explaining his strike strategy as peaceful enforcement of the law's intent by a quiet, big stick, Murphy maintained in a statement prepared by Kemp that, "of course" the sit-downs were illegal. Moreover, they had been "thoroughly discredited." Certainly he believed in property rights as "one of the main pillars upon which our economy, indeed our democracy is based." But protection of property did not require shedding blood of American workers with long-standing grievances. Rather than suspend the law he had merely postponed writs of bodily attachment over a weekend because "peace was imminent." To insure it, he had issued a private threat of force to the CIO president, which he implied had brought capitulation and swift settlement. At Senator Burke's request, Murphy read his letter to Lewis; it was a carefully balanced statement—almost a lecture—on the sanctity of property rights, the judicial process, and the supremacy of constitutional government. In fact, his letter to Lewis, which was written several weeks before the rest of the nation debated the sit-downs in these terms, used the very language which was so extensively praised in his later public statements. Apparently, his right-about-face on law and order had been only from private to public expression. Could there be any doubt that he was devoted to law? "I believe in vigorous law enforcement," he told the Senators; but an executive's duty was to maintain respect for law as well as to secure compliance. Since the sit-down crisis was deeper than disobedience by a few common criminals it called for conciliatory measures to obtain the ultimate end of all law—public order and safety—without undermining allegiances to free government.[12] As he wrote to Senator Josiah W. Bailey, who continued the debate in private, "I could not conceive it as being statesmanlike or responsible conduct for the Governor to ignore the potentialities of the crisis, as well as its sources, and in a purely mechanical fashion, to proceed to execute the order of the court." While there had been disappointments, Murphy added, the result was one of which no believer "in the reign of law need be ashamed."[13/a]

Murphy's primary object of conveying his concern for law and order was genuine enough. Never did he say in so many words that his Lewis ultimatum was the turning point of the strike, but he left that impression and repeated it so often that he apparently believed it himself. Unencumbered by those qualifications necessary for precise accuracy, the argument was doubly impressive. "Where are the bawlers?" queried the *Louisville Times*. "Have those who were ardent lambasters of Governor Murphy decided that, after all, they didn't do as much thinking as talking?" The testimony silenced most of his critics. And the Hearst press conceded that, "if, as he says, 'the sit-down now has been thoroughly discredited,' he seems fairly entitled to part of the credit." Still, the compelling question remained: why had he waited so long to disclose his strategy?[14]

In a worldly capital Murphy's answer was too virtuous for belief. He had remained silent, he said, in order not to impair his neutrality as a mediator. "I think a public official has to be accessible to both sides, and never say or do anything that might make either side lose confidence in him," he asserted. "There was no point in making the letter public while I was Governor—except in defense of myself personally. And my personal fortunes are a secondary matter."[15] That had been his answer to those who had begged its release in 1937 and he stuck to his guns. "However much I regret it now and have in the

---

[a] Roosevelt took the same position. Commenting on his constant dread of having to take drastic action, he told Judge Samuel I. Rosenman that he had faced a number of occasions when "it took real calm not to call out the troops. Little do people realize how I had to take abuse and criticism for inaction at the time of the Flint strike. I believed, and I was right, that the country including labor would learn the lesson of their own volition without having it forced on them by marching troops." FDR to Rosenman, Nov. 13, 1940, RL:PPF-64.

past," he wrote reporter Guy H. Hawkins, "the fact still remains that by a combination of circumstances my hands were tied. The letter should, of course, have been public then and there. But I did not want to jeopardize the peaceful settlement that I believed was near at hand, and that was actually achieved the next day, by disturbing either of the parties in making it appear in the public mind that I had lined up with one of them. It would have made no difference to me had their positions been reversed. I would still have done the same thing."[16]

That the people had been unable to judge his government on its merits, Murphy confessed, was "extremely unfortunate." "My own blame is no little one," he conceded, for popular misunderstanding.[17] He did not deny that release of the letter might have reelected him. "But I could not and do not now believe that it would have been right to use it to win votes in a political campaign. I would still prefer to remain silent and face defeat." Charges of political expediency would have been hurled at him in either case; and he was being called on to mediate disputes until the very end of his administration. Said Murphy: "We had to give priority to a comprehensive and long view of the whole situation."[18]

So righteous a defense strained credulity. "By what stretch of the imagination," snorted Senator Bridges, would a public stand for law and order have discredited the governor of a strike-torn state? Even those who had no quarrel with his General Motors strategy viewed his subsequent silence as a "cardinal error." Whether for statesmanly or for political purposes, Walter Lippmann observed, saving Lewis's face and delaying an unequivocal denunciation of sit-downs had "left in doubt something that no government ought ever for a moment to leave in doubt: where it stands on the issue of upholding the law." Failure to reveal his hand had not only encouraged mass disobedience, it had shaken public confidence, which resulted in a "dangerous tide of reactionary sentiment" that eventually victimized Murphy himself.[19]

"Why should any man object to taking blows in a struggle for Justice and for those inarticulate souls unable to give a blow for themselves?" he replied. However men appraised his judgment Murphy the showman was in his element. Disclosure of the Lewis letter had a sensational impact on the Senate and the public. Many former critics were deeply impressed, even converted, by his subcommittee appearance. Some experienced bureaucrats, struck by the contrast with the usual atmosphere of committee hearings, described the confrontation as "deeply spiritual."[20] Felix Frankfurter, having noted the "radiating spirituality" of his speeches and moved by its effect on the educational processes of a democratic society, observed that his accounting to the country "was in effect a means of taking the whole nation to school to an understanding of the knotty, obdurate factors of ill-will and misunderstanding in our industrial relations which came to you as an evil inheritance and which your fearless and wise conduct did so much to restrain from still further exacerbation and considerably to soften. I can hardly avoid language that may seem to carry an atmosphere of exaggeration were I to tell you how superb I thought your statement."[21] Even Harry Bennett, director of Ford personnel organization, expressed his confidence. The Judiciary Committee approved Murphy's nomination unanimously; and after an occasionally heated, but essentially pro forma debate, the Senate confirmed by a 78-7 vote. With the significant exception of Senator Vandenberg, who considered himself bound by the Michigan elections, most of the opponents were freshmen Republican arrivals from the debacle of 1938.[22]

Murphy's Senate performance was more than a play to assure confirmation. In one dramatic move the lame duck from Michigan recovered prestige and stole the spotlight as a politician who operated according to different rules. In effect, he was bidding for national confidence as a public servant with individual flair and definite ideas about law enforcement. Speed rather than severity, energy mixed with example, were his notions of administering justice. Murphy's appearance before the Senate was merely a prelude to the short, spectacular administration he envisaged for the agency under his command.

II

The attorney generalship in 1939 was an ideal base for the recovery of Murphy's political fortunes. The Department of Justice, a diffuse organization of over 10,000 employees including 1,200 lawyers, was a hub of important government activity. The Attorney General and the bureaucratic agencies answerable to him were responsible for much more than the crime-chasing with which they were identified in the public mind. Besides enforcing federal criminal law and operating federal prisons, the department was directly responsible for antitrust, tax, and public lands litigation and controlled government appeals to the courts. That function alone endowed the Solicitor General's office with a leading role in shaping the direction of federal law. In addition, the Attorney General was chief legal counsel to the President, and the department as a whole was increasingly drawn into delicate foreign policy issues by virtue of involvement in neutrality and counterintelligence programs. New legislation and the Supreme Court struggle consumed the lion's share of departmental publicity during most of the New Deal period. But the President's concentration of talent at high echelons of the agency was evidence of the fact that, in addition to its vital interest in an unfinished constitutional revolution being worked in the courts, the Justice Department was strategically located in the day-to-day process of policy development which, more than headlines suggest, determines the course of American government. No Attorney General on brief assignment could expect to affect either process profoundly. The web of legal institutions and bureaucratic alliances was too intricate. Nevertheless, the convergence of time and personality created unusual political opportunities for Murphy, who demonstrated again the strength of his personal style on a national scale.

For all his talk that "the progressive movement is inevitable," for all the internal battle of Hopkins, Ickes, and himself to keep the administration from passing into what Ickes called the "difficult, if not evil, days of conservatism," the New Deal had entered a period of consolidation.[23] Just as they influenced Roosevelt's third-term decision, recession and the threat of war suspended serious efforts at social engineering. The most that could be expected concretely was entrenchment of recent gains and rounding off the movement with less spectacular measures of reform. Consolidation did not imply inactivity so much as shifting gears, but it placed a premium on catching up with well-recognized government functions and stabilizing the new. The relative importance of the Department of Justice rose accordingly.

Innovation had been so rapid that stabilization was in order. Of high priority was adjusting government operations to the impact of great social change and threatening war. A lack of "order and system," as Murphy had indicated after his Michigan defeat, pervaded American life.[24] A common conviction which Murphy shared was that democracies urgently needed to improve their efficiency in a deadly contest with totalitarian powers. Though the image of monolithic Nazi efficiency proved to be a mirage, few believed that expanding government services were being matched by parallel improvements in public management. Whatever one's view of the much-criticized NLRB, the mushroom growth of regulatory activity had created severe problems of accommodating administrative processes to the rule of law. The rise of aggressive foreign dictatorships—and the abuses of petty ones at home—also posed difficult problems of national security and civil liberties. The disclosures of public wrongdoing by prosecutor Thomas E. Dewey of New York merely whetted the Attorney General's own strong appetite to fight corruption in politics. And after a frenetic period of governmental innovation, the people plainly yearned for respite.

No doubt seeking to restore his political standing, Murphy again perceived causes where personal ambition and important public interests meshed. While he never tired of preaching "economic reconstruction" as Attorney General, he took advantage of his post to crusade on behalf of two original articles of his faith—morality in government and civil liberties. The one was calculated to strengthen confidence where the 1938 elections had revealed greatest attrition: the small towns and the middle-class. The other was designed to organize a positive new force "for the preservation of the people's liberties."[25] Both were calculated to make a contribution as well as a name for himself, and both were conducted with publicity worthy of a professional public relations man. Temporary or not, Murphy gave Washington an object lesson in how quickly traditional government operations could be transferred onto the center of the political stage. Not until the Kennedy brothers captured the White House did the Department of Justice loom so plainly as a command post of political action. "The Lord's gift to struggling humanity is not a pompous public official," the new Attorney General remarked of his sumptuous office.[26] But Americans, in his view, felt "insecure and unsafe." Instead of the false security provided by dictators, they wanted the "sure certain safety" of effective democratic government: "That means civil liberties. It means clean, honest government. It means that the forces of vice and crime, with the money they command, and their unholy alliance with partisan politics, must be brought to trial and convicted in honest courts. . . . The present situation in America must be cleaned up."[27] A new scene-stealer had arrived from the New Deal outposts determined to freshen an old-line agency—and the movement —with a new broom.

As Attorney General, Murphy lost little time stamping the office with his personality. Although he refrained from speaking engagements, at Gordon Dean's suggestion, until the job was under control, his first moves gave every evidence that he intended to invigorate the Department of Justice and strengthen public confidence in the integrity of the New Deal. Ordering a docket survey, a study of federal civil liberties statutes, and departmental attorneys to work at nine o'clock sharp, he announced plans to take personal command of important Supreme Court cases and to visit each jurisdiction to speed up justice. Capitalizing on the work of his predecessors, he sponsored a series of studies and conferences. Within his first four months the department organized a National Parole Conference, along with a joint meeting of district attorneys, which included officials from the President down to California's attorney general, Earl Warren. Organized by the Bureau of Prisons at the urging of Sam A. Lewisohn, who underwrote the expenses, the conference aimed at public education and the establishment of realistic parole standards.[28] Legal problems in the administrative process, justifiably a subject of acute controversy, were handed to a study committee of distinguished lawyers headed by James W. Morris and Dean Acheson, whose membership, Murphy made sure, included men sympathetic to reform and whose recommendations ultimately resulted in revision of the Administrative Procedures Act.[29] Abuses in receivership fees, a personal project, went under the surveillance of a group headed, though reluctantly, by Jackson and then Robert P. Patterson.[30] The Attorney General also organized two new units in the Criminal Division, one devoted to civil liberties and the other to commercial frauds, and the department recommended legislation to create an administrative office of the federal courts, new federal criminal rules, and a public defender fee system.[31] All but the latter proposal were enacted.

Much of the activity, most notably the rules and organization of the federal courts, merely carried forward the plans of previous Attorney Generals. Major departmental enterprises, such as the FBI, the Bureau of Prisons, the Antitrust Division, and the Solicitor General's Office, which were in highly capable hands, Murphy left more or less alone.[32] Although Jackson sent him records of pending cases for study, the new Attorney General's widely publicized desire to argue before the Supreme Court remained just that.[b] Washington newsmen, as a result, frequently left Murphy's early press conferences incredulous about the sudden flurry of plans and confessing "a touch of nausea" at his self-serving cliches and "downright painful righteousness."[33] Over-advertising was bound to create skepticism, especially after his old *Detroit Times* friend, Joseph A. Mulcahy, joined the department in June to head a newly centralized press office.[34] Sensing that the prime loyalties of existing personnel were not to him and

---

[b] Murphy did ask for the record in *Pittman* v. *Home Owners' Corp.*, 308 U.S. 21 (1939), but never argued it. See memo, Jackson to FM, Jan. 20, 1939, Box 62. Memo, W.W. Gardner to Jackson, Jan. 30, 1939, Box 63.

eager to bolster the administration's flagging popularity, Murphy laid
great stress on public relations. But as purpose began to unfold in
action, it was also apparent that he was "not a flash in the pan."[35]
The new Attorney General was making a dent with three special
concerns he brought to the department—personnel administration,
municipal corruption, and civil liberties.

Murphy arrived in Washington fresh from a civil service fight
and eager "to make a contribution to the improvement of personnel
standards."[36] Only in part did that mean infusing the federal register
with Michigan men to counterbalance the dominance of easterners.
Murphy seriously hoped to project leadership and example from the
Department of Justice by capitalizing on a favorable climate for personnel reform. In 1939 reorganization of the federal bureaucracy was
the order of the day. The Brownlow Committee was then at work
on the first major overhaul of the executive branch in a generation,
and the White House was applying pressure on all departments to
improve administrative standards. Needing little encouragement and
perceiving that the performance of the Justice Department was
peculiarly dependent on the calibre of the assistant attorney generals
and bureau chiefs immediately below him, Murphy began to sweep
at the top echelon of his own agency. In short order he reshuffled
the Attorney General's personal staff by bringing in Kemp and G.
Mennen Williams from Michigan; with a strong assist from Thomas
G. Corcoran, who still maintained status as a special assistant to the
Attorney General though officially employed by the RFC, he launched
a talent hunt for new division heads. By summer only Jackson, Thurman Arnold, and the professional chiefs of the prison bureau and the
FBI, James V. Bennett and J. Edgar Hoover, remained in charge of
the major bureaus and divisions. A fresh crop of assistant attorney
generals—including O. John Rogge, Norman M. Littell, Samuel O.
Clark, Jr., and Francis M. Shea—began to make their impress on
national affairs. Viewing them as vital new blood, loyal neither to
himself nor to party professionals, Murphy was very proud of the
appointments. "I want the forces of this Department mustered to
strike lethal blows at real crime and corruption," he wrote Hearst
executive, Edmond D. Coblentz. "The men I have selected . . . are
clean and fine and scholarly. They will not be politically dominated—
yet will do responsible work in the public interest."[37]

Murphy also imported his Michigan civil service chief, William
Brownrigg, as personnel director in order "to move a great professional
department onto a 'merit system' of recruitment and advancement

and do it wisely."[38] This decision landed the new Attorney General
in a thicket of bureaucratic conflict, and in basic opposition to the
traditions and professional outlook of the Justice Department. As
part of the administrative improvement program, the President had
recently extended civil service to major departments by executive order.
The FBI and lawyers throughout the government had bucked, however,
and urged their exemption from the merit system on grounds of
special training, functions, and problems of recruitment. Acceding to
this viewpoint, Attorney General Cummings had recommended that
departmental lawyers and FBI personnel be exempt from civil service,
but the Civil Service Commission postponed decision pending study
of the issue by a newly appointed President's Committee on Civil
Service Improvement which was chaired by Justice Reed and composed of Justices McReynolds and Frankfurter, General Leonard
Wood, Leonard D. White, and the new Attorney General, who could
be expected to be friendlier than most to uniform classification.

During the infighting that followed, Murphy became the mouthpiece
of the Brownrigg–Civil Service Commission viewpoint that lawyers
were no more entitled to civil service exemption than other professionals in public service. Though he lost the battle, and incurred a
slap from Justice Frankfurter for intolerance on the subject, the
episode was an early barometer of key differences between two future
Justices. Instead of championing the "lawyerly" orientation of the
nation's top law enforcement agency, as did Justice Frankfurter, the
Attorney General supported "scientific" personnel experts.[39/c]

As if the civil service dispute were not enough to shake departmental
mores, Murphy also threatened to turn Brownrigg loose within the

---

[c] Although Murphy did not accept Brownrigg's views in toto he disagreed with
the majority position that lawyers required special procedures and filed a separate
report, which Brownrigg helped to write, defending the principle of recruitment and
examination of lawyers by modern personnel techniques. During the preparation of
his statement Murphy observed that the majority report "seems to me to be a studied
effort to circumvent Civil Service rather than keep it." He openly charged that the
Committee had avoided the issue of the adequacy of civil service standards as applied
to lawyers. His attitude, and proposal for a thorough recanvass of the issue, while commended as sound by most personnel experts and several newspapers, drew Justice
Frankfurter's rebuttal that one could be a passionate advocate of civil service without
absorbing the whole procedures and mentality of the Civil Service Commission. Frank-
furter was considered the prime mover behind Chapter Five of the report. Murphy, by
contrast, accepted exemption of the FBI until the "emergency" was over. See William
Brownrigg to FM, Dec. 23, 1940, Box 93; Jan. 13, 1941, Box 94; Jan. 24, 1941, Box 95.
Undated note FM to Charles J. Hedetniemi; FM to Stanley Reed, Jan. 18, 1941; FM to
FDR, Feb. 7, 1941, Box 95. Felix Frankfurter to FM, Oct. 24, 1941, Box 99. Cf. E.
Blythe Stason to FM, Oct. 22, 1941, Box 99; *St. Louis Globe-Democrat*, March 1, 1941.

the department. That departmental personnel practices were deficient was beyond dispute. The personnel section, as Kemp discovered, did little more than record-keeping for otherwise diffuse subdivisions which went their separate ways. While the FBI made perpetual claims for special treatment, the outgoing chief of the Lands Division, Carl McFarland, complained bitterly about the disgraceful record of the past in making his division a patronage dumping ground. After a nascent study of departmental organization and budgetary procedures, suggested by Harold D. Smith as a model for other departments, the Michigan team of Kemp, Williams, and Brownrigg recommended internal reorganization and centralization to bring greater cohesion to the manifold activities of the Justice Department.[40]

Needless to say, the plans of an interim group to overhaul the agency won few friends among departmental regulars, some of whom berated the newcomers as "Murphy's political pals." To attempt solution of personnel problems by appointing a nonlawyer personnel expert, moreover, was far too radical a break from traditional methods of recruitment throughout the agency. Government attorneys and the FBI, in a show of bureaucratic staying power, successfully resisted the innovation, and Congress eventually cut Brownrigg's position out from under him. The iconoclastic reformer, Thurman Arnold, might commend the personnel chief for the help given his division; but Murphy's efforts to bring scientific personnel classification and administrative reorganization to the Justice Department faltered almost before they began. What new brooming he accomplished within the agency, in short, was done by beating the bushes for talent in customary and largely informal ways.

Precisely because he made no attempt to overhaul the system, Murphy was more successful with judicial appointments. Candid recognition of political realities in practice, if not in rhetoric, and insistence that "we must make good" on bargains made, were responsible for impressive appointments to the federal courts. When Thomas E. Dewey broke the evidence in January 1939 that Federal Circuit Judge Martin T. Manton, a onetime contender for the Supreme Court, had been "selling justice" in New York, Murphy pounced on the case and turned the subject of judicial personnel into a personal crusade. Ordering a grand jury investigation, forcing Manton's resignation, and launching a broad inquiry of "unhealthy and irregular conditions" in the federal judiciary, the new Attorney General was in a strategic position to influence federal courts for years to come. New judgeships created by the omnibus Judiciary Act of 1938 enabled him to fill 50 vacancies in the federal system in less than a year.[41] Keenly conscious of the responsibility, he told Henry M. Bates, dean of the Michigan Law School, that "one of my first desires in this new work is to make a definite contribution to elevation of the character, integrity and ability of the Federal judiciary, if it is within my power to do. My very earnest intention is that every vacancy shall be filled with the best qualified man available."[42]

To do so ran against the political grain. Murphy might urge the President "that considerations of patronage are wholly irrelevant"; but for the White House as well as the Senate, nonpartisan selection of federal judges would remove the choicest plums from the political market.[43] On the other hand, the subject was too important to be left to partisan chance. Choosing judges, as William Howard Taft understood so well, was the time-honored way by which executives bring the judiciary and popular majorities into a rough harmony. With the aid of Corcoran's eye for talent and of Matthew F. McGuire's very able and discreet handling of senatorial relations, Murphy made surprising headway with quality selections to the federal bench. Despite CIO reservations about William O. Douglas's supposed corporate connections, he pressed hard for the Douglas appointment to the Supreme Court, his one close involvement in filling vacancies on the high court.[44] The appointments to the Courts of Appeals were unusually impressive. Besides Francis Biddle, Charles Alvin Jones, and Robert P. Patterson, there were Calvert Magruder of Harvard, Charles E. Clark of Yale, and law school deans Arant, Dobie, and Rutledge of Ohio State, Virginia, and Iowa. New district judges included Harry E. Kalodner, James W. Morris, and T. Alan Goldsborough, while John T. Cahill, whom Murphy regarded as a critical choice, was named federal district attorney in New York.

Not all of the nominees were nonpartisan. Selection of Frank A. Picard in Michigan, as well as other district judgeships in Kentucky and Louisiana, went to the politically deserving, though even they were a cut above the norm. Neither did his recommendations invariably end in appointments. Dean Acheson was one conspicuous recommendation for the circuit bench which failed; and Francis Biddle, who disliked judging, accepted appointment only on the understanding that he would succeed Jackson as Solicitor General. If there was a marked prejudice toward academic men, a prerequisite also existed, as Ickes put it, that they be "vigorous, young, and convinced New Dealers."[45] Considering the political pressures, which included warnings that the choice of Arant over a Michigan man would be injurious to himself, the way Murphy and the administration worked with rather than against traditional political processes was as impressive as the appointments themselves.[46]

The contrast with his personnel plans, in method and in results, could hardly have been more marked. Murphy pressured for the resignation of other judges suspected of corruption and for retirement of conservative ones over 70. He traded other federal jobs for judges, stalled when he had no other choice, as in the case of New Jersey where a senator was angling for a judgeship, and poured on the balm of personal charm and public conscience when the bargaining was tight. The new Attorney General seemed to have a way of appealing to a politician's better nature. "That Murphy," said South Carolina's "Cotton Ed" Smith, "—he's a great American."[47]

The Attorney General's effort to improve the administration of justice ranged beyond judicial appointments. The docket survey (the first of its kind) had the intended effect of reducing a backlog of civil cases.[48] Murphy barnstormed around the country to boost the crusading spirit of district attorneys; he recommended elimination of judicial patronage by placing deputy marshals under civil service; and he evangelized fervently to awaken interest in the administration of justice.[49] "A good judge does not want patronage; a bad one should not have it," he declared in a widely heralded maiden address to the Associated Press. "It is a bitter but undeniable fact," he asserted, "that our courts do not enjoy the unquestioned respect that they had a generation ago." Public identification of lawyers with the interests of property, judicial inefficiency, and the influence of politics and patronage, were all responsible, in his view, for weakening "a national bulwark."[50] But the heart of the matter, he knew, was judicial appointment. Despite admonitions that "it is impossible to take politics out of politics," he urged the President to proceed on the principle that the judiciary was "privileged ground into which ordinary political interests could not be permitted to intrude."[51] While no single individual could claim exclusive credit in the involved process of choosing judges, Murphy took justifiable pride in the concrete accomplishments and in the "very, very, very fine impression," as Jesse Jones described reactions to Roosevelt, which his speech-making created in public.[52] Once again he was making an impressive start by exhortation and the talent he was bringing into government. Felix Frankfurter, in one of several friendly overtures, wrote on the day after Biddle, Patterson, and Cahill were nominated for service:

The implications of the so-called lower Federal judiciary to our whole scheme of government—the ramifying but subtle authority which they wield—are only gradually being understood even by many who are otherwise well versed in government affairs. Happily, you sized up the situation promptly, courageously and imaginatively. To the historian of our institutions who sees below merely obviously dramatic conflicts, yesterday will be noted as the beginning of a process of profound importance.

I congratulate you warmly for having enlisted the President to the vindication of his own discernment, and his own high standards.[53/d]

III

The new broom in the Justice Department and the judiciary appealed mainly to small but strategically located elite groups of lawyers and journalists. But it was accompanied by a spectacular anticorruption campaign which captured the imagination of the general public. In April Governor Lloyd C. Stark of Missouri was pressuring President Roosevelt to authorize federal income tax indictments against members of the Democratic Pendergast machine in Kansas City. Rather than discourage the President, as Treasury Department officials cautioned until all the evidence was in, Murphy aggressively supported Stark and intervened in the case, even though the investigation was only two-thirds complete, because of its "great magnitude."[54] Criticizing the local district attorney for making witness bargains, and lashing out at "evil," "provincial powers," who allegedly attempted to block the indictments, he flew to the scene with J. Edgar Hoover and even made a speech to a startled grand jury, to show the government's earnestness in the case.[55]

Understandably, many viewed this step as a grandstand play. Suspicions increased in May when Murphy announced a national campaign to strike at the relationship between crime and politics. "The purge is on," he asserted melodramatically. "Where it will strike I cannot disclose, but it will strike hard."[56] Reporters snickered at his amateurish zest for cops-and-robbers, but Murphy was quick to demonstrate earnestness. "This is no light crusade of the moment," he wrote Arthur D. Maguire with an eye to his critics. "The record in Michigan is re-

d In 1940, Justice Murphy passed the following note to Justice Frankfurter: "There is no single official act as Attorney General that I am prouder of than recommending and moving the appointment of Magruder. He has single-handed—in an intellectual way—lifted the quality and direction of his circuit into a new eminence." Frankfurter commented by each sentence: (1) "And bringing to pass." (2) "That's just what he has done & proves just what one first-rate judge can do. You did it in the case of some 6 other judges. F.F." FM to Felix Frankfurter, undated, Box 91.

plete with evidence to show that the crusade for clean administration of law is no whimsie for me."[57] In rapid succession came investigation of two federal judges, Edwin S. Thomas and J. Warren Davis. Then came income prosecutions of underworld king, Louis "Lepke" Buchalter; the GOP boss of Atlantic City, Enoch Johnson; and, despite a plea from a Roman Catholic cardinal, the aging Philadelphia publisher and racetrack information king, Moses Annenberg.[58] "We are especially anxious to break down alliances between corrupt forces and municipal government in this country," said Murphy. "We know where we have to fight and what we have to fight, if city and State government won't clean up of their own accord."

There is no mystery how government is corrupted. It starts with slush funds amassed by vice . . . which makes its alliance with partisan politics.

What follows is corruption of elections, corruption of the courts, corruption of the whole government structure. The people, who are the backbone of any democracy, have no sense of safety any more. It must be restored to them.[59]

"Go It Frank!" cried the *El Paso Herald-Post*. No Attorney General had crusaded like this since muckraking days. No matter how much "Old Ironpants," General Hugh Johnson, might fume against federal intervention, Murphy's crime offensive drew enthusiastic newspaper support.[60] City editors, often lone crusaders against municipal corruption, had begun to perceive that organized crime, like commerce, had grown into an international business empire beyond the control of local governments. Federal authority was limited, to be sure; a national police force ran deeply against national tradition and FBI goals. But Justice Department leadership could do much to bolster local efforts against "the private government of crime," which overpowered public authority in some instances, and still does. As Governor Stark wrote Murphy following passage of legislation to clean up the Kansas City police force: "Thanks to your aggressive backing, I was able to accomplish 'the impossible.' "[61]

One substantial accomplishment of Murphy's in the spring of 1939 was to add glamor to an otherwise dour period of the New Deal. As the Attorney General and J. Edgar Hoover toured the country promoting law enforcement, the anticrime crusade became something of a national sensation. Flying to inspect facilities and to give pep talks in federal prisons and regional offices—and gathering, as J. Parnell Thomas charged, "a newspaper headline with each spectacular swoop" —bachelors Murphy and Hoover put on a show that delighted newsmen and the President's political managers. For Murphy's part, he was engaged in the very serious business of supporting local crusaders and generating public goodwill, which here, as elsewhere, he regarded as more important than organizational tinkering. The more he succeeded outside the department, however, the more the effort reverberated within.

The flamboyant Murphy was not merely tossing baseballs with prisoners in the Atlanta jail as a gesture of his sympathy, he was also playing with bureaucratic fire.[62] For one thing, his morale-building missions disrupted regular channels—as they were designed to do. For another, his impromptu speeches and press announcements were frequently overly dramatic and premature. One unannounced visit at the Leavenworth prison with Hoover at his side almost touched off a riot. He also embarrassed the Bureau of Prisons after visiting Alcatraz by denouncing the institution as "a place of horror" that created "stir crazy" men and a blot on beautiful San Francisco Bay.[63] "The Lord be thanked for an Attorney General possessed of an interest in the human spirit—may you go on!" commented John Collier, Commissioner of Indian Affairs, after the Attorney General revealed plans to relocate the prison and suggested that San Francisco erect in its place a memorial to the idealism and spirit of the West.[64] That Murphy reacted from Christian compassion and a well-developed philosophy of rehabilitation was not questioned, but an impulsive reaction on his part set him in opposition to a pet project of his predecessor and offended the Bureau of Prison's policy that the less publicity about prisons the better. Murphy revived an old controversy over the morality of maximum security institutions for "incorrigibles," which had lasting repercussions within Alcatraz itself until the prison was vacated in 1963. What was more, the episode gave rise to an ugly Washington rumor, in spite of eye-witness denials, that Alcatraz itself had not offended his sensibilities—merely the failure of harbor officials to fly the Attorney General's flag from his launch.[65] His vanity, even if inactive in this instance, had not gone undetected.

Regardless of the skepticism bred by his opportunism or his innocence (men found it difficult to decide which) Murphy's campaign against corruption and the accompanying publicity blitz made a deep popular impression. He was a fervent Irish crusader, whom reporters colored with choice nicknames, making good his pledges to attack crime in the cities. In the summer of 1939 federal agents were dispatched to prosecute the corrupt leavings of the Long regime in Louisiana, and mail fraud was brought to court in Los Angeles. When

Murphy ignored senatorial courtesy regarding district attorney appointments in Kansas City and dropped hints that the citadels of Democratic bossism, Kelly's Chicago and Hague's Jersey City, were next on the list, editorial hats flew. The Attorney General, putting "law enforcement above political expediency," apparently meant business.[66] "We tell you mates," commented the *Charlotte News*, "times change, and so do Attorney Generals."[67] The most impressive new broom, it seemed, was Murphy himself.

From a newsman's viewpoint Murphy was an ideal Attorney General. Colorful, cooperative, easy to caricature, he had a certain mystique and a sixth sense of what made effective copy. His weekly press conferences were second only to Roosevelt's in popularity. His work as Attorney General, consequently, was among the most highly publicized phenomena of the day. Behind all the hoopla, moreover, his actual performance was one of the biggest surprises of the late New Deal. As an aggressive public prosecutor, his special forte seemed to have been found. Flamboyant sensationalism had never been necessary, his press secretary Joseph A. Mulcahy advised, to reach the backbone of the nation's voters through the rural and small town press.[68] But the combination of high-powered publicity and concrete results spread his crusading image far and wide. Sophisticated columnists credited him with having "rejuvenated" the Department of Justice. Big-city editors hailed him for "doing one of the most remarkable jobs of public service an American has ever done in the cabinet." And catching the word where it meant the most, small-town weeklies, for example, the *Hammond* (La.) *Farmer's Friend,* interpreted that service as restoring the "confidence of the people of the entire nation in our Government."[69]

The Attorney General's actions were loaded with political implications. Once again he was being received on his own terms. Goodness was paying dividends. Journalists began to recall that as Governor he had brought Michigan one of the cleanest governments it had ever known. Those ironically inclined remembered that even Huey Long in the "Kingfish's" heyday had proposed him as the ideal Attorney General.[70] The sit-downs were forgiven as Murphy's alma mater, in an event which filled him with happiness, added to his string of honorary degrees for "outstanding service to his country."[71] While the columnists Pearson and Allen cited him as their Cabinet member of the year, others bemoaned his rumored transfer to War. "Keep Murphy Where He Is," the *Boston Traveler* advised. "Mr. Murphy is doing a magnificent job as attorney general."[72]

Presidential talk inevitably revived. His name again appeared in the Gallup poll.[73] James A. Farley rated him third, after Hopkins and Jackson, in the President's personal preference of successor; and columnist after columnist echoed the Alsop-Kintner argument that Roosevelt and his Catholic Attorney General would make a Democratic "dream ticket" for 1940.[74] With Corcoran doing the grooming and Mulcahy the press agentry, it looked as if the vice-presidency might be Murphy's next stop.[75]

The potentialities of a campaign against big-city corruption were particularly intriguing. The President was reportedly delighted with the lift Murphy was giving the New Deal. It was no accident that White House aides urged him to make speeches, especially in New York. Nor was it accidental that time and again the Attorney General's office raced to beat Thomas E. Dewey to the punch.[76] In a competitive duel against sin, Murphy was in a position to put the accomplishments of the leading GOP contender in the shade. "Never in our time," Raymond Moley commented, "have a Frank Murphy temperament and an opportunity of this magnitude coincided on the public stage." For the Attorney General not only could become a "super-Dewey," his drive against municipal misconduct also might block presidential aspirants such as Farley, who were identified with city machines, and enable new, pro-Murphy forces to rise in big electoral states.[77] Jersey City, as William Allen White noted, was "another lion's den that is crying for a Daniel." And if the move against Kelly were also given the clear light, as Chicago publisher Frank Knox urged the President, it would have political implications of utmost importance. What with both Murphy and Dewey her native sons, the *New York Herald-Tribune* observed, "Michigan seems to be foremost among expectant mothers of Presidents."[78]

Murphy was now a star in the big league. If he attempted to use the Justice Department as a base for building a national organization as distinct from his popular "image," however, the evidence was hard to find. His attorney generalship repeated the same old pattern of personalization at the expense of party relationships. His national preoccupations actually eroded his home base. Despite countless pleas from loyal supporters, Murphy did little to prevent control of state party machinery from passing to Murray Van Wagoner's highway department faction.[79] Nor could he prevent attacks on the state civil service. Although Murphy was willing to say, without making commitments, "I will be back in Michigan on the firing line in 1940," he refused to fight Van Wagoner or Senator Prentiss M. Brown over control of federal patronage.[80] His superiority in senatorial preference polls indicated that he was still Michigan's number one Democrat, a status which enabled him to bargain with party chieftains about the choice.[81] But the reluctant conclusion of Joseph M. Donnelly was amply justified, that Murphy's interest in party affairs was "too fitful and not sufficiently sustained" to obtain results.[82/e] Loyalties became overtaxed, for his attitude was all too plain: "I have job enough of my own to do."[83] Whatever his aspirations for higher office, the choice again would have to come from above.

Murphy denied having additional ambitions. "In light of international and domestic conditions," he said, "I should like to belong to that small company of public servants and others who are committed to do some of the homely and modest tasks of perfecting integrity in government and making government more efficient and orderly. We can leave the great and ambitious programs to those more competent to do them. . . . My only objective now is to be a good Attorney General."[84] These comments were typical of presidential aspirants, serving only to arouse rather than douse suspicions. All that goodness seemed "incredible, almost unhealthy." A modern counterpart of the early Jesuit zealots, as Ickes thought of him, was something new to Washington.[85] Granting Murphy a certain theatrical bent, was this man on the level? Particularly when such a teetotalling, religious individual was also one of the most dapperly dressed and active bachelors in the Washington cocktail circuit, it was easy to believe that Murphy was one of the "strangest paradoxes" in the New Deal.[86/f]

Murphy's position on larger issues of public policy reinforced his credentials as an independent force in the administration. Despite warnings to tread lightly between the conflicting views of Thurman Arnold and Robert H. Jackson concerning antitrust policy, Murphy vigorously backed Arnold, who attributed his success to that factor.[87] Issuing a major policy statement at Arnold's request that industrywide investigations to lower consumer prices were preferable to hit-or-miss individual prosecutions and business harassment, the Attorney General thus went

[e] To constant appeals from former supporters that he keep his hand in Michigan politics, Murphy's rebuffs were cold and sometimes cruel. Donnelly's criticism, for one, provoked an invitation to quit "snarling" and join the opposition. Then, after learning of the deep hurts caused, Murphy sent a characteristic apology: "Forget the letter—no man had a better friend than you." FM to Donnelly, July 26, 1939, Box 75; and telegram, Aug. 5, 1939, Box 76.

[f] Always sensitive to critics, Murphy was aware that his attempts at self-explanation were skeptically received. During preparation of a feature article for the *New York Times* he confessed to reporter Russell Porter: "It always seems to me that I try to make myself appear too virtuous and reveal an unfortunate inclination to preachments." But the very explanation of that characteristic was a resumption of form: "I have a real zeal for good government and am willing to give battle for it. . . . A crisis somehow or other always finds its way to my doorstep." FM to Porter, Feb. 26, 1939, Box 65.

on record that the antitrust statutes should be "discriminatingly enforced."[88] Though with reservations, he also supported Arnold's controversial decision to bring an antitrust indictment against the Carpenters' Union president, "Big Bill" Hutcheson; and he aggravated internal tension by a press conference remark that it was "the duty of the Department of Justice to enforce the law as it finds it," rather than base labor antitrust policy on Justice Brandeis' dissent to the *Bedford* decision as the Solicitor General preferred.[89] Upon requests from interested parties, Murphy even denounced the Chrysler "slow-down" strike as irresponsible, and threatened to jail WPA workers in Minneapolis for striking against their government.[90] Such things bred a "fascist psychology," he said; continued labor stoppages were "tragic and absurd." "We don't want any anti-government mentality; we don't want any anti-social mentality; we don't want any anti-business mentality." "Democracy today is in a fight for its life."[91]

Harmony, business responsibility, and admission of labor abuse—what kind of Progressivism was this? Careful reading of Murphy's speeches would have indicated no letup in his advocacy of social reform, yet businessmen regarded him as less radical than Roosevelt.[92] They also took comfort in the outcropping of his old Progressive impulses for nonpartisan administration. Prodded by Kemp, Murphy played a leading role in overcoming the President's reservations about the Hatch Act, which regulated the political activities of federal employees. Although the statute merely extended the rules then governing the classified civil service, its failure to cover state employees performing federal functions and its restrictions on political liberty raised sufficient doubts in the administration that a veto message was prepared for the President's signature.[93] Murphy, adding his weight to the Civil Service Commissioners, assured Roosevelt that the Act was constitutional, a step in the right direction, and that "if properly administered the measure can be made an effective instrument of good government." Personally Murphy preferred to extend civil service; but, realizing that fringe cases would be difficult, he pledged his "personal responsibility" to see that the measure was fairly enforced.[94] In the fall he took steps to secure compliance from recalcitrant district attorneys and federal marshals.[95]

"When the Congress convenes," he told James K. Pollock, "we must present a real corrupt practices act."[96] Apparently he also contemplated taking a lead in this field as another step in modernizing government. "The job is an enormous one," he observed to Edmond D. Coblentz, "but it is the sort of thing that I have always believed we must do in this country if democracy is to compete successfully with other systems." "Orderliness and efficiency in public affairs, as well as decency in public life, are indispensable if we are to halt the onslaught of the 'isms.' "[97]

To underscore his intentions Murphy made a strong speech before a civil service conclave advocating introduction of the merit system throughout American public administration. "We cannot forget the more commonplace and unspectacular, but tremendously important, task of placing the machinery of government in smooth running order," he declared. A public payroll that consumed an estimated 13 percent of average family income was an excessive luxury. The time had come to introduce "scientific" personnel management down the line.[98]

"Is a New Dealer out sailing alone, or what?" queried the *Helena* (Mont.) *Independent*.[99] The civil service speech, though its primary targets were state and local governments, which accounted for three-fourths of the public payroll, stirred a flurry of political speculation. Had the Attorney General joined the "economy bloc" against New Deal extravagance? Wishful thinking may have caused misunderstanding on that score, yet Murphy did speak against internal advice. Since he had already crossed swords with government attorneys and "the Brownlow crowd" over personnel management, administration liberals regarded his speech as an act of disloyalty. Was he building a 1940 political plank?[100] Throughout his stay in office Murphy's stock declined within the Department of Justice in inverse proportion to its rise in the country at large. But to the general public, policy differences within the administration appeared less important than the emergence of a "Strange New Dealer" of character and independence who articulated popular yearnings for order and repose. Administration leaders should be warned, the *Haverhill* (Mass.) *Gazette* commented, that "an earnest, courageous man, who obeys his conscience, can be just as dangerous as helpful to them."[101]

Little actually came of Murphy's civil service efforts as the national government passed onto emergency footing in the fall of 1939. Yet preachment alone enabled Murphy to add a new dimension to his public image as a liberal capable of tempering idealism with practical judgment. However much Washington sophisticates dismissed them as window-dressing, his Progressive streak and dedication to government service as a religious imperative, his new broom and crusades for political rectitude, caught the popular fancy after a long season of intense partisanship. To suggest a difference of personal style is not to criticize his predecessors; the Justice Department under Homer Cummings was better—if traditionally—led. Not even Murphy claimed that accomplishment matched the ballyhoo. "It isn't much," he conceded, "but whatever it is it has been done in earnest and for the public good." Handsome, eloquent, and at the peak of his powers, he cut a dashing figure as Attorney General. He also gave a striking display of the force of personality in politics. His energy and exhortation successfully activated intangible confidence in government at a time of genuine disaffection. While the price was attrition of his Michigan base and the creation of powerful Washington enemies, the personal dividends could not be gainsaid. As a result of his efforts to strike at the shortcomings which sowed distrust of the New Deal, the *Tulsa World* commented, "it is very apparent that Mr. Murphy has grown more in stature and public estimation than almost any other public man of our time. . . . The Attorney General now appears before the public as a real leader for morality and common sense in the larger affairs of the United States."[102]

Murphy, in six months of office, quite clearly had turned defeat into triumph by finding new causes for "moral leadership." Nor was recovery of prestige confined to the hinterlands. SEC Chairman Jerome N. Frank, conveying his loyalty after an interagency conflict, once asserted in an enthusiastic burst: "I know of nothing that has occurred in the history of the New Deal which has been as stimulating as the manner in which you have been administering the Department of Justice."[103] For those who knew him well, as for those who observed from afar, it was difficult to escape the conclusion that he had grown in power. And some, their idealism already fired by his performance in the labor wars, believed that he had found grace as well. Wrote Harvard theologian H. Richard Niebuhr:

I feel a warm glow of thankfulness whenever I remember the fact that the administration of justice in our country is, at least largely, in the hands of a man who has demonstrated in trying times his belief in a justice which is more than expediency and his faith that mercy is a part of justice. I think of you as belonging in the succession of Christian statesmen of whom Sir Thomas More is an outstanding example and though in doctrinal convictions I am something of an ultra-Protestant I hope I can recognize and be glad for demonstrations of Christian wisdom and divine grace without reference to ecclesiastical connections.

Pardon this note, if it is an intrusion. There's nothing I want to say save "Thanks for living."[104]

"Frank the Just," no doubt, was making a remarkable political comeback. Detecting still another ingredient responsible for it, Claude G. Bowers observed: "If you get disgusted with politics, try Hollywood."[105]

CHAPTER 9

SO MUCH TO BE DONE,

1939-1940

NOTHING contributed more to Murphy's stature as Attorney General than his attempts to strengthen civil liberties. Long a defender of minority rights, he arrived in Washington anxious to enlist the power of the Justice Department in this cause and to "help stimulate in our people a disposition to rediscover and embrace the civil liberties."[1] By virtue of his appointment, libertarian groups gained important access to the federal government. The new Attorney General was not only a board member of the NAACP and the ACLU, but a fervent libertarian evangelist who was eager to translate general attitudes into concrete action. That "something will be done" to bolster personal freedoms was among his premier resolves.[2]

The pogroms in Germany and purges in Russia, coupled in time as they were with the sit-down strikes and the anti-Semitic turn in Coughlin's movement, with notorious examples of local tyranny in the United States, and an atmosphere of threatening war—all had jolted from Murphy whatever assumptions he held that government neutrality was enough to safeguard fundamental freedoms. Prizing personal liberties as the "finest possession of the American people," and espousing "more democracy" as the answer to totalitarian threats from abroad, he embraced with unquestioning zeal the principle which distinguished modern libertarians from their classical liberal forbears—positive government protection of private rights.[3] Characteristically, his first initiatives as Attorney General concerned a program of "aggressive protection of the fundamental rights." As soon as he had assumed command of the department he held a series of discussions with libertarian leaders Roger Baldwin, Morris L. Ernst, and Arthur Garfield Hays concerning the labor conflicts in Harlan County, Kentucky, the muzzling of union organizers by the Hague machine in Jersey City, and other civil liberties problems.[4] Acting on a suggestion from CIO counsel Lee Pressman, who sought revival of dormant federal penalties to help enforce the rights conferred on workers by the Wagner Act, Murphy then ordered an exhaustive survey of federal civil rights statutes with a view toward establishing an administrative unit in the department devoted exclusively to civil liberties enforcement. Though it was problematic what the department could do beyond measures already taken,

Murphy wanted to explore every alternative. "Where there is social unrest—and I have been through no scant amount of that since 1930," he remarked to newsmen, "it is there that we ought to be most anxious, most vigilant to protect the civil liberties of a protesting and insecure people."[5] Civil liberties were more than personal privileges; they were insurance against revolution and the foundation of political security. Civil liberties were more than the nation's "spiritual strength"; they were the means of democratic renewal. And if enlarging them benefited the diverse minorities in the Democratic coalition, no one doubted the Attorney General's devotion to both principles.

The difficulty was a lack of federal authority. American institutions had been founded on classic liberal premises that government was the enemy, not the friend, of liberty. Constitutional guarantees in the Bill of Rights, as written, had restrained only federal action, not states or individuals. While the Civil War amendments had greatly enlarged federal authority against state deprivation of individual rights, Congress had not exercised its authority since Reconstruction and the Supreme Court had emasculated most of that. While the Justices were beginning to take a broader view of the Civil War amendments under judicial initiatives, executive authority rested on the slender foundations of two sections of the old Civil Rights Acts which the Court had left standing and which the Justices only now were being asked to revive. Progress, in other words, depended on untested judicial attitudes in cases being tried.

Traditionalists regarded separate civil liberties organization within the Criminal Division of the Justice Department as superfluous, if not favoritism. But in context, the idea of a special unit was a well-timed step in pushing the federal government over the threshold of activist commitment. A special unit could give organizational identity to libertarian interests and capitalize on work already done. For the past three years the Criminal Division had been exploring the potential of the Civil Rights Acts as a weapon against deprivation of rights. Section 19, which punished private conspiracies, underpinned indictments in the Harlan County peonage cases. Section 20, which punished acts "under color of law," provided the basis for the Jersey City investigation. Though the Harlan trial had resulted in a hung jury, and though a grand jury had refused to indict Hague, Murphy became Attorney General just as the Court of Appeals for the third circuit sustained an injunction against Hague in a civil suit and the department faced the question whether to resubmit criminal charges to another grand jury.[6]

Though he approved the Solicitor General's recommendation against filing an *amicus curiae* brief in the *Hague* case, in view of the thorough arguments of counsel, on February 3rd, he ordered into being a Civil Liberties Unit and appointed Henry A. Schweinhaut as its head. The resources at his disposal—a dozen lawyers and three assistants—were limited. Even more restricted was the agency's authority. The fact had to be faced, as Brien McMahon, the outgoing Criminal Division chief, reported to Murphy, that unless the Supreme Court could be persuaded to depart from earlier decisions, federal criminal statutes did not provide adequate legal remedies for deprivation of citizens' rights. Additional authority from Congress, given successive antilynch law filibusters, was out of sight. Within narrow statutory limits, however, the CL Unit could play a useful role. It could investigate critical situations involving the rights of substantial numbers; it could conduct defenses and select cases in order to develop a modern case law; it could also recommend legislation, refer individual complaints to proper federal authorities, and serve as a central clearinghouse of expertise and co-operation among interested private and governmental groups.[7] Small as it was, the Unit was the first organizational recognition of a civil liberties interest in the government, and Murphy took abundant pride in planting the germ. He wrote the President: "Through this unit for the first time in our history the full weight of the Department will be thrown behind the effort to preserve in this country the blessings of liberty, the spirit of tolerance, and the fundamental principles of democracy. . . . It is my personal opinion that the creation of this unit at your order, with all the emphasis it places upon protection of the civil liberties of the individual citizen and of minority groups, is one of the most significant happenings in American legal history."[8]

"I am delighted that at last some one has started to do something about civil liberties in this country," Treasury Secretary Morgenthau remarked after the Attorney General announced his plans to the Cabinet. Just as Murphy's new broom restored confidence in the hinterlands, so his civil liberties drive capitalized on growing liberal concern over the problem. In view of the CL Unit's limited scope, Murphy's optimism perhaps was unwarranted. Yet subsequent Supreme Court approval of the agency's expansive interpretation of federal authority in *Hague* v. *CIO* and in the landmark white primary case, *United States* v. *Classic*, gave powerful boosts to its prospects. The vagueness of the statute created vexing future dilemmas for the Supreme Court. But the organizational identity created and the experience gained were critical spadework for the expanded federal activity which became politically possible two decades later. Positive government protection of individual liberties, a seminal idea in 1939, was destined to enlarge the Unit into a full-fledged division of the Department of Justice and one of its central concerns.[9] In retrospect, creation of the Civil Liberties Unit was Murphy's single most significant contribution as Attorney General.

To reinforce "a program of vigilant action," Murphy brought his evangelical talents into play. He took advantage of the broad audiences available to him as Attorney General to preach the civil liberties gospel. These addresses, many of them nationally broadcast and carefully prepared by group effort involving himself, his speechwriter, and departmental brains such as Henry Schweinhaut, Alexander Holtzoff, and Paul A. Freund, still read as eloquent libertarian tracts. But to those who heard them live, the timeliness of the theme and the contagious intensity of the speaker generated great emotional force. With the passionate simplicity of a preacher (and the purple prose he loved) Murphy sought to awaken renewed devotion for individual rights and to explain government policy in an atmosphere clouded by war.

A public prayer meeting on behalf of civil liberty would have meant little had the Attorney General, following libertarian currents, evaded the problems of civil liberties by denying their existence. What made his evangelism so forceful was the way he faced up to critical issues. Neither falsifying history by holding out a golden age for emulation nor denying the need to control subversive threats from abroad, the Attorney General espoused a balanced policy and elaborated thereby a virtual deposition of his personal belief system as it was influenced by his office and impending war. In 1939 he was grappling in public with the everlasting dilemmas of security versus freedom.[10]

From the start, Murphy made plain the primacy of intangible personal freedoms in his scale of values. Whether a truism or not, he regarded the spirit of liberty as the animus of civilization. Civil liberty, he said, was simply "the idea of human dignity . . . translated into actuality. And measurably as we safeguard civil liberty, we enrich human dignity." Because he believed that principle was the core of religion and social progress, he could not help perceiving the totalitarian threat as a global struggle between civilization and barbarism.[11] On the other hand, Murphy did not believe that the liberal faith itself could be compressed into such simple antimonies. History taught that no era or religion, no class or group, had a monopoly of the free spirit—or of lapses from it. Intolerance was the common battle of all faiths because all men found it difficult to tolerate philosophies opposed to their own. "Yet apparently we must do this if we are to practice our faith in democracy," he declared.[12] "We need to be reminded what a tragic delusion it is to believe that justice and liberty can be denied to a part of a nation and maintained for the rest. In the last analysis, there is no halfway house between democracy and despotism. For persecution is a brutalizing force, and, once unleashed, it eventually destroys even those who brought it to life."[13] Roger Williams had imparted a vital truth in teaching that "freedom of thought was not freedom of thought until it was shared by all." The only way to preserve democracy, in short, was to practice it, "even when it hurts."[14]

The central theme of Murphy's message was the principle of security through freedom. Distilling the elements of the libertarian faith, he argued time and again that liberty was not an inefficient luxury but "spiritual wealth" more potent than material power. Free speech, far from producing weakness, was a source of strength—the mobilizer of free consent, the mechanism of achieving unity in diversity, and the means of escaping the predicament of human fallibility. The "immortal" Holmes had summarized the philosophy in a single concept: free trade in ideas. If every viewpoint is given "the opportunity to get itself accepted in the competition of the market," the Attorney General asserted, "ultimately—as our history shows—the true idea, the right policy comes out on top."[15] That was why civil liberty was not "a fair weather concept," and why its defense was always a "real test of patriotism." For the greater the social stress, the greater the need of free expression, free inquiry, and responsive government to resolve it. The genuine rather than pseudo-patriot would therefore insist that civil liberty is "a legal right in time of war as well as in time of peace— that, whatever the time, it is liberty for all, irrespective of the accident of birth." To weaken the Bill of Rights on grounds of emergency, said Murphy, would "destroy the very democratic principles we are seeking to preserve."[16]

There was double meaning in the Attorney General's plea that Americans reinforce democratic allegiances after the invasion of Poland. Unlike standard libertarian scripts, Murphy's speeches acknowledged the rise of subversive activity and hostile propaganda, and demanded their control. Attempting to reassure the population that "internal aggression" would be met, he argued that self-defense was the only rational course to follow given the fate of "other democracies that no longer live to tell the story." Even after leaving the post he held to the theme. "Unless we are pudding-headed," he told J. Edgar Hoover, "we will drive from the land the hirelings here to undo the labors of our Fathers."[17] A substantial part of his public speaking as Attorney

General thus was devoted to reconciling what many thought were contradictory policies—protection of civil liberties and propaganda controls—in a period of emergency.

For a world where "might is the test of survival," Murphy insisted on finding a middle ground: "I do not believe that a democracy must necessarily become something other than a democracy to protect its national interests. I am convinced that if the job is done right—if the defense against internal aggression is carefully prepared—our people need not suffer the tragic things that have happened elsewhere in the world and that we have seen, in less degrees, even in this land of freedom. We *can* prevent and punish the abuse of liberty by sabotage, disorder and violence without destroying liberty itself."[18] The question was, how? After Roosevelt proclaimed a state of limited emergency, the Attorney General refused the Senate's request to define the scope of executive powers implicit in the proclamation, for fear that it might drive a wedge between himself and the President.[19] Further, he went on record that the "best protection of our Constitution against dictatorship is not a *weak* but a *strong* constitutional executive." Resolute preparedness was not only consistent with democracy but a "deadly necessity."[20] How could individual liberties withstand these policies, also? Murphy answered with a triple set of principles—the *Milligan* rule; the clear and present danger test; and "responsible" administration. First, he maintained that the principle of *ex parte Milligan*—that the Constitution "is a law for rulers and people, equally in war and in peace, and covers with the shield of its protection all classes of men, at all times, and under all circumstances"—would be sufficient to hold executive authority in rein. That precept made good sense and "good constitutional law," the Attorney General asserted, without regard to the case's after-the-fact nature. "I want to give emphatic assurance that in this emergency, as well as in time of peace, the Department of Justice embraces that policy without reservation."[21]

Second, Murphy urged that the clear and present danger test as expounded by Justice Holmes in the *Abrams* case would provide the "true course" to reconcile liberty and authority. Under that test, there could be no restraint on utterances "unless they so imminently threatened immediate interference with the lawful and pressing purposes of the law that an immediate check is required to save the country."[22] Devotees of democracy had no reason to crush hated ideas or to deny them access to the marketplace, Murphy preached. "We have no reason to fear their competition. We have a better article to sell." But selling which wrecked the market was another matter. "We should and must be on guard" against covert agents and disguised propaganda, he insisted, "not just some of the time, but all of the time." Ample laws existed to control spies, saboteurs, and foreign propagandists without invading intellectual freedom; "we should be ready and able to use them."[23]

Finally, the way to avoid the "inhuman and cruel things" committed during World War I was to concentrate the effort in the hands of carefully prepared, "responsible" officials in the Department of Justice. With obvious reference to the FBI, Murphy sought to assure the populace that any antisubversive activity would be conducted "under responsible direction . . . not by over-zealous inexperienced laymen, but by men who have been equipped for the work by careful training —training that includes instruction in the rights of the citizen as well as in methods of crime suppression." "At the cost of whatever inconvenience and annoyance to individual citizens and government officials," he maintained, "enforcement officials will themselves obey the law of the land."[24]

Coming full circle, Murphy supported the Civil Liberties Unit as a means of meeting the government's "double responsibility of self-defense and preservation of civil liberty."[25] Defending positive government action to repel private assaults on liberty as a corollary of defense against foreign attack, he acknowledged that public sentiment was the ultimate guardian of civil liberty. "But it is not *entirely* a matter of public opinion," he said. "And until public opinion *does* reach the point where it will not tolerate the violation of civil liberties, there can be and will be such violation—*unless government takes a hand and refuses to permit it*."[26] In a speech at Jersey City, made against the advice of department regulars, he departed from a prepared text to explain: "We are trying in the Department of Justice to see to it in a sane, sensible, impartial way that the rights of every group . . . should be preserved—preserved even from being harassed by government itself and by those of us who speak for the government."[27]

Since the threats to liberty were multidimensional, so were the defenses. Free government not only had to guard itself against direct assault, it was obliged to protect the people from themselves and, indeed, itself. That was the supreme task of a free system to pluralists like James Madison; while Murphy articulated no sophisticated philosophy himself, he relied heavily on a complex of inherited controls. To judicial review, separation of powers, and "cooperative federalism" in administration, he merely added one new disease, economic insecurity, and one new remedy, positive federal protection of individual rights. That addition sufficed to distinguish the new liberalism from the old. "Government, by precept and example," he declared, could be a "powerful bulwark of civil liberty." In the last analysis, however, he had no illusions that government action would suffice. "The courts cannot review every denial of civil rights that may occur. . . . Tolerance cannot be enforced by law. No government, however strong, can guarantee complete observance of the spirit of the Bill of Rights."[28] Because ultimate responsibility rested on the daily practice of a free people, an impassioned Attorney General therefore implored: "We need, and we earnestly ask, from every citizen and every government an unswerving resolve that for as long as this crisis endures, we will keep our heads—that we will not abandon the Bill of Rights."[29] And in a flight of idealistic rhetoric, he lit the light in the window which American nativists traditionally proffer to wayward Europeans. The "thinkers of today—those who love justice and liberty—are looking to America to keep her system safe in a world gripped by war."[30] Americans had to prove "for all time that ours is a two-fold strength—the physical strength of self-defense and the moral strength of unflinching devotion to our ideals," so that one day, "other peoples, weary of strife, will turn to us for guidance in regaining the liberty they have lost."[31] Pleased by the fact or not, they were the "trustees of civilization."[32]

That his advocacy of a balanced civil liberties policy drew heavily on assumptions and truisms of the libertarian faith disturbed Murphy little. The substance of freedom, he maintained, was "something a democratic people should never stop pondering."[33] His purpose was to awaken interest in the problem and, after the outbreak of war in Europe, to ward off hysteria as the government embarked on a difficult control program. Judging by popular responses, he did succeed in allaying fears. The fact that the Attorney General, of all officials, would take the lead in so delicate a subject heartened men of many descriptions who were similarly disturbed. Eminent scholars and jurists, some of whom had reservations about the activist philosophy of the Civil Liberties Unit, applauded the use of his office as a platform of public education; and, like him, they regarded the effort as no less valuable than organization as such. Following his address on the responsibilities of municipalities to safeguard basic freedoms, American Civil Liberties Union official Roger Baldwin commented: "That does the cause more good than anything we do in months. You don't know how refreshing it is to have a man in your office with this major concern on his mind. I almost believe we should begin to feel that we could go out of business."[34]

Militant liberals might express displeasure over the FBI's prominence in his thought, but the Attorney General created a highly favorable impression for "wisdom" and "foresight" on a serious issue. Even Justice Stone, a man sparing in his compliments, congratulated Murphy following a foray against religious intolerance. On that subject, as the *Flint Journal* observed, Murphy "could and did rise to masterful heights."[35] Extensively reprinted, his civil liberties addresses lifted his standing among intellectuals and important liberals as did no other activity. In an introduction to a pamphlet of the speeches published by the American Council on Public Affairs, Charles A. Beard wrote: "All that Mr. Murphy says has a double force, for he is no mere preacher of doctrines. In his private and public life, he has exemplified them in practice at great cost of time and energy, and much vexation of spirit. . . . It is fortunate that he now heads the Department of Justice."[36]

II

In a few months Beard was not so sure. The various goals of the Attorney General were beginning to collide. Energetic prosecutions, for one thing, encouraged local district attorneys to use aggressive methods which Murphy's libertarian friends condemned as hypocritical.[37] Symbolic prosecution of foreign agents, for another, was being undertaken for the first time since 1917 to demonstrate government concern over the "growing menace of foreign espionage."[38] After Murphy announced in October that the administration would cooperate with the Dies Committee, suspicions flared among liberals that they had been betrayed by the Attorney General's rhetoric. In announcing cooperation with Dies, it was true, Murphy had been careful to say that the department would not participate in "Red hunts or brass band raids."[39] Skilled analysts, moreover, perceived an adroit Roosevelt maneuver to fend off repressive legislation and to silence Dies. Unknown to the public, Murphy also blocked several security control measures. He vetoed a suggestion to fingerprint known communists, for example. During one inning in the perennial Washington battle over wiretapping, he also supported J. Edgar Hoover against Treasury Department and congressional proposals to enlarge the federal wiretapping authority. The Justice Department took a position of neutrality toward the bills passed in Congress in hopes of preserving the FBI's current policy of limiting wiretaps to situations of aggravated criminal conduct or where human life was at stake. The department's resistance undoubtedly contributed to the failure of a House-Senate conference committee to approve the only legislation expanding wiretapping authority to pass both houses of Congress until 1968, though it was not long before positions reversed.[40]

The visit of "a splendid group of Protestant clergymen," led by Methodist Bishop G. Bromley Oxnam, even stimulated him to order a departmental study of the rights of conscientious objectors. "It is not the man who follows the dictates of his conscience who is a danger to the Republic," he remarked prophetically, "it is the man who doesn't."[41] Nevertheless, the alien agent prosecutions seriously compromised his libertarian credentials, especially after he greeted the Polish invasion with a widely publicized warning that there would not be a "repetition of the confusion and laxity and indifference of twenty years ago." "Foreign agents and those engaged in espionage will no longer find this country a happy hunting ground," said Murphy. "We are prepared."[42]

The effort had been "localized" in the FBI. Contrary to popular assumptions, the bureau had been quietly investigating communist and fascist activity since a secret presidential directive in 1936. It had also been training men in counterespionage since 1938. A prolonged bureaucratic struggle over control of counterintelligence had been resolved in June 1938, concentrating the effort in the FBI and the military services. Meanwhile, the Dies Committee stirred up controversy over violations of the Alien Registration Act; and the President, after a series of Cabinet meetings in early 1939, decided to investigate the charges largely to undercut Dies. After a prod from Sumner Welles, an interdepartmental investigation was launched in mid-1939 against the Bund, the Communist party, and the American League for Peace and Democracy.[43]

Murphy both inherited and supported this policy. Following the outbreak of European hostilities the President revealed that the FBI had been made the central agency for counterintelligence in the United States. The Attorney General appeared before a special grand jury called in the District of Columbia to investigate passport and registration irregularities by communists, and he authorized a series of controversial prosecutions of political suspects. Communist leader Earl Browder was indicted for passport fraud. Murphy, most likely with Roosevelt's personal approval, authorized prosecution of Spanish Loyalist recruiters in Detroit, whose activities in violation of neutrality statutes both the State and Justice Departments had heretofore ignored. Although it reflected a mixing of political priorities between their offices, as Kemp cautioned him, he also announced that John T. Cahill would investigate the Brooklyn Catholic Front and other anti-Semitic propaganda groups in New York.[44] At Murphy's urging, the President requested all citizens and local officials to cooperate with the FBI. To prevent the "confusion and irresponsibility" of the last war, which newly formed vigilante groups in Cleveland gave promise of repeating, the fight against internal enemies had to be centralized.[45/a]

Liberals took alarm. The Attorney General's well-known respect for J. Edgar Hoover, as well as his friendships among the dilettantes of high society, had long been suspect.[46] His assumed public silence about the third term until July (though actually his 1938 suggestion of a Roosevelt draft had caused some embarrassment for the White House) offended certain members of the President's inner circle. So did his speechmaking, particularly the plea for civil service.[47] Furthermore, as the administration publicly began to veer from a policy of neutrality to open support of the Allies, the independent-minded Attorney General seemed even more out of step by raising a voice of caution. Murphy had praised Roosevelt's pacifist utterance in 1938, and when the President asked him informally in 1939 whether German and Italian vessels could be seized in American waters prior to hostilities as a precaution against sabotage, his reply was a flat negative.[48] In July, prompted by Harold L. Ickes' impatient argument that the Neutrality Act should be ignored as an invasion of the President's constitutional authority as Commander-in-Chief, Roosevelt asked pointedly: "If we fail to get any Neutrality Bill, how far do you think I can go in ignoring the existing act—even though I did sign it?!" The Attorney General—influenced by the closely reasoned arguments of Kemp and Assistant Solicitor General Newman A. Townsend that it would be politically dangerous to flout the expressed will of Congress, irrespective of legalities—dampened the whole idea.[49]

Murphy, though eager for military preparedness and cognizant of the effects of rearmament on economic recovery, was skeptical about the President's drift to measures just short of war. Murphy's pacifist, neo-isolationist attitudes, which reflected his Progressive roots and reopened avenues to the Right, were forcefully expressed in a letter he wrote to broadcaster G. A. Richards following Hitler's invasion of Poland:

[a] For important use of the FBI's prewar arguments for centralized antisubversion control, see *Pennsylvania* v. *Nelson*, 350 U.S. 497 (1956), in which the Supreme Court held that the dominant federal interest in sedition against the United States precluded state prosecutions for the same crime.

This War isn't any stage fight. It is likely to be of long duration and when it is over with it isn't unlikely that great social and political upheavals will follow.

Individuals can go far minding their own business; so can nations. We ought to build our own country into a strong and prosperous land. We can do it. We are on our way right now. It is unfortunate that the misfortunes of others have brought us our chance but it would be doubly unfortunate for us to pass it by. Prepare, be ready, muster everything for any emergency but do our best to keep out. "Fear God and take your own part" isn't an unwise policy.[50]

Even though the Attorney General reflected broadly popular sentiments the combination of an antisubversion campaign and personal independence aggravated doubts whether he was a loyal member of the President's team. As Murphy increasingly appeared to fall out of character as a liberal, the press picked up rumors of friction within the Justice Department, and the glamorous reception of the spring faded into hostility and opposition. Moved to the back pages by the war, *Life* magazine stated, the Attorney General was seeking to recover the limelight by chasing spies, most of whom were "phony imaginings." In Ickes' view, he was being "buffaloed" by the Dies Committee and "weakened under pressure from Hoover."[51] After Hoover disclosed that the FBI had compiled a dossier of suspected subversives and the Detroit Loyalists were treated to wee-hour arrest and arraignment in chain-handcuffs, the liberal outcry was ferocious. Historian Beard disavowed Murphy for failing to practice what he preached, and the Civil Liberties Union accused him of "political prejudice." The *New Republic* labelled the FBI an "American OGPU" [Soviet secret police], and Senator Norris demanded that the agency be investigated. Though the FBI apparently was not responsible for the method of arraignment in Detroit, few people knew, its chief remarked, "how close they [the liberals] came to wrecking us."[52] The man responsible for the policy, moreover, could defend it no longer. On the day before the Loyalist affair, he became an Associate Justice of the United States Supreme Court.

III

Murphy's appointment to the Supreme Court was a paradox. On the one hand, he was a "natural" prospect for the vacancy created by the death of Pierce Butler in November 1939. A Catholic and a Progressive, a man of middle-class origin and a midwesterner, Murphy satisfied to an unusual degree the "representational" criteria of religion, section, and political background traditionally used by Presidents in making selections to the high court. What he lacked in judicial training could be balanced by political experience unmatched among eligibles. Swift recovery of prestige as Attorney General assured easy confirmation. And not least in importance, his elevation to the bench made it possible for the President to relieve a nagging personnel logjam caused by Woodring's resistance to the reshuffling scheme and by Roosevelt's own faintheartedness about firing people. By mid-December Murphy's appointment appeared so certain that speculation centered on whether Biddle would succeed Jackson as Solicitor General. To friends and foe alike, Murphy once again seemed to be Roosevelt's logical choice for higher office.[53]

Far from a Taft-like lust for the Court, however, the Attorney General exhibited an extraordinary resistance to his nomination. It was not easy for any lawyer to refuse membership among the elect. Loyalty to the President demanded that he accept the post if Roosevelt pressed. Refusal under the circumstances would not only embarrass the President but might leave a bundle of frustrated ambitions dangerously unstilled. Murphy also acknowledged frankly to friends that he had nowhere else to go. Yet he still aspired to be Secretary of War, a job already promised him; and he had genuine doubts, which cut far deeper than surface modesty, about his technical competence. Accustomed to the rough and tumble of politics, he had no pretense to intellect or learning. He thought of himself as a political executive with a forte for moral leadership, not as an advocate. He venerated the Court as an embodiment of virtues he felt he lacked. Would the Supreme Court anticlimax a meteoric career? Would it mean, as Norman H. Hill suggested, taking the veil?[54] Like a romantic bride caught in a match arranged by realists, Murphy responded to the speculation and overtures of support by the only thing he could safely do—berating his qualifications and calling for loftier motives.

Such had been his reaction when Roosevelt had asked him to run for Governor of Michigan in 1936. Now his equivocation was no less earnest. His fears were discernible even before the President spoke. Catholics had been appointed to the Court before, but never had their religion been considered relevant until now. Only four days after Justice Butler's death, the Attorney General, in contrast to his usual treatment of critical journalists, replied to Charles G. Ross's attack on the use of religious criteria by writing:

I particularly agree with the observation that there "are other men in the United States better fitted intrinsically to sit on the Supreme Bench"!

As I see it, the view that one of a certain faith should be succeeded by another of like faith is entirely unworthy.[55]

Roosevelt seldom hurried in making judicial appointments. His attorney generals commonly had to defend their Supreme Court recommendations against a barrage of political considerations; it was the President's way of enjoying himself while testing the soundness of the decision. Others privy to his personnel plans assumed in this instance that Murphy was not consulted. In fact he was. When it became apparent in early December that the President's mind was running in the same groove as virtually everyone else's, the Attorney General gave Roosevelt a list of prominent eligibles,[b] along with a letter carefully drafted by Kemp and himself, which contained a thinly disguised reproach. After listing the ideal qualities of mind and character desired in the post, he lectured the President: "We must think only of the nation itself. . . . Members of the Supreme Court are not called upon nor expected to represent any single interest or group, area or class of persons. They speak for the country as a whole. Considerations of residential area or class interest, creed or racial extraction, ought therefore to be subordinated if not entirely disregarded."[56]

Roosevelt received the letter in good humor, just as did Murphy's old college chum who contrasted his public reticence with his youthful Irish yarn about "thou sweet, but blasted lyre."[57] Roosevelt and Murphy had a certain rapport and shared an earthy humor which urbane professionals like Francis Biddle, who considered Murphy a pious fraud, failed to perceive. Roosevelt respected Murphy's dedication and political acumen, and seemed to be amused by his posturing, his moralizing —and his bachelorhood. "Frank," he had quipped when Murphy was sworn in as Attorney General "you will do a good job, for there is the Bible before you and the Constitution behind you." Murphy, for his part, also enjoyed teasing with "the chief." "Remember," he once wrote from the Court, "I don't want to lose the Tennessee widow because of laches—so function."[58] But there was no doubt about his reluctance to enter the Court. When the inevitable was announced on January 4, 1940, his anguish was unconcealed. "During the years I have tried hard, failed mostly . . . ," he wrote Dean Henry M. Bates. "A new honor has come to me which I did not seek and do not de-

---

[b] Names suggested were: Henry F. Ashurst, Francis Biddle, Sam Gilbert Bratton, John Joseph Burns, James F. Byrnes, John P. Devaney, Joseph C. Hutcheson, Jr., Robert M. Hutchins, James M. Landis, Patrick B. O'Sullivan, Robert P. Patterson, Harold M. Stephens, George F. Sullivan, and John D. Wickhem. Murphy did not include Robert H. Jackson, despite Kemp's suggestion, though he may have done so verbally. Memo, Kemp to FM, Nov. 22, 1939, Kemp Papers.

serve. I am entirely unworthy of it."[59]/[c] And with straightforward candor he unburdened himself to his former parish priest, Father William Murphy, to whom he wrote: "I am not too happy about going on the Court. A better choice could have been made. I fear that my work will be mediocre up there while on the firing line where I have been trained to action I could do much better."[60] "It has been a difficult decision for me," he added to publicist Stephen J. Hannagan, "but two decades back I put on a uniform and I am still a soldier."[61]

Resignation tinged with pride was the principal reaction of the Court's newest Justice, and even if it could be tacitly assumed, as Roosevelt did, that he would not remain on the bench for long, Murphy could not resist a parting shot at the process which put him there. "I appreciate the honor," he told newsmen. The Court was the country's "Great Pulpit." "But I consider myself unworthy of it and I think a far better selection could have been made."[62]

Compounding the paradox was the curious disparity in public and professional responses to the President's choice. Although a few leading dailies such as the *Los Angeles Times* concurred wholeheartedly with the nominee's own appraisal, Murphy's nomination was actually one of the most favorably received judicial appointments of the century.[63] Liberals, who did not know of the Detroit Loyalist presentments until February, expressed joy at the strengthening of civil liberties and the entrenchment of "our kind of folk" on the Court.[64] Conservatives and Southern Democrats, showing signs of relief that Roosevelt's fifth appointment was not worse, echoed the line that the independent-prone Murphy was the right man for the right place.[65] Indeed there was "something just a little bit queer about the whole thing." For while the nominee openly demurred, the President was praised in the mass media for setting "a peak of excellence in his judicial appointments."[66] "Distinguished," "a scholar and a philosopher," "a militantly honest man," "a master of the law," were phrases commonly used in describing the nominee's virtues.[67] That he quoted "his own qualifying stock bearishly" seemed to add the merit of modesty to the President's "splendid selection."[68] And when Murphy remarked during a mid-December press conference that a retiring Attorney General should be foreclosed from further office for two years because he wielded powers that "might be abused by a politically ambitious person," it was taken not as a prayer for escape but as additional evidence of his

[c] To Joan Foy he said: "I am not too sure that I am glad about my new job, but I no longer ask myself whether I am glad about things—only whether it is my duty and then I try in earnest." FM to Joan Foy, Jan. 11, 1940, Box 86.

refreshing subordination of "personal ambitions to a high conception of the public welfare."[69] "Frank Murphy belongs naturally to the Supreme Court," William Allen White commented. "Such men make the Court respected by their very presence there." Any regrets heard usually resembled J.P. Hallihan's lament over the loss of "the best educator and law enforcement officer of my time," or the mixed feelings of Arthur M. Schlesinger, Sr., and William G. McAdoo over the side-tracking of "such excellent live Presidential material."[70]

Time had finally given Roosevelt a majority on the Supreme Court, but the enigmas of Murphy's personality and his flirtations with the Right fed speculation about his likely ideological niche. Some Cabinet members predicted that he would be the first New Deal Justice to go conservative. Others pondered whether he could settle down to the quiet life of a jurist. The question was not that he lacked "judicial temperament," the *Detroit News* observed perceptively, but whether Murphy could reconcile his feelings for pure justice and the constraints of law. "He is not a great lawyer, as he himself would be the first to admit. He is studious and will learn, but for the present, one suspects, there will be occasions when his sympathetic nature will rebel at the finespun but galling chains of legal theory."[71]

Whatever the reservations about his slender judicial experience, his seven years on Recorder's Court was longer than any other Roosevelt appointee. And after an epic struggle over judicial qualifications, it was fashionable to believe that firsthand experience with social realities was more essential than technical proficiency.[72] Few went so far as the Mississippi editor who predicted that he would make a "great associate justice," but the public response to Murphy's appointment so soon after the sit-down strikes was an extraordinary tribute to his skills as a manipulator of public opinion.[73]

Reflecting popular sentiment, the Senate accorded him a remarkably unruffled reception for a crusader. There was no attack to block confirmation, as in the case of Brandeis, nor to frighten him into different ways, as in the case of Hughes. Though a screening subcommittee did require him to answer that, "of course," he believed in property rights, Murphy's appointment was confirmed without so much as a roll call vote.[74] The contrast with his reception as Attorney General was a striking demonstration of how well he had worn at the capital. In another tour de force of personality, Murphy had not only won over his critics but fairly well dazzled the country as a capable, even "ideal attorney general." By virtue of that performance, as the *New Orleans Times-Picayune* commented, his appointment to the high court was accepted "with the entire confidence and hearty good wishes of a vast American majority."[75]

The final oddity about Murphy's appointment is that, despite extravagant public approval, he also entered the Supreme Court under fire. The very reasons for his mass popularity—flamboyant activism and high-powered publicity in the Department of Justice—created a strongly adverse reaction among administration liberals and a strategically located group of New Deal lawyers, above all, Solicitor General Robert H. Jackson, which played no small part in his elevation to the Court. Given Murphy's new broom and indifference to legal affairs, it was to be expected that professionals in the Department of Justice and Supreme Court bar would resent his leadership and look upon his appointment to the bench as a bad mistake. Roosevelt, who must have had misgivings about choosing a pacifist and neo-isolationist as Secretary of War, was also considering the appointment of a Republican such as Frank Knox or Henry L. Stimson to head the War Department as a token of bipartisanship in emergency. Complaints from the Justice Department probably influenced his final decision. The death of Justice Butler thus gave him a chance to kill three birds with one stroke: appoint a Catholic Justice who would "be for us"; honor his pledges to Jackson and Biddle; and eliminate a serious source of friction among restive lieutenants.[76] The trouble was, appointing Murphy only intensified the friction and exposed a rift between Jackson and Murphy, which subjected both men to a barrage of public criticism just as they assumed office. Because Murphy was mending fences on the Right and Jackson was then the shining hope of a liberal palace guard, their collision was magnified by the politics of presidential succession.

The Jackson-Murphy clash of 1939, like so many of its kind, was a complex affair rising out of ambition, personality conflicts, and policy differences which were aggravated by common frustration over the President's stalled personnel plans. Although their relationship actually was more mutual aloofness than personal feud, two men of sharper contrast in character and personality would have been hard to find. Murphy was soft-spoken, sentimental, and an idealist who attempted to play the part of moral leader. Jackson was quick-witted, lean, and a realist who wrestled with a sharp temper. Murphy, working with uncanny instincts for the popular pulse, excelled on the public stage by dint of showmanship and ethical passion. Jackson impressed both friend and enemy by the brilliance of his pen and the power of his intellect.

Murphy was an aggressive public prosecutor, Jackson—as Brandeis said —an ideal Solicitor General. About the only thing they had in common, besides ambition and dedication to the New Deal, was the belief that Murphy was ill-suited for the Supreme Court.

Jackson opposed Murphy's appointment, even though it satisfied his own ambition to become Attorney General, because Murphy was "not interested in legal problems . . . nor in the law as a philosophy. He was not a man of studious habits"[77]—which is what the restless Murphy, whose prolix reading habits ranged from ancient history to ornithology, had already told the President. But Jackson's opinion of Murphy was damning in the extreme. For one thing, Murphy did not conduct the Justice Department as a holding action, which befitted the interim nature of his appointment. Nor did he conduct it as a professional law enforcement agency. Rather, he converted the post into a political spectacular in order to recover personal prestige, and Jackson had little love for Murphy's energizing or flamboyant crusades.

In Jackson's view, the outgoing Attorney General had an insatiable, almost pathological, passion for publicity and self-glorification. The first titters at Murphy's vaunted conscience and public piety rapidly changed to anger, for Jackson and his friends believed that the country was being hoodwinked by the Attorney General's self-advertised religion, sensational flying trips, and disingenuous exploitation of cases that would have been brought to bar in the usual way. For the most part, Jackson regarded the judicial appointments as commendable and the vigorous prosecution of Judge Manton by a fellow Catholic as a fortunate circumstance. Yet he also had serious policy differences with Murphy, which the latter made little attempt to resolve. Jackson, who was slighted in the policy-formation process of the Attorney General's office and stung by it, disagreed with his chief about civil service, Alcatraz, and permission to wiretap. He disagreed about antitrust prosecution of labor unions and regarded Murphy's press statement on the subject as indiscriminate. He opposed calling a sedition grand jury in Washington and the anti-Semitic inquiry in New York. Above all, Jackson opposed conscious manipulation of publicity, which he regarded as courting public opinion for political gain.[78]

Jackson's objections were not groundless. For example, after the Supreme Court refused to grant certiorari in the AMA antitrust suit, the department, without consulting him, issued a press release implying that the suit was without merit. Jackson objected strenuously, and justifiably, that the release broke faith with the Justices in order to save public face. Although his protest drew an apology from Thurman Arnold, the affair was one of several which led Jackson to believe that the Attorney General was willing to exploit the public relations potentialities of his post regardless of price.[79] And when Murphy publicized a list of planned investigations even after his Court appointment was settled, Jackson simply exploded. Courtesy demanded that a retiring Attorney General refrain from announcing plans which he knew his successor disapproved. Murphy's "improvident announcements," Jackson feared, made it difficult for him to make a decent showing. Indicating apprehension that his administration would be an anticlimax, he told the President: "Your next Attorney General cannot fail to disappoint public expectations and to suffer criticism of his motives and competency. In some respects expectations have been aroused which it is my belief that no one can fulfill, but in other respects there is a fundamental difference of approach to the work of the Department between Mr. Murphy and me, and some other person might satisfy public opinion better than I am willing to do."[80]

In particular, Jackson believed that prematurely announced plans in highly publicized subjects like Chicago left him facing a choice between defeat in court or abandonment of prosecution with consequent charges of political "fixing."[81] Furthermore, while Murphy had carefully qualified the alien agent announcements, and while even their mutual friend Ickes confessed that a successful effort to steal Dies' thunder would be worthwhile, the Solicitor General regarded the antisubversion and anti-Semitic prosecutions as irresponsible witch hunts. In a nutshell, he told the President that he wanted to run the department "in a lawyerly way, without premature publicity, with prosecutions based on criminal acts not merely reprehensible attitudes or opinions, and without yielding to or cultivating hysteria among our people."[82]

Roosevelt laughed at Jackson's fears. "All in all he made me feel a little contemptible and cowardly about it," Jackson admitted later.[83] But when Murphy told reporters that he wished to remain in charge of the department for another month to complete his program, that was the last straw. All his disclaimers could not remove the implication that he distrusted Jackson's willingness to complete his unfinished business. Further hints by the outgoing Attorney General at chasing Kelly, Hague, and other men "behind the throne" seemed to confirm his reckless headline-hunting.[84]

Administration leaders were disturbed over Murphy's last press conferences. Ickes exacted a vain promise that they would stop, because "in two or three matters Frank has already gone off the deep end."[85/d] After speaking with Jackson, the President ordered retraction of the remark about Hague and Kelly, which Corcoran helped to draft; and when it was delivered on the day he resigned, Murphy merely provoked additional speculation that he was being kicked upstairs on account of the Chicago probe. Frankly stating that he did not want "the bum's rush," he also offended the mediator. "Even Tom Corcoran is now convinced," Gordon Dean wrote in his diary, "that Murphy is a phoney." To prevent more press conferences and more anger, Roosevelt pushed Murphy off the fence on January 18th by having him take his constitutional oath of office with Jackson in an unprecedented White House ceremony, which an unsuspecting press presented as a happy New Deal gathering. And to top it off, the Murphys stole the show with the new Justice's tattered Bible and his sister's reported remark: "Frank looks more like Jesus everyday."[86]

But the damage was done. The fury that descended on Jackson over the FBI and the Detroit Loyalist case confirmed his worst fears. His pointed curtailment of press conferences, rapid staff changes, and cancellation of Murphy's Alcatraz plans indicated that he was sorely aggrieved. So were his orders cancelling the WPA strike cases, the authority to wiretap, and the Detroit Loyalist indictments. "I can see no good to come from reviving in America at this late date the animosities of the Spanish conflict," said Jackson; and though he could have quashed the case before the arrests, his statement was a signal for their partisans to open fire in public.[87/e]

---

[d] Ickes himself went off the deep end when he called for a third party of Progressives in the event a liberal was not nominated in 1940. Roosevelt's reaction was blunt:

> The easiest way to put it—please excuse the language and do not quote it—I am too damned busy [laughter], literally, to be talking about political events a long, long way off. . . . I . . . have, as some of you have been kind enough to intimate, two things, a sense of proportion and a sense of timing [laughter].
> Q. You sat up all night on that one?
> Yes [laughter].

RL:P.P.F.-Press Conferences, v. 14 (Dec. 22, 1939), p. 384.

Some newsman implicated Murphy in Ickes' proposal, but Murphy's reaction was swift. Although liberals would always be welcomed "with open arms" into the Democratic party, a third party would be "unnatural," "disastrous," and "a sure way of getting a reactionary in the White House." *Detroit News*, Dec. 25, 1939; *NYT*, Dec. 22, 1939, p. 1:1.

[e] Murphy and Jackson took their constitutional oaths of office on January 18, 1940; and Murphy was sworn in at the Court on February 5th. The 17 Spanish Loyalists were arrested and indicted on February 6th. Jackson dismissed the indictments on February 16, 1940, four weeks after taking office. Memo, Eleanor Bumgardner to FM, April 20, 1940, Box 90.

After Murphy delayed entry to the Court until February 5th, while taking two Florida vacations to cure bronchitis, a sudden rash of criticism, some spontaneous and some inspired, appeared in the mass media condemning his "witch hunts" as Attorney General and his personal qualifications for the Court. Although his trips actually were taken during a fortnight recess with the approval of Chief Justice Hughes, Murphy was accused of being personally unhappy with the job and of being chastised by Hughes for indifference and ineptitude in his work.[88] Although Palm Beach gossip columnists actually complained of his unusual seclusion there, he was condemned for preferring carousal with "economic royalists" to the judicial cloister. Although vice-presidents are seldom chosen that way, the Luce publications, which appeared to be prime outlets for his opponents, circulated reports that Murphy had begged Michigan party leaders to obtain the vice-presidential nomination for him, so badly did he want off the bench.[89] The *Macon* (Ga.) *News-Telegraph* commented: "To put it mildly, the people who pay Mr. Murphy a salary of $20,000 a year are wondering when he is going to work. . . . The fact of the matter is that the entire career of Murphy is one of the most discreditable in the history of American politics. . . . Maybe Black was not the last word in public indecency, after all."[90]

While Murphy replied privately that he had missed none of the work for which he was qualified, and broke public silence in mid-February to assert that he expected to be happy as a judge (it suits "my temperament"), his partisans counterattacked.[91] The Hearst press accused the Jackson forces of "smearing" and of letting up on communists; even Judge Paul V. Gadola defended Murphy for vigorous law enforcement—before "they" kicked him upstairs.[92] Innuendoes flourished in turn about the Court's "missing and misbehaving" new Justice, all of which led Henry A. Wallace to ponder sadly the propensity of New Deal idealists to war among themselves rather than with their common enemies.[93]

In retrospect, much of the criticism was petty gossip; it paled beside the regular feuds of the New Deal. And for the most part, Murphy took the criticism stoically. "Pay little attention to some of the news stories," he told his Detroit friend, Henry A. Montgomery. "Remember this is an election year—an old-timer like yourself knows how the daggers fly during such a period. I cannot conceive of my leaving the Court for any reason."[94]/[f] The persistence of the gossip, however, be-

---

[f] To Judge Frank A. Picard he observed: "That sort of thing can't be helped. It comes to those in high places and when one of my mediocrity is up then he singly

came a source of real concern. At the suggestion of his clerk, Murphy cancelled speaking engagements, publications, and memberships.[95] After another news story appeared in late February that he was "disinterested and lackadaisical" in judicial work, he wrote Chief Justice Hughes: "No one could be happier than I am to labor with you and my brethren in this vineyard. The statement is all untrue."[96] Ever eager to defend the reputation of his Court, the Chief Justice engineered a denial of his alleged criticism in the *New York Times* the following day, which substantially silenced most of the "groundless yarns."[97]

The uproar, just the same, had enduring effects. It aggravated in Murphy an already active sense of inferiority and self-consciousness, which significantly affected his work, along with egocentricity which strained personal relations. Murphy believed that stories circulated by Corcoran and others turned Harry Hopkins against him and colored relations with other Washington luminaries, such as Ickes, Frankfurter, and, to a degree, even Roosevelt. Consequently, reporters who had defended him, such as Blair Moody, were received warmly with "what a grand friend you are!" Critics of his absenteeism got the treatment, which in Joseph Alsop's case, required Justice Frankfurter's intercession to overcome."[98/g] His vanity wounded by a feeling of having been wronged, and his prestige weakened before he wrote an opinion, Murphy even unburdened part of his side of the story on paper, a rare thing for him. In April he wrote Joseph R. Hayden:

There will always be "smears" during election years. The one on Paul McNutt is the worst of all time. . . . Appointed a Supreme Court Justice I had the best press of any man in the land. For the first time a record vote was not asked on confirmation in the Senate. Two weeks later I was something of a cross between a mountebank and a bum. What had happened in the fourteen day interlude? There was no official act complained of. I was the same man. But here was my sin or error:—Knowing they were going to decapitate Hoover, competent, efficient, nonpartisan I undertook on my last

---

looms up as a greater target. It is the price one pays for distinction and those of us who are good stuff roll with the punches and thank the Lord for his manifold blessings. I don't like it but with the others I have to take it. Right now it is doubly offensive to me for I alone am not concerned—there is the Court to think of—the Supreme Court with its traditions and its place in the hearts of our people. Were it not for this the arrows would hurt little; experts have shot them at me in the past and thus far they have fallen harmlessly to the ground. FM to Picard, March 21, 1940, Box 89.

g After Alsop extended the peace pipe Murphy wrote but did not send this reply: "You wronged me. You already know how I view what you did and you have chosen not to do anything about it. And so I have nothing to discuss with you." FM to Alsop, March 22, 1941, Box 96.

act of office to defend him. That was an apostasy of some sort. It mined the plans of a little group of twitwits. They are not an entirely bad lot; they have a mistaken notion of their toughness. The discharge of Hoover would have been bad for the country and a serious injury to the President and I undertook to prevent it and accordingly stories were planted. There were other reasons but this is chief among them. The President . . . was furious about it.[99]

Thirdly, the episode colored the relations between two future Justices, Murphy and Jackson, and revealed noteworthy differences between them which transcended merely frustrated ambitions or personality conflicts. The episode highlighted fundamentally divergent approaches to leadership and to the role of the Department of Justice—the difference between Murphy's political activism and Jackson's "lawyerly way."

Whichever is more suitable for the agency is a matter of dispute, if not of temperament itself. While Murphy's methods exposed the weaknesses of crusades—flamboyance, unsatisfied expectations, and occasional intemperate abuses—the other is subject to the characteristic omissions of bureaucratic professionalism, losing popular contact, and political support generated from the center. No matter who heads the Department of Justice, either method creates difficulties. An Attorney General functions as a combination lawyer, administrator, high policymaker, and public spokesman. No individual has managed every task with equal skill, though in the twentieth century perhaps Stone, Mitchell, and Cummings came closest. Murphy was a master crusader; he had the qualities necessary for a fearless public prosecutor and the instincts of a political leader with mass appeal. Jackson was one of this century's greatest advocates. Neither actually enjoyed or excelled at the administrative functions of the office. After one experience in budgetmaking, Jackson himself confessed that he felt lost away from the solicitor generalship and the work of the Court.[100]

Murphy, far more than he realized, had administrative deficiencies which irritated associates. A purist, a restless soul whose span of attention ranged from crime and foreign policy to personal telephone calls at government expense, he did not have a mind for administrative detail. He delegated authority well and was attentive to professional advice—perhaps overly so to intellectuals—but he was impetuous. Assistants soon learned to dread his odd-hour checks on routine as well as his impulsive policy statements, which were prompted by a thirst for action and a sense of drama. Ill at ease among experienced professionals, he also tended to duck sticky problems by retreating behind his profile, a facade of other-worldliness, and the protective mantle of his staff. Even division heads complained about their difficulties cutting through the barriers erected by Kemp. And most had their favorite story of Murphy's amorous adventures.

Strong figures in the Jackson group—McMahon, Dean, Biddle—equated these qualities with incompetence and self-aggrandizement. But more neutral colleagues attributed them to a compelling activism and a talent at public relations which in fact interested them all. Neutrals regarded the interim Attorney General as a warm and dedicated human being who wished to make a contribution in the Department of Justice. Though most of them respected Jackson more, they rated Murphy on a par with the average Attorney General in performance and higher in integrity and purpose. They recognized also that he worked under severe handicaps. For he was new to Washington and its manifold power alliances; he had long been away from the law; and late in the New Deal he was placed in command of as strong-willed, yet capable a collection of characters as the department had ever known. A temporary replacement to start with, he occupied the office too briefly to establish a distinctive, let alone distinguished, record. Ironically, after years of anticipation, the same fate befell Jackson.

It is also true that the conflict was not serious until activated by policy disagreements. Murphy had Progressive impulses and a desire to control foreign agentry which at the time many New Dealers did not share. The Stalin-Hitler Pact, as he noted to Claude G. Bowers, "cleared up many things, left some people 'high and dry,' and I believe strengthened the genuine Progressive movement in this country." The sit-downs and war produced a natural emphasis on toleration, harmony, and efficiency. "Liberalism," he believed, "does not mean that we must be hostile."[101] Nor would it survive, he thought, without a supreme national effort to ward off disaster. "I am sickened with the apathy of our people," he told Joseph R. Hayden as he entered the Court. "Perhaps outside the government we need a Theodore Roosevelt trumpeting the gospel of sensible preparedness."[102]

Was that the role he had envisaged for himself as Secretary of War? As Attorney General, Murphy established himself as a gifted political evangelist. His most controversial policies, far more than his opponents conceded, were political errands for the President, consciously calculated to renew public confidence after a stinging defeat and to meet international crisis. Murphy's confidence in positive government, and in himself as a leader, permitted him to overextend himself, as always. The badgering over the start of an antisubversion drive in 1939, the

"Mr. Murphy Will Run" Pulling Roosevelt to Victory in 1936. *Detroit News*,
July 10, 1936.

Shoemaker in The Chicago News.

Governor Murphy, who arranged a settlement of the General Motors strike, now has further sit-downs on his roof.

"HOME TO ROOST IN MICHIGAN" Aftermath of the General Motors Sit-down Strike. © 1937 by the New York Times Company. Reprinted by permission. Also with permission from the Chicago Tribune–New York News Syndicate, Inc.

Chrysler Sit-down Strike, 1937. *Washington Star*, March 26, 1937.

'There Are Several Charming Young Men in My Cabinet'
—ROOSEVELT

Prospects for 1940 Democratic Presidential Nomination. *Detroit News,*
July 13, 1939.

Fait Accompli

Roosevelt Appoints a Majority of the Supreme Court. *Washington Star,*
January 6, 1940.

posthumous accusations of treason for not having done enough, and even the subsequent shifts of both men on issues of labor, wiretapping, and free speech, indicate what thorny subjects they were to touch. But if Murphy's plans were overly ambitious, he was quick with characteristic replies: "There is so much that needs to be done"; "it won't hurt to try."[103] In attempting to stimulate public opinion regarding corruption and civil liberties, he was both defending policy and attempting to generate the popular pressure which would sustain politically difficult undertakings such as the cleanup of Chicago. While political activism was not without its excesses, the very technique was something a man like Jackson, advocate more than politician, found impossible to exploit and hard not to suspect. Ickes and Roosevelt, even when they believed it carried to extremes, understood.

Thus Murphy left a fractured reputation as Attorney General—powerful politician, indifferent professional. For himself the year was an exciting interlude. "Even though so much remained to be done," he observed, "I like to think that at least we pushed the frontiers ahead—not far, I know, but ahead nevertheless."[104] Nor could the larger implications of his political activism be underrated. That so many people regarded him as an exceptionally able Attorney General was a mark of his ability as a showman—and of the press's vulnerability to it. That he was elevated to the Court was a product, not of crusades gone awry, but of customary political criteria working in curious ways. The fact is that Murphy's crusading made his appointment possible and broadly popular. From a politician's perspective, he was an obvious choice because he satisfied traditional standards of selection, plus contemporary demands for a modern outlook in a jaded institution. However disproportionate to his deeds, his mass popularity as Attorney General illustrated once more that talk alone has political significance, and that his combination of evangelism and political activism, while not of sufficient strength to sustain a presidential ambition, was a chemistry of more than local appeal.

The very reasons why he was an effective political crusader, however, spawned professional misgivings about Murphy's credentials for the high court. His appointment to the bench thus confronted him with a serious problem of levels which he had so far managed to avoid. Murphy all his adult life had excelled as a champion of moral rectitude before mass audiences; now the critical constituency had shifted to a professional elite. Murphy all his political life had won praise for attracting intelligence and integrity into government; now *his* were under fire. Having crossed swords with militant liberals as well as strategically placed lawyers who regarded him as an intellectual weakling and a political interloper in a professional world, he ascended the bench with a widely circulated reputation as a misfit. No one understood the change in store better than he. His differences with Jackson would have gone unnoticed had he not held back from the Court, continuing to press his crusades and almost tragically hoping that something would come along to save him for the war effort and the political life for which he felt himself equipped. By equivocating, he aggravated serious criticism about his fitness for a revered institution. Lacking confidence and concerned that he had landed out of his depth, Murphy for the first time in his life was making a bad beginning. Recovery would have to come from the quality of his opinions rendered in the sheltered confines which Holmes once called a "storm centre" and Murphy himself, in a prophetically impulsive moment, called "the Great Pulpit."[105]

PART II

CHAPTER 10

THE FRESHMAN MEMBER,

1940-1942

MURPHY joined the Supreme Court at a time of rich opportunity for the development of American law. As Roosevelt's majority appointee, he represented the triumph of the New Deal over the "Nine Old Men." Yet that victory had been substantially won as a result of the Justices' own strategic retreat in 1937. By the time Murphy took his seat on February 5, 1940, the long conflict over constitutional authority to regulate economic affairs was essentially finished. A new majority had formed in support of broad regulatory power at all levels of government, and the Court was taking its first fateful steps toward a new role in American life—the guardianship of unpopular political, racial, and religious minorities. Constitutional law, for all the doctrinal divergencies then evident and soon to come, was at the threshold of a major transformation.

That Murphy would fall outside the emerging judicial consensus appeared out of the question. Unlike other Justices, to be sure, he had not figured in the relatively small circle of lawyers, scholars, and would-be appointees who composed the Court's immediate constituency. Neither had he participated actively in the 1937 struggle against judicial supremacy. But as an alert liberal he had been cognizant of its import and in a general way had embraced the principles which accommodated New Deal programs to fundamental law. To Murphy, judges rather than the Constitution had created the "no-man's land" in which the states and the national government were powerless to cope with the "blind, ruthless operation of nature and uncontrolled economic forces" then ravaging the land.[1] By erecting unbridled individualism into constitutional dogma, he had declared in 1936, the Justices had forgotten that "the Constitution is not a fixed and rigid code of ancestor rule. It is a living document. Those who would subordinate its larger purposes and the evident needs of our people to the mere preservation of inherited traditions and doctrines are not the real friends of the Constitution. . . . The bedrock of the Constitution is recognition of the inherent right of the common man to govern and provide for himself."[2]

Basically, this outlook was a modern adaptation of John Marshall's philosophy that the Constitution was an organic instrument which invested generous powers and choice of means in Congress, a philosophy now refurbished to include all popular legislatures. Because the doctrine implied correspondingly narrow range for judicial review, reformers had been clamoring for its revival since the Justices had asserted special supervisory responsibility over economic policy 50 years before. When it carried the day in the *Jones & Laughlin Steel* case during the Chrysler strike of 1937, a troubled Governor of Michigan hailed the decision as "one of the most momentous in the history of the Court," and in so doing he absorbed the major principle which prompted the change.[3] Judicial power to nullify legislation, Murphy told a Senate confirmation committee in 1940, should be exercised "with great discretion."[4]

Apart from principles of judicial self-restraint, the new Justice's value system and conception of law conditioned him to accept new legal perspectives. If law is an instrument of social welfare, as modern schools of jurisprudence maintained, political adversity had thrust him solidly into the functionalist camp. "All rights," he asserted, "are derived, essentially, from the purposes of the society in which they exist."[5] The yardstick of successful law was the same as for "good government"—satisfaction of human needs. The sit-down strikes, especially, left Murphy with a healthy disrespect for "musty precedent" and "rigid legalism." Favoring them over "human rights," he believed, was the very way in which law fell into disrepute. A government of laws, of course, was the ideal of free men; but the upheavals of depression had convinced him that "where great social forces are at work, uncompromising legal views which do not reach deeply into questions of human justice are rather futile."[6] While respect for the rights of property he accepted as essential to free government, Murphy emerged from Michigan committed to the notion that "the great human rights that mean happiness to the masses must be given precedence." Failure to do so, he warned, was to "risk for democracy the fate of Lot's wife . . . death by petrification."[7]

Legal innovation was the obvious counterpart of social reform. Welcoming the change in 1939, Murphy observed that

The old conception of law as a system of purely negative rules designed primarily for the maintenance of order is giving way steadily to the broader view that the law is properly a positive instrument for human betterment.

Under the pressure of unprecedented economic problems, this transition to a broader viewpoint has been greatly accelerated within the present decade. There are some among us who view this change with anxiety, if not actual foreboding. Their concern is understandable, for man is ever reluctant to leave the tranquility and calm of old-established philosophies for the transitional confusion and uncertainty of the new.

I am not disposed to share these fears. The alteration, to my mind, is but a natural, evolutionary and inevitable process arising from the character of a changing social order.[8]

Murphy did not contemplate the overhaul of basic institutions. Unlike some young turks of the New Deal, he had never attacked judicial power in the name of democracy. Nor had he given more than lukewarm public support to Roosevelt's court-packing schemes.[a] To the extent that Murphy had a quarrel with judges, it had been confined to particular men and the values they served. To the extent that he had attempted judicial reform, his emphasis had been to make courts more independent than ever before. To the extent, in short, that Murphy had thought about the role of the judiciary in American society, he had valued courts with customary respect, if not a little awe.

Accepting the value of traditional institutions as self-evident, he entered the Court understanding, but not paralyzed by, the dilemmas of judicial power. For all the necessity of judicial circumspection in a democratic system, he had long thought it obvious as a general proposition that judges would play a large part in resolving the disputes inherent in a period of great social change. In particular, the federal courts were a "powerful bulwark" of civil liberty. That Murphy projected his own values into a conception of proper judicial goals was apparent even before his arrival on the high bench. Having dismissed liberty of contract as a "rhetorical absurdity" while Governor, and having openly appealed for "fearless" judicial protection of the Bill of Rights as Attorney General, he left little doubt that he believed courts should defend the "fine intangibles" more vigorously than traditional forms of economic enterprise. Without acknowledging any contradiction for the judicial function—much less offering a rationale to explain the difference—Murphy as a politician had echoed the standard libertarian demand that judges exchange their stewardship over property rights for positive protection of what he called "those imponderables—the precious liberties and rights—that to many of us are the most important things in life."[9]

The significant thing is that the Court he joined appeared responsive

[a] One of his few expressions of attitude ran as follows: "Your query as to my views on the present Supreme Court proposal is put in such a way that it is somewhat difficult to answer. Of course I do not believe it right for a political party to control the Supreme Court of the United States, nor even for the head of the Party to do so. To my mind that is not what the President aimed at. He is attempting to put through a constructive plan which will liberalize the Court and, of course, quite frankly, get rid of some of its dead timber. However, that is a big question and I haven't the time or opportunity to go into it extensively here." FM to Claude S. Hyman, March 9, 1937, Box 44.

to such a call. During the years following the court-packing clash, constitutional jurisprudence was undergoing a quiet revolution. At the same time that the Justices contracted their preoccupation with property, they began to expand their responsibility in field after field of personal liberty. Freedom of expression, racial equality, and criminal procedure, all gave rise to a quickening momentum of judicial intervention on behalf of individual rights. A momentous shift was occurring in Supreme Court values.

This great shift did not occur overnight and was not solely the work of New Deal judges. The new outlook, though given depth and permanence by Roosevelt appointees at all levels of the federal judiciary, was shared by sitting Justices. It also drew heavily from past struggles over the nature of liberty falling within the Constitution's shield. For the discerning, indeed, the Court's transition had been signalled even before 1937 by two conspicuous trends regarding freedom of expression: (1) the gradual extension of First Amendment guarantees of free speech and press to the states by their absorption into the word "liberty" of the Fourteenth, and (2) the imposition of stricter standards, such as the clear and present danger test, to measure restraints on those freedoms.[10]

Both developments, which began in the 1920s, were of prime importance. Application of the First Amendment to the states meant that the daily battles of freedom of expression, which occur mainly in the states and localities, for the first time fell within the jurisdiction of the federal courts. Stricter standards meant that the Supreme Court was enlarging the sphere of individual freedom, and its own power, at the expense of official discretion at every level of government. Coupled with parallel developments in race relations and criminal procedure, they also meant that the Supreme Court was embarking on a new role for itself—the protection of minorities which for reasons of race, poverty, or unpopular belief were denied equal chances in life and in law. Just as they had registered the dominant material urges of the population following the Civil War, the Justices were beginning to reflect the profound changes in group interests and social values of modern American society. The result—as then—would transform the Court's constituency, the politics of its support, and its impact on American life.

The radical changes at work, of course, were less obvious in 1940 than from hindsight. The Justices had yet to declare that First Amendment freedoms were "preferred." A generation awaited the pronouncement that "separate but equal" was a contradiction in terms. Sufficient steps were being taken, however, to raise anew the vexing issues over which the court-packing struggle had been fought. What was the proper function of the judiciary in democratic government? Specifically, how could courts favor First Amendment rights without falling into the same trap of enforcing private predilection which these very Justices had so vigorously condemned in their predecessors? If freedom of expression was so basic as to be enforceable against the states, by what logic could other constitutional rights be subordinated? And if all were to be enforced with equal vigor, what was the likely effect on the distribution of power between nation and the states, or between judges and popularly elected officials? It all boiled down to the dilemma of judicial review since its inception: who decides and by what standards?

For a generation of judges reared on Justice Holmes' admonition that "legislatures are ultimate guardians of the liberties and welfare of the people in quite as great degree as the courts," these were extremely troublesome questions. By the nature of the cases before them, the idols of the new jurisprudence—Holmes, Cardozo, Brandeis—had supplied few of the answers. At best their tests had a checkered history when they were alive, and insofar as these men had clarified their views, their legacy was a paradox for the judicial function: courts should give more favored treatment to First Amendment freedoms than to economic rights.[11]

Try as they might, when this philosophy began to win new converts during the 1930s, the disciples of Holmes and Brandeis were unable to explain away the paradox except by admitting that a hierarchy existed among constitutional values. Felix Frankfurter, for example, argued that the olympian Holmes had "attributed very different legal significance to those liberties of the individual which history has attested as the indispensable conditions of a free society from that which he attached to liberties which derived merely from shifting economic arrangements."[12] Roosevelt's protagonist in the court-packing struggle, Robert H. Jackson, took a similar position: there was no inconsistency between safeguarding the democratic method of making decisions and keeping hands off those decisions once made. To attack liberty of expression was to attack the primary means of defending all rights. Free speech, as Justice Cardozo explained for the Court in 1937, "is the matrix, the indispensable condition, of nearly every other form of freedom."[13]

Yet one man's liberty is usually another's restraint. Beyond natural justice concepts of "ordered liberty," Cardozo never offered a system to resolve a collision of rights. And colliding interests were the heart of this, as of nearly all, governmental problems. Justice Stone attempted to meet the difficulty in the *Carolene Products* case of 1938 by suggesting "narrower scope for the operation of the presumption of constitutionality" when legislation appeared on its face to invade express constitutional guarantees. More subtly, he also called for "more exacting judicial scrutiny" of enactments which threatened either the free political process itself or "discrete and insular" minorities which were powerless to protect themselves within it.[14] The Court, according to this conception, should act when political checks were absent or weak. For all its importance, however, Stone's suggestion was confined with a cautious verb "may" to a footnote; and the Justices were using quite different standards in other cases. Basically, the Court was still experimenting.

Hence, politicians like Murphy were in good company if they demanded extra judicial protection of civil liberty without resolving the implications for judicial review. All that could be said was that most of the Justices in 1940 held a similar solicitude for personal freedoms. How far and by what methods they could be expected to protect them was still uncertain. The same uncertainty, given his record as Attorney General, even existed about the new Justice. Novel questions were arising in response to the Court's expansion of responsibility over civil liberties. The chances of innovation were great. Murphy's arrival was significant, consequently, not so much because Roosevelt had finally appointed a majority which would approve his economic experiments, but because it coincided with a major transition in the value-laden art of judging. Murphy, to paraphrase Holmes on Marshall, became important because he was *there*.

II

Contrary to accumulated myths, Justice Murphy did not establish himself immediately as a libertarian firebrand on the Supreme Court. His initial influence on the development of law was ambivalent. Though he was determined, as he told President Roosevelt after his first day on the bench, "to give the best that is in me—to serve with credit to my country and yourself," probably no other Justice in this century began more conscious of "how inadequate are the abilities that I bring to this work" or more disquieted by the great changes of status and function which appointment to the high tribunal invariably entails.[15] The early Murphy, accordingly, was not the "activist" jurist of customary portrayal. He was a self-conscious freshman, restless over the personal and professional restraints of his new post, and diffident to the point of indecisiveness in exercising its responsibilities. Equivocation, not activism, was his primary trait.

Historically, a season of adjustment has been found necessary by virtually every new appointee, regardless of era or prior occupation, before he became a fully effective member of the Court. Despite frequent demands that the Justices have prior judicial experience, the very testimony of those who have had it suggests that, for all practical purposes, each one must be considered a novice in the unique decisional system of the Supreme Court.[16] First of all, the proprieties of the office, coupled with an always surprising workload, have usually compelled a personal discipline whose magnitude few men anticipated. Only a rare individual has failed to make the necessary adjustments, but it is also a rare man who escaped Chief Justice Taft's feeling of having entered a monastery. While Justice Murphy probably constricted his social life less than most, he expressed the newcomer's common reaction when he observed in 1941: "We are rushed beyond belief. . . ."[17]

Professional changes, secondly, have generally taxed new Justices of every background. The dynamics of decision by a relatively large group having ultimate appellate functions generate discrete decisional patterns that are seldom familiar. Power for some purposes may be supreme, but it is always shared, not only among nine judges but among a multitude of actors in a polycentric legal system. Most new Justices, moreover, have found the disputes to be resolved "infinitely more complex" and the responsibilities much more personal than those they have encountered before.[18] Most have been humbled thereby. While experienced lawyers or judges may have had initial technical advantages, as opposed to the politician's experience in making hard choices of public policy, a physical fact must also be faced that only a very few men with lengthy experience on a key federal Court of Appeals could possibly be intimate with the broad range of subjects rising for review. Justice Douglas's estimate of a decade on the Court to acquire that breadth, indeed, is not greatly less than the 13½-year average tenure of Justices since the Civil War.[19] And should these personal and professional considerations be inoperative in particular cases, the Court's own internal procedures, whereby junior Justices speak last and vote first during conferences, and receive relatively light assignments initially, would insure a "freshman effect" of varying intensity and duration. A transition stage of relatively light responsibility and influence has been the common lot (and source of frustration) of freshman Justices for generations.[20]

Finally, and more subtly, the newcomer's vote and role in the opinion-drafting process may be affected by his own personal responses to the transition itself. These reactions a simple vote cannot register; these reactions a Justice may be too proud to reveal; but in Murphy's case they were essential elements of his evolution as a jurist. Just as he started out guardedly in the Philippines, so he entered the Court reluctantly and with greater diffidence than normal. Just as Justices Davis and Black did before him, Murphy began his Court career under fire and with an aggravated sense of being on trial. First impressions only strengthened his feelings of inferiority. In February 1940 he wrote Reverend Leo T. Butler: "After three weeks now I have been a full-fledged Associate Justice—at least as far as the title is concerned—but otherwise I feel very much the 'freshman' member that I am and having had a taste of actual work on the Bench I am beginning to sense more fully the vast responsibility that this Court bears. I cannot hope to equal what others have done in meeting that responsibility, but even though I cannot be brilliant I can try to do the work that is before me thoughtfully and with devotion to the great cause that we all serve."[21] "To one like myself, who always thought of the Court as something venerable even though human," he added to Claude G. Bowers, "it is a strange, indescribable thrill to share in this work. I believe I am beginning to appreciate the magnitude of the responsibility that it entails, and I wonder all the more at the faith that the President and friends like yourself have placed in me. It is a new sea, and I do not know where my course will take me, but a 'mighty effort.' "[22]

Murphy made his "mighty effort," but at least three terms were required before he was able to assimilate himself confidently into the life and work of the Court. During that time not only did his substantive views undergo subtle change but his very "freshmanness" affected the judicial process—and the law of the land. Powerful feelings of inadequacy had potent and unexpected effects on some of the great civil liberties landmarks of the day.

It has been easy to assume otherwise. In his first major opinion, *Thornhill* v. *Alabama* and the companion case, *Carlson* v. *California*, Justice Murphy launched one of the Court's boldest and most controversial experiments with freedom of expression—the doctrine that constitutional guarantees of free communication include peaceful picketing.[23] The picketing doctrine, which was undoubtedly his foremost single contribution to the development of the First Amendment, justifiably caused commentators to brand Murphy as a "libertarian activist" from the start. Both the State of Alabama and Shasta County, California, had made it a misdemeanor for anyone to go near, to loiter, or to picket a place of business without just cause or legal excuse. Though no question of the peaceful, truthful, or limited character of the picketing existed in either case, Thornhill had been convicted for asking a worker not to cross a picket line and Carlson for carrying signs. When the convictions were appealed with AFL-CIO assistance, the Supreme Court responded with three unusual steps.

First, instead of merely reversing the convictions, the Court nullified the ordinances "on their face," on the theory that they were so broadly prohibitive of free speech as to amount to a prior restraint. Second, the assumption which established the Court's jurisdiction, that peaceful picketing is a form of communication, Justice Murphy made explicit in broad libertarian terms. "Free discussion concerning the conditions in industry and the causes of labor disputes appears to us indispensable to the effective and intelligent use of the processes of popular government to shape the destiny of modern industrial society," he declared.[24] In the circumstances of the times, as the Court ruled in *Carlson*, "publicizing the facts of a labor dispute in a peaceful way through appropriate means, whether by pamphlet, by word of mouth or by banner, must now be regarded as within that liberty of communication which is secured to every person by the Fourteenth Amendment." Finally, while reserving judgment as to the scope of state power to regulate picketing by narrowly drawn statutes aimed at specific evils, the Court offered the clear and present danger test, as strictly conceived by Justice Brandeis in *Whitney* v. *California*, to measure the breadth of this newly federalized freedom.[25] Justice McReynolds dissented alone without opinion.

The picketing decisions, though their outcome was expected, were a tour de force. Prior to the decision it was problematic whether picketing was even legal in many states, let alone a federal constitutional right. While a generation of union efforts had preceded the decision with mixed results, and while Justice Brandeis' *Senn* v. *Tile Layers Protective Union* opinion in 1937 had dropped a pregnant dictum that picketing might be speech, the question of federal limits on state power to control the practice was fresh. The *Thornhill* decision thus not only enlarged the concept of speech but also federalized "the voice of labor," and made picketing a matter of constitutional import, all at the expense of traditional state rules.[26] Rendered with surprising unanimity, the decisions had revolutionary effects.

Furthermore, the *Thornhill* opinion contained significant seeds for the development of civil liberties law generally. For the first time the Court applied the clear and present danger test beyond the problem of seditious utterance for which it was designed. The opinion also em-

braced the concept that the social value of ideas justifies their constitutional status, a concept which became a double-edged sword in subsequent censorship cases. And it strengthened a new stream of precedents which nullified overly broad statutes affecting free speech "on
their face."[27] This form of analysis, which was then in vogue, one suspects, largely because of Chief Justice Hughes, made serious inroads
into the Court's requirement of standing by relieving the challenger's
burden of proving that a statute was unconstitutional as applied to him.
All told, the Justices were clearly departing from their normal precautions of saving statutes by confining them to the facts or by reading
into them high standards of intent. The decisions, as the *Washington
Post* and the *Nation* then observed, were of "far-reaching importance."
"Justice Murphy has made a fine debut."[28]

Precisely because such sweeping decisions came so early in Murphy's
career, and produced such subsequent controversy, the picketing cases
spawned assumptions that Murphy followed libertarian values—without faltering and without thought—from his first day on the Court
to his last. The libertarian character of the cases, however, cannot be
explained merely on the grounds that the Justice was so simpleminded
or ideologically obsessed that the issues were dimly perceived. However justifiable the criticism of *Thornhill*, and much of it was, the case
is a relatively poor example of how "hyperactive concern for individual
rights" can lead to folly.[29] The *Thornhill* decision is better compre-
hended as a case of misunderstood intent, a problem not uncommon
for constitutional innovations where great forces stand to win or to
lose large stakes. *Thornhill* also provides a classic illustration of a freshman Justice at work and how his very newness on the Court may influence judicial decision. In the picketing cases the Supreme Court
faced a dual task of adjusting concepts on liberty to the industrial age
and of assimilating a new member to itself. That the two were related
in fact demonstrates anew the complexity of the judicial process.

An aftermath of misunderstood intent was perhaps inherent in the
substantive dilemma of the case. How could the element of communication in picketing be defended without weakening state power to
preserve other interests? Despite their neglect in subsequent debates,
the facts as presented by union counsel did not permit easy avoidance
of the question whether peaceful picketing was sheltered by the Constitution. Thornhill had been arrested after seven weeks of unmolested
picketing during a strike; arrest came only after he had asked an employee not to cross the picket line; and only Thornhill, the union

leader, had been arrested. There was no violence, no sign of intimidation, and no immediate threat of injury. There had been only, as Chief Justice Hughes argued in conference, an effort to persuade. The Alabama Supreme Court had construed Thornhill's verbal appeal, nonetheless, as proof of the harmful intent which was an essential element of the statutory offense. A clear consensus developed among the Justices, as the case was discussed, that state power to regulate labor relations had been used to cloak a suppression of free speech and that the Court had a duty to intervene against what the Chief called "arbitrary legislation."[30]

The only basis of intervention was the due process clause of the Fourteenth Amendment. Because of the sensitivity of recently appointed Justices to past restriction of state regulatory power by that route, however, consensus also formed that this new limitation on state authority should be held to a minimum. Beyond question, the intent of most Justices was to protect the communicative aspect of picketing while leaving the abuses of speech and the evils of the practice under traditional state control. "Our job as I see it," Justice Murphy noted to his clerk, "is to write a reversal without serious prejudice to the police power of the state which I believe is imperative to safeguard without unduly curtailing the right to free expression."[31] The real question was how.

To state the general proposition was easier than to accommodate the interests at stake. Murphy was a novice. Compounding the problems ordinarily presented by a delicate question of public policy was the fact that he was new to the decisional modes of the Court and, in a sense, abnormally on his own. While the assignment itself probably had resulted from his labor experience and the tradition that freshmen Justices cut teeth on the case of their choice, the same tradition also would soften internal criticism normally to be expected in a case of such moment. Labor experience would be of little real value to the precise issue. Neither, for that matter, would rich experience in law. Close precedents did not exist. Though he had no serious objection against using it, the Justice recognized that Brandeis' *Senn* statement was "dictum only" and not precisely apposite. All he had for guidance were the general sense of conference and analogous cases of overly broad ordinances governing handbill circulation and radical activities.[32] Fellow Justices, notably Frankfurter, Reed, and Stone, did their best to ease Murphy's adjustment to the Court. Frankfurter helped to arrange for a clerk during mid-season; all three patiently pointed out the logical flaws or procedural errors that are common to fledgling judges. Yet early in his career Murphy made Robert H. Jackson's discovery that the Supreme Court "functions less as one deliberative body than as nine, each Justice working largely in isolation, except as he chooses to seek consultation with others."[33] Early in his career, he also discovered serious practical limitations even to that. The upshot for him, as for his predecessors, was that his education as a Justice was largely self-education. Murphy had to learn on-the-job.

Cautious about an important issue of national policy, on the one hand, and personally diffident, on the other, the Justice responded in *Thornhill* by improvising a system of decision within his office which established a pattern for the "big cases" until about 1946, when confidence fully returned. This pattern of decision was at once a revival of past techniques, with its heavy delegation of authority, and a microcosm of the Supreme Court at work. The pattern was unusual, not only because of its heavy reliance on others, but because on a few occasions Murphy resorted to help from outside the Court, especially from his lifelong intimate, most trusted confidant, and Washington roommate, Edward G. Kemp, whose views, in the dozen or so cases in which he was consulted, bore a strong resemblance to those of Chief Justice Stone.

The normal sequence was that Justice Murphy, after discussing the case in conference and with his clerk, would set the clerk to writing on the basis of general direction in notes and memoranda prepared by himself. After soliciting criticism from the clerks, other Justices, and occasionally Kemp, Murphy would circulate the usual draft opinion among the Justices for the same process to begin again. His major opinions thus were collegial in a double sense. The clerks were chiefly responsible for research and the details of writing under his supervision. Kemp was used, as Murphy always had used him, as a conservative foil and as a guard against his own impulsiveness. Rarely, if ever, did Kemp's views influence the outcome. Murphy kept the power of decision to himself. His role as a Justice, though he invited a remarkable degree of internal debate among his staff, was that which he always had carved for himself—to make the policy decision and then to persuade. In his freshman years, particularly, his office resembled a kind of miniature court, in which he encouraged dialogue of opposing views before committing his vote or his pen. His very diffidence as a newcomer made Murphy all the more attentive to the differences of opinion which he stimulated in order to avoid error. The very strength of his consciousness of being a fledgling judge weakened whatever ideological com-

pulsion has been thought to exist. Judging, for Murphy, was an agonizing task.[b]

Though a full reconstruction is impossible because identities have
not been preserved, the process of self-persuasion had important consequences for the picketing doctrine. The problem of the case, as perceived by the opinion drafters, was not one of selling a policy, but how
to fulfill the official task of translating a general consensus about a result into a workable balance of interests. That problem rapidly reduced
itself to establishing the precise nature and scope of the right on which
Thornhill's reversal could be justified. Was it an assembly, was it free
speech, or could reversal be placed on a lesser and safer ground? Drafting the opinion became a process of choosing among alternatives, each
championed by a different spokesman around the Justice, and each to
a certain degree distasteful. The result, as frequently occurs for the
Court as a whole, was an opinion that suffered not so much because it
played policy favorites as because it was divided unto itself.

Upon receiving the case, the Justice provided his clerk with a general
outline of his views, which were inchoate. Then he fished for bait. "We
ought to review the true nature and extent of the right of assembly," he
wrote. "Does it include picketing as we know it?"[34] With the clerk's
reply on March 30, 1940, the real debate was on. The clerk replied: "I
agree entirely on the necessity of writing so as not to prejudice the
power of the state to keep the peace and set limits to the rights of contestants in an industrial dispute. The historical right of assembly *may
not* include picketing. I doubt that it does. It occurs to me, however,
that no right of *assembly* is involved where the statute is *construed* so
as to apply to *one man speaking to another in a public street*. The presence of two is an essential to any freedom of discussion. Can we not
avoid the extremely difficult point you raise? It seems to me that the
right of assembly is less well defined than any other."[35] In the clerk's
view, reversal could be justified on two possible grounds: (1) the fact
that guilt turned on purpose rather than on conduct, or (2) the fact
that petitioner was "being punished not for picketing, but for speaking." By concentrating on speech, the Court could narrow the opinion
by the usual disclaimers, and avoid the larger question of state power
to control picketing as such.[36] Apparently the Justice accepted the latter

---

[b] Murphy's tolerance of criticism is illustrated by the following note from his clerk
regarding the draft opinions in *Royal Indemnity Co.* v. *United States*, 313 U.S. 289
(1941): "Seems like this is briefly and rather well done. But if you are going to dissent,
I suggest that you do a little better job. . . ." Clerk to FM, No. 817, Box 130. Murphy
later withdrew his dissent.

proposal, and the opinion began to be drafted on that basis. Murphy also wrote some broad rhetorical paragraphs for the opinion, which he ultimately discarded, to establish his credentials in "the Great Pulpit."

When the first draft was completed, however, sober second thoughts set in. "I still think the act of speaking was only evidentiary of the purpose or intent that made the picketing unlawful, not the offense itself," came a rebuttal to the clerk's theory from an unknown critic, who might have been another Justice, but who sounded like Kemp. "You still have the problem whether the state can prohibit picketing, and it seems dangerous to view it (as union counsel would like) merely as a question of free speech. . . . It is unrealistic too. The decision would become a virtual bar to the effective exercise of public authority in these matters." How could the Court reverse without ignoring the fact that the statute did not outlaw speech or picketing as such but only picketing accompanied by specific intent to harm? How could the Court reverse without also ignoring the fact that Thornhill was picketing as well as speaking? Worse still, how could the Court reverse without immunizing all conduct accompanied by utterance from effective state control? Only two alternatives existed to overturn the conviction —ignoring the defendant's picketing or condemning the statute as vague—and neither seemed "feasible or realistic."[37]

Presumably the Justices, in voting for reversal, had rejected this either-or view of the problem. But the rebuttal, which closely resembled Alabama's position, was so clearly at odds with the theory of the draft opinion that Justice Murphy became worried. Broadening the consultations, he suggested visits by the clerk to Justice Stone and even to the retired Justice Brandeis, "if convenient," to help resolve doubts. The Justice took soundings himself, and in a long note to the clerk, he indicated the depth of his concern. "The opinion as drafted seems to me to be predicated upon a misconception of the true nature of the offense charged & the evil at which the statute is directed," he wrote. "I am not sure of this but am disturbed by it."

Are we to assume that the act complained of and prohibited was the act of speaking to a prospective employee, informing him there was a strike and saying that they didn't want anyone to go in there and work? Counsel for def. astutely drew our attention to that feature of the defendant's conduct to the virtual exclusion of the other features of the case and the main purpose of the statute.

Whether the mere act of speaking to a prospective worker, for the purpose prescribed by the statute could itself be made a penal offense or enjoined, without infringement of the broad fundamental right of free speech it is hardly necessary to decide.

Wasn't the actual offense loitering and picketing, for the purpose, etc.? And wasn't the conversation evidence only of the intent or purpose—I don't know—but we ought to answer this in our own minds before we get on to the wrong track. . . .

Read the provisions of the British Trade disputes and Trade Union Act of 1927. Of course the reference to intimidation in this act *is important*— But what about Legislative prerogative? Are we getting off onto a novel doctrine?

I am moved by Brandeis, great champion of labor unions in Duplex v. Deering. You will recall his admonition that it is the duty not of the judges but of the legislature to declare the limits of permissible contest and to declare the duties which the new situation demands. To go so far as to say that legislatures may not regulate the practices of picketing in the public interest because of *incidental* infringement on free speech and assembly, in an area of dispute, may be to extend Constitutional guarantees far beyond reasonable limits. I am not at all sure of this but we must think straight & clear about it.

Then came the fateful question of the Roosevelt Court:

Are we moving—in our desire to maintain free speech and assembly—the freedoms concerning which in my thought and actions I place above nearly every other consideration—in the direction of paralyzing popular government and making democracy if we go the full length—of such logic—ridiculous and impotent?

The notes you have prepared are careful & I believe correctly express the view adopted by the court in conference. But if on second sober breath we can steer this case away from the pitfalls & still keep fidelity to the freedoms that is just what we ought to do.[38]

To avoid the "pitfalls" required additional efforts to limit the new principle. The first problem was to describe the scope of affected conduct. Picketing, as the Justice noted during his conversations, "is a variable term," covering behavior that ranged from informational protests to outright coercion. While the opinion nowhere expressly equated all picketing with free speech, was it safe to leave implicit or in footnote references the Court's cognizance of those variations? "Haven't we got to analyze picketing?" the Justice asked. Some solace could be found, of course, in listing examples of conduct, *e.g.*, picketing en masse, which the Court had no intention of wresting from state control. Murphy's second draft added several such exclusions, among them the very situations which the Justices, after much travail, later exempted from the *Thornhill* rule.[39/c] To do so at the outset, however, raised a subsidiary difficulty: how could either picketing or its evils be precisely defined without deciding cases not before the Court?

A second and related problem was the remedy for the imprecision of Alabama's statute. The basic flaw, by common consensus, was its absolute character, its failure to distinguish the coercive aspects of picketing from harmless forms; and toward the final phase of drafting, greater attention was focused on this aspect of the case. "I agree," Murphy told his clerk, "that *part* of the answer is insistence on statutes precisely framed & free from nebulousness when they undertake to set limits on a citizen's right of expression."[40] That insistence had the additional advantage of being in the stream of recent precedents, such as *Lovell* v. *Griffin*, which nullified unrestricted public authority to license handbill distribution without upsetting it when narrowly focused.[41] Murphy thought the parallel clear because he believed an irreducible element of censorship was involved in Alabama's wholesale prohibition of picketing. Moreover, he was attracted to the notion that the Court should void overly broad ordinances affecting free expression "on their face." After all, if a statute admitted no exceptions, the whole people would be restrained by its coercive effects as much as the petitioner; and how better could the Court induce states to take a less destructive alternative than to nullify their blanket prohibitions outright and in suits in which the parties did not even have to show direct personal injury?[42]

In addition, Murphy had long advocated the clear and present danger test as the "true course" to follow in dilemmas of liberty versus authority. Thornhill's case offered an opportunity to advance a revival of the test already begun in *Herndon* v. *Lowry*.[43] The problem, he conceded, was essentially one of balancing interests. Where states failed to do so, the remedy was judgment "on the face." Where closer situations occurred, clear and present danger would provide ample guide to mark the boundary of individual freedom and state power. That mixture, however, was the rub. Out of zeal to explain both the principle and its limits as a total problem, the Justice left uncertain the basis of the particular judgment. Was Thornhill's conviction reversed because the statute was too broad, because his speech in fact had been suppressed, or because his picketing contained no threats of immediate

---

[c] On the margin of the second draft the Justice added a passage to foreclose any implication that "picketing in such numbers or otherwise conducted to present a threat of violence or injury or [which] constitutes annoyance or substantial interference with the right of privacy or free exercise of other rights may not be regulated by a statute narrowly drawn to cover the precise situation." No. 514, 1939 Term, Box 129.

injury? The opinion Murphy circulated among the other Justices said all three.

This characteristic, perhaps as much as the courtesy which Justices traditionally extend to new colleagues, accounts for the opinion's unruffled reception when it circulated among the others. The *Thornhill* opinion contained something for everyone. Only Justice Stone raised serious criticism and even his was not directed against the basic premise that Thornhill's conduct was speech and therefore constitutionally protected. While encouraging Murphy in making painstaking analysis, Stone had misgivings mainly about the wisdom of nullifying the statute on its face. It is doubtful that Stone had welcomed inclusion of that procedure in the first paragraph of his *Carolene* footnote, and this case illustrated the reasons for hesitation.[44] To void an ordinance "on its face" meant that it could never be applied to anyone under any circumstances, but Justice Stone had no difficulty imagining conduct to which Alabama's statute could be applied. What, for example, if Thornhill had picketed in order to throw a brick? Here, of course, he thought some measure of free speech was involved because Thornhill spoke while walking up and down, and Stone was inclined to go along with reversal on the basis of the Court's analogous conclusion in the *Stromberg* case. But preferring an opinion closer to the facts, he withheld agreement until assured that no one else had similar reservations.[45]

No one did. Four Justices—Hughes, Stone, Frankfurter, and Douglas—did object to Murphy's casual assertion that the workers' interest in industrial conditions "transcended" that of the employers. To make unnecessary comparisons would have been a serious tactical error, as Justice Stone cautioned, by inviting criticism of social bias and by rubbing the employers the wrong way.[46] But a quick patch suggested by the Chief Justice overcame the transgression and the case went to conference. "Well we are ready to proceed with our mutton," remarked the Chief, who seemed to be the driving force against the statute; and after Stone acquiesced, the Court agreed to accept language mutually agreeable to Justice Black and Murphy to express the result in *Carlson v. California.*[47] The only significant change wrought by the processes of collegial thought during circulation of that opinion was deletion of Murphy's string of examples of conduct on which the Court reserved opinion in favor of a tighter, general statement that state power to control specific evils by narrowly drawn statutes remained untouched.[48]

Otherwise, no record exists in Justice Murphy's papers that any Justice protested the conceptual basis of the picketing decisions, whether the association of picketing with speech or the clear and present danger test. No record exists that any Justice questioned the fusion of multiple analytical strands to link the doctrine to the small array of precedent available. And no record exists to suggest that other Justices besides Stone and McReynolds considered the Court's action to be precipitate. "I cannot agree! but I do not care to expand dissent," Justice McReynolds commented. The rest was a chorus of approval across the ideological spectrum. "A fine piece of work," "a grand expression of noble governmental policies," responded two New Dealers in the flattering vein typical among Justices. Yet Justice Roberts' reaction differed little: "Yes, sir! A carefully balanced and discriminating treatment of this troublesome subject."[49] Felix Frankfurter, the Court's labor expert and the colleague whose favorable opinion Murphy had long coveted, wrote on his *Carlson* slip opinion: "This gives me a chance to say what I put very inadequately on the *Thornhill* opinion—that this is work of the very best judicial quality. It decides extremely important issues fearlessly but also circumspectly, in language that rises to the heights of the great argument, appropriate to the profound issues canvassed & the best traditions of the Court. I warmly congratulate you & rejoice to be with you."[50]

Most striking, in view of the aftermath, was not what the other Justices said in reviewing the *Thornhill* opinion, but what they did *not* say. Even discounting their friendly encouragement to a newcomer, or their jockeying for his future support, the response of Murphy's colleagues made it difficult to believe that they were seriously dissatisfied with his attempt to strike a judicious balance between individual freedom and state control.

If the Justices of 1940 considered the *Thornhill* opinion to be sufficiently guarded, seldom have they miscalculated more. The initial press reactions commended the picketing doctrine as "good sense and good law," but the decision set off a spiralling controversy in professional circles which has yet to fade.[51] Denounced by eminent authorities for its "Jacobinism" and "label thinking," as "one of the greatest pieces of folly the Supreme Court ever perpetrated," the *Thornhill* case in fact became one of the most heavily criticized decisions since 1937.[52] Scarcely an aspect of Murphy's opinion, whether judging on its face, limiting state law, or the public information premise, escaped scholarly attack save the one of most contemporary interest—the casual application of the Fourteenth Amendment to private property.[53] Thornhill picketed in a company town.

From the perspective of a quarter century it is clear that much of the sound and fury was "jurisprudence by epithets," based on assumptions that picketing was either pure speech or pure coercion.[54] Obviously the Justices assumed otherwise and conceived their task as one of drawing lines. Given the nature of the economic interests and of the governmental relationships at stake, controversy was inevitable. Given the magnitude of the constitutional breakthrough, a degree of confusion regarding its scope was not unusual. Refinement case by case, as well as reading exaggerated hopes and fears into the opinion, were to be expected, especially when as here the Court's opinion was an analytical hybrid. However, it is also clear that the opinion's doctrinal eclecticism was partially, though not exclusively, responsible for the ultimate surgery it received. For *Thornhill* v. *Alabama* could be interpreted either as merely condemning blanket restrictions on picketing or as investing the practice with such constitutional status that it was removed from all local regulation except under conditions of clear and present danger, which proved to be an elusive test. Neither had the opinion precisely described the specific evils left to state control. While that imprecision may have been compelled by appellate restraints, and probably smoothed the opinion's passage through the Court, it was bound to create trouble when the Justices began the inevitable process of delineating its scope case by case.

Even so, the flaws of *Thornhill* cannot be explained as an accidental convergence of a doctrinaire Justice and a freshman status which led his colleagues to drown their misgivings in the customs of the Court. A routine tax immunities case, not *Thornhill*, was his "elegant commencer."[55] It is doubtful, in any event, that traditional amenities extended so far. The subsequent retreat from what many assumed to be the picketing doctrine was in large part an articulation of the very exclusions foreseen in Justice Murphy's second draft. And the main exception—the retreat on constitutional protection of "stranger picketing" (picketing by nonunion men or outsiders)—was led by Justice Frankfurter against his own opinion in *AFL* v. *Swing* of the following year, which was the Court's most explicit equation of picketing with free speech.[56] The main difficulty with Justice Murphy's handiwork, in other words, was not that no attempt was made to guard the *Thornhill* opinion, but that it was made by a freshman Justice who was unsure of himself and caught in a complex crossfire of rival doctrines and personalities, both among older Justices and the new. The main problem of craftmanship in *Thornhill*, it is tempting to say, was that Justice Murphy was trying too hard.

III

And so it went through his first two terms. The picketing cases, for all their significance, in no way removed Murphy's initial discomforts as a judge. If anything, the major landmarks of his first term, especially those concerning religious liberty, seemed to disquiet him all the more. Murphy entered the Court greatly agitated over the military unpreparedness of the United States and disturbed by popular apathy.[57] "Now terrible things are happening so rapidly in Europe," he noted to James K. Watkins in May 1940, "that even the great issues that come before the Court seem relatively trivial and unimportant." "I am a judge, and judges do not have to concern themselves primarily with matters of national defense and foreign affairs. But I am a believer in democracy, also, and it is an impossible thing not to be distressed and sick at heart at the awful news that comes from abroad. It is hard to keep from wondering if the question now is not merely who will win in Europe, but whether there will remain in this world a society where courts of justice as we know them are necessary." "I have no thought of joining the 'all-is-losters,' " he was quick to add.[58] But apparently it was going to take "an ordeal to teach men that they cannot have freedom without working for it—incessantly. . . ." Stern preparatory measures were necessary "to defend what we have. I pray," said the Justice, "that there will be time."[59]

Murphy also arrived fresh from battle and a mass education campaign to set a balanced civil liberties policy for national emergency, a policy which stood as a virtual deposition of his private beliefs. But a series of Jehovah's Witnesses cases, which placed both values of freedom and loyalty in conflict, seemed to shake well-settled views. In the first Flag Salute Case,[60] for instance, he did not share the view of Hughes and certain New Deal appointees that the framers would have considered the compulsory flag salute inoffensive to the First Amendment.[d] When Justice Frankfurter circulated his opinion, which followed the Chief Justice's analysis of the issue in conference with little apparent debate, Murphy's first reaction was to prepare a dissent on the ground that so "officious and unnecessary" an intrusion on religious conscience could only be made under national emergency power in

---

[d] During oral argument, Justice Frankfurter sent Justice Murphy the following note: "Is it at all probable that the framers of the Bill of Rights would have thought that a requirement to salute the flag violates the protection of 'the free exercise of religion' "? Note, April 25, 1940, No. 690, Box 129.

direst extremity. Yet his policy orientation was so blatant and untenable as a legal proposition that he held his tongue.[61] Apart from the appeal of "self-restraint," the controlling factor in his acquiescence seemed to be that the petitioner merely sought reinstatement into a public school following expulsion for refusing to salute. Had a penalty attached, a far more serious question would have resulted, along with a response that foreshadowed future reversals. Even in 1940, Justice Stone's discussion of accommodating interests struck Murphy as "sensible."[62]

In *Cantwell* v. *Connecticut*, on the other hand, while the Justice approved absorption of the right of free worship into the Fourteenth Amendment, he drafted a concurrence expressing the view that Justice Roberts' opinion inadequately protected state authority to control group coercion and public fighting by religious sects. He was willing to join the opinion on the question of licenses, he said, in contrast to the *Terminiello* situation of 1949, only because it lent no countenance "to the view that verbal attacks on particular races or creeds, inciting violence and breaches of the peace, have the sanction of the Constitution." Yet this opinion, too, he withheld after Justice Roberts strengthened support of state licensing power and his clerk advised that he "should not give the appearance of making a speech about civil and religious liberties especially in view of the fact [that] you already have expressed your stand on these matters in the Thornhill case." "There is always the danger," the clerk cautioned, "that a casual expression, intended to give the State power to control street fighting, may be used by an unfriendly court to deprive minority groups of all freedom of expression."[63/e]

While Murphy's recent experience as Attorney General made him sensitive to problems created by religious disorders, competing impulses to safeguard liberty and uncertainty how to make his influence felt threw him into ambivalence. Slowly the Justice was learning his trade throughout the first term, but indecisiveness was the main result, along with plain discomfort. Furthermore, as the administration stepped up its defense program, he found it difficult, "gaited as I have been, to take [my] hands from the plough."[64] At the beginning of summer recess he could hold his feelings no longer. Offering the President his services rather than taking a vacation, he wrote Roosevelt:

---

e Justice Stone likewise withheld a concurrence after Justice Roberts deleted sections of his opinion which questioned state regulation of solicitation as a prior restraint. For Justice Stone, state regulatory power was beyond doubt. Copy, Harlan F. Stone to Owen J. Roberts, May 2, 1940, No. 632, 1939 Term, Box 129.

I remain in Washington in the hopes that I might be of service to you. As a public servant I find it difficult to be away from the Capitol as darkness clouds a great segment of the earth and the immediate future of our own land, under certain eventualities, is not too bright.

My faith is of the militant kind. My gifts are modest and I know too well that there are many men of greater stature than myself available. But only a small company of officials have had my administrative experience. Energy, integrity and imagination, plus a zeal for all I believe in, are marks I can bring to a public errand. If needed this I can do.

It has been my hope that you would go forward with your original plans for me. But I myself would want those plans changed if it were in the country's best interest to do so. You must be free in judgment. You will be best served by men of humility and a will. You have always done me more than Justice. You owe me naught. I am your debtor.

History brings you another crisis. But when things go wrong men of high purpose do not wring their hands and sob. They act. I hope you will champion immediate *conscription*.[65]

Roosevelt found him no errand that summer. But the President apparently gave serious consideration to appointing him Attorney General, Secretary of Labor, or High Commissioner to the Philippines as vacancies loomed in 1941. Throughout that summer the restless Justice agonized over the possibilities, one of which—probably the Philippines post—he described as "one that tears right into the heart."[66] His sentimental ties to the Philippines were strong, and relations between President Quezon and High Commissioner Sayre were deteriorating as a result of continued concentration of executive authority in Manila. Even though it was rumored that Quezon had vetoed Murphy's reappointment, the Justice was informed privately that Quezon had requested Roosevelt to retain Sayre, rather than appoint an unknown, only after being informed that under no circumstances would the Justice accept the position.[67] The attorney generalship was another matter, however. After asking the President for more time to weigh alternatives, and after sending a gentle prod, Murphy drafted but did not send a letter to Roosevelt in July, signifying his willingness to descend from the bench. He wrote:

Viewing it as in the nature of a call to service at a time when the country is faced with a serious emergency . . . I think you should know that I was prepared to make the change suggested by you. While such a move might be construed unfavorably in some quarters, and while I prefer above all the work of the Court, at a time like this personal interests should not be allowed primary or exclusive consideration.

Because of my familiarity with the work of the Department . . . I felt that I could contribute more effectively for the time being there, than in my present position to the more pressing problems of law enforcement and national defense. Accordingly, I had decided to make myself available for such duty. While I do not want you to feel any obligation concerning it, I do want you to know that I was not, as it may have appeared, indifferent to the consideration. . . .[68]

Equivocation in the end cost Murphy his chance to leave the Court. In late August the President appointed Jackson's nominee, Francis Biddle, a man whom Murphy regarded as a "stuffed-shirt" and whose dislike Biddle reciprocated fully.

Rumors continued to fly about the Justice's unhappiness on the bench and about prospective jobs in store. Murphy added fuel to the fire by making a strong speech to recalcitrant Catholics, at Roosevelt's request, in support of Lend Lease to Russia.[f] But reports that he might be named ambassador to Mexico or Ireland, Murphy dismissed as "political gossip."[69] For one who had joined the Court reluctantly was showing signs of coming to terms with his office. Though Murphy was sensitive to criticism of his opinions and anxious "to stay ahead of the pack," a relaxed quality began to show through the strain. He thought it a fine joke, for instance, when a clerk sent him the score of a Michigan-Ohio State football game during a Saturday conference. Once during an oral argument by a particularly industrious lawyer he sent a clerk in the audience this note: "How would you like to be his wife? Perhaps with my own weaknesses, and failure too, I ought not—as a celibate—to ask such a question."[70] In 1941 the bachelor Justice even contemplated buying a Washington home in anticipation of long service ahead.

---

[f] This controversial address, which Murphy made before a national convention of the Knights of Columbus on August 19, 1941, placed the Justice in a double dilemma. On the one hand, he had to pull strings among friends in the National Catholic Welfare Conference to secure a reluctant invitation; but that forced him to accept obligations to speak elsewhere, contrary to his policy against making public appearances. Conservative Catholics, on the other hand, not only denounced him as a "religious traitor," but objected to his speaking against the policy of the Vatican. Administration leaders, nevertheless, were gratified. The President sent word that he was "tickled to death" with the speech, which Benjamin V. Cohen observed "cuts like a sun through a fog," and the State Department translated it into Spanish and Portuguese for distribution in Latin America. See materials, Box 98. Memo, FDR to Edwin M. Watson, Aug. 21, 1941, RL:P.S.F., Box 36. Cohen to FM, Aug. 20, 1941, Box 98. For domestic effects see Raymond H. Dawson, *The Decision to Aid Russia* (Chapel Hill: University of North Carolina Press, 1959), p. 232.

Throughout the 1941 term, nonetheless, a pattern of self-conscious irresolution continued to mark his work. His first year's assignments, following the custom in which assignments as well as speaking order are influenced by seniority, were heavily dosed with routine tax and statutory construction problems. While these opinions were received well enough, the odds and ends which fell to Murphy did not satisfy his restless energies. The first opportunity to test the reach of the picketing doctrine early in 1941 thus found the Justice champing at the bit. Because he had missed the conference in which the *Swing* case was decided, Murphy itched to write in defense of *Thornhill* when the majority of that case split for the first time in *Milk Drivers Union* v. *Meadowmoor Dairies, Inc.* There, in an opinion by Justice Frankfurter, the Court upheld state power to enjoin picketing, in itself peaceful, after prolonged violence had occurred in a dispute. Although Murphy voted in the majority against Justices Black, Reed, and Douglas, he was dissatisfied with the draft opinions of both Frankfurter and Black, whom he thought manifested "judicial jitters." "Both opinions," he told his new clerk, "are eloquent and emotional and as I view them not in good order." In Murphy's judgment, Frankfurter was excessively cautious about stressing the facts of violence. Black, on the other hand, minimized the violence and distorted the injunction in order to fit it under *Thornhill* and *Carlson*. Neither adequately applied the governing principles of those cases to the present facts. "We might even do it ourselves," Murphy hinted, to "indicate their true scope and meaning."[71] Quite simply, he believed, *Thornhill* confirmed rather than denied state power to control picketing in circumstances of violence.

Setting the wheels in motion to write, Murphy stimulated another debate in his own camp, which ranged from Kemp's unreconstructed argument, that peaceful picketing was not synonymous with free discussion, to doubts akin to Justice Black's, whether peaceful picketing, even when entangled with past violence, could be enjoined when other remedies were adequate to protect the interests of employers and of the state.[72] The advice of his clerk, heavy as it was with *Realpolitik*, kept the Justice quiet. Despite the clerk's lament that Murphy's junior position had lost him the assignment, the clerk advised him not to waste his strategic advantages by adding another opinion to those of Justices Frankfurter, Black, and Reed: "All three will try to woo you. Wouldn't it be better to work out your own views? Then pick the opinion that comes the closest. Then start work (a la Stone) on that. The name of Murphy in this case means much. It adds great weight to the opinion bearing it since you wrote Thornhill. I'd act accordingly."[73]

Needing little encouragement Murphy quietly went to work on Justice Frankfurter, whose opinion he thought basically followed "a sound legal path." The fruits of one of his first efforts at internal "bargaining" were sweet. Though anxious to avoid words that might heat up the atmosphere, Justice Frankfurter was willing to absorb Murphy's suggestions into his opinion.[74] "We do not qualify the *Thornhill* and *Carlson* decisions," he wrote for the Court. "We reaffirm them." "Peaceful picketing is the workingman's means of communication." "But utterance in a context of violence can lose its significance as an appeal to reason and become part of an instrument of force." The pattern of violence here was "precisely the kind of situation which the *Thornhill* opinion excluded from its scope."[75] No one could doubt the power of a state to protect the public peace.

Notwithstanding his libertarian image, Murphy began his Court career with that principle fully in view. While its concrete translation was still imprecise, both in his mind and in the Court's articulation of it from case to case, there can be no doubt that, as the Justices began to explore the reaches of the First Amendment, Murphy was operating on relativistic premises. While the judiciary had "no more solemn duty" than to protect freedom of utterance, he then wrote in an unpublished passage, "that guarantee, while precious, is not absolute at all times and places, and all circumstances"; while the Constitution afforded individual action wide latitude, he asserted in *Gobitis*, "in all things that are essential and appropriate for the maintenance of an orderly and healthy society and the protection of public morals, the acts of the individual are subject to the will of the group."[76] *Thornhill*, for all its subsequent reputation, had a restrictive side which the Justice thought of equal importance with the picketing doctrine. That he was not more vocal in articulating it was a function of the same factors at work in *Thornhill* now operating in reverse—his unsettled outlook as a newcomer and the interplay of principle and of personality on the Court.

The fact is, Murphy throughout his first two terms acted on a dual theory of the free speech problem. Some speech, such as "group defamation," was inherently "bad" and therefore beyond constitutional scope; all other speech depended on the context. Not only had his picketing opinions expressly exempted from their scope graduated ordinances aimed at specific evils, but his behavior in *Cantwell* and *Meadowmoor* was intended to strengthen state authority. Even when the Court dismissed *Thornhill* as irrelevant in *Cox* v. *New Hampshire*, which sustained licensing of religious parades, he joined in approving retroactive narrowing of the ordinance in order to squeeze it under the *Cantwell* rule.[77] Murphy's two main opinions in the 1941 term, in addition, were attempts to bolster public power all the more.

In *Chaplinsky* v. *New Hampshire*, an easy case involving a Jehovah's Witness who cursed a public officer, two restrictive themes of *Thornhill* dovetailed. Dismissing the claim to free worship out of hand, Murphy gave vent to some remarkable assumptions for an "absolutist." Of the free speech claim, he wrote: "Allowing the broadest scope to the language and purpose of the Fourteenth Amendment, it is well understood that the right of free speech is not absolute at all times and under all circumstances. There are certain well-defined and narrowly limited classes of speech, the prevention and punishment of which have never been thought to raise any Constitutional problem. These include the lewd and obscene, the profane, the libelous, and the insulting or "fighting" words—those which by their very utterance inflict injury or intend to incite an immediate breach of the peace. It has been well observed that such utterances are no essential part of any exposition of ideas, and are of such slight social value as a step to truth that any benefit that may be derived from them is clearly outweighed by the social interest in order and morality."[78]

Argument that these epithets fell into the class of "fighting words" was simply unnecessary. Yet what was the difference between them and the equally provocative insults used by Jehovah's Witnesses and fringe political groups which the Justice later voted to shelter? The unanimous *Chaplinsky* opinion, which was considered "well-executed" by his colleagues, has been cited frequently in support of less obvious censorship cases—and rightly so. Murphy's dismissal of certain words as inherently bad rested on the same assumptions of social value and of state control which he expressed in *Thornhill*, which have justified censors from time immemorial, and which both he and the Court, in other circumstances, later repudiated. Even though similar premises reign explicitly in the obscenity field and implicitly elsewhere, it was the early, not the late, Murphy who gave them voice.[79]

No better example of the contrast exists, for all its "pro-labor" overtones, than *NLRB* v. *Virginia Electric & Power Co.*[80] In that case, which presented the Court's first opportunity to reconcile the First Amendment and the Wagner Act, Justice Murphy was all set to advance *Thornhill's* restrictive force. To counter implications that the rights of workers and employers might differ, his draft opinion went out of its way to assert that picketing was subject to reasonable regulation or even outright prohibition as circumstances might dictate. Legislation fairly aimed at substantial public evils, he wrote—"and only so far as the necessities of the case require"—could not be nullified by the "mere circumstance" that "freedom of utterance is incidentally and indirectly curtailed." Otherwise, legislative power to protect any other social interest would be paralyzed.[81] The message was muffled, however, out of the necessity of "massing" the Court to agreement.

The *Virginia Electric* case was one of Justice Murphy's most difficult, ambiguous, and yet important opinions. In contrast to *Thornhill*, no consensus existed beyond the general proposition, which he freely expressed, that "language which merges with conduct does not necessarily place that conduct beyond legislative reach." Even a clear disagreement as to the facts, which characterized *Meadowmoor*, failed to emerge. Enmeshed with the free speech question raised by the company's bulletins to its employees were other issues regarding the agency's findings of company discrimination as well as its authority to order back wages and the disablement of a company-dominated union. All these issues fragmented the Court into several directions. Older Justices, such as Stone, who viewed the facts as close, stumbled on the question of company domination even before reaching the free speech problem. Justice Byrnes, who manifested the typical discomforts of a rookie out of step, was admittedly off-tangent on the wage issue. And a sharp division developed between Frankfurter and the rest of Murphy's majority, Black, Reed, and Douglas, regarding the Board's finding that the company bulletins constituted an unfair labor practice "on their face."[82] The multiplicity of issues meant that Murphy's task, in contrast to earlier opinions, was not merely to express a consensus, but to find one—to assemble a majority and keep it intact. The price was sacrifice of his own views.

To Murphy the problem of reconciling the *Thornhill* doctrine and the Wagner Act was not inherently difficult. Distinguishing *Thornhill* as a condemnation of blanket prohibitions on speech, he treated the *Virginia Electric* problem as simply another example of the exclusionary theme of *Thornhill* and *Cantwell*. And leaning heavily on Judge Learned Hand's analysis of the free speech issue in the *Federbush* case, he wrote a lengthy opinion in support of the Board's judgment, which Chief Justice Stone and Justice Frankfurter rightly criticized for resembling fact-finding rather than judicial review.[83]

The sticking point was the fact that the NLRB had found the company bulletins advocating company unionism to be coercive "on their face." Frankfurter, in a series of incisive memoranda, objected strenuously to basing the Board order on utterance alone. Failure to make a specific finding that the utterance was related to other evidence of coercion, he maintained, meant that an employer lost his right to speak about unionism merely because of his status as an employer. If speech unrelated to conduct were to be considered, then the same clear and present danger standards of *Thornhill* would have to apply. Justices Black and Douglas, with whom Murphy originally agreed, believed no less vigorously that the Board order was based on the totality of the company's conduct. "This will have to be handled deftly," Murphy commented to his clerk, after Frankfurter and Black responded to his request for elaboration of their views. "It is doubtful that they can be reconciled."[84] While Frankfurter's memoranda appeared to lay the basis of a forceful dissent, the Black-Douglas position created difficult issues of administrative review. As Murphy indicated to Justice Black, paraphrasing a memo by his clerk: "F.F. is right in saying that the Board did single out the bulletin and the speeches as violations of the Act in and of themselves. You will note that I admit this but attempted to duck the issue (which I don't like) by saying that it was part of a complex, adopting a somewhat unrealistic approach."[85] His opinion, in other words, considered what the Board omitted. Since several Justices rejected that procedure, and since the Court could hardly deny the Board's heavy reliance on the bulletins, Murphy was caught in a squeeze. The only alternatives were to stick to his guns that the bulletins alone coerced, thus pushing Hand's theory to the limit and risking the disintegration of Murphy's majority, or to duck the issue in still another way suggested by Frankfurter and agreeable to Stone and Byrnes—remanding the case for the Board's reasoned judgment whether, in context, the bulletins actually coerced.[86]

Seeking "to win as many of the Court as possible," Murphy chose the remand. That choice at least made it possible for a united Court to set the general contours of permissible employer speech, which was accomplished by borrowing language from both sides. In a word, utterance which merged with conduct could be considered as evidence of unfair labor practice, but utterance in isolation could not. Speech, to be restrained, required consideration in "the surrounding circumstances."[87]

But the price of articulating a vague general principle was heavy. What began as a major personal opportunity to resolve controversial issues of public policy ended in a substantial capitulation to the views of Frankfurter and retreat into obscurity. To assemble a majority favoring remand Murphy had to scuttle two-thirds of his own opinion dealing with the rest of the Board's judgment; and to justify that remand, he had to obscure what he himself had considered clear from the start. Remand was necessary, he explained for the Court, because the record left uncertain whether the Board had considered the bulletins in context or in isolation. That may have been true for the Court as a whole, but internal criticism was inescapable that the result seemed "incoherent and fumbling."[88] The Justices were altering the question into a hypothetical one they had not been asked; were they also inviting a different conclusion by the Board?

The *Thornhill* opinion lacked coherence because of Justice Murphy's own imprecision. In *Virginia Electric* the Court itself created ambivalence, where none existed before, for the sake of half a loaf. For Murphy the case was a sobering lesson of the cost of achieving cohesion. "If you can get the Court together on this," Byrnes observed even so, "you will render a real service."[89] The Supreme Court was beginning to divide unexpectedly and sharply over the scope of both the First Amendment and appellate review. The *Virginia Electric* case became an important germ in the development of labor law precisely because the Justices were willing to compromise. In the last analysis little of principle divided them; little was lost and much was gained by accepting the requirement of a reasoned judgment on the part of the NLRB. As Murphy's clerk commented when the case returned in 1943: "We did the Board a service by making it think."[90]

Together, *Meadowmoor* and *Virginia Electric* went a long way toward resolving the doubts created by the *Thornhill* decision. As applied, they contained a principle that worked both ways. The NLRB used it to restrain employer speech in contexts of coercion, which was easily established in the parent case; but the principle also upset a long line of decisions which assumed that employers had no permissible interest in employee self-organization issues. Its reasoning permitted lower courts to sustain employer speech qua speech and was eventually frozen into the Taft-Hartley Act to give a broad statutory guarantee to the employer's right to communicate. Curiously, Murphy's somewhat ambiguous *Virginia Electric* opinion, perhaps for the very reason that it did not proclaim the employer's right to speak with dramatic fervor, may have longer life as a precedent in the development of statutory and case law controlling labor relations than the sweep of the *Thornhill* doctrine where he started with the Constitution—and from scratch.[91]

After 1941 the Supreme Court's picketing doctrine underwent steady attrition. Because of factual disagreements it had been possible thus far for both sides to consider themselves the defenders of the *Thornhill* rule. But the stranger-picketing cases left little doubt that the Court, as a result of new perspectives and of new personnel, was in fundamental retreat. Not only did earlier pronouncements have to yield, as Frankfurter declared, "to the impact of facts unforeseen; or at least not sufficiently appreciated"; but the leadership of the minority which defended *Thornhill* passed to Justices Reed and Black.[92] The *Wohl* cases of 1942-43, while giving lip service to the doctrine, set the trend when Justice Jackson asserted that a state was not required "to tolerate in all places and all circumstances even peaceful picketing by an individual."[93] Then in *Carpenters Union* v. *Ritter's Cafe*, a narrowly divided Court confined free stranger-picketing to the same industry in which a dispute arose. Not to insist on some economic connection between pickets and picketed, Frankfurter maintained for the majority, when "other traditional modes of communication" were available to the workers and when their only object was "to conscript neutrals," would leave states without power to regulate picketing and would erect constitutional liberties into "doctrinaire dogma."[94]

This argument, to the minority, overstated the case. No one had ever denied state authority to regulate picketing with a discriminating eye. The issue was whether the Court still adhered to the *Thornhill* and *Swing* philosophy that public dangers in picketing should be balanced by the social interest in information or had substituted other criteria to expand state power. The criterion of economic interdependence not only contradicted the premise that workingmen were not to be restricted to traditional modes of communication, but, as Justice Reed asserted in a vigorous dissent, it seriously limited a doctrine originally advanced as a "limitation on State power to do as it pleased with labor disputes. . . ." The results, he predicted, could only be added uncertainty and a weakening of the very federal right of stranger-picketing which Justice Frankfurter himself had pronounced in *AFL* v. *Swing*.[95]

The consequences conformed to Reed's forecast. State judges soon resurrected "lawful purpose" to restrict stranger-picketing, and Congress made additional limits in the Taft-Hartley Act. In the *Giboney* case of 1949 the Supreme Court itself established another exception when it held in a unanimous opinion by Justice Black that a state may enjoin pickets attempting to force an employer to violate an antitrust statute.[96] Logically there was no difference between that situation and *Virginia Electric*, but it was plain that the Court's dominant mood was to permit states wider latitude in developing the ground rules of industrial combat. The denouement came in *International Brotherhood of Teamsters* v. *Hanke*, decided shortly after the deaths of Justices Murphy and Rutledge, which sustained an injunction against picketing of a self-employed business with Frankfurter's comment that "while picketing has an ingredient of communication it cannot dogmatically be equated with the constitutionally protected freedom of speech."[97] After that, the retreat became a rout. In the *Vogt* case of 1957 the Justices even upheld the prohibition of stranger-picketing altogether. The Court, as Douglas complained, had swung "full circle" to the dissents of Justices Roberts and Hughes in *AFL* v. *Swing*.[98]

The *Thornhill* doctrine underwent drastic surgery as a result of the stranger-picketing retreat. Today most of its analytical tools—judging on its face, the public information premise, and the clear and present danger test—have been shorn of strength in labor relations at the same time that labor picketing has passed under virtually complete congressional control. What had been the judiciary's main innovation in the development of a national labor policy has given way to the view that legislatures and state judges are primarily responsible for setting the rules of industrial combat. About all that remains of the Court's original handiwork is the prohibition against indiscriminate restrictions on peaceful picketing, a regulation against over-broadness which could have been made without the bold abstractions of the parent case. That residuum is of no small significance in view of the continuing opposition to labor's basic right and of the resort to picketing as a means of racial protest. It is ironic that just when *Thornhill* appeared to have atrophied, the Warren Court gave it new life as a tool against overly broad restrictions on nonlabor picketing and as a method of nullifying various restrictions of free speech on their face.[99] The subsidiary seeds of *Thornhill* thus have outlived the parent plant. For labor policy, the case stands only "as a monument to the Supreme Court's good intentions."[100] For civil liberties generally, however, it remains a potent weapon to protect transcendent social, as well as individual, interests in free expression. And it is not without interest that, in a so-called conservative swing, the most impassioned opponent of the offshoot is Hugo L. Black—one of the same Justices who had raised doubts about intrusions on local policy in 1940![101]

IV

Ultimately, whether the Court's intervention in picketing problems was a blessing or a curse depends on debatable value judgments concerning social policy and who should make it. While a discriminating association of picketing with speech still attracts defenders, the erosion and rebirth of the *Thornhill* doctrine was not untypical of the competing principles which the Court advanced to protect First Amendment freedoms in the 1940s. The Court of that day was at the threshold of a great debate over personal liberty which is not yet resolved. More than the *Thornhill* rule—the full *Carolene* rationale, for instance, or the clear and present danger test—has since fallen from favor. One of the ironies of the decade was simultaneous adjudication of First Amendment claims by use of inconsistent doctrines. Time was required for the Court's internal dialogue to harden, and what was true for the institution as a whole was also true for individual Justices. The Murphy of the first two terms was not the passionate defender of civil liberty of the postwar years, nor was he a judge, as so often pictured by his critics, who looked upon the judicial process as a simple projection of singular values. Justice Murphy, like the Court as a whole, was torn by the conflicts before him; and two final examples from the 1940-41 terms indicate that the result was frequently immobilism.

In *Hines* v. *Davidowitz,* which preempted the field of alien registration from state control, Murphy originally voted with the majority in favor of preemption. But under the badgering of his clerk that this conclusion conflicted with the Court's stand in commerce cases, the Justice began to waver toward Justice Stone's position that no conflict existed.[102] Murphy even began to prepare a dissent until he was persuaded that to do more than join Stone's dissent would be impolitic. Then, after having criticized Black's "tendency to spread into the field of policy," he ended where he had started—and convinced that Black's opinion was "exceptionally well done."[103]

A change of mind in *Hines* would not have altered the result, but similar wavering became critical in the *Bridges* and *Times-Mirror* contempt cases, the leading modern cases concerning press interference with fair trial. Two rights, both ardently believed in, there collided; and there Justice Murphy became an agonizing "swing-man." Voting in the fall of 1940 to quash the contempt citation against the *Times-Mirror,* as his clerk recommended for both cases, Murphy at the same time voted to approve Harry Bridges' contempt citation under the admitted influence of Frankfurter's "beautiful statement" in conference defending judicial power to protect fairness of trial. Toward spring, however, when the opinions were nearing completion, the Justice began to share his clerk's doubts whether the trial judge even had been aware of Bridges' threats, much less whether they presented a clear and present danger to the trial. Was the Court forgetting the facts?[104]

Justice Frankfurter, of course, believed the record was barren of such facts and that no liberty was of greater value than that of fair trial. Murphy had no quarrel with the proposition, but he was dubious about its concrete application in a factual setting he regarded as very close. Fine principle, he quipped, wrong case. Fully aware that to retrieve his vote would stalemate the Court after months of labor and would leave it with no alternative but to order reargument, he finally wrote Justice Frankfurter: "The still-new robe never hangs heavier than when my conscience confronts me. Months of reflection and study compel me to give it voice. And so I have advised the Chief Justice and Justice Black that my vote . . . must be in reversal."[105]

So to reverse had deep implications. Reargument in the fall of 1941, plus Justice Jackson's fresh vote, produced the opposite result. Reversal gave Justice Black an opportunity to write a leading opinion which, first, significantly reduced the power of state judges to control the press and, second, significantly advanced the clear and present danger test as a "working principle" to reconcile competing claims of liberty and authority. The Justices did not say in so many words that freedom of expression was "preferred" over other interests, but the momentum was plain. Finally, the *Bridges* case, along with Murphy's first dissent against limiting the discretion of the NLRB in the *Phelps Dodge* case, marked the beginning of a drift in which Justice Murphy, much to his own surprise, found himself veering from the leadership of Felix Frankfurter, whom he had assumed would be his spiritual and intellectual knight, to that of Hugo L. Black.[106]

The picketing doctrine and the *Bridges* case inevitably became exhibits in recurring disputes over the role of the Court in protecting First Amendment freedoms. Their symbolic and doctrinal importance, however, have tended to obscure both the frequently narrow factual divisions involved and a pertinent element of the Murphy story. The truth is that Justice Murphy's views underwent evolution on the Supreme Court, and the starting point of that evolution was surprisingly hesitant and nondoctrinaire. Murphy might admit, as he did to Chief Justice Stone in the *Bridges* case, that "conscience and judgment are inseparable, and the former allows the latter no alternative."[107] He might leave unrebuked his clerk's observation in *Hines* that judicial opinions in close cases perforce rationalize policy choices. But the very instability of his choices as a newcomer, the almost over-willingness to be persuaded, play havoc with customary explanations of his behavior, whether expressed by ideological identification or by quantitative inference from votes.[108] Justice Murphy as a beginner was not an activist automaton; he was a man of indecision—a man so cross-pressured by the complexities of choice, as aggravated by his own relation to it, that he found it difficult to make up his mind.

The ideological attrition of his freshman years was unusual only in its intensity. A "freshman effect" has moderated the positions of new Justices through history. Newness on the bench therefore looms as one of several intervening variables which qualify the force of personal belief systems in the judicial process.[109] Once he reached a conclusion, moreover, Murphy, like any trained advocate or evangelist, defended his position vigorously. But just as he hesitated before joining the Court, so he equivocated before exercising its awesome power. Several more terms were required before ideological values overcame self-doubt. Several more terms were required before he evolved a distinctive personal style. Both developments, not accidentally, awaited acute constitutional problems concerning religious liberty and war.

CHAPTER 11

FREEDOM TO ITS FARTHEST

REACHES, 1941-1943

THE assimilation of Justice Murphy into the Supreme Court was intimately related to the development of a great dialogue over civil liberty and American entry into World War II. No sooner had Murphy begun to settle into the job than a combination of circumstances altered his working environment and elevated personal freedoms to a dominant place in judicial concerns. By late 1941 the Roosevelt Court was entering the final stage of its transformation. Chief Justice Hughes, the towering figure whose defense of the Court in the clutches of 1937 had beaten Roosevelt at his own game, and Justice McReynolds, the last remaining member of the property-minded "Four Horsemen," both resigned for reasons of advanced age. In their places the President appointed James F. Byrnes and Robert H. Jackson as Associate Justices and promoted Harlan F. Stone to Chief. Of the embattled Court of 1937, only Stone and Roberts remained, the one strategically poised to preside over the withdrawal of the federal judiciary as a censor of economic regulation and the other, even while adjusting to the change, a somewhat lonely reminder of the chasm between Victorian liberalism and the new. Problems of public policy hardly imaginable as judicial issues a few years before, moreover, greeted the re-constituted Court as a result of radical extensions in government functions, the Justices' own expanded supervision of civil liberties, and the outbreak of war. The convergence of shifting personnel and issues strikingly illustrated the little observed phenomenon that the high court, though a symbol of stability for the better part of American history, has always been both subject and vehicle of continuous change.

"And so the hour came that I have been worrying about for a long time and hoped would never come so long as I remained on this Court," Justice Murphy recorded for history in June 1941, as Hughes, with tears in his eyes, announced his resignation at the term's closing conference. "All during the session, suspecting he was going to do it," Murphy noted, "I was very unhappy."[1] The junior Justice, while he and the outgoing Chief were never personally close, had reason for concern. For one thing, a Chief Justice's mode of operation is highly personal; Hughes's resignation meant a shake-up just as Murphy was beginning to adapt. In addition, the junior Justice shared the legal fraternity's awe of Hughes, whose bearded countenance resembled an artist's conception of Moses, and whose dominance of the Court no lawyer could help admire. It was more than rhetoric when, on joining Justices Frankfurter and Roberts in a radio tribute to Hughes, Murphy lamented his retirement as the passing of a giant. Regardless of their differences respecting economic policy and a burgeoning bureaucracy, which Murphy blessed as a necessary evil and Hughes as simply evil, the two men shared certain basic premises regarding the judicial function.[a] "Justice," for both, was the Court's fundamental cause, and, as *Thornhill* had shown, when "justice" was cast in the form of free speech claims, both men were willing to contemplate a policy of judicial boldness.[2]

By contrast, the new Chief Justice, though himself a champion of preference for First Amendment rights, advocated a more discriminating and circumspect philosophy. The essence of the judge's calling, to Stone, was accommodation—accommodation not merely of colliding social interests, nor of competing legal and ethical values, but of the Court's own functions and limitations in a pluralist political universe. The very fact that judging entailed choice, to Stone, meant that judicial power should be exercised with forbearance and restraint befitting a democratic order. However similar their private economic and social outlooks, undertones of rivalry also had marked the relations between Hughes and Stone since the latter bitterly attacked the judicial blockade of New Deal legislation in the mid-1930s. Stone's belief in broad popular power to govern and his mistrust of mechanical formulas of jurisprudence had often made him a supporter of New Deal policy in spite of himself, an irony Hughes enjoyed when he remarked after one conference vote: "You on [the] side of angels and there are more angels on this Court than there used to be!"[3] Because Stone had resented the byproducts of Hughes's tight reins over the Court—the slender time allowed for reflection and for discussion in conference, as well as the artificial agreements that were the price of compromise on a deeply divided bench—the new Chief could be expected to permit fuller and freer discourse in conference and to engage more actively as one among peers in debate. A more individualistic, and more discursive, Court was in the offing.[4/b]

---

[a] The NLRB apparently disturbed Hughes the most. Following his denunciation of the "highly technical and oppressive" behavior of the Labor Board during conference discussion of *Pittsburgh Plate Glass Co.* v. *NLRB*, Murphy noted: "I have not heard the Chief speak with greater feeling." Conference note, Nos. 521-23, Box 130. 313 U.S. 146 (1941).

[b] Murphy's notes reinforce the general impression that Chief Justice Hughes dominated conferences. That internal dialogue suffered was graphically illustrated by Mur-

Stone's appointment affected Murphy in still more personal ways. A Chief Justice and senior Associate Justices, because of their influence over assignments, play no minor part in the developing reputations of their colleagues. Advances in Murphy's seniority did not necessarily mean improved assignments from Chief Justice Stone. The New Deal crusader and the former Columbia Law School dean were poles apart in personality, philosophy, and method. If anything, Murphy's relations with Owen J. Roberts, the next senior Justice, were worse. Although Murphy followed Stone's leadership in the tax immunities and commerce fields, two of the most important areas of economic policy left in contention; and though he would be the only Justice to escape a Stone dissent in the latter's first year as Chief Justice, Stone regarded his younger colleague as a "weak sister."[5] Apart from frequent substantive disagreements, which few men find easy to explain without reference to the adversary's motivation or competence, Stone disapproved of Murphy's heavy reliance on law clerks and his rhetorical style. Stone struggled to be fair in assignments, but found it difficult to assign Murphy leading opinions—and frequently assumed a teacher's role even in those assigned.

"I have been resuming some of my law-teaching experience but with students not as receptive as some that I have known," the Chief Justice complained of the Roosevelt Justices generally.[6] Although Murphy greatly respected Stone's ability, the Chief was especially critical of him. "The English in this opinion is very bad in spots," he might say. "It ought to be thoroughly canvassed with that in mind."[7] Stone made constant appeals for the younger Justice to restrain his language. Even when Murphy's errors, such as incorrectly drafting orders to lower courts, repeated Stone's own past mistakes, the older Justice revealed his burdens in occasional bouts of impatience. "The job of the Court is to resolve doubts, not create them," he once observed of a Murphy opinion. Sensing the Chief Justice's low opinion of his talents, even while commending his appointment as well-deserved and as a reflection of Roosevelt's political genius, Murphy always labored self-consciously under Stone's critical eye.[8] Just as Stone himself had chafed under thin assignments from Chief Justice Taft, so Murphy and Wiley Rutledge, who joined the Court in 1943, were to feel slighted under Stone. Murphy knew that relations with the new Chief Justice, while always formally correct, would be distant and delicate.

phy's conference notes in *United States* v. *Darby*: "C. J. This is the most important case we have had by far in connection with the commerce power . . . (McReynolds is sound asleep mouth open—and Stone snores [or stares] away)." No. 82, Box 130.

The Court's other members offered scarcely greater empathy. Justice Byrnes, while friendly and talented, already had revealed relatively conservative colors during the Senate's sit-down debates and, in any event, would not remain in the fold for long. Justice Reed, while frequently in agreement on labor questions and especially helpful to Murphy concerning the intricacies of statutory construction and procedure, was too cautious a craftsman and courtly of manner for close alliance with anyone, let alone the flamboyant Irish reformer. Justice Jackson's hostility was well known. To make matters worse, the initial honeymoon with Justice Frankfurter, who more than any other influenced Murphy during his initial transition, was beginning to cool as a result of disagreements, some of which, as one clerk recalled of the *Phelps Dodge* dispute in 1941, set Murphy's eyes "sparkling with true Irish deviltry."[9]

The change in the Frankfurter-Murphy relationship alone was a fascinating litmus of a Court in transition. On the surface, the two Justices had much in common. Both were liberals and sensitive to minority status. Both were passionately devoted to idealized versions of the American dream. And no matter how heated their disputes, they managed to sustain a uniquely personal, almost love-hate understanding filled with frank discourse and frequent jokes about their personal idiosyncrasies and ethnic origins. Justice Murphy enjoyed Frankfurter's wit and acknowledged his superior intellect. Yet he felt defensive beside them. The agnostic Justice Frankfurter expressed respect for Murphy's religiosity and, when it furthered his cause, encouraged Murphy's evangelist impulses. "F. F. says I am 'too noble. No man is that good,'" Murphy reported during the *Williams* divorce tangle.[10] For all his professed disinterest in "angling for votes," Frankfurter time and again appealed directly to Murphy's conscience—a target seldom chosen in the others. Yet Frankfurter was an excitable and scrappy intellectual who had ill-concealed contempt for the Irishman's intellect and night life (though the Justice himself was probably more tolerant of both than were his disciples). Once Murphy began to assert his independence, he felt the sting of Frankfurter's trait in battle which one Harvard Law School dean described as making plainer than necessary that those who disagreed "were either stupid or venial."[11] Patience for an Irish ex-politician's moral posturings, or for his insistence that they concentrate on "the meat of the coconut," was too much to expect from an urbane sophisticate whose tiny body encased one of the century's most vibrant personalities and agile legal minds. "Us girls call him Murph," Justice Frankfurter was once heard to repeat one of the many tales that circulated of Justice Murphy's friendships along the chorus lines. For the scholar on the high bench, whose concerns were the absorbing interest of his life, that summed up fairly well the warmhearted but limited Murphy.

Justice Murphy in turn came to regard Justice Frankfurter's professorial habits as tiresome and tangential. The former law professor's campaigns for "self-restraint" and "law as the embodiment of reason," he found hard not to dismiss as masks for the same use of personal convictions that Frankfurter so readily condemned in others. While Frankfurter often accused Murphy of confusing his functions with those of a priest, Murphy twitted Frankfurter for confounding his with a professor's. And Frankfurter, he thought, was "bogged down by 'the confusion of his learning.'" While Frankfurter appeared to be offended by Murphy's rejection of his leadership, Murphy had difficulty tolerating what for Frankfurter was a commandment of collegial office and "one form of fun"—"intellectual ping-pong—discussing differences"—and their relentless exposure in a quest for reasoned decision. Felix Frankfurter thrived on argumentation.[12] Few Justices in history were better at it or quicker to change partners without rancor. But his sharpness in intellectual exchange, and his occasional resorts to flattery and sarcasm as if the recipient were unable to perceive either, pricked Murphy's abundant pride. Long after his early fascination with "F. F." was over, Murphy might readily dismiss Frankfurter's scholarly output as "elegant bunk." But not many battles were required before their differences became tinged with bitterness. Justice Frankfurter's switch from dissent to concurrence in a 1943 FELA case brought forth Murphy's irritated comment: "which means we are right but he has no taste for our pastry and that's mutual."[13] During an early war power debate in which Frankfurter made a passionate appeal for unanimous support of executive discretion as a patriotic duty, Murphy queried his clerk triumphantly from the sidelines: "Now do you believe me?"[14] And it was Frankfurter who provoked Murphy's half-jesting, yet incisive confession that he "really did not care much for Jews—until somebody jumps on them." However hopeful at the start, liaison between the Court's two minority members, whose differences recalled the contrast that Jefferson drew between the judgment of professors and plowmen, was inevitably shortlived.

By 1942 philosophic and personal ties with Justices Black and Douglas were beginning to fill the void. Murphy's relations with Black, who ranked second in seniority, were of particular significance, both for his rising self-confidence and for his improving caseload. Nearly every major assignment Murphy received during Stone's chief justiceship was dependent on Justice Black, who as the years passed regarded Murphy with brotherly warmth. Moreover, as the major battles of the decade began to take shape, the so-called liberal trio of Black, Douglas, and Murphy showed a close affinity of view that hardly would have been predicted in 1939. Sharing the Populist premises of the former Alabama Senator, Murphy vigorously supported Black's crusade to reduce judicial control of legislative reasonableness in the economic sector as well as his campaign, which began in *Betts* v. *Brady* in 1942, to extend the federal Bill of Rights to the states by wholesale "incorporation" into the Fourteenth Amendment.[15]

Contrary to popular thought, however, it was inaccurate to equate ideological affinity with formation of a judicial "bloc." Too many variables were at work within the judicial process to treat results as cause. Too much disagreement existed among the trio even within the areas of converging beliefs to assume that attitude and behavior were equivalents. Justice Murphy had not yet probed his own philosophy sufficiently to accept Black's unorthodoxies regarding the commerce clause and due process without qualification. Nor was he yet eager to assert his own. Troubled more by feelings of personal inadequacy than by the vagueness of natural justice or by the dangers of judicial supremacy, Murphy in the early 1940s was somewhat caught in the middle of the growing doctrinal struggle between Justices Frankfurter and Black. Just as he ran afoul of Justice Frankfurter's analytical brilliance and limited concepts of judicial power, so he felt constrained by constantly having to be on guard against using the traditional shorthand adjectives of the craft (for example, "unreasonable") which Black disapproved because of their proven potential for enlarging judicial discretion. Later Murphy might take impish delight at sneaking the offensive words past Black's watchful eye—which was seldom—but in the early 1940s he usually felt obliged to warn his clerk against the habit.[e] To indulge such concepts at that time was to open a Pandora's box, not only of protesting New Dealers but also of natural law Justices who thought it their job to discover reasonable legal norms. After all, if the Constitution itself forbade "unreasonable" standards, as Jus-

[e] During preparation of one opinion, for example, he told his clerk that the expression " 'we think it clearly reasonable' might get us in trouble," after which the clerk noted: "It did." FM to clerk, undated, No. 601, Box 130. *Magruder* v. *Washington, Baltimore and Annapolis Realty Co.*, 316 U.S. 69 (1942). For similar reasons, Chief Justice Hughes had deleted the adjective "reasonable," which he had used "out of abundant caution," in *Cox* v. *New Hampshire*, 312 U.S. 569 (1941). Memo, Hughes to FM, March 28, 1941, No. 502, Box 130.

tice Frankfurter was wont to say of criminal procedure, the legal system presupposed the existence of "reasonable" ones.[16]

Because of personnel changes, Justice Murphy could no longer be considered a freshman Justice by 1942. But just as he always had been a cautious soloist in politics, so he remained a "loner" on the Court, a man who hugged the center, dissented sparingly, and continued to manifest growing pains as a jurist. Murphy was still groping for his place on a Court itself "in search of a role."

II

War, even more than shifting personnel and hardening issues, was responsible for the continuation of Murphy's professional uncertainties and their ultimate resolution. Since the sit-down strikes, the notion that democracy was in a deadly contest with totalitarian isms had imbued his thinking.[17] How, during an era of crisis, could a free people compete against the assumed efficiency of totalitarianism without destroying the very freedoms they were fighting to preserve? As Attorney General, Murphy had attempted to chart a course through the dilemma; but after Pearl Harbor the guidelines he had set—the *Milligan* principle, the clear and present danger test, and "responsible" administration—struck most contemporaries as hopelessly impractical restrictions on emergency authority, which even he had refused to circumscribe in advance. If Charles Evans Hughes's dictum was correct, that war power is "the power to wage war successfully," the only test of its limits was necessity.[18] And who was the judge of that? "When it comes to a decision by the head of the State upon a matter involving its life," Justice Holmes once remarked of a domestic insurrection, "the ordinary rights of individuals must yield to what he deems the necessities of the moment. Public danger warrants the substitution of executive process for judicial process."[19]

Hopefully, there would be no such choice. But as the nation braced itself before the sweep of Axis conquest, as Americans adjusted themselves to government-imposed discipline as never before, there was obvious realism in Justice Murphy's observation that "we shall need vigorous and devoted public servants to safeguard our liberties."[20] The behavior of Supreme Court Justices did little to inspire confidence that judges were immune from loving liberty most "when it is under pressure least."[21] The emphasis on loyalty and national security in the first Flag Salute decision struck a discordant note that rang of war hysteria. Despite Chief Justice Stone's resistance, members of the Court also became increasingly involved in extrajudicial chores. Both Justices Roberts and Murphy spoke openly on foreign policy issues even before the outbreak of hostilities. When war came, Roberts headed the official investigation of the Pearl Harbor disaster; Justice Byrnes resigned to command the mobilization effort; and the somewhat restless energies of young New Dealers on the Court were put to extensive advisory use by their "gallant leader," FDR.

Justice Murphy was afflicted with so strong a case of war fever that he not only became the Court's most active propagandist but yearned for more active service throughout the conflict. His first reaction, in fact, was to contemplate entering the army. Within a week after Pearl Harbor, he wrote a letter offering his off-hour services to the Army Reserve, then decided not to send it. Afterwards he remarked to a friend: "No doubt like me you are asking to get back in uniform. A soldier is trained for action and for him action never ceases. In a sense we have never put our uniforms away."[22]

More was involved than a romantic gesture. Though he preferred an executive post and decided against resigning in midterm, the Justice wanted action. As summer recess approached he again took the problem of how to be of service to the President. "Nothing could distress me more than idleness while so many sacrifices are being made and the country is in its present grave position," he told Roosevelt.[23] In April 1942 they resumed discussions about possible errands for Murphy to the Philippines or to Ireland. Whether his resignation would have been necessary, it is difficult to say. Other than advisory and morale-boosting missions, the character of their plans is elusive. Murphy at the time was eagerly advocating organization of Filipino guerrillas and creation of an allied defense council to centralize political direction in the Far East. "As I see it," he told Roosevelt, "some of our setbacks in the political phase of the war need not have occurred had there been a vigorous and tenacious effort by the United Nations to hold the political lines."[24] Although the President throughout the war was cool to political direction of military decision in the field—"there are some advantages in the idea, but also a lot of headaches," he replied—administration leaders were anxious about Filipino loyalties in face of Japanese appeals to Asian nationalism. Roosevelt also was attempting to woo Ireland away from its policy of neutrality.[25] The delicacy of relations with Dublin and the military reversals in the Far East, coupled as they were with doubts about Murphy's relations with General MacArthur, soon undermined the prospect of special errands for the Justice. The war was becoming too implacable for one-shot trouble-shooters.

After reassuring the President that he would be available for either mission, or both, "at a moment's notice," Murphy indicated that, as an alternative, he desired to undertake military training.[26] He had already made overtures to army chief of staff, General George C. Marshall, outlining his World War I experience and requesting service with his old unit, the Fourth Infantry Division.

While I can claim no military proficiency [he wrote] I cannot help but feel that today there is no work more important for me than that of a soldier. Accordingly, I would like to return to military service, if the Army deems me qualified.

It is my thought, however, that it would serve no good purpose for me to leave my present duties unless I could be assigned to active duty with the Infantry and see action at the front. I wish, therefore, to advise you frankly that if such assignment is not possible I would be reluctant to interrupt or leave my work on the Court. . . .

It would seem to be in the interest of the service, however, that the rank be low. I desire no rank for which I am unprepared and which I do not deserve.[27]

Gently, but firmly, the general informed the Justice that he was too old for active military service.[28] Expressing keen disappointment and willingness "to take my place in the ranks again," Murphy then requested, "if it could be properly arranged—without creating difficulties or problems for the Army—" military training during the summer recess.[29] Marshall complied by inviting him to undergo training as a lieutenant colonel in the infantry reserve. Because an act of Congress prohibited federal employees except inactive reservists from holding dual offices, it was necessary for the Justice to be on inactive status, which precluded his exercising command. Without fanfare—or notice to the Chief Justice—Murphy jumped at the offer. To the surprise of most and the chagrin of some, when the Court adjourned in June he exchanged his robe for a uniform, saying, it was reported, "I have a date in Manila," as he took the oath.[30]

His action shattered judicial tradition. For the first time in recent memory, a Supreme Court Justice had accepted an additional federal position unconnected with problems of law or with those infrequent public inquiries so delicate as to tempt presidents to lean on judicial prestige. It was a period "when traditions are being broken everywhere," Murphy explained; with unforetold dangers ahead, "I wanted to be prepared for anything."[31]

"I am thrilled at your decision," the President responded; "I wish I were there with you." To many it was "a fine thing" and a "real inspiration" for a Supreme Court Justice to make such a display of patriotism. "Is this a comedown?" asked the *New York Times*. "Not in this democracy. Frank Murphy wanted to do some direct thing to help win the war. He chose the way open to him. He does not lose in stature or prestige by submitting himself to a hard discipline."[32]

The Justice, who insisted on living in regular quarters rather than receiving VIP treatment in officers clubs, was earnest about military training. Throughout the summer the press pictured a 52-year-old judge zestfully driving tanks and shooting machine guns on maneuvers, sweating in bivouac, reading certiorari petitions in his barracks, and issuing rousing declarations calculated to inspire confidence in a fighting machine which to date had suffered nothing but defeat. "The Army is all right," he proclaimed. "I know." "It is not with racial conceit that I say . . . ours is the greatest Army under the sun." The trouble with the war effort was "national complacency." The people had not awakened to "the gravity of our position."[33/d]

The war stimulated a certain chauvinist streak in Murphy. It also sparked an irrepressible urge to preach. At the same time that he urged Roosevelt to involve the American Legion in counterespionage and public morale activity, he indulged his thirst for public attention by ringing the war alarm. To shake the people from what he considered their "deadly lethargy," he made speeches at bond rallies and bar meetings as well as shortwave broadcasts to Filipinos and American troops. "No ordinary issue" could persuade a judge so to depart from the tradition of aloofness from political affairs, he said, but "our civilization is threatened with death." At a time "when the normal prob-

[d] Murphy, as elsewhere, made notes of his army experiences, which form an interesting journal of training methods and political moods during the early months of the war. For example, during June maneuvers in the Carolinas, he wrote: "Last night, black-faced, in the Jungle with the commandoes from 10:30 p.m. until 6:30 this morning. Marvelously trained men. . . . All armed with knives, hand grenades, and tommy guns. All of us blackfaced and in blue denim which protected us from briar brush barbed wire and the slide down various hills in the dark. We did stream wide over, hip high. Crawled through several ditches and along several little streams. Good thing for me it was dark. Snakes thrive in this but as long as I couldn't see them O.K."

Disappointed with his training at Fort Knox, largely because so much was made of his presence there, Murphy enjoyed most the sessions involving geopolitics, strategy, and inter-allied political problems. Following one chance meeting with Senator Henry Cabot Lodge, who had just returned from North Africa, he observed: "Why don't Republicans unite around him instead of Willkie & Dewey. He is really timber." Army notes, Box 104. By 1944, Murphy thought the GOP could not fail to win the White House by nominating General MacArthur, "a dream of a candidate." "Wealth, however," he said, "seems to convince Republicans that they have a monopoly on stupidity. Too much power has done the same to some Democrats I know." FM to John J. Adams, Jan. 25, 1944, Box 111.

lems of our day seem banal," every voice was needed to elicit from the population the material sacrifices, the Puritan courage, the outpouring of "untold riches of the human spirit," which were necessary "to win this war or any war." When the alternatives were "win or perish," a "new and fiery zeal" had to envelop the land.[34]

In tenor, the Justice sounded as if he had developed "a new and fiery zeal" himself. Damning the "blood money" of war profits, and the governmental debility resulting from "the spoils system, gangster politics and putrid politicians," he spared no group from his wrath.[35] Agitated by reports of strikes and jurisdictional conflicts in Michigan factories, he recommended a wartime labor conference to the President, gave public interviews on the subject, and stopped by Detroit to give labor executives a piece of advice: "Labor is not now fighting for its God-given right to collective bargaining. It is fighting for its right to exist. . . . The crisis we face is the darkest since the black days of the American Revolution." Curtailed production in total war amounted to cold-blooded murder of American troops, and Murphy minced no words in the equation. The plain fact, to him, was that unless the people rolled up their sleeves, the country could be "defeated, destroyed by indecision, [by] lack of unity."[36]

None of it sounded like a jurist. Heroic rhetoric combined with physical involvement in a younger generation's war compounded public bewilderment about the enigmatic Justice. Ordinarily Murphy spoke seldom in public. He also had a longstanding aversion to bar meetings and judicial conclaves, and made it a policy to avoid public speeches that might touch upon civil liberties or other matters before the Court. Unlike more professionally oriented colleagues, he even avoided informal discussion of legal problems with lower court judges and intimates. Hence, his evangelical war speeches were all the more exceptional. A listener could easily have inferred that the administration would find Justice Murphy no hindrance in waging war. But while his activities impressed many former critics and probably did some good in building army morale, the episode kindled substantial critical fire. Particularly after Murphy disqualified himself in the dramatic special hearing of the Nazi Saboteur Case—at which he stole some scenes by showing up resplendent in uniform—serious misgivings were voiced about his military service.[37/e]

e For example, when the Chief Justice invited him to lunch with the senior circuit judges, he remarked to his secretary, "Lady—how to make excuses." Harlan F. Stone to FM, Sep. 6, 1944, Box 113. On declining an invitation to officiate at the swearing-in ceremonies of Mayor Fiorello LaGuardia, Murphy explained that tradition restricted Justices to serving only at the ceremonies of Cabinet officials or above. "Of course, I need

"Can Justice Murphy legally enjoy the dual role of judge and a commissioned officer in the Army?" Congressman Emanuel Celler, chairman of the House Judiciary Committee, inquired of the Chief Justice and the Secretary of the Army. Attorney General Biddle had already raised the question with Stone just prior to announcement of the appointment in the press, whereupon the Chief brought the statute prohibiting dual positions to Murphy's attention.[38] Apparently both Biddle and Celler were unaware of the inactive character of Murphy's appointment and of the exemption for inactive reservists. Once informed of the detailed arrangements, Stone was satisfied that the Justice had a right to undergo military training, and he let the matter drop with a noncommittal reply to Celler.[39] The policy as distinct from the legal right was another issue, however. Murphy's failure to inform Stone of his plans embarrassed the Chief Justice, and his summer tour was criticized as patriotism misguided and misplaced.[f] However temporary, were the armed services or the civilian government well served by Supreme Court Justices—or Congressman Lyndon B. Johnson for that matter—mixing their functions in war? "With all sympathy for Justice Murphy and respect," the *Louisville Courier-Journal* commented, he "ought to have resigned."[40]

A summer in the army *was* a strange way for a Justice to spend his vacation. Although powerful voices continued to defend his service fling and his efforts to keep labor at the wheel, Murphy's conduct offended judicial proprieties at a time when New Deal Justices were being attacked for indifference to them. Whether "splendid example" or a case of "bumptuous" restlessness, his summer training revealed more than a melodramatic flair. It revealed a Justice attempting to improve his assets as a potential Secretary of War. It amplified in public his strange combination of flamboyance and personal asceticism. And at the cost of provoking renewed aspersions that he was "wretched on the bench" or, alternately, that his enemies were using the episode to oust him from it, the Justice exhibited an extraordinarily strong case of "the good old patriotic fervor."[41] Had he shown less, Theodore Roosevelt, Jr. remarked, Murphy's Irish ancestors would have cried

---

not tell you that tradition does not mean much to me," he said, "but it is a matter also of the views of the entire Court and the responsibility of being part of the team." FM to LaGuardia, April 22, 1941, Box 96.

[f] By contrast, the Justice had informed the President of his intentions and had leaked the idea to George Murphy, the actor and future Senator, with whom he conducted a casual "cousin Murphy" correspondence. FM to Murphy, May 14, 1942, Box 103.

from their graves, "the blood's running thin."[42] The important question was: did his war fever mean that he would permit the Constitution, like himself, to go to war?

III

The results soon spoke for themselves. Privately Murphy admitted to "the blues" about returning from soldiering. "Above all," he said, "I would like to go to the battlefront. I would make any sacrifice to achieve this. . . ."[43] Yet it is striking how little the army experience, which failed to convince him of his physical limitations, penetrated Murphy the judge. For all the emotional impact of the war, his conduct on the bench was the reverse of what might have been expected from his glorification of the military and damnation of war profiteers. Rather than perceiving judicial duty as legitimation of power in a struggle to the death, he conceived of his function as championing human rights in a war-weary world. Rather than immobilizing public philosophy for the duration, Murphy, as he always had done in crisis, drew sustenance from the libertarian goals of the American dream. War produced no retreat from favored constitutional values. Instead, war produced an almost messianic belief that Americans should maintain and invigorate their liberties in peril as a demonstration of superior moral strength. The American mission was thus the Court's mission and in that equation Murphy found his identity as a judge.

Idealism was obscured, at first, by a time lag before direct challenges to war power rose for review. It also was softened by considerations of internal strategy and by problems of assimilation, which continued to mute the libertarian strains of his thought. The contrast between Murphy's public philosophy and private thirst for action, nevertheless, was evident even at the height of his martial zeal. Preservation of traditional values as a burden of wartime government was a reigning concept in his work. Bombs hardly had fallen before the Justice began to resort to judicial opinions to preach the same gospel of individual freedom and government-by-example that had been his uniform philosophy for 30 years. Except for *Chaplinsky* virtually all of his wartime utterances bore the stamp of these themes.[44] Their articulation, which became clearer as war progressed, was not free from difficulty, however, because of internal pressures and professional biases against converting judicial opinions into sermons.

The earliest cases in 1942-43, though overshadowed by subsequent debates of a showdown nature, in some ways were the more revealing because Murphy was still in the process of resolving value commitments, personal relations, and institutional responsibilities into a working philosophy of judging. Because war sharpened his libertarian premises and emotional force, on the one hand, he manifested a new willingness to take isolated positions and to evangelize the libertarian faith. Because he perceived an opinion-writer's task to be in good part brokerage of multiple viewpoints, on the other hand, and because he still felt at sea as a jurist, he remained quite flexible about tailoring opinions to suit others and responsive to criticism of both style and substance. War was a catalytic agent in unleashing idiosyncratic traits, in other words, but continued personal diffidence, combined with processes of "bargaining" within the Court, softened those idiosyncrasies considerably. Murphy's early war years, consequently, were a period of gestation in which his attempts to assert personal views were self-conscious, tentative, and frequently frustrated. Only the gathering self-confidence of experience and the strongest convictions aroused by war exposed them.

Justice Murphy's concurring opinion in *United States* v. *Bethlehem Steel Corp.*, an excess profits case left over from World War I, was a harbinger of things to come. Murphy's concurrence, which denounced both war profits and rescission of government contracts, was the beginning of a long stream of opinions which combined heavy doses of ethical preachment with practical policy considerations the Justice could not put down.[45] Feeling strongly about the maintenance of public confidence in crisis government, he already had urged the President to create a special antiprofiteering agency to keep the defense program above suspicion.[46] But despite favorable press reactions to his *Bethlehem* opinion and his belief that Stone and Roberts thought well of it, Murphy had to overcome several obstacles before deciding to write.[47] Because the case had been under litigation during his attorney generalship, he first had to satisfy misgivings about his participation. When initially considered in October 1940, following disqualification by Stone, Roberts, and himself, the *Bethlehem* case had failed to muster the requisite vote of four Justices in favor of granting certiorari. After Chief Justice Hughes reversed his position and ordered a grant, Murphy then signified to conference that in view of the close vote he was "deeply worried" about his disqualification and wished also to reconsider. "We will have to carefully determine whether I am disqualified," he told his clerk, while instructing him to canvass Court customs thoroughly.

As a matter of fact I had naught to do with the case [he said] but even so I might be disqualified because my first duty is to preserve the reputation of the court and fastidiously preserve its impartiality and litigation was pressed while I presided over it.

It is a case I feel strongly about. But my feelings are deeper about the proprieties. So look into it carefully. . . .[48/g]

Since it was not unprecedented for Justices to sit in cases involving pro forma responsibility, Murphy decided to participate, a change of mind which made his vote decisive. He also decided to write a separate statement under the dual stimuli of Justice Douglas's last-minute dissent and his own overpowering impulse to preach. Though cautioned that emphasis on morals might weaken the majority position by implying that a 22½ percent profit rate was abnormal, rather than a customary and inevitable product of a contracting system which the majority attacked, Murphy could not resist temptation. "Douglas by implication and otherwise re-writes the contract . . . ," he remarked; and "22½% no matter how it is dolled-up is inordinate, against [the] public interest, destructive of the integrity so necessary to the winning of a war and I want to condemn it." "I simply cannot in the setting of the defense program today put my imprimatur on 22½% profit." Thus, while voting to sustain the contract in a "trap pass" move which virtually forced Congress to overhaul the procurement system, Justice Murphy also denounced the Bethlehem contract as immoral.[49/h]

Tension between private convictions and institutional restraints was more pronounced in the rising number of appeals which probed the Court's recently expanded jurisdiction over civil liberties. Not surprisingly, in view of his past crusades for public defenders, the right to counsel cases were among the first in which Murphy sought to achieve old objectives by exerting judicial power. In 1942 he joined Justice Black's prophetic *Betts* v. *Brady* lament against the Court's failure to absorb the right to counsel into the Fourteenth Amendment; and in his majority opinion in *Glasser* v. *United States*, which Justice Roberts assigned him at Black's suggestion, Murphy gave early indications that

[g] Murphy also worried about his qualification to sit in the *Appalachian Power* case, which Hughes assigned with the remark: "I assign to Roberts to do his damndest." Conference note, No. 674, Box 130. 311 U.S. 377 (1940).

[h] On one copy of Murphy's memorandum opinion was the notation, "F.F.'s idea." Since Justice Frankfurter opposed using the case to invite revision of the contracting system, it would have strengthened his position to have Murphy attack Bethlehem, rather than the system as a whole, but no other evidence exists in the Murphy papers that Frankfurter encouraged Murphy to write.

he was willing to lean very far to safeguard procedural rights.[50] In *Glasser* a 6-3 majority overturned a conspiracy conviction of a federal district attorney on the ground that appointment of his counsel to represent a codefendant abridged his Sixth Amendment right. In the face of Justice Frankfurter's protest, that reversal abused the appellate function by entertaining a "lawyer's afterthought," which had been raised only on final appeal, Murphy wrote feelingly about the responsibility of federal trial judges to enforce constitutional guarantees. He also went out of his way to warn against the dangers of undemocratic bias in federal "blue ribbon" juries, against Chief Justice Stone's advice against assuming unnecessary burdens and Justice Douglas's request to narrow the language.[51] His lone dissent in *Adams* v. *United States ex rel. McCann* the following term even refused to concede that the requirement of intelligent waiver to jury trial could be met without advice of counsel, a position which the Court is on the verge of taking but which Justice Frankfurter then denounced as a doctrinaire standard that would "imprison a man in his privileges and call it the Constitution."[52]

These early cases on the right to counsel and the scope of jury trial were forerunners of fundamental conflict over the meaning of due process and the role of federal appellate judges in developing standards of criminal justice. While they also opened up the broad vistas and bold strokes with which libertarian judges treated the rights of criminally accused, it is significant that neither characteristic was Murphy yet willing to indulge until encouraged to express himself by colleagues, especially Black and Douglas, who, on several occasions, also persuaded him to hold his fire. In fact, no major opinion by Murphy thus far had escaped modification at the behest of other Justices. Nor was it accurate to attribute the growing affinity of view among Justices Black, Douglas, and Murphy to concerted bloc action. The Court's own procedures, as Justice Jackson once observed, breed individualistic habits, no more so than among the hardy individualists on the Roosevelt Court.[53] Murphy was hesitant about isolated expression, but he began to assert his independence at the same time, and for the same reasons, that he joined Justices Black and Douglas in the Court's larger doctrinal concerns.

Disagreement within the liberal trio prevailed across a wide spectrum of the Court's business, including problems of federalism, taxation, and Indian claims; but the most prophetic deviations occurred within the areas of closest cohesion, such as administrative procedure and criminal law. In *Endicott Johnson Corp.* v. *Perkins*, for instance, Justice

Murphy landed into a lonely corner by opposing reduction of judicial controls over administrative subpoenas.[54] Although unrivalled as a defender of the discretion of the NLRB, and cautioned by New Deal colleagues that judicial controls on administrative subpoena power might permit judges to do what Congress had forbidden them to do by injunctions, Murphy wrote an effective dissent, which Justice Roberts unexpectedly joined, favoring retention of a "probable cause" requirement as a reasonable balance between administrative efficiency and private right. "I fear multiplying bureaucracy—the drift that way," he commented after conference, "—and the tendency to hamstring judicial authority in favor of loose or not well delineated authority." Initially, in an effort to be circumspect, Murphy had concurred. "But I don't like it," he told his clerk. "Explore the facts and see if there is not some fact or facts on which we can bluntly dissent. The Court is made up so as to forewarn me," he added. Lone dissents, he knew, seldom counted for much. But Murphy felt compelled to speak out against this administrative innovation. The Court, he said flatly, was "going overboard because of F.F.'s phobia on the subject and my friend Hugo and Bill's dislike for business."[55]

Regardless of individuals, strategic considerations among judges commonly compromise all but the most deeply felt convictions. The necessity of achieving consensus among powerful personalities, each of whom may be antagonist today but ally tomorrow, imposes forceful constraints. So does the Court's relations with other institutions. Except when he speaks alone, no Justice is a free agent. And even a soloist may be persuaded or cajoled into modulating his voice.[56] Two electronic eavesdropping decisions in 1942, *Goldstein* v. *United States* and *Goldman* v. *United States*, richly illustrate the counterforces Murphy faced as he struggled to establish his identity on the Court.[57] In both cases, which touched a field in which he regarded himself as experienced if not expert, the liberal trio split. Murphy joined Justices Stone and Frankfurter in opposition to extension of federal eavesdropping authority, and he elected to speak for the minority against the majority opinions written by Justice Roberts.

In *Goldstein* the question was whether Section 605 of the Communications Act, which forbade unauthorized use of information obtained by wiretaps, permitted third parties to object to the admission of such evidence in trials when authorized by another. Justice Roberts' opinion presented an easy target, because his argument that a third party lacked standing to complain against a violation of the statute conflicted with his own opinion in the better known *Nardone* case and a stream of decisions based thereon. Enthusiastically Justice Frankfurter urged Murphy to exploit the contradiction, which he did. Though Murphy withdrew personal reference to Roberts in response to the Chief Justice's lecture concerning the custom of impersonal debate, he wrote a tightly effective dissent in support of the minority view that Section 605 expressed an unequivocal "congressional command that society shall not be plagued with such practices as wiretapping."[58]

"I am fearful that we have agreement achieved by a technique beneath wire-tapping and the use of detectaphones," the Justice observed to his clerk after Stone and Frankfurter joined the dissent. "For my comrades in legal arms do not know that I am taking to the hustings in the [*Goldman*] case."[59] A dissent in *Goldman*, the first case in which the Court sustained the constitutionality of electronic "bugging," faced formidable strategic obstacles. On the one hand, the Court had refused to overrule the well-known *Olmstead* decision of 1928, that electronic penetration was not a physical search and seizure and therefore beyond Fourth Amendment control.[60] To repeat the masterly dissents of Justices Holmes and Brandeis in that case was appealing, but Chief Justice Stone was very anxious, as his clerk informed Murphy's, that the minority lie low for fear that defeat after two great battles would firmly entrench the majority's doctrine that new methods of invading privacy were beyond constitutional reach.[61] Not without difficulty, Stone persuaded Frankfurter to follow suit in a terse opinion which stated that had a majority been willing to overrule *Olmstead*, they would have gladly joined; but inasmuch as the Court declined to do so, "and as we think that this case is indistinguishable in principle from Olmstead's, we have no occasion to repeat here the dissenting views in that case with which we agree."[62]

On the other hand, the dissents of Justices Brandeis and Butler in *Olmstead* had simply assumed, without explanation, that wiretapping was an unreasonable search. Justice Murphy resisted Stone's strategy of reticence for at least three reasons. First, silence compromised the principle. Second, the Chief had passed remarks at conference, while attempting to find a basis of distinguishing cases, which inspired some doubt about his commitment to overruling *Olmstead*. Third, Murphy believed it important in wartime to impress on the public consciousness the urgency of striking a balance between the need and the dangers of electronic searches. To set this balance judicially posed additional difficulties. Expansion of the Fourth Amendment would be necessary because the privacy principle is not mentioned in specific terms and because the case involved offices, not homes. In addition, detectaphones were designed primarily to discover "mere evidence," and search warrants for that purpose were suspect under the Court's decision in the *Lefkowitz* case.[63] How, without legislating or repudiating Brandeis, could the Court offer a middle ground? Refusing to believe that the government was "powerless in the face of national peril or a crime wave to regulate through legislation" or that special warrant procedure could not be worked out to maintain judicial control, Murphy put aside technical difficulties for the sake of preaching a larger lesson. "In the detectaphone case have we made plain," he asked his clerk, "that the most important thing about government is that it is the exemplar of conduct?" "Privacy, a right as precious as any, does not mean that you have anything to conceal. But it certainly means that you have the decision of determining that which you want to disclose. Man's moral autonomy hinges on the indefeasible right to privacy."[64]

No one disagreed in principle. But notions of authority and timing differ. Justice Frankfurter, who ranked Fourth Amendment rights at the apex of constitutional values, urged Murphy to forbear with him and the Chief Justice in order to conserve their strength. But while cautioning Murphy against making advance commitments by citing *Milligan*, Justice Frankfurter could not resist criticizing his finale for being beneath his attainable lucidity. Murphy responded by "working on a little pastry," as he called his rhetoric, to strengthen the dissent.[65] But that move led Justice Jackson, who had disqualified himself in both cases, to strike a counterblow that eliminated much of the pastry and raised troublesome normative issues besides.

Irritated by the severe criticism of the government's conduct in the dissent, conduct which Murphy had done nothing to reprove as Attorney General, Jackson sent a memo to the conference requesting that he be permitted to make an oral explanation of his disqualification in order to remove uncertain implications regarding his own responsibility for the practice in question. Those facts were that the prosecution and the detectaphone recordings in *Goldman* were made under rules and regulations in force when he became Attorney General; because the prosecution was continued under his official responsibility he therefore deemed it appropriate to refrain from participation in the case.[66] Jackson's memorandum not only called attention to Murphy's reversal of position; by implication it impugned his integrity for failure to disqualify himself.

Disqualification ultimately is governed by custom and individual conscience. Because a majority of the Court at that time were former government attorneys, the criteria of disqualification and the problem of obtaining a statutory quorum of six members were beginning to figure increasingly as a source of external embarrassment for the Court as well as a touchstone of internal dispute. Eager to conform to tradition, Murphy, like the others, was quick to disqualify himself in cases involving personal connections, as he did, for instance, in one case of his friend, Doris Duke. He also disqualified himself in cases in which he had participated officially. Accordingly Murphy withdrew his signature from Frankfurter's opinion in the *Hutcheson* case after being reminded of his former defense of the indictment in 1939.[67] As a rule, he followed that pattern automatically even when past participation had been insubstantial or formal. Yet he sometimes felt obliged to make exceptions in the latter category, as both he and the Chief Justice did in the Holding Company Cases, out of a contrary aversion to denying a party, otherwise entitled to a hearing, his day in Court.[68] Exceptions were likely, as *Bethlehem* indicated, when quorums were tight and feelings high—but not always. Having supreme confidence in his own rectitude, Murphy occasionally permitted strength of conviction to overwhelm doubts. There is no evidence that either he or Jackson had personal contact with the *Goldman* litigation while Attorney General. Nor under prevailing standards was Murphy's decision to participate a reflection on his honor. *Olmstead,* after all, had been argued by Justice Butler's law partners and the indictment brought under Attorney General Stone without disqualification of either Justice. But wiretapping had provoked hot controversy while Murphy and Jackson were in the executive branch and Jackson made the most of it.[69]

Worked into an embarrassing corner by Jackson's memorandum to the conference, Murphy responded by signifying his willingness to reconsider the offensive language. Jackson then tightened the vise by sending him, and all the other Justices, the following statement of complaint:

My dear Frank . . .
    I will give you frankly all that is on my mind on the subject.
    This case presents a new question of law, on which difference of opinion is to be expected and upon which it is not inconceivable that one's attitudes as a prosecutor and as a judge might differ. However, the Department of Justice under several Attorneys General has assumed the law to be as the Court now holds it to be. Even so, any Attorney General was empowered to impose further limitations on investigative methods if he thought good morals or good government required it. None of us did so. In these circumstances, a characterization of a continuing policy in which we all participated as that of "overzealous officials" and "debasing to government" may well be un-

pleasant to those who were similarly situated with you.

But any discomfort of my own is small compared with the position of those who served under both of us and who looked to us—not as much as they should have, perhaps—for guidance and supervision. They are still trying to carry on the work of their department under increasingly difficult and baffling conditions. My grievance is only academic compared to the gravity of putting words such as I have quoted into the mouth of every criminal lawyer in the United States to be hurled at the Government as quotations from a former Attorney General and a present Justice, when it attempts to use evidence that the Court now holds to be its legal right, as well as on other occasions.

Now that you know how I feel in the matter, I shall leave the result to your own good judgment. Whatever you do, I think the interests of the Court would not be served by carrying the matter to the public. I commit myself not to do that in order to leave you free of any pressures in the matter except those of your own strong sense of justice.[70]

Faced with the ultimate threat of a public airing of the dispute, Murphy withdrew the offending language, including his lesson about government as the exemplar of conduct, and even admitted that police officials could have assumed in good conscience that their conduct was lawful. Jackson then retracted his statement, and the disqualification dispute blew over, only to resume each successive year until it eventually spread beyond them to engulf Stone and Roberts in the Holding Company Cases, and finally Jackson and Black in their ill-starred 1946 "feud."[71]

Insignificant though the *Goldman* case may have appeared in the stream of litigation over the difficult issue of electronic eavesdropping, it reflected a mode of internal "bargaining" that soon exacerbated personal relations on the Court. *Goldman* also offered a revealing glimpse of an inexperienced Justice attempting to break from a pattern of reticence. On the one hand, Murphy manifested several traits of his subsequent crusading style—indifference to doctrinal consistency under the influence of different offices, impatience for gradualist tactics, and impulses to preach. Divorcing personal war fever from public philosophy, he managed to salvage his essential sermon that law must be adapted to "a changing social order" and to advance the libertarian themes which became so prominent near the end of the war: "At a time when the nation is called upon to give freely of life and treasure to defend and preserve the institutions of democracy and freedom, we should not permit any of the essentials of freedom to lose vitality through legal interpretations that are restrictive and inadequate for the period in which we live."[72/1] In his first lone dissent, on the other hand, Murphy was hardly a model libertarian absolutist. Rather, he was an uncertain exponent of accommodation whose wings were easily clipped. In the warlike atmosphere of 1942 the few who noted his sermon dismissed it—along with the seminal theme of Justice Holmes' great *Olmstead* dissent: "it is less evil that some criminals should escape than that the Government should play an ignoble part"—as "innocent highmindedness" demonstrating why the Court remained unconvinced.[73] Justice Murphy himself stoutly defended his position as a compromise not dissimilar from the stated objective of the Justice Department's wiretap policy in 1939. He was also more tolerant of police eavesdropping in nonsecurity cases than the Johnson administration's privacy bill of 1967.[74] To Joseph A. Mulcahy, the Justice commented: "You will note in my opinion that I only oppose its irresponsible and abusive use, and that I take the view that it should be used only under such circumstances as a search warrant is used—that is within the lane of judicial authority. In this manner, kidnappers, espionage agents and the like may be easily apprehended and at the same time adequate protection can be given to the right of privacy to the general public. These indiscriminating and unauthorized invasions of privacy [are] becoming something of a plague in this country."[75]

Even though a search warrant procedure might provide imperfect protection, he conceded, a judicially imposed standard was better than none. Even though riddled by a nonparticipating adversary, which he did not concede, a lone dissent was "the sort of thing you enjoy when you know you are right."[76] Enjoyment cost a pretty price in effectiveness, nevertheless. For *Goldman* was partially undermined by gradualist tactics in 1957, President Johnson banned most federal eavesdropping by executive order in 1965, and the Warren Court in 1967 overruled both *Olmstead* and *Goldman* (Justice Black alone dissenting) in an opinion which struck essentially the same compromise Murphy had advocated in 1942—all without reference to his *Goldman* preachment.[77]

So strong a believer in the moral integrity of government that he called into question his own, Justice Murphy thus unveiled in *Goldman* the basic elements of his personal style—an itch to use dissents for evangelical purposes and a concomitant flamboyance of expression which offended professional traditions no less after softening within

---

[1] Cf. Black, J., who specifically repudiated the power of the Court to bring the Constitution into "harmony with the times" by stretching the words of the Fourth Amendment to include nonphysical searches. *Katz* v. *United States,* 36 *Law Week* 4080 (Dec. 19, 1967).

the Court. In 1942 these characteristics were shrouded under public preoccupation with war and under his de facto tractability in drafting opinions. But at the same time that he was pulling every string to enter active military service, Murphy revealed emerging concepts of the Court as a defender of liberty and a spokesman of public conscience in the face of intense pressures on both. The break-out became unmistakable during renewed battle over religious liberty.

IV

"I come up to this case like a skittish horse to a brass band," Charles Evans Hughes had said in 1940, while opening conference discussion of the first Flag Salute Case. In Murphy's notes Hughes is recorded as having observed:

I am disturbed that we have this case before us. There is nothing that I have more profound belief in than religious freedom so I must bring myself to view this case on the question of state power.

There is no legitimate impingement on religious belief here. What is required of those who salute the flag is a legitimate object.

We have no jurisdiction as to the wisdom of this. We have to deal with state power and consider whether this is a proper exercise of it. I don't want to be dogmatic about this but I simply cannot believe that the state has not the power to inculcate this social objective. . . . As I see it the state can insist on inculcation of loyalty. It would be extraordinary if in this country the state could not provide for respect for the flag of our land. It has nothing to do with religion—indeed it has to do with freedom of religion.[78]

Thus had Charles Evans Hughes, shortly before his own retirement intensified its emergence, posed a central dilemma of the Roosevelt Court. Conflict between judicial review and popular rule, antimony between values the judiciary is called on to protect, had marked the exercise of Supreme Court power since its inception. Following the landmark *Gobitis* decision, a rash of religious freedom cases raised the problem anew. The Jehovah's Witnesses sect, encouraged by absorption of rights of free worship into the Fourteenth Amendment and by the often repressive measures used by local authorities to control their militant activities, pressed so many claims that they precipitated one of the greatest dialogues over "the role of the Court" in judicial history. And well they might. The cases presented not only delicate issues of public policy but eternal conundrums of free government—liberty versus authority and majority rule versus minority right—conundrums that are intensified in the American scheme by localized issues of federalism and the judiciary's part in resolving the clash. Not without reason did Harlan F. Stone remark that the Witness "pests" deserved an endowment for their contribution to the law of religious liberty.[79]

The Jehovah's Witnesses cases were painful for Justice Murphy. Nothing in his beliefs seemed more fixed than his commitment to religious freedom. Yet his participation in *Gobitis* evidenced attrition of principle in the face of competing values. A prime target of Witness invective, moreover, was his own church. Whatever course he took would be interpreted by the misinformed as "the" Catholic viewpoint on the Court. Personal diffidence, symbols of self-restraint, and values of local autonomy, all had dictated his reluctant acquiescence in *Gobitis*. Time for reflection and the perspective of war now placed him in a position of reweighing the scales and in full public view. Two months after Pearl Harbor, while ruminating privately about the maintenance of freedom in wartime, the Justice observed: "We need unity, but that will never be accomplished by a purge. . . . We must always bear in mind that the denial of liberty to those with whom we heartily disagree makes easier the eventual denial of our own freedom. The remedy is education and more discussion—not repression or force."[80] It was not long before the general proposition was applied concretely, making Justice Murphy the Court's most ardent evangelist of "preferred freedoms."

The first public signal of the change, registered two days before Murphy entered the army, was *Jones* v. *Opelika*, a case which involved municipal license taxes on the door-to-door sale of Witness pamphlets. In upholding the taxes for the Court, Justice Reed emphasized that no difference existed among the Justices regarding devotion to the freedoms of press and religion. "We view these sales," he said, "as partaking more of commercial than religious or educational transactions. . . ."[81] But that perception tore the Court apart. Chief Justice Stone, who had hesitated initially for fear that the appeal was prematurely brought, rendered an unusually vigorous dissent warning the nation that a new way had been found to circumvent First Amendment guarantees. Rights of press and religion were not directed solely against wholesale attempts to "wipe them out," the Chief Justice asserted. "On the contrary, the Constitution . . . has put those freedoms in a preferred position."[82] And despite their participation in *Gobitis*, Justices Black, Douglas, and Murphy joined him.

For the lonely philosophy of his *Gobitis* dissent Stone had now won three converts. None was more vocal about the need of greater judicial action than the Court's Catholic Justice. In a companion dissent in which all minority members joined, he maintained that the religious literature was distributed "for religious reasons alone and not for personal profit." Taxation therefore offended three First Amendment guarantees—speech, press, and worship—and should be nullified "on its face." "The mind rebels at the thought," wrote Murphy, "that a minister of any of the old established churches could be made to pay fees to the community before entering the pulpit." Public solicitation did not absolve the taxes from taint unless the Court was prepared to restrict freedom to disseminate religious ideas to those financially able to "distribute their broadsides without charge." That he refused to do. Sounding the keynote of his credo from that day forward, the Justice declared: "Liberty of conscience is too full of meaning for the individuals in this Nation to permit taxation to prohibit or substantially impair the spread of religious ideas, even though they are controversial and run counter to the established notions of a community. If this Court is to err in evaluating claims that freedom of speech, freedom of the press, and freedom of religion have been invaded, far better that it err in being overprotective of these precious rights."[83]

The break with Frankfurter was now complete. At the very outset of their union, however, the proponents of preferred freedoms revealed serious divergencies that presaged their eventual inability to translate a general attitude into mutually satisfactory doctrine.[84] Justice Murphy's troubles in winning minority consensus for his laboriously prepared dissent indicated that the preference philosophy still lacked coherence. Eager to make an impression, and substantively more extreme than the rest, Murphy attacked taxation on religious literature with all stops out. Although the actual burden of taxation on free dissemination of ideas was neither pressed in the appeal nor consistent with judgment "on its face," Justices Black and Douglas had to restrain him from condemning the taxes on the practical but contradictory basis of empirical proof.[j] Instead, they urged that the dissent should take advantage of the opportunity to advance the *Thornhill* principle that overly broad ordinances should be invalidated on their face. Murphy's *Opelika* dis-

[j] In his first draft opinion, which he showed to Black and Douglas before circulation, Murphy argued prophetically: "having broadly attacked the ordinance as invalid under the Fourteenth Amendment, appellant is entitled to a decision in his favor if for any reason the ordinance runs afoul of the amendment. This Court does not fulfill its function when it deals with, and finds insufficient, only one of several possible defects." Failure to examine the question, merely because petitioners had not specifically attacked the amount "in so many words," he maintained, "is a perpetuation of the vagaries of such cases as *Morehead* v. *New York ex rel. Tipaldo*, 298 U.S. 587 . . . , to which I cannot subscribe." No. 280, Box 130.

sent, as a result, dropped reliance on burdensome amounts and became the last serious use of "on face" analysis until its revival by the Warren Court.[85]

Chief Justice Stone raised no objection to the device in the *Opelika* case, but he also had to restrain Justice Murphy from unnecessary discussion regarding taxation of the press and religious tax exemptions.[86] Both questions raised perplexing dilemmas of internal conflicts within the First Amendment which the Justices were just beginning to perceive. Easy to state, but difficult to solve, the dilemma was simply: how could judges "prefer" freedom to worship without discriminating among First Amendment guarantees and without themselves offending constitutional strictures against fusion of church and state?[87]

At some point the free exercise and establishment clauses of the First Amendment collide. Murphy broached that point during preparation of his opinion when he wrote the Chief Justice: "I note that you assume there could be a lawful non-discriminatory license tax of a percentage of the gross receipts of churches and other religious orders in support of their religious work. I have been constrained to go further and to state that no tax whatever, unless it is to defray the expenses of needed regulation in the public interest, can be imposed upon petitioner's non-commercial evangelization of their faith. Perhaps this point of difference will prevent our concurrence."[88] Since the practical problem in 1942 was achieving greater toleration of religious unorthodoxy, it is perhaps understandable how a novice could have been unmindful of a future quagmire in urging the Court to consider "every possible ground" of invalidating the tax, including the possibility that the First Amendment as distinct from legislatures required tax exemption for church activity. For all his emphasis on noncommercial evangelism so as not to exempt profit-making from taxation, however; and for all his fervent defense of the pamphlet as "an historic weapon against oppression," he can be faulted for having erected no guards against exalting the "perhaps more precious" right of worship above the rest. Libertarians in the next generation, after all, advanced the opposite argument that the establishment clause made tax exemptions *unconstitutional*!

Disagreement doubtless would have resulted had not Stone convinced him that equating taxation of church property with taxation of evangelism would weaken their protest. Stone also persuaded him to drop discussion of the constitutional basis of church tax exemptions, a question the Court still avoids.[89] More interested in strengthening his voice than in the lonely purity of a solo, Murphy willingly pruned his opinion, even though its internal coherence suffered as a result. Judging from outward appearances observers were left to ponder what, other than personal vanity, had moved Justice Murphy to write.

Circumlocutory by contrast to the Chief Justice's hard-hitting dissent, Murphy's opinion nevertheless drew uniformly favorable responses from the nation's press. At a time of scant attention to the Court, two powerful dissents successfully alerted the public to a precedent which many condemned as "latent with peril to personal freedoms."[90] While the narrow division of the Court gave some reassurance that the Justices had not lowered their guard in war, to the *Louisville Courier-Journal* the performance of the minority was "the more impressive for the fact that Justice Murphy is a devout Catholic whose faith has been subjected to scurrilous abuse by peripatetic Witnesses."[91]

The most striking aspect of the case, however, was the public recantation of Justices Black, Douglas, and Murphy for their part in the original Flag Salute decision. Calling the tax decision "a logical extension" of the *Gobitis* principle, the trio publicly announced that they viewed the salutary "self-restraint" principle inapplicable to religion. "The First Amendment does not put the right freely to exercise religion in a subordinate position," they asserted. "We fear, however, that the opinions in these and in the *Gobitis* case do exactly that."[92/k]

Unprecedented though it may have been for Justices to express views about issues not before them, their announcement was an open invitation for reconsideration of the Court's "repressive rulings" in the Jehovah's Witnesses cases.[93] The sect furnished them quick opportunity. With the replacement of Justice Byrnes by Wiley Rutledge, whose opinions in the Court of Appeals Murphy had cited for support in his *Jones* v. *Opelika* dissent, the law of religious expression so recently "found" was speedily overturned in some of the most dramatic reversals in recent times.

Invoking Stone's principle that First Amendment freedoms were in a "preferred position," and placing religion in the streets in "the same high estate" as the pulpit, the Court in an opinion by Justice Douglas struck down a series of license taxes in *Murdock* v. *Pennsylvania*.[94] Vacating its judgment and ordering reargument in *Jones* v. *Opelika*, the Court overruled the tax decisions in the spring of 1943. Then in *Martin* v. *Struthers* it invalidated an anti-doorbell ringing ordinance which was designed to protect the privacy of sleeping night-shift workers in an Ohio industrial town.[95] Justice Murphy, writing a concurring

---

k The Murphy papers contain no evidence, one way or the other, about the inspiration or authorship of this opinion.

opinion in *Struthers* which Justices Douglas and Rutledge joined, again expressed himself in righteous vein. Few, "if any, believe more strongly in the maxim, 'a man's home is his castle,' than I," he asserted. But freedom of religion had a "higher dignity under the Constitution than municipal or personal convenience." Privacy could be safeguarded by more carefully drafted time, place, and manner regulations which kept religious liberty intact. "In these days free men have no loftier responsibility than the preservation of that freedom," Murphy insisted. "A Nation dedicated to that ideal will not suffer but will prosper in its observance."[96]

Because his concurrence bore a heavy resemblance to Justice Black's opinion for the Court, commentators again pondered why the junior Justice replowed the same terrain. The reasons pointed to the hazards of inferring individual attitudes from group behavior. The *Struthers* case presented the first frontal clash between two favored libertarian values—privacy and free speech—to reach the Court. The difficulty of that issue encouraged multiple opinions. Both sides, according to Justice Frankfurter, recognized that the Witnesses cases were "probably but curtain raisers of future problems of such range and importance that the usual objections to multiplicity of opinions are outweighed by the advantages of shedding as much light as we are capable of for the wisest unfolding of the subject in the future." Furthermore, the difficulty of the issues unsettled preferred-freedoms ranks just as they began to form—and just as similar collisions have done on the Warren Court.[97] Chief Justice Stone, though he too expressed sympathy for the Sunday sleepers of Struthers, Ohio, was initially unable to attract a majority in support of preference for free expression. Justice Black saw the scales tipping toward privacy of the home and local control. With characteristic vigor he expressed prophetic fears in conference that the next case might be Jehovah's Witnesses invading Roman Catholic services if no restraints were approved. That view was accepted by a 5-4 vote; and after assigning himself the case, Justice Black circulated a forceful opinion to the effect that such a community, to protect privacy, could reasonably forbid doorbell-ringing altogether. Privacy of the home and personal control over private property, as subsequent picketing and sit-in cases showed, were fundamental to Black's jurisprudence. Not until after his second circulation in *Struthers* did he suddenly change his mind. The ordinance was overturned by a 5-4 vote, and the Chief Justice graciously permitted Black to write a new majority opinion which in effect invited the town to try again with a more carefully drafted ordinance that reconciled privacy and free speech. After all, as Stone argued behind the scenes, some room for accommodation remained before community action, at least until home-owners had an opportunity to listen or to object.[98]

Justice Black's about-face in *Struthers* went far toward explaining some of the puzzles in the opinions. For one thing, it accounted for Murphy's emotional concurrence which had originated as a strong Murphy-Douglas-Rutledge dissent against their colleague's failure to balance interests. In that context, there was special force in the protest which, once written, Murphy now addressed to the minority:

I believe that nothing enjoys a higher estate in our society than the right given by the First and Fourteenth Amendments freely to practice and proclaim one's religious convictions. . . The right extends to the aggressive and disputatious as well as to the meek and acquiescent. The lesson of experience is that—with the passage of time and the interchange of ideas— organizations, once turbulent, perfervid and intolerant in their origin, mellow into tolerance and acceptance by the community, or else sink into oblivion. . . If a religious belief has substance, it can survive criticism, heated and abusive though it may be, with the aid of truth and reason alone. By the same method those who follow false prophets are exposed. Repression has no place in this country. It is our proud achievement to have demonstrated that unity and strength are best accomplished, not by enforced orthodoxy of views, but by diversity of opinion, through the fullest possible measure of freedom of conscience and thought.[99]

Justice Black's shift also made more sense of the Frankfurter-Jackson complaints that the Court was "wanting in explicitness" and attempting to resolve tough practical issues by a "vague but fervent transcendental-ism." What the Court had decided was a narrow question of judgment, whether it was possible for a community to accommodate colliding interests by more carefully framed time, place, and manner regulations. What the public read, on the other hand, were heavily rhetorical out-pourings from both sides which obscured the precise rights involved and exaggerated the doctrinal split over preferred freedoms. While the Court's sudden reversals appeared to "restore order" in the gyrating law of religious liberty, dispassionate observers had reason to complain that its First Amendment output was becoming excessively ideological and abstract. Presenting conclusions as if none other were possible offered little help for vexing collisions among the rights of a militant minority to proselytize freely and those of the majority to live and worship in peace. Was the Court, as Jackson charged with an eye to 1937, paralyzing local authority and adding another top-heavy story "to the temples of constitutional law"?[100/1]

Ironically, what toppled next by Jackson's own hand was the compulsory flag salute, a feat which he executed for the Court in *West Virginia State Board of Education* v. *Barnette*—the apogee of preference doctrine.[101] As a result of the first Flag Salute Case, several communities had tightened their flag salute requirements by expelling children for noncompliance and by arresting their parents for truancy. Encouraged by the about-face of the minority in *Jones* v. *Opelika,* as well as by the refusal of the New Jersey Supreme Court to follow *Gobitis,* a West Virginia Witness challenged his state's program, won a reversal from a prescient Court of Appeals, and precipitated a great debate over the judiciary's role in a free society. Shrewdly, Justice Jackson skirted conflict among First Amendment guarantees by distinguishing the flag salute from doorbell-ringing and taxation as a simple clash between liberty and authority, not a collision of rights. By linking Stone's *Carolene* doctrine with the more stringent clear and present danger test, Jackson also authored a leading defense of the preferred freedoms philosophy that went beyond even what Justice Murphy thought necessary. Restrictions on religious liberty, Jackson argued, could not rest on slender grounds of deference to legislative policy, even if that policy was founded in reason and was correctable at the polls. The very purpose of the Bill of Rights was to remove certain rights from majority reach and to establish minority guarantees as legally enforceable interests. Furthermore, the explicit character of the First Amendment, as opposed to the vague contours of due process, reduced the dangers of judicial supremacy. "True," Jackson conceded, "the task of translating the majestic generalities of the Bill of Rights . . . is one to disturb self-confidence. . . . But we act in these matters not by

---

[1] Having complained of "mischievous rhetoric" and "miseducative" opinions by the majority, Justice Frankfurter joined Justice Jackson's sharp criticism of the licensing cases with the comment: "Dear Bob, . . . You did what it was high time for someone to do—and no one, to put it mildly, could have done it better. If one religion must call another a "whore," at least let them confine such manifestation of the Fatherhood of God and the Brotherhood of Man to their own temples and tabernacles, and not turn one's house into a scene of coercing and hating proselytising. Good for you!" Felix Frankfurter to Robert H. Jackson, April 9, 1943. One Justice related to Frankfurter a luncheon conversation with Murphy to the effect that the reason for his vote and voice in *Struthers* was his desire "always to err on the side of religion. I replied that as we are judges it is our business not to err on either side. This seemed a new thought to him. He made no reply, but rushed out!" Undated handwritten note, Box 19, Frankfurter Papers, Manuscript Division, Library of Congress.

authority of our competence but by force of our commissions. We cannot, because of modest estimates of our competence in such specialties as public education, withhold the judgment that history authenticates as the function of this Court when liberty is infringed."[102] That judgment was clear; compulsory affirmation of belief was unconstitutional.

"This is no dry, technical matter," Frankfurter replied in a moving, philosophical dissent. "It cuts deep into one's conception of the democratic process. . . . The whole Court is conscious that this case reaches ultimate questions of judicial power and its relations to our scheme of government." Delivering his first charge that the Court was taking Holmes' "felicitous" clear and present danger phrase out of context and converting it to a mechanical formula, Frankfurter threw Stone's argument that judicial power implied self-restraint back into his face, and explicitly denied the preferred freedoms concept. Judicial power, Frankfurter asserted, "does not vary according to the particular provision of the Bill of Rights which is invoked. The right not to have property taken without just compensation has, so far as the scope of judicial power is concerned, the same constitutional dignity. . . . In no instance is this Court the primary protector of the particular liberty that is invoked."[103]

To some extent, the Justice punched a strawman. No one had ascribed this primary function to the Court; no one had removed a specifically guaranteed property right from its aegis, though the preference of the entire bench for noneconomic values was obvious. But Frankfurter left no doubt that he considered his colleagues to have enforced their merely private prepossessions against the state of West Virginia and to have breached the democratic wall thereby. The great question, to him, was who should protect the most precious values of civilization, courts or the people? For his part, so long as the channels of political protest were open to minorities, the guardian was the people. "Only a persistent positive translation of the faith of a free society into the convictions and habits and actions of a community is the ultimate reliance against unabated temptations to fetter the human spirit," Frankfurter declared. As Jackson himself had observed in the tax cases, "if that faith should be lost, five or nine men in Washington could not long supply its want."[104]

Having recanted earlier, Justices Black, Douglas, and Murphy explained their reasons in open court. Rather than join the tightly reasoned statement of Black and Douglas, which posed the issue as extending liberty as far as order would allow, Murphy concurred alone.

In part, he carried on a side debate with Justice Frankfurter over the factual issue whether compliance with the salute was compulsory. Having already obtained a concession from Justice Jackson in the form of a deleted footnote that might have been construed as an attempt to scuttle his *Schneiderman* opinion, Murphy also wrote to outline those essential operations of government, for example, trials, which he believed might justify compulsory expression of belief.[105] But the heart of his opinion echoed the themes of the majority so clearly that the drama of the occasion appears to have moved the Justice to a solo. He wrote: "A reluctance to interfere with considered state action, the fact that the end sought is a desirable one, the emotion aroused by the flag as a symbol for which we have fought and are now fighting again, —all of these are understandable. But there is before us the right of freedom to believe, freedom to worship one's Maker according to the dictates of one's conscience, a right which the Constitution specifically shelters. Reflection has convinced me that as a judge I have no loftier duty or responsibility than to uphold that spiritual freedom to its farthest reaches. . . . It is in that freedom and the example of persuasion, not in force and compulsion, that the real unity of America lies."[106]

The Jehovah's Witnesses cases were hailed in the press as "a great victory for religious freedom and civil rights in general."[107] The Court had reached a turning point, and so had Justice Murphy. No longer disturbed by the spectre of group conflict, which had troubled him in *Cantwell* and which troubled Justices Frankfurter and Jackson still, he never again opposed a Jehovah's Witnesses claim accepted for review. No longer restrained by philosophies of judicial abnegation, he never again voted against a serious First Amendment claim. "I hope I am above all an American who knows the significance of his country's birth," he observed to former American ambassador to Germany, James W. Gerard. "It comforts me that with 800 years of Catholic background I can speak in defense of a people opposed to my own faith."[108] Coincident with the Jehovah's Witnesses cases, and in part because of them, Murphy was recovering the sense of mission, the identification with underdogs, which had always sparked his energies but so far had eluded him as a judge. And the effect on his serenity of spirit was marked. "Contrary to popular belief," he informed dean Henry M. Bates at Christmas 1943, "I am supremely happy on the Court." "I live now only to excel in the work of the Court. It is a joy to take my pen in hand and endeavor to write for the gracious and civilized society to which free men aspire."[109]

V

Henceforth "freedom to its farthest reaches" became his fervent cry. And in defense of personal freedoms, he often landed, with rhetoric blazing, in a lonely wilderness he hitherto had struggled to avoid. When procedural problems of conscientious objection rose for review, Murphy persistently held out for wider review of draft classifications than any of his colleagues.[110] When the federal Mann and Kidnap Acts were applied to itinerant Mormons, he was a strict constructionist, indignantly charging his brethren with judicial legislation to govern problems beyond Congress's design.[111] When Justice Roberts accused the Court of subsidizing religion and exempting church property from its share of tax burdens in *Follett* v. *Town of McCormick*,[112] he issued a hot concurrence to stress the "obvious" distinction between taxes on commercial church property and actual evangelism, which Stone had impressed on him, whereupon Roberts on opinion day denounced him by name.[m] Small wonder that the Justice inspired a popular wag: "If Frank Murphy is ever sainted it will be by the Jehovah's Witnesses."[113] With kindred evangelical fervor he fought to protect the unorthodox worship of an unpopular few who called his own church "a whore."

Murphy's libertarianism was not confined to religion. The Justice was just as uncompromising about freedom of speech and press. After *Bridges* he never voted to sustain a contempt of court citation against an editor.[114] In two important regulatory cases, *National Broadcasting Co.* v. *United States* and *Associated Press* v. *United States*, he dissented against assumed federal authority to regulate monopolistic practices in communications industries.[115] It should be noted that in both cases he graduated his attack according to the restrained principle that authority so potent should be expressed by Congress, not implied. Evangelism was not his only tactic; both opinions, as a result, attracted Justice Roberts' unexpected vote.

[m] Tempers must have flared on both sides. Murphy's published opinion was much tamer than his first draft, which answered Roberts' charge with the following deleted statements: "The fact that Jehovah's Witness doctrine may be personally distasteful to members of a court does not justify them in ignoring the right of the appellant to believe and practice those doctrines free from unconstitutional restraints." "Any other conclusion" than the one reached, he declared, "would force appellant to pay tribute for exercising a dear constitutional right." "If that be subsidizing religion, we should make the most of it. No price is too high to pay to retain freedom of conscience and worship." After Roberts' denunciation from the bench, Justice Rutledge remarked to Murphy: "The brother has lost all sense of restraint or consideration. I'd give it no more thought than a child's petulant outburst." Note, "Re Roberts reference to my name . . . ," March 27, 1944, No. 486, Box 133.

"Sursum Corda—as we say in the Faith!" Murphy remarked as Roberts registered his adherence in the Radio Case.[116] Support from the senior Justice, the colleague with whom he most disagreed and with whom disagreement came close to personal antagonism, not only strengthened his protest. A duo of "the Saint" and "the Senior Warden," as Murphy and Roberts nicknamed each other, was repeated in *Endicott* and demonstrated their independent streaks at the very emergence of libertarian cohesion. Consistently, Justice Murphy's refusal to sanction implied authority to regulate commercial communication split a libertarian grouping that was otherwise united in a Populist outlook toward business regulation. In one case he even opposed application of a highly favored New Deal statute, the Fair Labor Standards Act, to a small town weekly.[117] Disturbed less by restraints on trade than on freedom of expression—and undaunted by Justice Black's argument in the *Associated Press* case that the restraints were on both —Murphy as a judge was never far from the exuberant conception of freedom he advanced as Governor of Michigan: "I believe not only in the liberty, but the licence of the press. I hold that the press of America must have the right to do the wrong things."[118] And eccentric though he knew his views would be classified by label-makers, he remained adamant. Of the opinions which broke libertarian unity in 1943 he observed proudly: "They are the gospel as I know it."[119/n]

Justice Murphy erupted from deference to preference so vocally in 1942-43, that he acquired swift symbolic status as an "uncompromising liberal idealist" and an emotional "doctrinaire."[120] Neither notion, indeed, did he personally attempt to quash. Murphy continued to express preference for a political post and to badger the White House unsuccessfully about missions abroad until Roosevelt's death.[121/o] He

[n] After the *NBC* case Murphy commented: "I am unable to place the radio—after the lesson of horror in Europe—on the same status as securities, electrical power, etc." FM to James W. Gerard, May 10, 1943, Nos. 554-55, Box 132. "If the press isn't radio," he added to his college friend, Leland S. Bisbee, "what is it? . . . Should the Court in the absence of legislative authority fabricate it? I think not. What is the difference in determining what you hear and what you read? I am going to look with the eyes of reason open on all legislation affecting either." FM to Bisbee, May 17, 1943, Box 108.

[o] In 1943, after the War Department vetoed his proposals for a contact mission to Filipino guerrillas, General Marshall suggested a morale-building trip to Pacific outposts. Murphy rejected the trip on the ground that entertainers were better qualified. "The only morale that a field soldier trained as I have been recognizes," he told the President heartily, "is the kind that prepares a soldier to gain advantage over his adversary in combat." "I want to be really effective." FM to FDR, May 31, 1943, Box 108. See Marshall to FM, May 11, 1943; FDR to FM, May 20, 1943, Box 108. The Justice also turned down a trip proposed by Secretary of War Stimson to consult with military missions in Latin America regarding training programs in U.S. camps, after

continued to express concern to the Chief Justice about the quality of his opinions, and to compromise when confronted with competing loyalties.[122] But in the midst of a war he earnestly wished to join, Murphy began to find identity by perceiving judicial office, like all others, on his own terms. The Court became his "Great Pulpit," a secular agency having power to enlarge human liberties and a platform to preach his gospel while submerging himself under lofty goals. "What a supreme joy it is to have no other mission in life than to lift one's pen in defense of freedom of conscience and the security and equal justice to the inarticulate!" he sang of his role in a rosy mood at Christmas 1943.[123] If the price, as always, was sacrifice of group leadership, Justice Murphy's assimilation to the Court could not have been purchased for less.

To realists on the bench, whose own absorbing patriotism was projected into opposite directions of legitimizing national power, Murphy's idealistic outpourings thereafter were dangerous identifications and charts of a dangerous judicial course. The impetus to push liberty to its farthest reaches would soon convince other Justices, all liberty-loving, that libertarians erred in overly protecting precious rights, that they came close to falling "into a well from looking at the stars."[124] But for Justice Murphy the path of duty was clear. Civil liberties were more important than who protected them. "As long as I am able to hold a pen in my hand," he declared, "I'll write opinions on the basis that those freedoms must be maintained in our land." "If we come out of this war with less than these freedoms, then we have lost."[125]

Kemp saw through its synthetic character and FM was forced to undergo a nasal operation. Kemp to FM, June 27, 1943, Box 108.

CHAPTER 12

THE INESCAPABLE DUTY,

1943-1945

PROBLEMS of war power, even more decisively than issues of religious freedom, were responsible for the resolution of Justice Murphy's status and style as a jurist. Because he had disqualified himself in the Nazi Saboteur Case in July 1942, a decision which his staff believed was prompted by criticism of his army fling at conference, he missed World War II's first major challenge to executive discretion and the Court's basic determination that the judiciary lacked authority to review military judgments beyond threshold questions of proper jurisdiction.[1] Disappointed though he was at missing *ex parte Quirin*, Murphy's appetite for judging was whetted following his return from soldiering in the fall of 1942. The Court was embroiled in a sharp dispute over its power to review executive judgments in the Saboteur Case; more was bound to come. Cases probing the outer reaches of constitutional liberty were on the docket, and his personal confidence was plainly on the rise. The convergence of influences all but removed uncertainties about his place on the Court. Justice Murphy's third spring on the bench, a period in whch he emerged from the periphery to the forefront of battle over civil liberties, thus marked the pivotal turn of his judicial career.

The major stimuli, besides First Amendment cases, were a series of challenges to emergency policies that the Court encountered simultaneously with its great reversals over preferred freedoms. In an atmosphere already strained by religious issues, the war power cases inevitably aggravated the "role of the Court" dilemma. Unlike the Jehovah's Witnesses problem, in which a libertarian Court collided at most with state and local officials in an atmosphere of support from powerful editors and religious groups, the Justices now faced the prospect of unpopular clashes with Congress and Commander-in-Chief in contexts that affected inter-Allied relations and perhaps even national survival itself. So soon after the court-packing struggle not merely the propriety but the very power of judicial intervention was in the balance.

"When war comes the laws go" expressed a popular axiom of past experience, though Chief Justice Stone took pains in the Saboteur Case to keep the door of judicial review ajar. Yet when war finally reached the high tribunal in concrete form, Murphy's thoughts of leaving it abated. In June 1943, the same season of the second Flag Salute Case, he emerged as the Supreme Court's most ardent defender of constitutional limitations in war. And his distinctive judicial style was set.

It should be stressed that Murphy's starting point was not uncompromising libertarianism, but libertarianism compromised under pressure. Conflicting loyalties had the same constraining effects in war-power controversies that had occurred with preferred freedoms. The Justice not only failed to participate in the initial conscientious objection appeal, in the threshold test of military control over civilians—*Hirabayashi* v. *United States*—Murphy, against his better judgment, accepted a decisive compromise of the principle that guilt is personal.[2]

The Japanese relocation program, the most massive deprivation of personal freedom under federal authority in American history, had given rise to the case. Shortly after Pearl Harbor the fear of invasion, espionage, and sabotage on the mainland produced a clamor for control of the "Japanese menace" on the west coast. Although the Department of Justice had investigated thousands of aliens prior to Pearl Harbor and rounded up suspected individuals immediately thereafter, the President, yielding to popular pressures, pleas of military necessity by the War Department, and buck-passing by Justice Department civilians, issued executive orders on February 12, 1942, which Congress later endorsed with criminal penalties, authorizing Secretary of War Stimson and his designates to establish military zones in which the activities of aliens and suspected civilians could be regulated, to the point of outright exclusion and relocation from the zone. On the basis of these orders General J.F. DeWitt, the west coast commander whose dissatisfaction with civilian measures made him a leader in demanding such authority, issued a series of proclamations beginning in March 1942 which provided for: (1) an evening curfew confining all enemy aliens and "all persons of Japanese ancestry" to their homes; (2) the exclusion of "all aliens and non-alien Japanese" from California, parts of Washington, Oregon, and Arizona; and (3) their detention outside the zone in camps operated by an ad hoc War Relocation Authority, a move hastily improvised after the rest of the country likewise refused to accept the Nisei. Within eight months after the first edict approximately 112,000 persons, two-thirds of them native-born citizens and many of them the parents and relatives of men in the armed forces, had been relocated and detained after sustaining estimated property losses of $400 million. The burden on the national conscience was all the heavier because only a handful of unpopular libertarians, such as socialist Norman Thomas, braved a protest.[3]

Proponents of the relocation program justified it as an emergency measure under circumstances which permitted no time to determine individual loyalty and as protective custody of an unpopular minority. The program raised the most serious constitutional problems of the war. Although the Fifth Amendment contains no equal protection clause, could 70,000 American citizens be deprived of their homes and property and be incarcerated in relocation camps solely on the basis of ancestry? Unless judges turned into strategists, leading authorities such as Charles Fairman suggested in the typical argument, the policy had to be sustained as reasonable. Certainly not all the Nisei were disloyal, but fundamental differences in mores had made them so inscrutable that their "utter loyalty" was impossible to prove. Overriding dangers of disloyalty, "potential if not active," made wholesale evacuation expedient. However great the individual inconvenience, evacuation was merely "one of the unavoidable hardships incident to the war."[4]

Most Americans in 1942 doubtless accepted this view. As public hysteria spread, demands for action in the sensational press were strengthened by respected voices, such as Walter Lippmann and Earl Warren, who advanced the stock explanation that the very absence of disloyal acts by the Japanese minority was proof of ominous conspiracies afoot.[5] The administration, caught off guard, deferred to the military judgment, and Congress was in no mood to object. Still, disloyalty was not a crime. Even under doctrines of protective custody, was it necessary to evacuate and intern *citizens* without the individual screening which thousands of German and Italian *aliens* had received in England, Hawaii, and elsewhere in the United States? And some of those Germans and Italians had paraded with Nazi flags in New Jersey on the very eve of Pearl Harbor!

The first test to reach the Court offered little comfort to the Justices, because the appeal was by a hardly inscrutable senior at the University of Washington, George Hirabayashi, who had been convicted of misdemeanor charges for refusal to obey a curfew order and to report to a control center for evacuation. Besides a general challenge to the constitutional power of President and Congress to establish military zones outside theatres of combat, Hirabayashi's appeal attacked the regulations on two grounds—that the executive order entailed an unconstitutional delegation of authority to a military commander, and that General DeWitt's discriminatory policy against citizens of Japanese ancestry violated the due process clause of the Fifth Amendment.

Obviously not wishing to judge from hindsight or to interfere with military judgments in a struggle to the death, the Justices hewed a cautious line as the case moved to conference. Substantial agreement existed that the President and the Congress together could authorize establishment of military zones, but virtually uncontrolled discretion of designated commanders and, above all, discrimination by race on the west coast were bitter pills to swallow. While Justice Jackson expressed doubt whether the military could be bound by due process in emergencies, several Justices, such as Roberts, Reed, and Douglas, were sorely troubled by the failure to screen individuals once the Nisei were in custody at control centers. The Chief Justice, even though he expressed himself as being jarred by the treatment accorded to citizens and apprehensive about the power claimed, nevertheless contended that curfew, evacuation, and detention each were separable parts of the program and were supportable alone or in toto on a "rational basis" test. The fact that the trial judge had sentenced Hirabayashi on both counts concurrently proved to be a crucial technicality enabling Stone to separate the program, avoid the second count, and thereby satisfy the general demand for the narrowest possible ruling. Limiting review to "the curfew order as applied, and at the time it was applied," the Court thus ducked the hard issue by processes known as the "judicial stall."[6]

Several Justices conceded that compartmentalizing the relocation program was unrealistic. Whether Justice Murphy challenged that maneuver in conference is unknown because his notes seldom registered his own remarks. The notation of his vote in the *Resweber* case—"Loud R"—went as far as his personal references were likely to go.[7] But the Chief Justice's circulation for the majority in *Hirabayashi* could hardly have failed to prick the conscience of a romantic Irishman whose very rise to power had been based on ethnic appeals. However limited the Court's review, the Chief Justice now justified the orders by one of the most sweeping definitions of war power ever written. The war power was nothing short of Hughes' off-the-cuff definition—"the power to wage war successfully"—coupled with Stone's significant addition regarding judicial review: when authority to wage war is exercised by those on whom "the Constitution has placed the responsibility of warmaking," no court could "sit in review of the wisdom of their action or substitute its judgment for theirs."[8] However influential his advancement of racial equality in other cases, Stone now supported the rationality of the military judgment by reference to the "racial solidarity" of Japanese immigrants, as manifested by their close settlements, Shinto training, and special schools, which inhibited their assimilation into American society and made their loyalty suspect.[9]

Stone's argument was a far cry from "searching judicial inquiry" on behalf of discrete minorities. Both the breadth of his language and his racial references rubbed Murphy's ethnic nerves to the raw. What the Chief had said about Japanese-language schools, he remarked, could be applied equally to "Catholic and other church schools." Despite pleas for a show of unity he circulated a blistering polemic that not only followed Hirabayashi's brief down the line, but excoriated the Court for approving a program that "utterly subverts" individual rights in war.[10] Whatever deference Murphy had previously manifested toward Stone was now a thing of the past.

The gravamen of Murphy's dissent was the *irrationality* of the military decision. Rather than challenge the Court's rationality test, which would have required philosophic exploration, he worked within the Court's frame of reference. Conceding the power of Congress and the President to create war zones, the wide discretion of military commanders in wartime, and the gravity of the situation in early 1942, he maintained that the curfew order was insupportable even under the Court's limited review. "We can never forget that there are boundaries which it is our duty to uphold," Murphy declared. "The mere existence of a state of war" did not suspend the Bill of Rights. Martial law was the Constitution's remedy for emergency. And in his view, only martial law could warrant such extraordinary delegation of legislative authority to military commanders or abridgment of civil liberties outside of actual combat zones. Having elected to proceed without martial law, which was resorted to in Hawaii, the political authorities were still governed by constitutional limitations and should not expect the judiciary to relieve them of that responsibility by weakening constitutional safeguards. The Court, for his part, should stand by *Milligan* and rule that the statute was an unqualified delegation of power.[11/a]

Murphy also found the curfew order defective by due process standards. Though the Fifth Amendment contains no equal protection clause, all the Justices assumed, as they ultimately held in the School Segregation Cases, that due process at some point prohibits irrational discrimination. "Distinctions between citizens solely because of their ancestry," as the Chief Justice remarked in his opinion, "are by their very nature odious to a free people. . . ."[12] Yet Murphy believed that point was reached "when we have one law for the majority of our citizens and another for those of a particular racial heritage."

---

[a] The Justice's strong commitment to the *Milligan* principle was underscored by his scribbling during oral argument: "Ex parte Milligan 77 years governs this case. Counsel. *There was no suspension of the writ in this area*—No. 1." Note, Nos. 870-71, Box 132.

This discrimination [he wrote] is so utterly inconsistent with our ideals and traditions, and in my judgment so contrary to constitutional requirements, that I cannot lend my assent. It is at variance with the principles for which we are fighting and may well have unfortunate repercussions among peoples of Asia and other parts of the East whose friendship and good-will we seek. It bears a melancholy resemblance to the treatment accorded to members of the Jewish race in Germany and other parts of Europe. We cannot close our eyes to the fact that for centuries the old world has been torn by racial and religious wars, has been put on the rack and suffered the worst kind of anguish due to inequality and discrimination. There was one law for one and a different law for another. In the new world we conceived all men to be free and equal.[13]

It was no answer, as Justice Douglas suggested in concurrence, that curfew restrictions were less severe than those imposed by the draft. Draft laws, Murphy replied, did not discriminate on the basis of race.[b] It was no answer to plead emergency or insufficient time to screen individuals. The program was directed against special groups on the basis of racial inferences and concepts of group guilt. Emergency might have been the answer, he conceded, had the government presented substantial evidence of general disloyalty or aggregate individual acts which produced reasonable grounds to fear for the security of military installations. "But such evidence is lacking," he insisted, "and power should not be generated by the general considerations, applicable to many racial and cultural groups, mentioned in the opinion of the Court. The orders in question do not state the facts upon which they are based, and there is good reason to believe that the action of the military authorities, which I am confident was taken in the utmost of good faith, was based primarily if not solely on a widespread belief that persons of Japanese descent had not and could not be assimilated and that by and large they gave primary allegiance to the Empire of Japan."[14] Taking judicial notice of the program in detail—the lack of serious effort to segregate aliens, to isolate disloyal elements, or to apprehend propagandists, in spite of similar precautions already taken by civilian officials and in spite of a three-month delay while General DeWitt awaited authority from Washington, Murphy voiced the refrain which, like Frankfurter's theme of deference, drew virtually every wartime utterance into a solid unity:

[b] Until the Korean War, however, inductees were racially segregated. Recognizing one contradiction, Murphy deleted a remark about nondiscriminatory laws in the United States from his draft opinion. By an assertion that American law was racially neutral, he asked: "Is this so[?] How about laws in most states on marriages with Ethiopians?" Margin note, draft opinion. Nos. 870-71, Box 132.

To say that any racial or cultural group cannot be assimilated is to admit that the great American experiment has failed, that our way of life has failed when confronted with the normal attachment of certain groups of people to other lands. We have had foreign language schools in this country for generations, without considering their existence as grounds for racial discrimination. If people of Japanese extraction have shown an inclination to associate together and have not fully assimilated, it is due largely to restrictions which have been placed upon them by law and social custom. As a nation, we embrace many groups, some of them among the oldest settlements in our midst, that have isolated themselves for religious or cultural reasons.

Undoubtedly we must wage war to win, and do it with all our might. But the might of America lies in something else, something that is unique—the concerted purpose of free men of all faiths, of all creeds, of all extractions, to preserve our free institutions. It will avail us little to win the war on the battlefield and lose it at home. We do not win the war, on the contrary we lose it, if in the process of achieving military victory we destroy the Constitution and the best traditions of our country. What we want to do is win it on the field and also win it at home.[15]

Language so close to the bone, in the heat of war and at a time when tempers were frayed by *Barnette* and *Schneiderman,* appears to have stung Murphy's colleagues. To challenge the rationality of a decision which the Justices now sustained implicitly questioned their reason and explicitly their love of liberty. Justice Reed, who remarked—"It is appealing but I stay unconvinced"—warned Murphy against conceding possible group disloyalty. "F. M.," he observed, "if you admit this you give your case away. Military protection only needs reasonable grounds, which this record has. You cannot wait for an invasion to see if loyalty triumphs."[16] Justice Frankfurter, ardent advocate of national unity, and the Court's leading champion of executive discretion in waging war, peppered Murphy with notes and criticism calculated to dissuade him from dissent.[17] Following Murphy's statement of intention to conference on June 5, 1943, Frankfurter entreated the recalcitrant Justice: "Please, Frank—with your eagerness for the austere functions of the Court & your desire to do all that is humanly possible to maintain and enhance the *corporate* reputation of the Court, why don't you take the initiative with the Chief in getting him to take out everything that either offends you or that you would want to express more irenically."[18] "Felix, I would protect rights on the basis of ancestry—But I would never deny them," Murphy replied, after which Frankfurter retorted: "That's not good enough for me. I don't want any of my fellow citizens to be treated as objects of favor, *i.e.* as inferiors."[19] In conference the next day, Justice Frankfurter added: "F. M. Are you writing Indian cases on the assumption that rights depend on 'ancestry'? If so—I cannot give my imprimatur to such racial discrimination!"[20]

Overwhelming facts of racial discrimination, to Murphy, dissolved Reed's alleged contradictions and reduced Frankfurter's argument to sophistry. Sociological evidence then available, not to speak of subsequent research, makes irrefutable the accuracy of Murphy's hunch that the military orders were based on a priori assumptions of racial guilt. General DeWitt's reports to Congress, explaining his conduct on the basis of belief that the "Japanese race is an enemy race," whose "racial strains are undiluted," furnished internal evidence of prejudice. So did his resort to standard conspiratorial theory that "the very fact that no sabotage has taken place" was a "disturbing and confirming indication that such action will be taken."[21] The truth is, not one citizen of Japanese ancestry was convicted of sabotage or espionage during World War II. Over 5,000 persons of Japanese extraction did request repatriation to Japan in a wave of bitterness over camp conditions in California, but most of them were older generation aliens who were denied citizenship and who sought restoration of resident status soon after their return to civil life. Otherwise the Nisei record was one of valor and self-sacrifice second to no other identifiable group.[22]

By limiting review to the curfew order when rendered, the Court necessarily shunned the detailed record, which might have relieved it from hindsight judgment. Judges relied, as Murphy charged, on general considerations applicable to most American minorities. Penetrating as was his criticism, however, Justice Murphy was filled with nagging insecurities about a lone dissent in the middle of a war. There is no evidence that he took his doubts to Stone, who was having difficulties enough holding Justice Douglas to the racial overtones in his opinion, while at the same time satisfying Justice Frankfurter's strong convictions that waging war was an executive and legislative responsibility. To suit Douglas, Stone withdrew discussion of racial affinities and reemphasized the narrow scope of the Court's review.[23] As opinion day approached, Frankfurter then renewed the pressure on Murphy to close ranks; of the isolated protest in *Hirabayashi* he observed on June 10, 1943:

Of course I shan't try to dissuade you from filing a dissent in that case— not because I do not think it highly unwise but because I think you are immovable. But I would like to say two things to you about the dissent: (1) it has internal contradictions which you ought not to allow to stand, and (2) do you really think it is conducive to the things you care about, including the great reputation of this Court, to suggest that everybody is out of step except Johnny, and more particularly that the Chief Justice and seven other Justices of this Court are behaving like the enemy and thereby playing into the hands of the enemy? Compassion is, I believe, a virtue enjoined by Christ. Well, tolerance is a long, long way from compassion—and can't you write your views with such expressed tolerance that you won't make people think that when eight others disagree with you, you think their view means that they want to destroy the liberties of the United States and "lose the war" at home?[24]

Justice Frankfurter's biting remarks, which played on Murphy's deep patriotic feelings and hesitation about isolated utterance, had the desired effect. Already persuaded by Justice Reed that he had admitted too much and should withdraw the concession about group loyalties, Murphy decided to concur in the narrow holding that there was a rational basis for a discriminatory curfew during the critical period of early 1942.[25] "Whether such a restriction is valid today," he observed, "is another matter." Transforming his prepared dissent into a concurrence, the Justice made plain his abhorrence of the racial theories of the case and his limited agreement with the Court.

Today is the first time, so far as I am aware, [he declared] that we have sustained a substantial restriction of the personal liberty of citizens of the United States based upon the accident of race or ancestry. . . . The result is the creation in this country of two classes of citizen for the purposes of a critical and perilous hour—to sanction discrimination between groups of United States citizens on the basis of ancestry. In my opinion this goes to the very brink of constitutional power.

In voting for affirmance of the judgment I do not wish to be understood as intimating that the military authorities in time of war are subject to no restraints whatsoever, or that they are free to impose any restrictions they may choose on the rights and liberties of individual citizens or groups in those places which may be designated as "military areas." While this Court sits, it has the inescapable duty of seeing that the mandates of the Constitution are obeyed. That duty exists in time of war as well as in time of peace, and in its performance we must not forget that few indeed have been the invasions upon essential liberties which have not been accompanied by pleas of urgent necessity advanced in good faith by responsible men. . . .[26]

"Nor do I mean to intimate," he added with pointed reference to the rest of the program, "that citizens of a particular racial group whose freedom may be curtailed within an area threatened with attack should be generally prevented from leaving the area and going at large in other areas that are not in danger of attack and where special precautions are not needed." "When the danger is past, the restrictions imposed upon them should be promptly removed and their freedom of action fully restored."[27] Taking Stone's opinion at face value, Justice Murphy was willing to defer to past military judgment regarding an evening curfew —but no more. Institutional loyalties had their limits.

II

Murphy soon repented his last-minute retreat in *Hirabayashi*. Opportunity to speak his mind followed shortly, however, in one of the decade's most ideologically divisive cases, *Schneiderman* v. *United States*.[28] Some Supreme Court decisions generate greater heat than light because of the notoriety of the parties, the political importance of the outcome, or because clashing values permit perceptual differences so wide that dialogue never joins. The *Schneiderman* case, though properly speaking not a war power problem, became a turning point in Murphy's career for all these reasons. William Schneiderman, Communist party leader and erstwhile candidate for Governor of Minnesota, had been stripped of his naturalized citizenship in 1939 under a federal statute which authorized cancellation of citizenship certificates on proof of fraud or illegal procurement at the time of naturalization. Analytically the proceedings were difficult because the government, having dropped charges of fraud and having admitted that Schneiderman had violated no laws, advanced the theory that his citizenship had been illegally procured for failure to satisfy a statutory requirement of "attachment to the Constitution" in the five-year period prior to his naturalization in 1927. Imputing lack of attachment retroactively from his subsequent membership in the party and from his active dissemination of communist ideas, the proceedings presented an early forerunner of vexatious issues which plagued the Court for the next two decades. Schneiderman's case was the first appeal based on imputed belief to reach the Court. It was another episode in a simmering conflict over Congress's power to impose belief tests in the naturalization process, a problem which had harassed the Justices ever since they had first upheld denial of citizenship to an aging, female pacifist, Rosika Schwimmer, for refusing to bear arms.[29] And Schneiderman's case presented a far more explosive issue at the very peak of the nation's flirtation with its Soviet ally—did the Communist party advocate forcible overthrow of the United States government?

If an occasion ever existed for a dispassionate analysis of that recurrent question, it was the period of official stimulation of pro-Russian attitudes and of the epic siege at Stalingrad. But the timing and unavoidable political ramifications of the case enveloped the controversy in ever-spiralling agitation. Four years in litigation and twice heard by the Supreme Court, Schneiderman's appeal was argued without fee by a defeated presidential candidate, Wendell L. Willkie, who made easy political hay by criticizing the administration's illiberality in instituting the case.[30] During initial argument in February 1942 government attorneys, acting on an initiative from Undersecretary of State Sumner Welles, inflamed the issue by suggesting to the Chief Justice in an informal letter that the Court postpone consideration of the appeal in order to free the government from embarrassment vis-à-vis the Soviet Union. This request, which placed the Court's reputation for nonpolitical decision on the block, threw the Justices into a wrangle whether they should act independently of foreign policy or, in recognition that the judiciary *is* the third branch of government, should exercise discretion cognizant of extralegal realities. The Chief Justice, after reading the letters in conference, expressed his embarrassment and resentment at State Department pressure. To yield would invite criticism that judges were adjuncts of diplomatic policy. "The onus ought not to be placed on us," Stone observed. "It ought to be placed on the department. The only thing that keeps this Court alive and gives it its influence is that we are not influenced by things extrinsic to our job."[31]

Yet the nation was in danger, the government asked only for delay, and this was not the first time judges had considered political factors. If the Court was willing to assign racial discrimination cases to southern members in order to cushion the blow among white supremacists, one Justice asked, why should it hesitate taking its foreign policy from the State Department rather than from Willkie? Apparently only two Justices expressed willingness to delay. After "prolonged and heated discussion," as Murphy described it, the Justices decided to follow Byrnes' suggestion that they ask the Solicitor General to move in open court for a continuance, giving Willkie opportunity to reply, whereupon the government dropped its request.[32] Meantime, Justice Byrnes resigned and the Court ordered reargument for November 1942. Justice Murphy, who had sided with the Chief Justice in favor of taking the case, but later disqualified himself along with Justice Jackson, then decided to participate; and Justice Black assigned him the opinion which would reverse Schneiderman's denaturalization by a five-to-three vote.[33]

Preparation of opinions provoked another round of agitation within the Court. The Justices, no less than society at large, were deeply di-

vided over the democratic dilemma embedded in the case. Must a free
society extend its rights and privileges to those who spread doctrines
aimed at its destruction? Did the Constitution and Congress contemplate manipulation of citizenship status because of political beliefs?
Perceived according to deeply felt patriotic perspectives, the *Schneiderman* problem fired unusual emotionalism within the Court. For Chief
Justice Stone, who presented the issues in conference with exceptional
force, it was inconceivable that the Court could upset the judgments
of two lower courts on Schneiderman's record. Denaturalization was a
civil, not a criminal process; the Court consistently had defined Congress's authority over the subject as plenary; and the *Schwimmer* and
Macintosh decisions, the first of which he had joined in opposition to a
powerful dissent from Holmes, had upheld use of belief tests to
deny citizenship to pacifists. Surely the Court could not now take a
different position for communists; and surely, beliefs which Congress
could exclude originally could be reexamined upon proper proof. The
Chief Justice, while lamenting the Court's inability to consider some of
the stricken evidence regarding fraudulent concealment of communist
activities which he deemed conclusive and free from imputation, thus
regarded his colleagues' talk about preferred freedoms and clear and
present danger as irrelevant. That Schneiderman had violated no laws,
the Chief snapped, "has nothing to do with it."[34] "Those who go in for
force & violence could not be attached to the Constitution of the
U. S. . . . This is the guide & all the guide in determining whether he
is entitled to become a citizen." "If Congress has not excluded this
man . . . then it has excluded no one."[35]

Justice Murphy, by contrast, saw the case as a critical test of political
toleration. Dubious about beliefs tests in naturalization to start with,
he regarded the difference between withholding and revoking citizenship as controlling. Imputation of beliefs to denaturalize citizens, he
felt strongly, violated the very principles the nation was at war to defend. Imputation also ran against the grain of the distinction between
action and advocacy which all sides had accepted in free speech cases
since the 1920s. And imputation, as a practical matter, jeopardized the
freedom of all naturalized citizens with unorthodox political ideas.
While, granted, a naturalization proceeding was not a criminal trial,
the Justices could not be blind to the fact that loss of citizenship could
result in harsher consequences than criminal penalties and without the
same procedural safeguards. Neither could they ignore the effects of individual cases on the political security of other foreign-born citizens.
As Justice Rutledge argued cogently from this case forward, if citizen-

ship could be cancelled on the same evidence as granted, merely because individual beliefs were either too strong or too weak for subsequent judicial palates, no naturalized citizen could be secure in his
rights. Nor, despite the language of the Fourteenth Amendment, could
he be equal with the native-born. Denaturalization without more created an inferior class of citizens whose liberties hung on the ephemeral
balance of judicial discretion.[36]

Although the Chief Justice regarded Schneiderman's activities prior
to naturalization as conclusive, that anomaly seemed lost on Stone.[37]
Justice Frankfurter, himself a naturalized citizen, was sensitive to the
dilemma and to the distinction between granting and revoking citizenship according to political faith. Yet Frankfurter all his adult life had
transformed a patriotism of passionate intensity into support of plenary
congressional power to regulate immigration. Belief tests might be
illiberal and inevitably enlarge judicial discretion, but for the Justice
a complex of reasons—deference philosophy, fear of legislative reprisal
against immigration because of judicial interference, and hatred of de-
filing a status which he prized with the added ardor of a convert—
all led to the same conclusion: a man could serve only one master.
Party agent Schneiderman, unlike those loyal Americans "who found
in Communism a practical expression of their hopes for a better society," was a "political instrument of the Soviet regime." For Frankfurter, no less than for Murphy, Schneiderman's case was a test of
patriotism. "I have never registered in the primary in any party," Murphy's notes record him as having remarked. "I have voted in all of
them. I am a mugwump. Debs LaFollette & others I have voted for . . .
if you are going to do this about the Communist what are you going
to do with [me?] [Yet] keeping this country as a powerful example
of the last great hope of mankind as Lincoln said is as near to religion
as I know it. I have no formal religion. I am for affirming." "There is
no use saying you are within the Constitution if you mean to destroy
it. . . . This fellow had a dual loyalty."[38]

Incantations of upholding American citizenship as a symbol of freedom emanated from all sides of the Court with evangelical force.
Whether that goal could best be achieved by enlarging national power
or by judicially enforced tolerance, however, were frames of reference
so far apart that the *Schneiderman* case generated more personalized
conflict among the judges than the intrinsically more significant contemporary decisions, *Barnette* and *Hirabayashi*. Feelings restrained in
these cases, perhaps, spilled over in *Schneiderman*. Minority Justices
accused the majority of political motivations; they charged them with

being swayed by events at Stalingrad; they accused Justice Black of writing Murphy's opinion; and rumors of personal back-biting spread through chambers, with outcroppings in printed reports.[39] Seldom, as an opinion writer, was Justice Murphy to face a more acrimonious conflict.

Murphy himself fanned the flames. Rather than attempt to mediate differences, as in *Virginia Electric*; rather than attempt to win Justice Roberts' vote by a remand based on close statutory construction, a possibility Justice Black suggested should be explored; he widened the breach by invoking the broadest of constitutional concepts and language.[40] Both reflected the influence of Willkie's argument to the Court that, so long as legal means were employed and equal Senate representation were preserved, no belief contradicted constitutional principles. The amending clause, so Willkie's argument ran, was otherwise unlimited; and Schneiderman's professed interpretation of the party's revolutionary canons, as last-resort violence when legal means failed to remedy oppression, accorded with the traditional American precepts which Jefferson, Taney, and Lincoln all had affirmed of a natural right to revolution. In a preliminary memorandum which he called "face-lifting to introduce our not too sound views," Murphy conceded the force of the Lincoln analogy on his thinking and asserted that lacking a showing of clear and present danger to the state, cancellation of citizenship on the basis of advocacy and association alone violated the spirit of the Bill of Rights, if not its terms.[41] However unpopular, Schneiderman's case was to be an object lesson in American political toleration. "Once more," the Justice observed to his former secretary, Norman H. Hill, "I will stand for intellectual freedom and relief from interference with the conscience of men."[42]

That approach, from its first showing, was dismissed as a non sequitur; and the familiar pattern of narrowing opinions by internal debate and by posing polar arguments resumed. After all, as the Chief Justice maintained, Congress was not denying First Amendment rights to anyone, but merely withholding the privilege of citizenship. Even to hint that Congress lacked power to impose conditions of belief before granting those privileges threatened a partial dissent from one member of Murphy's majority.[43] Justices Douglas and Rutledge, on the other hand, urged him to say nothing that might close the door to a future (and successful) challenge to the *Schwimmer* rule regarding pacifists.[44] Facing crossfire on the issue of constitutionality even before circulating a first draft, Murphy retreated to a narrower theory, a stricter standard of proof for denaturalization as distinct from naturalization and other civil proceedings. Incorporating a test of "clear, unequivocal and convincing" evidence in a memorandum to his clerk, Murphy observed on May 22, 1943: "Here is what I believe is the right approach to this problem. It avoids any argument or question about constitutionality. It also avoids too much reliance on the very doubtful proposition that the government failed to prove that the party advocated the overthrow of the government by force and violence. It depends mainly on the proposition that the statute was not intended to apply to doctrinal utterances and academic or theoretical exhortations, otherwise one must conclude that Jefferson and Lincoln had not behaved as one attached to the Constitution. This, it seems to me, puts the opposition in a bit of a hole and presents the strongest front for our side of the argument, legally and otherwise."[45]

In essence, the narrower argument advanced two propositions. First, since the government conceded that disagreement existed about the meaning of communist principles of forcible overthrow, especially in the mid-1920s, and since the government offered no evidence that Schneiderman's advocacy and associations were in any way advocacy of action, the Court would refuse to impute these beliefs to an individual who denied holding them in the absence of confirming overt acts. Second, in order to safeguard political liberties of naturalized as well as native-born citizens, where alternative interpretations of party principles were possible, the Court would interpret the revolutionary passages of party literature as "more or less theoretical propositions," not incompatible with constitutional principles, so long as the line between doctrinal advocacy and a call to present action was not breached and time remained for counterdiscussion and reasoned thought. "While it is our high duty to carry out the will of Congress," Murphy argued, "in the performance of this duty . . . we should let our judgment be guided so far as the law permits by the spirit of freedom and tolerance in which our nation was founded, and by a desire to secure the blessings of liberty in thought and action to those upon whom the right of American citizenship has been conferred by statute, as well as to the native born . . . the facts and the law should be construed as far as is reasonably possible in favor of the citizen."[46]

Following circulation of his argument the sparks began to fly. "My brethren of the majority do not deny that there are principles of the Constitution," Chief Justice Stone commented in a scathingly sarcastic dissent. The question he regarded as far simpler than it had been made to appear, namely, whether Schneiderman's beliefs comported with the Constitution; and, to Stone, it was "a little short of preposterous" to suggest that an agitator of Schneiderman's memberships and activities believed in free government. The question was not whether he *could* be, but *was* devoted to the Constitution, argued Stone. "A man can be known by the ideas he spreads as well as by the company he keeps."[47]

Strong objections were not confined to the Chief. Another member of the minority, Justice Frankfurter, could not resist a sarcastic dig:

> Dear Frank:
> Thorough and comprehensive as your opinion in *Schneiderman* is you omitted one thing that, on reflection you might want to add. I think it only fair to state, in view of your general argument, that Uncle Joe Stalin was at least spiritual co-author with Jefferson of the Virginia Statute for Religious Freedom.[48]

After Murphy's next circulation on June 1st, Frankfurter then suggested that he adopt the following headnotes:

> The American Constitution ain't got no principles. The Communist Party don't stand for nuthin'. The Soopreme Court don't mean nuthin'. Nuthin' means nuthin', and ter Hell with the U.S.A. so long as a guy is attached to the principles of the U.S.S.R. Respectfully yours, F.F. Knaebel

Justice Murphy replied in kind:

> My dear F.F.
> Many thanks for your original and revised headnotes in the *Schneiderman* case. Not only do they reveal long and arduous preparation, but best of all, they are done with commendable English understatement and characteristic New England reserve.[49]

Murphy's essay on toleration provoked sharp challenge from all sides, however. The result was retreat on the great issue of party doctrine. "Isn't this Court falling into a logical morass?" queried one critic, who observed: "It seems to me that Wilkie [*sic*] has confused the issue and hornswoggled the Court by a line of specious reasoning. He has made it appear that the issue in this case is one of preserving freedom of opinion against unwarranted infringement (which it is not). He has also tried to make it difficult by contending that the choice is one of requiring 100% attachment to the Constitution as it stood in 1927 or attachment only to Art. V,—which it is not. The Court ought not to let Wilkie take it for a ride on his political wagon."[50] The question, as Stone insisted, was not freedom of thought or speech—whether alien or citizen, Schneiderman was entitled to both. The question was not the degree of change he could advocate in the Constitution. The only question was whether he met statutory qualifications for citizenship; and unless

the Court was prepared to rule that the Bill of Rights prohibited belief tests as a condition of citizenship, how could the Court ignore
Schneiderman's lifetime of activity in behalf of the communist cause?
Furthermore, as Stone argued from a provision of the Immigration
Act, was not membership itself an overt act and therefore an independent ground for lack of attachment? Assuming that the majority's main
object was to preach and to set an example of tolerance, rather than to
protect Schneiderman personally, the only tenable alternatives for
this critic were either to affirm, making absolutely clear the general
right to advocate political change, or to pursue the alternative advanced by Justice Douglas that, in view of the time lapse between the
proceedings and of denaturalization's impact on the political security
of naturalized citizens as a class, the government should produce evidence of fraud.[51] Otherwise the Chief Justice was right: the Court was
being trapped into a whitewash of the Communist party.

In contrast to Justices Douglas and Stone, Murphy did not have a
well-developed view of the naturalization problem until the *Schneiderman* case. His personal attitude evolved in the course of sharpening an
opinion that perforce reflected the viewpoints of his colleagues. Having
started with freewheeling doubts about constitutionality Murphy by
June 1st conceded to Justice Frankfurter that, while he was satisfied
with the result, his opinion as a matter of law "skates on the thinnest
possible ice." He was impressed by Justice Douglas's alternate theory
of fraud, and attempted to absorb it into his opinion before Douglas
found it necessary to file a separate concurrence, in part because he was
leaving Washington before opinion day.[c] Because of the buffeting he
had received Murphy by his third circulation in mid-June was no
longer willing to risk his majority by casting constitutional doubts on
denaturalization via imputed belief. Neither was he willing to hazard a
conclusive interpretation of party doctrine. Though he prepared a rebuttal to Stone's membership argument, as not having been pressed by
the parties, he refrained from publishing it at Justice Reed's urging
that the fundamental objection of insufficient evidence controlled both
membership and advocacy issues.[52]

According to Frankfurter, Murphy was also greatly perturbed by
Douglas's concurrence without notice and on the verge of shifting his

---

[c] After reading Douglas's draft opinion, he observed to his clerk: "This argument
has considerable legal merit and the government may have slipped in waiving the
charge of fraud. But I don't think the government ought to be foreclosed from claiming
that citizenship was obtained illegally if it can later show want of attachment by clear
and convincing evidence." FM to clerk, June 6, 1943, No. 2, Box 131.

own position. The day after Douglas's departure Murphy voiced renewed doubts to Frankfurter about the superiority of Stone's legal argument, whereupon Frankfurter attempted to persuade him to follow his legal conscience rather than his instincts for liberty. To do so would divide the Court 4-4 and leave adjudication of the denaturalization problem to the calmer atmosphere of the forthcoming Bundist case, a course Frankfurter had advocated all along. When Murphy indicated that his whole life was bound up with protecting freedom and expressed fear that so late a reversal would be unethical, Frankfurter reminded him of previous last-minute reversals and declared that he saw "nothing improper but everything that was most proper and honorable for a man to be acting on what his legal conscience tells him should be the result in a case." But while Murphy accepted Frankfurter's importunings in "the friendliest spirit," it was too late.[53]

Dualism, as a result of interior doubts and accommodating multiple viewpoints, thus pervaded the final *Schneiderman* opinion. Avoiding constitutional doubts altogether, avoiding a conclusive holding whether the Communist party advocated force and violence, Murphy's final version, in the style of his political past, combined the radical rhetoric of toleration with a very careful ruling. Using the case to establish a strict standard of "clear, unequivocal and convincing" evidence in denaturalization proceedings based on imputed beliefs, the Justice ruled for the Court: "We hold only that where two interpretations of an organization's program are possible, the one reprehensible and a bar to naturalization and the other permissible, a court in a denaturalization proceeding . . . is not justified in canceling a certificate of citizenship by imputing the reprehensible interpretation to a member of the organization in the absence of overt acts indicating that such was his interpretation. . . . Were the law otherwise, valuable rights would rest upon a slender reed, and the security of the status of our naturalized citizens might depend in considerable degree upon the political temper of majority thought and the stresses of the times."[54]

To preach the lesson of tolerance, on the other hand, Murphy turned on the rhetoric, with the result that many did regard the *Schneiderman* opinion as politically inspired. The government had failed to meet the evidence test, the Justice argued, for two principal reasons. First, the Court recognized in a much-quoted passage that "under our traditions beliefs are personal and not a matter of mere association, and that men in adhering to a political party or other organization notoriously do not subscribe unqualifiedly to all its platforms or asserted principles." Without overt acts, it was treacherous to impute what was in an 18-year-old's mind 12 years later by membership alone. Even though the Justice failed to mention that Schneiderman also had joined the party at approximately the same time, for him the analogy was clear: because a man broke a marriage vow, he later observed, was no proof that he did not mean it when taken.[55] Second, the Court recognized that the meaning of communist doctrine was debatable in 1927, making all the more speculative his allegiances at that time. "The Constitutional fathers, fresh from a revolution, did not forge a political straight-jacket for generations to come," Murphy declared. Many a principle avowed by communists in the United States had been shared by loyal citizens. Lincoln's Emancipation Proclamation had expropriated property without compensation. Neither unicameralism nor criticism of judicial review was unknown. In what surely must rank as one of the most radically naïve syllogisms ever advanced from the high bench, Murphy even asserted that a belief in "some form of world union of soviet republics" did not necessarily demonstrate hostility to constitutional principles, "unless we are willing so to hold with regard to those who believe in Pan-Americanism, the League of Nations, Union Now, or some other form of international collaboration. . . ."[56]

Outside the Court that statement alone blinded critics to the subtle distinctions between advocacy and action which the decision enforced. What was "theoretical force and violence" anyway? "We can only infer that Murphy and his associates are moved by political considerations, as usual," the Justice's old critic, the *Macon* (Ga.) *News-Telegraph*, observed.[57] Narrowing the ruling did little to allay similar suspicions within the Court. Justice Jackson, indeed, alerted the public to the issue by publishing what he had threatened in *Goldman*, an explanation of his disqualification, which effectually asked the embarrassing question: why had Murphy authorized this proceeding as Attorney General if only four years later he could find no clear, unequivocal, and convincing proof of a lack of allegiance to the Constitution?[58] The Court's discussion of party principles, for that matter, hardly squared with his previous denunciations of Soviet communism for its atheism or aggressions in Eastern Europe, its "denial and contradiction of elemental human wants," or its agents in the United States who have "sought with premeditation to undermine our democratic form of government."[59] Murphy had not simply failed to disqualify himself; he was pulling another switch.

It was "plain as pikestaff," for one dissenter, that wartime expediency was the decision's driving force. There was not the slightest doubt, for him, that his colleagues were being swayed by world politics and that "if the same kind of record had come up with reference to a Bundist, the opposite result would have been reached."[60] The Court's protection of the Bundist Baumgartner and the propagandist Hartzel in the next term quickly disposed of invidious comparisons.[61] Justice Reed, the principal target of the Stalingrad charge, had made plain all along that he supported reversal only because of inadequate government proof of *knowing* advocacy and membership.[62/d] In answer to Stone's innuendo that alliance politics compelled the result, Murphy added a vigorous opening paragraph to state his agreement with the Chief Justice that relations with Russia and the merits of communism were irrelevant. Then he repeated the denial to Hearst executive Richard E. Berlin. Soviet-American relations "had nothing to do with the case," he insisted.

In the absence of a single act of violence or a violation of the law, I did not believe that the government made out a case against a lack of attachment. . . . Religious and political liberty bottomed this nation and they are fast sloughing off.

Schneiderman by judicial decree had been made a citizen in 1927. Since that date there is not the slightest evidence of lawlessness against him. If he could be denaturalized, don't you see it would be easy to denaturalize countless others who don't conform?[63]

Motivation is impossible to impute with certainty, but the evidence points to the conclusion that liberal fashions regarding Allied cooperation had less to do with Justice Murphy's perception of the case than romantic ideas of his country as a sanctuary of liberty. One reason is that his attitude toward the Soviet Union fluctuated with the tides of battle throughout the war. In the fall of 1942 he noted with some irony that "the irreligious Russians are making religious freedom possible for the rest of us," though he was "quite sure those gallant people will not prevail" against the Nazis, whom he already had denounced as civilization's gravest threat.[64] In early 1944 he was still enjoying the irony that "Russia has saved the civilized world"; but "whether she will run amuck afterwards," he added, "no one knows."[65] As attention in Washington began to fix on problems of postwar planning, moreover, the neo-isolationist strain of midwestern Progressivism began to reassert itself in his thought, with all its overtones of native superiority and mission. "I don't believe in the inevitability of wars . . . ," he wrote a departing clerk at the end of the term. "Nor do I believe our destiny

[d] Murphy quoted Reed in conference: "I do not think there was enough for the trier of fact. If I felt otherwise I could not go along." Conference note, No. 2, Box 131.

is to lead in war. This country was conceived to lead man in the pursuits of peace and therefore to the state of grace and civilization he craves."[66] While assuming that Big Three partnership would be the cornerstone of peace, and while sharing the general optimism about the prospects, the Justice retained his prewar view that national strength depended less on alliance politics than on ethical force. Short of the universal collective security of Wilson's dream, his distrust of Europeans and the British was not far removed from the hemispheric premises of Robert A. Taft. Of a proposed Big Three alliance to secure the peace, he observed to a former clerk at Christmas 1943:

I am more anxious for collaboration with the family of nations than I am for alliances that will cause us to carry the burden of a hopeless group, a segment of the Old World. If I were to be practical about alliances I would do it in an exemplary way in the New World with all its hopes for men and its devotion to free institutions. The Old World I would be helpful and friendly with. But the New World I would never abandon.

Personally I believe that the United States and England ought to demand the settlement of all problems on a moral basis. Don Eduardo [Kemp] shrugs his shoulders when I say this. "Let's be practical," he replies but remember he is an Anglo Saxon and that explains all.[67]

In preparing his *Schneiderman* opinion even Murphy might question the accuracy of his assertion that American citizenship embodied "the highest hope of civilized men," a remark which may have been a gentle jibe at Justice Frankfurter. But he had no doubt that traditional American liberties symbolized universal aspirations or that "the new world with unflagging zeal will protect them."[68] *Barnette*, *Hirabayashi*, and *Schneiderman*, in this sense, were all of one piece. For Murphy, maintaining civil liberties was part of the nation's defense and historic mission in world affairs.

Whether *Schneiderman* was an instance when Murphy swept causes he hated under symbols he cherished, his evangelism played no small part in creating resistance to the lesson. Twice during circulation of his opinion he refused to heed Douglas's warning that comparison of the Comintern with internationalist groups was irrelevant and impolitic. The opposition interpreted the reference, probably correctly, as a personal slap at Justice Roberts, a proponent of Union Now.[69] Against Jackson's revival of the disqualification issue he likewise remained unmoved. Just as the Court majority appeared to go out of its way to bolster the political security of naturalized citizens, so Murphy defied aspersions about his consistency and personal motives in order to preach the principle of personal rather than group guilt. It may have been anomalous that the Court protected naturalized communists more than native-born Nisei, but the decision gave a powerful boost to his evangelical streak. Vainly, in reports home, he called the case "the most important one of the year"; and though he assumed the decision would be unpopular, he gauged it correctly as a milestone in civil liberties.[70]

Not long thereafter, the Justices would scramble down from their summit of political toleration, and in the next decade the Vinson Court had no trouble taking judicial notice of a revolutionary communist conspiracy.[71] The freedom of speech permitted in World War II thus contrasted vividly with the hysteria both before and after. The credit lay partly with Attorney General Biddle's calm policy toward criticism of the government, partly with the educational efforts of the mass media, and the Court's highly publicized *Viereck* and *Hartzel* decisions, all of which manifested a general desire to avoid the mistakes of the previous war.[72] Given the force of Stone's dissent and the subtleties of the issue, the "decency and common sense" of the Court's choice in *Schneiderman* was remarkably well received.[73] It is significant also that the judiciary was most effective when it avoided constitutional climaxes, an object lesson not lost on future courts. After efforts to loosen the evidence test in *Baumgartner* v. *United States*, and the nearly fatal inroads during the McCarthy era, the Warren Court resolved the same issues by reviving similar tactics. Minus its rhetoric, the *Schneiderman* rule lives on.[74]

Eventually Justice Murphy crossed the constitutional divide by challenging the power of Congress to exile naturalized citizens or aliens for political belief, even under the *Schneiderman* test.[75] Nevertheless, spring 1943 was his turning point. In *Hirabayashi* he reluctantly compromised personal protest. In *Schneiderman*, when his views were inchoate, he also smothered constitutional doubts for sake of "marshalling" the Court behind a substantial advance in the political security of the foreign-born. But his old duality of style—combining practical judgments with radical rhetoric—reared itself on the Court. So did his self-righteous enjoyment of a fight. The results were another parting of the ways within the institution and a major step in the development of his reputation as an ideologically compelled jurist. Taking notice of the mixed reactions about *Schneiderman* the Justice responded:

All I know is that my pen was lifted in the cause of intellectual liberty and freedom. I can't help how others see the issue. I don't want posterity to hate my views. But I won't have anything to say about that.

I have always found that swimming upstream when your object is a just
one pays great dividends in the future especially as far as inward peace
is concerned. Every unpopular but right thing I have ever done in the long
run paid off.[76]

Justice Murphy, as a libertarian evangelist, was making peace with
his post.

III

"This is a magnificent opinion." "You will be proud of this opinion
all your life," Justice Rutledge told Murphy during the *Schneiderman*
fight.[77] Rutledge's reaction was an early indicator that a duo was developing within a bloc and a symbol of the personal variations that
cut into the cohesion of the libertarian quartet just as it emerged. War,
of course, and the dramatic battle over preferred freedoms, overshadowed subtler differences that might have restrained sweeping generali-
zations about group behavior which became popular after 1943. Compared with the great First Amendment debate, individual variations
naturally paled in significance. Compared with conflicts over economic
policy, however, which fed much public speculation about seething
internal feuds, the essential agreement of Justices Stone, Black, and
Frankfurter regarding war power and the cracks in libertarian solidarity revealed by the narrow concurrences of Douglas and Murphy in
Hirabayashi easily ranked among the most important developments of
the term. Yet somehow they were ignored.

The business of the Supreme Court is so varied that selective interpretations of total performance are inescapable. No universally accepted
scale of values exists to measure the intrinsic importance of cases or of
shifting personal combinations. Yet Justice Murphy's performance
alone in the 1942-43 terms was suggestive of his rising confidence and
independence, independence which also demonstrated the limitations
of bloc analysis of judicial behavior. Three areas of litigation—Indian
claims, divorce, and war power—not only revealed Murphy breaking
the traces. They showed that even libertarian blocs are a matter of
more or less, congeries of men now cohering, now parting according
to varying issues, strategies, and personal perceptions.

Indian claims, which became a Murphy specialty, split the "activists"
with hardly less regularity than they cohered over preferred freedoms.
Since the cases frequently turned on interpretations of nineteenth-century statutes and treaties the decisions were too complex for easy cate-
gorization. Suffice it to say that Justice Black's antipathy for special tax
treatment commonly placed him in opposition to exemptions for Indian

tribes, while Justice Murphy vigorously urged that all doubts should be resolved in their favor, according to what he regarded as "the humane and liberal policy that has been adopted by Congress to rectify past wrongs." "Knowing the history—sordid, corrupt, and sometimes vicious—" he wrote to Indian folklorist, Chase S. Osborn, "I have insisted and will continue to insist on a policy of uncompromising morality toward our wards."[78]

In fairness, most Justices, including Stone and Frankfurter, took much the same position less sentimentally. Because Murphy manifested more interest in the subject than the others, there was reason for Frankfurter's observation in 1943 that Murphy was fast replacing Justice Van Devanter as "the Court's chief expert and guardian of Indian rights— an enviable role."[79] A notable example was the Choctaw-Chickasaw claim in which Murphy labored through a maze of conflicting facts, changed his mind, and led a unanimous bench to follow suit.[80] Even his dissents were apt to attract company. One austere dissent, which Justice Roberts urged him to write, moved Justice Frankfurter to comment: "I call this—I'm sorry—lawyerlike!"[81]

Yet Murphy's boast that "I am writing most of the Indian law for the Supreme Court" was not fully accurate.[82] Though he did not always support Indian claimants, his feelings were too strong for liberal colleagues who believed that sympathetic treatment was being pushed into privilege. Undaunted, Murphy followed defeat in one tax exemption battle with a note to the former clerk who had once urged him to break libertarian ranks in a close case for reputational purposes: "On Monday read a little of my gospel in dissent from my brother Black. Whenever the moral obligations of the country are involved I believe you know how exemplary I feel they should be executed without being puddin headed."[83]

Murphy also strayed from the fold over federalism problems, an area of explicit judicial arbitration that appealed to his experience and mediatory instincts. He had few opportunities to write until Stone's death, but the troublesome issue of conflicts of state divorce law was a revealing exception. Joining forces with Jackson and Roberts against Black, Douglas, and Rutledge in the *Williams* v. *North Carolina* cases, Murphy candidly believed that full faith and credit obligations should be qualified by considerations of state policy and social morality.[84] After reading Douglas's "closely reasoned" opinion for the Court in the first *Williams* decision, he felt that he had "stirred up a legal hornet's nest" with the issue of fraudulent domicile. As he noted to his clerk, "I sent a note to Jackson suggesting that he, Warden Roberts and myself (representing the apostolic succession) have a word or two to say about Douglas's Free Love opinion reversing Haddock." Justice Jackson replied to the note: "We must. Jointly or severally. I dictated something which I fancy will not be the same ground you and the Senior Warden (apostolic succession via Henry VIII) will take. My point is hard to develop without being a trifle gay with the case in the light of this record. That is dangerous. It's short and I'll get it around soon. But I'm sure one or both of you will want a graver note."[85]

While Murphy made no end of jokes about Nevada's "lustful decree" in the *Williams* case, conflict of divorce laws was the main instance, except *Chaplinsky* or in reverse, when Catholic attitudes affected his self-perception as a defender of morality. "I don't want to be 'Churchie,'" he remarked to his clerk as writing began, "but public morals and the sacred bonds must be appropriately even tho inadequately recognized in whatever I write."

The more I think the more I believe
1. There is a sound moral—public morality ground—that ought not to be ignored in this case.
2. That Douglas' opinion tries to preach morality and rests on cold legalism. This case is one or the other but not both.
3. What about this being an indestructible union of indestructible states? Marriage as Don Eduardo [Kemp] looks at it may be a snare and a delusion but a Reno divorce is a raucous fraud, a pure tourist racket and an indestructible state has its public morality destroyed.[86]

Along with the judges of the Victorian era Murphy felt strongly that the full faith and credit clause should not be applied automatically to actions "grounded in deceit," by which he meant temporary residence changes rather than divorces per se. Conflicting state policies, he felt, in substantial agreement with the Court's ultimate position, should be accommodated even at the cost of erecting domicile into constitutional status. Besides, he said, "the whole thing is a humbug on America. . . . Jurisdiction for home purposes is not really established in Reno. It is done for the ranch trade. If continued for a long time it will make definite inroads on our finest tradition—the American home."[87/e]

To qualify full faith and credit obligations in order to reconcile com-

---

[e] Justice Jackson, who frankly stated that full faith and credit obligations could not be divorced from policy considerations, observed to Murphy after the first *Williams* decision: "I agree that they have builded worse than they know in the Carolina case. I think the Roman Church has an accumulated wisdom, arising from age-long experience in social matters that makes its stand greatly to be respected even by those of us who do not concede it to be authoritative. Bad seed has been sowed. It will take some time for the crop to be harvested—but it will be bad I fear." Robert H. Jackson to FM, Jan. 2, 1943, Box 107.

peting state policies conflicted directly with Justice Black's crusade to reduce judicial influence over social policy. The Court hardly had reconvened in the fall of 1943 when Murphy broke customary alignments again on a subject of first magnitude—war power. By the 1943 term the Court was no longer able to withhold review of emergency measures or revelation of its own divide. At a time when the tides of battle ran in Allied favor, a bundle of war power cases, all of them unified by a common scope of review issue, became the Justices' preoccupation and prime source of fragmentation.

No stronger example of the gulf between Murphy and his colleagues existed than their conceptions of the judicial function during national emergency. Justice Frankfurter, on one side, was the most vigorous exponent of executive freedom of action and corresponding judicial restraint, a principle he advanced not merely as the commandment of the Constitution and the Holmesian tradition, but as obvious dictate of love of country. Justice Murphy, after *Hirabayashi*, espoused the opposing *Milligan* principle with kindred passion. Idealizing the American tradition in common, but differing radically about the judiciary's part in maintaining it, Frankfurter and Murphy represented with common emotional force the Court's opposite extremes. Both were too shrewd to permit disagreement to inhibit cooperation elsewhere; but after 1943 their former friendship and alliance were beyond recovery. The mantle of leadership thus fell to less emotional, senior Justices in the center—Stone, Black, and Douglas—whose support of the government when the chips were down earned them the misleading label of "war hawks." Given the pressures of popular feeling and his sensitivity to personal standing, Murphy's constancy to the *Milligan* philosophy was a remarkable display of judicial independence. Alone among the Justices he championed the well-nigh utopian view smothered in *Hirabayashi* that more, not less, judicial review would help "win the war."

The gulf between Murphy and his colleagues, it should be stressed, was not over constitutional ultimates. Not once did he dispute the *constitutional* capacity of the political authorities to wage war by martial law or, short of that, to impose conscription and economic controls over civilians during wartime. Although these measures represented to him "a grim and suggestive foretaste" of the consequences of defeat, Murphy, after all, had advocated both to the President before Pearl Harbor and was not now prepared to backtrack.[88] Neither did he dispute the general principle of judicial deference to the Commander-in-Chief and Congress, or more realistically, in whose name countless harassed bureaucrats and military commanders were acting. Only Justice Jackson, by the same token, went so far as to suggest judicial disassociation from military judgments and even his view reflected more a realistic assessment of the enforceable limits of judicial power than a normative ideal. But short of those ultimate questions of emergency powers, most of which, as Jackson later observed, remain unsettled, Murphy's dominant note was the judicial protection of individual liberties in war.[89]

Views so uncompromising were enigmatic even to those who knew Murphy well. After all, here was a man who still longed to be Secretary of War or a common soldier, now opposing military discretion with some of the most idealistic outpourings in the history of the Court. The enigma would have been easy to solve had it been simply a function of lessening danger or a reflection of liberal fashions. Yet neither explanation sufficed. Actually Murphy lost little of his war fever as victory neared. During summer recesses he badgered friends in the executive branch and the military establishments as hard as ever for foreign assignment. "All I have known during my adult life . . . has been one crisis and emergency after another," he commented to Grace Tully. "I do not want to stand by. I long to serve my country rather than take a holiday." "It saddens me that one of my administrative experiences in government and my experience in colonial affairs, limited as I may be, cannot be of some genuine help in South America, India or Russia during this emergency period."[90] His yearnings to return to the Philippines, indeed, bordered on desperation. After appeals to Hull, Marshall, and lesser officials met with failure at every turn, he even attempted to obtain a presidential reversal via the President's daughter and his secretary, who must have been embarrassed by his boasts about military training and physical prowess.[91]

Murphy's relationship with President Roosevelt had narrowed progressively in focus following his ascent to the bench. After 1942 he was seldom consulted about patronage and judicial appointments, but he continued to advise the President actively regarding labor policy and the Philippines.[92/f] In 1943 he was instrumental in obtaining Roosevelt's support for a congressional resolution renewing pledges of Filipino independence, though as a stroke of psychological warfare, he would have granted independence "here and now."[93/g] He also did yeoman service

---

[f] After Justice Byrnes resigned Murphy wrote: "I probably will not be consulted about the court appointment but I have been before and I might be again." FM to Ralph W. Aigler, Jan. 14, 1942, Box 106. His most vigorous effort to influence a judicial appointment was on behalf of Kemp. FM to FDR, Dec. 7, 1944, Box 114.

[g] After the President broadcast the pledge to the Philippines, Murphy observed: "He would do better if he would disregard the caution of the British and ask Congress to immediately declare the Republic of the Philippines. That would rock Japan back on its heels." FM to James W. Gerard, Aug. 17, 1943, Box 109.

by helping to organize Philippines relief, by raising funds for the Quezon family, and by mediating a troublesome squabble between Quezon and Osmeña over presidential succession in the Commonwealth government-in-exile.[94/h] Thus when he appealed to the President in 1944 to permit him to return to the Islands at his own expense, Murphy expected to cash in on old debts. "While heretofore you have made assurances to me that you have been unable to keep," he reminded Roosevelt, "I completely understand. . . . In addition, there are forces in and around Washington at work that are without liking for both my zeal and independence—allowing them proper appraisal of my inadequate abilities."[95]

Still the President refused. Though it was obvious to everyone but himself that Murphy was getting in the way, he renewed the pressure to reach Manila in the spring of 1945 with every conceivable plan, ranging from a personal vacation to a leave of absence to direct an aid mission, after finding himself unable to break the wall of silence surrounding Roosevelt's final illness.[96] Melancholy over the growing separation from his beloved chief, even as he recognized its inevitability, and longing for popular affection which he missed on the Court, Murphy explained himself to his brother George: "My heart is out there. . . . What we did in the Philippines is the symbol of everything lofty we struggle for today." "You, more than any other person, know how I despise social inequality and how devout I am in the belief that an ethnic group, its culture, religion and civilization, should be allowed to bloom."[97] Whatever his past doubts about American moral obligations, Filipinos were helpless pawns of great-power politics whose wartime sacrifices imposed prime moral and legal obligations on the United States. Self-determination was an article of American political faith which Murphy assumed had universal validity. Filipinos had given him love. He could no more help identify himself with their cause than he could avoid making well-founded sympathies sound vainglorious. "To my mind," he said, Philippines independence is "a symbol of this whole great struggle." "We must not turn back." And his candid admission that policy considerations should fill the interstices in *Hooven & Allison* v. *Evatt*, left no doubt that he carried that concept into Court.[98/i]

[h] The Justice's efforts strengthened his standing among Filipino leaders. Quezon, who asked him to head the Joint Economic Commission planned for postwar rehabilitation, once wrote: "You always make me feel that we are not alone in this world. Needless to say *I do count upon you*." Quezon to FM, Sept. 9, 1943, Box 109. Quote, Quezon to FM, March 29, 1943, Box 108.

[i] The essential issue in the *Hooven* case was whether Filipino goods imported into the United States were "imports" and thus exempt from state taxation. In view of

The Justice's moralist and Far East emphasis, while perhaps more attributable to personal involvements than to neo-isolationist roots, contrasted heavily with his private lust for military action. The approach of victory and the comfort of judicial independence also encouraged the outcropping of an idealist world-view. The result was sharper idiosyncrasy than ever. Murphy, for one, regarded the avowed goal of total victory as a pipedream. The United States would surely win military victories, he thought, but no nation ever *won* a total war.[99] For all his admiration of Roosevelt and Hull, and his not-so-silent frustration over personal distance from great events, he was even more skeptical of the forms national involvements were beginning to take. Especially the war crimes trials—which Justice Jackson was beginning to prepare in the belief that Nuremberg would crown a lifetime of legal achievement—Murphy condemned as a corruption of American traditions by vengeance and power politics. Nuremberg, he advised a friend, would be a lynching party "it is wise to be out of...."[100] Firmly convinced that projecting superior native standards was the path to international leadership, Murphy increasingly began to interpret the Court's work in light of world reconstruction and international events. Offering a lofty

---

conflicting evidence regarding federal practice and of Congress's general policy of favored treatment, Murphy argued that policy reasons supported the Chief Justice's position for the Court. During preparation of the opinion on these grounds he relayed the following message to his clerk, maintaining that:

1. In 1898 we invaded the Islands because of a war with Spain.
2. That the Japanese in 1941 and our forces in 1944 invaded the Islands because of the Japanese-American war.
3. The helpless Filipinos have been only the pawn of great powers.
4. Our obligations in the Islands are unique because of moral and legal commandments above that we have elsewhere.
5. [That the United States aided other nations via trade policy . . .]
6. That American integrity is involved. Accordingly we ought not to let special sugar or hemp interests interfere with weighty obligations that we have in the Philippines.

FM to Lady [Bumgardner], March 19, 1945, No. 380, Box 133.

During administration debate over Quezon's pressure for an accelerated declaration of independence, Murphy also wrote War Department official Evett D. Hester, whom Quezon had called an "imperialist" for resisting the plan:

You and I have, I fear, many conflicting views. That does not mean that you are in error.

I am not an imperialist. "White Man's Burden" to me is only a stuffed shirt way of covering up rapacity. Live and let live directs me. I will have no part of suppression or oppression. Nordics are not a super race. Nor do they have a monopoly on stomachs, hearts and souls. Our inability to defend the Philippines should not be an excuse to turn the clock back to 1898.

FM to Evett D. Hester, Dec. 30, 1943, Box 111.

moral example, if only by way of preachment, could be a judicial contribution to peace.

In short, midway in his judicial career Justice Murphy rejected the principle of judicial self-restraint as a blinding abstraction. Not once after *Hirabayashi* was he willing to accept the procedural shortcuts imposed by Congress in draft and price-control regulation which interfered with substantial individual rights. Not once did he fully embrace an opinion of the Court sustaining war power or military discretion unless the Justices—as in the *Cramer* treason trial or his own *Hartzel* opinion, which imposed rigorous evidence tests for Espionage Act prosecutions—imposed subsidiary safeguards.[101] As the Court became immersed in the concrete issues of war a new duality thus appeared in his opinions, a duality produced not by indecision, processes of mutual accommodation, or even by the old combination of a tongue in the heavens and an eye on earth. Defending decisions with lofty principles with which no one disagreed—that common failing of simplistic minds that had dogged Murphy's trail all his life—was not now the principal criticism of his opinions. Posing either-or alternatives in the war power field became the very object of his attack. A self-appointed apostle of the libertarian tradition while hostilities raged, Murphy alternated between graduated responses addressed to the Court and crusading polemics aimed at a larger public.

In first reactions, he frequently looked to the Constitution for argument as well as bearings. Prodding from colleagues, such as Stone's warning against use of the clear and present danger test in *Hartzel*, usually was necessary before Murphy narrowed his analysis.[102] Yet narrow he did, for no one could ignore the fact that the most successful judicial interventions in World War II—*Cramer, Viereck, Hartzel*, Rutledge's *Yakus* dissent—took largely procedural and circumspect form.[103] Because Murphy more often than not was out of step with claimed authority, he faced a chronic strategic dilemma whether his opposition should be broadly cast in order to appeal to mass conscience or scaled to the precise legal issues. As military victory appeared certain and his personal defeats accumulated, the rhetorical style predominated. But it is essential to understanding that style itself was a matter of situation and choice. Emotional appeals to high principle, for Murphy, had always been a means of defending decisions as much as reaching them, particularly when the going was rough. The Supreme Court, once personal diffidence was overcome, was no different. The greater the gulf between Justice Murphy and his colleagues, the war power cases make plain, the greater the likelihood of his resort to radical rhetoric—

and Huey Long's purported strategy note on the margin of a Senate speech: "Weak Point. Holler Louder!"

The sharpest contrast in options of style was set by the draft cases and return engagement of the Japanese relocation program in 1944-45. While clearly of lesser significance, in terms of numbers affected and issues raised, the problem of conscientious objection to the draft, which the Justices had managed to avoid until the *Falbo* case in January 1944, provoked a more passionate outburst from Murphy than did internment of Japanese-Americans.[104] Because Congress had exempted religious objectors from the draft, the essential problem in *Falbo* was not the privilege to object as such, but the point in the selective service process at which administrative remedies were exhausted and judicial review of draft classifications could begin. Technical though the issue may have appeared, the scope of review had important bearing on both the efficiency of the draft and the statutory right to object. Litigation, on the one hand, could easily obstruct manpower procurement, which presumably was Congress's reason for declaring draft board classifications to be "final." Limited review, on the other, meant that members of some religious sects, notably the Jehovah's Witnesses, who refused to report for induction, found themselves either inducted or jailed with opportunity to challenge the legality of their orders only in criminal trials, before unsympathetic juries, and in a field where appellate review remains "the narrowest known to the law." Under the circumstances, did Congress's declaration of finality restrict judicial review to habeas corpus after induction or did due process require additional avenues of judicial review?[105]

Despite evidence of prejudice by board members in the *Falbo* case, the Court, speaking through Justice Black, restricted review to the last step in the selective service process, that is, after induction, in order to prevent "litigious interruption" of the draft. However essential, Murphy would have no part of such procedure. While confessing that the case presented "another aspect of the perplexing problem of reconciling basic principles of justice with military needs in wartime," to him "common sense and justice" dictated wider opportunity for individuals to challenge administrative orders. Provoked by inroads on religious conscience in the name of unproven dangers, Murphy let fly a classic expression of judicial crusading: "That an individual should languish in a prison for five years without being accorded the opportunity of proving that the prosecution was based upon arbitrary and illegal administrative action is not in keeping with the high standards of our judicial system. Especially is this so where neither public necessity nor rule of law or statute leads inexorably to such a harsh result. The law knows no finer hour than when it cuts through formal concepts and transitory emotions to protect unpopular citizens against discrimination and persecution."[106]

The dissent highlighted the Hobson's choice facing religious objectors that brought modification near the war's end. Although Justices Stone and Burton still insisted that habeas corpus after induction satisfied due process, the Court, under the leadership of Justice Douglas in *Billings* and *Estep*, broadened opportunity for review at the point of taking induction oaths and by permitting habeas corpus after criminal trials. "We are dealing here with a question of personal liberty," Douglas observed; there was little point forcing courts "to march up the hill when it is apparent from the beginning that they will have to march down again." Neither could it be assumed that Congress intended judges to enforce orders that bordered on constitutional danger zones.[107/j]

Despite the gains, Murphy remained unsatisfied. The Court's compromise still left unpopular religious minorities with only two choices —induction in violation of conscience or jail. Waging a lonely battle for his *Falbo* view that review should obtain upon receipt of induction orders, he converted his original dissent into a concurrence in order to protest the needless hardship imposed. Murphy wrote:

There is something basically wrong and unjust about a juridical system that sanctions the imprisonment of a man without ever according him the opportunity to claim that the charge made against him is illegal. I am not yet willing to conclude that we have such a system in this nation. Every fiber of the Constitution and every legal principle of justice and fairness indicate otherwise.

We must be cognizant of the fact that we are dealing here with a legislative measure born of the cataclysm of war, which necessitates many temporary restrictions on personal liberty and freedom. But the war power is not a blank check. . . . As long as courts are open and functioning, judicial review is not expendable.

---

[j] In the *Estep* case Justices Murphy and Reed originally prepared dissents against Justice Douglas's position that the Selective Service Act permitted habeas corpus only after induction. That had been the assumption of the Court in *Falbo* and of most lower courts, which were influenced by World War I decisions. Though the point was not argued on appeal, Douglas became convinced that habeas corpus also was available after conviction; then he redrafted his opinion and carried a majority, including Justice Reed. Justices Murphy, Frankfurter, and Rutledge concurred separately; and Stone and Burton dissented. See Douglas memorandum opinions of Dec. 14 and 19, 1945; Jan. 11, 1946; and Feb. 1, 1946. No. 292, Box 135.

All the mobilization and all the war effort will have been in vain if, when all is finished, we discover that in the process we have destroyed the very freedoms for which we fought.[108]

These were strident words uttered in isolation. The draft cases, which revived his angry charges of *Hirabayashi* and coincided with a cluster of passionate opinions in defense of minority rights, magnified the Justice's growing reputation as a doctrinaire so obsessed with protecting underdogs that he was insensitive to competing national interests or to the tactical necessity of husbanding his fire.[109] Even his private explanations of purpose reinforced impressions that he was becoming trapped in his own public image as a champion of the minorities. "I have no thought, no desire other than to work and write in my modest way in defense of human liberty and justice," he would respond to the small audience of kindred spirits, such as Norman Thomas, who lauded his example in resisting the passions of war.[110] In June 1944 he wrote his brother George: "Court recessed a few minutes ago for this term. Wherever and whenever my pen struck it was to unshackle man, enlarge his freedoms and make articulate those whose views do not reach to the heights above. On the field of battle rights are often won soon to be surrendered by men without light in the courtroom. But there are others who with their pen achieve that which nameless heroes suffer and die for." Was Justice Murphy beginning to sublimate lessening stature as a jurist by identifying himself as spokesman for the underdogs no one else saw fit to defend?[111]

At the time, he was thought to have been a wild dreamer, willing to risk obstruction of the draft in order to protect the intangible rights of an unpopular few. Yet even as he unleashed the crusading style of Recorder's Court, Murphy was operating at more pragmatic levels than his rhetoric implied. Nearly 6,000 conscientious objectors were imprisoned during World War II. Could not room have been made for their unorthodoxy? During conference in 1946 one Justice conceded that the government was now pressing on inductees the same choice between induction and jail which in *Falbo* it had denied could occur. Although the scope of review of conscientious objection remains largely unchanged, with intensification of the Vietnam agony as one result, in calmer times the Justices have not been so hesitant about intervening in military matters. Over the protest of Murphy's successor, Justice Tom C. Clark, the Warren Court upset military discharge decisions and accepted the major principle for which Murphy had battled: judicial review can serve to help induce government officials to choose less destructive alternatives.[112/k] In retrospect, perhaps his lonely fight to limit military jurisdiction was not shadow-boxing after all.

IV

Was war power a blank check? Was judicial review expendable? Close on the heels of the draft cases came World War II's pivotal answer, *Korematsu* v. *United States,* which convinced many that Justice Murphy's warnings were not phantoms of a melodramatic imagination, but a Kafka nightmare come true.[113] And in contrast to the stridency of his draft dissents, his response was a model of forceful probing into the concrete.

Just as the relocation camps were being dismantled on the west coast the exclusion and detention features of the program, which had been so carefully avoided in *Hirabayashi,* rose for review. The Court, with Justice Black as its spokesman, upheld "the finding of the military authorities that it was impossible to bring about an immediate segregation of the disloyal from the loyal."[114] The Justices had upheld the curfew order for that reason; now they merely extended the *Hirabayashi* principle to sustain orders requiring Nisei to report to relocation centers. Although the Court did rule in the *Endo* case shortly afterwards that the statute did not authorize detention of individuals whose loyalty was known, the Justices never conclusively reached the internment issue. Basing his opinion on the danger of hindsight judgment and on the principles of review elaborated by the Chief Justice in *Hirabayashi,* Justice Black straddled the detention problem and dismissed charges of racial discrimination as confusing the issue. However regrettable the action, he observed, "hardships are part of war, and war is an aggregation of hardships."[115]

"Read this and perish! The Court has blown up on the Jap case—just [as] I expected it would," Murphy remarked to his clerk as Jackson circulated a powerful dissent.[116] In conference the year before it had been plain that once exclusion and detention were reviewed, Justices Roberts, Murphy, and probably Douglas would not approve the long delay in screening interned individuals. Justice Rutledge now acknowledged that when swallowing the curfew order he knew that he

---

[k] The Warren Court departed from the position of "no review" in two ways: (1) strict insistence that civilians are not subject to military trials, either as military dependents [*Reid* v. *Covert* and *Kinsella* v. *Krueger,* 354 U.S. 1 (1957)] or as honorably discharged ex-servicemen [*U.S. ex rel. Toth* v. *Quarles,* 350 U.S. 11 (1955)]; and (2) the ruling that unauthorized military discharges may not rest on the pre-induction activities of the individual [*Harmon* v. *Brucker,* 355 U.S. 579 (1958)].

would have to stomach detention for a reasonably necessary time; but after Jackson indicated that he stopped at *Hirabayashi*, "and no further," the Court split five-four in a landmark case and fragmented wildly.[117]

As the Justices retired to write, only Reed and Rutledge appeared willing to exercise the self-restraint of silence. In initial circulations, Justice Jackson took Justice Black to task for interpreting the Curfew Case as having decided "the very things we there said we were not deciding"; and in a brilliant fusillade he aired his belief that unconstitutional military measures in war could no more be restrained by judges than judges should be expected to legitimize military measures without inquiry into their reasonableness.[118] Although Murphy may have been the model for Jackson's attack on the "dangerous idealism" of contrary expectations, Jackson's point was the enforceable limits, as distinct from the propriety, of judicial power. Nervousness about the Court's authority to release individuals in *ex parte Endo* highlighted the problem vividly. Justice Roberts, however, invoked traditional review power to condemn exclusion and detention as inseparable parts of a "cleverly devised trap" to incarcerate Japanese-Americans in "a concentration camp."[119] Douglas, though finally persuaded to concur after Justice Black accepted the Chief Justice's unpublished contention that orders to report to control centers and actual detention were separable, prepared a dissent protesting failure to screen individuals.[120] And Frankfurter, while eager to sustain the entire program as an inseparable package, concurred to answer the rest.[121] As if to atone for *Hirabayashi*, Justice Murphy dug in where the others refused to tread. The military judgment, he declared, "goes over the 'very brink of constitutional power' and falls into the ugly abyss of racism." And that dissent, as the *Washington Post* observed, "went to the heart of the matter."[122]

Having the advantage of a fully prepared position, Murphy published a sharper and less rhetorical version of his original *Hirabayashi* dissent. Fighting again within the Court's premises, he accepted the Court's rationality test and its limited review. He conceded the gravity of the crisis in 1942 and the necessity of deference to military judgments by judges whose "training and duties ill-equip them to deal intelligently with matters so vital to the physical security of the nation."[123] He even risked contradiction by admitting that an undetermined number of disloyal persons of Japanese descent existed in 1942. But within those terms of reference he painstakingly sought to show that no reasonable relation existed between military necessity and wholesale exclusion on the west coast.

To Murphy the very record in the case, a record now replete with facts from General DeWitt's report and a congressional investigation, demonstrated the overwhelming loyalty of those suspected and the military's reliance on racial prejudice rather than reasoned decision. Citing the general's hapless remark that "a Jap's a Jap," regardless of citizenship; quoting the general's conspiratorial theory about forthcoming sabotage; and contrasting the program with the FBI's quiet roundup of individual suspects without regard to race—a roundup whose foundations, of course, rested on the controversial dossiers of 1939—Murphy wrote a devastating rebuttal to the majority's theory of the case as a simple application of administrative review. If there was a "military judgment," he asserted, it was not the kind "entitled to the great weight ordinarily given the judgments based upon strictly military considerations." Instead of producing evidence of actual military danger from the Nisei's conduct, General DeWitt's report justified the exclusion policy mainly on "questionable racial and sociological grounds not ordinarily within the realm of expert military judgment," grounds which, had the general cared to look, had been discredited long ago "by experts in these matters."

The Court's deference, in sum, was misplaced. The Court was deferring to reasons based on the accumulated "misinformation, half-truths and insinuations that for years have been directed against Japanese-Americans by people with racial and economic prejudices—the same people who have been among the foremost advocates of the evacuation." "I dissent, therefore, from this legalization of racism," Justice Murphy declared. "Racial discrimination . . . is unattractive in any setting but it is utterly revolting among a free people who have embraced the principles set forth in the Constitution of the United States. All residents of this nation are kin in some way by blood or culture to a foreign land. Yet they are primarily and necessarily a part of the new and distinct civilization of the United States. They must accordingly be treated at all times as the heirs of the American experiment and as entitled to all the rights and freedoms guaranteed by the Constitution."[124]

That paragraph "should be engraved in stone," the *Christian Century* commented. By "legalization of racism," Murphy coined one of those phrases which seemed to characterize the sober second thoughts of a growing number. In contrast to *Schneiderman* and the draft cases, he received an overwhelmingly favorable response in the mail and the public prints. "Even the highest Court in the land," observed the *Washington Post*, "has no absolute immunity from the winds of hysteria."[125]

As if to purge guilty consciences in the comfort of hindsight, an energetic band of liberals took up the hue and cry. Groups such as the American Civil Liberties Union, whose silence in 1942 had been considerable, denounced the Court for legitimating the "worst single wholesale violation of civil rights of American citizens in our history." Academics, whose protests had not been much louder, now condemned the Justices for having turned fear of retrospective judgment into approval of a "great and evil blotch upon our national history."[126] By approving a "policy of mass incarceration under military auspices," the Court began to bear as much blame for having set an "insidious precedent" as Congress or the Commander-in-Chief—a phenomenon which speaks volumes about American expectations concerning judicial review. In effect, the Court stood accused of having "betrayed all Americans" by surrendering constitutional limitations in war.[127]

So successful was the denunciation that within a decade belief that the Court had erred became a part of conventional peacetime wisdom. Even though assimilation of the Nisei into American society was probably accelerated by their coerced dispersal in World War II, Congress itself, in response to the agitation of a dedicated group led by Yale Law School dean, Eugene V. Rostow, acknowledged error by granting an indemnity (albeit less than a tenth of the losses sustained) to those injured in the relocation. The end of a tragic tale came in 1959 when Assistant Attorney General George C. Doub of the now full-fledged Civil Rights Division closed the settlements with an astonishing admission of hope—that a wronged people would "have the charity to forgive their government."[128]

Korematsu, not to mention *Schneiderman* and the draft cases, restored Murphy's hero status on the Left. In a period of prolonged Cold War, however, it is useful to remember that much as his dissent may win grudging professional respect, much as Justice Jackson's unorthodox realism may tease the mind, these Justices lost one of the rare, direct confrontations over judicial review of military judgments in war. The *Korematsu* decision, as Jackson warned, left the precedent of group guilt standing as a "loaded weapon ready for the hand of any authority that can bring forward a plausible claim of an urgent need."[129] And the Court, unlike Congress, has acknowledged no error. Only time and future exigencies may tell whether the persuasive power of the dissents may moderate the force of that precedent; but *ex parte Quirin* and the Japanese Relocation Cases, together with the Court's expansive interpretations of emergency authority in draft and price control regulation, give small comfort to those who see the judiciary as a dependable guardian of constitutional limitations in war. Rather, the cases provide sobering evidence that judges who find themselves "powerless in fact" are apt to declare themselves "powerless in law."[130] The dissenters' insistence on reasoned decision in *Korematsu* fell well within the lane of the judicial function as traditionally defined by lawyers. Yet the very failure to persuade the Court of the unreasonableness of military policy shows how far modern judges have retreated from the mechanical notions of constitutional checks reflected in *Milligan*. Strategies of circumspect intervention, after all, may be all that reasonably can be expected from the judiciary in crisis government.[131]

Because the Japanese Relocation Cases were Justice Murphy's first brush with ultimate issues of constitutional limitation, his responses became key elements in his personal story. In both cases he was fired by the same ideals of American society that he expressed in *Schneiderman*, but compromised in *Hirabayashi* for the sake of institutional loyalties. In *Korematsu* his vanity as well as his vision of America operated full-bore when he observed that "I will struggle for the right and for the helpless with daring and without fear to the end."[132] But for all his crusading impulses, Justice Murphy in the final *Korematsu* showdown kept his head. For a problem in which he was so sure of himself that rhetorical exegesis was unnecessary, he proved himself capable of making those discriminating calculations about "reasoned decisions" which he had rejected in previous sermons and to which his opponents normally made exclusive claim. And he showed that his policy judgment and style had their place on the Supreme Court. Until *Korematsu*, Justice Murphy's performance as a jurist had been ambivalent if not disappointing. Aloof by choice and by necessity from the profound philosophic conflicts over the Court's role in enlarging personal freedoms, he had made no great impact apart from registering essential votes. His bid for leadership in labor and criminal rights issues had been largely eclipsed by strong-willed men with greater professional skills. His evangelism and identification with underdogs, whether Jehovah's Witnesses, Indians, political dissidents, or even harassed businessmen, seemed to put him on a different wave-length; but now they were on the beam. The result in *Korematsu* was a classic in Supreme Court literature.

"If America is to continue to grow as a democracy," Norman Thomas then observed, "I believe your dissenting opinion will live as one of that democracy's great documents. You have put us all in your debt."[133] Posterity, of many shades of opinion, has come to affirm that judgment.

CHAPTER 13

TEMPERING JUSTICE WITH

MURPHY, 1944-1946

FRANK MURPHY hit his stride on the Court as World War II
closed and postwar reconstruction began. Quantitatively, and
in contrast to his relatively low initial output, Murphy's opinion
rate between 1943 and 1948 rose above the norm. His 37 opinions in
the 1944 term, in fact, set a numerical record.[a] Qualitatively, moreover,
his opinions appeared to have suffered little from the quickened pace.
While still responsive to substantive criticism and flexible about making
changes, the Justice by mid-career reached a plateau of performance
and style which bore small resemblance to the self-conscious freshman
of the past. By the end of the war Murphy was a judge in the thick of
the fight.

In part, his increased productivity resulted from improved assignments and plain experience. More willing to trust his own instincts, he
relished trading blow for blow, and not merely in printed reports.
Resisting expansive discussion when writing for the Court in order to
discourage internal dissension or additional litigation; voting against
certiorari petitions in order to forestall reversal of decisions below that
he approved; going to conferences better prepared—he became pro-
ficient in less obvious tools of the trade.[1] The rapid pace was made
possible by special empathy with his able third clerk, whose unusually
long service from 1943-1948 obviated time-loss in training new personnel and enabled the Justice to delegate even more the routine drudgeries
of opinion production. Still the convergence of issues and personality
was the major stimulus to outspokenness. The imminence of victory
in Europe and Asia only heightened his conviction that the Court
should strike all possible blows on behalf of human rights. A record
number of dissents in the 1944 term was but one illustration of the fact

[a] Murphy's opinion rate in his first five years was as follows:

Term	Majority	Concurring	Dissenting	Total
1939	5	0	0	5
1940	17	0	1	18
1941	14	1	4	19
1942	15	4	10	29
1943	13	2	6	21
1944	18	6	13	37
Total	82	13	34	129

Source: Review of Justice Murphy's opinions, 1944-1945 terms, Box 140.

that Murphy was becoming reconciled to his post by converting it into a pulpit.

Though Murphy was skeptical about the value of airing philosophies of the judicial function in public, his increasing outspokenness was also influenced by hardening ideological lines. Except for the establishment clause of the First Amendment, the Roosevelt Court by the close of World War II had staked out the rough boundaries of judicial guardianship over civil liberties. Now the Justices were beginning to explore penumbral areas where results were less obvious and traditional limits on judicial authority were taxed. Concepts and tempers were strained accordingly. Except for the Holding Company Cases the Court also had worked the major constitutional revisions in commerce, taxation, and due process necessary to approve New Deal experiments.[2] Overturning with rapidity, if not zest, the inhibiting precedents of the laissez-faire era, the Justices now found themselves deeply divided over their role in nonconstitutional forms of economic policy-making. However men might have anticipated a drastic reduction of judicial power after 1937, it was plain that the Supreme Court had not abdicated. However men might have anticipated consensus among New Deal Justices at least in economic affairs, the liberal trio's attack on Justice Frankfurter in 1944 for indulging natural law concepts in utility rate-making and the acid rejoinders of Roberts and Frankfurter against excessive legal change, were signals that a new equilibrium in constitutional authority did not free judges from exercising discretion. The battle over judicial power was not over.[3]

While Justice Murphy took greater interest in economic problems than is generally assumed, he exerted no more leadership in developing doctrine for the Court's role in the welfare state than for its creativity in civil liberties. Yet he took for granted that men would differ about concrete options and the function of judges in both sectors, because he believed that the country was undergoing profound social and political adjustments from which the judiciary neither could nor should escape. On the threshold of what he hoped would be a new era of peace and reconstruction, he felt he had a contribution to make by espousing a "humanistic and humanitarian philosophy" and by articulating the moral standards he identified with the American promise and its basic charter.[4] Public duty and Christian conscience compelled a judge to do no less. Explaining his anti-Semitism crusade to Francis Cardinal Spellman in 1946, Murphy voiced typical evangelist assumptions: "Theodore Roosevelt was inclined to use a pithy expression during his prime that many Americans might ponder with interest today. I was just a boy but I recall his statement: 'TO REMAIN SILENT IN THE FACE OF WRONG IS TO JOIN HANDS WITH THE DEVIL.' " "There are so many wicked things that responsible men and men of conscience cannot remain silent about," said Murphy; and he saw few reasons for silence as a jurist.[5] "What is the use of having convictions if one is to surrender them?" he asked Chase S. Osborn. "My convictions are profound. They have been hard won. They are not going to be surrendered or why should I remain silent about them."[6]

Obviously Justice Murphy took pride in personal opinion. But he also had a powerful sense of the Court's example and symbolic influence. Though sensitive to questions of adjusting style to case, though willing to withhold dissents against denials of certiorari petitions after Justice Rutledge questioned the propriety of the practice, he believed it improper to dissent without stating the reasons, "buttressed with arguments and authority."[7] And Murphy thrived in the limelight. "The Law Reviews are now writing in recognition of my legal work," he informed one friend in 1945, of what was becoming a minor truth.[8] A publisher who proposed an anthology of his civil liberties utterance reeled before a demand of $25,000 in advance royalties.[9] After productivity, vanity seldom lagged, above all in boyishly braggart reports to the folks back home.

Immersing himself in judicial work Murphy in mid-passage found deep satisfaction expressing what he regarded as the deeper meaning of America and advancing its egalitarian goals. But his choices, as always, landed him in the lap of controversy at heavy reputational cost. Treating the Supreme Court as a vehicle of the humane ideals of the American dream, he became a symbol of partisan and personal judgment that companion pragmatism never erased. Justice, so the saying went, was "tempered with Murphy."[10]

II

Three broad areas of litigation—minority rights, labor, and criminal justice—did most to freeze Murphy's reputation for personalized justice. In all of them, to be sure, criticism directed at the libertarian quartet generally rubbed off onto its most flamboyant member. Especially was this so of their Populist drift in the economic sector. Actually Murphy was the least consistent and committed libertarian in reviewing questions of monopoly and ICC regulation; but he shared and sometimes voiced the group's generous view toward small business and antipathy to Bigness, its restrictive view of patent privileges, and its expansive view of the Wagner Act.[11] Holding less than awesome attitudes about *stare decisis*, Murphy also supported the constitutional revisionism over regulatory power, including the *extremis* application of the commerce clause to unsold wheat in *Wickard* v. *Filburn*, and judicial revival of the Federal Employers' Liability Act.[12] He provided essential votes in controversial decisions, such as *Thomas* v. *Collins* and the much misunderstood *South-Eastern Underwriters* case.[13] And he seemed fated to author some of the Court's most questionable conclusions in the labor field.[14] Whether measured by votes or by vocalism, reformist philosophy seemed the obvious touchstone of decision.

Group action was far less influential in fixing Justice Murphy's libertarian image, however, than two distinctly personal traits—consistent civil liberties choices and crusading on the bench. After 1943 he made no bones about a highly personal approach to judging. His votes were virtually predictable in favor of individual claimants in civil liberties cases which divided the Court. Whether analysts proceeded intuitively or by quantitative techniques, Murphy invariably occupied the top of the civil liberties scale. Sheer libertarian consistency naturally led to parallels between him and Justice Field, the strong-willed Spencerian who symbolized judging by predilection. Lawyers soon learned that Murphy, like Field, could be expected to lend sympathetic ears to any plausible plea of infringed personal freedom.[15]

Justice Murphy just seemed incapable of voting against underdogs. He was the only Justice to find a possible fatherly motive in the *Haupt* treason trial, though initial votes showed considerable uncertainty.[16] He was the first to voice doubts about strict liability crimes, though one scholar, Jerome Hall, applauded his protest and the Court may yet restrict their scope.[17] And beyond consistency there were curious aberrations that observers attributed to temperamental quirks. The most revealing was his campaign to restrict prosecutions under the Mann and Kidnapping statutes for acts of general immorality. This effort, which included a veiled charge in the *Chatwin* case that Stone and Frankfurter evaded issues dishonestly, led to endless jokes about his priestly sympathies for a sinful flock, which the Justice himself enjoyed.[18/b] Still, his compassion for criminals generated perplexity even among his friends. Ordinarily a strict constructionist in defining crimes, he opposed one price-fixing indictment so vigorously during the war that

[b] Murphy remarked: "Someone must speak for sinners and reality. The law is for all and fortunately each of us is not in a position to claim infallibility in walking on the sunnyside of life's street without stumbling." FM to John R. Watkins, March 1, 1945, No. 620, Box 134. *United States* v. *Beach*, 324 U.S. 193 (1945).

his old Progressive ally, Fiorello LaGuardia, expressed the politician's frequent lament: "it is queer what the bench will do to a man."[19] Granted that the cases contained some room for doubt, did Justice Murphy always have to resolve it for individuals? Granted that the Court had latent functions of moral leadership, did Justice Murphy always have to assume the mantle of priest?

Pyrotechnics in a few great cases probably had more to do with his reputation for partisan judgment than the choices themselves. In regulatory fields commonly regarded as routine, such as income tax, Justice Murphy actually spoke with low-keyed professionalism on a plane with the rest of the Court. His *Associated Press* dissent, which was decibels lower than the Roberts-Stone charge of "government-by-injunction with a vengeance," also showed his capacity to proportion his blows in delicate strategic situations.[20] But Murphy's leaner side was overshadowed by an aura of doctrinaire emotionalism earned elsewhere. In disputes that disturbed his human sympathies or the core of his political faith, his fiery protest reinforced beliefs that for him the judicial process was a simple registration of self. It was not simply that Justice Murphy carved out special interests which most Justices have, though one who perceived himself as a champion of "equal justice for the inarticulate" was a rarity. The difference was that in defending those interests, he forthrightly rejected conventional tactics in favor of crusading technique.

The Court, in this sense, was not simply the resolver of legal disputes but a spokesman of national conscience and a protector of the weak. When these interests were sacrificed, a Justice was not limited to writing for the profession; he must freely express moral indignation in terms comprehensible to the public. A distinction exists between dissents circulated internally for bargaining purposes and published dissents aimed at outside reference groups; Justice Murphy seemed more interested in the latter. Evangelism was his most comfortable style. By 1945 he resorted to it so frequently that he told his clerk, "if this speed keeps up I won't have either eye left and you will be ready for an institution."[21] It seems not to have occurred to him that overuse and overstatement could cheapen the currency of dissent.

Devotion to civil liberties—even compassionate instincts or pride of opinion—was insufficient to explain Murphy's strident tones. The only explanation seems to be that his crusading impulses and political idealism, which peaked at the war's end, were being converted into judicial goals. For the "inarticulate and friendless," for causes he identified with the image of the United States as a sanctuary of freedom, he flayed the Court for defaulting a positive, protective role. Americans had to redeem their international leadership, he declared in 1944, by remaining steadfast to their national experiment. While playing a "manly part" in world affairs, the United States had to prove itself "a just power as well as a great one." Courts, within the confines of their constitutional powers, were not exempt from his country's "mission of justice."[22]

Exceptions to this frame of reference were too numerous to label Murphy's outlook a philosophy of judging. Fervor more often than not was righteous indignation aroused on an ad hoc basis and expressed in the freedom of dissent. But a cluster of minority right cases, ranging from First Amendment to racial equality and war crimes claims, regularly drew crusading responses, and illustrate well the strengths and weaknesses of the approach.

Few opinions were more suggestive of doctrinaire impulses, or more illustrative of the hazards of the label, than *Prince* v. *Massachusetts.*[23] There, on the basis of a stream of precedents upholding compulsory education and vaccination of children, the Court sustained application of a child labor statute to prevent a nine-year-old child accompanied by her guardian from distributing religious pamphlets on the streets at night. Murphy, who appears to have been stimulated to action by an agitated clerk, joined Jackson in goading the Court to full consideration of the case after an initial decision to dismiss the appeal as insubstantial; and following defeat, he went the way of the property-minded Four Horsemen.[24] Liberty was the rule, restraint the exception. Infringement of First Amendment freedoms, in flat contradiction to the Court's attitude toward economic rights, was presumptively unconstitutional. That Jehovah's Witnesses had tapped all his sympathetic instincts was plain in his "pastry":

No chapter in human history has been so largely written in terms of persecution and intolerance as the one dealing with religious freedom. From ancient times to the present day, the ingenuity of man has known no limits in its ability to forge weapons of oppression for use against those who dare to express or practice unorthodox religious beliefs. And the Jehovah's Witnesses are living proof of the fact that even in this nation, conceived as it was in the ideals of freedom, the right to practice religion in unconventional ways is still far from secure. Theirs is a militant and unpopular faith, pursued with a fanatical zeal. They have suffered brutal beatings; their property has been destroyed; they have been harassed at every turn by the resurrection and enforcement of little used ordinances and statutes. . . . To them, along with other present-day religious minorities, befalls the burden of testing our devotion to the ideals and constitutional guarantees of religious freedom.

We should therefore hesitate before approving the application of a statute that might be used as another instrument of oppression. Religious freedom is too sacred a right to be restricted or prohibited in any degree without convincing proof that a legitimate interest of the state is in grave danger.[25]

Even for liberals this was freedom at the outer reaches, and one of the Justice's most ill-advised opinions. Preaching; equating a child labor statute with religious oppression rather than attempting to accommodate colliding interests, which two separate critics reminded him was the function of courts; outspokenly inverting the burden of proof in the manner of Justice Sutherland for liberty of contract—all this was too much for his brethren. "Frank," said one, "wants the solitary glory of dissent."[26]

Whatever the appearances Murphy was well aware of the reputational risk of a lone dissent. Conference discussion indicated that nearly all the Justices considered the regulation reasonable on the merits. The *Prince* case was also one of the few occasions in which he and Justice Rutledge parted company on the First Amendment, and that shook confidence. "Wiley," Murphy noted after conference, "I am never happy disagreeing with you. And there is so little I can contribute here but I am a profound if not an adequate Jeffersonian on freedom of conscience. So I will write a note—inoffensive I'm sure—in the *Prince* case when it comes down."[27]

What agitated him to take the risk was the explicit assertion in Rutledge's first draft that the faith of an immature child had lower constitutional status than an adult's as well as private suspicions that fellow Catholics in Massachusetts were up to old tricks. The *Prince* case drew characteristic responses from several Justices on the question of faith. Subordination of the child's religion troubled Chief Justice Stone, who nonetheless argued in an unpublished concurrence that individual rights must yield in any reasonable accommodation to allow some scope for other constitutional interests.[28/c] The case also prompted Justice Jackson to repeat his contention that the line should not be drawn between ages, but between worship in private structures and "accosting"

---

[c] Many state courts held to the contrary. The New Hampshire Supreme Court, dismissing the ground of protecting the morals of minors as "not impressive," had unanimously interpreted a similar statute as applicable to commercial activity only, and not to sales of Witness magazines by a ten-year-old boy under the auspices of his mother. Although the Massachusetts Supreme Judicial Court conceded in *Prince* that First Amendment rights were accorded "a highly preferred position in the struggle of competing interests," it held that the statute applied to petitioners, whose First Amendment rights were subject to "slight" and "incidental" regulation in pursuance of other social interests. 313 Mass. 223, 46 N.E. 2d 755.

the public with money-raising activities in the streets, which he considered "Caesar's affairs."[29/d]

For Justice Murphy limitation based either on age or on the commercial aspect of Witness evangelism was odious. Both ignored, in his view, the central role of conscience in *commanding* believers to propagate their faith. Both ignored also the lack of any showing of specific harm. The facts concerning injury in the case were scant. During oral argument the Chief Justice had observed that the Court could take judicial notice of street dangers to children. In response, Witnesses counsel later asked it to take notice of a life insurance company study which found that public sidewalks were safer than private homes. And to Murphy, the absence of substantial injury was the critical point. "The vital freedom of religion," he said, could not "be erased by slender references to the state's power to restrict the more secular activities of children." Restrictions concededly unconstitutional if applied to adults could not be sustained by "vague references to the reasonableness underlying child labor legislation in general."[30] Social dangers making reasonable the regulation of newsboys were not present against a girl exercising her religion.

Although one internal critic thought that Murphy assumed too much about the child's faith—"Did the youngster just like to be out on the street, as you and I did when we were kids?" he asked—the record was undeniably thin.[31] Rather than rest dissent on that basis, however, and simply chide the Court for applying to children a different standard of review from the ones employed in every freedom to worship case since *Jones* v. *Opelika*, Justice Murphy phrased his protest in the condemned jurisprudence of the past, which openly placed him in the position, as it had the exponents of vested property rights, of substituting his judgment for that of state officials.[32] What was more, his distinction between children worshipping and selling newspapers smacked of elevating religious freedom over speech or press in the hierarchy of constitutional values. What was the difference?

Justice Murphy's unyielding defense of freedom of the press after *Bridges* v. *California* lends little support to any conscious differentiation on his part.[33] The *Prince* case was merely another indication that he was a man of action for whom doctrinal distinctions among First

---

[d] Frankfurter refused to enter Rutledge's opinion because his conclusion was guided by *Pierce* v. *Society of Sisters* and *Meyer* v. *Nebraska*. "Holmes' dissent in the latter case," Frankfurter commented, "still seems to me compelling, and I shall turn out to be a very bad prophet indeed if this Court will not come to rue the implications of *Pierce* v. *Society of Sisters*." Felix Frankfurter to Wiley Rutledge, Jan. 22, 1944, Box 34, Frankfurter Papers, Manuscript Division, Library of Congress.

Amendment freedoms were subtleties far from mind. Sharing the common propensity among modern judges to describe basic freedoms in lush superlatives without distinction, Murphy scoffed at innuendoes that protection of religious minorities beyond sectarian discrimination violated the establishment clause: "It was religion and morality," he said, which "our fathers wished to flourish in the land."[34]

Prince thus became a classic illustration of a common deficiency of libertarian protest—the disparity between the often complex calculus used in reaching decisions and a simplistic mode of explaining them. Behind an opinion that gave every appearance of devotion to absolutes, there lay a lengthy process of reasoning and internal argument to buttress a position Murphy knew would be considered eccentric but which he perceived to be substantially founded in social reality. In a pro-and-con debate similar to that followed in *Thornhill* and most of his major utterance to date, Murphy weighed opposing arguments. He even solicited private criticism from his polar opposite, Justice Roberts. "Am I awfully wrong or just wrong?" he asked.[35] In a long memorandum to his clerk he probed the dilemmas of a solo view. He wrote:

> After carefully examining the records and briefs and with no little reflection and the benefit of the Rutledge draft, it is not difficult to come out on the same side of the question that he does although all my instincts are against it and I want very much to be on the other side in dissent if I can stand on firm ground.
>
> I begin with constitutional protection of all religions in this country. Jefferson is an authority for the following statement. Of all my struggles the most difficult was the one to pass the Virginia resolution on religious liberty. . . .
>
> You are familiar, I know, with not only the religious wars of England but the fate of the Quakers and Mormons and the horrible practices they were subjected to all of which bears sad resemblance to the treatment of the Jehovah's Witnesses in this country today. . . .
>
> I start out with the constitutional protection in this case. And I start also with the belief that this was the religion of the guardian and the religion of the child. . . . Child Labor and Welfare laws were aimed at certain diseases and abuses. We know the realistic condition[s] necessitating such legislation but those conditions are not present in this case and for my part I cannot see how Massachusetts would be imperiled by religious devotion practiced by a few children in the streets. In the slums of all the great cities the streets constitute their main recreation center until dark comes.
>
> Rutledge has made something of an impressive case. I want you to see his side of it and clearly what we have to meet. He stands on the grounds of enlightened conception of control and responsibility for child welfare. As

he sees it it is modern democratic social legislation under the police power to which religious as well as secular organizations ought to be required to conform,—and to which the 'rights' of the parent or custodian must be subordinated for reasons outlined by Rutledge.

But I do not want to conform—I want to save all that can be saved for the individual in freedom of conscience and I want to save all that can be saved for the parent as against the state in the right to teach the religion to the child. This might sound a little Catholic but I assure you I have nothing in mind but liberty of religion in a country that was conceived as a sanctuary for oppressed people.

What motives are behind the prosecutions in this case? What is there in the record to support my suspicions? Very little. But I am confident I am right about it. We are up against a tough problem I know when we attempt to say that the public streets are a no-man's land where social legislation cannot operate and parents or religious bodies are free to do as they like, regardless of regulations adopted to safeguard public health or public morals and correct substantive evils. . . . How can we make out a case in defense of a minor exercising his religious rights when at war with the state police power?

It can hardly be disputed that this was a normal and reasonable exercise of the police power of the state. . . . If this sale of magazines and other articles by minors is a public evil which ought to be regulated as a means of safeguarding the health and morals of children, the mere fact that they are religious in character does not affect the need and propriety of the regulation. But I can't see how health or morals are in the case before us. Moreover there is a grave danger of religious persecution in what Massachusetts has done in this case. . . . I don't see a genuine or substantial evil in what the child did in this case. She was evangelizing her religion as she understands it (as well as her guardian). Their literature *on religion* must be offered to the public. . . .

Is the matter in issue the rights of the custodian, not the child? It is to be observed that the custodian herself thought the child should be left home, and took her along only because she cried. But out on the street she went to the defense of the child's legal right.[36]

A strong commitment to religious freedom, together with a practical perception that substantive evils were absent, led Murphy to question the very rationality of a state policy in the strident, black-and-white style of the advocate who admits none of the doubts that he has resolved. The "arresting parallel" he saw between the Jehovah's Witnesses and the dissident groups of Jefferson's day, a parallel which his brethren thought a false analogy, also fanned evangelical fervor in a Justice who conceded his inclination "to be a little maudlin." Eschewing doctrine in favor of dramatization, Justice Murphy by 1944 made unmistakably plain that he believed treatment of minorities—not national unity, as Justice Frankfurter urged—was the acid test of devotion to the nation's professed ideals in war. And the shift of focus to peacemaking only strengthened his resolve to proclaim it openly. Guided by a Constitution which embodied "the highest political ideals of which man is capable," the United States was the exemplar of conduct.[37]

Defending underdogs, by definition, risks unpopularity. Defending them from the nation's highest tribunal by invoking transcendentalist ideals in the idiom of Bryan, courts professional disaster. The more Murphy did so, the more his lawyerly stock sank—and for the same reasons that it rose among libertarians. The Justice was not alone in considering *Prince* "A Shocking Decision." A state whose interests could be endangered by a child selling religious literature, as Jackson's hometown paper observed, was hardly one to inspire confidence. Lost professional prestige was offset to a degree by the lowly homilies of the defended who might write, "thank you, Justice Murphy, for your time, and your stand for *our God*." "Men like you give me faith in Democracy."[38] The Justice's spirits soared over glowing libertarian tributes, such as the books of Milton R. Konvitz, which commended his leadership in civil liberties. Differing public and professional reactions to his crusading confirm the common observation that the Court's constituency is not "the public," but differentiated reference groups which assort themselves according to Al Smith's scale—"whose ox gets gored"—a scale which Justice Jackson once asserted was "the greatest principle of law I know."[39] Differing public and professional reactions further confirm that Supreme Court opinions serve as both legal and political documents. The more Murphy preached, the more his opinions suffered in the eyes of the bar. Yet the more he preached, the more his opinions took on symbolic significance in public policy disputes. Partisan responses, regardless of his own interior doubts, greeted evangelism inevitably.

The strongest single example of crusading and its effects was *Bridges* v. *Wixon*, a "trying case" in 1945, which upset a long-term congressional effort to deport Harry Bridges, west coast longshoreman leader, to his native Australia.[40] Torn by conflict between what they regarded as an injustice and settled law, the Justices stayed the deportation on grounds of inadmissible evidence. Within the Court, most of the Justices were repulsed by the treatment of Bridges. Though not everyone accepted libertarian contentions that he was being exiled because he was a successful union leader with radical ideas, even the Chief Justice acknowledged that it was "a rotten thing" for Congress to amend deportation statutes specifically to catch him, as the sponsor of the legislation had proudly announced for Bridges "and all others of similar ilk." Though no one questioned that Attorney General Biddle had acted in good faith, neither did anyone protest when one personal friend characterized him as a "damn fool" for having overturned reversal of the deportation order on questionable evidence. But given the overwhelming weight of precedent that Congress's control over aliens was plenary, and the fear of legislative reprisal against aliens generally if they intervened, the Justices faced a difficult dilemma and a very close case. Only with "the greatest reluctance" had some members of the minority concluded that Congress left the Court powerless; on the other hand, only because they believed that Bridges had been denied "a fair hearing when you sum it all up," were others in the majority willing to risk going as far as they did.[41] A procedural rather than constitutional solution in such inflammatory circumstances was the only tenable choice.

All such counsels of caution had little effect on Murphy. Rather than take comfort in the net gain a stay would mean for aliens, as distinct from other subjects of administrative proceedings; rather than heed Frankfurter's fervent plea in conference not to tempt Congress to cut a wider swath into immigration and the "American fellowship" as a means of banishing Bridges, Murphy unleashed a slashing attack against the "over-subtle niceties" by which the Court, and especially the dissenting trio of Stone, Roberts, and Frankfurter, treated the problem as "wholly administrative."[42/e] Throwing caution to the winds, he laid bare the ugly facts in the anti-Bridges campaign that had been deplored in the privacy of chamber. "The record in this case [he began] will stand forever as a monument to man's intolerance of man. Seldom if ever in the history of this nation has there been such a concentrated and relentless crusade to deport an individual because he dared to exercise the freedom that belongs to him as a human being and that is guaranteed to him by the Constitution." And in the sensational style of an accomplished crusader, he marshalled powerful libertarian argu-

[e] Emotions apparently ran high in conference on the retaliation point. Noting that he spoke from the "depth of conviction about this country and its future," Murphy recorded one Justice as pleading with the majority not to embarrass Congress or the nation's immigrants by inviting reprisal. "I consider the action of the A.G. as unwise and foolish. But don't reach judgment that will seriously hamper freedom of action of this country. It will be a great injustice to immigrants to this shore. They wanted a freer country. You will be doing a great injustice because members of Congress will say we will let no one come in. . . . I haven't reached [the] point that [it] is an outrage. I beg of your conscience not to write into law something born out of [a] special situation." Conference notes, No. 788, Box 134.

ments, drawn from the briefs of Lee Pressman, why the Court should hold that such an "empty mockery of human freedom" floundered "in constitutional waters."[43]

In conference, some libertarians had attempted to extend the *Schneiderman* standard of proof to deportation hearings, a standard the Warren Court has since adopted. Murphy went all the way by urging that aliens were protected by the Bill of Rights. In order to insure that the freedom of political refugees in the United States was not "dependent upon their conformity to the popular notions of the moment," he implored the Court to hold that deportation could be sanctioned only upon convincing proof of "a real and imminent threat to our national security." "Congress has ample power to protect the United States from internal revolution and anarchy without abandoning the ideals of freedom and tolerance. We as a nation lose part of our greatness whenever we deport or punish those who merely exercise their freedom in an unpopular though innocuous manner. The strength of this nation is weakened more by those who suppress the freedom of others than by those who are allowed freedom to think and act as their consciences dictate."[44] "Security through freedom," an idea long uppermost in his personal faith, was a strong motif in *Bridges*. So was his romantic attachment to the United States as a haven of the oppressed. In 1893, Justices Field and Brewer had denounced plenary power to expel aliens as "pure, simple, undisguised despotism and tyranny."[45] In defying settled law that resident aliens were entitled only to minimal due process rights, Murphy was hardly less vehement. If extension of the Bill of Rights to aliens reduced Congress's absolute power to govern them according to "legislative whim," as well as generations of supporting precedent, so be it. "Only by zealously guarding the rights of the most humble, the most unorthodox and the most despised among us," he declared, "can freedom flourish and endure in our land."[46]

"What a windbag he was," Francis Biddle recalled of Murphy's sermon on opinion Monday.[47] As legal argument the concurrence was too far afield to be persuasive. As political protest, it was undeniably potent. Because it exposed the prejudice and pretense against Bridges, the opinion thus enlivened partisan dispute. Ridiculed by Westbrook Pegler as soap opera "Mammy," the Justice's performance was heavily criticized by Bridges' opponents as well as by members of the bar. Murphy, in turn, was stung by criticism he regarded as unfair; and following a similar occurrence in *Craig* v. *Harney* two years later, he retaliated by giving a tongue-lashing to publisher Eleanor Patterson for employing Pegler, an act he promptly regretted in an "I was wrong" letter. A Justice who used the Court as a platform of protest could not have it both ways; theory also imposed counterpart restraints. Confessing that "I am unduly sensitive," Murphy observed of the episode: "You must bear in mind that first a case must be proved. Once you start this business of Siberia you never know when it is going to end. Most of our early antecedents came to this country as a result of political and religious exile. In free America I don't want anyone put in a religious or political strait-jacket including our columnist friend."[48/f]

Liberals rushed to the Justice's defense. Having brought to bear all his skills as a polemicist to publicize an injustice, he reaped more public attention and fan mail in *Bridges* than in any other case except *Yamashita*. Hailed as a "masterful attack" on a "classic of intolerance," his protest struck responsive chords of idealism among libertarians who were equally frustrated by judicial noninterference with an illiberal immigration policy.[49] Despite the Chief Justice's reminder (at Justice Frankfurter's urging) that the Court's only concern was power not abuse, that "under our Constitution and laws, Congress has its functions, the Attorney General his, and the courts theirs," respected liberal journals applauded Murphy's protest as a notable utterance. Recalling that an alien, Rosika Schwimmer, had occasioned Justice Holmes' classic remark that free thought meant "not free thought for those who agree with us but freedom for the thought that we hate," the *Washington Post* observed: "Mr. Justice Murphy eloquently restated this doctrine. . . . In the light of the Bridges case, this restatement seems highly salutary."[50]

Whether the message had any restraining effects on those who made immigration policy, however, was doubtful. Whether more restrained, and legally more effective, dissents might go unheard under the pyrotechnics also sank from view. In the great causes which befouled an idealized image of his country Justice Murphy and his public were operating on a different wave-length.

III

Of all his causes racial equality produced Murphy's most ardent crusading. In conjunction with the Japanese Relocation Cases, two themes became pronounced in his opinions—(1) antimilitarism, sparked by

---

[f] To Mrs. Patterson, he wrote: "I don't mind criticism. I believe that it is good for all of us but to state untruths is regrettable and he has done it often. But I am profoundly for freedom of the press. . . . It is your business to select your columnist. It is certainly none of mine and I am sorry that I ever mentioned the subject." FM to Eleanor Patterson, May 19, 1947, No. 241, Box 137.

suspicion of race prejudice lurking in the "military mind," and (2) rejection of "the passive virtues" in cases involving racial discrimination. Although Murphy had played down the former in *Korematsu* in order to concentrate his thunder, he never faltered thereafter from an expansionary view of judicial power to fight the latter.[51] Impatient for action he developed a special, symbolic theory to oppose racism. Nothing short of "constitutional condemnation," he declared again and again, was fit to denounce evidence of racial discrimination at the bar.

Sometimes Murphy's protest was penetrating, as in his recently vindicated *Akins* v. *Texas* dissent, which objected to the Court's inaction before evidence of systematic inclusion of a single Negro on a jury panel to meet equal protection standards.[52] Sometimes it appeared hypersensitive, as in his denunciation of a prosecutor in *Malinski* v. *New York*, for making alleged racial references to a jury.[53] And not infrequently he published concurring opinions for the express educational purpose of exposing the "virus of racism."[54] But judicial activism was never clearer than in his concurrence in *Steele* v. *Louisville & Nashville Railroad Co.*, an important labor decision which sustained federal prohibition of racial discrimination in railroad unions operating under the Railway Labor Act. Rejecting the Chief Justice's skillful blend of statutory and case law in support of the result, and the strong reasons for gradualism in breaking new ground, Murphy argued hotly that the constitutional issue "should be squarely faced." "No statutory interpretation can erase this ugly example of economic cruelty . . . ," he declared. "The utter disregard for the dignity and the well-being of colored citizens shown by this record is so pronounced as to demand the invocation of constitutional condemnation. To decide the case and to analyze the statute solely upon the basis of legal niceties, while remaining mute and placid as to the obvious and oppressive deprivation of constitutional guarantees, is to make the judicial function something less than it should be."[55]

Contrary to popular impressions, Murphy usually tempered such language before final publication. In *Oyama* v. *California*, for instance, after reading the relentless exposure of racism underlying California's exclusion laws in his first draft, Murphy cautioned his clerk that the language was "awfully strong." "People ought to have natural views," he remarked. "Their views are wrong ones. They bear melancholy resemblance to the persecution of the Jews. Nevertheless, they are understandable. . . . We shouldn't go out of our way to insult [the] people of [the] State."[56] Yet Murphy was "more and more anxious to assert my own legal philosophy" and cognizant that "I go further than the rest of the Court." "As a rule," he told his brother George, "the Court is ticklish about involving the Constitution if the case can be decided on any other grounds. For my part, I want to utilize the great charter wherever it is necessary to sustain the rights of man."[57]

That he invoked it more than necessary was simply additional evidence that racial equality was his last passionate crusade. Taking advantage of his position to fight the "moral epidemic" of racial prejudice, the Justice by speech and pamphlet, by organizing rallies and button-holing reporters, concentrated his extracurricular energies on the brotherhood movement. Typically his memberships were reduced to a Philippines relief society, an Indian protection league, and a Christian Committee Against Nazi Persecution of the Jews, which he agreed to head with Wendell Willkie. This organization, though reduced in ultimate effectiveness by conflicts among other members of the board, was an all-Christian group formed to combat anti-Semitic propaganda. Murphy, who thoroughly enjoyed retooling his oratory once the crusade began, became the group's ace evangelist at brotherhood rallies because of his conviction that "thus far no one has undertaken to put the problem before the American people as it should be put—that is as the burden of the Christian and the majority group to be solved in order that justice will be done in the land."[58] That he sometimes labelled anti-Semitism as racism spoke volumes about the speaker, who was awarded the American Hebrew Medal in 1945. But to Murphy and most listeners, such ironies mattered little. Jews were being "jumped on." Without distinction as to forum, and with only slight concessions of style, "a strong new champion for an imperative cause" preached the gospel at every opportunity that one who embraces the "virus" of prejudice "in reality makes war on the Christian faith and the Constitution of the United States."[59/g]

Doggedly, and sometimes savagely, he fought for recognition of this precept as a legal principle. It was a rare case having racial aspects that

g Gratified by the response after a mass rally at the University of California, Berkeley, Murphy commented to his brother George that "the experience on the Supreme Court hasn't weakened my rather inadequate oratorical gift." On the contrary, he maintained that four years of advocacy on the bench had sharpened it. "Yet I try to be thoughtful and make a real contribution as one in my position should always make," Murphy added. "I did not look at a note. You could have heard a pin drop while I was speaking because I think I espoused the gospel young people covet." There was no denying his impact. Of one brotherhood speech at Carnegie Hall, Judge John J. Parker was moved to observe: "A noble expression of our American philosophy of life, and it ought to do much good." FM to George Murphy, Oct. 17, 1944; Parker to FM, May 25, 1944, Box 112. Also Judge J.F.T. O'Connor to FDR, Sep. 16, 1944, RL: P.P.F.

Murphy did not press beyond precise issues to invoke the special phrase, "constitutional condemnation," to denounce any trace of racism in the record. It was a rare case in which he refrained from sprinkling opinions with sociological data and even the United Nations Charter, to bolster decisions that the Court, in a quieter way, was gradually building into case law that was essential groundwork for a larger federal role. Whatever may be said of his legal arguments, which in the case of UN treaty obligations spread a tremor of fear among right-wing groups, there could be little doubt that Justice Murphy was addressing himself far beyond the immediate constituency of the bar. Evangelizing the "deathless doctrines of brotherly love," Justice Murphy was addressing the world.[60]

The fact that he spoke infrequently for the Court on a subject of such personal concern was not merely a function of style but that his colleagues saw the problems of judicial action as far more complex. Crusading aired dirty linen in official reports when, as Justice Black cautioned in the California Exclusion Case, "softer blows" yielded the same results without displaying ugly facts that enemies abroad could use "to do us harm." Reciting ugly facts, as Justice Frankfurter reminded both Murphy and Rutledge, also stirred up Negro resentments without weaning whites away from habits of prejudice.[61/h] Furthermore, positive judicial action clashed with competing constitutional values that could not be ignored. The federal government, after all, was a latecomer in pressing for racial equality in its own house, not to mention in the states. Concepts and statutes required considerable

---

[h] Choosing opposite tactics, Frankfurter explained his position to Rutledge in the *Bob-Lo* case: "Before coming down here, when I was counsel for the Association for the Advancement of Colored People, considerable practical experience with problems of race relations led me to the conclusion that the ugly practises of racial discrimination should be dealt with by the eloquence of action, but with austerity of speech. Time has only deepened that conviction and it has compelling force, I believe, in regard to opinions by this Court within this field. By all means let us decide with fearless decency, but express our decisions with reserve and austerity. It does not help toward harmonious race relations to stir our colored fellow citizens to resentment by even pertinent rhetoric or needless recital of details of mistreatment which are irrelevant to a legal issue before us. Nor do we thereby wean whites, both North and South, from what so often is merely the momentum of the past in them. Forgive this little sermon." Justice Rutledge, reminding Frankfurter of their mutual recital of racial facts in *Fisher* v. *United States*, replied that he did not object to a *little* bit of preaching now and then, and that he doubted if Frankfurter did either. Frankfurter, while distinguishing the cases, shot back: ". . . I am glad to have you cling to a little bit of the golden fleece of Baptism—but must you do it in opinions? Quite seriously . . . this Court should avoid exacerbating the very feelings which we seek to allay. And if I myself at times betray this wisdom, so much the worse for me." Felix Frankfurter to Wiley Rutledge and replies, Jan. 2, 1948, Box 34, Frankfurter Papers, Manuscript Division, Library of Congress.

stretching to provide even nonconstitutional remedies, much less constant constitutional relief. Political implications alone were enough to caution judges from making war against racism, even though continued discrimination against Negro voters in the South after the White Primary Cases should have humbled all men about the potency of judicial decrees in altering deepseated social customs.[62] "Here is gross wrong," the Chief Justice remarked in *Steele*. "The only question is can courts handle it." But for Murphy the very statement carried its answer. "The light of human freedom burns far too dimly to warrant ignoring any opportunity, however modest, to increase its intensity," he declared in an unpublished reply. "The least we can do is voice the Constitution's disapproval of such action."[63] Because the cases invariably presented wrongs and opportunities for preachment Justice Murphy became a constant irritant on a Court engaged in probing the boundaries of its authority in race relations. Piercing the conscience with stubborn facts, he tore at traditional limits on federal judicial power.

The difficulties of judicial intervention were highlighted in 1945 by the *Screws* case, a landmark decision in which a divided Court upheld and then deliberately checked federal authority under the old Civil Rights Acts to punish state officials for depriving individuals of federal rights.[64] Claude M. Screws was a Georgia sheriff who with two accomplices beat to death an "uppity" Negro prisoner named Robert Hall. Although the case was clearly "a shocking and revolting episode in law enforcement," Screws was not brought to trial in state courts because, as the prosecutor explained, the sheriff filed no complaint.[65] The Civil Rights Section, hoping to develop a modern case law in support of federal protection of civil rights in the states, then prosecuted Screws under an archaic Reconstruction statute which punished deprivation of federal rights by state officers acting "under color of any law." In contrast to the usual outcome, the jury convicted Screws and the Court of Appeals affirmed, one judge dissenting.[66]

Since the Supreme Court itself had opened up "sweeping constitutional vistas" in *Classic* and *Smith* v. *Allwright* by expanding the scope of state action covered by the Fourteenth Amendment, the Civil Rights Section could hardly be blamed for asking the Justices to approve the next step in developing the civil rights statutes into a viable weapon against unpunished police brutality in the states. After all, the purpose of the Fourteenth Amendment had been protection of Negroes, not property rights or labor unions. The great Holmes himself had written approvingly that the conspiracy section of the statutes applied to "all Federal rights . . . and in the lump."[67] Every Justice except Rutledge had been involved in reviving the statutes after years of federal dormancy. Only Roberts, irritated by the *sub silentio* overruling of his *Grovey* v. *Townsend* opinion in *Classic*, appeared to have developed distaste for case-by-case expansion of federal remedies.[68] And the potential gains were filled with practical significance. Acceptance of the government's contentions in *Screws* would enable an activist federal executive and a responsive federal judiciary to punish criminal conduct that politically captive local officials and Congressmen were unable to condemn. Federal authorities would be able to punish official deprivation of constitutional rights even when such conduct violated state law. Expansion of Section 20 to include due process rights also would lead inexorably to expansion of parallel statutes which outlawed conspiracies and authorized private civil suits. And because these civil rights statutes were tied to rights "secured by the Constitution" and the Fourteenth Amendment, both of which were undergoing revolutionary libertarian expansion in the courts, federal prosecutors and judges would be armed with a "sword" whose potential was limited only by the discretion of judges and a legislative veto which liberals, too, could checkmate. Screws' case was a libertarian's dream of bypassing a filibustered Congress.[69]

Judicial action, however, raised painful dilemmas at every turn. In the first place, it threatened to split the Court over the basic principle of state action. The *Smith* case especially had provoked greater internal difficulty and debate than met the eye. Justice Murphy's conference notes, though they should be interpreted cautiously as one man's perceptions among nine, suggest that the Roosevelt Court had broached the limits of innovation. While most Justices agreed that *Grovey* should be overruled, for example, Frankfurter thought it should be done roundabout. While ultimately only Roberts dissented, Murphy recorded Black and Jackson as initially voting to affirm a demurrer against the claim. Justice Jackson expressed acute discomfort over the collision with rights of the people to form groups, and both he and Rutledge voiced concern over the implications of judicial supervision of state elections which the decision made possible. Even Chief Justice Stone, hesitant before entering that thicket, answered Jackson: "not all primaries but this primary." And manifesting common misgivings, Stone once exclaimed, "I wait for light."[70]

Furthermore, the next step in legal development was a leap into the unknown. The White Primary Cases, for all their boldness, had been based on fairly plain representation guarantees of the First Article and the Fifteenth Amendment, and involved rights which, it was thought, met the least Southern resistance. The *Screws* case, by contrast, was the first to prosecute state officials for violating due process rights of the Fourteenth Amendment. Given the broad coverage of that amendment, how could anyone have advance notice of the substantive offense? The vagueness problem, which had led Justices Douglas, Black, and Murphy to dissent in *Classic*, was now far more serious. The Court would have to incorporate a law library into the civil rights statutes, as one Justice remarked, to comprehend the rights which the Court itself could define only case by case. Surely Congress had not intended to make the statute so all-embracing; and if it did, at least three, and possibly six, Justices believed that the broad coverage sought would make the statute unconstitutionally vague.[71]

To strike down the statute as indefinite, or to escape via legislative history, on the other hand, offered a disturbing choice. "I shudder from declaring [the] statute unconstitutional," one Justice reportedly remarked. "When we go into legislative history it will go bad for us." Passage of neither the Fourteenth Amendment nor the Civil Rights Acts had impeccable history. Inquiry into legislative intent might well produce the conclusion, as another Justice put it, that the Radical Congress had intended a broad expansion of federal crimes, and "to hell with state courts." Nullifying the measure also would be the first major act of Congress struck down since the 1937 imbroglio. Politically, the chances of Congress's enacting another statute were nil. Moreover, how could the Court invalidate Screws' conviction without undermining the recently decided White Primary Cases? The Justices' overt change of front on the status of primaries in the electoral process had provoked a deep fissure over the meaning of state action and an acrid denunciation of the Court by Justice Roberts for treating prior decisions as restricted railroad tickets, "good for this day and train only."[72] The political and legal implications of those cases did not permit retreat. Some basis of distinction had to be found.

One method, favored by Justice Reed, was to hold that the phrase, "under color of any law," applied only to deprivations *by* state law, not deprivations *against* it.[1] The trouble was, nearly all the precedents,

---

[1] Section 20 of the Criminal Code then read: "Whoever, under color of any law, statute, ordinance, regulation, or custom, willfully subjects, or causes to be subjected, any inhabitants of any State, Territory, or District to the deprivation of any rights, privileges, or immunities secured or protected by the Constitution and the laws of the United States, or to different punishments, pains, or penalties, on account of such inhabitant being an alien, or by reason of his color, or race, than are prescribed for the punishment of citizens, shall be fined not more than $1,000, or imprisoned not more than one year, or both." 18 U.S.C. 52. Section 19 read: "If two or more persons con-

including *Classic*, had held that any act by a state agent or under state authority constituted state action, whether commanded by the state or not. "If you don't say that," the Chief Justice remarked, "you do not have any 14th Amendment."[73] A second alternative close to the first and embraced by Frankfurter, was to revive the theory of the *Barney* case, which withheld federal punishment from acts that violated state law for want of finality of state action. The trouble here was that the Court had expressly scuttled *Barney* long before *Classic*, for the obvious reason that state inaction would rob federal rights of their force.[74] A third possibility, which attracted Jackson and Rutledge, was to trim the offense by holding that the second phrase of Section 20, "on account of being an alien, or by reason of his color," was a qualifying phrase, which restricted the offense to acts motivated by racial discrimination. But in *Classic* the Court had also considered and expressly rejected that distinction when it concluded that Congress had created two separate offenses. Though the discrimination argument might have drawn new adherents were the question fresh, the Court was now past it.[75] Still another alternative was to admit that the statute covered the slaying, but to accept Screws' theory of self-defense. Yet that suggestion, which would have cut even deeper into state law, was merely a mark of how desperately most of the Justices sought to avoid the second and underlying dilemma, the effect on the administration of criminal law by state governments.

The *Screws* case posed a peculiarly delicate issue of federalism, because the Court was asked to approve federal indictment of a state official for conduct that violated state law and customarily was of primary state concern. If the federal government could punish every instance of police brutality in the states, as one Justice frankly stated, every officer in the Union could be indicted for searches and assaults on prisoners "unless we define due process finer than we have. . . ." If the federal government could discipline "every petty offender" who violated due

---

spire to injure, oppress, threaten, or intimidate any citizen in the free exercise or enjoyment of any right or privilege secured to him by the Constitution or laws of the United States, or because of his having so exercised the same, or if two or more persons go in disguise on the highway, or on the premises of another, with intent to prevent or hinder his free exercise or enjoyment of any right or privileges so secured, they shall be fined not more than $5,000 and imprisoned not more than ten years, and shall, moreover, be thereafter ineligible to any office, or place of honor, profit, or trust created by the Constitution or laws of the United States." 18 U.S.C. 51. These sections are now numbered 242 and 241 respectively. For clarity, they will be referred to as sections 19 and 20 here. For the evolution of the statutes, see the appendix to the opinion of Frankfurter, J., in *United States* v. *Williams*, 341 U.S. 58, 83-84 (1951).

process as well as state law, then what would prevent deterioration of local responsibility for criminal justice? Fearful of the same revolution in federalism that had led the post-Civil War Court to emasculate most of the statutes, New Deal Justices were no less sensitive to the fact that indefinite offenses also meant indefinite federal power. The essential problem was how, in the absence of state concern, federal power could stimulate local responsibility without replacing it. "You can't run these things from Washington," one Justice observed: "Problems of local justice must be left to their communities. If we sustain this every time a Negro is beaten you are going to have F.M. and others jumping on [the] State for action. And then your local officers will lay down on the Job—So will the local judge. They will say let Washington do it." When reminded that due process was an expansive concept in the 19th century the same Justice denied that the Radical Congress had grafted all due process rights onto the civil rights statutes. When reminded that Congress at least had in mind the deprivation of Negro suffrage, he replied: "I consider this period one of the most shameful of our times. Stephens and Sumner were not giving it this interpretation. This interpretation belongs to Frank," though he ruefully admitted, as Murphy appears to have charged, that "we are going to be misunderstood as favoring a beating."[76]

The Chief Justice at first seemed willing to affirm the conviction; but as consensus formed about the dual dangers of indefiniteness and expansive federal power, the question rapidly resolved itself into how much of *Classic* could be saved. Only Murphy and Rutledge supported Stone's position, and even Rutledge was attracted to the narrow, discrimination argument. Justices Douglas and Black objected to the vagueness of the indictment, and Black manifested the same resistance to federal control over local law enforcement that he exposed, much to the surprise of libertarian commentators, in the racial sit-in cases of the 1960s. Three Justices—Roberts, Frankfurter, and Jackson—appeared ready to reverse, if they could have "put it on grounds we could stomach." Thus Murphy's notes record the Chief Justice as giving a virtuoso performance in *Classic*'s defense. Against charges of vagueness, he retorted, "it is not as vague as Sherman Act cases." Against charges that federal prosecutors would preempt state rights to punish their own officials, he replied: "but here he is doing it under color of his office." "Here you have [a] command of Congress. It says take jurisdiction. It doesn't say to do it when the state fails to act. . . . We can't go back to [the] Barney case to emasculate the Amendment."[77]

Yet Stone himself was deeply troubled by the implications of the case. The Court had already blown up over state action in *Smith* v. *Allwright*, and litigants were pressing that principle to its limits. "Whoever writes this I hope will keep us out of state action," he commented at the outset. But recognizing that such hopes were vain, that retrenchment was inevitable, Stone urged his colleagues to "leave some of the specific things under the 14th." And in a clear case of persuasion he acknowledged the force of the indefiniteness objection. "It may be the key to this is its vagueness when applied to the 14th Amendment," said the Chief. "We should consider it very carefully."[78]

Eager to salvage as much of their handiwork as possible, Stone and then Reed swung behind a compromise solution presumably suggested by Douglas. Without qualifying *Classic's* broad interpretation of offenses the Court would narrow their effect by imposing a stricter standard of intent. Remanding the case for new trial the Court would hold that the statutory requirement of "willful" deprivation be construed as meaning that a defendant had a specific intent to deny a recognized constitutional right. Given the nature of southern juries, everyone knew that this construction of the statute would "leave mighty little scope for its application." But at least it would save the statute, and, as Douglas argued, preserve *Classic* as a rule of law "good for more than one day only."[79]

Yet compromise produced stalemate and a paradox of voting. One majority sustained the statute and another reversed the conviction, but the memberships differed. At first, indeed, Douglas's opinion for the Court attracted only three additional votes—Black, Stone, and Reed. Four other Justices dissented in opposing directions and Jackson hovered in between.

Justices Frankfurter and Roberts, who regarded the statute as unconstitutional, pounded away at the flaw that also troubled Reed. How could a broad definition of intent make indefinite offenses definite? "It is true also of a statute that it cannot lift itself by its bootstraps," Frankfurter observed in a hardhitting memorandum. "I can understand a statute prohibiting specifically the deprivation of enumerated constitutional rights," he wrote. "But . . . I do not see how we escape facing decision as to what constitutional rights are covered by [section] 20 by saying that in any event whatever they are they must be taken away 'willfully.'" Nor could Frankfurter understand "how the intrinsic vagueness of the terms of section 20 is removed by making the statute applicable only where the defendant had 'the requisite bad purpose.'" Did the Court's patchwork not amount to saying that the black heart of defendant enabled him to know what Congress did not, and the Court could not, define? While loathe to strike down an act of Congress for fear of restricting its freedom of action, Frankfurter saw "no difficulty in passing effective legislation for the protection of civil rights against improper State action." "What we are concerned with here," he said, "is something very basic in a democratic society, namely, the avoidance of the injustice of prohibiting conduct in terms so vague as to make the understanding of what conduct is proscribed a guess-work too difficult for confident judgment even for the judges of the highest Court in the land."[80]

Justice Jackson, though "reluctant to add what can be no more than a confession of personal bewilderment to a subject already in a state of impeccable confusion," blamed the Court rather than Congress for the *Screws* predicament. Since *Betts* v. *Brady* in 1942, Jackson had frequently voiced belief that the history of Reconstruction weakened any feeling of sanctity on his part for the Fourteenth Amendment. Though somewhat embarrassed by his responsibility for the *Classic* prosecution, which had led to his disqualification from that case, Jackson now summoned history and administrative necessity in defense of a much narrower view of the statute and state action than *Classic* had approved. "I am disturbed by no doubts as to the constitutionality of what Congress actually has done in enacting the statute under consideration," he observed in a memorandum to conference, "but I have considerable misgivings about what the Court has done to it. This legislation originated in the Reconstruction Period and its aim was a narrow one." The statute, he contended, was aimed only against acts of racial discrimination and "that class of wrongs against federal rights which state law or custom sheltered or at least ignored, and which therefore could be said to be state action under the Fourteenth Amendment." For those limited purposes, he maintained, congressional language was not inept. If construed narrowly to mean that a deprivation of federal rights was an offense only when committed by reason of color or race, the Act would require a specific intent to discriminate on account of race, and thus its coverage would be restricted to a fairly definite class of cases. Accordingly Jackson proposed that Screws' conviction be reversed on the ground that the deprivation of rights was not state action.[81]

Alternately, if the Court held to the broader interpretations of *Classic*, he then offered a fallback position of restricting the statute to deprivation of voting rights.

I would not extend the application of this statute beyond the ground already taken in the *Classic* case. While I cannot say that the logic of that decision cannot reasonably be made to include this one, the very indefiniteness which it introduces seems to forbid such an expansion, particularly when it is a criminal act we are construing. I agree with the opinion of the majority that if this Act means what it is contended to mean, it is dangerously indefinite and perhaps unconstitutionally so. But we must remember that a large part of all that ill-defined indecisiveness we are reading into the statute by the very decision that deplores it. The Court is first choosing the broadest among possible meanings, which makes the Act so indecisive we do not know what it may punish; then it holds the Act so vague that heroic measures must be taken to rescue it from unconstitutionality. . . .

My vote, therefore, is to hold that this deprivation of rights was not committed under color of any law or custom, was not the act of the State of Georgia, and therefore I would reverse the conviction. But if a majority of the Court overrules this ground of reversal, I cannot agree to reversal on the ground suggested. That is, if the Court is to hold this a proper case for prosecution under the Act, I find no error in the procedure which led to conviction. It impresses me as well prosecuted, vigorously and ably defended and presided over impartially.

It seems to me that the Court is introducing unwarranted procedural barriers to any conviction under the Act in order to compensate for unwarranted expansion of the substance of the offense. What, in short, it seems to me to do is to make more prosecutions possible and fewer convictions probable— about the most mischievous thing I can imagine.

Assurances by the Department of Justice that federal power would be used sparingly, he added, were doubtless well-intended but of uncertain duration. The argument that local law enforcement officers could not be trusted to do their duty was "an ominous sign indeed." "And if the whole burden of such law enforcement must be carried in the Central Government," Jackson noted, "at least the Department should be armed with something better for legal weapons than the old-fashioned scatter gun of Section 20."[82]

Ultimately the memoranda of Frankfurter and Jackson were woven into Roberts' dissent, which somehow lost the brilliance of both. Posing the issue broadly, whether states should be relieved from the duty of punishing their own errant officials, and expressing universal hope that "the cure is a reinvigoration of State responsibility . . . not an undue incursion of remote federal authority," the minority predicted that the statute could become a "dangerous instrument of political intimidation and coercion in the hands of those so inclined." The only way to preserve traditional federal balances, they argued, was to invalidate the statute or to narrow state action to activities directed or condoned by the states, if need be by resurrecting *Barney*. Section 20 was not co-extensive with the Fourteenth Amendment. Congress, not the Court, was the proper agency to define rights whose deprivation duplicated state criminal law.[83]

Posing the issue in reverse, whether local officials could violate con-stitutional rights with impunity, Murphy protested the remand and predicted that the decision would frustrate the small federal relief avail-able. "Knowledge of a comprehensive law library is unnecessary for officers of the law to know that the right to murder individuals in the course of their duties is unrecognized in this nation," he declared. The Constitution, the statute, and "their own consciences told them that."[84] And with "simple, but unanswerable logic," Murphy hammered both sides with "realities."[85]

While not denying that acute vagueness problems would arise even-tually, he reminded the brethren that the *Screws* case did not raise them. In contrast to *Classic*, the right deprived here was the right to life, a right specifically enumerated by the Fourteenth Amendment, and one abridged because of race. If elsewhere Murphy had earned criticism for discussing abstractions *in vacuo*, now the tables were turned. It would be time enough to consider the "vice of vagueness" when it arose.

Murphy's dissent was also a rebuke to minority contentions that the *Screws* indictment was a "needless extension of federal criminal authority into matters that normally are of State concern."[86] Angered by a challenge to the premises behind the creation of the Civil Rights Section, he asserted that the federal government had to intervene "un-less constitutional guarantees are to become atrophied." The precise purpose of the enactment was to protect "the inarticulate and the friendless" from "the cruelties of bigoted and ruthless authority" in the states. Congress, not judges, had decreed that this vacuum be filled. Yet federal intervention would be "futile if courts disregard reality." While Justices could hardly say so, state responsibilities would not be met without outside pressure. Expectations of resurging local responsi-bility or of congressional relief, suggestions which circulated through the Court of publicity or of private civil suits as alternative remedies, all were utopian. The real question here was a federal remedy or none.[87]

Justice Rutledge, in a separate dissent, agreed point by point. This was an act of murder, an abuse of authority which a long course of decision from *ex parte Virginia* to *Classic* had sustained as state ac-tion.[88] No petition, no brief raised questions of vagueness and criminal intent. Appellate courts had injected those. Nor were these issues fresh.

Classic had rejected a clearer vagueness claim; surely the due process right to life was as definite as the equal protection rights upheld in *Smith* v. *Allwright.* "There can be no judicial hack work cutting out some of the great rights the Amendment secures but leaving in others," Rutledge asserted. "The *Classic* decision must stand or fall by this one. There is no solid room for distinction. Only chaos of principle could result from the effort to maintain that decision while holding the statute impotent to cover these facts." For Rutledge, as for Murphy, "a deeper implication" was at work in the *Screws* case—an effort to undermine the fragile federal role only recently revived.[89] If the Court narrowed the meaning of state action in criminal statutes how could it resist doing the same for civil remedies and the Fourteenth Amendment itself?

There was another implication in *Screws*, however—the implication of the appellate function and of the Court's reputation in stalemate. However shocking the crime, however distorted Rutledge considered the compromise solution, deadlock in a criminal proceeding was worse. Forgoing personal opinion, as he did later in the Illinois reapportionment case, *Colegrove* v. *Green*, Rutledge swung his vote to Douglas in order to achieve a firm result.[90] The statute was saved, as a result, and Screws' conviction was reversed without an "opinion of the Court."

The consequences of the decision conformed to predictions in uncanny ways. On the one hand, a second jury refused to convict; and Sheriff Screws, suffering no loss of local popularity, was elected to the Georgia Senate in 1958. The refusal of the Court to retreat from the broad interpretation of state action, on the other hand, left *Classic* and *Smith* v. *Allwright* standing as critical underpinnings for the modern law of equal protection pioneered by the federal judiciary. For all the lament of libertarians over the surgery performed on criminal statutes in *Screws*, a retreat there along the lines proposed by Roberts, Frankfurter, and Jackson would have made much more difficult the Supreme Court's subsequent plunge into desegregation of public facilities, not to mention its supervision of voting rights and legislative reapportionment.[91] Whatever the price in statutory effectiveness, the *Screws* case can only be viewed as a major constitutional victory for federal protection of civil rights.

Practically speaking, however, there is no denying that the mode of salvaging Section 20 in *Screws* seriously blunted the "sword" of the Civil Rights Division. Finding legal remedies for the police brutality problem remained much as before—a troublesome void. Although the high court did invigorate civil remedies in *Monroe* v. *Pape,* an evenly divided bench narrowed the conspiracy section of the statutes so severely in 1951, that a weakened Section 20 remained the federal government's primary legal weapon against racial violence until the Warren Court cleared the conspiracy path in the *Guest* and *Price* decisions of 1966.[92] Even after a sustained season of civil disobedience in the streets made it politically expedient to break the impasse of a century, Congress did not enact additional criminal penalties nor a statute of enumerated rights until 1968, despite uncontroverted suggestions from the Justices that enumeration of rights, the form Section 20 took in the beginning, would free legislation of constitutional problems.[93] And the impact of *Screws* reverberated through the resulting administration of federal law.

The Civil Rights Commission report of 1961 manifested deep frustration over the practical obstacles to convictions. While potential federal action probably spurs local initiative, experience has shown that the specific intent standard is confusing to use and difficult to satisfy, even with nonsouthern juries.[94] Of the thousands of complaints received annually by the Civil Rights Division, no prosecution under the conspiracy section survived the high court after *Classic* until the Philadelphia, Mississippi trials of 1966. Results under the "color of law" section have been meager even during the quickening civil rights agitation of the 1960s. In the fiscal years 1961-63 the Department of Justice prosecuted a yearly average of 23 cases under both sections; indictments were returned in only 16 cases and convictions in only three. In 1964-65 the Department prosecuted a yearly average of 40 cases, with a total yield of 27 indictments and six convictions.[95] Justice Jackson's forecast has yet to be proved wrong.

Neither did the Supreme Court itself escape feedback from *Screws.* Justice Roberts, who was scathingly contemptuous of Rutledge's prescient reference to a "penumbra of rights," was further embittered by the case. Justice Frankfurter, who freely avowed that his *Screws'* research had changed his mind about "one aspect of the *Classic* decision," thereafter made war on the statute and refused to join the Court opinion in the Restrictive Covenant Case because of arguments drawn therefrom.[96] Libertarian Justices have also been wary through the years about defining the threshold of state action. Even Murphy apparently voted against granting certiorari in the *Enoch Pratt Free Library* case, a significant lower court decision expanding state action, for fear of risking defeat and "another mess like *Screws.*"[97] Even as they stretch the old statutes to cover "all rights" and private action, contemporary Justices

have drawn back from the collision of state-federal judiciaries inherent
in equally expansive interpretations of civil rights removal statutes.[98]
They have also exempted judges from civil liability and cast longing
eyes to Congress for aid. How else can one explain the advisory opinion
in *United States* v. *Guest*, that the enabling clause of the Fourteenth
Amendment would sustain a criminal statute punishing all conspiracies,
with or without state action, that interfere with Fourteenth Amendment rights?[99]

A generation after *Screws*, in sum, men are still hoping for a resur-
gence of local responsibility to punish shocking episodes in law enforcement, they are still saying "let Washington do it," and they are
still frustrated over unpunished police murders by that route. A generation later the struggle of the federal government to use the feeble remains of Section 20 as its principal weapon against local police brutality leads inescapably to the conclusion that in the *Screws* case *all* the
Justices were right. And for similar reasons, the case illustrates the
hazards of attempting to reduce complex decision-making to simple
dichotomies, such as liberal versus conservative attitudes, as a means of
explaining judicial behavior.

IV

The climax of Justice Murphy's crusading came in three military
jurisdiction cases in 1946. In each, a combination of suspected racism
and slipshod trial procedures provoked him to bitter denunciation of
"militarism," a term he did not define in an American context, and
to appeal for enlarged judicial control of military justice. To challenge
the traditional judicial policy of hands-off in military trials was highly
unpopular, both legally and politically. The public, which delighted in
General MacArthur's own symbolic stroke of shoving a surrendering
Japanese premier aboard the battleship *Missouri*, thirsted for vengeance.
Legal doctrine was equally firm that, except for jurisdiction, the conduct of military tribunals was beyond judicial review. The Constitution
not only empowered Congress to make rules governing the armed
forces, but expressly exempted military personnel from most of the
procedural guarantees of the Bill of Rights. Even the *Milligan* Court
had agreed unanimously that denial of jury trial to servicemen was
unaffected by "the fifth, or any other amendment."[100] Although the
Justices did rule in 1949 that double jeopardy safeguards applied to
courts-martial, Congress basically met the minimal due process standards that governed the domestic system of military justice. In the Nazi

Saboteur Case the Court had reaffirmed these general principles in what then appeared as an uphill battle to preserve even habeas corpus review for enemy combatants.[101] Only jurisdiction, that is, the authority of a military tribunal and the validity of a charge, not the procedures of trial, was reviewable. Military justice, as the Justice Department and Frankfurter took pains to emphasize throughout the war, was an executive and legislative responsibility.

After *Korematsu* Justices Murphy and Rutledge were convinced that the time had come to impose corresponding judicial checks on the growth of military power. Traditional doctrine restricting habeas corpus to jurisdictional questions, as their certiorari notes analyzed the issue, had been developed in ordinary criminal cases that presupposed the existence of other avenues of appeal. Since habeas corpus was the only means of reviewing military trials, the Murphy-Rutledge camp believed it imperative that the Court fashion broader habeas corpus law in this field; otherwise American military commanders would be free to make their own law in pursuance of their greatly expanded responsibilities over civilians and foreign nationals at home and abroad. If it was argued that the Court had never before asserted such power, the short answer was that it was high time it did.[102] For at the same time that Murphy and Rutledge challenged customary review as outmoded, government attorneys were suggesting the same of *Milligan*. At the same time that military tribunals functioned around the globe, Manila war crimes commissions were using shocking methods in trials of Japanese generals, and military commanders were justifying denial of jury trial to citizens in Hawaii on grounds of untrustworthy race. In *Yamashita*, *Homma*, and *Duncan* v. *Kahanamoku*, Murphy's differences with the Court over war powers and the judiciary's part in fighting racism came to a head.[103] The result was some of the most impassioned dissents of modern times.

The two Justices could hardly have picked a more inhospitable occasion to challenge military justice than the war crimes trials of the Japanese generals, Tonoyaka Yamashita, the "Tiger of Malaya," and Masaharu Homma, the commander of the Bataan death march. The war crimes trials, though the subject of considerable legal controversy, were popular for reasons other than vengeance. The Nuremberg trials were part of a sincere Anglo-American effort to strengthen international law as a force for peace by making individual leaders criminally responsible for their nation's aggressive conduct and crimes against humanity. The trials in the Far East were directed in part against so-called conventional war crimes, which were recognized in both domestic and international law. Rather than execute Axis leaders by right of conquest, however, the Allies wrapped the proceedings behind a facade of questionable legality. The charges of making aggressive war at Nuremberg smacked of retroactivity, which civilized legal systems condemn; and the trial procedures of the American military commission in Manila fell below elementary standards of fairness—not to mention the Bill of Rights.[104] Since most of the war crimes tribunals were international in character it was uncertain whether their judgments were subject to American judicial review. But since the trials of Yamashita and Homma were under American auspices, their habeas corpus petitions from the Philippines Supreme Court raised two basic questions: (1) under the laws of war, was a military commander criminally responsible for not preventing the crimes of his troops; (2) was a military trial of a foreign belligerent exempt from due process restrictions and therefore from review by civilian courts? In the context of international politics, and in an emotional postwar atmosphere, it was generally assumed that internationally speaking a pioneering series of trials would also create benchmarks of American constitutional law.

Chief Justice Stone, who privately referred to the Nuremberg trials as Jackson's "lynching party," assumed a heavy burden marshalling the Court to agreement in the *Yamashita* case.[105] For himself Stone had no great difficulty in refusing to overturn Yamashita's death sentence. In a memorandum circulated on January 22, 1946 the Chief Justice maintained that a charge making it a duty to prevent atrocities could be inferred from General Styer's directive establishing the Manila commission (a position which Kemp urged Murphy was sound), and that the procedural safeguards of the American Articles of War did not apply to a military commission trying an enemy belligerent for offenses against the laws of war. The trial, the Chief seemed to imply, was a dirty political business best left untouched.[106]

Centrifugal views were to be expected in a matter of such importance, and they were strong. Justice Reed and others flatly objected to Stone's argument that the Articles of War were inapplicable. They also opposed his dismissal of the Geneva Convention, which obliged signatory powers to treat enemy combatants according to the same procedures used in trying their own personnel.[107] To hold his majority Stone met these objections by making two distinctions which withdrew procedural protection from defendants—that the Articles of War covered only domestic offenders, not foreign belligerents; and that Article 63 of the Geneva Convention covered only prisoner-of-war offenses, not war crimes.[108] The result, however, was confusion about the basis of the charge. Was Yamashita being tried according to American Articles of War, treaty law, or international custom?

Stone's retreat on the substantive offense, by general consensus, led a divided Court into obscurity. Furthermore it beat a hasty retreat from the review the Court had taken such pains to preserve in *ex parte Quirin*. Given his ordinary attraction to legal innovations, his Filipino attachments, and his personal knowledge of atrocities from secret reports, Murphy for once might have been expected to acquiesce.[109] By the same token, in view of Rutledge's past willingness to swallow offensive doctrine for the sake of corporate loyalties, he especially might have been expected to close ranks. But the two Justices champed at the bit. Nowhere did the Chief's opinion even mention what to them was "the great issue," whether Fifth Amendment guarantees of a fair trial "follows the flag." Nowhere did Stone discuss the trial procedures—the absence of a jury, the lack of time to prepare defense, the use of hearsay evidence two and three times removed—which to them were "a national disgrace."[110] While the Chief Justice apparently had hopes of converting Rutledge to the view that these were military questions beyond review, the more he worked on him, the angrier Rutledge became. *Yamashita* was to be his greatest hour.

Working against time, Rutledge circulated a penetrating dissent which protested the procedural deficiencies of the trial and the neglect of the Fifth Amendment. Chief Justice Stone then recirculated an answer defending the procedural shortcuts by analogy to administrative review. Stone's discussion of the merits threatened to disintegrate the Court. Justice Black retorted that the challenged procedures could not be squared with any "fair trial" norm if the constitutional question were reached. The whole premise of the case was that trial procedures were beyond review. Justice Frankfurter was assumed to believe the reverse, and to be pressuring Stone to hold that while the Constitution applied, different standards controlled military trials of enemy combatants. Trapped by conflicting views regarding due process standards over military tribunals, which had been smouldering since *Quirin*, Stone acquiesced.[111] In a move Rutledge labelled "the Big Backup," the Court refused to consider the applicability of the Fifth Amendment on the basis of *Quirin*.[112] Review of trial procedures, if any, was the responsibility of the War Department and the President.

The conscientious Rutledge, who fretted over details almost to a fault, was incensed by the "run-around" on the Fifth Amendment issue. While prepared to concede that lower standards might govern war crimes trials, he regarded the Court's refusal to face the issue as a derogation of responsibility. Rutledge was also angered by pressures for a speedy decision, which denied him time to prepare adequate dissent. Losing two sleepless nights to meet the gruelling schedule, Rutledge recalled that the effort of Murphy and himself to obtain a hearing and minimum writing time "was a battle royal all the way." "The two ends of the table were in direct and irreconcilable clash."[113]

"How about this:" Rutledge queried Murphy regarding their tactics. "You take the charge; I'll take the balance. And then, perhaps, we can join each other."[114] In *Yamashita* the two Justices established a division of labor that foreshadowed working arrangements in battles to come. Concentrating on the legality of the charge, which the Chief Justice conceded was open to review, while Rutledge took trial procedures, Murphy followed his *Korematsu* strategy of boring from within. Though he voiced belief that the Court should expand habeas corpus review as an act of "judicial statesmanship," he accepted Stone's ostensible frame of reference. The Court, he began, had "taken the first and most important step toward insuring the primacy of law and justice" by repudiating the "obnoxious" government argument that a war crimes trial of an enemy combatant was a political act beyond judicial review.[115] Not quarreling with the legality of the commission's creation, which had troubled the Court in *Quirin*, and leaving procedural infirmities to the heated pen of Rutledge with whom he concurred, Murphy subjected the *Yamashita* charges to searching scrutiny according to the Geneva Convention and the Articles of War. And in a biting attack he accused the Court of permitting the United States Army to make its own law of nations without judicial review.

On examination, Murphy maintained that the charges against Yamashita boiled down to one issue: "Is it a crime to be a commander of soldiers who commit crimes?"[116] Without any evidence of personal culpability or even knowledge of atrocities, Yamashita was made criminally responsible for the conduct of troops that the American armies themselves had placed beyond his effective control. "The recorded annals of warfare and the established principles of international law afford not the slightest precedent for such a charge," Murphy declared.

This indictment in effect permitted the military commission to make the crime whatever it willed . . . a practice reminiscent of that pursued in certain less respected nations in recent years.

In my opinion, such a procedure is unworthy of the traditions of our people or of the immense sacrifices that they have made to advance the common ideals of mankind. The high feelings of the moment doubtless will be satisfied. But in the sober afterglow will come the realization of the boundless and dangerous implications of the procedure sanctioned today.[117]

Two dangers, in particular, spurred the dissenters on. First, they feared that Yamashita's case would set the stage for massive blood purges under American auspices. In the "interlude of lawlessness" immediately following the war, these apprehensions were not far-fetched.[118] Both sides had indulged mass purges on the Russian front. Vigilante reprisals against alleged collaborators was the bloody after-math of liberation in France. The American government had rejected the Morgenthau plan for repressing Germany; but in the Philippines, war crimes and collaboration trials had begun under directives that authorized mass trials, use of coerced and hearsay evidence, and impu-tation of evidence in mass trials to individual defendants. Should mili-tary tribunals be permitted to take these shortcuts against big game such as Yamashita, what was to prevent a repetition of mass purges of lesser men on the German and Russian models? Should the United States ever lose a war, indeed, or should concepts of military due process urged elsewhere in Court be extended to civilians, what would prevent such practices from being applied to Americans?

Second, Justice Murphy, especially, feared the political implications of war crimes trials. Not only did the "needless and unseemly haste" at Manila tarnish the American record, but bloody reprisals could hin-der "the reconciliation necessary to a peaceful world."[119] Should ven-geance reign against the vanquished, what was to prevent another dead-ly cycle of bitterness and war that had followed Versailles? The *Yama-shita* case was not the first time the Justice had espoused a live-and-let-live principle. Even at the height of his war fever in 1942 he had op-posed a policy of postwar force with the Wilsonian warning that "it will require men of strong character and integrity to reason and pre-vail against this understandable human reaction—to point out that we must live together in the same world . . . and that while banditry must be suppressed, real peace can be achieved only on the basis of equity and constant seeking for harmony among men. . . . An essential part of freedom is the liberty of a people to choose freely their own form of government. And while this country may by example encourage the adoption of democracy by other peoples, this liberty of choice must be preserved for all, or peace cannot endure."[120]

As Murphy's criticism of Stone's opinion regarding the legal basis of the charge was trenchant, so his address to the policy issue went to the heart of his faith in the universality of American ideals. Anxious that the United States not stray from the traditional guidepost of moral example to the easy path of physical power, he appealed for a judicial brake in a soaring flight of compassionate rhetoric. Because the Fifth

Amendment referred to "person," he maintained, the Constitution permitted no exception to the principle that due process protected every human being under American control.

Indeed, such an exception would be contrary to the whole philosophy of human rights which makes the Constitution the great living document that it is. The immutable rights of the individual . . . belong not alone to the members of those nations that excel on the battle field or that subscribe to the democratic ideology. They belong to every person in the world, victor or vanquished, whatever may be his race, color or belief. . . . They survive any popular passion or frenzy of the moment. No court or legislature or executive, not even the mightiest army in the world, can ever destroy them. Such is the universal and indestructible nature of the rights which the due process clause . . . protects when life or liberty is threatened by virtue of the authority of the United States.[121]

Equating Constitution with natural right, Court with immanent national conscience and universal hopes for peace, Murphy unleashed a fervent sermon on the American moral example in the quest ahead. "Today, more than ever," he wrote in a passage deleted on Kemp's advice, "mankind looks to America to exhibit compassion and understanding. . . . The better life that might be ours can easily be lost by the deadly crops of bombs engendered by the hatred and animosity planted today. It is because I believe with all my conscience that the result reached today fosters those feelings and bodes nothing but ill for the world of tomorrow that I am forced to dissent in these terms."[122] Vengeance, left "free to masquerade in a cloak of false legalism," he warned in his final draft, was far more dangerous to peace than "all the atrocities giving rise to that spirit." "The people's faith in fairness and objectiveness of the law can be seriously undercut. . . . The fires of nationalism can be further kindled. And the hearts of all mankind can be embittered and filled with hatred, leaving forlorn and impoverished the noble ideal of malice toward none and charity to all. . . . If we are ever to develop an orderly international community based upon recognition of human dignity . . . Justice must be tempered by compassion rather than by vengeance."[123]

Perhaps it was too early, as Rutledge suggested, for a revival of "Lincoln's great spirit." Ring as it might, Murphy's final appeal to the "spirit, not of Constitutionality, but of Humanity," was immaterial to the jurisdictional inquiry which he well knew was the central issue before the Court.[124/j] Some lawyers thus took offense at his sermon on peace-

---

[j] In an undated, handwritten note written perhaps during oral argument, Murphy observed: "Isn't this different from Nuremburg? . . . To me this [is] no different than

making. The charge of vengeance "should be considered attentively," Charles Fairman commented. "Bias and lack of objectivity are of course to be condemned—wherever they appear."[125] "No trial could have been fairer," General MacArthur reportedly opined from Tokyo; the dissenters either advocated "arbitrariness of process above factual realism" or shrank from "the stern rigidity of capital punishment." Leading dailies such as the *Washington Star* and the *New York Times* also objected that Yamashita's sentence was not "imposed haphazardly in thoughtless haste." Certainly General Homma was guilty.[126]

Yet, to Murphy, guilt missed the point. The question was not *what* Japanese generals had done, but *how* Americans were trying them; not how the Japanese military might have treated Americans in victory, but how far the American military would descend to that level. "We should not consider what men deserve but the preservation of our way of life," he observed to Corrine Marshall and Clare Booth Luce. "Whenever the flag flies and when one is put to trial under American authority . . . the Bill of Rights must be adhered to. Because our enemies did not do so is no answer for me." "Culpability must be personal under the American Flag. Besides, vengeance is not likely to build an enlightened tomorrow."[127]

Other Justices might drown distaste of the trials in hatred of "pernicious abstractions," including the old emotional slogan whether the Constitution "follows the flag," a slogan which had torn legal thought since the Spanish-American War. Realists might pause before the revolutionary, even dangerous, implications of that principle for the Court as institution, and rest content with the thought that the Constitution placed responsibility on others. The scope of review sought by the dissenters, after all, not only would expose a sore split over the meaning of due process in military trials, but could also invite extremely delicate issues respecting the relation of domestic courts to international engagements, namely Nuremberg. Moreover, the flood-of-litigation argument, which judges habitually raise to oppose legal change, for once had merit. The Court could hardly withhold the same relief to millions of American soldiers or foreign civilians under military control. Great issues of politics and judicial statecraft—whether power can and should have a counterpart check, the degree to which judges can and should supply it—ran deep in the procedural battle of *Yamashita*. Justice Brandeis used to say that the most important thing the Court de-

any case coming up from State Ct. . . . The simple inquiry is Jurisdiction." No. 61, Box 136.

cided was what it did not decide. Ample institutional reasons, perhaps overpowering ones, existed for ducking the "grave issue" of *Yamashita*.

To Justice Murphy, however, the norms involved were so elementary a part of the American tradition that he saw no reason why military courts should be exempt from standards the United States demanded of other countries in the treatment of its nationals. The sacrifice of principle was so unnecessary and so great a stain on the country's credentials for world leadership that he found it difficult to understand why contemporaries regarded his dissent as courageous. Though confessing himself as "often assailed by doubt," he remarked:

My course was a difficult one to take only because of popular opinion and the rising power of militarism. As far as the law is concerned and my instinct for liberty, which shall never abate in my lifetime, it was easy because I could not have done otherwise.

The world is burdened with hate and while I cannot condemn those who have their view other than my own I wrote out the law as I saw it for a brave new world where men have the love of God in their hearts. In that alone is our salvation.[128]

For their pains the dissenters were denounced as "Jap Coddlers." Murphy was ridiculed by eminent law professors for making "an absurdity" of the Constitution. Yet the priestly liberties taken tapped deep, almost unspeakable reserves of idealism that runs in American thought, regardless of class or politics. From self-styled realists, for example Hans J. Morgenthau, to conservative columnists George Sokolsky and Samuel B. Pettingill, from United World Federalists to Wall Street lawyers and members of what Rutledge called "the Taft tribe," Justice Murphy was showered with praise for a "magnificent" and "imperishable" dissent.[129] "You are heartening beyond most men and *all* judges!" wrote Roger Baldwin of the ACLU. "Of course Japanese generals have rights in U.S. courts, but how few, alas, can free themselves from prejudice and partisanship. Someday civilization may catch up with you."[130]

Justice Holmes demonstrated more than once the power of appealing beyond immediate issues to universal values and common experience, a technique since weakened by overuse and of which Murphy himself was not blameless. The *Yamashita* trial was one of those infrequent occasions when dissenters successfully turned Court into political tutorial by sheer moral force. For most lawyers the Rutledge dissent was the more impressive, and undoubtedly a great opinion. For some lawyers and most laymen, who perforce are dependent on the translation of complex choices into simpler terms, Murphy's plea for "the correct way" was dramatically compelling. In the words of a public utilities executive, it was "one of those remarkable judicial opinions" which would "live as long as men revere truth and justice."[131] Nor was the lesson lost on members of the Court. "Frank," Justice Frankfurter asserted in a "strictly private" note, "I want to put on paper two things: (1) I wholly disagree with your view as to the duty of this Court in *Yamashita* because of my deep conviction as to the limitations upon the *power* of this Court. BUT, (2) I wholly respect the utterance of your conscience taking a contrary view. This applies to Wiley. I wish I could say as much all around! ! F.F."[132/k]

Whatever a younger generation of realists thought of the rhetoric, to its own time and generation, Justice Murphy's dissent pricked the conscience with disconcerting force. *Korematsu* and *Yamashita* alone assured his immortality as a jurist.

Realistically, Justice Rutledge believed that dissents had little to gain except preventing the public from having an "occasion to crow" about the glories of American justice.[133] General Homma's appeal, which the Court declined to review on the basis of *Yamashita*, was a poor vehicle for spreading the message. Just the same, the dissenters felt an urgent need to protest, because the directives authorizing mass trials and the admission of hearsay, coerced, and imputed evidence had gone largely unnoticed. Luckily for the Court, the dissenters could not say that Homma had been the victim of such evidence, inasmuch as his petition was filed in Washington before sentence was imposed; but for Rutledge and Murphy the directives vitiated the entire proceeding.[134] Ruthlessly the two Justices needled their brethren about the possibilities. Since little doubt existed that Homma had knowledge of atrocities, the very contrast with Yamashita enabled them to twist the knife. "Did you hear the C.J. say to me in Conf. room that there was *no* evid. in Yama—that he had *knowledge* of the atrocities?" Rutledge asked Murphy on February 7th, 1946.[135] Even after losing the fight to obtain a hearing the dissenters took grim satisfaction in the discomfort caused. Said Rutledge: "I think the Homma thing hit the C.J. heavier than the Yama—. thing. Did you see him slump? And then hear him groan? He had not seen 'the record'—yet there was *nothing* in it not in Yama—." "The boys are over the barrel. The C.J. et al had the

---

[k] Murphy, scenting a chance to divide the opposition, apparently replied with a statement of objections, to which Frankfurter responded: "Frank, I did not want to re-argue the *merits* of your position. I simply wanted to respect its *morality*." Undated note, No. 61, Box 136.

most pained expressions I've seen in moons. They dared not yell more than 'Yamashita.' " To which Murphy added: "And [another Justice] said the day might come when he would repudiate that monstrous case."[136/1]

Breaking their self-imposed rule against *per curiam* dissents in order to publicize the dangers of mass bloodletting, Murphy prepared their protest with all the righteous fury expressed in conference. "It is not the man concerned," he began his notes during conversation with Rutledge. "It is a system fashioned to be a way of life for impoverished libertarians. . . . It could be done the correct way—the American way so dearly bought rather than to abandon those virtues we cherish. When law is bled and finally perishes. Then too a nation dies."[137] References by Murphy to the possibility that the procedures approved might someday backfire against Americans, led to Rutledge's word of caution: "Frank— With the changes indicated I can, and would like to join, your opinion. . . . But I do not want to say—even now—that even this Court can turn these precedents against our own soldiers and citizens."[138] With a vehemence so fierce that Rutledge feared weakened force, Murphy then bathed the *Homma* trial in blistering fire: "It involves something more than the guilt of a fallen enemy commander under the law of war or the jurisdiction of a military commission. This nation's very honor, as well as its hopes for the future, is at stake. Either we conduct such a trial as this in the noble spirit and atmosphere of our Constitution or we abandon all pretense to justice, let the ages slip away and descend to the level of revengeful blood purges. . . . A nation must not perish because, in the natural frenzy of the aftermath of war, it abandoned its central theme of the dignity of the human personality and due process of law."[139]

These principles could scarcely be dismissed as narrow technicalities. They were "the very life blood of our civilization." To forego them now was to set the stage for "a procession of judicial lynchings without due process of law." To forego them now was to discredit at the start the very effort to create higher standards of international conduct through law, to admit "that the enemy has lost the battle but has destroyed our ideals."[140]

"Which Being Taught," the *Washington Post* commented in the sober afterglow of 1949, Murphy's "prophetic" warnings returned, not as a "reckless forecast" as some still believed, but to haunt the trials of lesser Japanese figures who successfully pleaded that General Yama-

[1] Chief Justice Stone died a few days later, after having complained of the strain of *Yamashita*. Mason, *Stone*, p. 671.

shita had borne responsibility for acts of which they stood accused.[141] At the time, however, army prosecutors were so stung by Murphy's prophecy that Joseph B. Keenan, chief of the army's international prosecution section, publicly denounced the *Homma* dissent as "offensive." General MacArthur had instructed that every precaution be taken to insure fair trials, he said; a procession of judicial lynchings was impossible.[142] Justice Rutledge was almost grateful to Keenan for the extra publicity about mass trials and imputed evidence. "I hope the protest may be able to prevent the use of that type of evidence in any case," he remarked, "but that is about all I can hope for in the present state of things, so far as further trials of enemy belligerents may be concerned."[143]

Whether the dissents had any restraining effect on the Manila trials is difficult to appraise. Leading segments of the American press did "crow" about fair trial and fairer precedent, and the Court's review was lauded as evidence of American generosity.[144] The dissenters' predictions of purges were proven wrong as international bedfellows changed abruptly and Filipino revisionists declared an amnesty in the belief that many wartime collaborators were as nationalist as members of the American-sponsored government-in-exile. The sensational temper of the *Homma* dissent probably did weaken its message in the United States, but there is little question that the main Murphy-Rutledge protest in *Yamashita* did more than anything else to sober the popular mood. Had they not spoken, it is doubtful that so large a portion of the American liberal community would have awakened so soon to the nagging uncertainties about the war crimes trials. Only the White House had more alertive power. Politically and administratively its use was out of the question. It is scarcely exaggeration to say that judicial dissents filled a vacuum with a remarkably simple moral: the needless sacrifice of principle.

V

The "disquieting" and "really significant" thing about the military jurisdiction cases, as a few commentators then observed, was the carte blanche given to military justice. "As matters stand," Merlo J. Pusey concluded, "it appears that the Supreme Court has shifted the responsibility of maintaining civil liberties in wartime to Congress and Congress has shifted it to the Army. In face of the performance to date it would be pretty difficult to show that we have come through the war with our constitutional liberties unimpaired."[145] Despite articulation of a stricter policy of review over military trial of civilians in *Duncan* v.

Kahanamoku, the Court did little to dispel the belief that total war had eroded constitutional barriers irrevocably.[146] Neither did it dispel the belief that on the subject of war power, Justice Murphy had become a militant antimilitarist. For the Justice did more than refuse to join the Court's gingerly holding that the territorial Organic Act did not authorize military provost trials in Hawaii when civilian courts were functioning. In a lone concurrence he published a tirade against neglect of the *Milligan* "open court" rule and the Bill of Rights. To retreat from either, he declared, was to "open the door to rampant militarism and the glorification of war. . . ." The government's argument that the *Milligan* safeguards were obsolete, he said, was "as untenable today as it was when cast in the language of the Plantagenets, the Tudors and the Stuarts. It is a rank appeal to abandon the fate of all of our liberties to the reasonableness of the judgment of those who are trained primarily for war. It seeks to justify military usurpation of civilian authority to punish crime without regard to the potency of the Bill of Rights. It deserves repudiation."[147]

The *Duncan* case, to be sure, tempted fire and brimstone. The military commander had pleaded racial mixtures as well as inconvenience in withholding jury trials; the government contended that military discretion was unlimited once martial law was validly declared. Enlivening the dispute was a bizarre feud between the civilian governor and the military commander over criminal jurisdiction after the initial crisis had passed, a feud which had caused each to be cited for contempt of the other's court and a harassed President to dispatch a commission from Washington to negotiate a settlement. The basic issue for the Court was not the power to declare martial law, but its effect once invoked. Though Murphy apparently was the only Justice willing to resurrect *Milligan*, he was not alone in approaching the issue from constitutional perspectives. Justice Black's opinion for the Court, though resting ostensibly on the Organic Act, was grounded in the constitutional philosophy of civilian supremacy. The Chief Justice, who chided the Court for reading unnecessary limits into statutory power to invoke martial law, would have reversed on the principle that martial law cannot go beyond the necessities of the case. Another Justice maintained that, while civilians might be detained indefinitely under martial law, once subjected to trial they were entitled to full constitutional protection. To the Frankfurter-Burton objections that Hawaii was under lawful presidential authority in wartime, the Chief Justice retorted: "I don't think war was going on there any more than in Massachusetts."

And another Justice added: "I agree with you. I wouldn't go so far that we couldn't inquire into military judgment."[148]

Plainly the deference of *Korematsu* was over. More discriminating review of military trials, for American civilians at least, was on the way.[149] In defiance of Frankfurter's reminders of what they would have decided in 1942, the Justices were retracting the constitutional permissiveness of war. Still the *Duncan* case was a mark of the distance courts had travelled in two world wars since the days when judges could espouse the *Milligan* philosophy of constitutional limitations and still be believed. Justice Murphy's "elaborate *fortissimo*" in defense of that philosophy was also a mark of the distance he had come since *Hirabayashi*. When the Court finally faced the war crimes trials of Japanese civilians in *Hirota* v. *MacArthur*, after continuous deadlock over jurisdiction to hear appeals from Nuremberg, he not only joined Rutledge in another "battle royal" to obtain review, but appeared ready to go off the deep end. To a clerk's argument that "not a scrap" of law or reason supported imposition of the entire Bill of Rights on foreign cultures even if the Constitution followed the flag, Justice Murphy retorted: "Why not? Should we accept their culture under our Constitution?"[150]

Because Black and Douglas were satisfied that the *Hirota* tribunal was international in character and beyond review, Rutledge and Murphy were unable to secure a hearing on the merits. They did provoke Justice Jackson to break the deadlock by considering the matter, however, along with Jackson's charge that the libertarian quartet thus embarrassed presidential power in Oriental minds.[151] Weakened by illness, Murphy was forced to dissent without opinion. But the *élan* was clear and, as the Justice himself asserted, so was the voice of the past. By the end of World War II, Murphy had ceased to differ with his colleagues simply on issues of timing and strategy. In race and war power cases he conceived of the Court as a vehicle of ideological protest. Vehemently he met internal defeat on concrete issues by appealing to a wider audience with the ideological idiom that had flourished in his youth. Americans habitually called it "the dream," a bundle of partly political, partly religious ideals that had brightened the wreckage of Lincoln's time and the path of reformers since. Justice Brandeis had opposed New Deal flirtations with Bigness by one variant of it; Walter Lippmann, Archibald MacLeish, and Senator J. William Fulbright would oppose foreign policy options of the 1960s by another strain which viewed idealism as realism and insularity as national interest.[152]

But the source was a common fusion of idealism and nationalism, the vision of Lincoln and the midwest, that from the American experiment would emerge a "new and distinct civilization" of universal appeal because it rested on ethical force rather than physical power. In the Philippines Murphy had championed self-determination and opposed military solutions from those premises. Now as the nation assumed leadership as a superpower he summoned all his evangelical powers to alert the people to compromises being taken with their ideal self.

"Someone must speak out," he said in self-defense.[153] Speaking out had given meaning to his life far too long for silence, no matter how innocent contemporaries regarded his idiom. Impatient of evil, Murphy appeared oblivious to the sting of his words on others or to the limitations of his forum. Melodramatic in style, he appeared unconscious of the danger that evangelism would exaggerate his ideological commitments. On the credit side he managed to raise impressive protest against heavyhanded military power during a period of high emotion and stress. Sweeping minorities and outsiders of all descriptions into his protective net, he also managed to enlarge the legal rights of naturalized citizens and political dissidents, while encouraging racial minorities to seek judicial avenues of redress. Activism, by stimulating litigation and confidence in adjudication when political processes were otherwise blocked, undoubtedly helped to stir up a larger momentum that future judges turned into massive war on racial discrimination. Yet the gains of speaking out were small reward for an enormous personal loss—a reputation in legal and government circles that he was a mystic misfit in a court of last resort. When Justice Murphy's views on economic policy and criminal justice were considered along with his libertarian evangelism as the nation laid down its arms, it was not an uncharitable commentator who responded: "Murphy thinks with his heart rather than his head."[154]

CHAPTER 14

HUMANITARIAN AND REMEDIAL

MEASURES, 1944-1947

ECONOMIC crusading and libertarian evangelism enlarged Justice Murphy's reputation for personalized justice. But his economic record differed sharply from consistent voting and an outspoken radicalism in civil liberties. Murphy not only remained silent in the pivotal constitutional decisions which reduced judicial supremacy over public economic policy, he held highly pragmatic attitudes in such remaining areas of judicial supervision as interstate commerce. In contrast to his tendency to stray off the reservation in the area of minority rights, Murphy's economic opinions, even in dissent, commonly served as the medium of a group. His reputation in the economic sector was earned on center stage, not as a soloist in the wings.

Because of Murphy's dominant identification with civil liberties, the extent of his interest in economic problems has been underestimated. Murphy was a follower rather than innovator in constitutional litigation. Yet by the second half of his judicial career he had the opportunity to articulate constitutional doctrine in important closing chapters of a century-old struggle over vested property rights; and his influence was felt especially in the statutory conflicts which soon displaced constitutional problems as the Court's main economic concern. Because he served primarily as group spokesman Murphy conformed more closely to customary patterns of give-and-take in opinion production than might be supposed. But whether an organ of minority or majority his opinions reflected his individuality. They could not escape his uncanny affinity for controversy. The very choices made and their far-reaching effects, the very subjects of special interest and his candidly reformist expression, thrust him into the thick of some of the Court's most inflammatory battles over judicial policy-making and spread universal images of him as a partisan judge. For regardless of case, Murphy articulated his conviction that the judiciary was inescapably involved in achieving the great humanitarian goals of the New Deal. Law was a positive instrument of social welfare.

That opportunity for judicial involvement even existed, after a historic campaign to remove judges from economic policy-making, came as a surprise to most contemporaries. Surprise turned to dismay after an outbreak of judicial quarreling in early 1944 exposed a bitter rift within the Court over the scope of judicial discretion in economic affairs. Consensus on economic issues had been expected, and feared, among Roosevelt Justices. Now, from the virulence of language used, few could have guessed that this was the Court that made First Amendment freedoms "preferred." Formalistic in analysis, commentators had overrated the significance of judicial deference to unused constitutional authority and underrated the potential of judicial influence by nonconstitutional routes. The campaign to remove judges from the economic sector had resulted in a drastic withdrawal of judicial supervision over the subjects of Congress's reach, but it had not removed judicial discretion concerning applications of that power or the need of exercising it in the transition to the welfare state. The struggle over judicial functions merely shifted to a different front—statutory interpretation and administrative review.[1]

As the Justices sallied into combat over the meaning and reach of New Deal enactments it was apparent that the Court had not, and probably could not have, surrendered law-making functions. Economic regulation, no less than constitutional adjudication, was riddled with choice. Philosophies of deference or canons of interpretation provided no automatic gauge to construe Congress's broad and sometimes necessarily ambivalent commands. Acceptance of administrative adjudication as no "alien intruder" in the judicial process provided few formulas to resolve concrete jurisdictional disputes among agencies and courts or to define the standards of procedure and discretion to guide a multitude of administrators who, functionally speaking, wore executive, legislative, and judicial hats.[2] Conflicts between stable law and flexible rule-making, which the agencies were created to provide; conflicts between just results and orderly system, which itself is an ingredient of justice— all were inescapable products of unprecedented extensions of regulatory power into new realms of life. Concentrating on symptoms, observers made much of personal conflicts among judges and little of the underlying strain that absorption of New Deal measures into the legal order now placed on the judiciary as a whole. Constitutional choices of courts may have been inherently more awesome, but the practical obstacles to effective congressional oversight made statutory choices no less permanent. Statutes, also, are what judges say they are.[3] The wonder is that the courts of the 1940s absorbed so many so soon.

In statutory interpretation Murphy had no grand theory of judicial functions in a welfare state, nor any grand design to extend New Deal policies by judicial decree. Having an uncomplicated faith in official theories of judging, he accepted at face value the precept that the Court's object is to find legislative intent. But with a candor that shocked contemporaries Murphy expressed unorthodox premises that the remedial and humanitarian purposes of New Deal measures were better guides in resolving doubts than conventional interpretative devices of the lawyer's craft. The necessarily legislative aspect of the judiciary's interpretative role, though not even Murphy called it that, compelled conformity to the "plain will of the people."[4] And the will of the people, to him, was plainly reform. The duty of enlightened and democratic judges, accordingly, was not to obstruct public policy, as so often in the past, but within the range of discretion permitted by language and economic realities, to help realize legislative goals. That meant resolving doubts in favor of the recipients of ameliorative measures—the weak and poor, the unequal in life. Reform legislation was in a different league from the judge-made law of contracts.

II

Justice Murphy's unorthodox approach to statutes was fairly selective. The most telling examples were labor legislation in general and the Fair Labor Standards Act in particular. Unless civil liberties are lumped into a single category, he was more active in labor problems than in any other field. Because of his choices and his rhetoric, his notoriety spread as an uncritical pro-labor partisan. The total record is somewhat spotty, however. *Thornhill* v. *Alabama* was probably his most consequential opinion, but the Justice, as previously shown, participated in its retrenchment. A foe of administrative subpoenas of business records, he wrote several opinions remanding NLRB orders as insufficiently based. In *Hickman* v. *Taylor*, he gave short shrift to union arguments that liberal pretrial discovery policy would be a boon to worker-plaintiffs.[5] The opinion most vulnerable to charges of labor partisanship was probably *United States* v. *Carbone*, but even that case presented genuine doubt whether Congress had classified embezzled union dues as kickbacks. Cognizant that the decision could have been written to weaken labor organization, and believing that "in a sense all dues are a kickback of some sort or another," Murphy accepted the district court's conclusion that kickbacks and embezzled initiation fees were legally distinct, and a majority followed his reasoning in a decision that could have easily gone either way.[6] Counterbalancing such options, moreover, was his opinion for the Court in *United States* v. *White*, a case of "utmost importance" in subsequent control of labor racketeering. There the Court restricted the privilege against self-incrimination of union officials to their personal rather than their official capacity.[7] While writing generative language for liberalization of the right as a personal privilege the Justice maintained that the principles already developed for corporations should apply equally to unincorporated associations such as unions, and he caused some jitters along the way by sprinkling the opinion with generous references to older decisions supporting antitrust suits against trade unions. Justice Frankfurter, for that reason, concurred without opinion.[8]

The Fair Labor Standards Act aroused the most intrepid reformist passion. Having labored for a minimum wage plank in the Democratic platform of 1936, along with Hugo L. Black, its chief ramrod in the Senate, Murphy was an aggressive defender of the measure. The future would prove, he had declared in 1939, that its enactment was "one of the sanest, most intelligent steps yet taken by the American democracy for its own preservation."[9] Determined to prevent judicial erosion of the legislation he openly advocated that it be construed according to the original objective of extending "the frontiers of social progress," in President Roosevelt's words, by insuring to all "a fair day's pay for a fair day's work."[10] With Justice Black assigning most of the opinions, and his clerk having a heavy hand in the writing, Murphy authored more Fair Labor Standards Act opinions (eleven for the Court and seven in dissent) than any other Justice of his time. And his approach throughout was as unconventional as it was forthright: "humanitarian and remedial" objectives, rather than "linguistic purism" or "formalistic dogmas of interpretation," he asserted, should fill the interstices Congress left in the law.[11]

That the interstices were large was an inescapable characteristic of the numerous cases that reached the Court. In concept and purpose the FLSA was a revolutionary departure from the philosophy of the old order. To protect unorganized workers and to raise purchasing power generally, Congress established a minimum floor for hourly wages, restricted the flow of goods produced by child labor, and sought to discourage excessive working hours by the now familiar system of overtime pay. In specific terms, however, the statute was more limited. Enacted during the reaction against the New Deal in 1938, the Act did not exercise the full sweep of commerce power, or so at least the high court concluded from Congress's failure to invoke the same commerce power phrases of other New Deal statutes. The Act also failed to provide an expert administrative agency with rule-making power over the subject. As a result, the judiciary was made independently responsible for applying the statute's broad terms to the diversified structure of American business, without the aid of an advance judgment or of constitutional criteria developed in other regulatory fields. Enforcement of the Act, as Frankfurter said, forced judges into "the empiric process of drawing lines from case to case, and inevitably nice lines."[12] The generality of the statute compelled them to legislate, regardless of their choice.

Murphy's influence on the Act was threefold. First of all, his majority opinions in the aggregate significantly extended the Act. Always pressing for expansive coverage as the "mandate of the people," Murphy guided the Court to apply generous coverage tests already developed under the Railway Liability Act. A series of technical opinions concerning piece-rate wages and overtime pay also established rules that private contracts could not set wages below statutory minimums and that, for overtime, wages had to be proportioned according to actual hourly rates.[13] If the cases smacked of splitting hairs, and involved judges in higher arithmetic for which they were poorly equipped, the economic stakes were not trivial. The accumulated effect of Murphy's willingness to labor in an unglamorous field was enlarged coverage of considerable scope.

A second, though indirect, source of influence were hard-hitting dissents regarding statutory concepts. After the *Darby* case settled the Act's constitutionality the Court set the broad guidelines that Congress had not intended to preempt local regulations and that coverage depended on the character of the work rather than on the employer's business.[14] But within that framework, the Justices split into predictable patterns over the Act's coverage and its effects on wage agreements. The minimum wage legislation was rivaled only by the Wagner Act in dividing judges according to generation and policy values. What was so intriguing to followers of the Court was how, without blushing, the busy Justices of the Roosevelt Court fought these minor battles by resurrecting the recently interred corpses of constitutional struggle. Justices Roberts and Stone, the judges farthest from the social philosophy of the measure, were the first to balk when the Court extended the concept of "production of goods for commerce" to elevator operators. Expressing bitterness in conference over the Court's expansive tendencies the two older Justices became increasingly isolated as the libertarian quartet, who usually attracted another vote or two in particular cases, pushed the statute through the "farthest reaches of the channels of interstate commerce." And they responded by invoking concepts of *E. C. Knight*: production was a "physical process."[15]

Younger Justices, even as they agreed that Congress used broader concepts of coverage, were no more fearful of constitutional ghosts in setting concrete limits to indefinite words. Reed, for example, led one retreat in *McLeod* v. *Threlkeld* by limiting coverage of railroad workers under the phrase, "engaged in commerce," to those engaged directly in transportation.[16] Frankfurter, stating his belief that the statute should be interpreted with "regard to the implications of our dual system of government," led another retreat in the *Callus* case by offering as a practical compromise a geographical test of coverage according to "common understanding" of what constituted local commerce. When Douglas accepted the compromise, the libertarian ranks broke and tempers rose.[17] "Nebulosity v. Reality." "May I join you and the people?" two of Murphy's collaborators commented on his biting response.[18] A geographical concept of coverage, after all, veered from the functionalism which even Justice Jackson had previously advocated in conference —whether work was an integral part of the productive process—while "common understandings" resembled the discredited tests of *Lochner* v. *New York*.[19] Restriction of coverage to transportation workers in the *McLeod* case also recalled certain disreputable feats with the Tenth Amendment and led to statutory imbalance. Workers engaged "in production of goods for commerce" were sweepingly covered; workers "engaged in commerce" were not.

"Legislation has a constant struggle with the courts," one Justice observed tartly in conference regarding judicial resistance to reform measures, past and present. Even assuming that judges under pressure of time and indefinite language invoked concepts that made resistance *appear* worse than it was, was history not repeating itself in reverse? On the one hand, the impetus of the "wild horses" to correct past mistakes and to enlarge reform measures gave fair ground for the widespread impression, which the *New York Times* expressed, that some Justices interpreted their function as "not so much to apply the law as it stands, or in cases of doubt to interpret it objectively, but to apply a new 'social philosophy' in their decisions." On the other hand, were other Justices not importing "dual federalism" premises into reform statutes to blunt their force?[20]

A third of Murphy's minimum wage opinions were dissents, which usually castigated the Court for doing precisely that. Though many of them impressed academic specialists as trenchant, the most effective was in *Western Union* v. *Lenroot*, a case in which he challenged Jackson's conclusion for the Court that Western Union messenger boys were exempt from the child labor provisions of the Act.[21] Technically the question was whether the statute covered nontangible goods such as telegraph messages, but a basic problem was whether Congress intended

the sanction against use of child labor—a 30-day production stoppage—
to apply to a vital communications industry in war. The only thing
certain was that Congress had not considered the problem. Resolving
doubt according to statutory objectives and the ability of courts of
equity to moderate injunctions to prevent public hardship, the district
court had construed the statute as covering intangibles and then stayed
the sanction. The Court of Appeals (Hand, Hand, and Frank) affirmed.
Though most of the Justices considered the question close, Justice Jackson, who conceded that the legislative history was ambiguous, dismissed
the conclusion below as "a ridiculous job of construction," and then
reversed it for the Court with a highly linguistic analysis.[22] In hot response, Murphy retaliated with Justice Jackson's own acerbity. The decision gave Western Union a special dispensation, he charged, " 'by
a series of interpretations so far-fetched and forced as to bring into
question the candor of Congress as well as the integrity of the interpretative process.' " And charging the Court with sacrificing "social
gains for the sake of grammatical perfection," he defended the solution below as an exercise in restrained judicial creativity.[23] Fashioning
equitable remedies rather than importing exceptions into the statute,
"can and should be done," said Murphy, "without abdicating our judicial function and assuming the role of the legislature."

"Perfect!" one fellow dissenter commented. "Particularly do I like
to see a man's own weapon turned against him."[24] For all the sharp
talk, both sides were engaged in resolving an unforeseen conflict of
policy. The case was a classic example of the futility of using legislative
history as a tool in such situations. Since Congress had not contemplated
its own cross-purposes, under the circumstances any decision "legislated." The minority solution, because it furthered statutory objectives
without imposing hardship or ascribing spurious legislative intent,
struck most commentators as a "superior job of scientific statutory interpretation," while Justice Jackson's opinion, in rebutting the textual
analysis of the district court, seemed to be "a peculiarly unsympathetic
and drily linguistic" approach.[25] Were personalities and irritation over
larger disputes aggravating perceptions in minor ones, too? In any case,
concluded Max Radin, a noted authority on statutory interpretation, "I
am confirmed in my conviction that the ordinary 'interpretative process'
is rather a technical language to set forth a conclusion than an organon
for reaching one."[26]

The Portal Pay Cases, Murphy's third source of influence on the
Fair Labor Standards Act, made Radin's conclusion irresistible. A long
and complex story could be told about organized labor's struggle to

achieve compensation for time spent in travel and preparation for work in American industry, particularly in the mines. Payment for travel time had been granted in some industries by negotiation, but the miners had met with little success when the minimum wage statute was passed in 1938. Though it was clear that the Act superseded wage contracts which established substandard terms, what constituted "worktime" was nowhere defined and little was said about the relationship of the measure to industrial customs and wage agreements. Before 1938 compensation in the mining industry was based generally on the face-to-face method of computation and instead of time calculated from portal-to-portal. In 1940 the operators and the United Mine Workers had agreed to retain the traditional measuring rod of work at the face of the coal. To compute working time from portal-to-portal was considered an invitation to chaos in the industry. The wage-hour administrator accepted this accord as not unreasonable, but he modified his position in 1941 and portal pay was granted to gold miners in 1943. As part of a drive for general wage increases the same year, the coal miners began to press for compensated travel in the pits, though not necessarily computed according to the portal formula.[27]

At this point the Supreme Court intervened with Murphy's opinion in *Tennessee Coal, Iron & R.R. Co.* v. *Muscoda Local,* a decision handed down during the coal strikes of March 1944.[28] The central issue in the case was whether subterranean travel in iron mines constituted worktime, which would entitle the miners to retroactive payments for overtime. Finding an absence of prevailing custom as well as evidence of company coercion in the wage agreement, two lower courts had ruled that underground travel in the iron mines bore "in substantial degree every indicia of work" and therefore was compensable between the "portals." Murphy accepted that conclusion for a bare majority in melodramatic terms. "We are not here dealing with mere chattels or articles of trade," he said, "but with the rights of those who toil, of those who sacrifice a full measure of their freedom and talents to the use and profit of others." Guided by no statutory definition of worktime, judges should not resolve the issue in "a narrow, grudging manner" but should recognize that they were dealing "with human beings and with a statute that is intended to secure to them the fruits of their toil and exertion."[29]

Waxing poetic, the Justice drew on Milton's sonnet on his blindness in reminding the bar that miners "do more than stand and wait."[30] The mode of travel was prescribed by the employer, it was for his benefit, and it was dangerous. "Broken ribs, injured arms and legs, and bloody heads often result; even fatalities are not unknown," he wrote. Dank, dark, and badly shored, the pits were "filled with discomforts and hidden perils." These conditions stood "as mute, unanswerable proof that the journey from and to the portal involves continuous physical and mental exertion as well as hazards to life and limb." It was inconceivable that such activity was not work. Thus the lower courts had found, and the judges had properly ignored the coal industry in finding an absence of custom or bona fide agreement in iron mines. The Justices could not find error below.[31]

Concurring separately, Frankfurter and Jackson agreed that, while little issue existed at law, there was enough evidence for the Court to follow the "seasoned and wise rule" that concurrent findings of two lower courts be accepted in the absence of "very exceptional showing of error." Yet Murphy's *Muscoda* opinion contained a critical dictum they refused to accept. Defining work according to the district court and Noah Webster—as mental or physical exertion prescribed by the employer for his benefit—the Court declared *as a matter of law* that Congress intended to achieve a uniform policy guaranteeing compensation for all work. Though marginal or difficult variables in determining worktime could be adjusted by local or private agreement, any custom or contract falling short of that standard was irrelevant. Miners could not bargain away statutory rights.[32]

"Regardless of well-established understandings as to what constitutes compensable work?" Murphy asked on the margin of his first circulated draft. This crucial dictum, it appears, began as a trial balloon from another source which Murphy himself was not entirely sure of. Though one colleague in the majority considered his memorandum opinion "the best job you have done," others regarded it as merely a statement of what they hoped would attract a majority but doubted was obtainable.[33] The Justices were well aware of the ugly national response to coal strikes over the issue in wartime. They were also conscious of the fact that the UMW had resorted to a federal court to win their goal. Frankfurter, who sent Murphy a newspaper account and a copy of the Virginia district court ruling in the *Jewell Ridge* case, which denied the UMW claim to portal pay, observed to him: "You will want to see this if you have not already done so. It serves to underline the importance of deciding the portal-to-portal case now before us on the facts in the immediate record and to avoid saying anything that may be twisted by either side in other situations when those situations in due course may come before us."[34] Acceptance of the dictum by a bare 5-4 majority (the liberal quartet plus Reed) thus heralded a very large stroke of judicial policy-making.

"Frank Murphy Strikes Another Blow for Liberty," the labor press exulted when the decision was announced. But for business spokesmen and the Court's duo of Stone and Roberts, supplying definitions by judicial action threatened American enterprise with millions in penalties, if not the constitutional system itself.[35] Appalled by the Court's overt sympathies, Justice Roberts rebuked Murphy's opinion vehemently. The problem should be approached, he wrote,

not on the basis of any broad humanitarian prepossessions we may all entertain, not with a desire to construe legislation so as to accomplish what we deem worthy objects, but in the traditional and, if we are to have a government of laws, the essential attitude of ascertaining what Congress has enacted rather than what we wish it had enacted.

Much of what is said in the opinion, in my view, disregards this fundamental function of the judicial process and relies on considerations which have no place in the solution of the issue presented.[36]

Beyond striking at substandard wages and hours, the minority believed the Act had nothing to do with prevailing wage structures. Behind the scenes Stone urged Roberts to expose the "fallacy" that judges were empowered to define what custom, contract, and Congress left equivocal. Roberts went much further by openly weighing facts in the coal industry to show that face-to-face payment prevailed in all mining. That custom was common knowledge, he maintained, until Lewis began to press for portal pay in a series of "disastrous" wartime strikes. The inability of the lower courts to find the custom in the iron mines could be explained only by their "judicial fiat." To subject the company to retroactive overtime payments, doubled by way of penalty, for activities only now considered work, Roberts concluded, plainly justified the irate reaction of the dissenting judge below: " 'The injustice of it to me is shocking.' "[37]

The dissenters appeared on weak ground in contending that no substantial difference existed between the iron and coal industries. The evidence of company pressure and long-term turbulence in the iron mines, as Murphy replied, hardly represented a firm understanding of the parties on the issue. Why the trial of facts and the repeated reference to the coal miners in the dissent? Did the Supreme Court, like the rest of the government, labor under Lewis's strike gun? Virtually recognizing the flat wage increase for travel time in the Lewis-Ickes agreement of 1944, the inferential legislation in the decision caused the dissenters to react as if they expected an avalanche. In the *Jewell Ridge* case the next term, the avalanche came.

III

In *Jewell Ridge*, which was decided on May 7, 1945, the claims of the UMW to portal-to-portal pay in the bituminous coal industry were upheld on the basis of the *Muscoda* dictum. Murphy again wrote the opinion of the Court.[38] Reluctantly the Court of Appeals had been unable to distinguish the coal miners' claim from *Muscoda* because of the dictum, and five Justices now agreed. Factually, underground travel bore "all the indicia of work," according to the definition already established. Legally, the *Muscoda* case governed. Private agreements, even if fairly bargained, could not prevail over statutory policy requiring compensation for "all hours actually worked." Though contracts averaging out complex variables in individual travel could stand in national bargaining, travel time was work; ergo, it had to be calculated according to the time each miner actually spent travelling, not simply by flat wage boosts as in the Lewis-Ickes agreement. If that principle meant alteration of customary practices and a nationwide contract, wrote Murphy, it was to effect the congressional design that every man shall "receive his own reward according to his own labor."[39]

"I fear this may be regarded by enemies of the legislation as 'political,'" Rutledge observed.[40] And Rutledge was right. "'Lawless' Decision," rose the acrid cry. Although the method of developing law step-by-step was "a la Stone" in the White Primary Cases, the *Washington Post* and its readers expressed a common reaction: "Irresponsibility in the Supreme Court appears to have reached a new high mark." So "wanton" an exercise of judicial power made the nexus of division on the Court not "liberal versus conservative" ideology, but "adherence to law." Was the Court substituting its "own arbitrary view" of worktime in order to bestow on Lewis the fruits of the strikes? Could New Deal Justices have interfered so boldly with collective bargaining without the miners' own change of front on the portal pay issue?[41] From a common sense viewpoint, of course, travel in mines resembled work, but the Court was not starting from scratch. Decades of industrial practice and scores of other wage agreements, decades of legislation to shore up a sick industry and stop cutthroat competition via labor costs, all had to be reckoned with. And so did the reputation of the Court.

In a brilliant and ferocious dissent, which quoted assurances by Senator Black in 1938 that wage contracts would be left untouched, Jackson took issue with the Court's twofold conclusion that Congress had envisaged alteration of wage agreements and that *Jewell Ridge* and *Muscoda* were indistinguishable. Murphy's reply that Black was being quoted out of context did not deter Jackson. Though urged by Frankfurter to depersonalize his attack into "wholly neutral tints," Jackson declared for the minority: "The fact is that the *Tennessee* case differed from this as night does from day. . . . We doubt if one can find in the long line of criticized cases one in which the Court has made a more extreme exertion of power or one so little supported or explained by either the statute or the record in the case. Power should answer to reason none the less because its fiat is beyond appeal."[42]

Once again, charges of judicial usurpation thundered across the bench. And once again they resulted in "self-inflicted wounds." The *Jewell Ridge* case touched off the "Black-Jackson feud," the most rancorous display of judicial temper in nearly a century. Smoldering since 1943, disagreements over the interpretation of New Deal statutes flared into personal animosities which could not be repressed. The ostensible cause was an old canker—personal disqualification. After its defeat, the Jewell Ridge Coal Corp. petitioned the Court for a rehearing on the ground that Justice Black should have disqualified himself because the victorious counsel in both Portal Pay Cases, Crampton Harris, was his former law partner. The practice was not uncommon, as Black's defenders were quick to point out; but a formal challenge to a decision on this ground presented a new question. How, or even whether, the Court should respond set off an intense wrangle which Chief Justice Stone was unable to control. Determined not to take any more of Black's "bullying," as he termed it, Jackson appended a brief concurrence to the denial of the petition, explaining that disqualification was a matter for each individual conscience, not the Court's.[43]

Up to this point—June 1945—the conflict was hidden from public view. But more was to come. Justice Roberts, who had grown so embittered over the trends of decision that he refused to lunch with the others in their customary 30-minute break, resigned at the end of the term. And the Court, unable to agree even about the language of a customary letter of farewell, let his resignation pass in ungrateful, and ungraceful, silence until autumn.[44] Then on June 10, 1946, the day on which the Court extended the portal pay principle to surface industries and Fred M. Vinson was nominated to be Chief Justice, and not long after press reports circulated that Justices Black and Murphy had threatened President Truman with resignation should he honor Roosevelt's pledge to appoint Jackson Chief, Jackson exploded in public. Wiring the congressional judiciary committees from Nuremberg, the distraught Justice invited their attention to the practice of judges hearing cases in which former associates were interested. Such conduct, he asserted, jeopardized "the reputation of the Court for non-partisan and unbiased decision." If it happened again, he remarked to reporters, "I will make my *Jewell Ridge* opinion look like a letter of recommendation."[45/a]

Jackson's explosion shocked the country. Although he concentrated his fire on Black and disqualification, his chagrin reflected deeper grievances over the Court's Populist drift and irreverence for settled law. The *Jewell Ridge* case originally had been voted against the union, with the majority opinion assigned to him. Justice Reed, after narrowing the principle to the precise facts, had swung to the other side; and Justice Black, the undisputed leader in minimum wage cases, assigned it to Murphy.[46] Uncovering the inner workings of the conference room, Jackson openly denounced Black for pressuring the Court to hand down the decision before dissenting opinions could be prepared, in order to help Lewis win the coal strike. Murphy, who had informed Jackson that "some of the brethren" were thinking of offering a motion to hand down the decision without delay, had not favored that move. "I don't want you rushed," he told Jackson, ". . . take all the time you want. . . . Besides there is little to write about now." When Jackson asked the reasons for hurry, Murphy had replied: "Maybe they have changed their minds since negotiations ended. I rushed my opinion to accommodate others."[47] It should be stressed that even if Murphy's allegations were true, there was nothing irregular about rushing opinions for policy reasons. Frankfurter had done so in the Radio Case, Stone had done so in *Yamashita*, and Murphy would do so again in *Chenery*. But just as the losers in those cases resented the pressure of timing, so similar resentments inflamed the atmosphere in *Jewell Ridge*. "When I went away from there that thing was seething," Jackson recalled. "There was a question in my mind whether I would resign."[48]

After Jackson's "disgraceful" public eruption suggestions were rife

[a] Columnist Doris Fleeson, a friend of Murphy's and the source of the alleged threat to President Truman, had reported earlier that Murphy would resign if Jackson were named Chief Justice to replace Hughes. See *Kansas City Times*, June 7, 1941. Among the high-flying rumors of the day was Drew Pearson's report that Truman's advisers wanted Murphy to replace Stone! *Washington Post*, June 12, 1946.

that both Jackson and Black should quit. More importantly, the uproar stimulated public inquiry into the judiciary's political base. "We see now what happens when second-rate men are appointed to a first-rate Court," observed Raymond Moley. Roosevelt's "purely political concept of the Court's function," a concept which allegedly included spite appointments, had "irreparably injured a precious tradition" from Coke to Stone.[49] However judicial functions were conceived, "too many politicians" was the common explanation of the Court's seeming "disintegration."[50] By odd analytic twists, Roosevelt's attempt to pack the high court was found to have atomized it. His appointees, who supposedly lacked "proper legal background" and "judicial temperament," were accused of playing "sociological favorites." They were condemned for overruling nearly as many precedents in seven years as all their predecessors combined. They were damned for rending the bench with feuds and spreading disrespect for law. There was "no possible excuse for great lawyers so to divide," Senator James Eastland exclaimed in support of a fantastic constitutional amendment to "unpack" the Roosevelt Court. With little more sophistication, the movement grew among bar associations to limit Supreme Court appointment to men having prior teaching or lower court experience. Such criteria would have excluded past giants like Marshall, Taney, or Brandeis and, on the present Court, the lawyerly Roberts, Reed, and Jackson. Somehow, different professionals could be expected neither to legislate nor to divide.[51]

Whatever the cause, the Roosevelt Court clearly broke the aura of olympian objectivity on which judicial power in good part depends. For those with short historical sight, the Court's prestige had sunk to "an all time low."[52] Though Justice Murphy attempted to placate tempers in the *Jewell Ridge* disqualification dispute by suggesting delay, he was not unaware of the criticism heaped on the Justices following the first outbreak of judicial quarreling in January 1944. Denunciations in the press over the frequency of dissent, after all, were only sterner versions of the Chief Justice's private rebuke: "It is not necessary to play every fly speck in the music."[53] Condemnation by leaders of the bar for legal instability merely echoed the Court's own clashes over continuity and change. Charges that history was repeating itself in a leftward direction, that the Court was becoming a third legislative house, were simply less charitable interpretations of events that Murphy had been receiving from friends in private correspondence, particularly concerning labor decisions, which the dean of the University of Michigan law faculty and even a former clerk decried for "obvious partisanship."[54]

Having dismissed the 1944 outbreaks with levity—"don't you think the Court is showing a little life these days?"—Murphy was not noticeably disturbed that the high tribunal, as so often before, was a storm center.[55] The gentle-mannered Justice seldom took part in the personal warfare that kept a Roberts from the lunch table or the Court from good manners. Following the Court's failure to agree on a parting word to Roberts, Murphy, in a characteristic gesture that bespoke his own miseries, sent his former antagonist a private farewell:

I understand why of late you have not been as happy as the first three years I knew you in the Chambers and on the Bench. But others too have been unhappy. And in this sad work I felt that we could not look for too much in the way of surcease of the heart. I hope that the farm you love and your own hearth will sweeten the years for you.

I will remember you only as a man of superb character, a purist able and wise and as an exemplary citizen in the community.[56]

Yet personal tensions undoubtedly added a new element to Murphy's alternating moods of unhappiness and reconciliation on the bench. By fall 1945, Frankfurter observed, Murphy was "growingly unhappy," and the perception was not groundless. Frustration was obvious in one note handed to Frankfurter in early December 1945, in which Murphy wrote, "*a propos* of nothing,"

I confided to Brandeis one time that as a boy I thought about life and the part I wanted to play. I concluded that, Sir Galahad-like, I would thrust my lance at intolerance. And all the road I travelled between then and now I had 'Cyrano's' devotion to undoing those who would make life unnecessarily cruel and burdensome. I never wandered. I kept my boyhood pledge.
The ancient Persians according to Herodinces taught their youth:

    1st To hunt and spear
    2nd To ride the horse
    3rd To speak the truth

Now while not put-under, as is done to useless horses, I have been put to pasture on the Court after a life of decency and truthfulness. Sometimes I give a deceptive appearance of youth—not often—but I have never abandoned my youthful hopes. The most intolerant place I have been in is the Capitol. It is not so throughout the land. And one day the people will overtake those who have deceived them.[57]

Murphy's frustration in judicial pastures was compounded by Roosevelt's death which closed a promised escape. Personal animosities on the Court aggravated his discomfort, too. Although Justice Jackson actually treated him with restrained tolerance in their personal relations,

Justice Roberts had a low opinion of Murphy, as evidenced by Roberts' sarcastic response to "the Saint's" farewell note.[58] Since Roberts was even more critical of Rutledge and of Douglas's alleged presidential ambition, little love was lost all around. But Frankfurter's continued digs got under Murphy's skin—and not without reason. During consideration of *First Iowa Hydro-Electric Cooperative* v. *FPC*, for example, Frankfurter wrote:

Dear god:

Since a god is presumably all just, I assume he needs no conscience to keep him straight. However that may be, the considerations that follow are addressed not to the conscience but to that other and despised organ—the intellect.

. . . . Certainly before entertaining the god-like confidence that reversal in this case would be a benefit to the Federal Power Commission, it behooves even a god to read what the Federal Power Commission says in support of its position. . . . But then, this suggestion may make you laugh because, for all I know, a god does not have to read or study things in order to understand them.

I suppose it must be wonderful to be a god, but I remain, unenvyingly yours, F.F.[59]

Believing that Murphy abused the freedom of dissent for personal gratification, and goaded by his concentration on humanitarian instincts, Frankfurter sometimes rebuffed Murphy's attempts to meet him on his own ground. Murphy's vote in one price regulation case prompted Frankfurter's rebuke:

Dear Frank:

No one knows better than you that I do not 'caucus' to secure adhesion to any opinion of mine and that, while of course I prefer to have people agree rather than disagree with me, I do not use even the effort of mere persuasion to secure such agreement. But don't you talk to me any more about your desire to have me write "precise" "lawyer-like" opinions, with the implication that that is the kind of opinion you like. In *Felin* I have written the most "precise and lawyer-like opinion," after the most conscientious lawyer-like labor, that I think I have written since I have been on the Court. And what do you do? You agree with Stanley's opinion reaching my result, but on indefensible grounds.

Why do I say indefensible? . . . In short, Stanley rejects the findings of the Court of Claims as he should. But he rejects them as a matter of degree. I disapprove them as a matter of law. . . . Yours with a smile, F.F.[60]

In October 1945, Frankfurter even attempted to help Murphy find another job. The effort was touched off by a conference concerning

Bailey v. *Anderson*, another joust over economic due process, in which Justice Black apparently restated his view that, short of expropriation, the fairness of damages in state condemnation proceedings was a local question beyond review. Justice Frankfurter, who thought that Black's position would remove property rights from the Fourteenth Amendment, related that Murphy was equally distressed by Black's argument. Indeed, Frankfurter recorded in his notes that: "After going on the bench at 12 o'clock Frank Murphy said to me that that talk of Black's was 'the most revolutionary and destructive speech' that has probably ever been made in the history of the Supreme Court. He seemed to be greatly disturbed by it and said again and again it was terrible. I then wrote him a note saying that I quite agreed . . . but wondered why he did not say at Conference what he had just told me and why he left it for me always to have to take on Black when he takes such outrageous positions. It led me to wonder, I added in my note, whether Murphy really understood what was going on here. Whereupon he wrote me the following note. . . .

> You are wrong. I am doing my best.
> And I know all that is going on
> hereabouts. I wish I did not. The
> Recorder's Court in Detroit never knew
> the shannanigans I have witnessed here.[61]

Just whose shenanigans Murphy had in mind was unclear; but for Frankfurter, who noted that Murphy had had several encounters with Black in the previous term, the reply confirmed his suspicions "that he, Murphy, was more and more disturbed about the behavior of Black and Douglas and was too weak to release himself from their control." The next morning Frankfurter handed Murphy a letter, the substance of which "was that all appeasements lead to Munich" and that Murphy was " 'mesmerized' by Black." Murphy, according to Frankfurter, responded:

Felix, I am very unhappy here and have been now for some time. I think it is very important for the Court to be revamped, to have two new men on here who have courage and competence or otherwise, mark me, the Court and thereby the country will get into a disastrous situation. "I am very unhappy here and have been for some time," he repeated, [Frankfurter wrote] "and stayed on here because President Roosevelt promised me that I would be Secretary of War. Now that is out of the question. But I do not see why a man with my public service and my experience and ability should not be sent to represent this country either in France or Italy. If I were sent to either place, the President could then at once appoint Charles Fahy in my place and he would be a great addition and strength to the Court."[62]

Justice Frankfurter knew that Murphy was moody; but convinced that this time he was serious and "eager for an honorable way out that will not hurt his ego," Frankfurter contacted Secretary of State Byrnes about arranging such a move. When it was questioned how President Truman would react, since Truman had hardly been endeared to Murphy by the Pendergast prosecution and reportedly thought he was "a nut," Frankfurter pressed the main point. "After all," he said, "it is more mischievous for him to be a nut on the Supreme Court."[63]

Nothing came of the proposal, though Frankfurter thought Byrnes agreed to recommend Murphy for a looming vacancy in Italy. But the episode was symptomatic of prevailing moods. The closing days of Stone's chief justiceship ranked as one of the bitterest, most schismatic periods in judicial history. Attributing the worst to "Black & Co.," minority Justices regarded Douglas as motivated by political ambitions, Murphy and Rutledge as well-meaning pawns of their "bosses," and Justice Black himself as an intellectually powerful, but willful Populist who had to have his way. As Frankfurter wrote Murphy on June 10, 1946, the day of Vinson's appointment and Jackson's statement from Nuremberg:

Today ends another epoch in the history of the Court—the quinquennium of the 1941-1945 Terms. Of course there have been many shortcomings in the past and some striking instances of what Chief Justice Hughes so aptly called "self-inflicted wounds." But if I were translated into a classroom and had to tell my students what I thought about the period just closed, I would have to say the following—assuming, of course, that I lived up to Holmes' injunction "never lie to the young!":

1. Never before in the history of the Court were so many of its members influenced in decisions by considerations extraneous to the legal issues that supposedly controlled decisions.
2. Never before have members of the Court so often acted contrary to their convictions on the governing legal issues in decisions.
3. Never before has so large a proportion of the opinions fallen short of requisite professional standards.

It would relieve me of much unhappiness if I did not feel compelled to have these convictions. But they are based on a study of the history of the Court which began from the day I left the Law School just forty years ago and on first-hand detailed knowledge of what has been going on inside the Court during the last thirty-five years.

Of all earthly institutions this Court comes nearest to having, for me, sacred aspects. Having been endowed by nature with zestful vitality, I still look forward hopefully to the era which will open on the first Monday of October next.[64]

And that, too, was the point. However abrasive their divisions, the personal feuding of Roosevelt Justices blew over in the interest of larger responsibilities. Seeking to build bridges of essential cooperation, Justice Frankfurter later sent Justice Black a prompt denial of published reports that he had been Jackson's informant of the Fleeson story. He also sent Justice Jackson his sympathies and his hopes that Jackson would not resign. "I want you to know," he said, "that the facts as you set them forth in your Nuernberg statement gives an accurate account in every detail of what actually took place."[65] Not long after the uproar Murphy and Jackson themselves would be exchanging personal greetings.[66/b] Frankfurter would be sending an ailing Murphy advice on how to cure a virus—"capitulate completely to that bug—give him no fight—and then by one of those mysteries of the world the bug will be defeated."[67] Murphy in turn responded to one of Frankfurter's many invitations to clear the air between them with a statement of his personal grievances.[c]

[b] Sending Murphy a copy of his book, *The Case Against the Nazi War Criminals,* "with the good will and good wishes of his colleague," Jackson wrote on May 1, 1947: "You may think me oversensitive but I find it difficult to send my work around to others when they may not be interested or think I am trying to influence their views. I am glad you are interested and happy to have you have this book." Letter, Box 122.

[c] Murphy wrote: "My grievances against you grow out of 1st

1. My belief in you.
2. My many acts of friendship toward you.
3. That you, too believed statements, stories and rumors brought to [you].
4. That—as I see it—you were ungrateful and chose to undo me in the only ambition I ever entertained [Stimson's appointment as Secretary of War?] when my administrative experience was above that also of most any one in the Capitol and in face of the fact that good people believe in [me]. . . .
5. That you have espoused legal views that seemed to me not only wrong but contrary to all that your early gospel stood for.

That you have gifts above any of us I have always admitted; that despite your faulty judgments in achieving lofty purposes you trained your sights toward their horizons I have never doubted, and that you are a good man and of personal charm I have held no doubt.

Your circuitous and meandering route can be explained and understood when one considers that you have had to stand at the breach and give blow for blow for your faith in a world of awful revolution.

Undated, handwritten note, FM to Felix Frankfurter, Box 28, Frankfurter Papers, Manuscript Division, Library of Congress.

If privately their views of one another remained unchanged, there is no question that the Justices restrained them, both internally and externally, out of a common loyalty to the Court and their collective responsibilities. As personal bickering receded into the background the blow-up could be seen as an understandable, perhaps even necessary catharsis of poisonous tensions. In any event, its significance was exaggerated. And so were Justice Murphy's personal discomforts as a jurist.

While regretting that the explosion had occurred in public, Murphy knew from long exposure that criticism of public officials was a question of more or less. Dispute he took for granted because, by definition, the Court served to settle disputes in the grey areas over which men were bound to contend. Sooner or later most of the country's explosive issues would wind their way to Court. Besides, everybody criticizes umpires. The Court, Murphy knew, also was being blamed by the ill-informed and by losers at the polls for great transitions in public policy during an era of emergency and rapid social change. The Court was acquiring heavy burdens of bureaucratic oversight and of legal refinement in response to the same forces, as well as the shortcuts, the faulty language, and the inconclusive bargains made by other governmental agencies. Ready answers were not available for such problems. Chief Justices might chastise the brethren for tinkering with statutes, for assuming legislative garb; but that, too, was a matter of degree. Frankfurter condemned libertarians for upsetting legislative compromises, and Jackson bemoaned the "low estate of precedent" while advocating "moderation in change"; but hesitation about unsettling law had the effect of preserving past judicial compromises of reform legislation.[68] Libertarian Justices, as many believed, probably were overzealous in correcting the Court's past wrongs and oversensitive about preventing a recurrence, but all too often sloppy legislative work was what invited judicial action and what produced the common though reverse discomfort that Rutledge once voiced in a tax case: "I am constrained to concur, though I wish, and I have no doubt that you do, there was some tenable way to reach the opposite result."[69] Harsh results, inexorable though they may have appeared, were not easy for judges of conscience to swallow. All too often the Chief Justice himself was having to do so under salty expressions of separation of powers theory: "Why in hell Congress can't draw up bills better . . . I can't see but I can't strain my conscience. That you have to hold your nose has nothing to do with it. If Congress can hold its nose so can we."[70]

That the power to regulate meant the power to leave unregulated went without saying, but judicial legislation was inescapable. More than anyone cared to admit, the Justices, at the same time that they fashioned a revolutionary shift of responsibility over constitutional liberties, were becoming a council of legislative revision, functioning somewhat like the modern House of Lords, by polishing into workaday rules the statutory policies which the political arms of government were too overburdened and diffusely organized to do. The trouble was that finding the will of Congress was not unlike chasing the wild goose of due process. Policy preferences and inherited value systems were unavoidable substitutes. Concerning the questions pressed daily before the Court, concerning whether courts should choose in this void also, responsible men were bound to differ.

Labor legislation was the thorniest subject of all. Policies were novel and monetary stakes were high. Increased union power and pressure tactics during and immediately after the war produced strongly adverse public reactions that rebounded politically. The campaign of 1944, as Murphy analyzed it, revealed trends against the Democrats—"1932 in reverse"—which only fear of changing Presidents in midstream could check. Unless Roosevelt ran again, he believed, despite his antipathy on principle to the fourth term, "all his undertakings will be modified—they might even collapse."[71] New Dealism as a governing philosophy, outvoted in Congress and in abeyance through much of the executive branch, flourished mainly on the Court. Determined to do his part to prevent the great work from being undone in the judiciary, Murphy was convinced by 1945 that he should stay on the bench, "where within my limits, I can be on guard for the liberties of our people."[72] The result was persistence in construing New Deal statutes according to a spirit now out of popular favor. And that attitude produced inevitable charges of favoritism which Jackson expressed so well in *Hunt* v. *Crombach*, when he observed that, with the Court's aid, workers now enjoyed "the same arbitrary dominance over the economic sphere which they control that labor so long, so bitterly and so rightly asserted should belong to no man." The labor movement, whether judges realized it or not, had come "full circle."[73]

Regardless of appearances, Murphy was conscious of shifts in popular sentiment and private power. He had few illusions after 1937 about the headstrong Lewis or union aggressiveness. Personally, he was disgusted with wartime strikes. Urging President Roosevelt to stiffen his labor policy in 1943, he freely noted in a passage cut from *Carbone* that abuse of the closed shop by union leadership was a "fact beyond dispute."[74] Nevertheless, Murphy was wary of penalizing workers for the excesses of a few. Just as turmoil had been the aftermath of the sit-down crisis, he believed the country was still undergoing a long process of union maturation, a process now aggravated by the natural aftermath of war. Faced with choice, he simply could not square hazardous travel in coal mines with physical reality or Christian compassion. Nor could he see why courts were less qualified to decide the question in the silence of Congress than industrial customs which, in the past, were euphemisms for ruthless exploitation of workers. If the immediate beneficiaries were Lewis and his union rather than unorganized laborers for whom the statute was written, Murphy focused on the miners. The portal pay problem, to him, was simply another step of a responsive government to interests long unattended, another step in lightening "the load of those who toil for their bread by the sweat of their brow."[75] Recalling the principle that had made such an impression on him during the sit-down crisis, the Justice declared: "A laboring man's investment in his job is his flesh and blood. The investment of others is in dollars."[76] His allegiance to that principle in 1937, he told Chase S. Osborn after *Muscoda*, had been misunderstood; but it had settled a labor crisis according to "reason and Christianity and Americanism."[77] So would it now. Union power and judicial power were not the issues. The issues were human dignity and social equality.

The hopes of some that the summer recess might reveal the limits of humanitarianism as a legal principle were soon dashed. In June 1946 a 5-2 majority extended the portal pay principle to workers in surface industries. Time spent walking to and from work within the premises, Murphy ruled for the Court in *Anderson* v. *Mt. Clemens Co.*, constituted worktime and must be "compensated accordingly, regardless of contrary custom or contact." That rule, he explained in remanding the case for reapplication to the facts, should be interpreted "in light of the realities of the industrial world." "Split-seconds absurdities" were not germane; but when a substantial part of the employees' time was consumed in preparation for work, lower courts, with due regard for the *de minimis* principle, should order compensation and damages.[78]

With this declaration, the roof fell in. A flood of lawsuits, ranging from an estimated three to forty billion dollars in claims, rose across the country to recover retroactive damages for travel time.[79] "Mr. Justice Murphy once again, by his wisdom and sense of fair play, has performed a great service to the workers of this nation," the *Detroit Labor News* declaimed; but a shocked business world greeted the decision as an injustice "almost beyond comprehension."[80] The *Mt. Clemens* case brought criticism of the Court's interpretation of the minimum wage act to a crescendo. Denounced on the floor of Congress as another Murphy "gift" to the CIO, derided by Frances Perkins as "doctrinaire," assailed by the scholar Roscoe Pound as the kind of "spurious interpretation" which threatened constitutional democracy in the United States, Murphy's opinion provoked another outraged assault by Justice Jackson after his return from Nuremberg.[81] What with this reception in high places, it was a mild report that the high court was "doing something rather more meddlesome than occasionally legislating 'in the interstices' of the law." Merlo J. Pusey wrote: "By substituting its own amorphous concept of what is a workweek for the definitions customarily accepted by industry and labor in working out their own relations, the Court has made an absurdity of the 'Fair' Labor Standards Act."[82]

Statutory construction had become statutory reconstruction. District Judge Frank A. Picard, Murphy's former campaign manager and appointee in Michigan, added comic relief to the imbroglio, first, by asserting publicly that the Justices had injected the portal pay issue into the case and, second, by eliminating the claims in *Mt. Clemens* as *de minimis*.[83] An unhappy sideshow was also played in windfall lawsuits, many of them inspired by unscrupulous attorneys, and in bombastic public dispute. All the Court did was to establish the principle that substantial time spent in the employer's control constituted work. Lawyers, as they did after *Thornhill*, read more into the decision than was necessarily there. Although Murphy had gloated in his reports to home that the case "may be the turning point in the economy of this country," once the storm broke, he was much more defensive. "I cannot comment on it except to say it has been distorted and misrepresented," he remarked. "Read the paragraph on the *de minimis* rule."[84] Both union and management counsel knew that the chances to collect vast windfall payments were slim. Each side, as reporter Robert L. Riggs suggested, was carrying on "psychological warfare," labor for more advantageous contracts, industry for restrictive labor legislation. Considered alone, much of the portal pay controversy was synthetic. Its significance was mainly as part of larger struggles over labor relations and judicial power.[85]

It was strange, even so, that politically alert CIO unions slapped such high claims against industry, and stranger still that the so-called political judges on the Court defied the election returns. Resisting generally the pendulum-like movement against unionism, they read the statute in light of "remedial and humanitarian" purposes of its passage which, by the late 1940s, were less fervently shared. While few measures gave judges greater room for discretion than the Fair Labor Standards Act, the controversy over the meaning of worktime well illustrated the limits of judicial policy-making in the American political process. The effort of the Supreme Court to overcome a statutory hiatus introduced serious uncertainty into wage practices; it fanned partisan fires over labor's place in the postwar economy and played into the hands of opponents of both the Court and organized labor itself. When redefining the concept of work in the Portal-to-Portal Act of 1947, the Republican 80th Congress rebuked the Justices for interference with collective bargaining and amended some of their other "extreme" interpretations for good measure.[86] The simple factor that judges had left unstated all along was now exposed: the intent of the Congress of 1938 was not likely to be repeated, except by them.

Murphy's pride was wounded by the reversal in Congress, but he expressed little rancor. "Honest differences of viewpoint are one of the pleasures of life," he said.[87] Though he still found it hard to comprehend how anyone could conclude that "miners riding underneath the ground in a tram car, denied the light of day and fresh air, always in danger, were not working until they reached the face"; though he believed the *Mt. Clemens* formula was distorted for partisan purposes, he felt there was nothing sacrosanct about judicial construction of legislative intent.[88] Hauling and tugging between courts and legislatures he took for granted as part of the multiple balances of American politics. Dispute over worktime was part of the ups and downs of social progress. From the comfort of judicial independence, Murphy took the long view. The basic solution, as the UAW contended, was a guaranteed annual wage.[d]

Acceptance of that idea was at least two decades away. Congress, at the time, was busily enacting a contrary assessment of union power into the Taft-Hartley Act. But even as he recognized the reasons for that enactment, Justice Murphy remained unreconstructed. "I make no attempt to say that you are wrong and I am right. Only the impartial

---

[d] "Congress can perfect its legislation and Courts can express their views with more and more wisdom," Murphy wrote Arthur B. Cuddihy, Jr., a prospective law student in 1947. "Yet I believe that the annual wage is the solution to many of these labor problems. Congress may have a Wage and Hour Act which is imperfect and then the Courts may misinterpret what Congress did and the employers want to go back to the old days of the status quo which to me is only sad because that isn't so as life moves on. But if workmen only had an annual wage instead of weekly or hourly or piecework payment, many problems would be resolved." FM to Cuddihy, Feb. 12, 1947, Box 121.

judge of history can settle that," he replied to criticism by Henry M. Bates. Detroit, he confessed, "gave me an anxiety to be vigilant about the rights of the working man."[89] Blaming labor's setbacks on the indiscretions of its leadership, he asserted that "the labor movement is not going to go backward in this country; it is going to go forward for this is the most highly industrial country on earth and those in private and public affairs, who pounce upon labor affairs as something evil don't look forward into the future with much imagination." "Read the Encyclical of Leo XIII. I always based my labor views on the Encyclical in large degree. It is written as if it were today. . . ."[90]

Pursuing egalitarian goals on the nation's highest court, Justice Murphy helped to enlarge the economic security of countless workers by unsung, piecemeal, and thoroughly professional opinions. But his humanitarian frame of reference in the Portal Pay Cases, in view of their impact on employers and the federal judiciary, could not withstand rigorous analysis even as an ethical principle. A great gamble of judicial power in the name of justice not only failed; history may well judge it as Frank Murphy's closest brush with abuse.

IV

The Portal Pay Cases were merely part of a series of decisions which unveiled the tattered secret that judges are "as other men are."[91] They also coincided with significant changes in judicial personnel. On April 22, 1946, seven weeks before the *Mt. Clemens* decision and Justice Jackson's outburst from Nuremberg, Chief Justice Stone collapsed on the bench and died. President Truman, to calm a contentious Court, replaced Stone with a popular conciliator, Circuit Judge Fred M. Vinson. Easygoing, moderate in social philosophy, Vinson bore some superficial resemblances to Murphy that made personal communication with the Chief Justice easier than before. Vinson, who was born the same year in a Louisa, Kentucky jailhouse where his father lived as jailer, was also reared in a small town and warmly political environment. Like Murphy, Vinson made his way to the Court from politics, not from law, and with little design. No one familiar with his college record or his maneuvering through the labyrinths of Kentucky mountain and Washington politics could doubt his powers. But Vinson's very earthy love of baseball, which he had played as a semi-professional was suggestive of his lack of intellectual pretension. The new Chief's gifts were dealing with men rather than ideas. Though he had six years of experience on the Court of Appeals, he, too, would have transitional problems among the talented, but quarrelsome Roosevelt Justices.

Yet Vinson came from a tradition different from Murphy's, a tradition of moderation and of compromise which befitted the politics of a border state whose rural ways had been bypassed by the forces of urbanization and industrialization. That pocket of poverty had produced more than its share of national politicians, but stark necessity, not social theory, was the source of the federal focus. Harold H. Burton, whom Truman chose to replace Justice Roberts in October 1945, was even further removed from Murphy in social outlook. A genial Unitarian of low ideological key, the former Ohio Senator was a Republican, Harvard-trained lawyer who could be expected to stop short of the Court's current course. Personal relations on the Court, from Justice Murphy's viewpoint, would be more pleasant. The Court's liberal momentum, on the other hand, suffered a serious setback. The new appointments meant more than ever that he had to remain on the bench.

"The Great Issue" facing Vinson, Merlo Pusey observed after the new Chief's appointment, was whether the Court was going to be "a genuinely judicial body" or one that plunged itself "deeper into the muddy waters of judicial policy-making."[92] In the summer of 1946 thoughts of great issues were far from Justice Murphy's mind. Five years of agitation finally produced an errand to the Philippines as United States representative to the burial of Manuel L. Quezon. Outfitted with the aircraft carrier *Princeton* and a small entourage, Murphy embarked on a trip that was combination wake and glorious homecoming. His enjoyment was supreme. Circling the globe on his return, he visited Rome, where he served as altar-boy in a church near the Vatican and Pope Pius gave him the longest recorded interview with any American layman. In Paris he sounded off against stalled peace talks; and despite obvious physical toll, he had an energetic high time.[93] "My trip was a humdinger," he boasted to a former clerk. "I took three aides with me—all of them broke down and are hospitalized. I came home in good health."[94]

Returning to Court in a happy mood Murphy gave few signs that the Vinson Court would be torn by ideological cleavage. In the spring and fall of 1946, on assignment from both Stone and Vinson, he authored some of the most significant majority decisions of the season and of his career. Two of them, *North American Company* v. *SEC* and *American Power & Light Co.* v. *SEC*, upheld the last major piece of New Deal legislation challenged in Court, the "death sentence" clauses of the Public Utility Holding Company Act, which authorized dissolution of holding company empires into single, integrated utility systems.[95] Argued in November 1945, the cases had been subject to troublesome delays since 1943 because of their complexity and the Court's quorum problems. Murphy contributed to delay, out of desire to take plenty of time in preparing major commerce power opinions, because only *North American* was finished when the Chief Justice died, thus destroying a bare quorum and forcing the companion cases to be set over to the next term.[96] Few opinions received closer attention from the Justice than these, however, and few were stronger examples of how decisively the post-1937 Court had rejected "dual federalism" from constitutional jurisprudence. Virtually paraphrasing Marshall's *Gibbons* v. *Ogden* doctrine, Murphy wrote sweepingly of Congress's plenary power to regulate interstate commerce. Federal authority to regulate an integrated national economy under the commerce clause, he said, was "an affirmative power commensurate with the national needs." "And in using this great power, Congress is not bound by technical legal conceptions." "Commerce itself," as Justice Holmes had taught, was "an intensely practical matter."[97]

This generous description of regulatory power was no wayward flight of language, but a realistic assessment of the principles that now governed the Court. From whatever posture—indifference, outright crusading, or conceptions of the judicial function that had motivated Holmes to approve legislation which "makes me puke"—the result was deference to legislative will. The Constitution granted Congress authority over economic policy "as broad as the economic needs of the nation." Once used, it was not for courts to inquire into legislative wisdom.[98] Murphy again echoed the thoughts of the new dispensation in *Daniel* v. *Family Security Life Insurance Company*, when he rejected a due process challenge to a state regulation by saying: "We rehearse the obvious when we say that our function is thus misconceived. We are not equipped to decide desirability; and a court cannot eliminate measures which do not happen to suit its tastes if it seeks to maintain a democratic system. The forum for the correction of ill-considered legislation is a responsive legislature."[99] This philosophy was a world away from Justice McReynolds' credo: "But plainly, I think, this Court must have regard to the wisdom of the enactment."[100] It was also a world away from Murphy's own protective outlook toward other civil liberties. Yet the easy acceptance of his forthright language was a barometer of the Vinson Court's constitutional consensus in economic affairs. The "great issue" was essentially one of statutory dimensions.

In June 1947, Murphy wrote the Court's opinion in *Hickman* v. *Taylor*, a landmark decision under the new federal rules of civil procedure. The *Hickman* case demonstrated that statutory conflicts were far from bogus reflections of private will.[101] At issue was the scope of pretrial discovery under the procedural reforms of 1938, which collectively not only constituted one of the New Deal's most significant achievements but also affected the legal profession most directly. Capping nearly a century of effort to simplify civil procedure, the new federal rules were designed to replace the old common law pleading system, with its premium on technicality and surprise, with a new philosophy that concentrated litigation on the merits of a fully disclosed controversy. Central among the innovations was pretrial discovery, a mechanism which replaced the old "sporting theory of justice" by compelling disclosure of information in advance of trial for the sake of truth, economy, and full preparation by both sides.

Although the new system probably increased costs and court congestion, the loudest rumblings from the bar rose over the possible invasions of professional privacy. *Hickman* magnified those fears in the formative period of the new system because a district court had cited a defense counsel for criminal contempt for having refused to divulge information obtained in interviews with witnesses and to comply with an order that he prepare written memoranda of their oral statements. Since the plaintiff's counsel could have interviewed the same witnesses, and desired the information only to insure that he had overlooked nothing, the case had all the overtones of a deepseated professional fear, a "fishing expedition" into the adversary's mental impressions and strategy. Provoked by prospects of one lawyer relying on the wits of another, the Court of Appeals vigorously reversed in a holding that the "work-product of the lawyer" was privileged from disclosure. Discovery policy and professional privacy, it appeared, were antagonistic interests.

As agitation over disclosure policy took on some of the color of a union jurisdictional feud, Murphy's docket notes indicate that the Supreme Court was hardly less divided over disclosure policy than the bar. Five Justices, including Murphy, initially voted to affirm the Court of Appeals. Justice Jackson, who of all members of the Court was most attuned to the outlook of practitioners, was a particularly vigorous exponent of the policy that discovery should be limited to matters of evidence. The new rules, as the Court had conceded in *Palmer* v. *Hoffman*, had to be interpreted from a perspective of centuries of custom and practice. Otherwise, he contended, the profession would be demoralized, lawyers would be converted into witnesses, and the adversary system set askew. Justices Black, Reed, Douglas, and Rutledge, on the other hand, voted to reverse.[102]

The division perhaps explains why the Justices chose to resolve the conflict by decision rather than by legislating the amendments proposed by the Rules Advisory Committee, which would have limited disclosure to written statements on a showing of unfair prejudice. Accepting the concept of the lawyer's work-product, but rejecting it as privileged, the Justices were able to unify around a compromise principle that an attorney's written records could be discovered on a good cause showing of need, though his mental impressions of oral statements, under ordinary circumstances, could not. The compromise permitted wider discovery than the proposed amendments. Justices Jackson and Frankfurter, who reflected professional attitudes strongly felt in the bar, thus remained unsatisfied. Favoring the Court of Appeals conclusion, they were nettled especially by the failure to prohibit absolutely disclosure of oral statements. But while many questions were deliberately left for the future Murphy's opinion did not open up the "veritable Pandora's box" of compulsory disclosures that some judges predicted. The *Hickman* opinion, liberal in the spirit of disclosure while erecting safeguards around professional privacy, became a "living organism" in a continuous process of accommodating professional interests with a public policy of disclosure without destroying either.[103]

Each of these decisions, as Murphy observed of *North American*, was "the sort of case we used to study in law school."[104] They also were revealing examples of another, little appreciated side of Justice Murphy in action—plasticity when spokesman for the Court as compared to ideological rigidity in dissent. Flexibility in an opinion-writer, of course, is dictated by the inherent demands of role, especially in complex litigations in which tangential opportunities abound. Personal sensitivity about his assignments and his reputation as a temperamental soloist may also have influenced Murphy. The Justice seemed eager to write for the Court, even if it meant compromising his personal views. In *SEC* v. *Engineers Public Service Co.*, for example, he opposed (unsuccessfully) counsel's motion to have the case declared moot because of a reorganization, after he had done so much work on the Holding Company Cases in the previous term. Following his failure to hold a majority in *Central Greyhound Lines* v. *Mealey* in November 1947, he pointedly reminded the Chief Justice that the case was "my sole assignment to date."[105]

Whatever the weights among multiple causes, flexibility was the first of three noteworthy characteristics of Murphy in his prime. Regarding a Court opinion as a conduit of collegial thought, he appears to have assumed that the group spokesman should be more willing than others to sacrifice personal views for the sake of solidarity. The resulting changes were seldom as significant as those prompted by the irresolution of his freshman years, but they spoke volumes about the assumed doctrinaire compulsions of the Justice. In *Hickman* v. *Taylor*, for instance, Murphy first circulated an opinion which accepted "good cause" disclosure for oral as well as written statements. But Jackson penned a strong dissent, protesting the professional impact of disclosing oral statements and implying that the Court, in response to union briefs advocating wide disclosure, played favorites. Rutledge, while urging Murphy to drop discussion of the privilege concept and to answer Jackson's dig, also expressed doubts about requiring counsel to reduce to writing their recollections of conversations. Black, in turn, opposed any reference to "injustice." Cross-pressured, Murphy retreated on the question of oral statements, with the result that Jackson's vigorous opinion became a somewhat gratuitous concurrence.[106]

Similarly, in the *Yellow Cab* antitrust case, in which the Justices deadlocked over a final question whether taxi rides from the Chicago railway station were interstate commerce, Murphy responded to Frankfurter's pressuring that the Sherman Act was not coextensive with the commerce clause and that *de minimis* should apply, by changing his vote to get a firm result. "I think that is better," he informed the conference, "than merely stating the majority and minority views and letting the matter dangle inconclusively. And since the issue is a sufficiently close one in my own mind, I am willing to forego my personal views and join the majority on Part III."[107] As ideological lines hardened and he matured, Murphy's choices were more stable than in his freshman years, but his willingness to accommodate others and his mode of operation were not significantly different from his colleagues. Like them he passed and voted tentatively, then changed his mind and influenced others to do the same; like them he had his blindspots and idiosyncrasies—and sometimes compromised them too, to increase effectiveness. Qualified ideology was the result.[e]

---

[e] In several instances Murphy changed his mind while preparing opinions, and the Court followed. See, *e.g., West* v. *Oklahoma Tax Commission*, 334 U.S. 717 (1948); and *United States* v. *Seattle First National Bank*, 321 U.S. 583 (1944). No. 489, Box 139; No. 267, Box 133. After independent research by his clerk in a poor record revealed that one compensation award might jeopardize statutory rights of handicapped longshoremen as a class, the Justice persuaded all but one colleague to turn tail. Justice

A second and familiar characteristic, which made the task of achieving agreement harder for Murphy than for others, was strong language. In writing, the Justice strove for economy and clarity of expression without sacrificing bounce. Because he wrote for lay as well as professional audiences, Murphy was sometimes a hard taskmaster in demanding simplification. Routine phrases, such as "in this connection," he rejected as suitable only "to a first class board of commerce member."[108] "State the idea—make clear," he would tell a clerk. "Here will be the trouble." "When I was young I had to get kicked in the pants in order to do a good job," Murphy once said. "I guess you are like me."[109] The resulting opinions were usually clear, forthright, and thoroughly comprehensible to nonprofessional readers. But, as always, Murphy offended leaner tastes. Chief Justice Stone, who disliked the "journalistic" flourishes of Murphy's prose, complained in *North American* that a Roosevelt quotation gave the draft opinion the "color of a New Deal political speech."[110] "O. K. Senator," Frankfurter remarked of Murphy's explanation in *American Power & Light* why Congress had resorted to drastic methods in the Public Utility Holding Company Act.[111] Besides pungent style Murphy had a habit of dropping the pose that judges were indifferent to legislative purposes. Nearly all of his colleagues, at one time or another, had to remind him that the Court's job was not to pronounce on the reasons for policy, but merely to review power to make it.

A final, and related, characteristic was a sense of action, a conviction that the Court should face rather than avoid issues raised below. This trait also troubled colleagues such as Frankfurter who were wary of judicial action and "needless generalization." The very clarity of Murphy's memorandum opinion in one bankruptcy case led Frankfurter to argue—unsuccessfully—that no opinion should be written.[112] Resort to the *Shreveport* doctrine in a Pure Food and Drug Act opinion, which he succeeded in removing, served only to convince Frankfurter that the Court was borrowing trouble by invoking the extremes to which judges had gone in sustaining federal regulation of intrastate commerce.[113] More was involved in these differences, however, than the

---

Frankfurter, with considerable justice, then "crowed": "It seemed to me a compelled conclusion, if due respect is to be given to legislation—if, that is, we let Congress make laws and not re-make them. This opinion (and change of Conference vote) ought to be a lesson that merely because a particular case is decided for a particular employee the result on a fair & long view may be a great disservice to labor and to Law. I could 'document' this truth." Comment on slip opinion, No. 56, Box 139. *Lawson* v. *Suwannee Fruit & Steamship Co.*, 336 U.S. 198 (1949).

"Doric taste" or "the Blue Danube side of me," by which Frankfurter jocularly described his own stylistic variations.[114] The very discussion of *Shreveport* doctrine which he protested as unnecessary in *United States* v. *Walsh* impressed Justice Reed, who was seldom accused of the failing, as a "perfect opinion—not a useless word."[115] By the same token, the forthright discussion of patent philosophy which Frankfurter commended in another case, Rutledge thought should have gone out, while the procedural discussion in a "piddling" compensation case that Frankfurter regarded as "needless generalization" Rutledge regarded as "a most excellent opinion, among the very best I have seen on this subject."[116]

Underneath the refinements of taste were differing perceptions of fact and law that dovetailed with high philosophies of the judicial process. Justice Frankfurter, who defended judicial power to protect the national free market in lieu of congressional action at the same time he contended that positive exertions of federal authority had to be accommodated with "historic functions of the individual states," was convinced that result-oriented libertarians overrode legislative choices and took on too much business. The libertarians, who championed regulatory authority in either form, were fearful in turn that Frankfurter weakened reform measures in the name of legal stability and the states. After accepting Frankfurter's other suggestions in *American Power & Light*, Murphy insisted on retaining "my good Senate speech" in order to answer a due process argument and to close an opening for procedural erosion of the statute.[117] In short, there were reasons for full as well as spare tastes. Not least among them were policy implications, which, to Murphy, should be faced squarely in decisions that conformed to legislative goals and preserved the power to regulate—even at the cost of doctrinal purity. Such was his instinctive way of reconciling judicial power with democratic theory, and his tendency in interpreting statutes, at least until checked by contrary force.

All of these characteristics boiled down to doctrinal indifference and impatience with technicality. Sometimes Justice Murphy lost majorities because of them. A good example is *Central Greyhound Lines* v. *Mealey*, in which he resorted to outmoded "dual federalism" doctrine himself in defense of state taxing power.[118] On other occasions his practical bent won majorities, as in *California* v. *Zook*, an important preemption case in which his argument that the test of preemption should be conflicting policy, not federal occupancy, attracted the unexpected vote of Justice Reed to make a narrow majority.[119] Tentative conclusions and changing votes were not uncommon in the complex interplay of fact and law, taste and theory, reason and rationalizing that go into the making of judicial decision. Murphy's choices were more personally stated than most, but they were not greatly off-stride in degree of stability or in policy orientation. Instead, they were mirrors of a Court at odds over its legislative role. New personnel on the Vinson Court at first appeared to moderate ideological conflict by diffusing it. There was to be no diminution of "the great issue" over judicial law-making, however. Two key tests in the spring of 1947—*United States* v. *United Mine Workers of America* and *SEC* v. *Chenery Corporation* merely exposed alternating figures on the scale, along with Murphy's ability to smother routine accomplishments in a few *causes célèbres*.[120]

V

The *United Mine Workers* case was one of the hottest cases of the decade. In May 1946, after another paralyzing strike by the UMW, the government took over the bituminous mines, negotiated an agreement with the union favorable to the miners, and began operating the industry. In October the union and its leader, John L. Lewis, who by then was probably the most hated individual in the United States, resumed pressure on the government to renegotiate the Lewis-Krug agreement. The government, seeking a declaratory judgment to prevent revision of the contract, obtained a temporary restraining order against a threatened walkout, while the federal district court determined its jurisdiction. The miners defied the order. Judge Goldsborough then fined the union $3.5 million and Lewis $10,000 for both civil and criminal contempt. In the glare of a great national controversy, the Court invoked its rarely-used emergency power to hear appeals directly from a district court. And in confirmation of Justice Holmes' adage that great cases make bad law, the Court "split five ways from the Jack."[121]

Murphy's notes reveal no secrets in the *UMW* case. Although Justices Black and Douglas expressed their votes tentatively, and Jackson shifted position on the applicability of the Norris-LaGuardia Act, the preliminary voting reflected the diffuse configuration that ultimately prevailed.[122] Perceiving "a serious threat to orderly constitutional government and to the economic and social welfare of the nation," Chief Justice Vinson, with Black and Douglas concurring in part, sustained the contempt according to the theory that the anti-injunction provisions of the Norris-LaGuardia Act did not apply to strikes against the government. Justice Frankfurter, a leading architect of the statute, issued a powerful rebuttal to Vinson's theory, showing that the precise aim of Congress was prevention of judicial interference with labor disputes; but Frankfurter then concurred on an alternate ground, embraced by Vinson but not by Black or Douglas, of protecting the sanctity of the judicial process—to wit, the power of courts to protect by contempt their competency to decide their jurisdiction. Justice Jackson, concurring alone, agreed with Frankfurter. Though a bare 5-4 majority reduced the union fine to $700,000, after three circulations by the Chief Justice to reach that figure, Murphy and Rutledge dissented "in *toto*."[123] Hence the Court reached the awkward result in which a majority of Justices held that Lewis and the union could be punished for disobeying orders whose validity was left in doubt.

In the *UMW* case Murphy wrote one of his most effective dissents. He argued with compelling force that both seizure and safeguarding jurisdiction were untenable bases of contempt in the face of Congress's historic and unequivocal policy prohibiting injunctions in labor disputes. The crux of Vinson's theory was that miners were public employees; but Murphy believed it a dangerous fiction to say that the strike was against the government when seizure itself was an outgrowth of a private dispute that was "very much alive" between union and coal operators. The Lewis-Krug negotiators had admitted as much when they referred several union demands back "to the owners and private operators . . . rather than to the Government," which was only the "interim custodian" of the mines.[124] Seizure, in short, was an ill-founded means of escaping the Norris-LaGuardia Act's embarrassing presence.

The alternate ground of safeguarding jurisdiction presented a harder target, if only because precedent was so spare, but Murphy also punctured its "seductive attractiveness" with Congress's contrary policy.[f] The narrow class of contempt developed to protect "competency-competency" was one thing in common law or in the silence of Congress, but quite another in the teeth of an express congressional command against strike-breaking. "Time and time again," Murphy reminded his colleagues, judges had broken strikes with temporary injunctions purporting to maintain the status quo. What administration, possessing seizure and contempt power, could now be blocked from breaking strikes at will? The short of the matter was that the courts were con-

---

[f] Frankfurter's theory apparently was not momentary improvisation. Murphy's conference notes regarding *In re Bradley,* 317 U.S. 616 (1942); 318 U.S. 50 (1943), record him as expressing doubts about *In re Sawyer,* 124 U.S. 200 (1888), a leading precedent supporting the doctrine that orders of a court lacking jurisdiction could be disregarded without peril of contempt. No. 473, Box 132.

cocting some law to help surmount a fuel crisis, but to Murphy that job belonged to Congress. Expressing fears for the faith of workingmen in the integrity of the law, one of his major concerns as a "labor governor," he wrote: "A judicial disregard of what Congress has decreed may seem justified for the moment in view of the crisis which gave birth to this case. But such a disregard may ultimately have more disastrous and lasting effects upon the economy of the nation than any action of an aggressive labor leader in disobeying a void court order. The cause of orderly constitutional government is ill-served by misapplying the law as it is written, inadequate though it may be, to meet an emergency situation, especially where that misapplication permits punitive sanctions to be placed upon an individual or an organization."[125] If government was to return to strike-breaking, if the Norris-LaGuardia Act was to be abrogated for national emergency strikes, only one body was competent to decide such a fateful shift in public policy—Congress, not the Court.

"Begging Mr. Justice Murphy's pardon," the *St. Louis Post-Dispatch* commented, the issue was not "just another labor dispute," but a "gargantuan form of industrial warfare" that threatened the supremacy of government. "Lewis asked for it; and he has now got it," doubtless summarized prevailing public sentiment. Commonly dismissed as another outburst of a labor partisan, Murphy's dissent drew scurrilous abuse in the vein of "why don't you resign and remove some of the stench from the Supreme Court?"[126] More detached observers, however, found it hard not to agree with the dissenters that the Court's "flagrant" legislating made "incredibly bad law." To Charles O. Gregory, critic of the Court's picketing doctrine, the alternative ground of contempt for defying void orders was "downright alarming." The capacity of lawyers to think up jurisdictional questions was boundless; injunctive delay was a proven strike-breaking technique. The majority Justices probably believed with most people, Gregory observed, that "the country would be bound for hell in a hay-rick if Lewis and his union were not stopped in their tracks. But that, I humbly submit, is none of their business." If ever there was an occasion for leaving to political processes the onus of building legal standards in the vacuum of doubt, surely it was the vacuum Congress had *expressly* created forbidding "government by injunction again."[127]

Congress soon reset the balance in the inclusive Taft-Hartley Act. Although Murphy regarded the enactment as vindictive legislation which labor leadership had brought on itself, his dissent against anticipating it in court was an impressive protest against makeshift judicial legislation. The *UMW* dissent, nonetheless, probably cost him more by way of partisan reputation than the Portal Pay Cases, in which congressional intent at least was doubtful. It is a good question which decision—*Jewell Ridge* or *United Mine Workers*—made more or worse law. That both decisions legislated in the thicket of public conflict over labor policy is incontrovertible. Could cynics thus be pardoned for asking whether the dissenters' offense in the Miners' Case was restraint— of the kind that bucked popular sentiment? The *United Mine Workers* case was an eye-opener to observers who foresaw retraction of judicial policy-making by the Vinson Court or to those who took slogans of judicial activism and restraint seriously. It was also a revealing episode in the even-handedness of the Court's critics, whose dexterous shifts on the sins of judicial legislation were a sight to see. And the shocks of the case on popular categories hardly had been absorbed before conflicting attitudes toward the judiciary's creative role came to a head in another case of explosive potential, *Securities and Exchange Commission* v. *Chenery Corporation.*[128]

On its face, the *Chenery* litigation was one of those complex, noninflammatory problems of administrative law that attract only professional interest. The SEC, acting under authority of the Public Utility Holding Company Act, had forbidden the managers of a holding company reorganization from purchasing stock to retain their control of the company, on the theory that stock purchases by fiduciaries so close to the reorganization would produce inevitable conflicts of interest with other stockholders and the public. In 1943, the Court in an opinion by Frankfurter, with Black, Reed, and Murphy dissenting, reversed the order on the grounds that this new standard of business ethics lacked a reasoned basis, either in equitable precedents, in norms articulated from administrative experience, or in actual proof of abuse. Treating the problem as part of a larger goal of insuring reasoned decisions in administrative law, a subject close to Justice Frankfurter's heart, the Court remanded the case with an invitation that the agency proceed prospectively by its rule-making power rather than by adjudication, a course which would have freed the Chenery managers from its effect.[129/g] Upon remand, the Commission declined the invitation to pro-

---

g That feelings were intense behind the technical facade of the first *Chenery* case can be inferred from Frankfurter's reaction when Reed joined the minority. "Dear Stanley," he wrote: "Were I at Cambridge I would be saddened to note that you underwrote an opinion like Black's in the Chenery case. I don't think I should be less saddened because I am your colleague. I hate to see you 'bogged down in the quagmire' of Populist rhetoric unrelated to fact." Frankfurter to Reed, Jan. 29, 1943, Box 32, Frankfurter Papers, Manuscript Division, Library of Congress.

mulgate an advanced general rule or policy statement. Basing decision on its statutory duties, its expert judgment that conflicts of interest were inevitable and otherwise impossible to eradicate, and also on the belief that lost expected profits were business risks knowingly assumed, the Commission ordered the managers to divest their stock at cost plus four percent. The Court, on the last day of the term, upheld the second decision by a five-two vote, Vinson and Douglas not participating. Hence, in another awkward result, the Justices approved administrative discretion to fashion new standards of law case by case—retroactively and by an order identical to one previously reversed.[130]

Few cases of the decade focused more sharply the dilemmas of accommodating new forms of adjudication into the legal system. At a time of criticism of bureaucratic development the world over, when eminent legal figures in Great Britain and the United States were denouncing administrative processes as "the new despotism," the *Chenery* case posed a point-blank issue: could administrative law, like judge-made law, grow case by case?[131] If there were intrinsic differences between the law-making processes of legislatures, courts, and agencies— and most people felt differences should exist—what were they and how could judges articulate them without intrusion into specialized and flexible development of policy which Congress sought? Administrative imperatives demanded a less drastic alternative than restricting agencies to rule-making. Administrative adjudication, on the other hand, was fraught with retroactive possibilities, as Jackson warned the American Law Institute in 1944, if only because agencies were less inhibited by *stare decisis*.[132] Sharing the burden of supervising bureaucracy, both by judicial inclination and Congress's command, was becoming a central function of modern judicial review. That function itself was unfolding. The essential question for the Court in *Chenery* was how to articulate standards governing an extreme assertion of agency power without harm to administrative discretion. And compounding the problem was a reversal of attitude by the Court's controlling membership.

New arrivals were actually only a partial explanation of the apparent shift. The SEC, after remand, correctly interpreted Frankfurter's opinion as not having ordered promulgation of a rule. The agency also articulated reasons in the second case, emphasizing expert experience rather than judicial precedents, that were sufficient to distinguish the two cases. Argued on December 13, 1946, and assigned to Justice Burton 10 days later, the *Chenery* case lingered in the background through the first few months of 1947. Preliminary votes held solid, except for Frankfurter who passed. But after Burton was unable to satisfy a majority, the case was reassigned to Murphy on June 3rd.[133] The controversy then gathered steam.

Working hurriedly to finish before the end of term, after which he planned a European vacation, Murphy circulated a first draft that was even more forthright than usual. The subject, he argued, was one in which Congress had called for drastic remedies and one peculiarly suited to determination by specialists. The Commission's error in the first case was reliance on flimsy judicial precedents; since the Court had not insisted on a prospective rule, ad hoc adjudication was an appropriate way to set a new standard when reformulated on the basis of technical experience. "Thus administrative law grows like every other kind of law," wrote Murphy. Retroactivity doubtless resulted from formulating a new norm in a particular case, but that was true of any new standard created in case systems of law. "Such retroactivity," he said, "must be balanced against the mischief of producing a result which is contrary to a statutory design or to legal and equitable principles."[134] Murphy had already provoked Chief Justice Vinson to remark, "I can't have a statute grow," in what he regarded as the nub of the conflict concerning NLRB jurisdiction over foremen unions.[135] Again Murphy called a spade a spade. Law-making by quasi-judicial expert agencies was not intrinsically different from law-making by judges.

The parallel between administrative and conventional law, though commonly drawn in classrooms across the country, was too strong for candid pronouncement by the high court. On June 18th, perhaps in hopes of satisfying Justice Burton, Murphy circulated a tamer draft which repeated Frankfurter's earlier lecture on the desirability of proceeding legislatively. Since the agency, unlike a court, had the ability of creating law prospectively through its rule-making powers, he asserted, "it has less reason to rely upon *ad hoc* adjudication to formulate new standards of conduct. . . . The function of filling in the interstices of the Act should be performed, as much as possible, through this quasi-legislative promulgation of rules to be applied in the future." On the critical point, however, Murphy refused to budge. To hold that the Commission had only the one alternative of formulating a prospective general rule, while approving the proposed transaction, would prevent the agency from performing its statutory duties in the instant case and "stultify the administrative process." "That," said Murphy, "we refuse to do." Not every principle essential to effective administration was capable of being cast immediately into rules of generality; not every rule could operate without ad hoc adjustments. "There is thus a very definite place for the case-by-case evolution of statutory standards," he contended, in argument similar to Frankfurter's regarding due process. "And the choice made between proceeding by general rule or by individual, *ad hoc* litigation is one that lies primarily in the informed discretion of the administrative agency." To insist on one method to the exclusion of the other was to weaken the statute and "to exalt form over necessity."[136]

As reformulated, Murphy's opinion attracted three votes. Justice Burton concurred in the result, and the decision was set to come down on June 23rd, the final day of term.[h] Still perturbed that the SEC had singled out particular individuals to announce new principles under a murky mandate, and galled that only one week remained before adjournment, Frankfurter threatened a tempest by preparing a notice of dissent, which referred to the date of Murphy's first circulation on June 17th, in order to explain why he lacked time to prepare adequate response. Because revelation of the date would have broken tradition in such matters and perhaps revived adverse public comment about the Court's rate of producing opinions, which had already occurred in *North American*, Frankfurter quickly dropped reference to the date and attributed his postponement of dissent to the Court's "unavoidable lateness."[137] The implication, to Murphy, was the same in any case— and a personal affront. In a memorandum to conference on June 18th, he requested that Frankfurter delete any reference to the lateness of decision. "So far as the public is concerned," he said, "any decision rendered in the same term as that in which the case is argued is not 'unavoidably' late. . . .

It is not unknown for cases to be argued early and decided late in the term. To say that such a decision is "unavoidably" late is thus to stir up needless speculation and comment by the public.

As we all know, the case was given to me but a short time ago. But whether the case was assigned late or circulated late are matters which lie solely within the private corridors of this Court; the public has no legitimate concern with them. And any explicit or veiled reference (such as here proposed) to them is not in harmony with the Court's traditions.

I have no objection to the Court remaining in session until an adequate dissent is written, even though it means cancelling my previous arrangements.

[h] In a cryptic handwritten note in the fall, written perhaps while the dissent was being prepared, Burton suggested that his reason for concurring in the result was his belief that equitable principles supported the Commission's contentions, which were rejected in the first *Chenery* case, that a fiduciary relationship existed and forbade stock purchases by reorganization trustees. Note, dated Oct. 7, 1946, Box 123, Burton Papers, Manuscript Division, Library of Congress.

Nor have I any opposition to the filing of a dissent next fall. But if the latter course is followed, I suggest that it be done in the unobtrusive manner followed last term. . . .[138/1]

Justice Frankfurter, facing the same tactical problem of timing which had irritated Rutledge in *Yamashita*, was understandably frustrated by the alternatives open to him in *Chenery*. But his partial disclosure of the situation, as Rutledge reminded him in an attempted mediation, reflected unfairly on both Burton and Murphy. Besides, Frankfurter himself had talked Rutledge out of complaining publicly about the shortness of time in considering *Yamashita*. Though Frankfurter distinguished the situations, and expressed surprise that his disclosure was offensive, he revised his notice of dissent and the threatened storm blew over.[139] Yet Frankfurter never filed an opinion. Instead he joined the outraged dissent published by Jackson in October. In tones that resembled Murphy's protest in the draft cases, Jackson flayed the Court for approving "administrative authoritarianism" and "expropriation without compensation." Upbraiding the Justices for reducing judicial review to a "mere feint," Jackson exploded: "I give up." "Now I realize fully what Mark Twain meant when he said, 'The more you explain it, the more I don't understand it.'" "The truth is that in this decision the Court approves the Commission's assertion of power to govern the matter *without* law. . . ."[140]

The savage quality of the dissent perhaps was animated by the necessity of attracting attention to a late dissent as well as by clashing attitudes over substantive issues. The issues transcended personalities and tactics, however, and even the worn query whether judges legislate. Emphasizing the values of stability and of legal system, and sensitive to the value practitioners placed on both, the Jackson-Frankfurter viewpoint illuminated the valid reasons why the rule of law, in nearly all societies, is a conservative force. Accepting reformist principles being fashioned by law, and the inevitable retroactivity of case-developed standards, the Court's option highlighted the price of administrative discretion and new modes of law-making in the modern administrative state. *Chenery* was one of the most widely discussed cases among students of administrative law in the post-New Deal transition. While the consensus was that the SEC by *policy* might have spared the Court a painful choice regarding its *power*, Jackson's attack on the Court for "dispensing with law" was unfair, just as Murphy's attack on the patrio-

[1] In *RFC* v. *Denver, R.G.W.R. Co.* (328 U.S. 495), a case argued on March 5, 1946 and decided on June 10, 1946, the opinion of the Court was first circulated two weeks before adjournment. Justice Frankfurter filed his dissent on October 28, 1946.

tism of his brethren had been in *Hirabayashi*. Retroactivity is not always absent from promulgated regulations. The retroactivity in *Chenery* was limited to a situation of unsettled law. Windfall gains were likely to go to some party in any event. And the Court could hardly have refused to accept administrative adjudication when frontally challenged without striking at the heart of the administrative process— expert development of law.[141]

The unresolved question was whether more discriminating means of accommodating administrative discretion and the rule of law could have been offered by the Justices, short of denying legal efficacy to quasi-judicial decisions. Although the parameters of this question were not entirely under judicial control, was there no way of articulating clearer norms of administrative action without defeating legislative goals? Or was that merely asking for a little less agency-discretion and a little more traditional control as a matter of taste? The pity is that of the three Justices best equipped to probe differentiated alternatives— Douglas, Frankfurter, and Jackson—one was disqualified and two resorted to polemics.

However incisive his rapier-like thrusts and blunt policy pronouncements elsewhere, *Chenery* was not one of Justice Jackson's finer moments. Murphy's opinion, by the same token, magnified his vulnerability to professional criticism. Having already shown his lack of lawyerly orientation in the 1939 civil service dispute, and having incurred ridicule for not writing "to the profession" in civil liberties dissents, he now belittled sacred traditions of the bar in the black-and-white terms lawyers are trained to abhor. Together, *Hickman* and *Chenery* sowed suspicion of his professional competence among members of a specialized constituency in the same way that the Portal Pay and *UMW* cases spread popular mistrust of his motives. Whether as Court spokesman or as fiery soloist, in sum, Justice Murphy managed to convey the impression that law, for him, *was* the extension of self.

The New Deal struggle against the courts had been fought under the principle that the very necessity of judicial discretion demanded self-restraint. Responses to the post-New Deal Court showed that even that degree of volition in judging still struggled for recognition against the hoary fictions of the bar. Because Murphy advanced the highly unorthodox view that judicial discretion should be exercised forthrightly in pursuance of legislative purposes and humanitarian goals, he was bound to offend tradition. The Court he viewed not as an antidemocratic oligarchy forced to deny or to mask its legislative power, but as an arm of public policy and "the will of the people." The main strength of this viewpoint—it was hardly a philosophy of judging—was the realistic premise that the Court was not a law-finder *above* the governmental process, but one of several power centers *within* it. The main weaknesses, of course, were the certitude of his "justice" and his refusal to adapt to change. Hypersensitive to past judicial obstruction of reform measures, Murphy glossed over the competing demands of legal system. Selective in focus, he championed laboring interests as if they were still "inarticulate," with the result that he appeared to advocate double standards beyond tolerable popular pulse. The same historic phenomenon of judges enforcing the conventional wisdom of one generation onto another now enveloped him. Yet Murphy had pressed too long for remedial and humanitarian measures to assume a veil of serene doubt, especially when, in his frame of reference, the scales had turned. "There is a wave of reaction sweeping the country," he observed to Mrs. James Roosevelt at the end of the spring 1947 term. "One sees it in the White House, the Congress, and even in the Court. For my part, I have stood for the rights of man, for human liberty, and I will be unflagging about it as long as I remain...."[142]

As the Vinson Court plunged deeply into policy-making, the "great issue" clearly was not whether judges make law. The issue, as Felix Frankfurter had said so well in 1939, remained "when and how and how much."[143] Justice Murphy's contributions to the economic policy of his period were greater than his enemies conceded and smaller than his hopes. Because his economic options and mode of address ran so counter to professional and popular thought, however, the personal increment was perhaps more damaging than his lonely polemics for minority rights. Whether by helping the Fair Labor Standards Act to grow incrementally or aggressively, whether by opposing a grandiose but popular piece of judicial legislation in the *United Mine Workers* case, or whether by accepting agency-made law in *Chenery,* Murphy became his generation's symbol of a willful jurist, an advocate, as Madison defined a legislator, of the very causes he was called upon to decide. In a bout of horseplay in 1944, another Justice had passed around the bench a list of "F. M.'s Clients,"[144] which read:

Reds	R. R. employees
Whores	Pacifists
Crooks	Traitors
Indians and all	Japs
other Colored people	Women
Longshoremen	Children
M'gors and all other Debtors	Most men

Except for an attack on personal honesty, no more devastating commentary could have been made about an American judge. Because the yearning was so strong, so was the myth: "courts should find the law and not make it."[145] Measured by the interests offended or by the conventions of his craft, Murphy in the prime of his powers was failing the test.

CHAPTER 15

NOT MENTIONING THE CARDINAL,

1946-1949

J USTICE MURPHY's last years on the bench were an autumnal
period of solid achievement against a background of physical decline. Having made his peace with the Court by the end of the
war, Murphy by his late fifties exhibited a mellow (some thought mystical) outlook toward life and work. To be sure, he was still a highly
strung egocentric capable of fretting over the details of portraiture
being hung in his honor or of lashing out in anger at unflattering remarks in a *Fortune* article by Arthur M. Schlesinger, Jr., which he regarded as a calculated attack inspired within the Court.[1/a] The death of
Roosevelt had killed his lingering political ambitions and put a different
administration in power. Murphy also had to adjust to a rising generation of "practical idealists," men fresh from their own war and suspicious of high-sounding crusades. The romance of reform, along with
his influence, had waned.

Advancing years, even so, brought compensations. Whatever his
standing in the Court's inner circle, Murphy was warmed by the many
tributes received from minority groups as a champion of liberty and
tolerance. Though withdrawn from national politics, he took pleasure
in watching the climb of younger men he had encouraged in public
service, the most prominent of whom, G. Mennen Williams, observed
of his decision to run for Governor of Michigan—"See what you
started."[2] Reelection of his brother George to Detroit's Recorder's
Court, the one exception Murphy made to his rule against political
involvements, served to confirm his belief that "Detroit is still my
town."[3/b] And his own work increasingly became a source of personal
gratification. "As for the Court," he remarked in 1948, "it is great. More

[a] Returning copies of the Schlesinger article to *Fortune* editors, Murphy remarked:
"I am left with the impression that the attack was conceived beforehand or was inspired by others. A lifetime of devotion to one's ideals certainly leaves some impressions
other than those which were set forth in the article." FM to William D. Geer, Jan.
8, 1947, Box 121. Justice Frankfurter, after Murphy accused him of seeing Schlesinger's
manuscript before publication, vigorously denied that he had a hand in the article.
Memorandum to conference, Jan. 7, 1947, Box 28, Frankfurter Papers, Manuscript
Division, Library of Congress.

[b] Apparently Murphy put the heat on the *Detroit Times* for its lukewarm support
of his brother's campaign. Richard E. Berlin to FM, April 22, 1947; Jack Manning to
Richard E. Berlin, May 2, 1947, Box 122.

than any other Court it has formulated law significant to our people. I trust it is not immodest of me to say that I have taken the lead in rights under our Constitution."[4]

Incurably romantic, Murphy continued his best efforts to maintain euphoria in spite of declining prestige and the onset of the Cold War. Reliving memories was one comfort, and he found another in early 1947—love. Beneath his frenetic social pace, Murphy through the years had suffered loneliness and a melancholy sense of having missed the simpler pleasures of home and family. "I am not much of an authority on matrimony," he told Charles B. Warren, Jr., in 1942, "but I write with singular appreciation when I tell you that the life of a bachelor is much less than a full, rich life."[5] Tiring of bachelor quarters in the Washington Hotel, he indulged a pastime in the mid-1940s of looking for an elegant house in the capital, a dream he could not afford. After years of flirtation with many females, few of whom he took seriously, and years of fixation with Murphy women, whom he took very seriously—first his mother, his sister, and then his niece—Murphy at the age of 57 found romance. Joan Cuddihy, granddaughter of a former *Literary Digest* executive, was a young woman of gentle charm. Quietly they became engaged and made marriage plans. "Do you realize how many parties you have regretted in the past ten days?" his secretary asked as the affair progressed—"Joan must be the answer."[6]

Intense interest followed his late-blooming romance within the Justice's circle of friends. Justice Rutledge wrote Murphy's fiancée: "As your attorney, I have been keeping a close eye on this man Murphy. He is very astute, as you know. But I have the real goods on him—so much that whenever you may be ready to take action he will have no way out but to walk the straight and narrow path, for the first time in his life." "I dissent," Murphy retorted. "Your lawyer is a professor and does not know the facts of life."[7]

Besides a new happiness outside, Murphy also found in Rutledge close friendship on the Court. His relations with Justices Black and Douglas, though hardly the conspiratorial pact some outsiders assumed, likewise developed into warm rapport. But Rutledge was special, something Murphy had seldom known in office—a friend with whom he easily shared power. The two Justices, who were identified as the Court's left wing after *Yamashita*, became more than allies in conjunction with that showdown; they became pals. Sensing their mutual status as outsiders in professional regard, both men relieved the strain of work with lusty humor reserved for the other. Murphy delighted in teasing the unpretentious Rutledge about his slang and his drinks; Rutledge poked fun at Murphy's romanticism toward Indians, the midwest, and "that little pond which you presume to call a lake."[8] "Michigan is not a state. It is a desert of barren sand and industrial blight," Rutledge quipped beside Murphy's reference to the state in the *Yellow Cab* antitrust case.[9] And in retaliation, Murphy invited Rutledge to Harbor Beach during summer recess for "a real old fashioned baptism in the sweet waters of Lake Huron." "In return," he said, "you can sprinkle a little holy water on me."[10]

The very personal nature of their ribbing reflected a deeper friendship than the playful banter that commonly ripples through the Court. Bonds developed between them that sustained candid criticism and support, even in disagreement. After one battle, an angry Justice Rutledge observed to his friend: "Nobody but a Murphy would fully understand a Rutledge's independence or his respect for a Murphy's. And were it not for you, this place would be damn nigh intolerable for me. This Court makes a great show of standing for free thought and tolerance with it. (I think they go together) But we—I mean the Court—do not know what tolerance means in the freedom of speech, within its own walls—except for you and *perhaps* two others of our brethren."[11] Rutledge, recognizing Murphy's strengths as a fighter, but also his weaknesses of overstatement, often took it upon himself to keep his cohort out of trouble. Complaining that an attempted straddle in a railroad regulation case "muddies all the waters, holy and unholy," Rutledge once advised him "to tone down the certitude of your wording . . . in view of all the trouble you've taken to make plain what after all isn't so terribly plain. And with these remarks my Brother (the word is used in non-religious sense) Murphy, I bid you again—get on *one* side of the line & stay there even tho its a thin one."[12] Murphy did not always follow the advice; the views of others also had to be accommodated. But increasing agreement strengthened their fellowship as the pressures mounted. "I do not know how I would have gotten on this year unless you were in the corner next to me. Your kindness and congeniality made the burdens of the Court bearable," Murphy remarked to Rutledge after the grueling spring term in 1947. "I hardly need to reiterate the sentiment . . . ," replied Rutledge. "Without you here, I do not know how I could stand the grind."[13]

Though neither Justice would leave his favorite watering spot to share summer vacations—Rutledge his simple cottages and Murphy the "unsalted seas"—their companionship was welcome respite. The beginning years of the Vinson Court, in response to new pressures and personnel, were a season of transitional tension. Conflicts long brewing among Roosevelt Justices climaxed at the same time that delicate problems of the postwar era—church-state relations, criminal justice, and Cold War—flared. As a result, judicial alignments took unexpected, sometimes bewildering turns. Rates of diffusion and dissent, though lower than in the Stone Court, remained high. While libertarian cohesion strengthened regarding preferred freedoms and economic policy, criminal procedure splintered the quartet decisively. While the output of Justices Douglas and Jackson in 1947-48 equalled Murphy's earlier peak, Justice Frankfurter's rates of 40 and 45 opinions set new highs. Murphy's production, by contrast, dropped to 29 opinions in the 1946 term and then, as illness set in, to the teens.[14] By virtue of his religion and long-standing interests, however, the outspoken jurist was anything but a bystander as his productivity declined; personal mellowing, even failing health, meant no change of public philosophy. In Murphy's last years on the bench, the Supreme Court came to grips with the same problems of criminal law and religious freedom on which his difficulties of assimilation had centered. Now, Murphy's philosophy was no longer qualified by freshman insecurities. As the Court regeared itself for a plunge to the Right, Justice Murphy, more determined than ever, veered to the Left.

II

Criminal justice, Murphy's earliest governmental interest, occasioned a burst of individuality on the Vinson Court. Although he made no claim to learning in criminal law, it was not by accident that Murphy asserted independence over the rights of criminal defendants or that the subject generated a great debate. Having campaigned to "modernize and humanize" the machinery of criminal justice since 1923, partly in response to the claims of urban minorities and partly to public ideals, he brought to the bench a well-developed philosophy of the criminal process and a practical experience with the problems of assembly-line trials in city courts that only Justice Black, with three years as a Birmingham solicitor and police judge, could match. Murphy, as a proponent of rehabilitation as the goal of criminal justice, was perhaps the first champion to reach the high court of what law enforcement interests often regard as a "flabby" and "sentimental" outlook on crime and punishment.

The Supreme Court, furthermore, had long been heading for an explosion over its supervision of criminal procedure. Though the Justices still adhered to the doctrine that the due process clause of the Fourteenth Amendment applied only "fair trial" standards to the states, not the entire federal Bill of Rights, the trend of decision had been steadily interventionist since the mid-1930s, when pre-Roosevelt Justices, after a long period of judicial dormancy, began to stiffen standards of federal and especially state conduct. By the early 1940s the Court had outlawed the most glaring deficiencies—physical torture, systematic exclusion of Negroes from juries, and capital punishment without counsel.[15] Roosevelt appointees had barely gained control of the bench, however, when they broke into bitter dispute over the basis and extent of judicial control, as criminal defendants, encouraged by the Court's responsiveness, pressed ever closer issues for decision. What came late in Murphy's judicial career was merely the climax of civil liberties and social equality issues long smoldering.

In contrast to the preferred freedoms debate, which had unfolded gradually and tentatively, the dialogue over criminal procedure had matured early. In retrospect the watershed was *Betts* v. *Brady,* a 1942 right-to-counsel case that not only marked the emergence of a libertarian bloc but set the frame of reference for the ensuing struggle.[16/c] The Court, reaffirming the *Palko* v. *Connecticut* doctrine that the due process clause imposed only "fair trial" obligations on the states, upheld a Maryland armed-robbery conviction of an indigent farm laborer who had waived jury trial without advice of counsel, which he had requested but was denied.[17] Justice Roberts' opinion for the Court, which emphasized the reputation of the trial judge and the fact that only 18 states then required counsel in noncapital cases, seemed calculated to arrest a contrary momentum begun by Justice Sutherland's vigorous language in *Powell* v. *Alabama.*[18] But armed robbery convictions in

---

c Indeed, one letter from Felix Frankfurter to Hugo Black, if accurately dated—Oct. 31, 1939—anticipated the *Betts* debate by almost three years. Frankfurter wrote:

Dear Hugo: Perhaps you will let me say quite simply and without any ulterior thought what I mean to say, and *all* I mean to say, regarding your position on the "Fourteenth Amendment" as an entirety.

(1) I *can* understand that the Bill of Rights—to wit Amendments 1-9 inclusive—applies to State action and not merely to U.S. action, and that *Barron* v. *Baltimore* was wrong. I think it was rightly decided.

(2) What I am unable to appreciate is what are the criteria of selection as to the nine Amendments—which applies and which does not apply.

This is not written to draw any comment from you—not that I should not have pleasure in anything you may say. But I have written the above merely to state as clearly as I am capable of, what is in my mind.

Box 4, Frankfurter Papers, Manuscript Division, Library of Congress. This letter could have been occasioned by consideration of *Chambers* v. *Florida*, which the Court agreed to hear on Oct. 23, 1939. Justice Black's opinion for the Court raised, without deciding, the question of incorporation. 308 U.S. 227, 235-36n (1940).

many states carried either life or death penalties. The result was so offensive to libertarians that Justice Black, repudiating his earlier participation in the fair trial formula, advanced the thesis that the Fourteenth Amendment applied the entire Bill of Rights to the states. Heretofore only one "eccentric exception," Justice Harlan, had embraced the "wholesale incorporation" doctrine. Now the Black-Douglas-Murphy trio advanced it and Rutledge soon made a foursome, thus giving the libertarians control of certiorari and leaving them only one vote shy of a fundamental revolution in American criminal law: nationalization of the Bill of Rights.

Formation of the libertarian bloc in *Betts* v. *Brady* touched off one of the most important legal struggles in this century. A central issue throughout was how to produce procedural progress without weakening traditional local responsibilities for criminal law. Yet the debate in *Betts* and contemporary confession cases revealed how deeply entwined were competing variables. Cutting across the perpetual need to balance private rights and public safety were values of federalism and decentralized administration of criminal law, delicate power relations among vested federal and state interests spread among divided branches of government, links between trial and appellate courts—and even opposing conceptions of the nature of law itself. Debate over these issues, in contrast to other areas of litigation, posed well-defined alternatives from the start. And the clash over the scope of review of substantive economic regulations in the next term sharpened the due process conflict all the more.

In *Betts* Justice Frankfurter charged that wholesale incorporation of federal procedural safeguards would uproot the criminal law of the states and freeze criminal procedure within the limited experience of the 18th century. Ardently defending due process as a progressive concept containing ascertainable standards of reason, Frankfurter thereafter became the Court's most devoted champion of the fair trial rule, natural law, and the states. There was no paradox for him that judges should reject preferred freedoms as predilection and yet enforce natural justice notions of criminal procedure, no paradox that judges should retain due process supervision over substantive economic rights. Both policies manifested a consistent concept. Due process, as he later maintained, was "the most majestic concept in our whole constitutional system," a concept which the Constitution purposely "left to gather meaning from experience." Due process, in effect, was an objective standard of society's sense of justice. To divine that consensus without personalizing law required the same system of judgment he advocated to reconcile judicial authority with majoritarian democracy—self-restraint, rigorous detachment, and "alert deference" to the judgment of other officials. However rigorous this system of review, he asserted, "apply we must, warily, and from case to case."[19]

The fair trial formula, on the other hand, was avowedly a standard of reasonableness and of natural justice, concepts which Justice Black, with an eye to the past, regarded as having been imported by judges into the Constitution at the expense of legislative power and private rights. Charging that Frankfurter's concept of due process would convert the Court into an overlord without fixed standards, Black blistered the majority for resting civil liberties on the vagaries of judicial opinion rather than on specific constitutional guarantees. Specific prohibitions, he argued fervently, were the only defense against unbridled judicial discretion and fluctuating liberties.[20]

Frankfurter, who had labored for two decades on a book about the Fourteenth Amendment before his appointment to the Court aborted it, never denied that due process would vary according to the make-up of the Court. Indeed, so long as the clause was taken to have substantive content, it was "inconceivable" to him that courts would not fluctuate as they had throughout the past. Moreover, he doubted whether specific prohibitions would check judicial discretion, given "the resourcefulness of interpretation"; and since Black shied away from applying every minute detail of the federal Bill of Rights against the states, Frankfurter believed that Black's position ultimately rested on the same core of fundamental justice he was at pains to reject. Thus, precisely because he assumed that judicial discretion was inevitable, for specific prohibitions as well as for substantive guarantees, Frankfurter drew the same inference about the judicial function for the due process clause as an entirety—"very narrow scope of judicial power to strike down political action."

Very narrow scope meant some scope, however, for economic as well as procedural rights, and Frankfurter drew on legal tradition and professional discipline to reconcile that amount of judicial review with democratic theory. Amplifying his views to Black, apparently in conjunction with their clash over review of public utility rate-making, he explained on November 13, 1943:

My starting point is, of course, the democratic faith on which this country is founded—the right of a democracy to make mistakes and correct its errors by the organs that reflect popular will—which regards the Court as a qualification of the democratic principle and desires to restrict the play of this undemocratic feature to its narrowest limits. I am aware that men who have power can exercise it and too often do—to enforce their own will, to make their will, or if you like their notions of policy, the measure of what is right. But I am also aware of the forces of tradition and the habits of discipline whereby men entrusted with power remain within the limited framework of their professed power. More particularly, the history of this Court emboldens me to believe that men need not be supermen to observe the conditions under which judicial review of political authority—that's what judicial review of legislation really amounts to—is ultimately maintainable in a democratic society. When men who had such background and such relation to so-called property interests as did, for instance, Waite, Bradley, Moody, Holmes, Brandeis and Cardozo, showed how scrupulously they did not write their private notions of policy into the Constitution, then I am not prepared to say that all that a court does when it adjudicates in these constitutional controversies is an elaborate pretense, and that judges do in fact merely translate their private convictions into decisions and call it the law and the Constitution.

I appreciate the frailties of men, but the War is for me meaningless and Hitler becomes the true prophet if there is no such thing as Law different from and beyond the individuals who give it expression. And what I am talking about is that if each temporary majority on this Court—and none is very long—in fact merely regards its presence on this Court as an opportunity for translating its own private notions of policy into Decisions, the sooner an educated public opinion becomes aware of the fact the better not only for truth but also in the true interest of democracy. For myself I think the years that are ahead make more and not less important the tribunal for which the wise founders of this country provided, acting however within the very narrow limits within which it was deemed appropriate that it should function.

Expressing doubts that specific prohibitions would bridle judicial discretion, Frankfurter asked Black to show him the materials which justified the conclusion "that the Fourteenth Amendment was in fact a compendious statement of some or all of the earlier first nine Amendments."

Are all nine so incorporated? Did the Fourteenth Amendment establish uniform systems of judicial procedure in all the states and freeze them for the future, both in criminal and civil cases, to the extent that the Constitution does for federal courts? Is it conceivable that an amendment bringing about such a result would either have been submitted to the states, or, if submitted, would have been ratified by them? And if not all the nine Amendments, which of the prior nine Amendments are to be deemed incorporated and which left out?

Believe me that in writing this nothing is farther from my purpose than contention. I am merely trying to get light on a subject which has absorbed as much thought and energy of my mature life as anything that has concerned me. I ask you quite humbly to lead me to the materials that show that the Fourteenth Amendment incorporated by reference the provisions—any or all—of the earlier nine Amendments.[21]

Later Black produced historical evidence to buttress the wholesale incorporation thesis, evidence which Frankfurter rejected as both scholarship *and* law.[22] But the net result of the early debate over due process was a structuring of the doctrinal problem from *Betts* onward. Libertarians, even while lying low on the doctrinal front in order to avoid another defeat, attracted sufficient votes in particular cases to sustain a general "activist" trend. The conscience of the bar began to sting over the right to counsel, and the Justices themselves gave *Betts* the silent treatment. The Court's intervention to improve federal search and seizure standards, an effort led by Frankfurter, also fueled controversy over judicial discretion. Contrary to the objective standards that words in the Constitution might imply, the Justices, repeating their performances in the Fair Labor Standards Act Cases, began to peel off into essentially personal patterns. Constitutional clauses gave no relief from judgment. And contrary to popular assumptions, the effects were not polar, but plural.

The federal confession techniques condemned in *McNabb* v. *United States*, for example, moved one Justice to remark: "My instincts are outraged." Were instincts the standard? Justice Roberts, by contrast, took issue with the Court for releasing criminals, regardless of guilt, as a means of reforming police. Nine men were too limited, physically and functionally, to supervise the entire criminal justice system, he argued; "we must stop it." Suggesting the alternative, which Jackson later repeated in state cases, of notifying the Justice Department about police abuses, Roberts began to stand pat against further Supreme Court intervention. With increasing regularity in state cases, Stone, Frankfurter, and Jackson followed suit.[23]

Whatever their consistency respecting Civil Rights Act prosecutions of errant policemen after the *Screws* case, it was inherent in the fair trial rule that no satisfactory accommodation of the cross demands on criminal law administration was forthcoming, or even possible, except by after-the-fact elaboration of principle case by case.[24] The rationality of that process presupposed, if not objective perceptions, at least steady ones, a condition difficult to attain in a court whose common lot was fringe cases and fluctuating personnel. Because the fair-trial principle was no more precise than its statement, few fields of law were more dependent on minute factual differences or on autobiography as a touchstone of judicial decision.[25] So had it been in the heyday of substantive due process, when judges attempted to supervise the reasonableness of economic legislation; so would it be in the 1940s, when judges, without resolving the doctrinal base, began to assert new tenderness for the rights of the criminally accused.

Murphy became a symbol of the issue because by World War II; no other Justice was more consistently libertarian, or more candidly personal in approaching due process problems. Consequently he wrote few major opinions for the Court; but aided by Black's assignment power, he pulled his weight within the bloc, particularly regarding jury trial and in dissent. He authored the majority opinion in *Thiel* v. *Southern Pacific Co.*, which forbade conscious exclusion of day laborers from jury service, and wrote effectively for the minority when the Court finally approved "blue ribbon" juries by a 5-4 vote. Repeating the attack made in *Goldman*, and emphasizing statistical evidence that special juries have a stronger tendency to convict, Murphy struck at the premises of the system: "The vice lies in the very concept of 'blue ribbon' panels—the systematic and intentional exclusion of all but the 'best' or the most learned or intelligent of the general jurors. Such panels are completely at war with the democratic theory of our jury system, a theory formulated out of the experience of generations. One is constitutionally entitled to be judged by a fair sampling of all one's neighbors who are qualified, not merely those with superior intelligence or learning. . . . Any method that permits only the 'best' of these to be selected opens the way to grave abuses. The jury is then in danger of losing its democratic flavor and becoming the instrument of a select few. . . . Appeals to administrative convenience do not soften that violence."[26]

Even as he collaborated within a group, however, the Justice's personal idiosyncrasies were sharply etched. By 1947, Murphy and Rutledge had emerged as a left-wing duo. Murphy, impatient of procedural concerns that stood in the way of compassionate goals, frequently soloed with a crusader's theme.[27] Though he accepted wholesale incorporation of the Bill of Rights as a minimum standard of due process, the Court's Catholic Justice was not persuaded by Justice Black's objections to natural law. The notion of due process as a progressive juridical concept, covering both written and unwritten procedures and permitting experimentation, appealed to his common sense. Specific prohibitions as a practical matter might reduce judicial discretion, but they would never eliminate it altogether. Justice, not literalness, was his central philosophic premise. Compassion and equality, not judicial forbearance, were his dominant motifs. Thus while needling the Court for failure to acknowledge that, "in effect," it had applied the right against self-incrimination against the states, Murphy commonly walked a stylistic tightrope between the jargon of "justice," which was stock personal coin, and Black's efforts to peg the Court's intervention on express constitutional rights.[28] Otherwise easy unanimous decisions, such as the *Lee* v. *Mississippi* confession case, consequently proved to be difficult tasks of linguistic reconciliation in spite of his having a foot in each camp.[29]

Murphy's radicalism also produced seemingly doctrinaire outcroppings in which he and Rutledge, who objected that the right to counsel must prevail "at each and every step in a criminal proceeding," anticipated controversial decisions such as *Escobedo* v. *Illinois* and *Miranda* v. *Arizona*.[30] Emphasizing individual rights over states' rights, and "justice" over system, moreover, Murphy ran afoul of less-appreciated procedural interests which Justice Rutledge shared with Justice Black. A case in point was *Carter* v. *Illinois*, in which the Court, over the separate dissents of Douglas and Murphy, upheld a defendant's waiver of counsel as having been intelligently made. Ignoring warnings received through his clerks that he should not take notice of facts outside the record reviewed below or imply that there could never be waiver in a capital case; and recognizing that the votes of Black, Douglas, and Rutledge were unobtainable anyway, he concluded: "I like it best as it is. . . . Why shouldn't there always be counsel in a capital case?"[31] And then on opinion Monday, he issued a salvo of the *compleat* crusader: "Legal technicalities doubtless afford justification for our pretense of ignoring plain facts before us, facts upon which a man's very life or liberty conceivably depend. . . . But the result certainly does not enhance the high traditions of the judicial process. In my view, when undisputed facts appear in the record before us in a case involving a man's life or liberty, they should not be ignored if justice demands their use."[32]

An instrumentalist, a crusader who looked on the Court's role with a layman's eye to "justice" rather than to "rights," Murphy made plain his belief that orderly administration of the judicial system was subordinate to tenderness toward human life—above all, when the claimant numbered among "the friendless, the ignorant, the poor and the despised."[33]

These personal variations would have mattered little had not the Court been so closely divided that decision often turned on the eccentricities of a single judge. Personal variations also dislodged erstwhile ideological barriers. Murphy, whose impulse to preach was nearly as predictable as his vote, was viewed as emotionally committed by his colleagues; but that quality did not impede their cultivation of his talent at impassioned dissent. No subject was more instructive than a series of federal search and seizure cases in the late 1940s. Here Frankfurter and Murphy once again found themselves in agreement, and Frankfurter, far from having his Doric tastes offended, repeated his *Goldman* tactic of stoking Murphy's fires.

Justice Frankfurter was without peer as an advocate of judicial leadership in elevating *federal* standards of criminal procedure, a subject over which he felt the Court had supervisory responsibilities free from the restraints of federalism.[d] And by his own confession, Frankfurter was "nuts about" searches and seizures.[34] Believing that the rights of privacy protected by the Fourth Amendment were central to the enjoyment of other constitutional guarantees and that they were in need of greater judicial protection than First Amendment freedoms, which aroused greater public support, Frankfurter had already written sharp dissents in the *Zap* and *Davis* cases against lowering of federal search standards in cases involving automobiles and public papers. Because Stone had died before dissents were filed in those cases, because the Court's changing membership had required a rehearing in *Zap*, and because he refused to consider himself bound by prior decisions on close constitutional issues, Frankfurter became the driving force behind protesting further inroads on Fourth Amendment guarantees.[35] The result was a strange alliance of "activists"—Frankfurter and Jackson, Murphy and Rutledge—which shook standard categories.

Harris v. *United States* was easy to be nuts about.[36] The Court, by a 5-4 vote, sustained search of an apartment and seizure of illegal draft cards without warrant as an incidence of a lawful arrest for an unrelated crime. Although Chief Justice Vinson justified the search and seizure of contraband goods as merely extensions of customary police authority to search the person during a lawful arrest and to seize contraband in plain sight, the minority regarded the decision as "a deplorably retrogressive step." Extension of the "incidental search" and "plain sight" rules to cover both search and seizure in the premises without warrant, they believed, obliterated the distinctions between lawful arrest, search, and seizure, each of which rested on different considerations and separate judicial authority. The practical result was to make

---

[d] In *Fisher* v. *United States*, for example, Frankfurter, Murphy, and Rutledge protested the Court's refusal to impose a broader standard of mental incapacity in the District of Columbia, while the majority preferred to await development of the rule by the courts below. Conference notes, No. 122, Box 135. 328 U.S. 463 (1946). Cf. *Griffin* v. *United States*, 336 U.S. 704 (1949).

search warrants unnecessary, indeed a hindrance to police making a valid arrest. "It means you trump up a charge then ransack the whole place," Rutledge said bluntly in conference. "I think this is making new law." Police could go in for murder and come out with sedition, Murphy added to his clerk, which was "awfully dangerous." Private papers were safe from unauthorized search, in effect, only when people were away from home.[37]

Repugnant as those consequences were to the minority, Frankfurter appears to have had some difficulty arousing the others to his level of intensity. Jackson had expressed some doubts in conference. Rutledge, who distinguished between seizures in homes and in vehicles, and between open and hidden contraband, drew back from attempts to undermine *Zap* and *Davis*.[38] Murphy's original circulated dissent, in comparison with Frankfurter's charge that *Harris* was "the most indefensible violation of the prohibition of the Fourth Amendment that any record has presented to this Court," was routinely restrained.[39] Reviving the cooperation maintained in *Goldstein* and *Goldman*, the animated Frankfurter, who apologized to conference for his zeal and confessed that general propositions could decide concrete cases if convictions were strong enough, encouraged dissents worthy of the cause. Unable to woo Jackson into a joint statement he wrote a powerful protest of his own and, in the manner of *Goldman*, urged Murphy to make his dissent an "impressive document."[40] After Murphy's first circulation Frankfurter outlined how he thought such a dissent should be composed: "All the inadequacies and what I believe to be the deep fallacy of the Court's opinion is for me adequately set forth in your opinion. But you are not writing for the converted. This is a protest opinion—a protest at the bar of the future—but also an effort to make the brethren realize what is at stake. Moreover, a powerful dissent in a case like that is bound to have effect on the lower courts as well as on the officers of the law, just as failure to speak out vigorously against what the Court is doing will only lead to further abuses. . . . It is terribly important to drive home the moral of this decision. The moral is that it is far better to have no search warrant than to have one. A search warrant merely authorizes a search for the things set forth with particularity in the warrant. But according to this decision a warrant of arrest for a particular crime authorizes a search of one's home from cellar to attic for evidence of anything that such a search may reveal. If that is not outlawed by the Fourth Amendment, James Otis lived in vain."[41]

Murphy revised his opinion, incorporating phrases from Frankfurter. It was not "a novel principle of our Constitutional system," he asserted, "that a few criminals should go free rather than that the freedom and liberty of all citizens be jeopardized." The "key fact" of the case was that "the search was lawless. A lawless search cannot give rise to a lawful seizure, even of contraband goods."[42]

Though the essentials were unchanged, Murphy's *Harris* dissent was an impressive document, and in Frankfurter's view, "none too strong." After suggesting that the opinion be held over in hopes of catching other votes, Rutledge quipped: "I hope these principles apply in cases of arrest for unlawful left turns." (While preparing *Harris,* Murphy had made unwelcome headlines by arguing with Washington police about a traffic violation—an inevitable defeat which impressed delighted journalists as a demonstration of evenhanded justice.[43]) The *Harris* case gave little merriment, however. Though the dissents penetrated public consciousness, most commentators thought the Court had "unreasonably stretched" the doctrine of incidental search. To determine basic questions of liberty by such narrow dialectics and thin majorities, opined the *St. Louis Post-Dispatch*, indicated that "not all is well in our great temple of justice in Washington."[44]

The vacillation of the Court aggravated concern. In the *Trupiano* case the following term, Justice Douglas's swing gave the *Harris* majority opportunity to cut back the incidental search doctrine.[45] Frankfurter assigned the majority opinion to Murphy, a task accepted "with enthusiasm and deep interest."[46] Holding that seizure of contraband goods, even in plain sight, required a warrant "whenever reasonably practicable," Murphy's opinion was a tight recapitulation of the *Harris* dissent. Chief Justice Vinson's argument that the Court encumbered police without strengthening privacy, he met with language suggested by Justice Jackson. The requirement of a warrant to search premises and seize contraband during valid arrests, he replied, "partakes of the very essence of the orderly and effective administration of the law." Without it police officers would be free "to determine for themselves the extent of their search and the precise objects to be seized. This is no small difference. It is a difference upon which depends much of the potency of the right of privacy. And it is a difference that must be preserved. . . ."[47]

The *Trupiano* decision came as close to overruling *Harris* as could be done without acknowledgment. It also demonstrated the price of piecemeal development of law from differing factual contexts. If *Trupiano* compounded "confusion in a field already replete with complexities," as Vinson charged and Black later hinted, part of the problem was that the "plain sight" rule was less in need of repair than the original stretching of "incidental search."[48] Within a year after the death of Murphy and Rutledge, the Court retreated on seizure of contraband, flatly overruled *Trupiano,* and aggravated the confusion all the more. Respect for *stare decisis* alone, Frankfurter complained, ought to have preserved the decision. In a revealing passage he wrote: "Especially ought the Court not reenforce needlessly the instabilities of our day by giving fair ground for the belief that Law is an expression of chance —for instance, of unexpected changes in the Court's composition and the contingencies in the choice of successors."[49]

The gyrations of the Court on federal searches and seizures also played into the hands of proponents of more specific standards of due process. If standards of reason were so elusive as to occasion a change of federal law once a year, what kind of guidance could Justices expect to give to law enforcement officers of the states?

In the spring of 1947 this was no idle question. In two cases, *Louisiana ex rel. Francis* v. *Resweber* and *Adamson* v. *California,* the due process struggle came to a head.[50] The *Resweber* case was an executioner's nightmare. Malfunctioning equipment in Louisiana had failed to execute Willie Francis, a Negro sentenced to death for murder. Was it cruel and unusual punishment, and thus a violation of due process, for the state to try again? Six Justices, though disquieted by the human horror of the case, voted to affirm judgment denying his claim. But Douglas then shifted position, making the division 5-4 and the lines wavered badly before finally solidifying.[51] Justice Reed wrote an opinion for the Court, which at first only Vinson and Frankfurter joined. Jackson wrote a concurring opinion emphasizing that due process embodied impersonal standards of law, but withheld it after deciding to support Reed. Frankfurter, resisting the Chief Justice's pressure against multiple opinions, which Vinson argued confused bench and bar, concurred alone in order to stress that Reed's opinion was a manifestation of Jackson's objective and to render a characteristic lecture that the "consensus of society's opinion" enjoined by the Constitution permitted no alternative.[52] The great issue of due process, no less than of preferred freedoms, was the judge's function.

Murphy and Rutledge prepared dissents, but stifling them in an unaccustomed maneuver, they joined with Douglas in Justice Burton's protest. This tactic of strengthening the hand of an unexpected participant, which perhaps explains Murphy's own assignments in *White* and *Hickman,* had the desired effect.[53] Yet it cloaked their characteristic responses to the problems of due process—Rutledge's resort to negligence concepts to hold states to higher standards of care in executions, and Murphy's appeal to "a civilized sense of justice" and "highest humanitarian ideals."[54] In direct opposition to Frankfurter's contentions that cruel punishment and due process were objectively determinable norms, Murphy defended instinct forthrightly: "More than any other provision in the Constitution, the prohibition of cruel and unusual punishment depends largely, if not entirely, upon the humanitarian instincts of the judiciary. We have nothing to guide us in defining what is cruel and unusual apart from our own consciences. A punishment which is considered fair today may be considered cruel tomorrow. Our decision must necessarily be based on our mosaic beliefs, our experiences, our backgrounds and the degree of our faith in the dignity of the human personality. . . . And it is not without significance that this cruel and unusual punishment is about to be inflicted upon a helpless and inarticulate member of a minority group."[55] For all their alliance in *Harris* and *Trupiano*, on the central nerve of judging, Murphy's and Frankfurter's views were irreconcilable.

The *Adamson* case showed why.[56] At issue was the question whether California's rule permitting a jury to draw inferences from a defendant's failure to testify constituted self-incrimination and a violation of due process. In *Twining* v. *New Jersey*, 40 years before, a redundancy-minded Court, while virtually excluding all federal guarantees from due process, had held that the privilege against self-incrimination was not essential to justice.[57] The Court's spokesman in *Adamson*, Justice Reed, had no difficulty sustaining California's rule in view of *Twining*, the steady reaffirmation of the fair trial rule since then, and the checkered treatment given the privilege by the several states. Yet Justice Black, who at first had passed, but who had done his best throughout the 1940s to rest confession cases on incrimination rather than due process, now mounted a full-scale offensive against the fair trial principle, which provoked between himself and Justice Frankfurter one of the greatest debates over the judicial function since the importation of natural law into the due process clause nearly a century before. Summoning history and literalism to the defense of wholesale incorporation, Black denounced the natural law formula as an "incongruous excrescence" that gave judges boundless power to "roam at large in the broad expanses of policy and morals and to trespass, all too freely, on the legislative domain of the States as well as the Federal Government."[58] Summoning federalism, *stare decisis*, and natural justice to his side, Frankfurter defended organic due process as a concept em-

bodying the wisdom of generations and the core of law of many jurisdictions, to which individual judges in a federal system must defer.
"Twining," he said, "is cloudless."[59]

Waged as an extension of past crusades to restrict judicial discretion,
and in terms of elusive standards of objectivity, the Black-Frankfurter
argument overshadowed both the workmanlike opinion of Reed and
the separate statement of Murphy and Rutledge. Just as Murphy had
drifted to the periphery over preferred freedoms, so he found it necessary in *Adamson* to make "one reservation and one addition" to the
literalist arguments of Black. In an opinion which Rutledge joined,
he laid the foundation of what came to be known as the "incorporation plus" doctrine. "I agree that the specific guarantees of the Bill
of Rights should be carried over intact into the first section of the Fourteenth Amendment. But I am not prepared to say that the latter is
entirely and necessarily limited by the Bill of Rights. Occasions may
arise where a proceeding falls so short of conforming to fundamental
standards of procedure as to warrant constitutional condemnation in
terms of a lack of due process despite the absence of a specific provision
in the Bill of Rights."[60]

Brief though it was, Murphy's *Adamson* dissent was a remarkable
performance. Part of Frankfurter's reasoning was grafted onto Black's
in a way that undercut both. Due process encompassed the federal Bill
of Rights plus the "incongruous excrescence," natural justice. The standard for state trials was both the federal Constitution and "fundamental
fairness," neither of which meant deference. Whether advanced as a
serious effort to sway the Court or merely as additional evidence of
Murphy's radicalism in defense of personal liberty, his *Adamson* opinion was a mark of his instrumentalism and distrust of doctrine. Un-
perturbed by Frankfurter's charge that incorporation would "tear up by
the roots much of the fabric of law in the several States" and unmoved
by warnings that lack of "alert deference" would permit the "idiosyncrasies of a merely personal judgment" to carry a judge outside the
"limits of accepted notions of justice," Murphy was guided by one principle: that any attempt by government to deprive men of life and liberty
should be "tested by the highest standards of justice and fairness that
we know." "In Adamson, while agreeing with Hugo," he told his
clerk, "we ought to go further for the accused suffers for exercising a
right under the Constitution."[61]

Regardless of the merits, Murphy's *Adamson* alternative was not offered haphazardly. After circulating his first draft on June 19, 1947 he
had solicited the criticisms of other members of the libertarian quartet,

whose replies made plain that his opinion left three unintended implications: (1) that it might be necessary to go beyond the Fifth Amendment to bar all coerced confessions; (2) that Black's opinion for the Court in the *Chambers* v. *Florida* confessions case had rested on the "fundamental justice" test of *Twining*; and (3) much more important, that they would tie procedural due process exclusively to the specific prohibitions of the Bill of Rights rather than include other procedural guarantees of the federal Constitution. In response Murphy withdrew the *Chambers* citation and for added safety cut reference to due process as such; but he refused to retreat on the vital point. "It is hard for me to agree with all that Hugo writes," he told his clerk. "He may be right but I doubt it."[62]

Murphy's published dissent did leave the undesired implication, however. Not until 1965 did Black fully articulate his belief that due process meant, in its ancient sense, " 'the law of the land,' including all constitutional guarantees."[63] Not until the civil liberties revival of the 1960s, moreover, when the Court overruled *Betts* and *Adamson*, and absorbed into due process specific guarantees regarding counsel, self-incrimination, cruel punishment, and confrontation, along with unwritten rights of association, travel, and privacy as well, did Murphy's reputation begin to recover from the *Adamson* confessional.[64] And that is so even though the Court reversed *Adamson* for the very reason Murphy gave for "going further"—the accused was being penalized for exercising his constitutional privilege against self-incrimination. Contemporaries, their imaginations fixed by the striking categories of the Frankfurter-Black debate, and their sensibilities offended by the sympathetic overtures, equated the Murphy-Rutledge refusal to accept either doctrine as a straitjacket with the very subjectivity both Frankfurter and Black were at pains to deny. Did the two Justices wish to make crime "a legally-protected industry"?[65] Was due process, for them, the Sermon on the Mount?

Although Murphy's *Adamson* dissent was considered highly aberrant in his own time, many things happened between *Adamson* and the civil liberties revival of the Warren Court to cause revised judgment. Contemporaries could not have foreseen the pressures that burst upon the proffered systems—the inability of the Court to formulate fair-trial standards beyond outraged instincts, on the one hand, and the elusiveness of even specific prohibitions, on the other. They could not have foreseen the de facto cohesion between Black and Frankfurter in opposing Jackson's "just deserts" philosophy in state confession cases.[66] Nor could they have foreseen a changing consensus on the right to counsel—a consensus which, it was rumored, Frankfurter himself acknowledged before his death as proof of due process's capacity for growth.[e] Few commentators foresaw that the Court would legislate a new system of rules governing police interrogation as an implication of the Fifth and Sixth Amendments and the Court's "supervisory powers."[67] Few also foresaw that literalism worked both ways, that, relentlessly in the Birth Control and 1967 Eavesdropping Cases, Justice Black would oppose absorption of unwritten rights of privacy into due process for want of a specific constitutional referent, and that Justice Douglas would part company by embracing "incorporation plus." And certainly few would have predicted that three Justices—Goldberg, Warren, and Brennan—would repeat Murphy's belief in "fundamental standards" independent of express guarantees, much less find additional support for them in the forgotten Ninth Amendment![68] While the doctrinal basis of incorporation *versus* absorption remains unresolved, Justice Black thus remains the only advocate of wholesale incorporation in criminal procedure who would not "go further."

Unlike the Warren Court trio Murphy adhered to wholesale incorporation of specific guarantees as well as immanent rights; and for them he made plain his willingness to subordinate procedural regularities to achieve a "just" result. Dual radicalism toward the appellate function and the tempo of change were enough to leave his criminal procedure dissents unmentioned even when in substance vindicated. For Murphy, in truth, was operating on a different frequency from

[e] If the rumor was true, the change came in subsequent decades. Of the Court's silent treatment of *Betts*, Frankfurter once observed to Reed:

> No wonder we get memos from the Chief's office from time to time in which the lads indiscriminately treat the Court's opinions and dissenting opinions as though they were equally significant, carrying the same weight. Why don't you overrule *Betts* v. *Brady* while you are about it—indeed that would be much better than what you are doing, for it would have the sanction of candor and clarity, and conformity with past traditions in dealing with cases. Instead, you give notice to the bar that there isn't any real difference between a Court opinion and a dissent—some think one thing and some another, and what de hell difference does it make anyhow whether some are only dissenters and some constitute the Court! Why do we bother to have Court opinions anyhow? Why not let each fellow get rid of his own guff and call it a day!
>
> I suppose the Chief's feeling about dissents indicates the real remedy for this situation. If we had no dissents and no concurrences there could only be a Court opinion!
>
> Yours for the New Look. P.S. The above is merely the froth of my feeling about your Uveges opinion. In due course you will have the blast.

Frankfurter to Reed, Dec. 1, 1948, Box 32, Frankfurter Papers, Manuscript Division, Library of Congress.

the others, the same frequency of Christian idealism which had caused the gulf over *Yamashita* and the grief over portal pay, and which made him on this subject, the most radical figure in the history of the Court.[69] Compassion and equality, the twin themes of his priestly outlook, Murphy had articulated all his adult life as ethical imperatives in a civilized system of criminal law. Unapologetically and without dialectical dodge, he advanced them now as primary judicial goals. In the process he offended a multitude—all those who favored order, system, and circumspect judicial power.

However deviant his position from dominant professional thought, to Murphy these standards were transcendent, not personal. Natural justice and natural rights, he believed, were of the same cloth. Neither was capable of inclusive statement nor of sustaining the sophisticated distinctions between "fundamental fairness" and "selective absorption" of specific rights, which future Justices would read into Cardozo's *Palko* formulation of the fair trial test. As highly as Murphy regarded Black, to say that the Constitution did not presume higher law concepts beyond its written terms, Murphy considered a denial of its history and the nub of Western experience. Catholicism was behind his radicalism. So was the old amalgam of religion and politics—and the impatience with theory—which had marked his decision-making for years. Zestfully Murphy had once described his belief system as a twinfold faith in the "Goddess of Reason, and the Sermon on the Mount."[70] Zestfully he also had distilled both into a secular faith in "democracy," an ideological construct into which the catalytic agent of personal activism swept a host of specifics. It would have been surprising had he failed to do the same on the Court. What made the merger of Thomistic and natural right elements intriguing was not so much its emergence in constitutional forms but that the merger coincided with problems on the opposite face of the coin, the relationship between church and state.

III

Spring 1947, the season of *United Mine Workers, Hickman,* and *Chenery,* of *Harris, Resweber,* and *Adamson,* was a time of rich productivity for the Court and of unusual stress for Murphy. Cancelling European travel plans in June so as not to press other Justices who needed more time "on these vital matters of conscience," he confided that "more than one" of his 29 opinions that term "was an opinion of anguish in an effort to seek the ends of justice." Two religion cases, *United States* v. *Ballard* and *Everson* v. *New Jersey,* added to the strain.

These decisions were the opening rounds of a prolonged church-state conflict and raised such delicate issues of public policy that the Justices, for all the apparent stability of their choices, were in an unusual state of tension and flux.[71]

Especially was this so of Murphy. The church-state cases, which reflected his uncanny gift for being in critical spots of decision, buffeted him between deeply felt principles. As the Court's only Roman Catholic and the ranking American layman, he was acutely conscious of his church's interest in the outcome and of his personal visibility. Historically, of course, the high court has been free from those wild, Know Nothing fears of papal domination that have marred presidential politics. Roman Catholic jurists, including two Chief Justices, Taney and White, served with distinction without giving rise to thoughts of conflicting interests. Yet the fact remains that a major reason for the absence of such fears was lack of opportunity. Except for Taney, White, and McKenna, the Court had no Catholic membership until the twentieth century. Except for the famous Mormon polygamy case and a smattering of parochial education cases assimilated under property rights, it had relatively little occasion to pass on religious questions until the absorption process began in the 1930s.[72] Not once, in fact, had a case turned on the establishment clause as such until *Everson* in 1947. Just as Murphy was the first Roman Catholic Justice to have been appointed from explicitly religious criteria, so he was the first Roman Catholic Justice to participate in full-dress battle over the establishment clause of the First Amendment. Even in silence his conduct was significant, because in groundbreaking decisions a devout Catholic, who had regarded his own faith as an insurmountable obstacle to the presidency, embraced the Jeffersonian principle of rigid separation between church and state. His example at the threshold thus strongly reinforced a paradoxical judicial tradition—immunity from sectarian influence in a system which accepts religious affiliation as a legitimate criterion of Supreme Court appointment.

The very prominence of religion in his philosophical universe added significance to Murphy's performance. It goes too far to assert that his judicial behavior was unaffected by religious faith. Highly self-conscious about religion, for one thing, he leaned over backwards to avoid any implication of "representing" his church. This trait, though common enough among Catholic officials in a predominantly Protestant country, was probably easier for him because of anticlericalism in his upbringing. But indirect religious influences were observable in his assumptions about Christianity in politics as well as in his precise attitudes toward obscenity control, family law, and "quickie" divorce. Because of his own spirituality, Murphy was especially empathic to the claims of unorthodox religious conscience. Because of his ardently Jeffersonian political philosophy, which was reinforced by practical perceptions of what sectarian diversity required in the United States, he also espoused the separation principle as "essential" for the health of the polity and of American Catholicism itself.[73] Action had followed principle, moreover, in the past occasions when he had faced choice as a policy-maker. In tempering secular and ecclesiastical conflicts according to the motifs of American liberalism, Murphy actually was the Court's most experienced hand.

Still, considering his experience and strong convictions, his judicial responses to religious problems were surprisingly fluid. His "judicial philosophy," contrary to popular belief, was not a simple registration of set, pre-Court attitudes; his philosophy unfolded between *Gobitis* and *McCollum* in a cross-rough of conflicting claims.[74] That was important because Murphy's evolution, including his underestimation of the internal tension within his own value system, was merely the sharpest instance of a wider experience. General principles, the Court soon discovered, seldom decided the concrete case.

The potential clash between the two religion clauses of the First Amendment, it is true, had been implicit in the early Jehovah's Witnesses cases. Murphy's own radicalism toward taxation of religious enterprise had sharpened cognizance of it. But frontal consideration of church-state issues made plain that more judges than Murphy had been thrown off balance by the single-faceted perspective produced by free worship claims. Discomfitted by the dearth of precedent on church-state issues, the whole Court appeared to be in transition and groping for bearings as the focus shifted from abridgment to establishment. The Supreme Court's religion doctrine, accordingly, became a forceful example of the strengths and weaknesses of "incremental" decision-making, that is, the elaboration of principle by *ad hoc* adjustments of theory to factual situations.[75] In contrast to the due process conflict, doctrine itself was emergent and positions were tentative.

The church-state cases also highlight the role that litigants may play in generating constitutional principles. Until *Everson* the Court managed to avoid a direct ruling on the relationship between free worship and establishment guarantees. But the *Ballard* case, which spanned the Stone and Vinson periods, offered a difficult preview only a month before *Everson*. In *Ballard* the Court faced two successive appeals by members of the "I Am" sect convicted under federal mail fraud statutes for misrepresenting religious experience. The trial judge, troubled by the First Amendment implications of the indictment, had withdrawn all issues concerning the truthfulness of the beliefs from the jury and had instructed it to follow a subjective test that honest belief in alleged miracles required acquittal. The Court of Appeals then reversed, holding that the jury should have considered whether the alleged religious experiences had occurred in fact. In light of that ruling, the Justices concentrated on freedom of worship aspects of the first appeal in late 1943; and a 6-3 majority, while remanding the case on other grounds, reversed in accordance with the subjective test.[76]

That disposition, nevertheless, masked internal questioning that approached consideration of the relation between the two clauses of the First Amendment. While the minority—Stone, Roberts, and Frankfurter—regarded the convictions as solid on other grounds, two vocal Justices of the majority argued in conference that the indictments were inherently bad, since fraud involved allegations of fact, and any inquiry into the truthfulness or sincerity of religious beliefs collided with the First Amendment. Observing that most religions proclaimed miracles and that jury determination of religious belief would vary according to dominant local orthodoxies, one Justice commented: "If we hold you can submit to Judges or Juries what they believe then the First Amendment is destroyed. This was forseen by [the] 1st Amendment. There is a degree of fakery in all of them. But I am not going to let some one determine the belief of another. . . . This is exactly the same as Christ when he was on this earth. They found it out centuries ago that you couldn't trust one group's beliefs to another."[77] Urging the Court to dismiss the mail fraud indictments as irreconcilable with free worship guarantees, this Justice came close to the implication left by Jackson that courts could not decide questions of spiritual faith without "establishing" religion. After all, how could inquiry be made into what was believed without determining what was believable? How could courts examine other people's faiths without defining faith?[78]

Justice Jackson was the only one to express those doubts publicly, and even his reference to establishment was oblique. When the case returned in December 1946 the Court found an ironic escape via sex-and-jury trial, by ruling that conscious exclusion of women from the federal grand jury in California vitiated the indictment.[79] Even so, the jury trial issue, which rested on an extension of Murphy's *Thiel* opinion, was not reached without fluctuating alignments. In preliminary balloting Murphy voted to reverse on all issues. Yet both he and Reed, who supported jury trial reversal, also echoed the minority's view that fraud under the guise of religion was punishable. A majority, in effect, appears to have rejected Jackson's original position that the First Amendment prohibited all mail fraud prosecutions for matters of faith. But conclusions were highly unstable. Justice Jackson, seeing infirmities in the fraud statute, thought it unnecessary to reach the constitutional issue. Frankfurter and Rutledge, who soon emerged as ardent separationists, eventually switched their initial positions on jury trial reversal; and Frankfurter, in contrast to his usual posture, urged the Justices to pronounce the controlling legal principles to settle the substantive issue once and for all. Libertarians, in turn, opposed that solution as "too much of a trap." Erstwhile defenders of jury trial rights now argued that entrusting subjective religious beliefs to different prosecutors, judges, and jurors from place to place would wipe out the gains of the Jehovah's Witnesses cases and strike at the free worship of religious minorities.[80] Because juries were not to be trusted with questions of religious faith, in sum, the Court would insist that women be on them. "Passive virtues" worked in wondrous ways.

Ultimately Rutledge's shift gave jury trial advocates a narrow majority. What could have been a confrontation over the relationship between the First Amendment's dual safeguards was skirted by some deft judicial legislation concerning federal jury service and by some sage observations of Douglas for the Court. "The truth is," he said, "that the two sexes are not fungible; a community made up exclusively of one is different from a community composed of both; the subtle interplay of influence one on the other is among the imponderables."[81]

Avoidance of constitutional issues normally may strain statutes and public understanding. But in California the *Ballard* case provoked more than its share of professional criticism. The *Thiel* decision itself, which had overturned a decision on day laborer exclusion after the practice was discontinued, had already offended members of the state bar.[82/f] Now Murphy's friend, Federal District Judge J.F.T. O'Connor, who had attempted to arouse his interest in the *Ballard* problem for years, jumped him for accepting the jury trial rubric. When the Supreme Court had to amend an act of Congress requiring federal conformity to state jury qualifications, overrule all California Supreme Court decisions on the subject, and ignore its own decisions which had accepted female exclusion from state juries for 70 years, was the price of constitutional avoidance not too high?[83]

"Earnestness is a precious virtue and you are possessed of it in no

---

[f] In *Thiel* the Justices were unaware that the practice had been discontinued. See Justice Burton, Memorandum to Conference, Jan. 2, 1947, No. 37, Box 138.

small measure," Murphy responded to O'Connor, then let the matter drop.[84] But a month later in *Everson* v. *New Jersey*, neither he nor the Court was able to escape the First Amendment trap in perhaps its most treacherous form—public aid to parochial education. A New Jersey township heavily populated by Catholics, in recognition of the share of its educational burden borne by parochial institutions, and acting on the basis of the "child benefit" theory used by the Court to approve textbook and school lunch programs in Louisiana, reimbursed parents for the public transportation fares of children attending public and parochial schools. The New Jersey high court had upheld the expenditure in a taxpayer's suit as fulfilling a predominantly secular purpose. On appeal the federal Supreme Court absorbed the establishment clause into the Fourteenth Amendment, interpreted the clause as imposing a "high wall of separation" between church and state, and then sustained the school bus subsidy by a 5-4 vote.[85]

Despite the close result the Justices were united on fundamental principles. Taking their cue from Jefferson and Madison, rather than from contrary evidence that the Amendment had been aimed at preventing federal tampering with state establishments, they all agreed that the establishment clause controlled the states and that it forbade not only official religions or sectarian preference but even nondiscriminatory state support. The high-wall principle prohibited the blending of secular and spiritual policy in order to preserve individual conscience within a no man's land of mutual neutrality and to insulate both church and state from mutual pressure. Neutrality, on the other hand, could not mean hostility to religion without violating free exercise guarantees. In a society in which secular and religious affairs have long been mixed, no one assumed that the establishment clause was absolute. The real question, as Frankfurter later remarked, was what the high wall separated.[86]

Application of the principle in *Everson* renewed the *Ballard* flux. Only two Justices, Frankfurter and Rutledge, would have nullified the school bus subsidy in preliminary voting. Frankfurter, who frankly voiced absolutist attitudes toward separation, expressed his conclusion "with difficulty." Murphy, torn by conflicting principles and doubt whether he should disqualify himself, passed. Jackson voted to affirm on first impression, but not without criticizing the "child benefit" theory as a subterfuge. Reviving his disagreement over the tax cases Jackson pressed the Court to enforce the two religion clauses equally. Establishment was the reverse side of abridgment. Religions could not have it both ways. What the state could aid, the state could also regulate.[87]

Everson, like *Classic* and *Screws*, opened such infinite vistas of immersion in public controversies; the difficulty of drawing lines was so readily apparent that judicial reticence was understandable. Justice Rutledge, fearful of taking the plunge, toyed with absolutes. "First it has been books, now buses, next churches and teachers," he said bluntly and presciently in conference. "Every religious institution in [the] country will be reaching into [the] hopper for help if you sustain this. We ought to stop this thing right at [the] threshold of [the] public school." Accordingly, Rutledge would have voided the statute on its face and, to prevent discrimination, would have ruled out state aid to private as well as parochial schools.

Rutledge's medicine was too strong for the others. They saw distinctions between private and parochial institutions that they were unwilling to read into the Fourteenth Amendment. Still others saw gradations of aid and a paramount public purpose sufficient to sustain a school bus subsidy, despite incidental church aid. Some, in all good faith, may have been willing to accept this compromise for the sake of making the high-wall principle more palatable to its enemies. Besides, did appellate functions not require leaving future questions to the future? The Chief Justice expressed the common anxiety when he said, "I try to think of [the] case in front of me."[88]

Clearly, with the exception of Frankfurter, Jackson, and possibly Rutledge, the Justices in their earlier rush to defend freedom of worship had not constructed a frame of reference apposite to the whole problem.[89] The development of the Court's religion doctrine supports the view that judicial decision-making is not enclosed by traditional models of logical exegesis from *stare decisis* to transcendental targets, nor even by newer attitudinal theories in which ideology dominates. However committed ideologically, most Justices paused before the implications of *Everson*. Attitudes were inchoate and options highly fluid. The Justices conformed to official theories of collective decision-making as they probed and criticized the multiple drafts behind the scenes. They also jockeyed for votes. Frankfurter, writing from home on a Sunday, appealed to Murphy in highly personal terms.

Dear Frank,
You have some false friends—those who flatter you and play on you for *their* purposes, not for your good. What follows is written by one who cares for your place in history, not in tomorrow's columns, as lasting as yesterday's snow. At least your sister and your brother would acquit me of anything but disinterestedness. I am willing to be judged by them.
The short of it is that you, above all men, should write along the lines—

I do not say with the phrasing—of Bob's opinion in *Everson*. I know what you think of the great American doctrine of Church and State—I also know what the wisest men of the Church, like Cardinal Gibbons thought about it. You have a chance to do for your country and your Church such as never come to you before—and may never again. The things we most regret—at least such is my experience—are the opportunities missed. For the sake of history, for the sake of your inner peace, don't miss. No one knows better than you what *Everson* is about. Tell the world—and shame the devil.

Anyhow—this comes to you from one who writes because the truth within him is insistent.[90]

Much of the sharp ideological divisions over church-state relations, in other words, appear to have hardened during and after *Everson* rather than before it. The case stands as a classic illustration of the disparity between rhetoric and reality in judicial decision—and of Brandeis' command to "go ahead" when the probabilities of certainty are no more than 51 percent.

When Jackson and Burton changed their votes, Murphy's signature gave Black's opinion the decisive margin. After an excursus of separationist principles, the Court held that a school bus subsidy involved merely incidental support in a primarily secular program, a conclusion which drew Jackson's brilliant riposte that only one precedent supported the contradiction between principle and application, Lord Byron's report of the lady Julia, who "whispering 'I will ne'er consent,'—consented."[91] Given the flux, it would be inaccurate to suggest that Murphy was the swing-man in the sense that he, more than the others, controlled the decision or held the balance of power. *Everson* was one of those pathfinding decisions in which unstable options were to be expected. His vote was a critical datum for a different reason, however —the fact that the Justice most commonly regarded as a predictable ideologue also embraced general principles unreservedly, yet paused in uncertainty. Among intimates, Murphy confessed that he had prayed long and hard over the church-state issue and replying to Judge O'Connor's criticism of *Ballard*, he gave some hint of his personal agonies when he wrote:

Have you read the School Bus decision? It came down from the Court 5 to 4 so you may gather how deep the feelings are about that case.

Today my religion is powerful and I am afraid too rich in this country. I know of the day in American history when convents were burned and churches leveled to the ground, not alone because of Romanism but because the bigots believed and still do that many of the beliefs of the church are frauds. It's a very delicate subject and for my own part I will struggle to be right. If I err I want to err on the side of freedom of religion.[92]

While the decision coincided with Catholic institutional interests, Murphy understood from the start that the high-wall principle would lead inexorably to unpopular results, not only among fellow Catholics but among most American denominations. The anticipated conflict was soon forthcoming. In *McCollum* v. *Board of Education* the following term, he participated in a decision which collided not only with the position of his own church, but with most organized religions in the United States.[93] And in the nightmare of criticism that followed—a nightmare which included denunciation of him by name from Catholic pulpits—Murphy became so agitated that he organized indirect replies.

The *McCollum* decision itself, though vigorously opposed by Justice Frankfurter for not going far enough, caused Murphy no particular grief.[g] At issue was a program in the public schools of Champaign, Illinois in which pupils on a nonpreferential basis were released from study halls to attend classes of religious instruction in public classrooms conducted by the clergy of their parents' choice. Even the appellants, in asking the Court to reconsider *Everson*, conceded that this program of religious instruction could not be reconciled with the high-wall principle. Murphy, along with the entire bench, was not prepared to retreat to a "no preference" doctrine; nor could he accept Reed's view that the wall in fact had not been breached. Released-time programs were a far cry from the incidental effects of educational subsidies or the indirect blending found in public symbols and oaths. Here the state aided evangelism itself. Debating the issue with his clerk on January 19, 1948, Murphy explained his position thus:

If you accept the thesis that the First Amendment was intended to erect a "wall of separation between church and state," and that it should be so construed, then it seems to me that Black's opinion is correct on the facts

---

[g] Frankfurter apparently attempted to use the *McCollum* case to close the dike opened in *Everson*. After Black circulated his opinion for the Court Frankfurter called a meeting of the *Everson* dissenters to exchange views in hopes that he would become their spokesman. See Fowler V. Harper, *Justice Rutledge and the Bright Constellation* (Indianapolis: Bobbs-Merrill, 1965), pp. 348-51. Felix Frankfurter to Justices Jackson, Rutledge, and Burton, Jan. 6, 1948, Box 19, Frankfurter Papers, Manuscript Division, Library of Congress. The willingness of Frankfurter to caucus in *McCollum* was one barometer of his intensity of conviction that the establishment clause should be rigidly enforced. So were his disagreement with the jurisdictional dodge offered by Justice Jackson in *McCollum* and his note to the lone dissenter, Justice Reed: "As an opinion . . . from your point of view, I think it is one of the very best things that you have done since you have been on the Court. Moreover, considering the Court's opinion in the *Everson* case, your present dissent stirs in me a respect which the proposed Court opinion in *McCollum* is far from generating." Frankfurter to Jackson, Feb. 12, 1948, Box 19; Frankfurter to Reed, Jan. 16, 1948, Box 32, Frankfurter Papers, Manuscript Division, Library of Congress.

of the case. The public school system of Champaign School District No. 71 is being used, under authority of State law, [by] organized religious groups to propagate their faith. The operation of the school system is integrated with a program of religious instruction conducted by representatives of various church groups.

You ask, is it really "union" of church and state? Perhaps not in the manner and form at which the amendment was originally aimed, namely a single established church, one to which all are required to adhere or which the state supports. And possibly it is too strong to say that this arrangement actually presents a case of *union*. It does, however, seem to violate to a considerable degree the principles of separation. It is cooperation and collaboration of a very direct sort, by school authority, in a program of sectarian instruction conducted by sectarian agents, and it involves a further measure of public support by providing facilities and services. This is obviously not the same as a course in comparative religion or ecclesiastical thought conducted under nonsectarian auspices.

If the classes were held after regular hours and on extra time, without coercion, it might be less objectionable. But it would still involve the regular and systematic utilization of public facilities by sectarian and religious groups in the propagation of their doctrines, plus a measure of collaboration with the public school authorities. It would be something less than complete separation.

Would this preclude the temporary or occasional use of public school property by religious groups for religious or social purposes, when their own facilities are temporarily unavailable, as distinguished from regular and systematic use? I would not think so. But you don't have that situation here.[94]

What grieved Murphy about *McCollum* was the unmodulated clerical attack on the Justices for alleged hostility toward religion. Stung by the unfamiliar reproval of men of the cloth, he was unable to let the *McCollum* criticism pass when Cardinal Mooney of Detroit joined the public assault. Discreetly, he planted rebuttals among reporter friends and Michigan clerics; and to Bishop William Murphy of Saginaw, his friend and former priest, he lowered his customary guard. He wrote on May 10, 1948:

The United States Supreme Court opens its session each day with the supplication "God save the United States and this Honorable Court."

Cardinal Mooney I know to be a good and holy man. Also I know of his vast experience in the Far East. In addition, he has been brave about the poor because I happen to know that many of his rich parishioners may not be disposed to give freely because of the Cardinal's honest and correct views.

One cannot explain an opinion of the Court. It speaks for itself.

Every member who signed that opinion save one is a believer.

Justice Burton has been layhead of his church.

These men I know to be competent and to be good men. Certainly they are not the type who would in any way assail religion.

Cardinal Mooney has chosen to make what I think is a political speech in a city where I was Mayor and in a state where I was Governor. I regret that he did this but the right of free speech belongs to him although I suppose when other priests speak about politics he dislikes it.

According to the Detroit News: "25 years ago, when he was a teacher of logic, he would have flunked any student who submitted the majority report of the court, because the 'pivot' idea—separation of church and state, which has become the shiboleth of the secularists—is 'wobbly.' " That is an unfair statement about me.

It seems to me that a man of the cloth is held to higher moral obligations than even the Court Justices letting alone the others who make up our country.

This is written to you as a friend and one who is possessed of a devout belief and because I know that a reply is going to be made to these attacks.

In Michigan I will have to say something, not mentioning the Cardinal of course, about the lack of wisdom and unattractiveness of the clergy who enter the political field to the extent that it belittles the ablest court in the land. Except for the Cardinal's reckless statement I would not have to do it.

Time is a great leveler and priest or cardinal would be wise to wait before they interpret something as the final word of the Supreme Court.[95]

Justice Murphy did not live to face released-time programs outside public classrooms, which he pondered in 1948, and the Court approved in *Zorach* v. *Clauson*.[96] He also left no record of how he regarded insistence on strict standing requirements, which Justice Jackson suggested in *McCollum* and the Court followed in the 1950s, to avoid scrutiny over innumerable church-state variations, frivolous and otherwise. Sunday closing laws, not to mention prayers and Bible reading in the public schools, were a long way off.[97] Even so, Murphy's views of church-state relations were sufficiently elaborated to characterize them as essentially middle-of-the-road. Qualifying Catholic orthodoxy according to Jeffersonian theory, he tempered separatism in practice to avoid hostility to religion. However much he had underestimated internal tensions within the First Amendment, Justice Murphy adhered to the view that establishment as well as abridgment guarantees should be interpreted according to the practical effects on the primary interest —freedom of conscience. That outlook toward establishment, regardless of doctrinaire appearances in the abridgment cases, was the antithesis of the absolutism commonly associated with the "libertarian activists." Inevitably the Black-Murphy position would draw judges into degree judgments which libertarians spurned in fair trial litigation and seldom acknowledged for free speech. And the necessity of making those degree judgments in church-state relations was precisely why Justices Frankfurter, Jackson, and Rutledge regarded the high-wall principle as nearly an absolute as was possible in law. Only the Supreme Court, they believed, was capable of resisting perennial group pressures for public aid. Only uncompromising resistance at the outset, they believed, would enable the Justices to avoid review of countless individual variations which, in effect, would convert the Court into the nation's school board. Only judicial activism, in short, would preserve the American doctrine of separation—an absolute, one Justice later observed, as American as the Red Indian.

That the establishment clause produced such topsy-turvy alignments regarding the judicial function was symptomatic of the difficulty of the issue. But the issue did turn the tables of absolutism and relativism. Murphy did not deny it. The touchstone of his own life was conviction that conscience *commands* action. Because he projected that principle onto others he believed that courts, consistently with the dual objectives of the First Amendment, should give greater room for free exercise claims, in which individual conscience is the primary interest, than claims under the establishment clause, whose dominant objective is institutional neutrality. Some observers have condemned this distinction as unneutral, as aiding religion judicially. But the anomalies were washed away in Murphy's view by the theory of judicial review and by a critical distinction in the First Amendment between belief and institutions. Near absolutism toward free worship, near relativism toward the relations of church and state, were but means of safeguarding private conscience from both.[98]

Officially Murphy added little public light to the Court's troublesome disposition of the religious question. Lacking a coherent philosophy of the problem at the outset, he probably confused matters, under pressures of time and short sight, by resort to radical rhetoric and standing arguments that obscured his pragmatism and the distance travelled between *Gobitis* and *McCollum*. Nevertheless, he played a substantial, strategic, and symbolic role in the germinal period of the Court's religion doctrine. Strategically the Court's most radical defender of freedom to worship supplied a decisive vote for an attempted accommodation of principle and reality. Symbolically his example refuted suspicions that sectarian commitments necessarily create higher loyalties in government service, a fact not neglected by Kennedy supporters in the 1960 presidential campaign.[99] Nor was it without significance that the Justice most suspected of fanaticism on the subject of religion was so evolutionary or centrist in fact. For regardless of their merits, his concrete responses bear surprising resemblance to the Court's emerging doctrine that the state may neither burden nor benefit religion. They even resemble the method of reaching conclusions. Murphy solved the *Chaplinsky* problem by labelling it, as both Black and Jackson appear to have done in *Everson*.[100] He gave smaller scope to burdens on religion than to benefits, as substantial majorities have continued to do. He deviated from the dominant center only in *Prince*, and even there his de facto differences with the Court resemble recent judicial insistence that civil authority choose policy alternatives that least intrude upon free religious practice.[101] The irony with Justice Murphy's position was not that his judicial activism regarding free worship breached the high wall; the irony was the way he scaled centuries of conflict over the place of religion in the secular state.

Since boyhood Murphy's religion had been tinged with anti-clericalism. Since boyhood he had synthesized Christian activism and liberal ideals to the point that what others regarded as deep philosophical conflicts posed no problem for him. "The essential faith of Christianity and the essential faith of democracy," he lectured time and again, "are one and the same."

It is the faith that the human personality is inherently free, that every man is endowed with certain rights founded in the very nature of human living, and that there is a code of justice—of wrong-doing and right-doing—that is not subject to change by the laws of man.[102]

Viewed as manifestations of ideological themes rather than of set policy attitudes, his votes might have been predictable. As the Supreme Court struggled to steer a course between the First Amendment's dual thrust Justice Murphy found his bearings, as he always had, by fusing American political ideology and religious faith.[h]

[h] *McCollum* was not the first time that clergymen attacked Murphy for subordinating theology to politics. Father Coughlin, charging him with fomenting a "naturalistic front," took umbrage at a 1937 speech in which Murphy declared: "Christian and Jew have in common a goal which, in a sense, is larger, more vital, than religion itself. That goal is the fulfillment of the ideal of democracy in its every phase . . . political, social, and economic. It is the task of carrying over into our social and economic order what in religion is called brotherhood. . . . Democracy as conceived and expressed in the American constitution is something more than a method of government. It is a passionate political faith. It is a faith in the natural capacities and inherent possibilities of the common man, in his essential worth and dignity. In the scheme of democracy, as in the code of Christianity, all men are on a common level of dignity and importance." "Selected Addresses," p. 73. *NYT*, Jan. 29, 1940, p. 4:8.

IV

The uproar over *McCollum* coincided with, and perhaps aggravated, a period of melancholy late in Murphy's life. The Justice, who continued to put down brushfires among Catholics to the limits permitted by his office, was far too experienced with Roman Catholic diversity to assume that his critics spoke for the whole church. The disapproval of clergymen fed his anticlerical feelings, nevertheless; and when a Washington cleric chastised him for serving as godfather to a child of the divorced Protestant, James Roosevelt, Murphy's verbal reply was rumored to have been a classic in a rich repertoire. Humanism, at the same time, became more prominent in his thought. Synthesis, emphasis on harmony and unity, however much Marxist-influenced liberals were perplexed by them, had long been staple ingredients of his optimistic faith. Serving as a bridge to conservatives, enabling Murphy to mend his fences in the 1940s with General MacArthur and Henry Ford, these elements strengthened with age and the loss of innocence that even he acknowledged during World War II.[103] Dampening ideological conflict, telling the truth about his age, distilling the essence of his religious and secular faith into the great ethical themes of Western tradition—brotherhood and equality, human dignity and natural rights—Murphy gave evidence of personal maturation in a host of ways, small and large.

Reduced energies could be seen in a gradual narrowing of his friendships to a few intimates, Thurman Arnold, Benjamin V. Cohen, Evalyn Walsh McLean. Mellowing could be seen in his joy at discovering the popularizer Will Durant, the neo-Thomist philosopher Jacques Maritain, and ecumenical elements in the Roman Catholic Church, all of whom expressed thoughts that Murphy, in his own way, came to in the process of self-discovery. Mellowing was also observable in his rediscovery of nature and of Old Testament minor prophets, as well as in a melancholy strain that crept into his utterance. There was no loss of evangelical identification with the poor or with the "American mission," to be sure. As perspectives cleared about the revolution in the underdeveloped world, the Justice became so agitated about wasting the country's "spiritual forces" that he considered writing a book about the power of "just example." Yet even Murphy acknowledged the inroads of international events on the innocence of "my Messiah years."[104] As he aged he was struck by the "strange alteration of progress and reaction," the "sequence of tragedy and uplift" in history. There was less talk about "making better men," and more of "the good things come hard," less complaint against reactionaries and more against the "jungle breed" loose on the earth.[105] "All my life," he remarked, "I have known nothing but depressions, upheavals, revolutions and wars." The American experiment, clearly, was never done but always in the making; the good things of life were "*kept* only by toil and pain."[106] But, he was quick to assert, "these things *are* worth fighting for." Inverting the jingoism of his Populist origins, he maintained that "as human beings, we have an obligation to take an interest in the greater errands that concern the entire family of men in this nation and in this world."[107] If observers were perplexed by his priestly demeanor and his uncompromising idealism on the Court, the clue was his characteristic fighting response. Greater dangers called for grimmer determination. Totalitarian successes only wove his militancy into a tighter web. "If our way of life is to survive," he said, "our ideology must be a fighting faith."[108]

Outsiders, to whom Murphy was an enigma or a caricature, attributed all this to a sentimental screen that hid discomforts on the bench. Sublimating inadequacies of mind and temperament by identification with underdogs, it was thought, the Court's misfit became more mystical and visionary than ever.[109] Judicial affairs, however, played only a small part in Murphy's periods of gloom. Messianic impulses, after all, were nothing new in romantic moods; and those moods were followed often as not by tortured feelings of inadequacy. Removal from active politics may have accentuated his needs for compensating approval, but Murphy was hardly unaware of his strategic location in furthering lifelong goals of public policy. If he seemed isolated on the Left, the reason was mainly that the Court's center of gravity shifted while he stood still. He was virtually penniless, partly because of extravagance with his family, but Murphy insisted, "I don't mind that."[110] Rejecting lucrative offers, which sought his name rather than his services, he found congenial the image of himself as a devoted public servant and a libertarian leader. Asceticism and egocentricity were both of a mold set long ago; and Murphy, like Harry S Truman, was usually first to do the reminding. "The great satisfaction that is mine these troubled days," he told his former Detroit aide, Josephine Gomon, in 1948, "is that I have never deviated from the path I set for myself when I first started in public life."

So many public servants are new born liberals only to be found conservatives the next day forgetting entirely the inarticulate and the plundered poor.

Three things I am proud of: We were the first to care for the poor during the depression. While freeing a people in the Orient we introduced woman suffrage. And then we authored the Civil Liberties Division in the Department of Justice. It is the cardinal issue before the American public today.

I do not seek any other office and would not accept one. I am content to write for the freedom of man.[111]

Part of Murphy's melancholy drift doubtless resulted from judicial isolation, partly from dreams shattered by Cold War, but the bulk was purely personal. Relations with his family, some of whom opposed his marriage plans, began to deteriorate at the same time he found less solace in the church. Estrangement reached the point in the summer of 1948 that the Justice, who hesitated about returning to Harbor Beach, spent most of the recess in Detroit's Ford Hospital. For all the front of good cheer and happiness he tried to maintain, Murphy was deeply wounded by these events, which probably affected his health. An attack of sciatic neuralgia, a nervous inflammation, forced him to cancel a scheduled trip to Manila in 1948, and even to miss the fall opening of Court.[112] Some of his relatives, even as they saw no alternative, saw a Greek-like tragedy being played as the head of a romantic clan found himself, estranged at home and unable to arrange a wedding in suitable glory in the Manila cathedral, with no place to save pride but a hospital in Detroit. And in the familiar Murphy manner, a few kinsmen believed he was dying of a broken heart.

None of Murphy's ailments at the time were critical, but all were painful and debilitating. Bouts of shingles forced him in and out of the hospital all year. Murphy, as a result, voiced thoughts of retirement, which he might have seriously considered except that eligibility under federal law required a judge to have 10 years of service or be 70 years of age. "What is the use of retiring at 70?" he remarked to his brother. "At that date in life the Lord retires everyone anyway. It seems to me when federal service takes the best years of one's life—years you cannot capture—the public servant should be allowed to retire without reference to disability or age."[113]

Financially he had little choice but to remain on the bench awhile longer. Politically the tight power balance on the Court made retirement even less palatable. "It is much more important for your long-run service here, invaluable to the causes we seek to serve, that you safeguard your health even at the expense of taking further time," Rutledge reminded him, while offering to help with his two new clerks. Though it added to his own burden, Rutledge and Murphy's clerks improvised a system of communication and opinion production which enabled the absent Justice, who kept up with written briefs, to give

Rutledge his vote in November conferences and not to fall behind.[114] Murphy also maintained contact by correspondence with other Justices, including several notes commending the "superb" quality of Frankfurter's opinions, which evidenced a nostalgic sense of missing the Court.[i] Returning to the bench in January 1949 he was hospitalized again for short spells in February, April, and June. The disruption did no observable damage to the quality of his published opinions, but it is nevertheless likely that illness affected his work.[115]

For one thing, Murphy was assigned no weighty opinions in the 1948 term, with the possible exception of *California* v. *Zook*; and two major efforts—*Eisler* v. *United States* and *Griffin* v. *United States*—were stillborn.[116/j] In addition, his clerks had a larger hand than usual in opinion writing and as emissaries within the Court. The Justice, as in his fledgling years, even enlisted a former clerk in preparing his *Wolf* v. *Colorado* dissent. His illness also made for closer liaison with Rutledge, especially during the lengthy fall absence when Murphy was virtually dependent on Rutledge's strategic assessments. In *Taylor* v. *Dennis*, for example, he supported Rutledge's strategy of granting certiorari, despite predictions of stalemate, on the remote chance that a vote of four Justices might tip the scales to clemency in Alabama.[117] Missing oral arguments and especially the give-and-take of personal exchange among judges, moreover, appears to have led to forming isolated initial impressions. Some of Murphy's most extreme options occurred during his final term. And despite his own self-imposed rule to the contrary, he was forced in the *Hirota* and Right-to-Work cases to dissent without opinion.[118]

Illness, in other words, revived some of the instabilities of his fresh-

---

[i] Despite his troubles Murphy retained his sense of humor. On returning to Washington, he had his secretary write columnist Doris Fleeson: "My chief wants to know what you mean by being stuck on another Judge?" Mrs. Fleeson replied, "You know I shall never be faithless to you. I hope you can say the same." Eleanor Bumgardner to Doris Fleeson, Feb. 17, 1949, and reply, Feb. 22, 1949, Box 126. After being rehospitalized he told Justice Douglas, "Fortunately, I am not very ill. The fact is I am in fine fettle. Upon returning to the Hospital for a checkup the nurses crowded in the hall to meet me and petition me to remain. I don't know why but I am fundamentally of a kindly nature and I am no one to say 'no' to such supplications so, here I am. One of the nurses said, 'Oh, I would like to meet that Justice Douglas. Don't you think he would be an interesting man to know?' I replied, 'Miss, he might have been acceptable and interesting 15 years ago.' Best wishes to you, dear Bill, and my Baptist Brother." FM to William O. Douglas, Jan. 6, 1949, Box 126.

[j] Eisler's escape from the country accounted for the first abort. 338 U.S. 189 (1949). In *Griffin* Murphy lost a majority after several unsuccessful efforts to win Black's support of appellate rather than trial-court development of evidentiary standards in the District of Columbia. See No. 417, Box 139. 336 U.S. 704 (1949).

man period—and with fewer restraints. The evidence is inferential, but some of Murphy's colleagues may have concluded that he was "burning out." Besides prolonged absence, his unpredictability increased. Even Rutledge expressed surprise at his objection to the broad language of Black's closing paragraph in *Kovacs* v. *Cooper*, which emphasized that some regulation of sound trucks was acceptable.[119] Against strong contrary advice from a clerk, Murphy published a solo dissent in *Williams* v. *New York* protesting the use of a probation report to lift a criminal sentence from life to death in a felony-murder case. Then he apparently expressed some uncertainty in conference, to which one opponent replied: "You will not ever be ashamed of your *Williams* dissent. It will enjoin caution in re-sentencing."[120/k]

In any event, the disruption was one of degree. Murphy in illness was a far cry from Justice McKenna, whose deterioration imposed burdens so heavy on an aging Taft Court that he was asked to resign. There is no evidence of senility or breakdown, no evidence even that his illness slowed the Court appreciably. Murphy's output at its lowest ebb was still ahead of Vinson and Burton.[121] But sensitive about productivity, he was eager to pull his weight. Making early arrangements for his 1950 clerks in hopes of carrying a redemptive load in the coming year, he returned from the hospital in April anxious "to go down the home stretch in fine style."[122] And, for all the discomforts, there is no doubt that he succeeded. Four opinions in the closing weeks of June 1949 capsuled his nine years on the high court as if in theatrical reprise.

In two search and seizure cases, *Wolf* v. *Colorado* and *Lustig* v. *United States*, Murphy wrote powerful protesting opinions, which Douglas and Rutledge joined, that since have become reigning law.[123] At issue in both was the rule excluding illegally obtained evidence from trials as a sanction against police violation of Fourth Amendment rights. Since the *Weeks* decision of 1914 the exclusionary rule had governed federal trials as an implication of both the Fourth and Fifth Amendments and of the Court's authority over federal procedure.[124] In *Wolf* the Court unanimously absorbed the "core" of the Fourth Amendment—the "security of one's privacy against arbitrary intrusion by police"—into the Fourteenth Amendment. But while declaring a federal right against unreasonable search and seizure by state officers, a six-three majority refused to extend the federal exclusionary policy to the states. State courts, as a result, were free to admit evidence that

k The Warren Court refused to extend the *Williams* rule in *Specht* v. *Patterson*, 386 U.S. 605 (1967).

violated the Constitution; and by implication in *Lustig*, federal courts also could accept such evidence so long as state officials handed it over on a "silver platter."

The *Wolf* case was a striking illustration of clashing philosophies of judicial action. Perceiving the problem as a variation on organic due process in the federal system, Justice Frankfurter, the majority spokesman, took a position that contrasted sharply with his views toward federal searches. The Court refused to nationalize the federal exclusionary rule, he explained, because it was "a matter of judicial implication," taken under the Supreme Court's supervisory authority over federal procedure, which Congress could abrogate. A canvass of the English-speaking world indicated, furthermore, that the exclusionary rule was not considered essential to the core concept. And in contrast to his *Harris* argument Frankfurter now contended that other remedies were available to protect private rights—civil suits, internal police discipline, and an "alert public opinion." If the result seemed asymmetrical, majestic concepts of justice imbedded in due process and respect for American federalism created the difference. Federal rules of evidence were not in the class of fundamental constitutional rights.[125]

The contrast with Murphy's sense of action could hardly have been sharper. Viewing the newly declared rights as meaningless without the exclusionary sanction, Murphy mapped a full-scale assault on Frankfurter's position. He also planned to rebut Justice Jackson's contention that federal police tactics were more to be feared than those in the states; in view of superior federal training methods and lower susceptibility to "Boss rule," he believed that the dangers were reverse. Ultimately Jackson and Murphy silenced their side debate. Since the whole bench assumed that the instant search was illegal by federal standards, the issue boiled down to the effectiveness of remedies.[126]

"It is disheartening to find so much that is right in an opinion which seems to me so fundamentally wrong," Murphy observed. "Of course I agree with the Court that the Fourteenth Amendment prohibits activities which are proscribed by the search and seizure clause of the Fourth Amendment. . . . Quite apart from the blanket application of the Bill of Rights to the States, a devotee of democracy would ill suit his name were he to suggest that his home's protection against unlicensed governmental invasion was not 'of the very essence of a scheme of ordered liberty'. . . . It is difficult for me to understand how the Court can go this far and yet be unwilling to make the step which can give some meaning to the pronouncements it utters."[127] Analyzing the available remedies in detail, he presented a formidable argument that exclusion was the only effective means of securing police compliance with constitutional commands. So the Justices had reasoned in the *Weeks* case; now that the Fourth Amendment controlled state action, had their reasoning lost its force?

The greatest difficulty with Murphy's argument was the theoretical, as distinct from the practical, basis of applying the federal sanction to the states. Even Justice Black concurred with Frankfurter that federal exclusion policy was "not a command of the Fourth Amendment but a judicially created rule of evidence which Congress might negate."[128] On the larger due process issue, however, Murphy landed effective blows. "I cannot believe that we should decide due process questions by simply taking a poll of the rules in various jurisdictions, even if we follow the *Palko* 'test,' he observed of Frankfurter's lengthy compilation of Anglo-American practice. Gibes from his side about the relevance of evidentiary rules in Allahabad and Rangoon may well have prompted their removal from the list. Admittedly there was no substitute for local regulation, but Murphy insisted that searches and seizures were fields in which "judicial action" would have "positive effect upon the breach of law," while forbearance would produce opposite results. The Court's refusal to carry over the exclusion rule, in effect, permitted government-by-example in reverse. Voicing a lifelong theme, he predicted: "Today's decision will do inestimable harm to the cause of fair police methods in our cities and states. Even more important, perhaps, it may have tragic effect upon public respect for our judiciary. For the Court now allows what is indeed shabby business: lawlessness by officers of the law."[129]

In *Weeks* the Court had not been deterred by fuzzy doctrinal underpinnings for the exclusion rule; in *Wolf* Murphy was not deterred by federalism. As he observed in *Lustig*, which reaffirmed the silver platter doctrine, "the important consideration is the presence of an illegal search. Whether state or federal officers did the searching is of no consequence to the defendant, and it should make no difference to us."[130] "States' rights" were not a license to experiment with or to subordinate individual rights.

With almost identical language, but without attribution, the Warren Court overruled both cases in the 1960s. Taking notice of a "seemingly inexorable" trend toward exclusion in the states and declaring that absorption of the Fourth Amendment had logically undermined part of the *Weeks* rule, a narrow majority overruled *Lustig* and the silver platter doctrine in 1960.[131] Then in *Mapp* v. *Ohio* the next term the

Court flatly overruled the exclusionary section of *Wolf* and imposed the federal policy on state courts. "There is no war between the Constitution and common sense," Justice Clark remarked in defense of the surprise move. Because experience had shown other remedies to be "worthless and futile," what *Wolf* had considered a rule of evidence beyond the core of the Fourth Amendment was now "an essential part of the right to privacy."[132]

The aggressive mode of reversal in *Mapp*, which scuttled *Wolf* without full argument in a case that rose on a different point, produced an understandable shock. The *Mapp* decision also intensified the old debate whether the judiciary, by its preoccupation with individual rights and social equality, coddled criminals at society's expense. *Mapp*, in any case, was a milestone in the nationalization of the Bill of Rights and a victory for the "activist" outlook that the Court's sophisticated doctrinal occupations weakened its effectiveness in the criminal process, that judicial leadership depended on relatively simple standards derived from experience. After two decades of variegated scrutiny over state searches and seizures, the Court finally chose to override "dialectical niceties" to establish what Justice Black now accepted as a "precise, intelligible and more predictable constitutional doctrine."[133] Only Justice Douglas referred to Murphy's words, but the Court vindicated his belief in judicial action, along with his pragmatic view that "practicality is a sturdy guide to the preservation of Constitutional guarantees."[134]

Clearly Murphy's *Wolf* dissent ranks among his most forceful opinions. If stylistically it was not "one of the rare great documents to emerge from the judicial process," as John P. Frank would have it, its restrained blend of idealism and practicality was Justice Murphy at his best, making a virtue of doctrinal indifference.[135] Moreover, *Wolf* was joined at the end of term by two congressional investigation cases which pointedly illuminated other forms of judicial action—"passive virtues" and ideological fervor. In *Christoffel* v. *United States* Murphy wrote a taut little opinion for a narrow Court, which upset a perjury-before-Congress conviction on the ground that the House Education and Labor Committee had failed to follow its own quorum rules concerning competency to exact testimony. Regarded by Frankfurter as a sound opinion, "thriftily expressed," *Christoffel* was one of the first demonstrations of nonconstitutional technique to control this contentious subject and the kind of routinely effective performance Justice Murphy was capable of doing to achieve a conclusive result.[136] Yet he came close to smothering the effect in the case of communist spy Gerhard Eisler by attempting to rear another facet of judicial action, radical preachment, in order to flay his old antagonist, the House Un-American Activities Committee, for invading freedom of political belief.[137]

Had Eisler not fled the country during its deliberation of his appeal, the Court probably would have exploded over congressional investigations at a time when liberal forces were relatively strong. Cited for contempt of Congress for refusing to be sworn in by HUAC, Eisler raised a battery of objections on appeal, ranging from procedural flaws to the First Amendment, which placed reversal of his conviction within reach. In conference, three libertarian members, including Murphy, accepted Eisler's allegation that he had been cut off from making objections to the Committee, and Frankfurter appeared willing to reverse on the failure of trial judge Alexander Holtzoff to disqualify himself for alleged prejudice.[138] Eisler's escape before opinions solidified resulted in removing his case from the docket without decision. Yet, as both Murphy and Jackson implied, the case still threatened to revive the *Schneiderman* fireworks, and for similar reasons. Having directed his clerks to explore all tenable grounds for reversal short of weakening Congress's power to inform itself, while he underwent hospital checks, Murphy circulated a protest opinion even after Eisler escaped that became the first known attempt to crack the "tough nut"—First Amendment limits on congressional investigation.[139]

This opinion, which was written at the urging of his clerks in hopes that a strong protest might have some restraining effect on Committee behavior, apparently irritated Jackson, even though Murphy carefully qualified his First Amendment attack.[140] In contrast to the absolutist dissents of Black and Douglas in the 1950s, Murphy expressly conceded that the First Amendment admitted matters of degree, that "the limits upon the investigative process are few, and that even those limits require judicial tolerance."[141] Without apologies to doctrinal consistency, he also rejected "on its face" and "clear and present danger" as proper tests of legislative inquiries and offered as a trial balloon a special test developed by his clerks—the total inroads into community freedom of thought. This line of reasoning, though implicit in *Thornhill* and in later loyalty oath and picketing cases, then had little support in law or popular thought. The fact that Murphy circulated it was significant, however, because it showed his colors as the Justice quickest to respond to First Amendment claims, the one most prone to using opinions for public preachment, and yet the one least concerned about doctrine. Further, his dissent advanced the same chain of argument against the chilling effect on free speech which was followed by Judge Howard F.

Corcoran in his celebrated injunction against the Committee in 1966.[142/1] As an instrumentalist Murphy was groping for a middle ground unencumbered by the antinomies of the preferred freedoms debate. Pegging his arguments to Madison's theory of constitutional restraints, he wrote his fullest response to the Hamilton-Hand-Frankfurter view that courts and constitutions were illusory safeguards against illiberal majorities. "Of course a court can do little to protect against what Mill called the 'tyranny of prevailing opinion and feeling,'" said Murphy. "But whatever the impact of 'paper barriers' upon society, the First Amendment became part of the Constitution. And the First Amendment is peculiarly an injunction upon courts. It is more than that, of course. It is a declaration of our country's faith in the dignity of the individual, the expression of an ennobling conviction that the people of our country will not stoop to the persecution of the dissident. But it has special meaning for courts. . . . *The First Amendment declares a policy of judicial action.* . . . We would ill serve its purposes were we to limit the 'abridgement' it proscribes to the penalties of fine, tax, or jail. . . . If freedom for the thought that we hate means anything, it means that the petitioner's personality, his political and religious views, have no relevance.[143]

"This is a court, not a political institution," Frankfurter retorted in an unfiled memorandum which urged the Justices to deny any further petitions on Eisler's behalf.[144] Even as qualified, Murphy's overt activism highlighted the "role of the Court" issue once more. Justice Jackson, strengthening impressions that he was being agitated by personalities as well as by issues, rose to the bait by publicly denouncing judicial interference with Congress's responsibility for its own conduct, for example, *Christoffel*, as "usurpation."[145] Could every vacuum be filled by courts?

[1] Taking its cue from Madison's defense of the Amendment in the first Congress (1 *Annals of Congress* 439) and from Stone's *Carolene* footnote, the opinion disposed of standing and self-restraint issues as follows: "The very presence of restrictive legislation upon the statute books has coercive effects upon citizens who do not wish to be jailed for their failure to predict judicial results with accuracy. The pervading importance of untrammelled discussion, or the free exercise of religion, makes us less reluctant to decide whether a statute can stand beside that part of the Constitution. The First Amendment does not restrict the exercise of free speech to the hardy or defiant. There is greater room for judicial protection of the process by which democratic decisions are reached than in the results of those processes . . . thus the statutes which abridge First Amendment liberties demand correspondingly less injury by the particular defendant who attacks them. We made that clear in *Thornhill* v. *Alabama*. . . ." Draft opinion, circulated June 3, 1949, No. 255, Box 139. Cf. Brennan, J., in *Dombrowski* v. *Pfister*, 380 U.S. 479, 486-87 (1965). Corcoran injunction, *NYT*, Aug. 16, 1966, p. 1:1; and Aug. 17, 1966, p. 24.

Offsetting his desire to preach were strategic lessons about the uses of judicial power that Murphy had long since learned. Having failed to attract any support for a sermon after Eisler's escape, he bowed to reality by withdrawing his opinion. He then wrote an alternate version urging reversal on a small evidentiary point, only to withhold it from circulation under advice from Rutledge.[146] Murphy was hospitalized again during the final week of the term, joking as usual with the Chief Justice that "whether you believe it or not, I am *not* going to the ball game this afternoon, although you know how much the prospect tempts me."[147] But his work was finished. On June 27, 1949, the final day of term, he delivered a forceful dissent in *Wolf* that was solidly within the modern judicial role, a little noticed variation on the "passive virtues" in *Christoffel*, and a final riposte from the pulpit. Whether Eisler escaped or not, the Court had a duty to decide, he declared. "Law is at its loftiest when it examines claimed injustice even at the instance of one to whom the public is bitterly hostile."[148]

Here in a nutshell was a crusader's credo. Here, too, was a dramatic exit worthy of Murphy. His last day on the Court, as if guided by some theatrical genie, laid bare the unresolved nature of his character—the passionate ideologue advertising the lofty absolutes of the American dream, the pragmatic man of action so untroubled by doctrine that he even joined Justice Jackson's *Brinegar* dissent, which challenged preferred freedoms doctrine for fear that it subordinated rights of privacy.[149] And after the work was done he penned a note wishing Frankfurter and his wife a pleasant summer amid their books and music. The swansong, like the opening, was highly symbolic of an evangelist, galled by the "chains of legal theory." Three weeks later he was dead.

CHAPTER 16

A MILITANT FAITH

FRANK MURPHY died of a coronary occlusion in Detroit's Ford Hospital on July 19, 1949. Although the 59-year-old jurist had been ailing for months his death came as a surprise, and the public response was full of characteristic contrast. A perfunctory air pervaded the official mourning. Observing the proprieties of the occasion, the President and most Justices paid tribute to his virtues. Congress suspended operations for a day.[1] On his home territory, however, the expression of loss was unique in American judicial history and an eye-opener for his enemies. While Murphy's family invited Father Coughlin to preach at his funeral in Harbor Beach—an invitation which the priest declined—the Justice's body was laid in state at Detroit city hall prior to burial services. Over 20,000 mourners—mostly "little people," as reporters described them, Negroes, immigrants, and men in "dirty overalls"—gathered to pay their last respects to the champion of "dew and sunshine." Having died virtually without estate Murphy received from the "inarticulate" a muted reply to his reported death bed query: "Have I kept the faith?"[2]

Dramatic flair did not escape him even in death. Murphy departed from the Court, as he had entered it, a richly symbolic figure. Just as his appointment in 1940 had heralded the New Deal triumph over the Nine Old Men, his departure, which was followed in September by the death of Justice Rutledge, signaled its demise. At a time when national energies concentrated on international upheaval and the ugly whiplash of fear and reaction which accompanied it domestically, the replacement of Murphy and Rutledge by Tom C. Clark and Sherman Minton shifted the Court's balance further to the Right and closer to popular moods. Only Justices Black and Douglas were left to struggle for the governmental philosophy that had flourished in the high court throughout the 1940s. Whether a "Great Loss" to "liberal jurisprudence" or the end of a period of "looseness—wildness" under the sway of judges "drunk with power," as Justice Jackson described them, the significance of Murphy's death could not be doubted. The strength of the liberal quartet was broken. Libertarianism as judicial philosophy was fading into partial eclipse.[3]

The public at large, and the legal profession particularly, saw little to lament in the waning influence of "the children of light." A decade of momentous legal change, in which the Court not only approved and advanced New Deal measures but also set in motion a revolution in civil liberties, had generated powerful resentments. It made little difference that the Justices had been unusually passive toward the constitutional powers of the federal government. It made little difference that legislatures, not courts, had been chiefly responsible for the great innovations in public policy or the profound readjustments among claimant groups in American society. The fact that the Supreme Court had legitimized and sped both processes exposed it to flanking attacks in which losers at the polls vented their spleen on a relatively defenseless body and capitalized on public yearnings for stability and repose.

Had Court-baiting been confined to the thinning "fighters" of the Liberty League or to those who confused their ideology with legal competence, the public censure could have been dismissed as variants on customary reactions, and tamer ones at that. However, as judicial disagreement skyrocketed and personal feuding broke into the open, the widespread negative responses made plain that deterioration of the Court's public relations was the price of rapid legal change. The campaign of the Roosevelt Court to correct past wrongs, rather than restore confidence shaken by the court-packing struggle, aggravated tension, especially between bench and bar, which ultimately weakened the judiciary's defenses against retaliatory pressures in Congress. Law, the archstone of social stability, had become the "New Guesspotism" to leaders of the organized bar. Groups formed in part to defend the federal judiciary now were in the forefront of the high court's critics, and from there disaffection spread.[4] The Supreme Court, symbol of neutrality, seemingly had fallen prey to a new band of partisan judges united behind a principle of positive judicial action to redress the imbalances of life. After a crusade against judicial supremacy, even liberals challenged that tendency. The short of it was that the New Deal capture of the high tribunal after 1937 converted the Court's traditional role of protecting property to championing social equality. And the upshot was reversal of the institution's traditional array of supporting and antagonistic client groups, including lower court establishments, in less than one generation.[5]

The tension also revived the old controversy over judicial qualification. In retrospect it is easier to see how wide was the room for honest disagreement among judges and how small the popular understanding of their difficulties in absorbing great political and social changes into the legal order. Yet, it is striking how uniformly political appointment became the stock explanation for troubles on the Roosevelt Court. Between the thunderings of the Hearst press, which charged "New

Deal lackeys" with leading the country away from "CONSTITUTIONAL government by LAWS to UNCONSTITUTIONAL government by MEN," and the aphorism of the liberal *St. Louis Post-Dispatch*—"partisan appointees are prone to be partisan judges"—there were differences only of style, not substance.[6] That judging is a value-laden art was a proposition easily deducible from the history of the common law and the American Constitution. That federal judges are recruited almost invariably from the political arena, doubtless in hopes that partisan appointees will be partisan-prone, has been the overwhelming national practice, and one reason in the past for the rough harmony between judicial directions and popular tolerances. But in defiance of experience, only a few voices resisted the temptation of blaming the ills of the Supreme Court on one root evil: "too many politicians" on the bench. Somehow Roosevelt's unsuccessful attempt at packing the Court had undermined it. Somehow a remedy had to be found, as the *Washington Post* suggested, by selecting judges "whose basic loyalties are to the law and its objective interpretation," judges who still clung to "the seemingly old-fashioned idea that . . . the courts should find the law and not make it."[7]

Clearly the mantle of impartiality had fallen from the Justices. Rather than replace the idea as a relic of a more certain past, critics found fault with men, not concepts. Prior judicial experience as a prerequisite of Supreme Court service has become a persistent professional demand ever since.[8]

II

The very comment after his death indicates how thoroughly Murphy symbolized the issue of judicial qualification. In the press, editors recalled that "as a politician, he fought with ability, courage and a deep sincerity on the side of those whom he regarded as the underprivileged"; and they generously reported, though with scant reference to his judicial record, that even in controversy "his goodness of heart and sincerity of purpose won him respect on every side."[9] But while an old enemy, the *Detroit Free Press*, admitted that he had displayed "seeds of greatness" as a reformer, the overpowering consensus was that he was badly miscast on the Supreme Court. "There with an air of martyred misery," wrote *Time*, "Frank Murphy sat out the afternoon of his life," functioning with little distinction or grace. "It was not his game."[10]

Others, in substantial agreement, probed for the reasons. Although his "heart invariably was in the right place," the *Detroit News* observed, few disagreed that he was a partisan who "lacked the intellectual stamina and depth of the great jurist."[11] Murphy was seen as a highly strung, "intensely subjective" crusader, who subordinated law to personal compassion. Even the *New Republic*, which argued that his "extreme humanitarianism produced an unusual ability to arrive at true justice," confessed that he had done so by unorthodox routes; and *America*, one of the few Catholic journals to comment, echoed the subjectivity charge. In particular, his critics considered him "handicapped by two conspicuously unfortunate tendencies": his inclination, when confronted with conflict between law and his sympathies, "to make the principle of law conform to his own predilections"; and his "weakness for extravagant language," both of which were manifestations of a fatal flaw—judicial partisanship.[12] Citing the sit-down strikes as proof of how his "humanitarianism predominated over his attachment to law and order," the *Washington Post* summarized prevailing sentiment when it commented: "His special talent was not that of the judge but that of the crusader, and his record might well have been more notable if he had not attempted to reconcile his humanitarianism with a judicial robe."[13]

"Mercy needs no justification beyond itself, but it is often wisdom," the Justice's admirers retorted. His memory would "serve ever to remind us that justice need not be tempered either with mercy or morality, but that it springs directly from them both." A curious disparagement at his death rankled kindred spirits who regarded him as "an intrepid soldier of democracy."[14] But defend him as they might, Murphy's friends could not salvage his reputation as a jurist. Neither a series of articles and encomiums which appeared in legal periodicals after his death, nor the customary memorial held at the Court in 1951, could escape a mold of apology and defense.[15] The fact is that the reputation of few Justices has been more heavily impugned than his, especially in the verbal traditions of the law school circuit and the practicing bar. Murphy, so the story goes, was a Justice whose clerks were chosen by Michigan Law School deans with extraordinary care—for the good of the country. Murphy, so the imagery goes, was a libertarian automaton with a one-tracked mind—"the McReynolds of the left." Decision after decision he opposed has since fallen under the Court's continuing preoccupation with individual rights; but seldom do contemporary judges cite him for support, and in scholarly literature he stands as a prime exhibit of judicial eccentricity. Murphy, as John P. Roche has lampooned dominant professional opinion so well, is regarded as "a legal illiterate, a New Deal political hack who approached the sacred arcana of Law with a disrespect that verged on blasphemy, who looked upon hallowed juridical traditions as a drunk views a lamppost; as a means of support rather than a source of light."[16]

Belittlement of Murphy's legal talents, of course, was in vogue even before he reached the Court. Murphy radiated an aura of radicalism and restlessness. He established a political rather than professional orientation early in the Department of Justice; and following the Jackson feud, professional disparagement spread scarcely before he wrote a line. Even after the *Thornhill* decision reports still circulated that he had yet to produce a significant opinion.[17] Nearly a decade in office, and continuing controversy over the role of the Court, only made matters worse. In the midcentury dispute over the judicial function, a dispute that has divided courts and commentators, professors and public alike, Justice Murphy has become a symbol of the political activist in judicial clothing and of the awkward consequences that result. "Tense, dramatic, self-intoxicated," as Arthur M. Schlesinger, Jr., once described him, he was a judge whose peculiarities of temperament were thought to have produced "a semi-mystical urge toward isolated positions"; and to C. Herman Pritchett, he illustrated how "hyperactive concern for individual rights can lead a judge into ventures little short of quixotic."[18] Few were so bold as to print that the Justice was a dunce, but appraisals by spokesmen of the Frankfurter school came close to it. Philip B. Kurland, a Chicago Law School professor and former Frankfurter clerk, once described Murphy and Vinson as follows:

Neither had any great intellectual capacity. Both were absolutely dependent upon their law clerks for the production of their opinions. Both were very much concerned with their place in history, though neither had any feeling for the history of the Court as an institution. . . . Each had desires for a non-judicial role in government. Neither dealt with the cases presented as complex problems: for each there was one issue which forced decision. Each felt a very special loyalty to the President who had appointed him. Both were more impressed with the office which they held than with the function they were called upon to perform.[19]

The sharpness of the indictments sheds light on the controversy surrounding the post-1937 Supreme Court. Some of the attacks are so contradictory that many of Murphy's supporters frankly believe he has been "smeared" and victimized by a "conspiracy of silence."[20] A germ of truth may be involved, because he has been damned for the partisan bias of opinions which he was accused of not having written. While derided for battling windmills on his own temperamental island, he also was charged with having seduced an unwary bench into raw judicial usurpations, for example, *Thornhill, Jewell Ridge*, and *Christoffel*, even though all of them were majority decisions, and two were supported by leading proponents of judicial self-restraint.[21] Was Murphy an inept jurist, below the intellectual and ethical standards of the Supreme Court? Was he a libertarian cipher, hopelessly bereft of lawyerly skill?

The facts are these. Much criticism of his technical competence collapses under close scrutiny. Any implication that his great admiration for Roosevelt equalled rubber-stamp subservience flounders on his war power dissents. Murphy's defense of minority creeds he detested, even his friendship with members of high society whose economic interests he opposed, belie the notion that he followed personal loyalties rather than articulate public philosophy. Opportunism may have figured in his rise to power as a liberal politician, but libertarianism did not slacken when, as in the Portal Pay or the war power cases, expediency demanded otherwise. In contrast to the changes often observed in other Justices after their ascent to the bench, the only difference to be discerned from his acquisition of judicial independence was that, after freshman insecurities were overcome, his radicalism increased. Public ideals, not personal vagaries, dominated his official conduct so clearly that the more reasonable complaint was against Murphy-as-ideologue.

Justice Murphy obviously had passionate ideological commitments and expressed them evangelically. That they became the sole factor in his decision-making, however, cannot be squared with the actual fluidity of his options, his malleability in concrete bargaining situations, or the gap between radical rhetoric and pragmatic calculations that always marked his public career. Just as he had upset categories as a politician, so Murphy the judge gave small comfort to simplistic explanations of either his behavior or the symbolic place he occupies in judicial controversies. Both the character and the decisional process are too complex for that.

His record regarding judicial traditions, for example, is mixed, partly because the traditions themselves are unfixed. Murphy, in some respects, did not measure up to the perfectionist standards he demanded of others in government. He retained the curious blind spot about his family while extracting small favors for them from his Court vantage point. At least a question might be raised about his conduct in purchasing a limousine directly through Chrysler Corporation connections. His attitude toward disqualification in cases of prior nominal responsibility, while not improper or unique by prevailing standards, was hardly purist. The closest he came to breaching judicial ethics, however, was consulting an outsider, his confidant, Edward G. Kemp, in several major cases between 1940 and 1946. Enlisting outside aid, especially from the general counsel of the Budget Bureau, raises serious normative issues in an adversary system. Yet even this was not the first instance of a Justice seeking expert advice. The motivation so plainly was to guard against his own deficiencies, and the substantive advice was rejected so uniformly, that objections in the circumstances may fade into formalities, though there is no record that the Justice considered the potential conflicts of interest involved.

Murphy, on the other hand, was dubious about the propriety of two common practices—discussing pending issues with lower court judges or with lawyers in the Court's inner circle, and philosophizing *ex cathedra* about the judicial function. Considering his personality, he also remained remarkably silent about feuding on the bench. Reining in his temper and refusing to indulge publicly in the personality conflicts that he felt quite strongly, he did not permit disagreement to overstep common courtesy. Nor did he fall into the easy habit of questioning the moral integrity of those with whom he differed. Though a fighter, and reputedly a voluble one behind the scenes, he seldom indulged petulant backbiting in opinions. Equally important, he normally refrained from the pressure tactics which soured personal relations beyond recall. Indeed, Murphy sometimes acted as peacemaker, as in the *Jewell Ridge* and Roberts letter disputes, for the same phenomenon occurred on the Court as in the Department of Justice: however they rated his technical proficiency and flamboyance, Murphy's colleagues regarded him as a well-meaning and warm-hearted person who struggled to maintain an atmosphere of cordiality. Even Justice Jackson, with whom agreement in the same dissent was a rarity, once observed: "You have never put into an opinion, however much we disagreed, anything that a Christian gentleman would not properly say. . . . I have no resentments now or at any other time about your opinions—just at times disagreements."[22]

In sum, judicial traditions are a cluster of norms having different functional bases in custom, professional ethics, and personal proprieties, all of which are subject to change. The observer can conclude merely that: (1) Justice Murphy offended no tradition that would call into question the integrity of decision, with the possible exception of using his roommate as internal critic; and (2) his conformity to the proprieties differed from his colleagues at most only in degree.

A similar conclusion holds for his dependence on law clerks. Although the exact scope of his reliance on them is unknowable, Murphy undoubtedly gave his aides a larger role in opinion-writing and negotiation than was customary. What other Justices might occasionally permit, having a clerk draft an opinion under his supervision, was for him routine. Only for major opinions or subjects in which he took a special interest—for instance, the Holding Company, war power, Mann Act, or Indian treaty cases—did he reverse his habitual decisional pattern of delegating details while reserving to himself the policy or substantive choice. Consequently his opinions sometimes served as vehicles to lift the trial balloons of others. The Justice, who eagerly sought to attract Michigan alumni into government, also chose his clerks with a careful eye to their writing ability and political views.[23] They in turn developed the affectionate loyalty for "their" Justice that has become one of the Court's grand traditions.

Whether his reliance on clerks was excessive is difficult to answer because working methods are personal and because average practice is shrouded in mystery. Indications are that clerks have substantial influence even with the greatest of technicians; certainly no clerk of Murphy's figured so importantly as did Louis Lusky in Stone's *Carolene* footnote.[24] The Court's rising workload appears to have compelled greater delegation than was considered normal by judges of the previous generation, and the trend will probably accelerate. The important question, as with all "ghosting" in government, is how well the work of the subordinate reflects the views of the superior. Except during his final illness, when the conference itself took command of a few opinions with Rutledge serving as coordinator, there is no evidence to suggest that Murphy, or any other Justice, failed to have command of the output of his office. Consistency of writing style, as well as the protests of Murphy's clerks about the matter, suggest the reverse. Forensic thrusts such as "the accident of birth" came from treasured rhetorical stores.[25]

One consequence of Murphy's organization of the office was that he carried an above-average share of the workload. Numerically he published 219 opinions in a decade—130 majority opinions, 20 concurrences, and 69 dissents—to which must be added 13 dissents without comment. Even considering the relatively low productivity of his opening and closing years, his annual average of 24 opinions was above the norm. Having reached that rate by 1943 he hit his stride in 1943-47, when he was usually third behind Black and Douglas in total volume and in the thick of the fight more than is generally assumed. Numbers, of course, tell little of craftsmanship. What with Stone and Vinson at the helm, many of Murphy's opinions were undoubtedly light assignments. Almost a third involved tax questions, usually decided unanimously and in favor of the government. The tax and antitrust opinions, which were written with routine competence, if not with distinction, indicate that the Justice was capable of functioning as a conventional jurist when he chose. And it is well to recall that even in some of the great cases (*e.g., Korematsu*) it was Murphy who remained close to the ground of appellant's briefs.[26]

In drafting opinions he strove for brevity and simplicity, neither of which is the equivalent of simplemindedness. While he was obviously not a model craftsman, the belief that he was a crude one, which usually derives from a few flamboyant dissents, is hard to support. Archibald Cox expressed expert consensus when he observed: "No careful reader of his opinions could deny the force of his writing or question his competence to deal with legal doctrines or complex facts."[27] Murphy's painstaking analysis of complex Indian claims alone refute contrary notions; and time and again he cut through to the nub of the issues, as Stone conceded to Reed in *Akins* v. *Texas*, when Murphy chastised the Court for approving systematic inclusion of lone Negroes on juries to meet equal protection standards.[28] Strong language gave fair ground for criticism, yet that also presents a stylistic matter intimately related to agreement. Few Justices seriously questioned his rhetoric—sometimes they stimulated it—when they shared his judgment. So did commentators outside. Some spare-minded authorities considered the California racial exclusion concurrences that troubled Black, for example, as "masterful" exposures of race prejudice lurking in legal forms. Even his severest critics concede that his Japanese Relocation opinions reached levels of "eloquence and power in keeping with the best traditions of the Supreme Court."[29] And matching every evangelical exercise were noninflammatory performances, *e.g., Daniel* v. *Family Security Life Insurance Co.* and *California* v. *Zook*, which drew from Jackson and Reed the plaudits—"fine opinion," "interesting and excellent opinion"—that Justices customarily use to register their assent. Murphy's writing, in short, albeit individualistic and pungent, was hardly "below par for the Court."[30]

How then could the legend have grown that he was an intellectually deficient misfit, a prototype of the "gastronomic jurisprude" who judges by visceral response? Much of the answer lies in substantive disagreement. Whether the Court is praised or damned depends largely on the disposition of interests. The sheer fact that Murphy helped to transform the historic preserve of American conservatism into "a bulwark of radicalism" would have been controversial enough.[31] Murphy, by word and deed, was the most radical Justice in the nation's history. Criticism was inevitable. Attacks on the form of his opinions was a convenient mask for dislike of their content.

But guilt by ideological association does not tell the whole story. Murphy's own behavior, his restless personality and his emotionalism on the bench, left him vulnerable to assault. War fever and war fervor, both of which followed closely a period of damaging publicity and open restiveness, kept alive rumors that he was unhappy as a jurist. Furthermore, they reinforced impressions among critical constituents in the capital, the law schools, and the Supreme Court bar that he lacked the requisite "judicial temperament." Exactly what qualities produce superior judges, of course, lacks consensus. Yet, for all the fuzziness of the concept of an inherently judicial personality, it is doubtful whether any Justice was more poorly endowed by nature to satisfy conventional stereotypes of the judge. The matter was significant because his instinctive approach to legal problems magnified the personal element. And Murphy's personality, a basic ingredient of his prior success, was always on the verge of overshadowing his judicial performance.

A person of bewildering complexity, he had a temperament almost calculated to inspire professional mistrust. That he was an honest and earnest reformer, to be sure, not even his enemies denied. That government for him was a ministry came very close to the truth. But, like other flamboyant characters on the bench whose experience had been primarily politics and criminal law, he never shared the dominant professional outlook. Murphy rose to power on an unusual combination of assets—political instinct, showmanship, and ethical passion—all highly personal rather than "lawyerly"; and in the pinch the differences showed. Moreover, there was always something unsettling about his contradictions of character that reduced respect. Part puritan and priest, part Irish romantic and hail-fellow-well-met rolled into one, even he confessed that he never "learned how to live" a normal life or to reduce frenetic energies to routine order.[32] Murphy was always the showman, a moody and insecure man who attempted to hide a tough inner core behind an exterior of saintliness, a lonely man talented at pouring on the butter, as Harold Ickes observed, and one who went out of his way to do it. Words instinctively attuned to the listener, along with public preachment, had to be taken as part of the Murphy style. Radical rhetoric and flag-waving had to be discounted as means of expressing decisions dramatically, as well as of making them, for an instrumentalist with an unfaltering sense of theatre. In the nature of things, men with leaner tastes were inclined to discount the whole package.[33/a]

The Justice's extracurricular life, which spawned the same rumors of sexual promiscuity and perversity in Washington gossip mills that followed Murphy everywhere, also exacted its toll. While the talk was the low and conflicting kind that commonly circulates about bachelors in high office, talk which even he would have been hard put to match in performance, Murphy hardly squelched the gossip by his active party-going or by the female company he sometimes kept in public. If anything, he seems to have taken devilish delight in fanning curiosity. Some of his friends, as a result, though they rejected the construction of psychic instability that enemies put on it, accepted emotional immaturity as part of his make-up. Traditionalists, without begrudging his activities in behalf of Philippines relief or the brotherhood movement, regarded his social pace as incompatible with judicial proprieties. And even those who understood why a product of Harbor Beach could mix asceticism with celebrity-chasing or why the unusually young members of the Roosevelt Court could not be expected to lead a cloistered life, wondered aloud, as observers always had, how Murphy found time for his post's heavy homework.

Other Justices, of course, also had their difficulties conforming to popular expectations, including some Murphy did not have. Practical-minded men who actually met him often expressed surprise at his level-headedness.[34] But all things considered, it was easy to believe that he was temperamentally unsuited for the Supreme Court. Murphy's very person exuded a tension of spirit at once too eerie and too rich for the relatively colorless mold of judges past. In popular imagery, the robe had changed nothing: Frank Murphy was still "Wild Mustard."

Important as temperament was in weakening popular trust, its effects on his judicial performance were overplayed, if only because one facet of his complex character was unusual ability to divorce private from public life. The Justice, it is true, did yearn for active politics for several years, though he rejected one opportunity to return to the Philippines in 1941. His problems of assimilation were greater than most, particularly during the war in which he itched "to serve." "If any experience or knowledge of mine can be helpful," he told Roosevelt in one of numerous notes, "command me."[35] But Murphy was not alone in being emo-

---

[a] Note the similarities with the ideal-type, dramatizer, sketched by Harold D. Lasswell, *Power and Personality* (New York: W.W. Norton, 1948), pp. 61-88.

tionally affected by the conflict; and after a period of awkwardness and diffidence, his discomfort faded in proportion to his perception of a useful place for himself on the bench. The lures of judicial power, observable in past Justices like Taft, who refused to resign lest the "Bolsheviki" and Progressives—Holmes, Brandeis, Stone, and Herbert Hoover—gain control, enveloped Murphy like the rest.[36] The great debate over First Amendment freedoms marked the turn. Just as the Court was evolving doctrine befitting its own new role as a guardian of minorities, so he developed self-confidence and a sense of filling a much-needed niche as their special champion. "It worries me sometimes that I am so inadequate," Murphy observed romantically to his clerk at the time. "For every hour—even every moment of from dawn to dusk—there is before me the God-given privilege to enlarge men's freedoms and make them content with justice."[37] Roughly translated, there was before him the opportunity of extending the work of the New Deal in the legal sector and of responding to needs only then beginning to win judicial recognition. Murphy had his ups and downs in personal reconciliation with the role, but in the final analysis he became reasonably content with the opportunity and prestige of the nation's highest tribunal, knowing full well that his personal star would pass.

Although sheer personal distrust can never be ignored in his relations with the practicing bar, it was precisely *how* Murphy came to terms with judicial office—his identification with underdogs and tactics in their defense—that in the long run was his own worst enemy. The fault was not simply that he believed in "judicial action" or "just results." Legal progress, after all, depends on reconciliation of general rule and particular needs, on a healthy tension, to paraphrase Pound, between rule and discretion.[38] Great jurists invariably have been innovators. But between Murphy and giants such as Brandeis and Black, who pursued the same goals without impairment of legal reputation, there were critical differences of technique. Brandeis, who entered his crusades "from" the law rather than from politics, was a master technician and a stickler for "procedural regularity." Black became an acknowledged "great" in his own lifetime because he defended unorthodoxy so forcefully, after prodigious work and thorough preparation, on the lawyer's own ground. The essential fact to be grasped about Murphy is that, while he was capable of functioning in conventional terms and did so more often than not, he *chose* different tactics when battling for principles he felt most deeply. Leaving legal refinements to his teammate Rutledge in many a vain battle, he *chose* to fight with the same moral fervor and radical rhetoric that had been familiar weaponry for years.[39] And that choice became critical because it exaggerated his ideological dogmatism and made his most widely read opinions stand for the antithesis of rationality in resolving disputes, the presumed goal of all legal systems and the presumed function that judges and practicing bar alike profess. Small wonder that Justice Murphy offended a profession that prides itself on principled accommodation of competing values. By his own proclamation in Supreme Court Reports, he subordinated ideas to ideology, legal reasoning to emotion, and appeared thereby as the epitome of a "lawless" judge.

If Murphy was aware that his tactics abetted the cause of his antagonists he apparently was undisturbed. Over and over again he announced the reigning concepts of his intellectual configuration. The art of judging reached its peak, he felt, when men cut through "complicated and twisting labyrinths of the law" to correct injustice "whenever it occurs."[40] Result-oriented, he did not disguise the fact that "just results" were the civil liberty and social equality which had inspired his energies for years. There was no necessity for a chapter-and-verse recital of his judicial philosophy. Boldly outspoken and frankly instrumental, he did attempt to make the less equal in life more equal in law—and was proud of it. Unfearful of change and undaunted by the "awesome" authority of judicial review, he left no doubt that his prime loyalties were to justice rather than to law, to results rather than to process, to ends rather than to means. Because he had uncomplicated faith in both the natural law tradition and popular conceptions of the Supreme Court as a "haven of justice," Murphy might well have rephrased the canon, Justice Under Law, to Justice Through Law. "My gifts are few," he wrote Chase S. Osborn in 1944, "but my hunger for justice does not abate"; in satisfying the hunger Murphy was willing, if necessary, to reaffirm the maxim he had invoked in Michigan: "We must love justice rather than its form."[41]

"Justice," in short, conceived in terms of Christian morality and democratic principle, was Murphy's pursuit as a judge. It was his style to defend it with all the crusading techniques at his command. That he was also a pragmatist who bargained and differentiated with the rest escaped notice under the glare of overpowering personality and rhetoric. Yet that was inevitable. How else could opinions that read like essays in fundamentalist homiletics be explained except by reference to inferior training, intellectual equipment, and self-discipline? Even if his motives were taken at face value, how could any man who felt so deeply judge dispassionately? Justice Brandeis had been the target of similar charges, but Murphy's own colleague, Justice Frankfurter, cut deeper when he observed:

Your biographers in 1986 will be confronted with many problems—e.g., the problem that Al Smith dealt with, in that wonderful article on the Americanism of a Catholic, and also the problem of a man with a sensitive conscience when confronted with his duty as a judge and his feelings as a humanitarian. Specifically, your biographers will have to face this question: which is the more courageous character—a sensitive humanitarian who has taken the oath as a judge, with the resulting confined freedom of a judge to give expression to his own compassion and therefore does not yield to his compassion, or the same person who thinks his compassion is the measure of law?

What is the difference between you and Louis XIV, who said "I am the law," when you say "I am the law, jurisdiction or no jurisdiction"?

After long meditation and the most merciful suspension of judgment, the aforesaid biographers will conclude that their Justice failed to keep in mind the vital doctrine of separation of Church and State, more particularly in that he exercised the compassionate privileges of a priest when in fact he was only a judge.[42]

Here was the heart of the issue. Did Murphy substitute personal compassion for law? If his unorthodoxy was not so much a function of technical inadequacy as of tactical options, did he offend in the more fundamental sense of making judgments that, functionally, he had no right to make?

For most lawyers, and those who value legal reasoning as a process of objective discovery, the verdict was guilty. However battered with age and exceptions, however refined by modern theories of jurisprudence which admit of judicial discretion but confine it within notions of "legal science," the official theory of the judicial process is that judges do not "will" but merely "reason," an exercise supposedly kept in bounds by the discipline of a professional craft and the multiple limits inherent in the adversary process, appellate functions, and a complex governmental system. Philosophically Justice Murphy accepted rather than rejected that tradition. In action, however, he embarrassed it—much as the freshman law student who queries his professor, "is that just?" and keeps on asking. In place of an ideal of law as a body of norms discovered through objective inquiry, an ideal Frankfurter defended with great depth of mind and feeling, Murphy offered intuition, idealism, and morality. It was no accident that he was pronounced a misfit on the country's highest court. Professionally he was a heretic. Without calculated intent and with only passing interest in jurisprudence, he personified ageless tuggings between law and justice, between rule and discretion, at a time of exceptional judicial creativity and agitation over the proper boundaries of judicial choice. Consequently, Justice Murphy has become a symbol of issues that transcend his personal impact on law. And by the same token, only in the perspective of these issues can his significance as a judge be accurately assessed.

III

The social upheavals of the 20th century have exploded once and for all the myth that judges discover, rather than make, the law. If the secret had slipped out from time to time before, the topsy-turvy legal developments since World War I have made it a matter of conventional wisdom that "law as it *is* is a continuous process of becoming."[43] To have believed otherwise by midcentury was either wishful thinking or concealment of policy disagreements behind a facade of ancient aspirations—the search for infallibility, objectivity, certainty. Though fundamentalists still decry the volitional quality of judicial decision, the fact is that whichever way they decide cases, judges affect public policy, much in the manner that bankers perforce create money. Law, the formal expression of authoritative policy choices, has unavoidable political implications and judges have unavoidable political power. That is why the public philosophy of prospective appointees is considered carefully, why judicial biographies are written, and why the system of political appointment has worked as well as it has. Political perception on the Supreme Court, as distinct from lower courts with predominantly private law concerns, is an indispensable element of success.

There is no secret why this is so. The Constitution is specific to the point of pedantry regarding procedures, but the clauses which distribute and limit authority are fraught with generality. As Felix Frankfurter once explained in his professorial days, "the words of the Constitution . . . are so unrestrained by their intrinsic meaning, or by their history, or by tradition, or by prior decisions, that they leave the individual Justice free, if indeed they do not compel him, to gather meaning not from reading the Constitution but from reading life."[44] Discretion is called for throughout public law. Statutes are seldom free from ambiguity; and not infrequently, the so-called legislative compromises which judges theoretically should respect pass along the issues to judicial chambers unresolved. Moreover, in the hard, close cases, which by definition the Supreme Court monopolizes, the problem is commonly selection from conflicting values and contradictory precedents. Burdened with the additional task of keeping law abreast of changing needs, a judge sometimes must reject "the gloss which his predecessors have put on it," even at the price of unsettling established relationships.[45] *Stare decisis* can no more be absolute than judicial restraint or any other single variable in a process that teems with choice.

The result, as Holmes said, is that "judges do and must legislate." The central question is "when and how and how much."[46] Judicial policy-making, however essential a part of the governmental scheme, thus presents a twofold dilemma—the institutional dilemma of reconciling judge-made law with popular government and separation of powers, and the personal dilemma of exercising discretion within tolerable limits of subjectivity. Nineteenth-century jurists avoided both quandaries by denying their existence, by appealing to law-finding notions popularized by Blackstone and to mechanical theories of constitutions as popular sovereignty written down. The fact that judges in a common law country felt compelled to deny personal power while exercising it was a testament to the force of the government-of-laws ideal. Judges still take refuge behind an immanent Constitution, "the will of the people," or simply "the law"—and Murphy did so, too. But nearly a century of legal positivism and legal realism, with their shifting emphasis from the rational consistency of decisions to the process of decision-making, has so successfully debunked traditional theory that it no longer carries credence. Frank recognition of the volitional elements and policy ingredients of judicial decisions have become the single common denominator of every major school of legal thought since the turn of the century. Only in bar association rituals would anyone today seriously dispute Justice Cardozo's observation that the judicial process "in its highest reaches is not discovery, but creation."[47]

Americans, despite occasional educational forays by judges about the creativity of their work, do not like to admit these truths. One reason why the Roosevelt Justices provoked popular wrath was that they shattered thriving myth. By making it clear that judging connotes discretion, they revealed that there is no Santa Claus.[b] Contemporaries, already shaken by the revelation of humanity in the Court and disturbed by its ideological cleavages, were shocked by the starkly candid

[b] For forthright choosing cf. Murphy, J., in *Hooven & Allison Co.*, v. *Evatt*, 324 U.S. 652, 691-94 (1945); and Frankfurter, J., in *United States* v. *United States District Court*, 334 U.S. 258, 265 (1948).

choosing, the refusal to hide behind the traditional guises which Learned Hand once described as "a protective veil of adjectives such as 'arbitrary,' 'artificial,' 'normal,' 'reasonable' . . . whose office usually, though quite innocently, is to disguise what they are doing and impute it to a derivation far more impressive than their personal preferences, which are all that in fact lie behind the decision."[48] Judicial power had seldom been so honestly exposed. For a people nursed on a mystique of law as objective discovery, and still eager to believe it, such behavior bordered on the scandalous. Even professionals, who knew better, expressed dismay. Judges might make law, judges might seek just results, but never should they confess it. Otherwise, the very power to do so might be lost in a wave of popular retaliation.

To make matters worse, no one was able to replace shopworn official theory with a functional explanation of the Court's new role that satisfied both political realities and the conventional normative categories of the practicing bar. Legal realism had been a negative catharsis, not a positive system; in the heat of battle it was all too easy for busy judges to resort to standing arguments that understated their doubts and overstated their differences. The result was to invite further distortion of a complex process so that differences of degree were depicted as differences of kind. Regardless of the Court's membership, a number of factors made it impossible to reduce the judicial process to simple antinomies, whether the terms be activism versus restraint, collective reasoning versus private principle assumptions of the Hart-Arnold debate, or sophisticated mathematical models in which votes are used to infer attitudes and blocs. The appellate process, for one thing, carries its own correctives against free-wheeling discretion. Intricate procedures governing issue-formation, argumentation, and opinion-writing, all of which focus on questions rather than interests and on reasoned arguments rather than group bargaining or mediation, channel inquiry and narrow alternatives into highly institutionalized forms. Appellate courts, as a result, probably achieve greater rationality in their decision-making than legislative or executive organs, whose processes of resolving disputes necessarily require negotiation, unprincipled behavior, and secrecy which judges must eschew.[49] By the same token, however, Supreme Court Justices are heavily dependent on other actors to structure their choices and, in the last analysis, their power rests on one thing—ability to persuade.

The effect of personal ideology is also limited by competing perceptions and strategies, both among the Justices and between the Court and its constituents.[50] While room doubtless remains for the play of predilection, ideological commitments are likely to be lower and fluidity of choice greater than opinions imply. That was the lesson of Justice Murphy's freshman years, the lesson of the Court's First Amendment gyrations, and if it ever needed repetition, Justices Black and Douglas furnished classic illustrations in two landmarks of assumed libertarian dogmatism, *Colegrove* v. *Green* and *Terminiello* v. *Chicago*.[51] In the *Colegrove* case Black not only changed his vote after having expressed noninterventionist sentiments in conference; he handed back his assignment as spokesman of a majority opposed to entering the reapportionment thicket and thus structured a fateful enlargement of judicial responsibility in the nation's political affairs.[52/c] In *Terminiello*, after having voted initially to sustain police control of a volatile political rally, Douglas authored one of the most radically libertarian judgments of the day.[53] And the opinions in both instances read as if doubts had never existed at all!

The disparity between rigid ideological appearance and fluctuating choices in these and other cases may be explained by a number of factors —*experimentation*, in which ideological commitments are a victim of novel situations; *conversion*, in which judges who reverse tack after further analysis write with a conviction that acknowledges none of the misgivings they have resolved; *workload*, in which busy decision-makers reach into pigeonholes for standard arguments to support conclusions more discriminatingly reached; *a milieu of advocacy*, in which the demands of persuading colleagues and country in pathbreaking cases coalesce with professional skills and personal antagonisms to transform opinion-writing into special pleading. Among the myriad influences at work on the Roosevelt Court, surely advocacy by judges flowered with unaccustomed brilliance. Whatever the cause, the effect was exaggeration of doctrinal conflict among the Justices to a point, it is tempting to say, that outside ideologues preferred. Fashionable though it became to depict judicial struggles as dualities, it is useful to remember that judging, like most American decision-making, is situational. Libertarians had no monopoly on concern for results. Activist shoes were on other feet. The problems that divided the Justices could not be stated simply as choice versus no choice, security versus freedom, or justice versus orderly legal development. The problems involved the

---

[c] On first impression, only one Justice voted to intervene. Murphy passed, and Rutledge echoed general doubts whether congressional reapportionment presented a justiciable issue. Rutledge later changed his mind on the issue, but then cast the decisive vote against intervention because of difficulties perceived in equitable remedies. Conference notes, No. 804, Box 136. See 328 U.S. 549, 564; and Docket Book, 1945 Term, Box 92, Burton Papers, Manuscript Division, Library of Congress.

proper weight to be given colliding values in contexts of ravelled fact. And though it is understandable why those issues generated heat, they were inherently problems of degree for the simple, final reason that no Justice, certainly not Murphy, challenged the basic functions of the institution or the test of its performance. As Frankfurter once remarked to him: "The decisive factor regarding work on this Court is whether a man is completely disinterested or not—meaning by 'disinterest' regard *exclusively for* (1) the result that judicial conscience and right require *and* (2) expressing that result as carefully as the best craftsmanship can achieve."[54]

What did judicial conscience and right require? It was here, in the framework of a narrower conflict in which all sides admitted choice and acknowledged limits, that Murphy's symbolic significance came into focus. To say that he abused the judicial function by indulging personal compassion presupposes that law leaves no room for ethics, a proposition that neither history nor functional theory support. To say that he exceeded proper bounds of discretion presupposes universally accepted standards of performance which do not exist. Murphy was unorthodox, not because of technical incompetence or because choice was improper, but because of the radicalism and outspoken instrumentalism of his judgments. Both characteristics made him a useful symbol in several running controversies in modern jurisprudence. In the public mind he became a prototype of judicial partisanship during a period of legal upheaval. He also typified wide-open choice in a Court torn with conflict over the limits of its choosing. And without attesting it, he approximated the position of extreme legal realists who argue that policy considerations are not only legitimate considerations but more trustworthy guides to decision than the law-finding theories of the craft.[55] Recalling disputes in scientific circles, whether it is more objective to make one's biases explicit or implicit, Murphy seemingly placed into question the traditional object of the judicial process—enlarging the rationality of social life.

The image, however, was larger than the man. At bottom, Justice Murphy had no well-rounded philosophy of the judicial function. What he resembled most was the old-fashioned and, according to popular mythology, worthy type of judge who seeks justice less in law books than through the instinctive application of public principles, private sympathy, and a heavy dose of preaching from the bench. This may have been heresy in an age of specialization, but it was not new. Murphy mirrored an old cleavage between faith in feeling and in learning. Jefferson preferred the ethical judgment of the plowman to the professor;

so have Grand Dragons of the Ku Klux Klan.[56] In modern versions of the conundrum a few contemporaries saw in Murphy's bold choosing the best means of averting judicial self-deception, just as others saw "lawlessness." Many would contend that the day has passed for "substantial justice" judges on the high court, that technical superiority is a *sine qua non* of effective performance; but there is no doubt where he stood—squarely in the native tradition which distrusts "legalism," scholastics, and theoreticians.[57/d]

Murphy's outlook was not necessarily anti-intellectual, nor was it simpleminded. Instead of emphasizing the complexity of decision, he regarded his job, like all statesmanship, as the translation of complex problems to simpler moral terms. Rather than logic, he emphasized goals. Rather than belabor the possible taint of judicial interference in the politics of the people, he accepted the system of expectations that has grown in response to judicial power and drove on, assuming that courts could "do something" to remedy abuses without perverting the democratic process.[58] Unlike Stone he did not forge a cautious philosophy of accommodation out of the complexity of choice. Unlike Frankfurter or Jackson, who had been deeply influenced in the 1930s observing the Court's self-inflicted wounds, he did not conceive of the judiciary as a fragile institution necessarily removed from the rough and tumble of governing men. Murphy was fundamentally an emotionalist rather than a craftsman, a man of action who applied crusading techniques to virtually everything he touched. While he may have underestimated the risks he understood the opportunities of judicial power in a pluralistic political order. And in method he simply applied to judging the approach he recommended in politics: inquiry, first, in the context of history and "stubborn facts"—"what are we trying to do here?"—before worrying about "legal technicalities."[59] The sheer fact that he was one of the few forthright exponents of legal instrumentalism to reach the Supreme Court explains the cool reception he met there, but it does not diminish the force of that tradition in American life or the contribution that he made to the solution of legal problems. "I liked his approach," one elder statesman of constitutional criticism, Edward S. Corwin, commented later. "There was common sense—and morality—there."[60]

d Congratulating Justice Byrnes on his appointment to the Court, Murphy himself observed of judicial qualification: "And while adequate knowledge of the law is basic in the make-up of the good judge there are other qualities high over that. . . ." FM to James F. Byrnes, June 15, 1941, Box 97. Experience on the Court did not dissuade him from the belief that "the cardinal virtue of a public servant is character. . . ." FM to Edward R. Stettinius, Jr., Dec. 1, 1944, Box 113.

This is not to argue that Murphy was a "great" jurist. Personally he lacked the olympian serenity that marked poetic innovators like Hand or Cardozo, not to mention those qualities of prudence and balance which for want of other criteria have become the hallmark of a "judge's judge" like Stone. Professionally he carried slight influence. But it is to argue that he is usually regarded as a weak Justice for the wrong and certainly overblown reasons, that there was a place for a Murphy on the Court of his day, and that his judicial import has generally been misconceived under the weight of his rhetoric and of issues larger than himself.

Murphy's weaknesses as a jurist were a function of his strengths. He brought to the judicial process qualities of eloquence and courage, a deep commitment to democratic principles, and a remarkable compassion for lowly litigants not always felt in judicial councils. He had a keen eye for political implications of decision as well as for the uses of Supreme Court opinions as instruments of warning, example, and public instruction. In subject matters involving his experience, such as criminal justice and intergovernmental relations, he infused decision with refreshing practicality. Few Justices in history had their sights more firmly fixed on "the final cause of law," as Cardozo put it—"the welfare of society."[61] And there is no denying his talent at protest. Dissent was his forte.

These qualities enriched the judicial process at a time of great legal flux and intense pressure on courts. Murphy played a useful part on the high bench as a counterpoise to system-oriented professionals, because he seldom permitted them to lose sight of the law's normative aspirations. It will always be a credit to his instincts and courage that he seldom muffed the big ones. Especially was this so in wartime. Repeating his sit-down performance, he stood fast while most of the country succumbed to momentary passions that he accurately predicted they would later regret. But just as dedication to principle enabled him to withstand his own war fever, so he was prone to neglect the claims of system. The weakness was not that he attempted to reconcile humanitarianism and law. That effort was commendable in itself. The weakness was method.

The contrasting judgments of Hughes and Murphy, both of whom announced "justice" as their cause and savored "on the face" judgments, point to the limitations of reliance on instinct and abstract principles.[62] The chief difficulty is that their content varies with the user. Although Murphy's "justice" was informed by widely shared ideals, in one important respect his judging resembled the practices of the property-minded McReynolds. Uncompromisingly both Justices equated a set of constitutional values with the whole fiber of the Republic, at the expense of other principles and with only token recognition that the Constitution itself bridged conflicting aims. There, of course, the resemblance ceased. Their characters were opposites; Murphy's doctrinaire qualities were expressed mainly in dissent where, as Chief Justice Stone once observed, a judge is a "free-lance" who "can go as far afield as he likes"; and his discretion was exercised mainly in novel situations.[63] Yet Justice McReynolds' answer to Stone's charge of prejudice would have suited them both: "Our ideas may be influenced by some social predilections but they are so strong within us that we cannot consider this a petty offense."[64]

The legal and political consequences of such deep convictions, for Murphy as for McReynolds, were not always salutary. The same ideological commitments that sustained him under pressure, also enabled him to drift into stentorian isolation and the habits of the doctrinaire. There were times when Murphy placed under broad labels issues that called for more careful differentiation—though it is always questionable whether ideology or showmanship was the cause.[65] While amenable to softening by his colleagues he permitted his rhetoric to get the best of him, so that he probably wrote too much. The Court's ultimate sanction, it is generally agreed, is community consensus. Justice Murphy thus shares responsibility for the drop in public confidence that resulted from making judicial power appear so personal.

Unorthodoxy always exacts a price. The certainty that law provides, after all, is an element of justice. Arriving at a just result for one litigant by a cavalier attitude toward means can create injustice for countless others. Using cannon shots instead of "softer blows" also rejects in advance the cumulative advantages of case-by-case development of law. Incremental growth has disadvantages, too, both from the standpoint of litigants and of public policy. But the genius of the case-law system, its empiricism and inductive development of principle, carries special significance for courts having powers of judicial review. Aggressiveness by the Supreme Court not only brakes popular rule; it risks the institution's omniscience in the public mind and rubs against what is perhaps the severest limitation of all—law, and the strategic problem of guiding its growth without undue upset to an established and highly complex legal order.

Solid reasons, in other words, support the self-restraint philosophy. Preservation of judicial power may well depend on its careful expenditure, even on the maintenance of a mystique. Justice Murphy was not unaware of the intangible nature of Supreme Court authority or of the need to husband it. A large part of his crusading, indeed, stemmed from a different calculus of the Court's public support—assumptions that its prestige did not derive from *withholding* power, like the British monarchy, but from *exercising* it according to popular expectations that courts would defend what was right. Much of his self-righteous moralism was advanced precisely because he attempted to live up to popular assumptions about the Court as the national conscience. Supreme Court Justices, irrespective of personal deficiencies, could not afford to slip from the loftiest public standards. The office, in this sense, stimulated already generous preconceptions of himself as a moral leader. His audience for the same reason was neither a professional elite nor traditional recipients of judicial protection, but a mass public and segments of society only then beginning to achieve effective access to and confidence in the national judiciary. Hence, the confidence question may boil down to a matter of whose was sought.[e] So may the question of technique. It is by no means certain that traditional lawyerly discourse is the most effective means of reaching the Court's newer constituents or of securing compliance with its commands. Certain impact studies suggest that great publicity—even the exaggerated publicity over which Justices fret—has been instrumental in alerting both officials and citizens to newly declared rights. And since occasions did exist when evangelism was appropriate, the question whether Murphy carried preachments too far is a function of a larger and seldom analyzed issue—how far a court of law can pioneer legal change and still "legitimate." Roles of government agencies change and notions of legitimacy with them. In rejecting the strategies of the past, Murphy may well have been a prophet of the future, not merely in libertarian choices subsequently vindicated, but even in role and technique.[66/f]

[e] Compare Frankfurter's conception of audience: "I hope I do not fool myself into thinking that when we write opinions we should keep our minds singularly free from thinking about the lay public." Frankfurter to Stanley Reed, April 7, 1943, Box 32, Frankfurter Papers, Manuscript Division, Library of Congress. Similarly, when Chief Justice Vinson argued that multiple opinions tended to confuse the public and practicing bar, Frankfurter observed: "If there is one thing that the history of this Court proves it is that very little attention should be paid to the ephemeral griping of an uninformed laity, and too often, of an unlearned or narrowly preoccupied bar." Frankfurter to Vinson, Dec. 2, 1948, Box 40, Frankfurter Papers, Manuscript Division, Library of Congress.

[f] Concerning the appropriateness of emotion, Rutledge once complained to Murphy about another colleague: "He may feel strongly but I've never seen emotional evidence of it. That lack of *intense* feeling is why he can't see some of these biggest things right. There are times when emotional force *must* be added to intellectual. So I'm all for your occasional volcanic eruptions. They do you, me and all others good." Quoted in Gressman, "The Controversial Image of Mr. Justice Murphy," p. 652n.

In the final analysis, however, Justice Murphy displayed an emotionalism and an impatience with procedural limitations that did him great damage. The impulsiveness which marred his executive career also affected his work on the bench. Murphy wrote quickly and forcefully. One senses that he made statements that sober reflection might have removed. Murphy delegated too much of his homework to others. One senses that he might have carried more weight had he graduated his blows, relying more on preparation and less on public display of feeling. Emotionally explosive, he detracted from otherwise solid workmanship by overstatement and histrionics. The tactical Murphy, in short, was overdone.

As a result, he occupies a discrete and highly ambivalent place in Supreme Court history. On the one hand, while still a beloved hero of libertarians, he is one Justice whose public stature not only declined as a result of Supreme Court appointment, but failed to recover even after substantial vindication of his judgment in subsequent action of the Court. His pragmatic streak and his actual contributions to legal growth, while light compared to Stone, Frankfurter, or Black, continue to be underrated. Murphy actually had substantial influence on the labor law of his period and more on economic affairs and federal relations than is commonly credited. Certain isolated opinions, such as *United States* v. *White* and *Hickman* v. *Taylor*, which appear to have been assigned to him because of unexpected votes, laid important legal cornerstones.[67] Above all, his vote and impassioned pen were key elements in a revolutionary development of civil liberties. The Murphy of concrete cases was far more in the stream of the judicial process than generally assumed, and a judge whose outlook, incidentally, was not greatly different from the relative handful of judges of similar background who have since risen to high judicial office.[68] He is remembered by most professionals, nevertheless, as a starry-eyed utopian whose appointment was a mistake.

On the other hand, the very evangelism most responsible for his low professional standing has acquired political stature of its own. Whatever his preachments lost in legal force, they gained as libertarian propaganda and as political documents.[69] Revered jurists, such as Learned Hand, have demurred from the "benign function" of judges serving as political tutors no less than as Platonic guardians.[70] But regardless of equipment the Supreme Court has never served simply as a court of law in American life. As a byproduct of resolving disputes, it has become a major source of normative political theory in the United States, a forum for the deliberation and articulation of principles that guide, and divide, the polity. The institution was transformed from a property-protecting agency into a kind of national conscience in Murphy's lifetime. For libertarians, at least, he became "the conscience of a Court."[71] Among the most civil liberties-conscious Justices in history, this was not a painless task. Murphy's didactic performance raises the question why, if it was so aberrational, has he not been relegated to the limbo of forgotten Justices where most remain? Did he become a symbol of great issues because he nettled? And did he nettle because of ability to spotlight the law's imperfections, the prices being paid, the values surrendered, those things which men in a hard world prefer to forget? The chore, however flamboyantly and self-righteously performed, does not appear to have been lightly undertaken. Late in life, a public servant who had weathered much public peril without loss of faith could be heard proclaiming: "The greatest duty of a statesman is to educate."[72] In the "Great Pulpit," he did just that.

IV

Murphy, even beneath his shell of modesty, never pretended to greatness. Like heroes of classic tragedy who succumb to fatal flaws of character, he was aware, perhaps overly so, of the deficiencies of intellect and temperament that kept him from the select company of 20th-century giants whose lives he touched. Unlike Roosevelt, he lacked the charisma, and perhaps the cunning, to build a political coalition capable of sustaining reform movements and of surviving himself. Unlike Black and Frankfurter, he lacked the intellectual drive and the patience to structure the central juridical options of his time. For Murphy as a political phenomenon was always a personal phenomenon, a lay preacher *cum* politico who, for all his talent at energizing bureaucracies and mass opinion, had little beyond personal magnetism and moral fervor with which to climb.

Because his career depended less on party and program than on personal force and preachment, Murphy was one of his generation's most colorful exhibits of the power of personality, and yet its limits, in American politics. "I follow no isms of any kind," he told an audience of Young Democrats in 1938. "They call me a radical and a dreamer. I am not a radical, though I am not afraid of a new idea. I have had to face too many realities in my life to be a dreamer. I am simply a believer in democracy, with an ambition to make it work."[73] Simple as it sounds, and with personal ambition added, his self-appraisal contained a surprising measure of truth. The most impressive features of his career were how solidly it fit within the American reform tradition, and how constant he remained to his roots. In ideas and assumptions, he was heir to a native idealism whose vernacular was drawn from the romantic and transcendentalist thought of an agrarian past. In politics he was a lone wolf of Progressive derivation, transformed by ambition and events into a champion of urban minorities and the humanitarian social goals of the New Deal. His very transition from the Hearst-Legion-Coughlin alliances of nonpartisan Detroit to the liberal forefront was indicative of sure political instincts and a harbinger of shifts within a larger reform movement. And if he sounded more starry-eyed than most it should be remembered that Murphy's talk always was more radical than he. Rhetorical excess was merely the occupational hazard of an Irish evangelist who pushed his comparative advantage in an inherited and congenial oratorical style. Even moral certitude was a Victorian habit only a few of his contemporaries escaped. However they differed otherwise, neither a Roosevelt, a MacArthur, nor a Frankfurter would have disowned his animating postulate—men of conscience cannot "remain silent" in the face of evil—or his assumption that statesmanship, in the end, is ethical leadership.[74/g] A moralistic universe, too, was only a matter of degree.

Yet Murphy always defied the easy political label. Although he fit closest the loose grouping of indigenous militants whose spokesmen were the *Nation*, the *Progressive*, and the *Catholic Worker*, he differed significantly from categorical norms.[75] Alienation was not his starting point; neither was Marxism. Violence he decried as "a revolt against reason and God."[76] Class struggle he berated in the same breath that he inveighed against "a socially irresponsible system of laissez faire."[77] Murphy actually had no ideology other than the democratic principles most Americans profess. He struggled to reform political and economic conditions precisely because he took for granted the need of preserving "essential institutions" and inherited values. Even his perception of self, however egocentrically linked to the underprivileged,

g Arguing that "mere toleration" of religious diversity was not enough, Murphy described his concept of Christian activism as follows:

> The true Christian cannot stain his conscience with hatred of those of differing religious beliefs or ancestry. Nor can he remain indifferent to their sufferings under the tyranny of others. . . . To remain silent while the forces of evil are abroad is to give those forces aid and comfort, and this the true Christian cannot find in his conscience to do.
>
> Today, of all times, is not a time for silence.

"Race Hate—The Enemy Bullets Can't Stop," *Liberty* (Jan. 6, 1945), reprinted *Cong. Rec.*, v. 91, pt. 10, App. 230.

seldom strayed from the routine assumptions of an interest-oriented political environment that demands pragmatic remedies and strong egos. And his test of achievement was no more utopian than "doing something constructive" for country and client groups according to time-tested ideals of the "American dream."

Fundamentally Murphy was a humanist turned social activist. Because he was reared to think of himself as a moral champion, offices were incidental to his self-assumed role of ethical leadership. Changing emphases, even contradictory policy decisions, followed inevitably from the shifting institutional perspectives of each job. Action dominated blueprints for a soloist temperamentally disposed to evangelism. His economic thought, for the same reason, reflected the inconsistencies of an eclectic parent movement that attempted "partnership" with Bigness while nurturing the Populist tradition of "sympathy with the pains and heartaches of workers, small farmers and small businessmen."[78] But unifying the whole was a deep humanist faith in the dignity and "precious uniqueness of the individual," and quick empathy for the problems of the lowly. "Trust people," he would say. "Man at heart is good."[79] Over and over again he preached that the free American was caught in de-humanizing conditions beyond his control—"it is our task to free him." Over and over again he preached that positive government was merely application of the Christian obligation of the strong toward the weak.[80] For Murphy, like churchmen, regarded faltering values, not decaying institutions, as the crisis of his time. Remedies, accordingly, would come less from institutional tinkering than from thinking "a great deal less in terms of the Almighty dollar, and a great deal more in terms of the human family living in peace."[81] And in the process of renewal and restoring confidence, he perceived of himself as a political organizer who could serve as a broker between idea men and the mass, as a nonpartisan dealer in the vital intangibles of social trust and goodwill, who made up in fervor what he lacked in intellect or grand design. "Government will be the great friend, for the Government loves justice," he preached repeatedly. "The New Deal has sought to dignify life."[82]

Murphy became a militant crusader, in other words, not because he embraced alien ideologies, but because traditional American ideology itself had revolutionary implications, both in its egalitarian promise and its faith in men. The cardinal fact of his political socialization was that he took conventional idealism seriously. In an act of creative synthesis, he converted patriotism and the Social Gospel into a passionate secular faith that was readily displaced onto political objects because it served as animus, standard, and outlet for a passionate personal temperament. The cardinal fact of his subsequent development was that, during an era when countless numbers were stripped of idealism, he held onto his. He held onto it furthermore, not only for rhetorical support, but for guidance in a succession of battles that would have wearied lesser men, with the result that principles themselves acquired new and deeper meaning. Not without reason, in the Detroit relief battle, the sit-down crisis, or in the *Yamashita* case, did men regard him as a prophet.[83] Murphy revealed to them undisclosed recesses of strength in common ideals, which is the essence of moral leadership.

This process of projecting religious idealism onto political objects, and of refining principles thereby, in many ways was a personal equivalent of the function ascribed to American theology by Paul Tillich, the Protestant theologian, in contrasting European and American differences.

The difficulties, [he observed] stressed by Continental theology, in applying the absolute principles of the Christian message to concrete political situations, were met by American theological ethics in a rather ingenious way. One found that between the absolute principle of love and the ever-changing concrete situation, middle axioms exist which mediate the two. Such principles are democracy, the dignity of every man, equality before the law, etc. They are not unchangeable in the sense in which the ultimate principle is, but they mediate between it and the actual situation. This idea prevents the identification of the Christian message with a special political program. It makes, on the other hand, possible for Christianity not to remain aloof from the actual problems of man's historical existence.[84]

The "middle axioms," for Murphy, served as spiritual and secular ideology every bit as commanding as the "isms." God, country, and family, to paraphrase Francis Biddle, were his Trinity. Government became his ministry.[85] By adulthood, he could no more have spurned those ideals than any man could take an axe to his roots, negate what had given life meaning, and discard his most effective weapon. "My faith is of the militant kind," he told Roosevelt in 1940, while asking for more active assignment.[86] That was the key, more than any single factor, to his life as a reformer.

Moral fervor found an odd, and to many an incredible, locus in Frank Murphy. Irish Catholic politicians, who first broke into national prominence from their city strongholds in his generation, were easier to locate with urban machines than with the militants. Theatricality, romanticism, and false modesty also lay so heavily on his idealism that it was not always easy to take him seriously or to be amused, as his friends were, by quirks so outsized as to match virtues larger than life. Only the most insecure of men could have developed a self-assuring vanity so intense that he could write a journalist in 1935 without blushing—"you may not believe this, but it is the truth that from the first day I was in public life, I have always shuddered at the sight of my name in headlines"—and then in the next breath send him some clippings.[87] Only the most complex of men could have perceived of statesmanship and self through the prism of the great moral absolutes of the Western tradition, and then alternate them so readily with raw humor and pangs of inadequacy. About Murphy there always lurked suspicion that he was a *poseur* more interested in posturing than performance, an actor caught up in his own image as poor man's priest, a man of over-abundant heart and constant pretense.

These were not attractive images, especially among urbane professionals and intellectuals who in the same period staked out special claims to influence in modern government. Collision with intellectuals and lack of credibility, however Murphy gravitated toward intellectuals and utilized their talents, were inevitable because, as a vote-getter and professional generalist, he operated from a different plane of responsibility than the specialist. And that is why his performances usually exceeded expectations. In government, the stuff of heroes is what the Romans called *gravitas* and he called "character," qualities which have more to do with conviction, strength, and courage than with intellect. Because he was romantic and florid in style, the temptation is easy to dismiss him as only a sentimental liberal—too easy. No matter how innocent his sound, no matter how flawed the character, Murphy's judgment met tests of depression, crisis, and war. In a lifetime of wielding power, when many men lost faith and some jumped out of windows, he was responsible for little abuse and considerable translation of common ideal into concrete good. Standing out in his political career were the pioneering of public relief in Detroit and the organization of municipal interests; an administration in the Philippines that effectuated, without sentimentalizing, the anticolonial traditions of the United States; and a performance in the labor wars that can only be described as statesmanlike.

Murphy's strongest qualities appeared as defects after his shift into a more specialized world of law. But even there he gave organizational identity to the civil rights movement and a stronger performance on the Court than anyone had a right to expect. To say that he was miscast as a jurist overstates the case for the simple reason that a standard cast does not exist. To say that he was *relatively* miscast, however, in the sense that he could not make best use of his talents in the role, Murphy was the first to admit. Yet, at a time when the legal order was undergoing a much needed overhaul, it was healthy having a moralist on the high bench who perceived of law from outside the system, and even within it. John P. Frank's contemporary estimate was probably accurate that he was "the most underestimated member of the Supreme Court in our time."[88] For Murphy did assimilate to the judiciary in his fashion; and given his personality, it is striking how the judicial process constrained him more than he personalized it. Nine years of Supreme Court service, after all, is less than an average span. As Justices go, he had at least an average imprint on the growth of law and his share of "finer hours." Of the strong-willed men who have occupied the high bench, how many had the luck to participate in so creative a period of American public law? How many authored opinions with such enduring qualities in the literature of democracy as *Korematsu* and *Yamashita*? And how many could have looked to the future with confidence that so many of his guesses would prevail, as Murphy did when he exclaimed, with ego glowing: "I'll be remembered in the books"?

History will record that Frank Murphy was an apogee of the libertarian idealism which helped transform the role of government in the New Deal era. History may record that as a Justice he became a symbol of larger issues regarding the judicial function in the American governmental system. But it should record that Murphy also was a highly personalized variation of a favorite American romance—the tale of the small-town idealist of modest origins who grows up believing the impossible dreams of his country, fights for its egalitarian promise, and wins power with an extraordinary mixture of ethical passion and common sense. The tale would be truer to form had he been a rustic creature with lyre tuned down and with personal foibles masked. But after all the complexities of character have been examined and the "pastry" has been swallowed, Murphy's public career resolves into an impressive unity. It was a life of unwavering defense of human rights, a witness both to the vitality of the ideals he championed and to his personal credo of action: " 'Faith without works is dead.' So it is with democracy."[89]

OPINIONS BY ASSOCIATE JUSTICE

MURPHY, 1940-1949

DOCUMENTARY FOOTNOTES

CHAPTER 1

[1] Cf. *Cong. Rec.*, v. 79, pt. 3, p. 3,050; "The Labor Governors," *Fortune* (June 1937), p. 81; *Decatur* (Ill.) *Herald*, Jan. 3, 1939; H.C. Garrison, "Murphy's Stormy Career May Find Its First Calm," *Detroit News*, Jan. 4, 1940, reprinted *Cong. Rec.*, v. 86, pt. 13, A-534.

[2] Baptismal certificate, Box 1, Murphy Papers, Michigan Historical Collections of The University of Michigan. Unless otherwise cited, all correspondence comes from this source.

[3] "Selected Addresses of Frank Murphy, Governor of Michigan, January 1, 1937, to September 30, 1938" (Lansing, 1938), p. 81. Hereafter cited as "Selected Addresses." FM to Arthur B. Cuddihy, Dec. 17, 1945, Box 117.

[4] Frederic S. Marquardt, *Before Bataan and After* (New York: Bobbs-Merrill, 1943), pp. 167-69; address before Advertising Club of Boston, Nov. 5, 1942, *Cong., Rec.*, v. 88, pt. 10, A-4025-27.

[5] FM to Joseph Hanlon, Sep. 5, 1946, Box 120. FM to James Roosevelt, Dec. 5, 1945, Box 117.

[6] Daniel C. Roper, *Fifty Years in Public Life* (Durham: Duke University Press, 1941), p. 132.

[7] "Selected Addresses," p. 101.

[8] Andrew M. Scott, "The Progressive Era in Perspective," *Journal of Politics*, v. 21 (Nov. 1959), 700.

[9] Carl Sandburg, "For 'All Men, In All Lands, Everywhere,'" *New York Times Magazine* (Feb. 8, 1959), p. 11.

[10] Quote, Edward McNall Burns, *The American Idea of Mission* (New Brunswick: Rutgers University Press, 1957), p. 1.

[11] "The Physician's Responsibilities," reprint, *Journal of the Philippine Islands Medical Association*, v. 14 (Jan. 1934); *Manila Tribune*, Sep. 3, 1935.

[12] "Selected Addresses," p. 42. *Manila Post*, July 31, 1946.

[13] "Selected Addresses," p. 9; "The World We're Coming To," *Commonweal*, v. 42 (Aug. 10, 1945), 400.

[14] Souvenir Section, *Detroit Times*, April 23, 1933, p. 2.

[15] FM to G. Mennen Williams, Dec. 13, 1942, Box 106. Marguerite Teahan to FM, undated note, 1930, Box 6.

[16] Cf. "Murphy: New Broom," *Newsweek* (April 24, 1939), p. 14; Russell Porter, "Our No. 1 Trouble Shooter," *New York Times Magazine* (April 16, 1939), p. 3. Richard Hofstadter, *The Age of Reform* (New York: Knopf, 1952), pp. 15-17.

[17] Quoted, E.K. Higdon, "Manila Welcomes New Governor," *Christian Century* (Aug. 23, 1933), p. 1,070.

[18] Letter from "Marion," Box 1.

[19] See William V. Shannon, *The American Irish* (New York: Macmillan, 1963), pp. 343-46.

[20] FM to Leo M. Franklin, Nov. 24, 1924, Box 2.

[21] Letters, May 25, 1923 and July 12, 1923, Box 1.

[22] *Harbor Beach Times*, June 26, 1908.

[23] "Labor Governors," *loc. cit.* Joseph R. Hayden to James R. Fugate, April 8, 1933, Hayden Papers, Michigan Historical Collections of The University of Michigan.

[24] *Lansing State Journal*, Aug. 3, 1937. *New York Herald Tribune*, July 20, 1949, p. 16:2. Cited hereafter as *NYHT*.

[25] Chase S. Osborn to Edward G. Kemp, Feb. 14, 1940, Kemp Papers, Michigan Historical Collections of The University of Michigan.

[26] Copy, FM to Francis Biddle, Dec. 7, 1944; J. Weldon Jones to Edward G. Kemp, March 27, 1939, Kemp Papers.

[27] Henry F. May, *The End of American Innocence* (New York: Knopf, 1959), p. 40. *Michigan Daily* (Ann Arbor), May 30, 1914, and Nov. 9, 1916, as quoted in Eugene Gressman, "The Controversial Image of Mr. Justice Murphy," *Georgetown Law Journal*, v. 47 (Summer 1959), 652n.

[28] Photostated copy of transcript, 1911-14, courtesy Dean Francis A. Allen, Michigan Law School.

[29] "Selected Addresses," p. 42.

[30] Hofstadter, *Age of Reform*, p. 167. Scott, "Progressive Era," p. 697.

[31] City of Detroit, *Journal of the Common Council*, Sep. 23, 1930, p. 2,442.

[32] Alpheus T. Mason, *Brandeis: A Free Man's Life* (New York: The Viking Press, 1946), p. 147.

[33] Leland S. Bisbee to FM, April 26, 1937, Box 45.

[34] *Detroit News*, Sep. 11, 1945.

[35] *Harbor Beach News*, June 28, 1918, p. 4.

[36] *Detroit News*, May 11, 1918, p. 7. Quotes, *Harbor Beach News*, Jan. 11, 1918,

p. 1, and *Harbor Beach Times*, June 28, 1918, p. 1.

[37] *Harbor Beach News*, Aug. 9, 1918, Aug. 17, 1917, and Jan. 11, 1918.

[38] FM to "Aunt Maggie" [Margaret Brennan], Dec. 20, 1918, Box 1. Application for veterans insurance, July 2, 1927, Box 4. Copy, Col. F.C. Bolles to the Commanding General, 4th Division, Jan. 16, 1919, Box 1. FM to George C. Marshall, April 15, 1942, Box 102.

[39] Copy, FM to A.C. Baird, Jan. 5, 1940, Box 85.

[40] "Selected Addresses," p. 101.

CHAPTER 2

[1] *NYT*, Dec. 14, 1919, VIII, pp. 1 and 12:1. Henry F. May, "Shifting Perspectives on the 1920's," *Mississippi Valley Historical Review*, v. 43 (Dec. 1956), 406.

[2] Keith Sward, *The Legend of Henry Ford* (New York: Rinehart, 1948), pp. 199-202. Walter Galenson, *The CIO Challenge to the AFL* (Cambridge: Harvard University Press, 1960), pp. 127-30.

[3] *NYT*, Dec. 14, 1919, VIII, p. 12:1, and Dec. 14, 1930, III, p. 6:2. Sidney Fine, *The Automobile Under the Blue Eagle* (Ann Arbor: University of Michigan Press, 1963), pp. 21-24.

[4] "The 1925 Detroit City Census," *Detroit Educational Bulletin* (October 1925), p. 14. *NYT*, Nov. 7, 1923, p. 3:5; Oct. 22, 1924, p. 1:4; and Nov. 3, 1925, p. 8:1.

[5] Chester E. Rightor to Arthur J. Lederle, Dec. 12, 1933, Box 17. Budget Message, *Detroit Legal News*, March 11, 1931, p. 19. City of Detroit, *Journal of the Common Council*, Jan. 12, 1932, p. 3. C.E. Rightor, "Comparative Tax Rates of 290 Cities, 1931," Municipal Administrative Service, p. 707, Box 4, Mayoralty Papers, Detroit City Archives, Burton Historical Collection of the Detroit Public Library. Hereafter cited as BHC.

[6] FM to William C. Lehr, Dec. 19, 1932, Box 12, BHC.

[7] See Arthur S. Link, "What Happened to the Progressive Movement in the 1920's?" *American Historical Review*, v. 64 (July 1959), 833-51; and Clarke A. Chambers, *Seedtime of Reform* (Minne-

apolis: University of Minnesota Press, 1963).

[8] *NYT*, Dec. 2, 1919, p. 17:7; *Detroit Times*, April 23, 1933, Souvenir Section, p. 7. See Blair Moody, "High Commissioner to Manila," *Survey Graphic*, v. 24 (Dec. 1935), 610.

[9] Woodbridge N. Ferris to FM, Nov. 1, 1920, Box 1.

[10] See instructor's report and copy of examination, June 1922, Box 1. Asher L. Cornelius to FM, June 30, 1934, Box 19. *The Legionnaire* (Charles A. Learned Post, Detroit) (Dec. 10, 1921).

[11] *NYT*, Aug. 2, 1964, IV, p. 3:3. FM to A. E. Dale, April 17, 1934, Box 18.

[12] Byron C. Foy to FM, July 18, 1925; FM to Harold Murphy, Oct. 22, 1925, Box 2. Marguerite Teahan to FM, undated, Box 3.

[13] See Arch Mandel, "Appraising Detroit's New Criminal Court," *National Municipal Review*, v. 10 (Nov. 1921), 552.

[14] *Detroit Times*, March 3, 1923, p. 1. FM to George Miller, March 15, 1923, Box 1. *Detroit News*, March 22, 1923. *The Legionnaire*, March 15, 1923. *Detroit Free Press*, April 8, 1933. Copy, election returns, April 2, 1923, Box 1.

[15] Handwritten notes on a copy of address by A. Lawrence Lowell, 1923, Box 1. FM to Phelps Newberry, May 17, 1928, Box 5.

[16] Quoted, Eugene Gressman, "The Controversial Image of Mr. Justice Murphy,"

Georgetown Law Journal, v. 47 (Summer 1959), 641.

[17] Undated, handwritten memoranda; Fred R. Johnson to FM, Jan. 14, 1924; report, Jan. 24, 1924; and Charles F. Chute to FM, Feb. 8, 1924, Box 2.

[18] Copy, remarks to American Crime Study Commission, May 30, 1927, Box 4. Fred R. Johnson to FM, January 22, 1929, Box 5. *Detroit News*, March 22, 1923.

[19] Remarks to American Crime Study Commission, May 30, 1927, Box 4. Alvin D. Hersch to FM, Dec. 29, 1924, Box 2. *Detroit Times*, April 23, 1933, Souvenir Section, p. 8. "Only the Helpless Hang," *Detroit Times*, Feb. 1, 1927.

[20] Fred R. Johnson to FM, May 14, 1930, Box 8. R.H. Ferriss to FM, Sep. 28, 1925, Box 2. Undated remarks, "A Bonding Bureau for Recorder's Court," Box 3. Percy Montreat to FM, July 1, 1930, Box 8.

[21] Signed letter, April 13, 1926, Box 3. Undated newspaper fragment, *circa* Sweet trial, 1926.

[22] Report, Fred R. Johnson to FM, Jan. 22, 1929, Box 5.

[23] See Moley, *Tribunes of the People* (New Haven: Yale University Press, 1932), p. 247. FM to Reinhold Niebuhr, Jan. 9, 1932, Box 10, BHC. Frank T. Doremus to FM, Nov. 26, 1923, and Casey D. Ferguson to FM, July 28, 1925, Box 2. William J. Griffin to Longlay & Middleton, attys., June 6, 1929, Box 7.

[24] FM to Henry M. Bates, Jan. 31, 1925; copy, Grand Jury Report, April 25, 1925, Box 2. "Corruption in Detroit," *Literary Digest* (May 16, 1925), pp. 14-15.

[25] *Ibid*. George Murphy to FM, April 30, 1925, Box 2.

[26] *NYT*, July 12, 1925, II, p. 2:4.

[27] Irving Stone, *Clarence Darrow for the Defense* (Garden City: Doubleday, Doran, 1941), p. 476. White to FM, Sep. 2, 1930, Box 9. Lilienthal, "Has the Negro the Right of Self-Defense?" *Nation* (Dec. 23, 1925), pp. 724-25.

[28] Josephine Gomon, quoted in Stone, *Darrow*, p. 485. Arthur Weinberg, ed., *Attorney for the Damned* (New York: Simon & Schuster, 1957), pp. 260-62.

[29] Josephine Gomon, quoted in Stone, *Darrow*, p. 484.

[30] Murphy, handwritten notes and instructions to jury, Box 3. Clarence Darrow, *The Story of My Life* (New York: Scribner's, 1932), pp. 306-307. Copy, Clarence Darrow to FM, Oct. 9, 1935, Box 28.

[31] May, *The End of American Innocence* (New York: Knopf, 1959), p. 182. "Only the Helpless Hang," *Detroit Times*, Feb. 1, 1927, reprinted in *True Detective*, v. 50 (Nov. 1948), 50.

[32] Clarence Darrow to FM, July 29, 1927, Box 4. Clarence Darrow to FM, Aug. 12, 1928, Box 5.

[33] FM to Bradford Newell, May 5, 1927; FM to F.J. McCarthy, Sep. 1, 1927, Box 4.

[34] FM to Sanford Bates, June 27, 1929, Box 5. *Detroit Times*, May 6, 1928. *Pittsburgh Sun-Telegraph*, May 20, 1928.

[35] J.A. Fellows, "Detroit's Crime Clinic," *Nation* (May 14, 1930), pp. 568-70. Ulman to FM, May 26, 1930 and White to FM, May 20, 1930, Box 8.

[36] Edward G. Kemp to E.G. Chapman, and reply, Aug. 2, 1934, Box 19. Chapman to FM, Oct. 11, 1934, Box 20.

[37] FM to Franz Pettinger, April 1, 1929, Box 5.

[38] FM to David M. Wellenz, May 7, 1929, Box 5. The author is grateful to Henry D. Brown, Director, Detroit Historical Commission, for the data on Ward 21. See Charles R. Adrian, "Some General Characteristics of Nonpartisan Elections," *A.P.S.R.*, v. 46 (Sep. 1952), 766-76; "A Typology of Nonpartisan Elections," *Western Political Quarterly*, v. 12 (March 1959), 449-58; and Raymond E. Wolfinger, "The Development and Persistence of Ethnic Voting," *A.P.S.R.*, v. 59 (Dec. 1965), 896-908.

[39] FM to Peter Quinn, May 15, 1929, Box 5.

[40] *NYT*, July 24, 1930, pp. 1:5 and 20:3.

[41] Frank X. Martel to FM, July 30, 1930; and unsolicited letters, Box 8.

[42] John P.M. Nichols to FM, July 31, 1930 and Joseph A. Mulcahy to FM, July 31, 1930, Box 8.

[43] Leo Dretzka to FM, Aug. 11, 1930, Box 8. Copy of speech, Box 10. *Detroit Times*, Aug. 30, 1930, p. 1.

[44] *Detroit Times*, Aug. 30, 1930, p. 1. *NYT*, Oct. 12, 1930, p. 5:6. See Blair

Moody, "Murphy's Brilliant Career," *Detroit News*, July 20, 1949, reprinted in *Cong. Rec.*, v. 95, pt. 15, A-4,932-33.

[45] *Detroit Times*, Aug. 30, 1930, pp. 1, 14. *Sugar News* (Manila), v. 14, Nov. 1935.

[46] *NYT*, Sep. 11, 1930, p. 24:4. Detroit Board of Commerce, Résumés of Local and General Business Conditions, Jan. 8, 1932 and April 8, 1932, Box 4, BHC.

[47] Alfred J. Murphy to FM, Sep. 12, 1930 and Frank A. Picard to FM, Sep. 10, 1930, Box 9.

[48] City of Detroit, *Journal of the Common Council*, Sep. 23, 1930, p. 2,441.

[49] Executive Order No. 1, supplement, Vouchers Box, 1931, BHC. Joseph E. Mills to FM, Jan. 3, 1933, Box 9, BHC.

[50] FM to Charles Casgrain, Aug. 15, 1932, Box 11. Mauritz A. Hallgren, "Detroit's Liberal Mayor," *Nation* (May 13, 1931), pp. 526-28. John H. Reynolds to FM, Jan. 1, 1931, Unnumbered Mayor's Office Box, 1931, BHC.

[51] See Richard D. Lunt, *The High Ministry of Government: The Political Career of Frank Murphy* (Detroit: Wayne State University Press, 1965), pp. 40-42. FM to John L. Brennan, Sep. 29, 1930, Box 10.

[52] City of Detroit, *Journal of the Common Council*, Sep. 23, 1930, p. 2,441-42.

[53] *NYT*, Oct. 12, 1930, p. 5:6-7. "Schedule of Case Loads and Expenditures," Detroit Department of Public Welfare, enclosed in Norman H. Hill to Edward G. Kemp, Feb. 1, 1951, Kemp Papers.

[54] Josephine Gomon to J. Walter Fay, Feb. 24, 1932, Box 4, BHC. FM to Martin Hayden, Aug. 27, 1934, Box 19. See Beulah Amidon, "Detroit Does Something About It," *Survey*, v. 65 (Feb. 15, 1931), 540.

[55] *Ibid.*, p. 540. "Detroit's Employment Plan," *Literary Digest* (Oct. 25, 1930), p. 11.

[56] Statistics, "Proceedings of a Conference of Progressives," March 12, 1931, p. 112, Mayor's Office Box 1, 1931, BHC. Detroit Board of Commerce, "Résumé of Local and General Business Conditions," Jan. 8, 1932, Box 4, BHC. William Haber to Frank D. Adams, Nov. 2, 1932, Box 5, BHC. Quote, City of Detroit, *Journal of*

the *Common Council*, Jan. 13, 1931, p. 3.

[57] Memorandum, Oliver Baker to Harvey Campbell, "Source of Welfare Figures from Leading Cities," Nov. 21, 1932, Box 4, BHC. Edward H. Pence to FM, Feb. 3, 1931, Mayor's Office Box 1, 1931, BHC. "Detroit's Duel over Doles," *Literary Digest* (July 11, 1931), p. 11.

[58] *NYT*, Dec. 14, 1930, p. 6:2. "Three Months of Mayor Murphy," *Civic Searchlight* (Detroit Citizens League pub.), v. 27 (Dec. 1930).

[59] W.J. Curran to FM, Jan. 30, 1931; and Committee on City Finances to Common Council, April 14, 1931, Vouchers Box, 1931, BHC. Controller to Department Heads, Aug. 1, 1931, Mayor's Office Box 1, 1931, BHC. *Detroit Legal News*, March 11, 1931, p. 19.

[60] Ralph Stone to FM, Jan. 2, 1931, Mayor's Office Box 1, 1931, BHC; FM to Henry Hart, Feb. 19, 1931, Vouchers Box, 1931, BHC. Budget Message, *Detroit Legal News*, March 11, 1931, p. 19.

[61] See note 59 above. Ralph Stone to FM, Jan. 2, 1931, Mayor's Office Box 1, 1931, BHC. FM to Department Heads, July 13, 1931 and July 31, 1931, Vouchers Box, 1931, BHC. Executive Order No. 5, Jan. 29, 1931, Box 2, 1931, BHC.

[62] FM to Frank D. Adams, Feb. 2, 1932, Box 4, BHC. *Detroit News*, April 22, 1933.

[63] *NYT*, March 26, 1932, p. 22:3.

[64] See note 61 above. FM to Department Heads, Aug. 12, 1931; FM to Andrew P. Biddle, Aug. 22, 1931; and copy of speech, March 4, 1931, Mayor's Office Box 1, 1931, BHC.

[65] FM to Ray S. Corliss, Dec. 12, 1932, Box 12, BHC.

[66] Murphy, "The Moral Law in Government," *Commonweal*, v. 18 (May 19, 1933), 63.

[67] "Proceedings of a Conference of Progressives," pp. 114-15. FM to James H. Cromwell, Dec. 21, 1938, Box 59.

[68] FM to George W. Trendle, April 29, 1931, Mayor's Office Box 1, 1931, BHC. James K. Watkins to FM, Nov. 16, 1932, Box 5, BHC.

[69] City of Detroit, *Journal of the Common Council*, Jan. 13, 1931, p. 5. Joseph

T. Clark to FM, April 2, 1931, Box 1, 1931, BHC.

[70] Gertrude Springer, "The Burden of Mass Relief," *Survey*, v. 65 (Nov. 15, 1930), 201. Edward H. Pence to FM, Feb. 3, 1931, Mayor's Office Box 1, 1931, BHC. Irene Murphy to FM, April 23, 1931, Box 10.

[71] John J. Gorman to FM, May 3, 1932, Box 5, BHC.

[72] *NYT*, May 3, 1931, p. 5:4. Telegram, Josephine Gomon to FM, March 10, 1931, Unnumbered Box, 1931, BHC.

[73] FM to William L. Stidger, April 9, 1931, Unnumbered Box, 1931, BHC. Copy of address, March 4, 1931, Box 1, 1931, BHC. *NYT*, Feb. 15, 1931, p. 5:3.

[74] "Proceedings of a Conference of Progressives," p. 112. See Ralph Stone to FM, Sep. 14 and 24, 1931, Mayor's Office Box 1, 1931, BHC. W.J. Curran to FM, Sep. 16, 1932; G. Hall Roosevelt to FM, Sep. 1, 1932, Box 12, 1932, BHC. City of Detroit, *Journal of the Common Council*, Jan. 12, 1932, p. 3.

[75] *Ibid.*, p. 3. H.R. Stackpoole, "Background Data for Urban Current Change Survey," May 26, 1936, Box 36, BHC. Guy A. Durgan to FM, Aug. 8, 1932, Box 5, BHC. FM to Wilber M. Brucker, June 15, 1932; Wilber M. Brucker to FM, July 29, 1932, Box 3, BHC. Paul V. Betters to FM, Oct. 19, 1932, Box 11, BHC. FM to Burnet R. Maybank, Aug. 12, 1932, Box 13, BHC.

[76] See note 73 above. *NYT*, May 3, 1931, p. 5:4. For a full account, see Sward, *Legend of Henry Ford*, ch. 17.

[77] *Ibid.*, p. 226. *NYT*, July 8, 1931, p. 29:5. Quote, "Detroit's Duel Over Doles," *Literary Digest*, p. 11.

[78] FM to H.Y. Potts, July 18, 1931, Mayor's Office Box 1, 1931, BHC. "Detroit's Duel over Doles," *Literary Digest*, p. 11.

[79] Undated address over WJBK Detroit, Unnumbered Box, 1931, BHC.

[80] *NYT*, Nov. 8, 1931, p. 5:8. Louis B. Ward to FM, June 24, 1931, Box 10. FM to Matthew Woll, Nov. 19, 1931, Water Board Box, 1931, BHC.

[81] Congratulatory messages of Pinchot, Baker, and LaFollette, Box 10. Vandenberg to FM, Oct. 19, 1931, Mayor's Office Box 1, 1931, BHC.

CHAPTER 3

[1] *NYT*, Sep. 8, 1931, p. 24:5.

[2] Committee on City Finances to Mayor and Common Council, July 7, 1931; FM to Department Heads, July 13, 1931 and August 12, 1931, Vouchers Box, 1931, BHC. Budget Message, *Detroit Legal News*, March 11, 1931, p. 19.

[3] *Ibid.*, p. 19. Clarence E. Wilcox to FM, Nov. 2, 1931, Box 2, 1931, BHC.

[4] FM to Benjamin C. Marsh, Sep. 26, 1931; James Couzens to FM, Aug. 21, 1931, and reply Aug. 24, 1931, Box 2, 1931, BHC.

[5] Alvan Macauley to FM, Oct. 8, 1931; FM to Charles Fisher, Nov. 4, 1931, Mayor's Office Box 1, 1931. H.R. Stackpoole, "Background Data for Urban Current Change Survey," May 26, 1936, Box 36, BHC.

[6] FM to Ralph Stone, Nov. 19, 1931, Vouchers Box, 1931, BHC. John L. Lovett to FM, Jan. 27, 1932, Box 2, 1932, BHC. City of Detroit, *Journal of the Common Council*, Jan. 1, 1932, p. 2. *Cong. Rec.*, v. 75, pt. 2, p. 1,686. FM to Dudley Field Malone, Jan. 12, 1932, Box 10, BHC.

[7] Arthur H. Vandenberg to FM, Jan. 12, 1932, Box 13, BHC. Budget Message, *Detroit Legal News*, March 11, 1931, p. 19.

[8] Henry F. Vaughan to FM, Feb. 5, 1932; and associated reports, Box I-B, 1932, BHC.

[9] Chester E. Rightor to Arthur J. Lederle, Dec. 12, 1933, Box 17. W.P. Lovett to FM, April 5, 1932, Box 4, BHC.

[10] Detroit Board of Commerce, "Résumé of Local and General Business Conditions," April 8, 1932, Box 4, BHC. Ralph Stone to FM, March 25, 1932 and Paul C. Smith to FM, March 28, 1932, Box I-B, 1932, BHC.

[11] For the Dearborn Hunger March, see Ford Riot Folder, Box 13, BHC. Quote, FM to Roger Baldwin, June 24, 1932, Box 7, BHC.

[12] William G. Woolfolk to FM, April 12, 1932; and associated materials, Box 10, BHC. FM to Clem Norton, Aug. 3, 1935, Box 27.

[13] Ralph Stone to FM, March 28, 1932, Mayor's Office Box, BHC. Hill to Charles W. Burton, Oct. 31, 1932, Box 7, BHC. Fred Wardell to FM, June 6, 1931, Vouchers Box, 1931, BHC. FM to Vincent H. Conlogue, Nov. 14, 1932, Box 2, 1932, BHC. FM to G.E. Bowman, July 13, 1932, Box 7, BHC.

[14] City of Detroit, *Journal of the Common Council*, Jan. 12, 1932, p. 6.

[15] Press release, Feb. 23, 1932, Box 13, BHC. *NYT*, Feb. 7, 1932, p. 1:2.

[16] *NYT*, April 7, 1932, p. 3:2, April 8, 1932, p. 34:1. Ralph Stone to FM, March 23, 1932; quotes, press statement enclosed with Ralph Stone to FM, May 20, 1932, Mayor's Office Box, 1932, BHC.

[17] Copy, Ralph Stone to Common Council, May 20, 1932, Mayor's Office Box, 1932, BHC.

[18] Undated press statement, Box 13, BHC. Copy, Daniel W. Hoan to William Borah, June 9, 1932, Box 3, BHC.

[19] Undated press statement, Box 13, BHC.

[20] FM to Carl F. Clarke, May 23, 1932, Box 4, BHC. Ralph Stone to FM, April 21, 1932, Box I-B, 1932, BHC.

[21] G. Hall Roosevelt to FM, March 28, 1932, and April 13, 1932, Box 12, BHC.

[22] FM to Carl F. Clarke, May 23, 1932, Box 4, BHC. FM to James F. Murphy, March 10, 1932, Box 2, 1932, BHC.

[23] City of Detroit, *Journal of the Common Council*, July 5, 1932, p. 1,163. *NYT*, July 21, 1932, p. 9:3. G. Hall Roosevelt to Ethelbert Stewart, June 9, 1932, Box 12, BHC. Guy A. Durgan to FM, June 27, 1932, Box I-B, 1932, BHC.

[24] FM to August Bastuda, Nov. 4, 1932; John F. Ballenger to FM, Nov. 11, 1932, Box I-B, BHC. Annual Report of the Department of Public Works, 1932, p. 9, Box 5, BHC. *NYT*, Aug. 2, 1932, p. 7:3. Josephine Gomon to J.R. Nix, Box 5, BHC.

[25] Clyde H. Burroughs to FM, Jan. 19, 1932, Box 12, BHC. Stackpoole report, note 5 above.

[26] City of Detroit, *Journal of the Common Council*, July 5, 1932, p. 1,163. *NYT*, Sep. 25, 1932, p. 6:6. Ralph Stone to FM, Sep. 9, 1932, Mayor's Office Box, 1932, BHC.

[27] Report of an Investigation of the Welfare Department, July 27, 1932, Box I-B, 1932, BHC. Copy of unpublished ms. by Joe Creighton, Aug. 1938, Box 55. FM to George Murphy, Sep. 17, 1934, Box 20.

[28] Ralph Stone to FM, July 29, 1932, Box I-B, BHC. FM to Reverend Williams, July 29, 1932, Box 5, BHC. Norman H. Hill to Sherman Brown, Oct. 13, 1932, Box 3, BHC. FM to H.T. Weber, July 27, 1932, Box I-B, 1932, BHC.

[29] Ralph Stone to FM, July 20, 1932, Box 4, BHC. *NYT*, Sep. 4, 1932, p. 6:6. FM to Charles W. Casgrain, Aug. 15, 1932, Box 11.

[30] W.J. Curran to FM, Sep. 16, 1932, Box 12, BHC. Guy A. Durgan to FM, Aug. 8, 1932, Box 5, BHC. FM to Wilber M. Brucker, Dec. 7, 1932, Box 3, BHC.

[31] FM to Theodore Roosevelt, Jr., Nov. 22, 1932, Box 11, BHC.

[32] Lent D. Upson to FM, Jan. 25, 1933, Box 11, BHC.

[33] Copy, Daniel W. Hoan to Benjamin C. Marsh, Sep. 14, 1931. Mayor's Office Box 2, 1931, BHC. FM to Hoan, Aug. 12, 1932, Box 3, BHC. Telegram, James M. Curley to FM, Jan. 18, 1932, Box 4, BHC.

[34] FM to Anton J. Cermak, May 19, 1932; draft telegram, FM to Dudley Field Malone; FM to George W. Welsh, May 26, 1932; FM to the President and members of Congress, May 23, 1932, Box 5, BHC.

[35] Copy of remarks, and transcript, Conference of Mayors, Detroit, June 1, 1932, pp. 12, 118-19, 2-5, Box 2, BHC.

[36] *NYT*, June 9, 1932, p. 3:5. Glenn Leet to FM, June 2, 1932, Box 7, BHC. Paul V. Betters to FM, Sep. 23, 1932, Box 5, BHC. Paul V. Betters to FM, Jan. 30, 1933, Box 8, BHC. Quote, FM to Mrs. Edward Anderson, Dec. 13, 1932, Box 11.

[37] *NYT*, Dec. 25, 1932, p. 5:3. City of Detroit, *Journal of the Common Council*, Jan. 10, 1933, p. 1,933. FM to Ray S. Corliss, Dec. 12, 1932, Box 12, BHC. FM to Wilber M. Brucker, Dec. 7, 1932, Box 3, BHC. *NYT*, Feb. 19, 1933, p. 7:2.

[38] Radio address, April 14, 1933, Box 8, BHC. FM to Fred G. Croxton, Feb. 2, 1933, Box 7, BHC.

[39] *NYT*, Feb. 14, 1933, p. 32:4.

[40] *NYT*, Feb. 19, 1933, II, p. 9:1.

[41] Royal T. McKenna to FM, Feb. 16, 1938, Box 50. Telegram, FM to Raymond Moley, March 20, 1933, Box 8, BHC.

[42] Royal T. McKenna to FM, May 28, 1934; FM to Standish Bachus, June 28, 1934, Box 18. Paul V. Betters to FM, May 10, 1939, Box 70. *Ashton v. Cameron County Water Improvement District*, 298 U.S. 513 (1936).

[43] Elliott Roosevelt, ed., *FDR: His Personal Letters* (New York: Duell, Sloan & Pearce, 1950), v. 3, p. 144. G. Hall Roosevelt to Louis M. Howe, Aug. 12, 1931, Group 27: Democratic National Committee Papers, Michigan, Franklin D. Roosevelt Library, Hyde Park. Hereafter cited as "RL:DNC-Mich."

[44] G. Hall Roosevelt to FDR, filed April 7, 1933. RL: President's Personal File—285. *NYT*, Jan. 3, 1932, p. 3:2.

[45] G. Hall Roosevelt to Louis Howe, Aug. 12 and 19, 1931 and Howe to G. Hall Roosevelt, Nov. 16, 1931, RL:DNC-Mich.

[46] Charles R. Adrian, "Some General Characteristics of Nonpartisan Elections," *A.P.S.R.*, v. 46 (Sep. 1952), 766-76.

[47] FM to Charles Casgrain, Aug. 15, 1932; copy, Dudley Field Malone to Louis Howe, April 30, 1932; quote, FM to Dudley Field Malone, May 6, 1932, Box 11.

[48] FM to James Roosevelt, Dec. 5, 1945, Box 117. Address, "The Procession of Forgotten Men," Nov. 7, 1932, Box 8, 1933, BHC. FM to William J. Davitt, April 6, 1932, Box 11.

[49] Frank Freidel, *Franklin D. Roosevelt: The Triumph* (Boston: Little, Brown, 1956), pp. 284-85; G. Hall Roosevelt to FDR, Feb. 20, 1932, RL:DNC-Mich. *NYT*, April 10, 1932, p. 3:1. Telegram, FM to Charles E. Coughlin, April 18, 1932, Box 11.

[50] Freidel, *Roosevelt*, p. 285. G. Hall Roosevelt to FDR, March 7, 1932, RL:DNC-Mich. Farley to FM, April 11 and May 3, 1932, Box 11.

[51] G. Hall Roosevelt to FDR, Feb. 20 and April 19, 1932, RL:DNC-Mich. Cf. Elliott Roosevelt, *FDR*, pp. 258-59.

[52] FM to Charles Casgrain, Aug. 15, 1932, Box 11. "The Procession of Forgotten Men," note 48 above.

[53] Frank X. Martel to FM, Nov. 17, 1932, Box 1, BHC. Quotes, FM to Casgrain, Aug. 15, 1932 and FM to W.J. Niederpruen, Aug. 12, 1932, Box 11.

[54] G. Hall Roosevelt to FDR, April 19, 1932 and G. Hall Roosevelt to Howe, undated, RL:DNC-Mich.

[55] G. Hall Roosevelt to Howe, undated; and Howe to G. Hall Roosevelt, Sep. 30, 1932, RL:DNC-Mich. FDR to FM, Nov. 2, 1932 and G. Hall Roosevelt to Howe, Oct. 24, 1932, RL:Group 12, Governor Roosevelt file. Telegram, Patrick H. O'Brien to FDR, Nov. 9, 1932, RL:DNC-Mich.

[56] Telegram, FM to FDR, Nov. 9, 1932, Box 11. FM to Benjamin F. Comfort, Nov. 15, 1932, Box 4, BHC.

[57] Moley, *After Seven Years* (New York: Harper, 1939), p. 124. G. Hall Roosevelt to FDR, filed April 7, 1933, RL: President's Personal File—285. *Philippines Herald* (Manila), April 8, 1933.

[58] See notes 41 and 42 above. Also FM to Homer S. Cummings, April 19, 1933; telegram, John L. Lovett to Royal T. McKenna, March 6, 1933; telegram, FM to James Couzens, May 26, 1933, Box 8, BHC.

[59] Copy, Frank Couzens to Joseph Steidle, July 12, 1933, Box 8, BHC.

[60] *Detroit Free Press*, May 27, 1936, p. 10.

[61] *Detroit Labor News* and *Detroit Times*, April 22, 1933.

[62] *Detroit Times*, April 22, 1933; *Marquette Daily Mining Journal*, Oct. 22, 1932; *Detroit Times*, April 20, 1933; address, "The Procession of Forgotten Men."

[63] FM to C.N. Maycock, April 12, 1932, Box 2, 1932, BHC.

[64] FM to Arthur J. Lederle, Jan. 15, 1934; Rightor to Arthur J. Lederle, Dec. 12, 1933, Box 17.

[65] FM to Bowers, Feb. 28, 1940, Box 89.

[66] Radio address, Oct. 31, 1931, Box 1, 1931, BHC.

CHAPTER 4

[1] W. Cameron Forbes to FDR, April 10, 1933, Roosevelt Library: Official Files 400—Philippine Islands; hereafter cited as RL:OF-400-PI.

[2] Hayden to James R. Fugate, April 8, 1933; and Hayden to John A. Hackett, May 17, 1933, Hayden Papers, Michigan Historical Collections.

[3] Hayden to James R. Fugate, April 8, 1933; and May 12, 1933, Hayden Papers.

[4] Speech materials, undated. Press release, Dec. 16, 1934, Box 22. This chapter and the next are heavily indebted to three excellent studies: Joseph R. Hayden, *The Philippines: A Study in National Development* (New York: Macmillan, 1942); George E. Taylor, *The Philippines and the United States* (New York: Praeger, 1964); and Theodore Friend, *Between Two Empires: The Ordeal of the Philippines, 1929-1946* (New Haven: Yale University Press, 1965).

[5] *NYT*, June 16, 1933, p. 4:2. José Gil to Charles W. Franks, June 28, 1933, Box 13.

[6] Draft of cable, Evett D. Hester to FM, Aug. 5, 1933, Box 14.

[7] Joseph R. Hayden, "The Philippine Public Schools; A Brief Appraisal," Box V, Hayden Papers. Evett D. Hester to FM, Aug. 5, 1933, Box 14.

[8] Ralston Hayden, "China, Japan and the Philippines," *Foreign Affairs*, v. 11 (July 1933), 711-15. See Taylor, *Philippines and U.S.*, pp. 81-85; and Friend, *Between Two Empires*, ch. 2.

[9] Quoted, *Philippines Herald* (Manila), June 15, 1933, p. 1.

[10] Friend, *Between Two Empires*, p. 2.

[11] Copy, Newton D. Baker to Francis B. Harrison, Aug. 18, 1916, Box 16.

[12] George A. Malcolm, *The Commonwealth of the Philippines* (New York: Appleton-Century Company, 1936), pp. 68, 77-81. Copy, Frank McIntyre to Henry L. Stimson, June 16, 1926, Box 16. For example, see Evett D. Hester to FM, Sep. 16, 1933, Box 15.

[13] *Ibid.*, Box 15. Copy, Frank McIntyre to Henry L. Stimson, June 24, 1926, Box 16. Robert Aura Smith, *Philippine Free-*

dom (New York: Columbia University Press, 1958), pp. 15-17, 31-32.

[14] *Ibid.*, pp. 15-17, 31-32. Joseph R. Hayden to Evett D. Hester, Sep. 29, 1933, Hayden Papers. Copy, Frank McIntyre to Henry L. Stimson, June 24, 1926; Memorandum, Judge Advocate General to Chief, Bureau of Insular Affairs, Feb. 2, 1933, Box 16. Cable, FM to Creed F. Cox, Nov. 25, 1933, Box 15. Friend, *Between Two Empires*, p. 169.

[15] *NYT*, Jan. 14, 1933, p. 6; and Jan. 18, 1933, p. 2:5.

[16] Evett D. Hester, "Notes on the Hare-Hawes-Cutting Bill," undated, Box 22. Cable, FM to Creed F. Cox, Nov. 28, 1933, Box 15.

[17] Copy, Frank McIntyre to Henry L. Stimson, Dec. 1, 1927, Box 16. Taylor, *Philippines*, pp. 81-85.

[18] Hester to Governor General, Sep. 1, 1931, Box 12. "Notes on the Hare-Hawes-Cutting Bill," undated, p. 19, Box 22. Cable, FM to Creed F. Cox, Nov. 28, 1933, Box 15.

[19] Cable, FM to Creed F. Cox, Dec. 1, 1933, Box 16.

[20] See Grayson Kirk, *Philippines Independence* (New York: Farrar & Rinehart, 1936); Friend, *Between Two Empires*, ch. 5.

[21] *Ibid. NYT*, Nov. 26, 1933, p. 3:1. Norman H. Hill to Joseph R. Hayden, July 22, 1933, Hayden Papers.

[22] *Ibid.*, Hayden Papers. *NYT*, June 16, 1933, p. 4:2.

[23] Roosevelt Library: President's Personal File, Press Conference, v. 1 (April 28, 1933), 203. *Florida Times-Union* (Jacksonville), April 22, 1933. Roosevelt letter, enclosed George H. Dern to FM, May 13, 1933, Box 13.

[24] *Philippines Free Press* (Manila), Nov. 30, 1935. John J. Burke to FM, May 6, 1933, Box 13.

[25] *Manila Mail*, Aug. 21, 1933. FM to John Murphy, Sep. 19, 1933, Box 15. FM to Sam Ledner, Aug. 10, 1933, Box 14.

[26] *Manila Daily Bulletin*, June 15, 1933. Gouverneur Frank Mosher to Joseph R. Hayden, July 20, 1933, Hayden Papers.

FM to George Renchard, Aug. 14, 1933, Box 14.

[27] FM to Frank L. Riordan, undated, Box 14. FM to Homer S. Cummings, April 2, 1934, Box 18. FM to John Murphy, Sep. 19, 1933, Box 15.

[28] *Philippines Herald*, June 16, 1933; *La Opinion* (Manila), June 15, 1933.

[29] *Shanghai Evening Post & Mercury*, June 9, 1933; *Japan Chronicle* (Kobe), June 7, 1933.

[30] Trans., *La Vanguardia* (Manila), June 16, 1933. Manuel Roxas to FM, July 19, 1933, Box 14.

[31] Inaugural address, FM to Secretary of War, June 16, 1933, Box 13. Also, *Manila Daily Bulletin*, June 15, 1933, p. 3. First message to Philippines Legislature, *Philippines Herald*, July 17, 1933. Louis J. Van Shaick to FM, July 17, 1933, Box 14. *Manila Daily Bulletin*, July 18, 1933.

[32] Quote, Inaugural address, *loc.cit.;* *Manila Tribune*, Jan. 20, 1934.

[33] First message to Philippines Legislature, *loc.cit.*, note 31 above.

[34] Friend, *Between Two Empires*, p. 146. *La Vanguardia*, July 14, 1933.

[35] Cable, FM to Creed F. Cox, Dec. 1, 1933, Box 16.

[36] Quoted, *NYT*, Jan. 14, 1933, p. 12:1.

[37] FM to José M. Albertson, May 10, 1933, Box 13. Joseph R. Hayden to James R. Fugate, May 3, 1933, Hayden Papers. Cable, FM to Cox, Dec. 1, 1933, Box 16.

[38] Inaugural address and first message to Philippines Legislature, *loc.cit.*, note 31 above. *China Press* (Shanghai), June 10, 1933. Gouverneur Frank Mosher to Joseph R. Hayden, Nov. 4, 1933, Hayden Papers.

[39] Francis LeJ. Parker to FM, May 10, 1933, Box 13. Unsigned personal memo, April 1, 1933, Box 12.

[40] Louis J. Van Shaick to FM, July 3 and July 5, 1933, Box 13. Council of State Minutes, July 24, 1933, Box 14. FM to Charles W. Franks, Dec. 30, 1935, Box 31.

[41] Memorandum, Edward G. Kemp to author [Oct. 1961]; J. Weldon Jones to FM, Dec. 9, 1936, Box 39. FM to Kemp, Sep. 1, 1936, Box 37. The author is grateful to Professor Alejandro Fernandez of the University of the Philippines for sharpening these concepts.

[42] John J. Burke to FM, May 16, 1933; Council of State Minutes, June 21, 1933, Box 13. Minutes of July 24, 1933, Box 14. Cabinet Minutes, Sep. 12, 1934, Box 20.

[43] Quezon to FM, July 23, 1934, Box 19.

[44] Gouverneur Frank Mosher to Joseph R. Hayden, July 20, 1933; Charles E. Griffith to Hayden, Nov. 7, 1933; letter to Hayden, April 27, 1934; and Hayden to Frank L. Crone, Feb. 27, 1934, Hayden Papers.

[45] Hayden to Herbert Lyons, Jan. 16, 1934; Hayden to Herbert G. Watkins, March 1, 1934; and Charles E. Griffith to Hayden, Nov. 7, 1933, Hayden Papers.

[46] FM to John Murphy, Sep. 19, 1933, Box 15. Council of State Minutes, July 24, 1933, Box 14. Cabinet Minutes, Dec. 12, 1934, Box 21.

[47] *Manila Daily Bulletin*, July 28, 1933; and Feb. 3, 1934. Executive Order No. 437, Aug. 18, 1933; Budget Circular No. 5, April 17, 1934, Box IV, Hayden Papers. Cabinet Minutes, Dec. 20, 1933, Box 16. Quezon remark, J. Weldon Jones to FM, June 7, 1936, Box 36. Also, see *NYT*, Dec. 24, 1933, p. 8:5; and Hayden, *Philippines*, pp. 294-96.

[48] Council of State Minutes, June 21, 1933, Box 13. Minutes of July 24, 1933, Box 14. FM to Joaquin Elizalde, Oct. 10, 1934, Box 20. Edward G. Kemp to FM, July 9, 1935, Box 26.

[49] Evett D. Hester to FM, Feb. 20, 1935, Box 24. Press release [1934], Box 16. Narrative Report of Department of Public Education, Alejandro Albertson to Joseph R. Hayden, Sep. 16, 1935, Box V, Hayden Papers.

[50] FM to Millard E. Tydings, Sep. 4, 1934, Box 20. Press release, undated, *circa* 1934, Box 16. J. Weldon Jones to FM, "Figures on Philippine Government Finance," Oct. 25, 1935, Box 29. Joseph R. Hayden to Herbert Lyons, Jan. 16, 1934, Hayden Papers.

[51] *Manila Daily Bulletin*, July 18, 1933. FM to Evett D. Hester, April 23, 1934, Box 18. *La Vanguardia*, dateline Manila, Dec. 26, 1933.

52 FM to McIntyre, Feb. 19, 1934, RL: OF-400-PI.

53 Message to the 10th Philippines Legislature, *Philippines Herald*, July 17, 1934, p. 6:4. *Philippines Herald*, March 20, 1934.

54 Hayden to Harry J. Hayden, Oct. 30, 1934; and quote, Hayden to Jesse H. Reeves, June 14, 1934, Hayden Papers.

55 *NYT*, March 2, 1935, p. 12:1. See U.S. Congress, *Annual Report of the Governor General of the Philippine Islands: 1934*, 74th Cong., 2d Sess., House Doc. 411, p. 4.

56 For details see *Philippines Herald*, July 17, 1933; and Aug. 10, 1935. *NYT*, Dec. 3, 1933, p. 8:1. Executive Order No. 501, Aug. 24, 1934, Box 19.

57 Cabinet Minutes, July 31, 1935; and FM to Charles Edward Russell, Aug. 5, 1935, Box 27.

58 Press release, Dec. 26, 1934. George C. Dunham to FM, March 14, 1934, Box 22. Dunham to FM, June 20, 1935, Box 26. For general accounts see *NYT*, Dec. 3, 1933, p. 8:1, and Aug. 19, 1934, p. 2:1. Message to 10th Philippines Legislature, *loc.cit.*, note 53 above. Hayden, *Philippines*, pp. 648-66; and the *Annual Reports of the Governor General* for 1934 and 1935. The best sources are Hayden, *loc.cit.*; and memorandum, "Public Health and Welfare Activities, 1932-1935," George C. Dunham to FM, Oct. 26, 1935, Box 29.

59 *Ibid.*, Box 29. Notes of Staff Meeting, July 22, 1934, Box 19. FM to Manuel L. Quezon, July 6, 1935, Box 26. Cable, FM to D. C. McDonald, Aug. 24, 1935; and quote, FM to Charles Edward Russell, Aug. 5, 1935, Box 27. *Manila Daily Bulletin*, July 24, 1935.

60 Hayden to Jesse S. Reeves, Feb. 9, 1934, Hayden Papers. Memorandum by Hayden, enclosed, F. LeJ. Parker to FM, May 9, 1933, Box 13.

61 *Ibid.*, Box 13. Hayden to FM, Jan. 22, 1934, Box 17. Louis J. Van Shaick to FM, Aug. 5, 1933, Sep. 7 and 8, 1933, Box 14. Hayden to Jesse H. Reeves, Feb. 9, 1934, Hayden Papers. FM to Secretary of Interior, Feb. 19, 1934, Box 17.

62 *Ibid.*, Box 17. Hayden to James R.

Fugate, May 31, 1934; Hayden to Harry J. Hayden, Oct. 30, 1934; and Hayden to Caroline Spencer, Oct. 31, 1933, Hayden Papers.

63 Hayden to Frank L. Crone, Feb. 27, 1934; Hayden to Herbert G. Watkins, March 1, 1934; Hayden to Eugene A. Gilmore, July 11, 1934; and quote, Hayden to Reeves, Feb. 9, 1934, Hayden Papers.

64 Hayden to FM, Nov. 27, 1935, Box 30. Hayden to Willis J. Abbot, May 15, 1934; and Hayden to James K. Pollock, Jr., July 2, 1934, Hayden Papers.

65 Dunham to FM, April 14, 1934, Box 18. Memorandum, Dunham to FM, Oct. 26, 1935, Box 29. Dunham to FM, Sep. 18, 1934, Box 20. Dunham to FM, March 16, 1934, Box 17.

66 Undated memo, "Brief Statement of Social Welfare Activities in the Philippines Today," Box 12. Dunham to FM, March 8, 1934; and March 16, 1934, Box 17.

67 Executive Order No. 436, Aug. 18, 1933, Box 14. Stanton Youngberg to FM, Feb. 17, 1934, Box 17.

68 Dunham to Murphy, Nov. 10, 1933, Box 15; and Dec. 14, 1933, Box 16.

69 FM to Dunham, Feb. 16, 1934, Box 17; and Aug. 30, 1934, Box 19; and Cabinet Minutes, Oct. 20, 1934, Box 20. Smith, *Philippine Freedom*, p. 61.

70 Memos: Dunham to FM, Dec. 14, 1933, Box 16; June 8, 1935, Box 26; Oct. 26, 1935, Box 29.

71 Dunham to FM, June 17, 1935; and FM to Quezon, July 6, 1935, Box 26.

72 Dunham to FM, Sep. 18, 1934, Box 20. Thurman Arnold to FM, Jan. 4, 1935, Box 23. Edward G. Kemp to FM, June 14, 1935, Box 26. FM to Henry A. Wallace, March 14, 1935, Box 24. *United States* v. *Butler*, 297 U.S. 1 (1936). Stanton Youngberg to FM, Feb. 17, 1934, Box 17. Friend, *Between Two Empires*, pp. 269-70.

73 Dunham to FM, Oct. 26, 1935, p. 6, Box 29.

74 FM to Millard Tydings, July 16, 1935, Box 27. *Annual Report of the Governor General: 1934*, p. 4. *Manila Daily Bulletin*, July 23, 1934.

[75] *Manila Daily Bulletin,* Oct. 31, 1934. Notes of staff meeting, July 27, 1934, Box 19.

[76] FM to Roger Baldwin, Dec. 23, 1933, Box 16. FM to Secretary of the Interior, March 3, 1934, Box 17. Quote, *Philippines Herald,* Feb. 23, 1934.

[77] Smith, *Philippine Freedom,* p. 25. See memo and attached materials, Kemp to FM, Oct. 1, 1935, Box 28. Dunham to FM, Aug. 15, 1934; and J. E. Kiernan, Aug. 17, 1934, Box 19. William A. Fletcher to FM, Nov. 24, 1934, Box 21.

[78] *Philippines Herald,* June 15, 1935.

[79] *Manila Daily Bulletin,* May 24, 1934. *Philippines Herald,* Jan. 12, 1935. *Manila Tribune,* Aug. 31, 1933. *NYT,* April 13, 1934, p. 7:3.

[80] FM to Jones, May 25, 1936, Box 36.

[81] *La Vanguardia,* June 10, 1935; and Dec. 21, 1933. *Philippines Herald,* Nov. 1, 1935.

[82] Memorandum, "Conversations between the Secretary of War and Senator Quezon," Dec. 18, 1933, RL:OF-400-PI.

[83] *Philippines Herald,* June 22, 1934. *La Vanguardia,* Dec. 21, 1933. Quezon, quoted in *Manila Tribune,* Jan. 22, 1935. See *Philippines Herald,* March 28, 1934; and *Manila Tribune,* Nov. 17, 1934. Quote, Juan F. Hilario, *Manila Daily Bulletin,* March 28, 1934.

CHAPTER 5

[1] FM to Homer S. Cummings, June 2, 1934, Box 18. FM to Farley, May 16, 1933, Box 13.

[2] See for example, John D. Dingell to FM, May 12, 1934, Box 18. Thomas F. McAllister to FM, March 28, 1934; Frank X. Martel to FM, Jan. 26, 1934; and Kavanagh to FM, Feb. 12, 1934, Box 17.

[3] FM to James A. Farley, May 23, 1933; and George Bushnell to FM, June 30, 1933, Box 13. Telegram, FM to Arthur J. Lacy, Sep. 9, 1934, Box 20. Quote, FM to James K. Watkins, Oct. 8, 1935, Box 28.

[4] Telegram, FM to Charles E. Coughlin, Feb. 19, 1934; and William M. Walker to FM, Jan. 19, 1934, Box 17. Charles E. Coughlin to FM, Jan. 5, 1934, Box 16; and July 26, 1934, Box 19. James P. Shenton, "The Coughlin Movement and the New Deal," *Political Science Quarterly,* v. 73 (Sep. 1958), 352-73.

[5] Telegram, FM to John D. Dingell, March 3, 1934, Box 17. FM to John D. Dingell, April 18, 1934, Box 18.

[6] For example, John E. Kinnane to FM, March 9, 1934, Box 17. Edmund C. Shields to FM, June 21, 1934; and George J. Burke to FM, July 18, 1934, Box 18.

[7] Cable, FM to FDR, July 5, 1934, Box 18.

[8] FM to Edmund C. Shields, April 22, 1934, Box 18. FM to George W. Welsh, Jan. 25, 1934, Box 17.

[9] FM to William J. Davitt, April 22, 1934; and FM to Edmund C. Shields, April 22, 1934, Box 18.

[10] Cable, FDR to FM, June 30, 1934, RL:P.P.F.-1,662. Arthur H. Vandenberg to FM, Aug. 21, 1934, Box 19.

[11] "Conversations between the Secretary of War and Senator Quezon," Dec. 18, 1933; George H. Dern to FDR, Dec. 20, 1933; and draft of letter to Quezon, Dern to FDR, Jan. 30, 1934, RL:OF-400-PI. See cables, "Alunan" to "Yulomike"; and Mike "Ynchausti to Manolo," Jan. 3, 1934, Box 16.

[12] Harry B. Hawes to FM, May 5, 1933, Box 12. W. Cameron Forbes to FM, Jan. 3, 1935, Box 23. Theodore Friend, *Between Two Empires: The Ordeal of the Philippines, 1929-1946* (New Haven: Yale University Press, 1965), chs. 5-6.

[13] For the army position see memoranda, Fred W. Manley to FM, Aug. 14, 1934, Box 19; and Copy, Stanley D. Embick to Gen. Nolan, Jan. 12, 1935, Box 23. See generally, Dorothy Borg, *The United States and the Far Eastern Crisis of 1933-1938* (Cambridge: Harvard University Press, 1964), pp. 235-54.

[14] George A. Malcolm, *The Commonwealth of the Philippines* (New York: Appleton-Century, 1936), pp. 119-31.

[15] Theodore Roosevelt, Jr. to FM, March 23, 1934, Box 17.

[16] Joseph R. Hayden, *The Philippines: A*

Study in National Development (New York: Macmillan, 1942), p. 789.

[17] Cables, FM to Cox, Nov. 25, 1933; FM to Cox, Nov. 28, 1933, Box 15. FM to Cox, Dec. 1, 1933, Box 16.

[18] Handwritten notes, "When Governor General talked with President," April-May 1935, Box 25. Also *Philippines Herald*, May 2, 1934.

[19] *Ibid.*; "Notes on G.G.'s Speech Detroit February 20, 1935," Jan. 19, 1935, Box 23. Copy, Frank Parker to the Adjutant General, Aug. 16, 1934, Box 31. Also report, "Military Aspects of the Situation . . . ," Dec. 2, 1935, Box 50.

[20] Handwritten notes, *loc.cit.*, notes 18 and 19 above.

[21] FM to Francis B. Sayre, July 26, 1935, Box 27. FM to W. Cameron Forbes, Oct. 16, 1935, Box 29.

[22] FM to Edward G. Kemp, May 21, 1936, Box 36. Also, FM to Millard E. Tydings, July 16, 1935, Box 27.

[23] FM to Kemp, May 2, 1935, Box 25. FM to W. S. Gilmore, March 17, 1934, Box 18.

[24] Handwritten notes, *loc.cit.*, note 18 above. Hayden, *Philippines*, p. 40; Robert Aura Smith, *Philippine Freedom* (New York: Columbia University Press, 1958), p. 80.

[25] FM to George W. Norris, Jan. 5, 1935, Box 23. Manuel L. Quezon to Claro M. Recto, Nov. 2, 1934, Box 21.

[26] Claro M. Recto to FM, Jan. 7, 1935; and cables, FM to Cox, Jan. 5, 1935, and replies Jan. 9 and 22, 1935, Box 23.

[27] FM to Hayden, Hester, and Kemp, Dec. 12, 1934, Box 21. FM comment on draft cable to Cox, Jan. 11, 1935, Box 23. *Manila Tribune*, Jan. 26, 1935; and Hayden to FM, Dec. 31, 1934, Box 22.

[28] Hayden, *Philippines*, p. 43. *Manila Tribune*, March 1, 1935, and Jan. 26, 1935.

[29] *Manila Tribune*, Nov. 14, 1935.

[30] Excerpts from *Manila Tribune*, Jan. 26 and March 1, 1935; *Philippines Herald*, Jan. 23, 1935; *Shanghai Times*, Jan. 29, 1935; and *Manila Daily Bulletin*, Jan. 26, 1935.

[31] Engagement book, Box 24.

[32] *Manila Daily Bulletin*, March 3, 1935.

[33] *Washington Post*, Feb. 28, 1935. George H. Dern to FDR, March 9, 1935, RL:OF-400-PI.

[34] Cordell Hull to FDR, March 18, 1935, RL:OF-400-PI. FM to Francis B. Sayre, July 26, 1935, Box 27. Creed F. Cox to FM, May 9, 1936, Box 35. Cox to FM, May 23, 1935, Box 25. Executive Order No. 780, July 9, 1935, Box 26.

[35] Kemp to FM, April 3, 1935, Box 24. Cable, Creed F. Cox to FM, Oct. 9, 1934, Box 20. Cox to FM, May 16, 1935; and FM to Manuel L. Quezon, July 9, 1935, Box 26.

[36] FDR to FM, April 10, 1935, Box 24. Quote, *Manila Daily Bulletin*, March 9, 1935. Also FM to Blair Moody, May 11, 1935, Box 25.

[37] FM to Hayden, May 23, 1935; and Staff meeting notes, May 25, 1935, Box 25. *Manila Daily Bulletin*, Jan. 23, 1935.

[38] *Philippines Herald*, April 13, 1935.

[39] FM to Frank X. Martel, Oct. 14, 1935, Box 29. Cabinet Minutes, April 17, 1935, Box 24. Cable, Hayden to Cox, May 8, 1935, Box 25. For reports of Agent 110 on the activities of Aguinaldo to prevent the inauguration of Quezon, see Fred W. Manley to FM, Oct. 10, 1935, Box 28. Also report, Agent 110, Oct. 22, 1935, Box 29.

[40] Cables, Hayden to Cox, May 8 and 9, 1935, Box 25. Report of Investigation Committee, May 18, 1935, Box 10, Hayden Papers. For general accounts see Hayden, *Philippines*, pp. 361-89; and David R. Sturtevant, "Sakdalism and Philippine Radicalism," *Journal of Asian Studies*, v. 21 (Feb. 1962), 209-11.

[41] Cable, FM to Cox, Aug. 3, 1935, Box 27. FM to Millard E. Tydings, July 16, 1935, Box 27. FM to Blair Moody, May 11, 1935, Box 25.

[42] Joseph C. Grew to Hayden, May 13, 1935, Box 25. Cable, Quezon to FM, May 12, 1935; FM to Quezon, May 14, 1935, Box 25. FM to Francis B. Sayre, Dec. 4, 1935, Box 32.

[43] Cabinet Minutes, Aug. 7, 1935, Box 27.

[44] Cabinet Minutes, Aug. 28, 1935, Box 27.

[45] José Yulo to FM, July 12, 1935, Box

26. Cabinet Minutes, July 24, 1934, Box 27.

[46] FM to Cordell Hull, May 13, 1936, p. 3, RL:OF-400-PI. Hayden to Wilfred B. Shaw, June 30, 1934, Hayden Papers.

[47] FM to Francis B. Sayre, Jan. 20, 1936; and Evett D. Hester to FM, Feb. 27, 1936, Box 35. Quote, *NYT*, July 14, 1935, p. 5:7.

[48] Fred W. Manley to FM, Oct. 10, 1935, Box 28. Hayden, *Philippines*, pp. 428-32.

[49] FM to G. Donald Kennedy, Nov. 22, 1935, Box 30. *NYT*, Oct. 15, 1935, p. 4:5. Quote, Sturtevant, "Sakdalism," p. 209n.

[50] *Manila Tribune*, Nov. 14, 1935. Address to the 10th Philippines Legislature in its Final Session, *Annual Report of the Governor General of the Philippine Islands: 1935*, 75th Cong., 1st Sess., House Doc. 100, p. 19.

[51] Edward G. Kemp to author, Oct. 1961. Memoranda by Quezon and Murphy on the Tydings Act, Nov. 2, 1935, enclosed FM to Dern, Dec. 4, 1935, RL:OF-400-PI.

[52] Quezon memorandum, *ibid.*, p. 6. J. Weldon Jones to Edward G. Kemp, Aug. 18, 1936, Box 37.

[53] Quezon memorandum, p. 6, see note 51.

[54] Kemp to author, October, 1961; and FM to George H. Dern, Dec. 4, 1935, Box 30. Murphy comment on Quezon memorandum, Nov. 21, 1935, p. 2, see notes 51 and 52. Arthur H. Vandenberg to FM, Dec. 24, 1935, Box 31.

[55] As summarized in Harry H. Woodring to FDR, March 22, 1935, RL:OF-400-PI. Murphy comment on Quezon memorandum, pp. 4 and 7. Viceroy notion, memo to Fred W. Manley, Aug. 14, 1934, Box 19.

[56] Cable, FM to Creed F. Cox, May 21, Box 19.

[57] *Ibid.* FM to Harry H. Woodring, Dec. 31, 1936, Box 39.

[58] Cox to FM, Feb. 23, 1935, Box 24. Cable, Quezon to FM, enclosed, J.D. Hopkins to FM, March 6, 1935, Box 24.

[59] Cable, Cox to FM, Sep. 6, 1935, RL:OF-400-PI. Cox to FM, Sep. 10, 1935, Box 28. Cox to FM, Aug. 16, 1935, Box 27.

[60] Dern to FM, Aug. 16, 1935, Box 27.

[61] Richard D. Lunt, *The High Ministry of Government: The Political Career of Frank Murphy* (Detroit: Wayne State University Press, 1965), p. 117.

[62] Cables, FM to Cox, Sep. 11 and 23, 1935, Box 28. Kemp, comment on Quezon memo concerning Tydings Act, *loc.cit.*, note 51 above.

[63] Draft instructions, cable, FM to Cox, Sep. 13, 1935; and cable, FM to Cox, Sep. 11, 1935, Box 28.

[64] Cable, FM to FDR, Sep. 22, 1935; and Stanley Reed to FDR, Sep. 26, 1935, RL:OF-400-PI.

[65] Douglas A. MacArthur to FDR, Sep. 26, 1935, RL:OF-400-PI.

[66] Woodring to FM, Oct. 12, 1935; FM to Dern, Oct. 7, 1935, Box 28. FM to FDR, Dec. 16, 1935, RL:OF-400-PI.

[67] Hayden notes, undated [Nov. 1935], Box 29. Kemp to author, Oct. 1961; FM to Kemp, April 15, 1936, Box 35.

[68] Memo, "Message to Sec War might say," Sep. 30, 1935, Box 28. Memo, Nov. 27, 1935, Box 30.

[69] FM to Dern, Dec. 4 and 10, 1935, Box 30. FM to Dern, Oct. 7, 1935, Box 28.

[70] Dern to FDR, Aug. 16, 1935, Box 27. FM to Blair Moody, May 11, 1935, Box 25.

[71] FM to Dern, Nov. 9, 1935, Box 29. Cable, Cox to FM, Sep. 6, 1935, RL:OF-400-PI.

[72] FM to Dern, Nov. 9, 1935; and cable, Dern to FDR, Nov. 9, 1935, Box 29.

[73] Cable, FDR to Dern, Nov. 9, 1935, Box 29. FDR to Dern, Nov. 12, 1935, RL:OF-400-PI.

[74] Cable, FM to FDR, Nov. 16, 1935, Box 30. Cable, Dern to FDR, Nov. 16, 1935; and memo, FDR to acting Secretary of War, Nov. 22, 1935, RL:OF-400-PI. Quote, *NYT*, Dec. 1, 1935, p. 32:2.

[75] FM to Kemp, Oct. 13, 1936, Box 37. Cable, FM to Hayden, Nov. 26, 1935, Box 30.

[76] FM to Hayden, Dec. 5, 1935, Box 30.

[77] Dern to FM, Nov. 13, 1935, Box 30.

[78] FM to Cox, April 16, 1935, Box 24. FM to Dern, Dec. 6 and 10, 1935, Box 30.

[79] FM to FDR, Dec. 16, 1935, RL:OF-

400-PI. FM to Hayden, Feb. 9, 1936, Box 33.

[80] Dern to FM, Jan. 21, 1936; and Kemp to FM, Feb. 20, 1936, Box 33.

[81] Quotes, *NYT*, Dec. 1, 1935, p. 32:2; and *Manila Daily Bulletin*, April 14, 1936. Frederic S. Marquardt, *Before Bataan and After* (New York: Bobbs-Merrill, 1943), pp. 180-81.

[82] Quezon to FM, Dec. 1, 1935, Box 30. FM to Norman H. Hill, Dec. 30, 1935, Box 31.

[83] J. Weldon Jones to FM, Oct. 10, 1936; Creed F. Cox to FM, Oct. 28, 1936, Box 38. FM to Cox, Dec. 10, 1936, Box 39.

[84] Quezon to FM, Jan. 21, 1936; FM to Dern, Jan. 30, 1936, Box 33. Dern to FM, March 12, 1936, Box 34.

[85] Belo Fund: Quezon to FM, May 4, 1936; FM to Quezon, May 10, 1936, Box 35. Philippines National Bank: J. Weldon Jones to Kemp, Aug. 18, 1936; Jones to FM, Aug. 21, 1936, Box 37.

[86] Quezon to FM, Jan. 21, 1936, Box 33; May 4, 1936, Box 35.

[87] High Commission Report, Feb. 1, 1936, Box 32. Cf. reaction to Quezon's Rotary Speech, Norman H. Hill and J. Weldon Jones to FM, July 5, 1936, Box 36. FM to Jones, May 19, 1936, Box 36.

[88] FM to Kemp, Sep. 1, 1936; Jones to Kemp, Aug. 18, 1936, Box 37.

[89] Kemp to FM, July 8, 1936; and Jones to FM, July 15, 1936, Box 36.

[90] George A. Malcolm to FM, Nov. 5, 1936, Box 38. Jones to FM, July 15, 1936, Box 36. Draft, FM to Woodring, Dec. 10, 1936, and final draft, Dec. 31, 1936, Box 39.

[91] Jones to FM, Jan. 8, 1936, Box 32. High Commission Report, July 14, 1936, Box 32. Jones to FM, Nov. 8, 1936, Box 41. Hayden to FM, Dec. 2, 1936, Box 39. FM to Dern, Feb. 3, 1936, Box 32.

[92] Kemp to FM, Feb. 7, 1936, Box 34. Fred W. Manley to FM, Dec. 10, 1935, Box 31.

[93] Draft of Veto Message, H.R. 735, Box I, Hayden Papers. Handwritten notes, "When Governor General talked with President," April-May 1935, Box 25.

[94] Jones to FM, Jan. 8, 1936; FM to Richard R. Ely, Jan. 2, 1936, Box 32. FM to Kemp, Dec. 20, 1935, Box 31.

[95] Copy, orders of Sep. 18, 1935, Box 28. Memo, Office of Military Adviser to High Commissioner, Jan. 17, 1936, Box 33.

[96] FM to Kemp, Feb. 1, 1936, Box 33.

[97] *Ibid.* Elliott Roosevelt, ed., *FDR: His Personal Letters* (New York: Duell, Sloan & Pearce, 1950), v. 3, p. 507. Kemp to FM, Feb. 7, 1936, Box 34.

[98] FM to Jones, Feb. 13, 1936, Box 34.

[99] FM to Kemp, Feb. 1, 1936, Box 33. Memo, Office of Military Adviser to High Commissioner, Jan. 17, 1936, Box 34.

[100] Douglas A. MacArthur, *Reminiscences* (New York: McGraw-Hill, 1964), p. 107. Fred W. Manley to FM, Dec. 10, 1935, Box 31. FM to Kemp, March 15, 1936, Box 35. Kemp to FM, Feb. 7 and 20, 1936, Box 34. FM to Francis B. Sayre, July 26, 1935, Box 27. Friend, *Between Two Empires*, pp. 160-66.

[101] See note 95 above. J. Weldon Jones to FM, Dec. 12, 1935, Box 31. Kemp to FM, Feb. 7, 1936, Box 34. Kemp to FM, Jan. 23, 1936, Box 33.

[102] Copy, E. T. Conley to MacArthur, Jan. 11, 1936; cable, Cox to FM, Jan. 16, 1936, Box 33. FM to Kemp, Feb. 1, 1936, Box 33. FM to Kemp, March 23, 1936, Box 34.

[103] Cable, FM to Cox, Feb. 3, 1936, Box 33. FM comment on Hester memo, Feb. 24, 1936, Box 34.

[104] Edwin L. Neville to FM, Dec. 7, 1935, Box 31. Cables, FM to Cox, Jan. 21 and 29, 1936, Box 33.

[105] FM to Kemp, May 10, 1936, Box 35.

[106] FM to Kemp, April 15, 1936, Box 35. Quote, FM to Kemp, Feb. 1, 1936, Box 33.

[107] Stanley D. Embick to FM, Aug. 5, 1936; FM to Malin Craig, Aug. 10, 1936; and Kemp to FM, Aug. 19, 1936, Box 37.

[108] Borg, *United States and Far Eastern Crisis*, pp. 235-42. Malin Craig to FM, Aug. 13, 1936; and Stanley D. Embick to FM, Aug. 5, 1936, Box 37.

[109] *Ibid.*, Box 37. FM to FDR, May 8, 1936. RL:File 178 makes a cross-reference to this 41-page report, but it could not be

found in the Roosevelt Papers, the Murphy Papers, or the National Archives.

[110] FM to Malin Craig, Aug. 12, 1936; and Craig to FM, Aug. 13, 1936, Box 37.

[111] *Ibid.*, Box 37. Kemp to FM, Aug. 19, 1936; and FM to Kemp, Aug. 16, 1936, Box 37.

[112] FM to Kemp, Sep. 1, 1936, Box 37.

[113] Woodring to FM, Sep. 19, 1936, Box 37. See FDR memo of conference, Sep. 12, 1936, RL:File 178.

[114] Borg, *United States and Far Eastern Crisis*, pp. 245-49.

[115] *Ibid.*, p. 247. Quezon opposition, High Commission Report, Jan. 10, 1937; undated handwritten notes on press release of Quezon visit, Box 39.

[116] On honors: cable, Cox to FM, Oct. 28, 1936, Box 38. On trade: Cox to FM, May 7, 1936, Box 35. Sayre to FM, Dec. 21, 1936; FM to Quezon, Dec. 22, 1936, Box 39. Sayre to FM, June 14, 1937, Box 46.

[117] FM to Woodring, Dec. 31, 1936; and Cox to FM, Dec. 29, 1936, Box 39. Memo, "When Discussing National Defense Matter with State Department," July 1936, Box 36.

[118] Friend, *Between Two Empires*, pp. 191-207.

[119] *Manila Daily Bulletin*, Jan. 25, 1936.

[120] FM to George Murphy, Sep. 17, 1934, Box 20. Frank X. Martel to FM, Oct. 29, 1934, Box 21.

[121] Memo, Louis M. Howe to Mr. Stanley, Feb. 12, 1935, Box 23. Howe to James A. Farley, March 24, 1935; and FM to Farley, April 15, 1935, Box 24.

[122] FM to Arthur D. Maguire, March 5, 1935, Box 24. FM to Raymond Moley, May 14, 1935, Box 25. FM to William Murphy, Oct. 16, 1935, Box 29. Charles E. Coughlin to FM, March 13, 1936, Box 34.

[123] See, for example, FM to A.E. Dale and Harry Bitner, Feb. 17, 1936, Box 34. FM to William Randolph Hearst, Aug. 4, 1936, Box 37.

[124] Telegram, Emil Hurja to FM, May 29, 1936, Box 36. Report, enclosed in G. Donald Kennedy to FM, June 1, 1936, Box 40.

[125] For example, Edmund C. Shields to FM, March 7, 1936; and Edward F. Thomas to FM, Feb. 20, 1936, Box 34.

[126] *NYHT*, May 5, 1936, p. 5.

[127] *Philippines Herald*, Feb. 24, 1936. Also *Manila Tribune*, Feb. 25, 1936.

[128] FM to Harry Bitner, Feb. 17, 1934, Box 34. FM to Louis M. Howe, Jan. 30, 1936, Box 33. FM to Emil Hurja, March 31, 1936, Box 34.

[129] FM to John D. Dingell, June 22, 1935, Box 26.

[130] FM to Joseph A. Mulcahy, Feb. 7, 1936, Box 33.

[131] FM to Dern, Feb. 28, 1936, Box 34.

[132] Henry A. Montgomery to FM, Nov. 20, 1935, Box 30. FM to Norman H. Hill, Jan. 4, 1936, Box 29.

[133] FM to Adelaide Williams, Dec. 30, 1935, Box 31.

[134] FM to Frank A. Picard, Feb. 15, 1936, Box 34. FM to Edward H. Williams, Feb. 27, 1936, Box 34.

[135] FM to Charles E. Coughlin, Feb. 27, 1936, Box 34.

[136] FM to FDR, March 3, 1936, Box 34.

[137] FDR to FM, July 8, 1936, RL:OF-400-PI. *NYT*, July 5, 1936, p. 7:5. Marquardt, *Before Bataan and After*, p. 181. Frederic S. Marquardt to FM, May 16, 1943, Box 108.

[138] Marquardt, *Before Bataan and After*, p. 181. FM to Carlos P. Romulo, July 1, 1947, Box 122.

[139] See R. A. Smith, *Philippine Freedom*, pp. 62-67. Friend, *Between Two Empires*, pp. 268-69. Borg, *United States and Far Eastern Crisis*, p. 253.

[140] FM to Carlos P. Romulo, Dec. 28, 1938, Box 59.

[141] Hayden to FM, March 12, 1936, Box 36. *Philippines Herald, Mid-Week Magazine*, May 6, 1935, p. 15. Romulo to FM, Oct. 13, 1943, Box 109.

[142] *NYT*, Dec. 1, 1935, p. 32:2.

[143] FM to Marguerite LeHand, May 12, 1935, RL:OF-400-PI.

[144] Quote, FM to Millard E. Tydings, July 16, 1935, Box 27.

[145] *Philippines Herald*, July 4, 1935. *Manila Daily Bulletin*, Nov. 15, 1935.

[146] FM to FDR, Nov. 20, 1935, RL: Group 13. See *Hooven & Allison Co. v. Evatt*, 324 U.S. 652, 691 (1945).

[147] *Manila Tribune*, May 13, 1936.

Quote, "Selected Addresses of Frank Murphy, Governor of Michigan, January 1, 1937, to September 30, 1938" (Lansing, 1938), pp. 80-81.

CHAPTER 6

[1] FM to Lee Kreiselman Jaffe, Sep. 17, 1936, Box 37.

[2] FM to Frank A. Picard, March 6, 1935, Box 24. See Samuel T. McSeveny, "The Michigan Gubernatorial Campaign of 1938," *Michigan History*, v. 45 (June 1961), 97-127; James K. Pollock and Samuel J. Eldersveld, "Michigan Politics in Transition," *Michigan Governmental Studies*, No. 10 (Ann Arbor, 1942); and Richard D. Lunt, "Frank Murphy's Decision to Enter the 1936 Gubernatorial Race," *Michigan History*, v. 47 (December 1963), 327-34.

[3] Telegram, Edmund C. Shields to FM, July 6, 1936; and reply, July 7, 1936, Box 36. *Detroit Free Press*, June 27, 1936, p. 3.

[4] FM to FDR, July 9, 1936, RL:OF-400-PI. *NYT*, July 10, 1936, p. 9:4.

[5] *Detroit Times*, July 9, 1936, p. 1. *Detroit Free Press*, July 11, 1936, p. 1.

[6] Mrs. James H. McDonald to James A. Farley, Aug. 5, 1936, RL:OF-300-DNC-Mich. *Detroit News*, Aug. 28, 1936. *Houghton* (Mich.) *Mining Gazette*, Aug. 26, 1936.

[7] *Detroit Times*, Aug. 7, 1936, p. 34. *Detroit Free Press*, July 11, 1936, p. 1. Letter to FM, Sep. 21, 1936, Box 37. FM to P.H. Callahan, Oct. 28, 1936, Box 38.

[8] Undated memo, FM to Mead and Van Auken, Box 39. James A. Farley to FM, Aug. 7, 1936, Box 37.

[9] *Detroit News*, July 10, 1936, p. 18.

[10] George J. Burke to Farley, Aug. 3, 1936, RL:OF-300-DNC-Mich. FM to Kemp, July 14, 1936, Box 36.

[11] Undated platform notes, Box 37. *Detroit News*, Aug. 17, 1936, p. 8.

[12] Undated memo to Mead and Van Auken, Box 39. Joseph R. Hayden to FM, Nov. 14, 1936, Box 38. George A. Schroeder to FM, Aug. 11, 1936, Box 37.

[13] *Detroit Times*, July 18, 1936. *Detroit News*, July 19, 1936, p. 10. Kemp to FM, Oct. 23, 1936, Box 38. FM to Kemp, Sep. 11, 1936, Box 37.

[14] *Detroit Free Press*, July 11 and 29, 1936, p. 6; Oct. 12, 1936; Oct. 31, 1936; and Sep. 3, 1936, p. 1.

[15] FM to Frederic S. Marquardt, Oct. 10, 1936, Box 37. Picard to Farley, Sep. 17, 1936, RL:OF-300-DNC-Mich.

[16] *Lansing State Journal*, Sep. 16, 1936. "Complete Summary of Votes Cast in the State of Michigan," Nov. 1936, Box 38.

[17] G. Donald Kennedy to FM, Sep. 10, 1936, Box 37. Kemp to Fred W. Manley, Oct. 21, 1936, Box 38.

[18] FM to Norman H. Hill, Oct. 25, 1936, Box 38.

[19] *Detroit Times*, Oct. 7, 1936, p. 10.

[20] "Official Tabulation of Votes by Counties," Nov. 1936, Box 39. Wise to FM, Nov. 4, 1936, Box 38.

[21] Telegrams, William Randolph Hearst to FM, Nov. 5 and 23, 1936, Box 39. FM to Joseph P. Kennedy, Dec. 17, 1936, Box 39. FM to Hill, Dec. 7, 1936, Box 39.

[22] "Message to the 59th Michigan Legislature," Jan. 7, 1937, p. 3. Telegram, FM to Harry Mead, Sep. 18, 1936, Box 37. Edward F. Thomas to FM, Nov. 24, 1936, Box 38. G. Donald Kennedy to FM, Nov. 21, 1936, Box 38.

[23] Hayden to FM, Nov. 14, 1936, Box 38. James K. Pollock to FM, Dec. 8, 1936, Box 39. William Haber to FM, Dec. 24, 1936, Box 39. FM to Hilmer Gellein, Nov. 11, 1936, Box 38.

[24] FM to Frank D. Fitzgerald, Dec. 15, 1936, Box 39. *Detroit News*, Nov. 6, 1936; and Jan. 2, 1937.

[25] Inaugural address, quoted in *Detroit Free Press*, Jan. 2, 1937. *Detroit News*, Jan. 4, 1937.

[26] Message to 59th Michigan Legislature, *loc.cit.*, see note 22 above. *Detroit Free Press*, January 8, 1937.

[27] *Grand Rapids Herald*, Jan. 9, 1937.

Muskegon Chronicle, Jan. 9, 1937. *Lansing State Journal*, Jan. 1, 1937.

[28] See Walter Galenson, *The CIO Challenge to the AFL* (Cambridge: Harvard University Press, 1960), pp. 121-34; and Sidney Fine, *The Automobile Under The Blue Eagle* (Ann Arbor: University of Michigan Press, 1963), pp. 377-428.

[29] Fine, *Automobile*, pp. 407-15. Galenson, *CIO Challenge*, pp. 127-31.

[30] Galenson, *CIO Challenge*, pp. 134-35.

[31] *NYT*, Feb. 12, 1937, p. 18.

[32] Kemp to FM, March 12, 1937, Box 43. Memo, Labor Commissioner to Governor's Office, Dec. 23, 1938, Box 59. Sen. Wagner, *Cong. Rec.*, March 31, 1937, p. 2,943.

[33] *Selections from the Writings and Speeches of William Randolph Hearst* (San Francisco: published privately, 1948), p. 368.

[34] As quoted in *Macon* (Ga.) *News-Telegraph*, March 6, 1940.

[35] Galenson, *CIO Challenge*, p. 134. Murray Kempton, *Part of Our Time* (New York: Simon & Schuster, 1955), ch. 9.

[36] *NYT*, Jan. 5, 1937, p. 15:1.

[37] *Manila Tribune*, July 13, 1933; and *Detroit Labor News*, Sep. 14, 1936.

[38] *Detroit Times*, Feb. 25, 1936; and Inaugural address, Jan. 2, 1937.

[39] *NYHT*, Jan. 29, 1937, p. 9:3; *NYT*, March 20, 1937, p. 4:4; and FM to Octave P. Beauvais, quoted in *NYT*, Jan. 29, 1939, p. 9:3.

[40] "Message to the 59th Michigan Legislature," *loc.cit.*, see note 22 above.

[41] *Cleveland Plain Dealer*, Feb. 12, 1937.

[42] *NYT*, Jan. 12, 1937, p. 10:2.

[43] *NYT*, Jan. 6, 1937, p. 1:8. See Edward D. Black Papers, Michigan Historical Collections of the University of Michigan. *NYT*, Jan. 8, p. 1:8, 9; p. 18:3; and 10, 1937, p. 1:1. For stock holdings and sale, see Hayden, Stone & Co., to FM, Oct. 3, 1936, Box 37. Eleanor Bumgardner to FM, Dec. 31, 1936, Box 39. Sidney Fine, "The General Motors Sit-Down Strike: A Re-examination," *American Historical Review*, v. 70 (April 1965), 706-707n.

[44] *NYT*, Jan. 12, 1937, p. 1:8. George D.

Blackwood, "The Sit-Down Strike in the Thirties," *South Atlantic Quarterly*, v. 55 (Oct. 1956), 438-48.

[45] *Detroit News*, Jan. 12, 1937.

[46] *NYHT*, Jan. 12, 1937, p. 1:4. *NYT*, Feb. 12, 1937, p. 18:2.

[47] *Detroit Free Press*, Jan. 13, 1937.

[48] *NYT*, Jan. 16, 1937, p. 8:3. Undated speech notes [March 1937], Box 45.

[49] *NYT*, Jan. 15, 1937, p. 1:2. *NYHT*, Jan. 14, 1937, p. 21:7.

[50] *NYHT*, Jan. 16, 1937, p. 14:1. *Lansing State Journal*, Jan. 17, 1937. *Phoenix Gazette*, Jan. 20, 1937.

[51] Galenson, *CIO Challenge*, p. 138. *NYT*, Jan. 18, 1937, p. 1:8; and Jan. 19, 1937, p. 8:6.

[52] *NYHT*, Jan. 18, 1937, p. 1:8.

[53] *NYT*, Jan. 22, 1937, pp. 1:8 and 6:4.

[54] *The Secret Diary of Harold L. Ickes* (New York: Simon & Schuster, 1954), v. 2, p. 57. *NYT*, Jan. 23, 1937, p. 1:1.

[55] *NYT*, March 26, 1937, p. 20:5.

[56] See Mark Sullivan, William Knudsen, and Homer Martin, in *NYT*, Feb. 10, 1937, p. 2:4; *NYHT*, Jan. 14, 1937, p. 21:7; and *NYT*, Jan. 24, 1937, p. 1:1.

[57] *NYHT*, Jan. 19, 1937, p. 16:8. *Cong. Rec.*, Jan. 14, 1937, p. 247.

[58] *NYT*, Jan. 27, 1937, pp. 1:1 and 2:7. See *NYHT*, Jan. 30, 1937, p. 13:1.

[59] *NYT*, Feb. 3, 1937, p. 1:6; and Jan. 28, 1937, p. 1:2.

[60] *NYT*, Jan. 31, 1937, p. 2:5; Feb. 2, 1937, p. 2:3; and Jan. 30, 1937, p. 1:8.

[61] *NYT*, Jan. 24, 1937, p. 2:4. Lawrence P. Fisher to FM, Jan. 25, 1937, Box 42.

[62] Galenson, *CIO Challenge*, p. 139. *NYT*, Jan. 27, 1937, p. 3:1.

[63] *NYT*, Jan. 30, 1937, p. 4:2; Feb. 13, 1937, p. 5:3; and Jan. 29, 1937, p. 4:2, respectively.

[64] FM to Kemp, Jan. 27, 1937, and attached reply, Box 42.

[65] Kemp to FM, Jan. 27, 1937, Box 42.

[66] *NYT*, Jan. 29, 1937, pp. 1:2 and 4:2. Text of injunction, Feb. 3, 1937, p. 13:1.

[67] Galenson, *CIO Challenge*, p. 139. FM notes on GM strike, Feb. 1-8, 1937, Box 42. Hereafter cited as "Strike Notes."

[68] Strike Notes, Feb. 1, 1937.

[69] Strike Notes, Feb. 2, 1937.

[70] *Ibid.*

[71] *Ibid. NYT*, Feb. 3, 1937, p. 1:8.

[72] Conversations with Frances Perkins, Strike Notes, February 5 and 2, 1937.

[73] Conversations with Lawrence P. Fisher and John Brophy, Strike Notes, Feb. 2, 1937. Fine, "General Motors Sit-Down Strike," p. 704.

[74] Strike Notes, Feb. 5, 1937.

[75] *Ibid.* Fine, "General Motors Sit-Down Strike," p. 701.

[76] *NYT*, Feb. 7, 1937, p. 1:1. *Cong. Rec.*, Jan. 29, 1937, p. 589.

[77] Garner to FM, Dec. 24, 1936, Box 39. *NYT*, Feb. 4, 1937, p. 20:5. See Elliott Roosevelt, *FDR: His Personal Letters*, p. 694.

[78] Strike Notes, Feb. 5, 1937.

[79] U.S. Congress, Senate, Subcommittee of the Committee on the Judiciary, *Hearing, Nomination of Frank Murphy to be Attorney General of the United States*, 76th Cong., 1st Sess., Jan. 13, 1939, pp. 9-10. Hereafter cited as *Hearing*.

[80] Strike Notes, Feb. 5, 1937. Fine, *Automobile*, p. 397.

[81] Strike Notes, Feb. 5, 1937.

[82] *Ibid.*

[83] *Ibid.*, Feb. 6, 1937. Also telegram, William Green, J. W. Williams and John P. Frey to FM, Feb. 6, 1937, RL:OF-407B-Labor:Automobile Strikes.

[84] Fine, "General Motors Sit-Down Strike," pp. 710-12. Strike Notes, Feb. 5-7, 1937.

[85] *Ibid.*, Feb. 8, 1937.

[86] *Ibid.*

[87] *Ibid.*, conversation with Lawrence P. Fisher.

[88] *Ibid.*, conversation with Frances Perkins.

[89] *Ibid.*, conversation with Marvin H. McIntyre.

[90] *Ibid.*, conversation with Edward F. McGrady.

[91] *Detroit News*, Feb. 11, 1937; and *NYT*, Feb. 12, 1937, p. 1:8.

[92] *NYT*, Feb. 12, 1937, pp. 19:2, 1:2, and 1:7.

[93] FM to Lewis, Feb. 9, 1937, Box 42. See *Hearing*, pp. 7, 10-12.

[94] Blackwood, "Sit-Down Strike in the Thirties," p. 446. Also interview, George Murphy (by Sidney Fine and Robert M. Warner), March 28, 1957. Michigan Historical Collections of The University of Michigan.

[95] United Automobile Workers, *Proceedings of the Fifth Annual Convention* (July 24–Aug. 6, 1940), p. 104.

[96] *Detroit News*, Jan. 18, 1939. Also George H. Maines to FM, Dec. 6, 1937, Box 49.

[97] Memorandum for the President: telephone conversation with Governor Murphy, Feb. 8, 1937, RL:OF-407B-Labor: Automobile Strikes. Also, Microfilm, General 9:Murphy 32-40.

[98] Thomas W. Wolcott to FM, Aug. 17, 1938, Box 54. Copy, Arthur Krock to P. H. Callahan, May 3, 1937, Box 45. Prentiss M. Brown to Robert M. LaFollette, Jr., Aug. 23, 1938, Box 55. Joseph H. Creighton to FM, May 11, 1938, Box 52. See Creighton's manuscript and Murphy's notes, Aug. 1938, Box 55.

[99] *Atlanta Constitution*, Feb. 14, 1937. *NYT*, Feb. 12, 1937, pp. 19:2-5 and 18:1. *Hearing*, pp. 5-8. *NYT*, Feb. 12, 1937, p. 22:5.

[100] *NYT*, Feb. 13, 1937, p. 5:2. Galenson, *CIO Challenge*, pp. 143-48.

[101] *NYT*, Feb. 12, 1937, p. 16:2. *Detroit News*, Oct. 29, 1937.

[102] *El Paso Times*, Feb. 19, 1937. *Time*, Feb. 22, 1937, p. 1. Also see *Emporia Gazette*, Feb. 11, 1937; *Springfield* (Mo.) *Leader and Press*, Feb. 23, 1937; and *St. Petersburg Conciliator*, Feb. 25, 1937.

CHAPTER 7

[1] *NYT*, March 3, 1937, p. 1:8; and March 21, 1937, p. 1:6.

[2] Walter Galenson, *The CIO Challenge to the AFL* (Cambridge: Harvard University Press, 1960), p. 145. FM to Kemp, Feb. 18, 1938, Box 51. Boris Shishkin to FM, Aug. 14, 1937, Box 47.

[3] *NYT*, March 28, 1937, p. 29:1. McReynolds quoted in *Cong. Rec.*, March 29, 1937, p. 2,841.

[4] *NYT*, Feb. 16, 1937, pp. 1:3 and 11:3; Feb. 23, 1937, p. 9:2; and Feb. 27, 1937, p. 16:4.

[5] *NYT*, March 12, 1937, p. 4:1; March 14, 1937, p. 6:3; March 10, 1937, p. 2:6.

[6] *NYT*, March 16, 1937, p. 22:5; and March 21, 1937, p. 3:1.

[7] *NYT*, March 13, 1937, p. 18:4.

[8] *NYT*, March 12, 1937, p. 5:1; March 13, 1937, p. 7:2.

[9] *NYT*, March 19, 1937, p. 4:4.

[10] *NYT*, March 21, 1937, p. 31:6.

[11] Galenson, *CIO Challenge*, p. 149. *NYT*, March 16, 1937, p. 2:5.

[12] *NYT*, March 17, 1937, p. 2:3. Foy message, Kemp to FM, March 17, 1937, Box 44.

[13] *NYT*, March 20, 1937, p. 1:2; March 21, 1937, pp. 1:6, 34:4, and 7:3.

[14] Press Statement, March 13, 1937, Box 44.

[15] Kemp to FM, March 12, 1937; E. Blythe Stason to FM, March 18, 1937, Box 43.

[16] Press Statement, March 13, 1937, Box 44. Text, *NYT*, March 18, 1937, p. 5.

[17] *Ibid*.

[18] See editorials of *Washington Post* and *Detroit Free Press, Cong. Rec.*, March 19, 1937, pp. 2,472 and 2,485. Telegram, Martin to FM, March 17, 1937, Box 43.

[19] *NYT*, March 18, 1937, pp. 1:5 and 4:2; March 21, 1937, p. 1:8.

[20] *Cong. Rec.*, March 17, 1937, pp. 2,337-38.

[21] *Cong. Rec.*, March 18-19, 1937, pp. 2,471-72 and 2,476-95. Quotes, pp. 2,478 and 2,484.

[22] *NYT*, Feb. 12, 1937, p. 18:5.

[23] Martin, quoted in *Cong. Rec.*, March 24, 1937, p. 2,728. Sen. George, *Cong. Rec.*, April 2, 1937, p. 3,075. Sen. Burke, *NYT*, April 5, 1937, p. 4:5.

[24] *Cong. Rec.*, March 23, 1,937, pp. 2,639, 2,665; April 8, 1937, pp. 3,293-94; April 1, 1937, p. 3,022; and April 2, 1937, p. 3,075. Galenson, *CIO Challenge*, p. 145.

[25] *Cleveland Plain Dealer*, March 25, 1937.

[26] *NYT*, March 20, 1937, p. 1:2; March 21, 1937, p. 31:1. Quote, "Selected Addresses of Frank Murphy, Governor of Michigan, January 1, 1937, to September 30, 1938" (Lansing, 1938), p. 8. Text, *NYT*, March 22, 1937, p. 2:3.

[27] RL:President's Personal File, Press Conferences, v. 9 (March 23, 1937), p. 211.

[28] *NYT*, March 21, 1937, p. 30:3.

[29] "Rebellion in Michigan," *America*, v. 56 (April 3, 1937), 613. *NYT*, March 21, 1937, p. 3:1.

[30] *NYT*, March 23, 1937, p. 16:5.

[31] FM to Kemp, March 22, 1937; K.T. Keller to FM, March 19, 1937, Box 44.

[32] Kemp to FM, March 22, 1937, Box 44.

[33] *Ibid*. Also memos, Kemp to FM, March 20, 22, and 23, 1937, Box 44.

[34] Telegram, FM to Lewis, March 23, 1937, Box 44. Text, *NYT*, March 24, 1937, p. 21:2.

[35] Telegram, Lewis to FM, March 23, 1937; Chrysler to FM, March 23, 1937, Box 44. Texts, *NYT*, March 24, 1937, p. 21:4.

[36] *NYT*, March 25, 1937, p. 1:8 and 10:3. Galenson, *CIO Challenge*, p. 149.

[37] *NYT*, March 25, 1937, p. 24:1. *San Francisco Chronicle*, March 28, 1937. Sandburg to FM, March 29, 1937, Box 45.

[38] *NYT*, March 26, 1937, p. 1:1.

[39] *NYT*, March 29, 1937, p. 1:8; *Cong. Rec.*, March 25, 1937, p. 2,774; Senate debate, April 1-7, 1937, pp. 3,017-43. Quote, p. 3,082.

[40] *Ibid.*, p. 3,082; Maverick, June 22, 1937, p. 6,162. Leon Green, "The Case for the Sit-Down Strikes," *New Republic*, v. 90 (March 24, 1937), pp. 199-200.

[41] Dixon Wecter, *The Age of the Great Depression* (New York:Macmillan, 1938), p. 114. *Cong. Rec.*, v. 81, pt. 9, App. 595-96. *NYT*, March 30, 1937, p. 22:2.

[42] Text, *NYT*, March 27, 1937, p. 1:7.

[43] Quoted in *Cong. Rec.*, April 2, 1937, p. 3,074.

[44] FM to Hill, March 31, 1937, Box 44. Undated, speech notes, Box 45. *NYT*, March 26, 1937, p. 12:4; and April 1, 1937, p. 12:2-3.

[45] *NYT*, April 4, 1937, p. 38:4; March 26, 1937, p. 12:5; and April 1, 1937, p. 12:2.

[46] *NYT*, March 26, 1937, p. 12:5; April 1, 1937, p. 12:2; and March 20, 1937, p.

4:4. Undated speech notes, Box 45. *New York American*, April 1, 1937.

[47] *NYT*, April 7, 1937, p. 1:8. Galenson, *CIO Challenge*, pp. 149, 150ff.

[48] *Ibid.*, pp. 149, 150ff. *NYT*, April 8, 1937, p. 18:1. *Cong. Rec.*, April 8, 1937, pp. 3,280-3,300; April 7, 1937, pp. 3,233-43.

[49] *NYT*, April 7, 1937, p. 4:7.

[50] S.L.A. Marshall to FM, April 7, 1937; Chrysler to FM, April 7, 1937, Box 45.

[51] *Shanghai Evening Post & Mercury*, March 27, 1937. *Los Angeles Times*, April 11, 1937. *New York Daily News*, July 16, 1937.

[52] *NYT*, Jan. 9, 1938, p. 22:6.

[53] *Washington Post*, Jan. 13, 1938. *New York Daily Mirror*, Oct. 12, 1938. Frederic Siedenberg to FM, Sep. 26, 1938, Box 55.

[54] FM to Elinor Greene, Jan. 18, 1938, Box 50.

[55] FM to Kemp, Dec. 30, 1937, Box 49. *Detroit Times*, Jan. 8, 1938. See Lee Kreiselman Jaffe to FM, undated, Box 46. Archibald MacNeil to FM, May 18, 1938, Box 52. Louis Brustein to FM, Aug. 22, 1937; Frederic C. Schouman to FM, Aug. 24, 1937, Box 47.

[56] Hayden to FM, Feb. 7, 1938, Box 50.

[57] Daniels to FM, March 26, 1937, Box 44.

[58] *NLRB* v. *Jones & Laughlin Steel Corp.*, 301 U.S. 1 (1937). See Edward S. Corwin, *Constitutional Revolution, Ltd.* (Claremont: Claremont Colleges, 1941), p. 73. *Detroit News*, April 15, 1937.

[59] Galenson, *CIO Challenge*, p. 147. Boris Shishkin to FM, Aug. 14, 1937, Box 47.

[60] *NYT*, May 31, 1937, p. 5:1; and June 12, 1937, p. 3:5.

[61] *NYT*, April 11, 1937, p. 1:6; June 28, 1937, p. 2:2; March 28, 1937, pp. 1:6 and 30:1.

[62] *NYT*, June 1, 1937, p. 1:1; and June 10, 1937, p. 12:1.

[63] *NYT*, June 23, 1937, p. 21:4; and June 10, 1937, p. 15:2.

[64] *NYT*, June 15, 1937, p. 14:2.

[65] FM, "The Shaping of a Labor Policy," *Survey Graphic*, v. 26 (Aug. 1937),

pp. 411-13, and comments, pp. 465-68. *Emporia Gazette*, Aug. 4, 1937.

[66] *Nation*, v. 146 (Jan. 1, 1938), 735; *NYT*, July 12, 1937, p. 5:2. Peale quoted, *NYT*, June 14, 1937, p. 21:2.

[67] *NYT*, April 8, 1937, p. 1:8; April 9, 1937, p. 1:6; April 11, 1936, p. 1:1; and April 8, 1937, p. 17:1.

[68] Galenson, *CIO Challenge*, p. 154. *NYT*, April 7, 1937, p. 1:6. Martin quoted, *NYT*, June 13, 1937, p. 7:8.

[69] Galenson, *CIO Challenge*, p. 145.

[70] Frances Perkins to FM, April 7, 1938, Box 51.

[71] Galenson, *CIO Challenge*, pp. 158, 162.

[72] *NYT*, April 2, 1937, p. 14:3; April 4, 1937, p. 38:4. Also see *NYT*, July 11, 1937, p. 2:4.

[73] FM to James W. Clapp, Dec. 19, 1938, Box 59.

[74] *NYT*, April 2, 1937, p. 14:3. *Detroit Times*, May 20, 1937.

[75] *NYT*, June 8, 1937, p. 1:8. *Detroit Times*, June 8, 1937.

[76] *Grand Rapids Herald*, June 9, 1937.

[77] *NYT*, June 12, 1937, p. 5:7. *Cong. Rec.*, June 30, 1937, p. 6,638.

[78] Norman H. Hill to FM, June 10, 1937, Box 46; *NYT*, June 10-14, 1937, p. 1; June 15, 1937, p. 14:2; *Cong. Rec.*, June 22, 1937, p. 6,161.

[79] FM, "The Shaping of a Labor Policy." *NYT*, June 29, 1937, p. 1:8.

[80] *NYT*, May 4, 1937, p. 17:4. *Detroit Free Press*, April 30, 1937. *Cong. Rec.*, June 30, 1937, p. 6,638.

[81] *NYT*, June 12, 1937, p. 5:7; June 16, 1937, p. 7:1.

[82] *NYT*, June 29, 1937, p. 7:1. *Muskegon Chronicle*, July 7, 1937. Also, "Selected Addresses," pp. 53-57.

[83] *NYT*, July 1, 1937, p. 5:4; July 28, 1937, p. 6:5; and July 30, 1937, p. 1:3.

[84] FM to Jaffe, Aug. 13, 1937, Box 47.

[85] *NYT*, July 31, 1937, p. 1:3; June 30, 1937, p. 22:1; and *Iron Age*, quoted in *NYT*, June 24, 1937, p. 2:3.

[86] *NYT*, June 30, 1937, p. 1:8, and Sep. 4, 1937, p. 1:2.

[87] *NYT*, Nov. 22, 1937, p. 1:5.

[88] *Lansing State Journal*, Sep. 26, 1937.

Detroit Times, Oct. 18, 1937; Dec. 30, 1937. *NYT*, Nov. 25, 1937, p. 33:1.

[89] *NYT*, Nov. 22, 1937, p. 1:5. FM to John M. Connolly, Nov. 27, 1937, Box 49. Quote, *NYT*, Nov. 25, 1937, p. 33:1.

[90] *Ibid.*, p. 33:1. *Cong. Rec.*, v. 82, pt. 3, App. 211-12. *Lansing State Journal*, Dec. 1, 1937.

[91] Charles J. Hedetniemi, Sr. to author, July 20, 1959.

[92] Unsigned memo, "School Aid," Sep. 8, 1938, Box 55. Harold D. Smith to C. L. Crawford, Sep. 29, 1938, Box 56. *Detroit Times*, Jan. 2, 1938. *Detroit News*, Jan. 2, 1938. *NYT*, Nov. 5, 1938, p. 4:2. Winfred Overholser to FM, Jan. 13, 1939, Box 61. FM to Salvador Areneta, Oct. 25, 1937, Box 48.

[93] Harold D. Smith to John Brennan, Aug. 2, 1940, Box 90. See report of Public Administrative Service to Harold D. Smith, Aug. 6, 1937, Box 47.

[94] See report, Arthur W. Bromage to FM, April 23, 1938, Box 52. Kemp to FM, Aug. 5, 1938, Box 54.

[95] Harold D. Smith to Eugene Johnson, June 15, 1938, Box 54.

[96] *NYT*, Feb. 3, 1939, p. 14:5.

[97] See note 94 above. FM to Norris, Sep. 9, 1937, Box 48.

[98] FM to George W. Norris, Nov. 18, 1937, Box 49. *Lansing State Journal*, Nov. 4, 1937.

[99] FM to Bowers, May 27, 1938, Box 53.

[100] *Detroit News*, Sep. 9, 1937. Also *St. Louis Post-Dispatch*, Aug. 21, 1937. "Uprooting the Spoils System," *Capitol Bulletin* (Lansing), Nov. 9, 1937, p. 2.

[101] Frank A. Picard to FM, Sep. 10, 1938, Box 55. Pollock to FM, Sep. 8, 1937, Box 48. See Pollock, "Michigan's First Year of Civil Service," *National Municipal Review*, v. 28 (Jan. 1939), 29ff.; and Edward H. Litchfield, "Michigan's Experience with Civil Service," *Personnel Administration*, v. 2 (Dec. 1939), 1-9.

[102] *Cong. Rec.*, Jan. 11, 1939, pp. 658-59.

[103] *Detroit News*, Oct. 17, 1937. Address to State Convention of Young Democrats, Muskegon, Oct. 16, 1937, reprinted by Democratic State Central Committee, Lansing, p. 5.

[104] Edward J. Fry to FM, June 7, 1938, Box 53.

[105] FM to Edward J. Fry, June 30, 1938; FM to Norman H. Hill, undated, Box 53.

[106] For example, Louise Henderson to Farley, Dec. 16, 1938. Martin R. Bradley to Farley, Dec. 23, 1938, RL:OF-300-DNC-Mich.

[107] Malcolm Hatfield to FDR, June 4, 1937, RL:OF-300-DNC-Mich.

[108] Joseph M. Donnelly to FM, July 22, 1938, Box 54.

[109] *Detroit News*, April 29, 1938. FM to Van Wagoner, May 6, 1938, Box 52. *Detroit Free Press*, Aug. 25, 1938. Samuel T. McSeveny, "The Michigan Gubernatorial Campaign of 1938," *Michigan History*, v. 45 (June 1961), 99.

[110] John C. Calahan, Jr., to FM, Feb. 25, 1938, Box 51. Frederic C. Schouman to FM, Nov. 3, 1938, Box 40.

[111] Raymond W. Starr to FM, Feb. 27, 1939, Box 65. *Detroit News*, dateline Oct. 13, 1938.

[112] FM to Claude G. Bowers, Jan. 3, 1938, Box 50. See relief reports, George Granger and Fred E. Levi to FM, April 12, 1938, Box 52.

[113] Frank A. Picard to Blair Moody, Nov. 28, 1938, Box 58.

[114] *Detroit Times*, Oct. 21, 1938. Telegram, FM to Martin Dies, Oct. 23, 1938, Box 56. Paul V. Anderson, "The Loaded Dies Committee," *Nation*, v. 147 (Oct. 29, 1938), 443. See House of Representatives, Special Committee to Investigate Un-American Activities and Propaganda in the United States, Report No. 2, 76th Cong., 1st Sess., 1939.

[115] RL:President's Personal File, Press Conferences, v. 12 (Oct. 25, 1938), 184. August R. Ogden, *The Dies Committee* (Washington: Catholic University Press, 1945), pp. 80-82. See RL:OF-320-Dies Committee Investigation.

[116] Copy, FDR to Hannah C. Hull, Oct. 29, 1938, Box 57.

[117] Copy, Wolcott statement, Oct. 21, 1938, Box 56.

[118] *Detroit Times*, dateline Oct. 25, 1937. Arthur D. Maguire to FM, Oct.

21, 1938, Box 56. *Detroit Times*, Nov. 3, 1938.

[119] Norman H. Hill to FM, Aug. 11, 1938; Raymond W. Starr to FM, June 20, 1938; and G. Mennen Williams to FM, Aug. 1, 1938, Box 54. Press release, Oct. 13, 1938, Box 56.

[120] FM to Hill, Dec. 15, 1937, Box 49. For example, see Carl Muller to FM, Oct. 11, 1938, Box 48; and Nov. 15, 1937, Box 49.

[121] FM to Frank C. Walker, Aug. 17, 1938, Box 55. *Flint Journal*, Oct. 22, 1938.

[122] Copy of speech at Flint, Oct. 21, 1938; and Kemp to FM, May 14, 1937, Box 46.

[123] FM to Chaplin, Nov. 3, 1938, Box 57.

[124] FM to Dale, July 23, 1938, Box 54.

[125] FDR to FM, Sep. 2, 1938, Box 55. Stephen Early to FM, Sep. 30, 1938, Box 56.

[126] *NYT*, Nov. 5, 1938, p. 5:3. *Detroit News*, Oct. 31, 1938.

[127] *Cong. Rec.*, Jan. 11, 1939, p. 211. State of Michigan, *Official Directory and Legislative Manual*, 1943-44, p. 267.

[128] FM to Doris Fleeson, Nov. 11, 1938; FM to Thomas G. Corcoran, Nov. 10, 1938, Box 57. Frank A. Picard to Blair Moody, Nov. 28, 1938, Box 58. See Mc-Seveny, "Michigan Gubernatorial Campaign," pp. 118-27.

[129] *NYT*, Nov. 10, 1938, p. 26:5. Cf. William E. Leuchtenberg, *Franklin D. Roosevelt and the New Deal* (New York: Harper & Row, 1963), p. 271.

[130] F. Murphy, "Tragic Interruption," *Nation*, v. 147 (Dec. 3, 1938), 589-90. FM to Doris Fleeson, Nov. 11, 1938, Box 57.

[131] FM to David Dubinsky, Nov. 21, 1938; FM to Richard A. Richards, Nov. 19, 1937, Box 57.

[132] FM to Murray, Nov. 23, 1938, Box 57.

[133] FM to A. E. Dale, Nov. 15, 1938, Box 57. Quote, FM to J.A. Wolfson, Dec. 13, 1938, Box 58.

[134] FM to Josephine Gomon, Dec. 5, 1938, Box 58.

[135] Ickes to FM, Nov. 10, 1938, Box 57. Wheeler to FM, Nov. 25, 1938, Box 58.

[136] Haber to FM, Nov. 16, 1938, Box 57.

[137] Galenson, *CIO Challenge*, pp. 147-48. Victor Riesel, *Los Vegas Sun*, Feb. 12, 1957.

[138] S.L.A. Marshall to FM, April 7, 1937, Box 45.

[139] Sandburg to FM, Oct. 2, 1937, Box 48.

[140] Murphy, "Tragic Interruption," p. 589.

[141] See *Cong. Rec.*, Jan. 19, 1939, pp. 421-22. Quote, *Annual Report of the Governor General of the Philippine Islands: 1935*, 75th Cong., 1st Sess., House Document 100, p. 19.

[142] FM to Osborn, June 13, 1944, No. 409, Box 133.

[143] *Kalamazoo Gazette*, April 5, 1938.

[144] Quoted by Dorothy Day, *The Catholic Worker*, Oct. 1937. "Selected Addresses," pp. 56, 20-21; *Hearing*, p. 3.

[145] "Selected Addresses," pp. 33-40. Quote, *NYT*, April 15, 1937, p. 15:3.

[146] *NYT*, Dec. 30, 1938, p. 3:8. "Selected Addresses," p. 50. "The Shaping of a Labor Policy," p. 451.

[147] "Selected Addresses," p. 101.

[148] *Ibid.*, pp. 37-38, 7, and 51. FM to Hayden, April 8, 1937, Box 45.

[149] Memo, "Stoppage of Work," Feb. 18, 1938, Box 51. FM to Kemp, July 20, 1938.

[150] Speech note, undated [March 1937], Box 45.

[151] FM to Francis B. Sayre, Oct. 5, 1938, Box 56.

[152] *NYT*, Nov. 21, 1938, p. 6:4. "Michigan's Responsibility to Education," address before Michigan Congress of Parents and Teachers, May 5, 1938. *MS*.

[153] "Ex-augural Message to the 60th Michigan Legislature," January 5, 1939, p. 3; and "Progress in Democracy," *American Labor Legislation Review*, v. 29 (June 1939), 61.

[154] "Selected Addresses," p. 30. "Progress in Democracy," *loc.cit.*; and *Wayne County Democrat*, Oct. 15, 1938.

[155] "Selected Addresses, p. 60.

[156] *Ibid.*, p. 9.

[157] John Locke, *Two Treatises of Civil Government* (Everyman's Library edn., 1924), p. 160.

[158] "Selected Addresses," pp. 13-14.

[159] Edward H. Litchfield to FM, Jan. 19, 1940, Box 87. See FM to Norman H. Hill, Jan. 9, 1945, Box 114.

[160] FM to Frankfurter, Nov. 23, 1938, Box 58. *Emporia Gazette*, Aug. 4, 1937.

[161] FM to Thomas W. Lanigan, Nov. 5, 1938, Box 57. "Selected Addresses," p. 16.

[162] *Ibid.*, p. 57.

CHAPTER 8

[1] FM to Thomas G. Corcoran, Nov. 10, 1938, Box 57. FM to Carlos P. Romulo, Dec. 28, 1938, Box 59.

[2] FM to James H. Cromwell, Nov. 19, 1938, Box 57.

[3] Eugene C. Gerhart, *America's Advocate, Robert H. Jackson* (Indianapolis: Bobbs-Merrill, 1958), pp. 161-64, 168. *The Secret Diary of Harold L. Ickes* (New York: Simon & Schuster, 1954), v. 2, pp. 537, 539, 628. Francis Biddle, *In Brief Authority* (New York: Doubleday & Company, 1962), pp. 79-80.

[4] Gerhart, *America's Advocate*, pp. 484n and 162. Ickes, *Secret Diary*, v. 2, pp. 527, 539, 628.

[5] *NYHT*, Jan. 3, 1939, p. 11:7.

[6] *Raleigh News and Observer*, Jan. 3, 1939. *Nation*, v. 148 (Jan. 7, 1939), 22.

[7] *Chicago Daily Tribune*, Jan. 4, 1939. *Traffic World*, reprinted, *Cong. Rec.*, Feb. 17, 1939, p. 1,542.

[8] *Cong. Rec.*, Jan. 17, 1939, pp. 409-17; and Jan. 11, 1939, pp. 189-202.

[9] *Gary* (Ind.) *Post-Tribune*, Jan. 12, 1939. *NYT*, Jan. 2, 1939, p. 22:5. *Kansas City Journal*, Dec. 2, 1938.

[10] *NYHT*, Jan. 3, 1939, p. 14:2. Matthew F. McGuire to FM, Jan. 9, 1939, Box 61. Prentiss M. Brown to FM, Jan. 5, 1939, Box 60. FM to Garner, Dec. 23, 1938, Box 59.

[11] Matthew F. McGuire to FM, Jan. 9, 1939, Box 61. *Detroit News*, Jan. 6, 1939; FM to Marvel M. Logan, Jan. 12, 1939, Box 61.

[12] U.S. Congress, Senate, Subcommittee of the Committee on the Judiciary, *Hearing, Nomination of Frank Murphy to be Attorney General of the United States*, 76th Cong., 1st Sess., Jan. 13, 1939, pp. 3-7, 10-12.

[13] FM to Josiah W. Bailey, March 7, 1939, Box 65. *Hearing*, Jan. 13, 1939, p. 8.

[14] *Louisville Times*, Jan. 11, 1939. *Knox-ville News-Sentinel*, Jan. 16, 1939. Also *Topeka Capital*, Jan. 17, 1939. *Davenport* (Iowa) *Democrat*, Jan. 13, 1939.

[15] *Washington Post*, Jan. 14, 1939, quoted in *Cong. Rec.*, Jan. 17, 1939, p. 410.

[16] FM to Hawkins, Jan. 28, 1939, Box 63.

[17] *Ibid.* FM to Tom Ferriss, June 27, 1939.

[18] FM to Hawkins, Jan. 28, 1939, Box 63. FM to P.H. Callahan, May 25, 1937, Box 46.

[19] *Cong. Rec.*, Jan. 17, 1939, pp. 410-11. *NYHT*, Jan. 17, 1939, p. 17:1.

[20] FM to David T. Boguslav, Jan. 27, 1939, Box 63. *NYT*, Jan. 18, 1939, p. 18:3. Walter J. Munro to FM, Jan. 16, 1939, Box 62. Joseph Lawrence to FM, Jan. 13, 1939, Box 61.

[21] Frankfurter to FM, Jan. 16, 1939, Box 61.

[22] Harry H. Bennett to FM, Jan. 10, 1939, Box 61. *Cong. Rec.*, Jan. 17, 1939, pp. 409-29. *NYHT*, Jan. 18, 1939, p. 1:6. Arthur H. Vandenberg to FM, Jan. 16, 1939, Box 62.

[23] *NYT*, Nov. 13, 1938, p. 42:2. Ickes, *Secret Diary*, v. 2, pp. 606-607, 685.

[24] *Eau Claire* (Mich.) *Advocate*, Jan. 13, 1938.

[25] FM to Roger Baldwin, Jan. 17, 1939, Box 62.

[26] Quoted by Bruce Catton, *Pittsburgh Press*, Jan. 17, 1937.

[27] Murphy, quoted in *NYT*, Aug. 27, 1939, IV, p. 7:1; and May 30, 1939, p. 3:5.

[28] Departmental memo, Jan. 26, 1939. James V. Bennett to FM, Jan. 17, 1939; FM to FDR, Jan. 24, 1939, Box 62.

[29] Press release, Feb. 24, 1939. FM to Kemp, Feb. 28, 1939, Box 65. Order No. 3,215, March 15, 1939, Box 66. See *Washington Post*, Feb. 25, 1939.

[30] Press release, March 23, 1939. Rob-

ert H. Jackson to FM, March 17, 1939, Box 66; and March 29, 1939, Box 67.

[31] Order No. 3,205, February 4, 1939, Box 63. *NYT*, Feb. 4, 1939, p. 2:2. Memo, Alexander Holtzoff to Kemp, March 8, 1939, Box 66. Press release, Feb. 8, 1939, Box 63. Press release, March 18, 1939, Box 66.

[32] Homer S. Cummings, "Memo to be handed to my Successor," Jan. 1939, Box 63. Press release re FBI, Jan. 21, 1939, Box 62.

[33] Alsop and Kintner, *Washington Star*, March 25, 1939. Krock, *NYT*, Feb. 3, 1939, p. 14:5.

[34] *Baltimore Sun*, Feb. 16, 1939. Lewis Wood to FM, Sep. 15, 1939. Order No. 3,280, July 26, 1939, Box 75.

[35] Ernest K. Lindley, *Brooklyn Eagle*, undated.

[36] FM to Ralph W. Aigler, Feb. 2, 1939, Box 65.

[37] Memo, Gordon Dean to FM, May 11, 1939, p. 3, Box 70. FM to Coblentz, July 21, 1939, Box 74. See Richard Polenberg, *Reorganizing Roosevelt's Government* (Cambridge: Harvard University Press, 1966).

[38] FM to Russell Porter, March 13, 1939, Box 66.

[39] Memo, FDR to FM, Jan. 12, 1939, Box 61. Memos, Gordon Dean to FM, and Linton M. Collins to Kemp, Jan. 19, 1939, Box 62. See Report of the President's Committee on Civil Service Improvement, House Document No. 118, 77th Cong., 1st Sess., Feb. 1941. William Brownrigg to FM, May 4, 1939, Box 70.

[40] Kemp to FM, Feb. 9, 1939, Box 64. McFarland to FM, Jan. 31, 1939, Box 63. G. Mennen Williams to FM, Dec. 6, 1939, Box 82. Kemp to FM, June 29, 1939, Box 73.

[41] Memo, Joseph B. Keenan to FM, Jan. 12, 1939, Box 61. FM to Matthew F. McGuire, Oct. 17, 1939, Box 79. Press releases, Jan. 28 and 30, 1939, Box 63. *NYT*, Feb. 4, 1939, p. 3:1. Memo on judicial appointments, Nov. 10, 1942, Box 105.

[42] FM to Bates, Feb. 11, 1939, Box 64.

[43] Draft statement for FDR, FM to FDR, Jan. 30, 1939, Box 63.

[44] Memo, Lee Pressman to John L. Lewis, March 8, 1939, Box 66.

[45] Biddle, *In Brief Authority*, pp. 79-80. *Washington Times-Herald*, Feb. 23, 1939. Ickes, *Secret Diary*, v. 2, pp. 570-71.

[46] Prentiss M. Brown to FM, Feb. 2, 1939, Box 63. Harry H. Woodring to FM, May 18, 1939, Box 70.

[47] Press release, April 12, 1939, Box 68. FM to Matthew F. McGuire, Oct. 17, 1939, Box 79. Memos, McGuire and Brien McMahon to FM, March 22, 1939, Box 66. Also McGuire to FM, March 24, 1939, Box 67. Quote, *Dallas Times-Herald*, May 28, 1939.

[48] Memos, Alexander Holtzoff to FM, March 9, 1939, and Brien McMahon to FM, March 23, 1939, Box 66.

[49] Alexander Holtzoff to FM, March 8, 1939. Press release, March 10, 1939, Box 66.

[50] "The Courts—A National Bulwark," *Vital Speeches*, v. 5 (May 1, 1939), pp. 436-37. *Detroit Times*, May 1, 1939. Also "The Lawyer and the Economy of Tomorrow," reprinted *Cong. Rec.*, v. 84, pt. 13, App. 2,684-85.

[51] Malcolm Hatfield to FM, April 7, 1939, Box 68. FM to FDR, Jan. 30, 1939, Box 63.

[52] Telegram, Jones to FDR, April 24, 1939, RL: OF-10-Attorney General. FM to Joseph M. Donnelly, April 25, 1939, Box 69.

[53] Frankfurter to FM, Feb. 10, 1939, Box 64.

[54] Memo, Kemp to FM, March 28, 1939, Box 68. *St. Louis Post-Dispatch*, April 6, 1939.

[55] *Ibid. St. Louis Star-Times*, March 30, 1939.

[56] *NYT*, May 30, 1939, p. 3:5.

[57] Unsent letter, FM to Maguire, June 12, 1939, Box 72.

[58] *NYT*, May 12, 1939, p. 7:3. Letter to FM, May 1, 1939, Box 69.

[59] *Los Angeles Examiner*, May 25, 1939; *NYT*, May 30, 1939, p. 3:5-6.

[60] *El Paso Herald-Post*, May 23, 1939. *Charlotte News*, June 4, 1939. For example, *Tampa Tribune*, June 11, 1939; *Chicago Daily News*, June 22, 1939.

[61] See Daniel P. Moynihan, "The Private Government of Crime," *Reporter*, v. 25

(July 6, 1961), 14-20. Stark to FM, July 19, 1939, Box 73.

[62] "St. Francis," *Time*, June 5, 1939, p. 16. *NYT*, Oct. 23, 1939, p. 1:1. FM to Jerome Nadonley, Jan. 10, 1939, Box 61. *Atlanta Constitution*, June 1, 1939.

[63] Delos G. Smith to FM, April 20, 1939, Box 69. *NYT*, June 8, 1939, p. 3:3.

[64] Collier to FM, June 22, 1939, Box 73. Also Angelo J. Rossi to FM, June 7, 1939, Box 72. Memo, Joseph A. Mulcahy to FM, June 22, 1939, Box 73. *NYT*, June 23, 1939, p. 15:3.

[65] James V. Bennett to FM, July 27, 1939, Box 75. *Washington Post*, May 5, 1946. Gerhart, *America's Advocate*, p. 177.

[66] *NYT*, Aug. 4, 1939, p. 2:2. *St. Louis Post-Dispatch*, July 18, 1939, and Sep. 15, 1939. *Kansas City Star*, Oct. 11, 1939.

[67] *Charlotte News*, Aug. 21, 1939.

[68] *Pontiac Press*, April 24, 1939. Mulcahy to FM, May 28, 1939, Box 71.

[69] Alan Barth, *Charlotte Observer*, undated. *Miami Daily News*, Dec. 29, 1939. *Farmer's Friend*, July 31, 1939.

[70] *NYT*, Feb. 3, 1939, p. 14:5. *Detroit Times*, Sep. 20, 1935.

[71] FM to Alexander Ruthven, June 6, 1939, Box 72. *Detroit Times*, June 17, 1939.

[72] *Washington Times-Herald*, Dec. 31, 1939. *Boston Traveller*, Aug. 30, 1939.

[73] *Washington Times-Herald*, June 13, 1939.

[74] *Jim Farley's Story* (New York: McGraw-Hill, 1948), p. 153. Cf. Robert E. Sherwood, *Roosevelt and Hopkins*, rev. edn. (New York: Harper & Bros., 1950), pp. 94-95. *NYT*, May 28, 1939, p. 10:6.

[75] *Philadelphia Inquirer*, June 12, 1939. *Kansas City Star*, June 16, 1939. *United Progressive News* (Los Angeles), Sep. 18, 1939.

[76] Stephen Early to FM, March 4, 1939, RL:OF-10-Attorney General. Kemp to FM, May 3, 1939, Box 70.

[77] Moley, "Mercy and the Big Chance," *Newsweek*, v. 13 (May 15, 1939), p. 56.

[78] White to FM, Aug. 14, 1939, Box 76. Ickes, *Secret Diary*, v. 3, pp. 93-94. Frank Knox to FM, Sep. 6, 1939, Box 77. *NYHT*, May 31, 1939, p. 20:3.

[79] *NYT*, Feb. 19, 1939, p. 6:2. Frank A. Picard to FM, Feb. 20, 1939, Box 64. Joseph M. Donnelly to FM, Feb. 27, 1939, Box 65; and July 26, 1939, Box 75. Raymond Wesley Starr to FM, March 3, 1939, Box 65.

[80] Note, FM to Charles J. Hedetniemi on telegram, Michigan Young Democrats to FM, Oct. 16, 1939, Box 78. G. Mennen Williams to FM, Sep. 12, 1939, Box 77. Frank A. Picard to FM, Aug. 16, 1939, Box 76.

[81] Copy, W.M. Gibb to G. Donald Kennedy, Nov. 12, 1939, Box 80. Telegram, FM to Murray D. Van Wagoner, Dec. 29, 1939, Box 83.

[82] Donnelly to FM, July 26, 1939, Box 75.

[83] FM to G.A. Richards, July 21, 1939, Box 74.

[84] Russell Porter, "Our No. 1 Trouble Shooter," *NYT Magazine* (April 16, 1939), p. 20:2. *NYT*, June 23, 1939, p. 4:7.

[85] "Lay Bishop," *Time*, Aug. 28, 1939, p. 16. Ickes, *Secret Diary*, v. 2, p. 372.

[86] *Buffalo News*, Dec. 26, 1939.

[87] Arnold to FM, March 8, 1939, and March 20, 1939; Letter to FM, March 17, 1939, Box 66. Arnold to FM, May 25, 1943, Box 108.

[88] Thurman Arnold to FM, March 8, 1939, Box 66. Press release, May 18, 1939, Box 70. *Louisville Courier-Journal*, April 28, 1939.

[89] Thurman Arnold to FM, Oct. 21 and 25, 1939, Box 79. FM to William Green, Dec. 1, 1939, Box 82. Memo, Alexander Holtzoff to Kemp, Dec. 27, 1939, Box 83. *Bedford Co.* v. *Stone Cutters Assn.*, 274 U.S. 37 (1926).

[90] *Flint Journal*, Nov. 3, 1939. *NYT*, July 14, 1939, p. 1:1. Hugh A. Fisher to FM, July 11, 1939, Box 74.

[91] *NYT*, July 21, 1939, p. 3:2. *Nashville Tennessean*, July 21, 1939. Address, "The Higher Duty," Jan. 14, 1940, *MS*. Address, "The Democratic Crisis in America," text, *Philadelphia Record*, April 14, 1939. Address, "Civil Liberties," March 27, 1939, *Cong. Rec.*, v. 84, pt. 12, App. 1,352.

[92] Moley, "Mercy and the Big Chance," p. 56. *Business Week*, March 27, 1937, p. 14.

[93] Carl A. Hatch to FM, July 28, 1939; Kemp to FM, July 28, 1939; and draft of veto message, July 31, 1935, Box 75.

[94] FM notes on draft presidential message, Aug. 1, 1939; Civil Service Commissioners to FDR, July 31, 1939, Box 75. *NYT*, Aug. 4, 1939, p. 4:7.

[95] Department Circular 3,285, Aug. 10, 1939, Box 76. FM to Kemp, Oct. 17, 1939, Box 79. Press release, Oct. 26, 1939, Box 79.

[96] FM to Pollock, Aug. 3, 1939, Box 75. FM to Alexander Holtzoff, Oct. 17, 1939, Box 79.

[97] FM to Coblentz, June 29, 1939, Box 73; and April 3, 1939, Box 67.

[98] Address, "Better Servants for Democracy," June 15, 1939, *MS*. Partial text, *NYT*, June 16, 1939, p. 3:6.

[99] *Helena Independent*, June 17, 1939.

[100] Lee Waters to FM, April 5, 1939, Box 68. Charles J. Hedetniemi to Matthew F. McGuire, June 21, 1939, Box 73. *Time*, June 26, 1939, p. 18. *Detroit News*, June 17, 1939.

[101] *Haverhill Gazette*, June 20, 1939. Also *Bakersfield Californian*, July 11, 1939. *Baltimore Sun*, June 18, 1939.

[102] FM to Boake Carter, July 10, 1939, Box 74. *Tulsa World*, June 17, 1939.

[103] Frank to FM, Sep. 20, 1939, Box 78.

[104] J. Weldon Jones to Kemp, March 27, 1939, Kemp Papers. Niebuhr to FM, April 16, 1939, Box 68. Also see Reinhold Niebuhr to FM, Jan. 8, 1940, Box 86. Joseph E. Davies to FM, April 6, 1939, Box 68; and James K. Pollock to FM, Sep. 21, 1939, Box 78.

[105] Claude G. Bowers to FM, Nov. 27, 1939, Box 81.

CHAPTER 9

[1] FM to Morris L. Ernst, Jan. 9, 1939, Box 61.

[2] *New York Journal-American*, Jan. 25, 1939.

[3] Address, "The Test of Patriotism," reprinted in *National Lawyers Guild Quarterly*, v. 2 (Oct. 1939), 165. Address, "The Return of Religion," June 13, 1939, *MS*. Partial text, *NYT*, June 14, 1939, p. 18:4.

[4] *NYT*, Feb. 4, 1939, p. 2:2. Roger Baldwin to FM, Jan. 3, 1939, Box 60. FM to Morris L. Ernst, Jan. 9, 1939, Box 61.

[5] Lee Pressman to FM, Jan. 17, 1939, Box 62. Quote, *New York Journal-American*, Jan. 25, 1939.

[6] Memo, Brien McMahon to FM, Feb. 3, 1939, Box 63.

[7] Memo, Gordon Dean to FM, Feb. 14, 1939, Box 64. Order No. 3,204; press release, Feb. 3, 1939, Box 63. Memos, Brien McMahon to FM, Feb. 3, 1939, Box 63; and March 4, 1939, Box 65.

[8] FM to FDR, Report on the Activities of the Department of Justice, July 7, 1939, reprinted, *Cong. Rec.*, v. 84, pt. 14, App. 3,310.

[9] Henry A. Morgenthau, Jr., to FM, Jan. 27, 1939, Box 63. 307 U.S. 496 (1939); 313 U.S. 299 (1941). See *Screws* v. *United States*, 325 U.S. 91 (1945), and Robert K.

Carr, *Federal Protection of Civil Rights: Quest for a Sword* (Ithaca: Cornell University Press, 1947).

[10] *NYT*, Feb. 4, 1939, p. 2:2. Address, "The Evolution of a Century," May 29, 1939, *MS*.

[11] "The Test of Patriotism," p. 165. Address, "Civil Liberties and the Cities," May 15, 1939, *Vital Speeches*, v. 5 (June 1, 1939), 543.

[12] Address, "Civil Liberties," March 27, 1939, *Cong. Rec.*, v. 84, pt. 12, App. 1,352-53.

[13] Address at 104th anniversary of the N.Y.U. Law School, March 2, 1940, *Cong. Rec.*, v. 86, pt. 14, App. 1,588-89.

[14] "Civil Liberties and the Cities," pp. 543-44; "The Democratic Crisis in America," *Philadelphia Record*, April 14, 1939.

[15] "Test of Patriotism," p. 169; "Civil Liberties and the Cities," p. 544.

[16] *NYT*, Nov. 12, 1939, p. 29:1. "The Test of Patriotism," pp. 168-69.

[17] *Ibid.*, p. 166. FM to Hoover, Sep. 7, 1940, Box 92.

[18] "The Test of Patriotism," p. 167.

[19] FM handwritten note, undated, Box 84. Kemp to FM, Oct. 3, 1939, Box 78.

[20] "The Democratic Crisis in America,"

Philadelphia Record, April 14, 1939; undelivered draft address, Joseph A. Mulcahy to Stephen Early, Sep. 23, 1939, RL: OF-10-Attorney General.

[21] 4 Wall. 2, 120-21 (1866). "Test of Patriotism," pp. 168-69.

[22] *Ibid.*, pp. 168-69. *Abrams* v. *United States*, 250 U.S. 616, 630 (1919).

[23] "Civil Liberties and the Cities," p. 544.

[24] *NYT*, Oct. 1, 1939, p. 38:3. "Test of Patriotism," pp. 167-68. FM to Martin Dies, *NYT*, Nov. 4, 1939, p. 9:6.

[25] "Test of Patriotism," p. 168.

[26] "Civil Liberties and the Cities," p. 544.

[27] Gordon Dean to Kemp, June 9, 1939, Box 72. Cf. Herbert Bayard Swope to FM, June 23, 1939, Box 73. Quote, *NYT*, June 22, 1939, p. 14:5. For full address, see "The Meaning of Civil Liberty," *Cong. Rec.*, v. 84, pt. 13, App. 2,921-22.

[28] "Civil Liberties and the Cities," p. 544; "Civil Liberties," App. 1,353.

[29] "Test of Patriotism," p. 168.

[30] "The Meaning of Civil Liberty," *NYT*, Sep. 26, 1939, p. 12:6.

[31] "Test of Patriotism," p. 170; "The Right Use of Democracy," address before Second National Catholic Social Action Conference, Cleveland, June 14, 1939, *MS*.

[32] "Civil Liberties and the Cities," p. 543.

[33] Address, "The Substance of Freedom," May 23, 1939, *MS*.

[34] See Peter H. Odegard to FM, May 8, 1939, Box 70. Justin Miller to FM, April 8, 1939, Box 68. Quote, Baldwin to FM, May 16, 1939, Box 70.

[35] *Nation*, v. 150 (Jan. 13, 1940), p. 29. See *Cincinnati Post*, Dec. 12, 1939; *NYT*, May 16, 1939, p. 22:2; *Washington Post*, Jan. 9, 1940. *Philadelphia Record*, Oct. 17, 1939. Harlan F. Stone to FM, January 8, 1940, Box 86. *Flint Journal*, Jan. 14, 1940.

[36] *Chattanooga Times*, May 17, 1939. Introduction to "In Defense of Democracy," reprinted, *Cong. Rec.*, v. 86, pt. 13, App. 60. Also see *International Conciliation* (May 1940).

[37] Copy, Morris L. Ernst to Ernest Cuneo, Aug. 29, 1939; and Ernst to FM, Sep. 7, 1939, Box 77.

[38] Report on the Activities of the Department of Justice, App. 3,309.

[39] *NYT*, Oct. 27, 1939, p. 13:4.

[40] Morris L. Ernst to FDR, Dec. 11, 1939; FDR to FM, Dec. 13, 1939, Box 82. Note on Joseph A. Mulcahy to FM, Nov. 2, 1939, Box 80. Morris L. Ernst to FM, April 17, 1939, Box 68. Kemp to FM, May 4, 1939, Box 70. See Walter F. Murphy, *Wiretapping on Trial* (New York: Random House, 1965), pp. 130-35.

[41] FM to Alexander Holtzoff, Nov. 9, 1939; quote from G. Bromley Oxnam to FM, Nov. 13, 1939, Box 80. Holtzoff to FM, Nov. 29, 1939, Box 81.

[42] *NYT*, Sep. 7, 1939, p. 8:1; Oct. 1, 1939, p. 38:3.

[43] Don Whitehead, *The FBI Story* (New York: Random House, 1956), pp. 161-65. Homer S. Cummings to FDR, Oct. 20, 1938; FM to FDR, June 17, 1939; FDR memo to the Secretary of State and related agencies, June 26, 1939, RL:OF-10-Attorney General.

[44] Whitehead, *FBI Story*, pp. 161-65, 170. *NYT*, Oct. 23, 1939, p. 1:1; Jan. 3, 1940, p. 3:4; Jan. 4, 1940, p. 14:7. Memo, Matthew F. McGuire to FM, Nov. 16, 1939, Box 81. Memo, O. John Rogge to FM, Dec. 6, 1939, Box 82. Teletype extract, Dec. 14, 1939, Box 84. Kemp to FM, Oct. 2, 1939, Box 78; Oct. 19, 1939, Box 79.

[45] FM to FDR, Sep. 6, 1939, RL:OF-10-Attorney General. Memo, J. Edgar Hoover to FM, Dec. 4, 1939, Box 82. Press release, Sep. 6, 1939, Box 77.

[46] *The Secret Diary of Harold L. Ickes* (New York: Simon & Schuster, 1954), v. 3, p. 139. Frank R. Kent, *Baltimore Sun*, July 9, 1939.

[47] Ickes, *Secret Diary*, v. 3, p. 139. George Murphy to James Roosevelt, July 27, 1938, and memo attached, July 29, 1938, RL:OF-300-DNC-Mich.

[48] FM to FDR, Sep. 30, 1938, RL:P.P.F.-1,662. FM to FDR, Aug. 19, 1939, Box 77.

[49] FDR to FM, July 1, 1939; Kemp to FM, June 7, 1939, and July 13, 1939, Box 74.

⁵⁰ FM to Richards, Sep. 13, 1939, Box 77.

⁵¹ "America and the War: A Washington Letter," *Life*, Oct. 9, 1939, p. 22. Ickes, *Secret Diary*, v. 3, pp. 54, 76.

⁵² *NYT*, April 3, 1940, p. 22:6; April 7, 1940, p. 2:5; and Whitehead, *FBI Story*, pp. 170-78.

⁵³ Claude G. Bowers to FM, Nov. 27, 1939, Box 81. Josephus Daniels to FM, Dec. 14, 1939, Box 82. Francis Biddle, *In Brief Authority* (New York: Doubleday & Company, 1962), pp. 86-87. *NYT*, Nov. 21, 1939, p. 22:5.

⁵⁴ Ickes, *Secret Diary*, v. 3, p. 97. Hill to FM, Jan. 5, 1940. Also Stephen J. Hannagan to FM, Jan. 5, 1940, Box 85.

⁵⁵ FM to Ross, Nov. 20, 1939, Box 81.

⁵⁶ Biddle, *In Brief Authority*, pp. 92-93. FM to FDR, Dec. 9, 1939, Box 82.

⁵⁷ Porter Sims to FM, Jan. 6, 1940, Box 86.

⁵⁸ Biddle, *In Brief Authority*, p. 93. FM to Grace Tully, Feb. 11, 1942, RL: P.S.F., Box 36. FM to FDR, March 22, 1940, Box 89.

⁵⁹ FM to Bates, Jan. 17, 1940, Box 87.

⁶⁰ FM to William Murphy, Jan. 8, 1940, Box 86.

⁶¹ FM to Hannagan, Jan. 6, 1940, Box 86.

⁶² Ickes, *Secret Diary*, v. 3, p. 110. Press release, *MS*, Jan. 4, 1940. *Fort Wayne Journal Gazette*, dateline Jan. 4, 1940.

⁶³ *Los Angeles Times*, Jan. 5, 1940.

⁶⁴ Roger Baldwin to FM, Jan. 9, 1940, Box 86. David K. Niles to FM, Jan. 5, 1940, Box 85.

⁶⁵ *Winchester* (Va.) *Evening Star*, Jan. 5, 1940. See Wright Patman to FM, Jan. 5, 1940, Box 85.

⁶⁶ *New London* (Conn.) *Day*, Dec. 27, 1939. *Gadsden* (Ala.) *Times*, Jan. 7, 1940.

⁶⁷ *Houston Chronicle*, Jan. 6, 1940. Sen. Ashurst, *Washington Star*, Jan. 4, 1940. *Decatur* (Ill.) *Herald & Review*, Jan. 7, 1940. *Fort Wayne Journal Gazette*, Nov. 18, 1939.

⁶⁸ Krock, *NYT*, Nov. 21, 1939, p. 22:5; *Miami Herald*, Jan. 5, 1940.

⁶⁹ *NYT*, Dec. 16, 1939, p. 10:2. *Cleveland Plain Dealer*, Dec. 17, 1939; *New Orleans Times-Picayune*, Dec. 24, 1939; *Washington Post*, Dec. 17, 1939.

⁷⁰ *Emporia Gazette*, undated. Hallihan to FM, Feb. 8, 1940, Box 88. Schlesinger to FM, Jan. 24, 1940, Box 87. McAdoo to FM, Nov. 28, 1939, Box 81. Also, Adolph A. Berle, Jr. to FM, Jan. 4, 1940, Box 85. Edgar N. Durfee to FM, Feb. 2, 1940, Box 88. Michael A. Musmanno to FM, Jan. 8, 1940, Box 86. *Chicago Daily News*, Jan. 5, 1940.

⁷¹ Ickes, *Secret Diary*, v. 3, p. 70. Quote, *Detroit News*, dateline Jan. 4, 1940. Also, *Washington Post*, Jan. 7, 1940.

⁷² See Henry M. Bates to FM, Jan. 31, 1940, Box 88. Also *Boston Transcript*, undated; *Philadelphia Record*, Jan. 5, 1940.

⁷³ *Vicksburg Herald*, Jan. 6, 1940. *NYT*, Jan. 5, 1940. *Detroit Free Press*, Jan. 6, 1940.

⁷⁴ Press release, *MS*, and *NYT*, Jan. 12, 1940, p. 10:4. *Cong. Rec.*, Jan. 15, 1940, p. 329. See Arthur H. Vandenberg to FM, Jan. 16, 1940, Box 87.

⁷⁵ *NYT*, Nov. 19, 1939, IV, p. 3:1. *Miami Daily News*, Jan. 5, 1940. *New Orleans Times-Picayune*, Jan. 9, 1940.

⁷⁶ *Jim Farley's Story* (New York: McGraw-Hill, 1948), p. 216. Ickes, *Secret Diary*, v. 3, pp. 12, 51-54. Biddle, *In Brief Authority*, pp. 92-96.

⁷⁷ Eugene Gerhart, *America's Advocate, Robert H. Jackson* (Indianapolis: Bobbs-Merrill, 1958), p. 183.

⁷⁸ *Ibid.*, pp. 170-77, 182-87. See memo, G. Mennen Williams to FM, Oct. 9, 1939, Box 79.

⁷⁹ Jackson to FM, and Arnold to Joseph A. Mulcahy, Oct. 24, 1939; Arnold to FM, Oct. 25, 1939, Box 79.

⁸⁰ Gerhart, *America's Advocate*, p. 185.

⁸¹ *Ibid.*, p. 186.

⁸² *Detroit News*, Dec. 12, 1939. *NYT*, Oct. 27, 1939, p. 1:2. Gerhart, *America's Advocate*, p. 187.

⁸³ *Ibid.*, p. 185.

⁸⁴ *Washington Star*, Jan. 4, 1940. *Chicago Daily News*, Dec. 7, 1939.

⁸⁵ Ickes, *Secret Diary*, v. 3, p. 104.

⁸⁶ *NYT*, Jan. 18, 1940, p. 17:6. Gerhart, *America's Advocate*, pp. 189, 486n, 190. *NYT*, Jan. 19, 1940, p. 3.

⁸⁷ Whitehead, *FBI Story*, pp. 175-76.

Baltimore Sun, Feb. 27, 1940. *NYT*, Feb. 29, 1940, p. 18:5.

[88] *Ibid*. See memo, Eleanor Bumgardner to FM, April 20, 1940, Box 90. Matthew F. McGuire to FM, Jan. 9, 1940, Box 86. Hughes approval: FM to Hughes, Jan. 20, 1940, Box 87. Kemp memo of telephone call, Jan. 20, 1940; Kemp to FM, Jan. 22, 1940, Kemp Papers. Charles Evans Hughes to FM, and reply, Feb. 1, 1940, Box 88.

[89] Blair Moody, *Detroit News*, dateline March 1, 1940. Nancy Randolph, *Washington Times-Herald*, Feb. 19, 1940. See *Detroit Free Press* and *Kansas City Star*, Feb. 28, 1940. "Even Hand," *Time*, (Feb. 26, 1940), p. 14. Alsop and Kintner, *Washington Star*, Feb. 17, 1940.

[90] "Loafing on His Job," *Macon News-Telegraph*, undated *MS*, reprinted, *Detroit News*, Feb. 27, 1940.

[91] FM to W.T. Anderson, March 14, 1940, Box 89. *Flint Journal*, Feb. 23, 1940.

[92] *New York Journal-American*, Feb. 23 and March 6, 1940. *Jackson* (Mich.) *Citizen-Patriot*, Feb. 27, 1940. Cf. "Frank Murphiwell," *New Republic*, v. 99 (July 12, 1939), 279.

[93] Wallace to FM, Jan. 23, 1940, Box 87.

[94] FM to Montgomery, Feb. 27, 1940, Box 89.

[95] Clerk to Eleanor Bumgardner, March 25, 1940, Box 89. Memo by Lee Waters, March 2, 1940, Box 90.

[96] FM to Hughes, Feb. 28, 1940, Box 89.

[97] *NYT*, March 1, 1940, p. 12:6.

[98] Undated note, FM to Felix Frankfurter, Box 28, Frankfurter Papers, Manuscript Division, Library of Congress. FM to Moody, March 2, 1940, Box 89.

[99] FM to Hayden, April 9, 1940, Box 90.

[100] Jackson to FM, June 18, 1941, Box 97.

[101] FM to Bowers, Feb. 28, 1940, Box 89. Address, Jackson Day Dinner, Detroit, Jan. 6, 1939, *MS*.

[102] FM to Hayden, April 9, 1940, Box 90.

[103] See "Who Covered up for Reds?" *Chicago Daily Tribune*, Feb. 24, 1954. Quotes, "The Higher Duty," *loc.cit.; Baltimore Sun*, Feb. 16, 1939.

[104] FM to Jacabo Zobel, March 8, 1940, Box 89.

[105] *Buffalo News*, Jan. 5, 1940.

CHAPTER 10

[1] "Selected Addresses of Frank Murphy, Governor of Michigan, January 1, 1937, to September 30, 1938" (Lansing, 1938), pp. 3-5.

[2] *Detroit News*, Aug. 6, 1936, p. 6.

[3] *NLRB* v. *Jones & Laughlin Steel Corp.*, 301 U.S. 1 (1937). *Detroit News*, April 15, 1937.

[4] Undated *MS*, press release of Hearing, Senate Judiciary subcommittee on his nomination to the Supreme Court. See *NYT*, Jan. 12, 1940, p. 1:2.

[5] "Selected Addresses," p. 50.

[6] *Ibid.*, pp. 17, 45. *NYT*, July 7, 1937, p. 6:4.

[7] "Selected Addresses," p. 95. Address, "The Democratic Crisis in America," *Philadelphia Record*, April 14, 1939.

[8] Quoted, Russell Porter, "Our No. 1 Trouble Shooter," *NYT Magazine* (April 16, 1939), pp. 3, 20.

[9] Address, "The Courts—A National Bulwark," *Vital Speeches*, v. 5 (May 1, 1939), 436. "Selected Addresses," p. 30.

[10] For cases and discussion see John Raeburn Green, "The Supreme Court, the Bill of Rights and the States," *University of Pennsylvania Law Review*, v. 97 (April 1949), 608-40; C. Herman Pritchett, *The American Constitution* (New York: McGraw-Hill, 1959), ch. 22.

[11] *Missouri, K. & T. Ry. Co.* v. *May*, 194 U.S. 267, 270 (1904). Vincent M. Barnett, Jr., "Mr. Justice Murphy, Civil Liberties and the Holmes Tradition," *Cornell Law Quarterly*, v. 32 (Nov. 1946), pp. 177-221.

[12] Frankfurter, *Mr. Justice Holmes and the Supreme Court* (Cambridge: Harvard University Press, 1938), p. 51.

[13] Jackson, *The Struggle for Judicial Supremacy* (New York: Alfred A. Knopf,

1941), pp. 284-85. *Palko* v. *Connecticut,* 302 U.S. 319, 327 (1937).

[14] *United States* v. *Carolene Products Co.,* 304 U.S. 144, 152, note 4 (1938).

[15] FM to FDR, Feb. 5, 1940, Box 88.

[16] See Frankfurter, "The Supreme Court in the Mirror of Justices," *University of Pennsylvania Law Review,* v. 105 (April 1957), 785.

[17] See, *e.g.,* Merlo Pusey, *Charles Evans Hughes* (New York: Macmillan, 1951), v. 1, p. 276. Alpheus T. Mason, *Brandeis: A Free Man's Life* (New York: The Viking Press, 1946), p. 514. Henry F. Pringle, *The Life and Times of William Howard Taft* (New York: Farrar & Rinehart, 1939), v. 2, p. 961. FM to G.A. Richards, Dec. 16, 1940, Box 93.

[18] Arthur J. Goldberg, "Reflections of the Newest Justice," *Cong. Rec.,* v. 109, pt. 11, p. 15,233.

[19] Douglas, "The Supreme Court and Its Case Load," *Cornell Law Quarterly,* v. 45 (Spring 1960), 401, 413. Charles L. Black, Jr., *The People and the Court* (New York: Macmillan, 1960), pp. 180-81.

[20] See, *e.g.,* Alpheus T. Mason, *Harlan Fiske Stone: Pillar of the Law* (New York: The Viking Press, 1956), p. 260.

[21] Willard L. King, *Lincoln's Manager, David Davis* (Cambridge: Harvard University Press, 1960), pp. 191, 201; John P. Frank, *Mr. Justice Black* (New York: Alfred A. Knopf, 1949), p. 108. FM to Butler, Feb. 28, 1940, Box 89.

[22] FM to Bowers, Feb. 28, 1940, Box 89.

[23] 310 U.S. 88; 310 U.S. 106 (1940).

[24] 310 U.S. 88, 101-103.

[25] 310 U.S. 106, 113. 274 U.S. 357, 376-77 (1927).

[26] Ludwig Teller, "Picketing and Free Speech," *Harvard Law Review,* v. 56 (Oct. 1942), 180. *Senn* v. *Tile Layers Protective Union,* 301 U.S. 468, 478 (1937). Louis L. Jaffe, "In Defense of the Supreme Court's Picketing Doctrine," *Michigan Law Review,* v. 41 (June 1943), 1,054. Joseph Tanenhaus, "Picketing as Free Speech," *University of Pittsburgh Law Review,* v. 14 (Spring 1953), 397-418; and "Picketing-Free Speech: The Growth of the New Law

of Picketing from 1940 to 1952," *Cornell Law Quarterly,* v. 38 (Fall 1952), 1-50.

[27] See *Lovell* v. *Griffin,* 303 U.S. 444 (1938); and *Schneider* v. *Irvington,* 308 U.S. 147 (1939). Cf. Brandeis, J., in *Whitney* v. *California,* 274 U.S. 357, 372 (1927).

[28] *Washington Post,* April 23, 1940; *Nation,* v. 150 (May 4, 1940), 553.

[29] C. Herman Pritchett, *The Roosevelt Court* (New York: Macmillan, 1948), p. 285. See Wallace Mendelson, "The Neo-Behavioral Approach to the Judicial Process," *A.P.S.R.,* v. 57 (Sep. 1963), 596; "Neo-Behavioralism—A Rebuttal," *A.P.-S.R.,* v. 57 (Dec. 1963), 952.

[30] Conference notes, undated, No. 514, 1939 term, Box 129.

[31] *Ibid.* Note, FM to clerk, dated April 1940, No. 514, Box 129.

[32] See note 27 above. Marginal note on draft opinion, No. 514, Box 129.

[33] Jackson, *The Supreme Court in the American System of Government* (Cambridge: Harvard University Press, 1955), p. 16.

[34] Note, FM to clerk, dated April 1940, No. 514, Box 129.

[35] Clerk to FM, March 30, 1940, No. 514, Box 129.

[36] Unsigned memo, March 30, 1940, No. 514, Box 129.

[37] Unsigned five-page memo, March 30, 1940, No. 514, Box 129.

[38] Handwritten memos, FM to clerk, undated, No. 514, Box 129.

[39] Handwritten note, undated, No. 514, Box 129.

[40] Handwritten note, FM to clerk, undated, No. 514, Box 129.

[41] See note 27 above.

[42] Note, "Inseparability in Application of Statutes Impairing Civil Liberties," *Harvard Law Review,* v. 61 (July 1948), 1,208.

[43] "The Test of Patriotism," *National Lawyers Guild Quarterly,* v. 2 (Oct. 1939), 165-70. 301 U.S. 242 (1937).

[44] Harlan F. Stone to FM, April 19, 1940, No. 514, Box 129. *United States* v. *Carolene Products Co.,* 304 U.S. 144, 152, note 4 (1938). Mason, *Stone,* pp. 512-16.

George D. Braden, "The Search for Objectivity in Constitutional Law," *Yale
Law Journal*, v. 57 (Feb. 1948), 580n28.

[45] Stone to FM, April 19, 1940, No.
514, Box 129. *Stromberg* v. *California*,
283 U.S. 359 (1931).

[46] *Ibid*. Comments on first circulated
slip opinion, No. 514, Box 129.

[47] Conference note, April 20, 1940, Box
90. Undated note, FM to clerk, No. 514,
Box 129.

[48] *Ibid*. Draft opinion, No. 667, Box
129.

[49] Comments on final circulation, No.
514, Box 129.

[50] Comment on slip opinion, No. 667,
Box 129.

[51] *San Francisco Chronicle*, April 25,
1940. Also, *Mankato* (Minn.) *Free Press*,
April 26, 1940; *St. Louis Star-Times*,
April 23, 1940.

[52] Joseph C. Hutchinson, Jr., Book Re-
view, *A.B.A.J.*, v. 30 (Feb. 1944), 160n.
Charles O. Gregory, "Peaceful Picketing
and Freedom of Speech," *A.B.A.J.*, v. 26
(Sep. 1940), 714. Quote, Gregory, *Labor
and the Law*, 2nd rev. edn. (New York:
W.W. Norton, 1958), p. 328. Also see
Edward S. Corwin, Book Review, *Harvard
Law Review*, v. 56 (Nov. 1942), 486;
Charles O. Gregory, "Constitutional Limi-
tations on the Regulation of Union and
Employer Conduct," *Michigan Law Re-
view*, v. 49 (Dec. 1950), 199; Teller, "Pick-
eting," pp. 200, 204.

[53] Paul A. Freund, "The Supreme
Court and Civil Liberties," *Vanderbilt
Law Review*, v. 4 (April 1951), 539-40.
John Raeburn Green, "The Supreme
Court, the Bill of Rights and the States,"
University of Pennsylvania Law Review,
v. 97 (April 1949), 624-25. Barbara N.
Armstrong, "Where Are We Going with
Picketing?" *California Law Review*, v. 36
(March 1948), 1-40. Cf. Archibald Cox,
"The Influence of Mr. Justice Murphy on
Labor Law," *Michigan Law Review*, v. 48
(April 1950), 767-810; E. Merrick Dodd,
"Picketing and Free Speech: A Dissent,"
Harvard Law Review, v. 56 (Jan. 1943),
513-31.

[54] Edgar A. Jones, Jr., "Picketing and
Coercion: A Jurisprudence of Epithets,"
Virginia Law Review, v. 39 (Dec. 1953),
1,023.

[55] *Tradesmens National Bank* v. *Oklahoma Tax Commission*, 309 U. S. 560
(1940).

[56] *AFL* v. *Swing*, 312 U.S. 321 (1941).
Cf. Mendelson, note 29 above, at 952n,
and Martin Shapiro, *Law and Politics in
the Supreme Court* (New York: The
Free Press, 1964), p. 79.

[57] FM to Joseph R. Hayden, April 9,
1940, Box 90.

[58] FM to Watkins, May 23, 1940, Box
91.

[59] FM to J. Weldon Jones, July 12,
1940, Box 91.

[60] *Minersville School District* v. *Gobitis*,
310 U.S. 586 (1940).

[61] "Observations of Chief Justice
Hughes," April 25, 1940; Murphy, handwritten draft, No. 690, Box 129.

[62] Typed draft and unsigned, undated
memo, margin comment, slip opinion, No.
690, Box 129. See *Jones* v. *Opelika*, 316
U.S. 584, 611 (1942); *West Virginia State
Board of Education* v. *Barnette*, 319 U.S.
624, 645 (1943).

[63] 310 U.S. 296 (1940); undated draft
concurrence; clerk to FM, May 3, 1940,
No. 632, Box 129.

[64] FM to J.F.T. O'Connor, June 18,
1940, Box 91.

[65] FM to FDR, June 10, 1940, RL:O.F.–
41A–Supreme Court.

[66] Joseph R. Hayden to FM, June 4
and June 10, 1941, Box 97. Telegram,
FDR to FM, June 26, 1941, RL:P.P.F.—
1,662. Copy, FM to Joan Sattley, June
4, 1941, Box 97.

[67] Copy, telegram, Manuel L. Quezon
to Joaquin M. Elizalde, June 16, 1941,
Box 97.

[68] Unsent letter, FM to FDR, July 28,
1941, Box 98. Cf. Francis Biddle, *In Brief
Authority* (New York: Doubleday &
Company, 1962), pp. 164-65.

[69] Address, "The Greatest Danger—the
United States and the Russo-German
War," August 19, 1941, reprinted *Cong.
Rec.*, v. 87, pt. 13, App. 4,041. FM to
Gordon E. Taylor, Nov. 4, 1941, Box 99.
FM to Frank Schwartz, Feb. 25, 1942,
Box 101.

[70] FM to clerk, Dec. 21, 1940, Box 93. Copy, notes, FM to clerk, *MS*.

[71] *Milk Wagon Drivers Union* v. *Meadowmoor Dairies, Inc.*, 312 U.S. 287 (1941). FM to clerk, undated, No. 1, 1940 term, Box 129.

[72] Kemp to clerk, Feb. 7, 1941; clerk to FM, Feb. 10, 1941, No. 1, 1940 term, Box 129.

[73] Clerk to FM, Feb. 7, 1941, No. 1, 1940 term, Box 129.

[74] FM to clerk, undated; Felix Frankfurter to FM, Feb. 7, 1941, No. 1, 1940 term, Box 129.

[75] 312 U.S. 287, 297, 293 (1941).

[76] Unpublished, first circulated opinion, p. 11, *NLRB* v. *Virginia Electric & Power Co.*, 314 U.S. 469 (1941), Nos. 25-26, 1941 term, Box 130; handwritten draft in *Minersville School District* v. *Gobitis*, No. 690, Box 129.

[77] 312 U.S. 569, 578 (1941).

[78] 315 U.S. 568, 571-72 (1942).

[79] Comment on slip opinion, No. 255, 1941 term, Box 130. See Harry A. Kalven, Jr., "The Metaphysics of the Law of Obscenity," *The Supreme Court Review* (1960), p. 9.

[80] 314 U.S. 469 (1941).

[81] See note 76 above.

[82] *Ibid.* Undated conference note; comments on first circulated opinion; note, James F. Byrnes to FM, undated; copy, Felix Frankfurter to Hugo L. Black, Dec. 18, 1941, Nos. 25-26, Box 130.

[83] *NLRB* v. *Federbush* Co., Inc., 121 F. 2d 954 (2d Cir., 1941). See note 76 above. Harlan F. Stone to FM, Dec. 20, 1941, Nos. 25-26, Box 130.

[84] Note, Felix Frankfurter to FM, undated; copy, Frankfurter to Black, Dec. 18, 1941; memos, FM to clerk, undated, Nos. 25-26, Box 130.

[85] Memo, Dec. 16, 1941; handwritten note, FM to Hugo L. Black, undated, Nos. 25-26, Box 130.

[86] Unsigned memo to FM, Dec. 16, 1941; memos, Harlan F. Stone to FM, Dec. 18 and 20, 1941; note, James F. Byrnes to FM, undated, Nos. 25-26, Box 130.

[87] FM to Hugo L. Black, undated, Nos. 25-26, Box 130. 314 U.S. 469, 477-79 (1941).

[88] Unsigned, undated memo regarding rider to second draft, Nos. 25-26, Box 130.

[89] Comment on slip opinion, final circulation, Nos. 25-26, Box 130.

[90] Cert. note, No. 709, Box 132.

[91] Cox, "Influence of Murphy," p. 785.

[92] *International Brotherhood of Teamsters, Local 695* v. *Vogt*, 354 U.S. 284, 289 (1957).

[93] *Bakery and Pastry Drivers* v. *Wohl*, 315 U.S. 769 (1942).

[94] 315 U.S. 722, 728 (1942).

[95] *Ibid.*, p. 729.

[96] Gregory, "Constitutional Limitations," pp. 200-205. Note, "Picketing and Free Speech Since the *Ritter's Cafe* Decision," *Harvard Law Review*, v. 59 (Sep. 1946), 1,123. *Giboney* v. *Empire Storage & Ice Co.*, 336 U.S. 490 (1949).

[97] 339 U.S. 470, 474 (1950). Also *Hughes* v. *Superior Court of California*, 339 U.S. 460 (1950).

[98] *International Brotherhood of Teamsters* v. *Vogt*, 354 U.S. 284, 295 (1957).

[99] See *Edwards* v. *South Carolina*, 372 U.S. 229, 242 (1963); *NAACP* v. *Button*, 371 U.S. 415, 432 (1963); *NLRB* v. *Fruit & Vegetable Pickers*, 377 U.S. 58, 76 (1964); *Baggett* v. *Bullitt*, 377 U.S. 360, 379 (1964); *Aptheker* v. *Secretary of State*, 378 U.S. 500, 514, 520 (1964); *Dombrowski* v. *Pfister*, 380 U.S. 479 (1965).

[100] Gregory, *Labor and the Law*, p. 329.

[101] *Cox* v. *Louisiana*, 379 U.S. 536, 580 (1965). Conference notes, No. 514, Box 129.

[102] 312 U.S. 52 (1941). Memos, clerk to FM, Jan. 4 and 14, 1940; also undated memo, clerk to FM, No. 22, Box 130.

[103] FM memos to clerk, undated; comment on slip opinion, No. 22, Box 130.

[104] 314 U.S. 252 (1941). Conference note, undated; "memorandum on the merits," undated, Nos. 19, 64, Box 130.

[105] Note, clerk to FM, undated; FM to Felix Frankfurter, May 29, 1941, Nos. 19, 64, Box 130.

[106] 314 U.S. 252, 263 (1941); *Phelps Dodge Corp.* v. *NLRB*, 313 U.S. 177, 200 (1941).

[107] FM to Harlan F. Stone, May 29, 1941, Nos. 19, 64, Box 130.

[108] See note 29 above. Also, Glendon Schubert, *The Judicial Mind* (Evanston: Northwestern University Press, 1965).

[109] Eloise Snyder, "The Supreme Court as a Small Group," *Social Forces*, v. 36 (March 1958), 236-38. See Walter F. Murphy, *Elements of Judicial Strategy* (Chicago: University of Chicago Press, 1964), ch. 3; and the author's "On the Fluidity of Judicial Choice," *A.P.S.R.*, v. 62 (March 1968), 43-56.

CHAPTER 11

[1] Copy, memorandum regarding Hughes's resignation, June 2, 1941, Box 97.

[2] Merlo J. Pusey, *Charles Evans Hughes* (New York: Macmillan, 1951), v. 2, p. 691.

[3] See Alpheus T. Mason, *The Supreme Court from Taft to Warren* (Baton Rouge: Louisiana State University Press, 1958), pp. 124-29, 105-106. Hughes remark, conference note, April 12, 1941, No. 671, Box 130. *Olsen* v. *Nebraska*, 313 U.S. 236 (1941).

[4] Alpheus T. Mason, *Harlan Fiske Stone: Pillar of the Law* (New York: The Viking Press, 1956), pp. 794-96.

[5] *Ibid.*, pp. 583, 793.

[6] *Ibid.*, p. 487.

[7] Comment on slip opinion, No. 377, Box 134. *Precision Instrument Mfg. Co.* v. *Automotive Maintenance Machinery Co.*, 324 U.S. 806 (1945).

[8] Mason, *Stone*, p. 793. Cf. *ibid.*, p. 220, and *Riggs* v. *Del Drago*, 317 U.S. 95 (1942), No. 30, Box 131. FM to Harlan F. Stone, June 15, 1941, Box 97.

[9] John J. Adams to FM, Jan. 25, 1944, Box 131.

[10] FM to clerk, undated, No. 142, Box 132.

[11] Felix Frankfurter to Wiley Rutledge, Jan. 1, 1949, Box 34, Frankfurter Papers, Manuscript Division, Library of Congress. Erwin N. Griswold in "Felix Frankfurter—Talks in Tribute," Feb. 26, 1965, Occasional Pamphlet Number Eight, Harvard Law School, p. 4. FM to clerk, No. 280, Box 130. *Jones* v. *Opelika*, 314 U.S. 593 (1942). See Felix Frankfurter to the President, Aug. 28, 1962, 9 L. ed. 2d *li*.

[12] Felix Frankfurter to FM, May 7, 1945, Box 28. Frankfurter to Owen J. Roberts, May 11, 1944, Box 33, Frankfurter Papers, Manuscript Division, Library of Congress.

[13] Comment on Frankfurter draft opinion in *Griffin* v. *United States*, 336 U.S. 704 (1949), No. 417, Box 139. FM to clerk, Nov. 11, 1943, No. 124, Box 132. *Lilly* v. *Grand Trunk Western R.R. Co.*, 317 U.S. 481 (1943).

[14] *Ex parte Quirin*, 317 U.S. 1 (1942); handwritten note on "F.F.'s Soliloquy," Nos. 1-7, 1942 Special Term, Box 132.

[15] 316 U.S. 455 (1942).

[16] Conference notes, No. 837, Box 132. *Betts* v. *Brady*, 316 U.S. 455 (1942).

[17] "Selected Addresses of Frank Murphy, Governor of Michigan, January 1, 1937, to September 30, 1938" (Lansing, 1938), p. 67.

[18] *NYT*, Oct. 6, 1939, p. 12:5; and address before Hibernian Society, Baltimore, March 17, 1939, reprinted *Cong. Rec.*, v. 84, pt. 11, App. 1,109-11.

[19] *Moyer* v. *Peabody*, 212 U.S. 78, 85 (1909).

[20] "The Challenge to our National Character," reprinted *Cong. Rec.*, v. 88, pt. 8, App. 347.

[21] John P. Frank, "Review and Basic Liberties," in Edmond N. Cahn, ed., *Supreme Court and Supreme Law* (Bloomington: Indiana University Press, 1954), p. 114.

[22] FM to George C. Marshall, Dec. 13, 1941, Box 99. FM to Harry Levinson, Dec. 25, 1941, Box 100.

[23] FM to FDR, May 13, 1942, Box 103.

[24] FM to FDR, Jan. 14, 1942, and Feb. 19, 1942, Box 101. FM to FDR, May 6, 1942, Box 103. Quote, FM to FDR, May 13, 1942, Box 103.

[25] FDR to FM, May 7, 1942, Box 103.

[26] FM to FDR, April 10, 1942, Box 102.

[27] FM to Marshall, April 15, 1942, Box 102.

[28] Marshall to FM, April 20, 1942, Box 102.

[29] FM to Marshall, April 25, 1942, Box 102.

[30] Marshall to FM, May 18, 1942, Box 103. *NYT*, June 11, 1942, p. 25:7.

[31] *NYT*, Sep. 18, 1942, p. 13:5; June 16, 1942, p. 10:6.

[32] FM to FM, July 13, 1942, RL:OF-41A-Supreme Court. *Washington Times-Herald*, June 11, 1942; *NYT*, June 18, 1942, p. 20:1.

[33] *NYT*, Sep. 18, 1942, p. 13:5.

[34] FM to FDR, Jan. 5, 1942, RL:OF-41A-Supreme Court. Address, "Challenge to Our National Character," pp. 346-48. *NYT*, Aug. 12, 1942, p. 8:5.

[35] *Washington Star*, Sep. 20, 1942. *NYT*, Sep. 15, 1942, p. 16:3.

[36] FM to FDR, June 7, 1943, RL:OF-407B-Labor:Strikes. *Detroit Free Press*, Sep. 29, 1942; *NYT*, Sep. 18, 1942, p. 13: 5; and Sep. 15, 1942, p. 16:3.

[37] See letters declining speaking invitations from the ACLU and the Association of the Bar of the City of New York, FM to Roger Baldwin, Jan. 29, 1945, Box 114. FM to Lloyd Laporte, March 15, 1948, Box 124. J.F.T. O'Connor to FDR, Sep. 14, 1942, RL:P.P.F.-1,662.

[38] *NYT*, Aug. 14, 1942, p. 34:4. Francis Biddle to FM, Aug. 1, 1942; and Charles Fahy to FM, Aug. 10, 1942, Box 105.

[39] Kemp to FM, Sep. 9, 1942, Box 105. Mason, *Stone*, pp. 648, 708-709. Clerk to Eleanor Bumgardner, undated, Box 106.

[40] *Louisville Courier-Journal*, June 12, 1942. Also, *Washington Star*, June 11, 1942.

[41] *NYT*, Sep. 19, 1942, p. 14:3. *Quincy* (Ill.) *Herald-Whig*, June 11, 1942. *Time*, Oct. 26, 1942, p. 20. Pearson & Allen column, *Los Angeles Daily News*, June 22, 1942.

[42] Theodore Roosevelt, Jr., to FM, undated, Box 128a.

[43] Undated note, FM to Jacob Devers, courtesy Eleanor Bumgardner Wright. FM to Wallace Packard, July 10, 1942, Box 105.

[44] *Chaplinsky* v. *New Hampshire*, 315 U.S. 568 (1942).

[45] *United States* v. *Bethlehem Steel Corp.*, 315 U.S. 289, 310 (1942). See *Penn Dairies, Inc.* v. *Milk Control Commission of Pennsylvania*, 318 U.S. 261, 279 (1943); *Pacific Coast Dairies, Inc.* v. *Department of Agriculture of California*, 318 U.S. 285, 303 (1943); and *Hooven & Allison Co.* v. *Evatt*, 324 U.S. 652, 691 (1945).

[46] FM to FDR, Dec. 3, 1941, Box 99.

[47] *Chicago Sun*, Feb. 20, 1942; FM to Leland S. Bisbee, Feb. 25, 1942, Box 101.

[48] Conference note; and FM to clerk, Oct. 12, 1940, Box 130. See clerk to FM, Nov. 26, 1941, Box 99.

[49] See memo to FM, Jan. 14, 1942, Box 115. Memos, FM to clerk, Feb. 9, and undated, 1941, Box 130. For "trap pass" maneuver, see Walter F. Murphy, *Elements of Judicial Strategy* (Chicago: University of Chicago Press, 1964), pp. 129-30.

[50] 316 U.S. 455 (1942); 315 U.S. 60 (1942). Conference note, No. 32, Box 130.

[51] 315 U.S. 60, 75, 86, 89 (1942). Harlan F. Stone to FM, Jan. 7, 1942; Douglas comment on slip opinion, Nos. 30-32, Box 130.

[52] 317 U.S. 269, 286 (1943).

[53] See, *e.g.*, *Adams* v. *United States ex rel. McCann*, No. 79, Box 131. Robert H. Jackson, *The Supreme Court in the American System of Government* (Cambridge: Harvard University Press, 1955), p. 16.

[54] 317 U.S. 501, 510 (1943).

[55] Memos, FM to clerk, undated, and Jan. 2, 1943, No. 142, Box 132.

[56] See Murphy, *Elements of Judicial Strategy*, ch. 3.

[57] 316 U.S. 114, 122 (1942); 316 U.S. 129, 136 (1942).

[58] Felix Frankfurter to FM, March 31, 1942, and comment on slip opinion; Harlan F. Stone to FM, April 3, 1942, No. 256, Box 130. 316 U.S. 114, 127 (1942).

[59] FM to clerk, March 31, 1942, No. 256, Box 130.

[60] *Olmstead* v. *United States*, 277 U.S. 438 (1928).

61 Clerk to FM, undated, No. 962, Box 130.

62 316 U.S. 129, 136 (1942). Chief Justice Stone, "Memo for Justice Frankfurter and Justice Murphy," Feb. 27, 1942, No. 962, Box 130.

63 Conference notes; unsigned, undated "memo re revision of dissent," No. 962, Box 130. *United States* v. *Lefkowitz*, 285 U.S. 452 (1932). Cf. 316 U.S. 129, 140, notes 7-8; and Black, J., in *Berger* v. *New York*, 388 U.S. 41 (1967).

64 Notes, FM to clerk, undated, No. 962, Box 130.

65 Frankfurter to FM, April 3, 1942; FM to clerk, undated, No. 962, Box 130.

66 Robert H. Jackson, "memo for the Chief Justice and the Associate Justices," April 6, 1942, No. 962, Box 130.

67 Clerk to FM, Jan. 17 and 31, 1941, No. 43, Box 130.

68 See clerk to FM, Nov. 26, 1941, Box 99. Mason, *Stone*, p. 703.

69 Walter F. Murphy, *Wiretapping on Trial* (New York: Random House, Inc., 1965), p. 142.

70 Robert H. Jackson to FM, April 6, 1942, No. 962, Box 130.

71 Cf. draft opinions, April 6 and April 27, 1942, No. 962, Box 130. See Mason, *Stone*, pp. 640-45.

72 316 U.S. 129, 142 (1942).

73 *Baltimore Sun*, April 28, 1942. Cf. *Detroit News*, May 10, 1942.

74 See H.R. 5,386 (1967). Cf. White, J., in *Berger* v. *New York*, 388 U.S. 41 (1967).

75 FM to Mulcahy, May 12, 1942, No. 962, Box 130. Cf. Brennan, J., in *Lopez* v. *United States*, 373 U.S. 427 (1963).

76 FM to George Murphy, April 27, 1942, No. 962, Box 130.

77 *Jencks* v. *United States*, 353 U.S. 657, 680 (1957); *Louisville Courier-Journal*, Dec. 23, 1966. *Katz* v. *United States*, 36 *Law Week* 4080 (1967). Cf. *Berger* v. *New York*, 388 U.S. 41 (1967).

78 *Minersville School District* v. *Gobitis*, 310 U.S. 586 (1940). "Observations of Chief Justice Hughes," No. 690, Box 129.

79 Mason, *Stone*, p. 598.

80 FM to George B. Eberenz, Feb. 25, 1942, Box 101.

81 316 U.S. 584, 598 (1942).

82 Conference note, No. 280, Box 130. 316 U.S. 584, 601, 608.

83 *Ibid.*, pp. 611, 615-23.

84 For a critique of preference doctrine, see George D. Braden, "The Search for Objectivity in Constitutional Law," *Yale Law Journal*, v. 57 (Feb. 1948), 571-94. Also, Walter F. Murphy, "Deeds Under a Doctrine: Civil Liberties in the 1963 Term," *A.P.S.R.*, v. 59 (March 1965), 72-79.

85 Unsigned, undated memo, "Mr. Justice"; and Murphy remark on first draft, "Black thinks we ought to have this out," No. 280, Box 130. See *NAACP* v. *Button*, 371 U.S. 415 (1963); *Baggett* v. *Bullitt*, 377 U.S. 360 (1964); *Aptheker* v. *Secretary of State*, 378 U.S. 500, 516 (1964); *Dombrowski* v. *Pfister*, 380 U.S. 479 (1965).

86 FM to Harlan F. Stone, May 28, 1942; Stone to FM, May 29, 1942, No. 280, Box 130.

87 Philip B. Kurland, "Of Church and State and the Supreme Court," *University of Chicago Law Review*, v. 29 (Autumn 1961), 1-96.

88 FM to Harlan F. Stone, May 28, 1942, No. 280, Box 130.

89 316 U.S. 584, 619-21 (1942). See *Horace Mann League* v. *Maryland Board of Public Works*, 385 U.S. 97 (1966); and *Murray* v. *Goldstein*, 385 U.S. 816 (1966).

90 Clerk to FM, July 1, 1942, Box 105. *Richmond Times*, June 12, 1942. *St. Louis Globe-Democrat*, June 10, 1942.

91 *Louisville Courier-Journal*, June 10, 1942.

92 316 U.S. 584, 623-24 (1942).

93 *St. Louis Post-Dispatch*, May 4, 1943.

94 319 U.S. 105, 109, 115 (1943).

95 319 U.S. 141 (1943).

96 Conference notes, No. 238, Box 132; No. 966, Box 131. 319 U.S. 141, 151-52.

97 Felix Frankfurter to Stanley Reed, Jan. 6, 1943, Box 32, Frankfurter Papers, Manuscript Division, Library of Congress. Cf. *Time, Inc.* v. *Hill*, 385 U.S. 374 (1967); and Glendon Schubert, *The Judicial Mind* (Evanston: Northwestern University Press, 1965), pp. 171-74.

[98] Conference notes, No. 238, Box 132; No. 966, Box 131. *Cox* v. *Louisiana*, 379 U.S. 536, 580 (1965); *Bell* v. *Maryland*, 378 U.S. 226, 344 (1964). Cf. Justice Black's second and final circulation on May 3, 1943, No. 238, Box 132.

[99] 319 U.S. 141, 149-50.

[100] *Baltimore Sun*, May 4, 1943. 319 U.S. 141, 152, 179-81.

[101] 319 U.S. 624 (1943).

[102] *Ibid.*, pp. 638-40.

[103] *Ibid.*, pp. 651, 667.

[104] *Ibid.*, p. 671 and 319 U.S. at 182.

[105] 319 U.S. 624, 642-46. See successive draft opinions, No. 591, Box 132. Clerk to FM, March 30, 1943, No. 591, Box 132.

[106] 319 U.S. 624, 645-46.

[107] *St. Louis Post-Dispatch*, June 15, 1943.

[108] FM to James W. Gerard, April 15, 1943, Box 108.

[109] FM to Bates, Dec. 25, 1943, Box 110.

[110] See *Falbo* v. *United States*, 320 U.S. 549, 555 (1944); *Billings* v. *Truesdell*, 321 U.S. 542 (1944); *Estep* v. *United States*, 327 U.S. 114, 125 (1946); *Cox* v. *United States*, 332 U.S. 442, 457 (1947). Also see *Sunal* v. *Large*, 332 U.S. 174, 193 (1947); *Singer* v. *United States*, 323 U.S. 338, 346 (1945); and *In re Summers*, 325 U.S. 561, 573 (1945).

[111] *Cleveland* v. *United States*, 329 U.S. 14, 24 (1946); and *Chatwin* v. *United States*, 326 U.S. 455 (1946). Also, *Musser* v. *Utah*, 333 U.S. 95, 98 (1948).

[112] 321 U.S. 573, 578 (1944).

[113] Wesley McCune, *The Nine Young Men* (New York: Harper & Bros., 1947), p. 143.

[114] *Pennekamp* v. *Florida*, 328 U.S. 331, 369 (1946); *Craig* v. *Harney*, 331 U.S. 367, 383 (1947); *Fisher* v. *Pace*, 336 U.S. 155, 166 (1949).

[115] *NBC* v. *United States*, 319 U.S. 190, 227 (1943); *Associated Press* v. *United States*, 326 U.S. 1, 49 (1945).

[116] FM to clerk, undated, Nos. 554-555, Box 132.

[117] *Mabee* v. *White Plains Publishing Co.*, 327 U.S. 178, 185 (1946).

[118] 326 U.S. 1, 20 (1945); *Detroit News*, dateline Lansing, Sep. 24, undated fragment.

[119] FM to J.P. McEvoy, May 11, 1943, Nos. 554-55, Box 132.

[120] *Washington Post*, July 20, 1949, p. 1:2.

[121] FM to Alex J. Groesbeck, Dec. 25, 1943, Box 110. See memos, George C. Marshall to FM, and Henry L. Stimson to FDR, April 1, 1943, Box 108. FDR to FM, April 8, 1943; and FM to FDR, May 31, 1943, Box 108.

[122] FM to Harlan F. Stone, Sep. 15, 1943, Stone Papers, Manuscript Division, Library of Congress.

[123] FM to clerk, Dec. 25, 1943, Box 110.

[124] Jackson, J., in *Terminiello* v. *Chicago*, 337 U.S. 1, 14 (1949).

[125] Quoted in *Wayne County Democrat*, Sep. 25, 1943.

CHAPTER 12

[1] *Ex parte Quirin*, 317 U.S. 1 (1942). Clerk to Eleanor Bumgardner, July 31, 1942; clerk to Edward G. Kemp, Sep. 10, 1942, Box 105.

[2] *Bowles* v. *United States*, 319 U.S. 33 (1943); *Hirabayashi* v. *United States*, 320 U.S. 81 (1943).

[3] See Morton Grodzins, *Americans Betrayed: Politics and the Japanese Evacuation* (Chicago: University of Chicago Press, 1949); Jacobus ten Broek, *et al.*, *Prejudice, War, and the Constitution* (Berkeley: University of California Press, 1954); John P. Roche, *The Quest for the Dream* (New York: Macmillan, 1963), pp. 193-99.

[4] Fairman, "The Law of Martial Rule and the National Emergency," *Harvard Law Review*, v. 55 (June 1942), 1,301-1,302. Also Maurice Alexandre, "The Nisei—A Casualty of World War II," *Cornell Law Quarterly*, v. 28 (June 1943), 385-413.

[5] Roche, *Quest for the Dream*, pp. 194-95.

[6] Conference notes, No. 870, Box 132. John P. Roche, "Judicial Self-Restraint,"

A.P.S.R., v. 49 (Sep. 1955), p. 767. 320 U.S. 81, 100-102.

[7] Conference notes, No. 142, Box 137.

[8] 320 U.S. 81, 93.

[9] Draft opinion, No. 870, Box 132. Cf. *United States* v. *Classic*, 313 U.S. 299 (1941).

[10] Handwritten comment on Stone's draft opinion; Murphy draft opinion, p. 3, No. 870, Box 132.

[11] *Ibid.*, p. 2. *Ex parte Milligan*, 4 Wall. 2 (1866).

[12] *Bolling* v. *Sharpe*, 347 U.S. 497 (1954); 320 U.S. 81, 100.

[13] Draft opinion, p. 5, No. 870, Box 132.

[14] *Ibid.*, pp. 4-5.

[15] *Ibid.*, pp. 5-6.

[16] Note on circulated dissent, p. 4, No. 870, Box 132.

[17] See "F.F.'s Soliloquy," Oct. 23, 1942, Nos. 1-7, Box 132.

[18] Felix Frankfurter to FM, June 5, 1943, No. 870, Box 132.

[19] Notes, FM to Felix Frankfurter, and reply, June 5, 1943, No. 870, Box 132.

[20] Felix Frankfurter to FM, June 6, 1943, No. 870, Box 132.

[21] See note 3 above. Quotes, *Korematsu* v. *United States*, 323 U.S. 214, 236, 241 (1944).

[22] *NYT*, May 21, 1959, p. 5:1. See *Korematsu* case, 323 U.S. 214, 219. Roche, *Quest for the Dream*, p. 199.

[23] Cf. Stone's circulated drafts and memorandum to conference, June 4, 1943, No. 870, Box 132.

[24] Felix Frankfurter to FM, June 10, 1943, No. 870, Box 132.

[25] FM to clerk, June 8, 1943, No. 870, Box 132.

[26] 320 U.S. 81, 109, 111, 113.

[27] *Ibid.*, pp. 113-14.

[28] 320 U.S. 118 (1943).

[29] See *United States* v. *Schwimmer*, 279 U.S. 644 (1929). Also *United States* v. *Macintosh*, 283 U.S. 605 (1931).

[30] *NYHT*, June 22, 1943, pp. 1:1, 8:3.

[31] Conference notes, April 22, 1942. Murphy dated Welles' letter Feb. 25, 1942, No. 2, Box 131. See *Smith* v. *Allwright*, 321 U.S. 649 (1944); and Alpheus T. Mason, *Harlan Fiske Stone: Pillar of the Law* (New York: The Viking Press, 1956), pp. 614-15.

[32] Conference note, April 22, 1942, No. 2, Box 131.

[33] Cert. memo; conference notes, No. 2, Box 131.

[34] Conference notes, No. 2, Box 131.

[35] Conference notes, undated and March 28, 1942, on notes for No. 500, 1941 term, Box 131.

[36] 320 U.S. 118, 165 (1943). *Knauer* v. *United States*, 328 U.S. 654, 677 (1946).

[37] Mason, *Stone*, p. 688.

[38] "Notes on the Schneiderman case," p. 4, Box 28, Frankfurter Papers, Manuscript Division, Library of Congress. Conference notes, undated, No. 2, Box 131.

[39] *Ibid.* Note to Harlan F. Stone, July 27, 1943, Stone Papers, Manuscript Division, Library of Congress.

[40] 314 U.S. 469 (1941). Note, March 15, 1943, No. 2, Box 131.

[41] Note to clerk on typed draft opinion, No. 2, Box 131.

[42] FM to Hill, April 24, 1943, Box 108.

[43] Unsigned, undated memo, No. 2, Box 131. See undated partial dissent and deleted section of first circulated master opinion, rider 7, *ibid.*

[44] William O. Douglas to FM, June 4, 1943; Rutledge comment on first circulation, June 3, 1943, No. 2, Box 131.

[45] FM to clerk, May 22, 1943, No. 2, Box 131.

[46] Draft memorandum, *ibid.*, 320 U.S. 118, 120, 122.

[47] *Ibid.*, pp. 181, 170, 195-97.

[48] Note to FM, May 31, 1943, No. 2, Box 131.

[49] Felix Frankfurter to FM, and reply, June 2, 1943, Box 28, Frankfurter Papers, Manuscript Division, Library of Congress.

[50] Unsigned, undated memo on which Murphy wrote, "This is the other side as I see it"; two unsigned, undated memos criticizing Murphy's first circulated opinion, No. 2, Box 131.

[51] *Ibid.* 320 U.S. 118, 165.

[52] "Notes on the Schneiderman case," p. 1. FM memo to the "Brethren," June 14, 1943; Stanley Reed to FM, June 14, 1943, No. 2, Box 131.

[53] "Notes on the Schneiderman case," p. 5.

[54] 320 U.S. 118, 158-59.

[55] *Ibid.*, p. 136. FM note, undated, No. 493, Box 133. *Baumgartner v. United States*, 322 U.S. 665 (1944). See *Aptheker v. Secretary of State*, 378 U.S. 500, 510 (1964).

[56] 320 U.S. 118, 137, 145.

[57] *New Bedford* (Mass.) *Standard-Times*, June 27, 1943. *Macon News-Telegraph*, June 23, 1943.

[58] 320 U.S. 118, 207. Robert H. Jackson to FM, June 18, 1943, No. 2, Box 131.

[59] Address, "The Greatest Danger—the United States and the Russo-German War," Aug. 19, 1941, reprinted, *Cong. Rec.*, v. 87, pt. 13, App. 4,041.

[60] Mason, *Stone*, p. 689.

[61] *Baumgartner v. United States*, 322 U.S. 665 (1944). *Hartzel v. United States*, 322 U.S. 680 (1944).

[62] See note 53 above.

[63] Memorandum to conference, June 18, 1943; 320 U.S. 118, 119. FM to Berlin, June 28, 1943, Box 109.

[64] FM to George Murphy, Oct. 23, 1942, Box 105. Copy FM to Mrs. Walter Hoving, Aug. 27, 1941, Box 98.

[65] FM to John J. Adams, Jan. 25, 1944, Box 111.

[66] FM to John H. Pickering, July 4, 1943, Box 109.

[67] FM to John J. Adams, Dec. 25, 1943, Box 110. FM to Adams, undated [1944], p. 2, Box 114.

[68] Memo to the "Brethren," undated, No. 2, Box 131. FM to John H. Pickering, July 4, 1943, Box 109.

[69] Memoranda, William O. Douglas to FM, June 4 and June 14, 1943, No. 2, Box 131.

[70] FM to Norman H. Hill, April 24, 1943, Box 108.

[71] See, *e.g.*, *Joint Anti-Fascist Refugee Committee v. McGrath*, 341 U.S. 123 (1951); *American Communications Assn. v. Douds*, 339 U.S. 382 (1950); *Dennis v. United States*, 341 U.S. 494 (1951).

[72] Robert E. Cushman, "Civil Liberties," *A.P.S.R.*, v. 37 (Feb. 1943), 49-56. *Viereck v. United States*, 318 U.S. 236 (1943). See Mason, *Stone*, pp. 683-85.

[73] *Kansas City Star*, June 26, 1943; *Birmingham* (Ala.) *Age-Herald*, June 24, 1943; *Norfolk Virginian-Pilot*, June 24, 1943. Cf. *Washington Star*, June 25, 1943.

[74] *Baumgartner v. United States*, 322 U.S. 665, 675, 678 (1944). Cf. Murphy memorandum to the Court, May 17, 1944, No. 493, Box 133. See *Maisenberg v. United States*, 356 U.S. 670 (1958). Also *Nishikawa v. Dulles*, 356 U.S. 129, 135 (1958); *Keyishian v. Board of Regents*, 385 U.S. 589 (1967); and *Woodby v. Immigration & Naturalization Service*, 385 U.S. 276 (1966).

[75] *Knauer v. United States*, 328 U.S. 654, 676 (1946); *Klapprott v. United States*, 335 U.S. 601 (1949); *Bridges v. Wixon*, 326 U.S. 135, 157 (1945).

[76] FM to clerk, on copy of *Fordham Law Review*, v. 12 (Nov. 1943); FM to G. Mennen Williams, April 27, 1943, Box 108.

[77] Comments on circulated majority opinions, No. 2, Box 131.

[78] FM to Osborn, June 28, 1943, No. 321, Box 132. Cf. *Creek Nation v. United States*, 318 U.S. 629 (1943); *Oklahoma Tax Commission v. United States*, 319 U.S. 598 (1943).

[79] *Ibid.* See Harlan F. Stone to FM, June 11, 1943, No. 623, Box 132. Frankfurter remark on slip opinion, No. 556, Box 132. *Board of County Commissioners v. Seber*, 318 U.S. 705 (1943).

[80] Cf. draft opinions, No. 80, Box 131. *Choctaw Nation of Indians v. United States*, 318 U.S. 423 (1943).

[81] Felix Frankfurter to FM, March 8, 1945, No. 63, Box 134. *Northwestern Bands of Shoshone Indians v. United States*, 324 U.S. 335 (1945).

[82] FM to Chase S. Osborn, June 28, 1943, No. 321, Box 132.

[83] FM to John J. Adams, March 31, 1943, Box 108. Cf. Adams to FM, Jan. 31, 1942, Box 101.

[84] 317 U.S. 287 (1942); 325 U.S. 226 (1945).

[85] Notes to clerk, undated and Nov. 19, 1942; Jackson to FM, undated, No. 29, Box 131.

[86] FM to clerk, Nov. 19, 1942, and undated note. *Ibid.*

[87] FM to Clarence B. Hewes, Aug. 15, 1947, Box 123.

[88] See *Yakus* v. *United States*, 321 U.S. 414, 460 (1944); *Bowles* v. *Willingham* 321 U.S. 504 (1944). "The Challenge to Our National Character," reprinted, *Cong. Rec.*, v. 88, pt. 8, App. 347.

[89] See *Korematsu* v. *United States*, 323 U.S. 214, 242 (1944); *Youngstown Sheet & Tube Co.* v. *Sawyer*, 343 U.S. 579, 634 (1952).

[90] See FM to George C. Marshall, May 26, 1944, Box 111. Dictated notes to Grace Tully, undated, Box 109. Quote, FM to Grace Tully, June 15, 1943, Box 108.

[91] Dictated notes to Grace Tully, undated, Box 109. FM to Anna Boettiger, Dec. 5, 1944, Box 114.

[92] For some of the few consultations on judicial appointments, see FM to FDR, May 23, 1942; FM to Charles E. Winstead, May 22, 1942, Box 103. FM to Robert E. Hannegan, June 21, 1945, Box 116.

[93] Manuel L. Quezon to FM, Dec. 5, 1942; FM to FDR, Dec. 8, 1942, Box 106. Quezon to FM, Sep. 2, 1943; dictated notes to Grace Tully, undated; FM letter to Tydings Committee, Sep. 28, 1943. Box 109.

[94] Evett D. Hester to FM, Dec. 23, 1943; Edward G. Kemp to FM, undated, with enclosed draft letter to FDR, Oct. 30, 1943, Box 110. See Joint Resolution, No. 95, 78th Congress, Nov. 12, 1943.

[95] FM to FDR, March 27, 1944, Box 111.

[96] FM to Norman H. Hill, March 8, 1945, Box 115. FM to Gerald J. Cleary, March 16, 1945; FM to Will Durant, April 27, 1945, Box 115. See FM to Robert P. Patterson and Harry S. Truman, Nov. 6, 1945, Box 117.

[97] FM to George Murphy, Oct. 17, 1944, Box 113.

[98] FM to George C. Marshall, May 10, 1943, Box 108. FM to Manuel L. Quezon, Aug. 17, 1943, Box 109. 324 U.S. 652, 692 (1945).

[99] FM to John J. Adams, March 31, 1943, Box 108.

[100] FM to Frank M. McHale, June 21, 1945, Box 116.

[101] See note 88 above. *Cramer* v. *United States*, 325 U.S. 1 (1945); *Hartzel* v. *United States*, 322 U.S. 680 (1944). Also, *Haupt* v. *United States*, 330 U.S. 631, 646 (1947).

[102] Harlan F. Stone to FM, and reply, June 1, 1944, Stone Papers, Manuscript Division, Library of Congress.

[103] See notes 101 and 72 above.

[104] *Falbo* v. *United States*, 320 U.S. 549 (1944).

[105] Conference notes, Nov. 22, 1943, No. 73, Box 132. *Blalock* v. *United States*, 247 F. 2d 615, 619 (1957).

[106] 320 U.S. 549, 553-55, 555-61.

[107] Harlan F. Stone to William O. Douglas, Nov. 24, 1945, Stone Papers, Manuscript Division, Library of Congress. *Billings* v. *Truesdell*, 321 U.S. 542 (1944); *Estep* v. *United States*, 327 U.S. 114, 121-25 (1946).

[108] *Ibid.*, pp. 125, 128, 130-32.

[109] See *Tennessee Coal, Iron & Railroad Co.* v. *Muscoda*, 321 U.S. 590 (1944); *Prince* v. *Massachusetts*, 321 U.S. 158 (1944).

[110] FM to Thomas, March 3, 1944, No. 73, Box 132.

[111] FM to George Murphy, June 12, 1944, Box 112. Cf. William V. Shannon, *The American Irish* (New York: Macmillan, 1963), pp. 352-53.

[112] Robert E. Cushman, *Civil Liberties in the United States* (Ithaca: Cornell University Press, 1956), p. 96. Conference notes, No. 221, Box 136. *Gibson* v. *United States*, 329 U.S. 338 (1946).

[113] 323 U.S. 214 (1944).

[114] *Ibid.*, p. 219.

[115] *Ibid. Ex parte Endo*, 323 U.S. 283 (1944).

[116] FM to clerk on Jackson slip opinion, Nov. 30, 1944, No. 22, Box 133.

[117] Conference notes, No. 22, Box 133.

[118] 323 U.S. 214, 244-47.

[119] *Ibid.*, p. 232. Conference notes, No. 70, Box 135.

[120] See Douglas draft dissent, circulated Dec. 1944; Stone undated memorandum; Black memorandum to conference, Dec. 8, 1944, No. 22, Box 133.

[121] Frankfurter memoranda, Dec. 1 and 13, 1944. *Ibid.* 323 U.S. 214, 224-25.

[122] *Ibid.*, p. 233. *Washington Post*, Dec. 22, 1944.

[123] 323 U.S. 214, 234.

[124] *Ibid.*, pp. 236-42. Roche, *Quest for the Dream*, p. 196.

[125] "Racism in the Constitution," *The Christian Century*, v. 62 (Jan. 3, 1945), 9. *Washington Post*, Aug. 5, 1945. See letters, No. 22, Box 133.

[126] See notes 3-4 above; Grodzins, *Americans Betrayed*, p. 374. Cf. Harrop A. Freeman, "Genesis, Exodus, and Leviticus —Genealogy, Evacuation, and Law," *Cornell Law Quarterly*, v. 28 (June 1943), 414-41. *Washington Post*, Aug. 5, 1945.

[127] *Ibid.* Also see, *e.g.*, Eugene V. Rostow, "The Japanese American Cases— A Disaster," *Yale Law Journal*, v. 54 (June 1945), 533; Eugene V. Rostow, "Our Worst Wartime Mistake," *Harper's Magazine*, Sep. 1945, p. 193. Nanette Dembitz, "Racial Discrimination and the Military Judgment: The Supreme Court's *Korematsu* and *Endo* Decisions," *Columbia Law Review*, v. 45 (March 1945), 239.

[128] Roche, *Quest for the Dream*, p. 199. *NYHT*, May 21, 1959, p. 1:1.

[129] 323 U.S. 214, 246.

[130] Clinton Rossiter, *The Supreme Court and the Commander in Chief* (Ithaca: Cornell University Press, 1951), p. 17.

[131] See Alexander Bickel, "Forward: The Passive Virtues," *Harvard Law Review*, v. 75 (Nov. 1961), 64-79. Also the author's "Constitutional Limitation and American Foreign Policy," in Gottfried Dietze, ed., *Essays on the American Constitution* (Englewood Cliffs: Prentice-Hall, 1964), pp. 167-84.

[132] FM to Chase S. Osborn, Jan. 19, 1945, Box 114.

[133] Thomas to FM, Jan. 6, 1945, No. 22, Box 133.

CHAPTER 13

[1] See, *e.g.*, FM to Stanley Reed, Nov. 9, 1942, No. 30, Box 131. *Riggs* v. *Del Drago*, 317 U.S. 95 (1942). Also, memorandum to conference, No. 198, Box 135. *Kraus & Bros., Inc.* v. *United States*, 327 U.S. 614 (1946).

[2] *North American Co.* v. *SEC.*, 327 U.S. 686 (1946); *American Power & Light Co.* v. *SEC.*, 329 U.S. 90 (1946).

[3] See *FPC* v. *Hope Natural Gas Co.*, 320 U.S. 591, 619 (1944); *Mercoid Corp.* v. *Mid-Continent Investment Co.*, 320 U.S. 661, 672 (1944); *Mahnich* v. *Southern S.S. Co.*, 321 U.S. 96, 112, 113 (1944); *Smith* v. *Allwright*, 321 U.S. 649, 669 (1944).

[4] FM to George Murphy, Sep. 9, 1946, Box 120.

[5] FM to Spellman, Oct. 8, 1946, Box 120.

[6] FM to Osborn, June 8, 1945, Box 116.

[7] Wiley Rutledge to FM, Oct. 16, 1943, Nos. 247 and 302, Box 132. FM to E. Blythe Stason, June 26, 1947, Box 122.

[8] FM to Chase S. Osborn, Jan. 19, 1945, Box 114.

[9] Arthur W. Wang to FM, May 14, 1945, Box 115.

[10] Wesley McCune, *The Nine Young Men* (New York: Harper & Bros., 1947), p. 137.

[11] See C. Herman Pritchett, *The Roosevelt Court* (New York: Macmillan, 1948), pp. 177-82, 191-97. Also *United States* v. *Columbia Steel Co.*, 334 U.S. 495, 543 (1948); *State Bank* v. *Brown*, 317 U.S. 135, 142 (1942); *Bruce's Juices, Inc.* v. *American Can Co.*, 330 U.S. 743, 757 (1947); *Dow Chemical* v. *Halliburton Oil Well Cementing Co.*, 324 U.S. 320 (1945); *NLRB* v. *E. C. Atkins Co.*, 331 U.S. 398 (1947).

[12] 317 U.S. 111 (1942). See *Daniel* v. *Family Security Life Insurance Co.*, 336 U.S. 220, 224 (1949); *Wilkerson* v. *McCarthy*, 336 U.S. 53 (1949); *Lavender* v. *Kurn*, 327 U.S. 645 (1946).

[13] 323 U.S. 516 (1945). *United States* v. *South-Eastern Underwriters Assn.*, 332 U.S. 533 (1944).

[14] See, *e.g.*, *United States* v. *Carbone*, 327 U.S. 633, 644 (1946). Cf. *New York Daily Mirror*, March 29, 1946.

[15] See Wallace Mendelson, "The Neo-Behavioral Approach to the Judicial Process: A Critique," *A.P.S.R.*, v. 57 (Sep.

1963), 596. C. Herman Pritchett, *Civil Liberties and the Vinson Court* (Chicago: Chicago University Press, 1954), p. 190. Glendon Schubert, *The Judicial Mind* (Evanston: Northwestern University Press, 1965), p. 123. Carl B. Swisher, *Stephen J. Field, Craftsman of the Law* (Washington: The Brookings Institution, 1930).

[16] *Haupt* v. *United States*, 330 U.S. 631 (1947).

[17] *United States* v. *Dotterweich*, 320 U.S. 277, 285 (1943). Jerome Hall to FM, March 4, 1944, No. 5, Box 132. See *Robinson* v. *California*, 370 U.S. 660 (1962).

[18] FM to Harlan F. Stone, Dec. 4, 1945, Stone Papers, Manuscript Division, Library of Congress. *Chatwin* v. *United States*, 326 U.S. 455 (1946). See *Nye and Nissen* v. *United States*, 336 U.S. 613, 630 (1949). See *Cleveland* v. *United States*, 329 U.S. 14, 29 (1946); *Mortensen* v. *United States*, 322 U.S. 369 (1944); *United States* v. *Beach*, 324 U.S. 193, 196 (1945).

[19] *M. Kraus & Bros., Inc.* v. *United States*, 327 U.S. 614 (1946). "The Garbage Tie-In Sales," *P.M.* (New York), April 7, 1946.

[20] *Associated Press* v. *United States*, 326 U.S. 1, 46 (1945).

[21] Pencil note, FM to clerk, No. 84, Box 134. *Williams* v. *North Carolina*, 325 U.S. 226 (1945). See Walter F. Murphy, *Elements of Judicial Strategy* (Chicago: University of Chicago Press, 1964), pp. 63-64.

[22] Pamphlet, "Anti-Semitism is Un-Christian and Un-American!" (reprint of address to B'nai B'rith, New York, May 8, 1944), p. 11.

[23] 321 U.S. 158 (1944).

[24] Memoranda to "Mr. Justice Murphy," and note, Oct. 8, 1943, No. 98, Box 133.

[25] 321 U.S. 158, 175-76 (1944).

[26] See conference notes and unsigned memo, Jan. 24, 1944, No. 98, Box 133. Fowler V. Harper, *Justice Rutledge and the Bright Constellation* (Indianapolis: Bobbs-Merrill, 1965), p. 57.

[27] *Ibid.*

[28] Harlan F. Stone to Wiley Rutledge, Jan. 24, 1944, Stone Papers, Manuscript Division, Library of Congress.

[29] 321 U.S. 158, 177-78. Cf. *In re Gault*, 387 U.S. 1 (1967).

[30] Harper, *Rutledge*, p. 58. 321 U.S. 158, 174, 173 (1944).

[31] Undated "Notes" on typed draft, No. 98, Box 133.

[32] 319 U.S. 103 (1943).

[33] 314 U.S. 252 (1941).

[34] Pencil note, No. 486, Box 133. *Follett* v. *McCormick*, 321 U.S. 573 (1944). Cf. Walter F. Murphy, "Deeds Under a Doctrine: Civil Liberties in the 1963 Term," *A.P.S.R.*, v. 59 (March 1965), 72-73.

[35] Undated note, FM to Roberts, No. 98, Box 133.

[36] FM to clerk, Jan. 22, 1944, No. 98, Box 133.

[37] Undated note to clerk, *ibid. Oyama* v. *California*, 332 U.S. 633, 663 (1948).

[38] *Jamestown* (New York) *Post-Journal*, Feb. 1, 1944. See letters to FM, No. 98, Box 133, and No. 73, Box 132.

[39] Milton R. Konvitz to FM, Jan. 10, 1947, Box 121. FM to Eugene Gressman, undated, Box 122. Robert H. Jackson to FM, Feb. 16, 1942, Box 101.

[40] 326 U.S. 135 (1945).

[41] *Ibid.*, p. 159. Conference notes, No. 788, Box 134.

[42] *Ibid.*

[43] 326 U.S. 135, 157, 162, 165.

[44] *Ibid.*, p. 165. See *Woodby* v. *Immigration & Naturalization Service*, 385 U.S. 276 (1966).

[45] *Fong Yue Ting* v. *United States*, 149 U.S. 698, 755 (1893).

[46] 326 U.S. 135, 161, 166.

[47] Francis Biddle, *In Brief Authority* (New York: Doubleday, 1962), p. 307.

[48] *Washington Times-Herald*, June 20, 1945. FM to Thomas J. White, May 19, 1947, No. 241, Box 137. *Craig* v. *Harney*, 331 U.S. 367 (1947).

[49] See letters, No. 788, Box 134. McCune, *Nine Young Men*, p. 147. *P.M.* (New York) June 25, 1945; *St. Louis Post-Dispatch*, June 19, 1945.

[50] 326 U.S. 135, 166. *Washington Post*, June 23, 1945.

[51] *Korematsu* v. *United States*, 323 U.S. 214 (1944).

[52] 325 U.S. 398, 407 (1945).

[53] 324 U.S. 401, 433-34 (1945).

[54] See *Oyama* v. *California*, 332 U.S. 633 (1948); *Takahashi* v. *Fish and Game Commission*, 334 U.S. 410 (1948).

[55] 323 U.S. 192, 208-209 (1944).

[56] Undated note on typed draft, No. 44, Box 138. 332 U.S. 633 (1948).

[57] Copy, FM to Leland S. Bisbee, Feb. 6, 1948, No. 44, Box 138. FM to George Murphy, Sep. 9, 1946, Box 120.

[58] FM to Edmond D. Coblentz, May 31, 1941, Box 112.

[59] *Chicago Sun*, Feb. 1, 1944; *NYT*, Jan. 29, 1945, p. 15:7. See "Interdependence for Americans," *Cong. Rec.*, v. 91, pt. 12, App. 3,836; "Race Hate—The Enemy Bullets Can't Stop," *Liberty*, Jan. 6, 1946. Reprinted, *Cong. Rec.*, v. 91, pt. 10, App. 229-31.

[60] *Oyama* v. *California*, 332 U.S. 633, 673 (1948). Draft of statement on acceptance of American Hebrew Medal, Feb. 13, 1945, Box 115.

[61] Eugene Gressman, "The Controversial Image of Mr. Justice Murphy," *Georgetown Law Journal*, v. 47 (Summer 1959), 651. Felix Frankfurter to FM, Jan. 3, 1947, Box 28, Frankfurter Papers, Manuscript Division, Library of Congress.

[62] *United States* v. *Classic*, 313 U.S. 299 (1941); *Smith* v. *Allwright*, 321 U.S. 649 (1944).

[63] Conference notes and Murphy's first slip opinion, No. 45, Box 133.

[64] *Screws* v. *United States*, 325 U.S. 91 (1945).

[65] *Ibid.*, pp. 92, 160.

[66] 140 F. 2d 662 (1944).

[67] See note 62 above. *United States* v. *Mosley*, 238 U.S. 383, 387 (1915).

[68] 295 U.S. 45 (1935).

[69] See Robert K. Carr, *Federal Protection of Civil Rights: Quest for a Sword* (Ithaca: Cornell University Press, 1947).

[70] Conference notes, Nov. 13, 1943, and undated, No. 51, Box 133.

[71] Conference notes, No. 42, Box 133.

[72] *Ibid.* 321 U.S. 649, 669 (1944).

[73] Conference notes, No. 42, Box 133.

Cf. *Barney* v. *City of New York*, 193 U.S. 430, 438 (1904); and *United States* v. *Raines*, 362 U.S. 17, 25-26 (1960).

[74] *Barney* v. *City of New York*, 193 U.S. 430 (1904). Cf. *Home Tel. & Tel. Co.* v. *Los Angeles*, 227 U.S. 278, 294 (1913).

[75] Conference notes; memorandum opinions of Reed and Jackson, JJ., No. 42, Box 133.

[76] Conference notes, No. 42, Box 133.

[77] *Ibid.* Cf. Black, J., in *Cox* v. *Louisiana*, 379 U.S. 536, 580 (1965); and in *Lance* v. *Plummer*, 384 U.S. 929 (1966).

[78] Conference notes, No. 42, Box 133.

[79] Alpheus T. Mason, *Harlan Fiske Stone: Pillar of the Law* (New York: The Viking Press, 1956), p. 638. 325 U.S. 91, 112 (1945).

[80] Memorandum to conference, Dec. 13, 1944, No. 42, Box 133.

[81] Conference notes, No. 837, Box 132. 316 U.S. 455 (1942). Quotes, memorandum to conference, circulated Feb. 2, 1945, No. 42, Box 133.

[82] *Ibid.*, pp. 5-6.

[83] 325 U.S. 91, 160-61.

[84] *Ibid.*, pp. 136-37.

[85] Julius Cohen, "The *Screws* Case: Federal Protection of Negro Rights," *Columbia Law Review*, v. 46 (Jan. 1946), 104.

[86] 325 U.S. 91, 145.

[87] *Ibid.*, pp. 134-38.

[88] See 100 U.S. 339 (1880). Draft dissent, Feb. 20, 1945, No. 42, Box 133.

[89] *Ibid.*, p. 11.

[90] Memorandum to conference, Feb. 24, 1945, No. 42, Box 133. See 328 U.S. 549, 564 (1946).

[91] *Brown* v. *Board of Education*, 347 U.S. 483 (1954); *Baker* v. *Carr*, 369 U.S. 186 (1962).

[92] *Monroe* v. *Pape*, 365 U.S. 167 (1961). Cf. *Williams* v. *United States*, 341 U.S. 97 (1951); *United States* v. *Guest*, 383 U.S. 745 (1966); and *United States* v. *Price*, 383 U.S. 787 (1966).

[93] See Roberts, J., in 325 U.S. 91, 153.

[94] *Justice*, 1961 Commission on Civil Rights Report, Book 5, pp. 8-9, 46-52. See also Carr, *Federal Protection*, pp. 114-15; and Harry H. Shapiro, "Limitations in Prosecuting Civil Rights Violations," *Cor-*

nell Law Quarterly, v. 46 (Summer 1961), 532-54.

[95] Figures are from Department of Justice sources.

[96] Felix Frankfurter to Wiley Rutledge, May 10, 1945, Box 34; Frankfurter to Fred M. Vinson, April 27, 1948, Box 40, Frankfurter Papers, Manuscript Division, Library of Congress. See cases, note 92 above; and *Shelley* v. *Kraemer*, 334 U.S. 1 (1948). Also, Dean Alfange, Jr., "Under Color of Law: Classic and Screws Revisited," *Cornell Law Quarterly*, v. 67 (Spring 1962), 395-428.

[97] 383 U.S. 745, 756. Cert. note, No. 113, Box 136. *Enoch Pratt Free Library of Baltimore* v. *Kerr*, 326 U.S. 721 (1945).

[98] *Georgia* v. *Rachel*, 384 U.S. 780 (1966); *City of Greenwood* v. *Peacock*, 384 U.S. 808 (1966).

[99] *Pierson* v. *Ray*, 386 U.S. 547 (1967). See 383 U.S. 745, 782. *NYT*, April 3, 1966, IV, p. 10:1.

[100] *Ex parte Milligan*, 4 Wall. 2, 137 (1866). See discussion by Justice Reed, *U.S. ex rel. Toth* v. *Quarles*, 350 U.S. 11, 35-43 (1955).

[101] *Wade* v. *Hunter*, 336 U.S. 684 (1949); *ex parte Quirin*, 317 U.S. 1 (1942).

[102] See undated cert. note by "H.I.P.," and unsigned memorandum, No. 61, Box 136.

[103] *In re Yamashita*, 327 U.S. 1 (1946); *Homma* v. *Patterson*, 327 U.S. 759 (1946); and 327 U.S. 304 (1946).

[104] See Adolf Frank Creel, *The Case of General Yamashita* (Chicago: University of Chicago Press, 1949); Sheldon Glueck, *The Nuremberg Trial and Aggressive War* (New York: Alfred A. Knopf, 1946).

[105] Mason, *Stone*, p. 716.

[106] "Memorandum for the Court," Jan. 22, 1946; undated pencil note, Edward G. Kemp to FM, No. 61, Box 136.

[107] Mason, *Stone*, p. 667.

[108] Memorandum to conference, Jan. 23, 1946; and memorandum for the Court, Jan. 31, 1946, No. 61, Box 136. Mason, *Stone*, pp. 667-68.

[109] *Ibid.*, p. 671. Cf. Edward S. Corwin, *Total War and the Constitution* (New York: Alfred A. Knopf, 1947), p. 121.

See note, Jan. 23, 1946, Box 118.

[110] 327 U.S. 1, 79. FM to George Murphy, Sep. 9, 1946, Box 120.

[111] Mason, *Stone*, pp. 667-68. Memoranda to conference, Jan. 26 and 31, 1946, No. 61, Box 136.

[112] Harper, *Rutledge*, pp. 184-85.

[113] *Ibid.*, pp. 188, 185-87. Wiley Rutledge to Harlan F. Stone, Feb. 1, 1946, Stone Papers, Manuscript Division, Library of Congress.

[114] Undated note, No. 61, Box 136.

[115] 327 U.S. 1, 30.

[116] Comment on cert. note by "H.I.P.," undated, No. 61, Box 136.

[117] 327 U.S. 1, 28.

[118] Harper, *Rutledge*, pp. 185-89.

[119] 327 U.S. 1, 28, 29.

[120] *Detroit News*, June 14, 1942. *Omaha Evening World-Herald*, June 4, 1942.

[121] 327 U.S. 1, 26-27.

[122] Draft opinion, p. 10, No. 61, Box 136.

[123] 327 U.S. 1, 40-41, 29.

[124] *Ibid.*, p. 41. Milton Mayer, *Progressive*, Feb. 25, 1946, p. 4.

[125] Fairman, "The Supreme Court on Military Jurisdiction," *Harvard Law Review*, v. 59 (July 1946), 869.

[126] Quotes, *Washington Star*, March 21, 1946, and editorial, Feb. 6, 1946. *NYT*, Feb. 13, 1946, p. 22:2.

[127] FM to Mrs. George Marshall, Feb. 12, 1946; FM to Clare Booth Luce, Feb. 12, 1946, No. 61, Box 136.

[128] FM to Fred Wieck, May 23, 1949; FM to Roger Baldwin, Feb. 6, 1946, Box 117. FM to W. Earl Ledden, Feb. 8, 1946, No. 61, Box 136.

[129] See letters in No. 61, Box 136, from: Hans J. Morgenthau, March 1, 1946; Samuel B. Pettingill, March 2, 1946; Eugene L. Garey, March 20, 1946; Hulbert Taft, Feb. 7, 1946. Sokolsky column in *Washington Times-Herald*, March 7, 1946. Wiley Rutledge to FM, Feb. 9, 1946, No. 93, Box 135.

[130] Baldwin to FM, Feb. 6, 1946, No. 61, Box 136.

[131] Copy, letter of William Chamberlain to "William," June 21, 1948, *ibid.*

[132] Undated, pencil note, *ibid.*

[133] Harper, *Rutledge*, pp. 185-89.

[134] *Ibid. Homma v. Patterson*, 327 U.S. 759 (1946). Undated note, Wiley Rutledge to FM, No. 93, Box 135.

[135] Note, Rutledge to FM, Feb. 7, 1946, *ibid.*

[136] Undated pencil note; and note, Feb. 9, 1946, *ibid.*

[137] Memo, FM to clerk, Feb. 9, 1946, *ibid.*

[138] Comment on typed draft, *ibid.*

[139] 327 U.S. 759, 760-61.

[140] *Ibid.*, p. 760; 327 U.S. 1, 29.

[141] *Washington Post*, Nov. 20, 1949. Cf. *Washington Star*, July 20, 1949.

[142] *Washington Star*, Feb. 13, 1946.

[143] Harper, *Rutledge*, 189.

[144] See editorials, *NYHT* and *St. Louis Post-Dispatch*, Feb. 6, 1946. Also *NYT*, Feb. 5, 1946.

[145] *Washington Post*, Feb. 6, 1946. Merlo J. Pusey, in *Washington Post*, March 5, 1946.

[146] 327 U.S. 304 (1946).

[147] *Ibid.*, pp. 334, 329.

[148] Conference notes, Nos. 14, 15, Box 135.

[149] See *Johnson v. Eisentrager*, 339 U.S. 763 (1950); *Harmon v. Brucker*, 335 U.S. 579 (1958); *Reid v. Covert*, 354 U.S. 1 (1957).

[150] Fairman, "Supreme Court," p. 852. 335 U.S. 876 (1948). Murphy comment on clerk's "interim report," No. 239, Box 140.

[151] 335 U.S. 876, 877-78 (1948); 338 U.S. 197 (1949). Cf. Douglas, J., in *Mitchell v. United States*, 18 L. ed. 2d 132 (1967).

[152] Copy, FM to Leland S. Bisbee, Feb. 6, 1948, No. 44, Box 138. *Oyama v. California*, 332 U.S. 631 (1948). See Walter Lippmann, "Declining Influence of the Great Powers," *Durham Morning Herald*, Oct. 17, 1965; Archibald MacLeish, "What is 'Realism' Doing to American History?" *Saturday Review*, v. 48 (July 3, 1965), 10-12; and J. William Fulbright, *The Arrogance of Power* (New York: Random House, 1967).

[153] FM to John R. Watkins, March 1, 1945, No. 620, Box 134.

[154] Fred Rodell, in *Progressive*, Oct. 4, 1943, p. 9.

CHAPTER 14

[1] Cf. *Mercoid Corp. v. Mid-Continent Investment Co.*, 320 U.S. 661 (1944); *FPC v. Hope Natural Gas Co.*, 320 U.S. 591 (1944); *Mahnich v. Southern Steamship Co.*, 321 U.S. 96 (1944). See Martin Shapiro, *Law and Politics in the Supreme Court* (New York: The Free Press, 1964).

[2] *United States v. Morgan*, 307 U.S. 183, 191 (1939).

[3] Merlo J. Pusey, *Charles Evans Hughes* (New York: Macmillan, 1951), v. 2, pp. 204-205.

[4] *International Union of Mine, Mill & Smelter Workers v. Eagle-Picher Mining & Smelter Co.*, 325 U.S. 335, 356 (1945).

[5] See, *e.g.*, *NLRB v. Express Publishing Co.*, 312 U.S. 426 (1941); *NLRB v. Stowe Spinning Co.*, 336 U.S. 226 (1949); *Hickman v. Taylor*, 329 U.S. 495, 506 (1947).

[6] 327 U.S. 633 (1946). FM to George Murphy, Sep. 9, 1946, Box 120.

[7] 322 U.S. 694 (1944). Victor Riesel, in *Las Vegas Sun*, Feb. 12, 1957; Walton Hamilton, "The Supreme Court Today,"

Nation, (Aug. 19, 1944), p. 207; *International Association of Machinists v. Gonzales*, 356 U.S. 617, 619 (1958).

[8] See comments of Justice Rutledge on slip opinions; and Felix Frankfurter to FM, undated, No. 366, Box 132.

[9] "Progress in Democracy," *American Labor Legislation Review*, v. 29 (June 1939), 61.

[10] *A. H. Phillips, Inc. v. Walling*, 324 U.S. 490, 493 (1945).

[11] *Morris v. McComb*, 332 U.S. 422, 439 (1947). See Archibald Cox, "The Influence of Mr. Justice Murphy on Labor Law," *Michigan Law Review*, v. 48 (April 1950), 793-809.

[12] *10 East 40th Street Bldg., Inc. v. Callus*, 325 U.S. 578, 579 (1945).

[13] *Overstreet v. North Shore Corp.*, 318 U.S. 125 (1943); *Walling v. Helmerich & Payne, Inc.*, 323 U.S. 37 (1944); *United States v. Rosenwasser*, 323 U.S. 360 (1945); and *Walling v. Harnischfeger Corp.*, 325 U.S. 427 (1945). Cf. Irving J.

Levy, "Belo Revisited," *George Washington Law Review*, v. 15 (Dec. 1946), 39-62.

[14] *United States* v. *Darby*, 312 U.S. 100 (1941); *Opp Cotton Mills* v. *Administrator*, 312 U.S. 126 (1941); *A. B. Kirschbaum Co.* v. *Walling*, 316 U.S. 517 (1942); and *Walling* v. *Jacksonville Paper Co.*, 317 U.S. 564 (1943).

[15] *Ibid.*, p. 567. See, *e.g., Warren-Bradshaw Drilling Co.* v. *Hall*, 317 U.S. 88, 93 (1942); *Borden* v. *Borella*, 325 U.S. 679, 685 (1945). Cf. *United States* v. *E. C. Knight Co.*, 156 U.S. 1 (1895).

[16] 319 U.S. 491, 502 (1943).

[17] See the *Kirschbaum* case, 316 U.S. 517, 520 (1942); 325 U.S. 578, 583 (1945).

[18] Comments on typed draft, No. 820, Box 134.

[19] Conference notes, No. 608, Box 134. 324 U.S. 490 (1945). *Lochner* v. *New York*, 198 U.S. 45 (1905).

[20] Conference notes, No. 379, Box 135. *NYT*, Feb. 4, 1944, p. 14:3. See Charles S. Lyon, "Old Statutes and New Constitution," *Columbia Law Review*, v. 44 (Sep. 1944), 637.

[21] See, *e.g.*, Cox, "Influence of Murphy," p. 799; E. Merrick Dodd, "The Supreme Court and Fair Labor Standards, 1941-1945," *Harvard Law Review*, v. 59 (Feb. 1946), 338, 345, 363. The *Lenroot* case, 323 U.S. 490, 509 (1945).

[22] Conference notes, No. 49, Box 134, 52 F. Supp. 142 (1943); 141 F. 2d 400 (1944).

[23] 323 U.S. 490, 509-10.

[24] Comment on slip opinion, No. 49, Box 134.

[25] Dodd, "Supreme Court," p. 345. E. Blythe Stason to FM, Feb. 21, 1945. Louis L. Jaffe, "Mr. Justice Jackson," *Harvard Law Review*, v. 68 (April 1955), 988.

[26] Radin, "A Case Study in Statutory Interpretation: *Western Union Co.* v. *Lenroot*," *California Law Review*, v. 33 (June 1945), 229.

[27] Dodd, "Supreme Court," pp. 352-54.

[28] 321 U.S. 590 (1944).

[29] *Ibid.*, pp. 597, 592.

[30] FM to Frank Nolan, April 3, 1944, Box 111.

[31] 321 U.S. 590, 596-99, 601.

[32] *Ibid.*, pp. 603-605, 602-603.

[33] Marginal notes on slip opinions, No. 409, Box 133.

[34] Frankfurter to FM, Feb. 3, 1944, No. 409, Box 133.

[35] *Detroit Labor News*, March 31, 1944. Cf. David Lawrence, *Washington Star*, March 30, 1944.

[36] 321 U.S. 590, 606.

[37] Stone to Roberts, March 16, 1944, Stone Papers, Manuscript Division, Library of Congress. 321 U.S. 590, 606-607, 615-17, 619.

[38] *Jewell Ridge Coal Corp.* v. *Local No. 6167*, 325 U.S. 161 (1945).

[39] *Ibid.*, pp. 163-66, 167-69, 170.

[40] Comment on slip opinion, April 5, 1945, No. 721, Box 134.

[41] Merlo J. Pusey, " 'Lawless' Decision," *Washington Post*, undated. *Washington Post*, May 13 and 18, 1945. Dodd, "Supreme Court," p. 355.

[42] 325 U.S. 161, 170-73, 194-96. Murphy reply, memorandum to conference, May 5, 1945, Stone Papers, Manuscript Division, Library of Congress. Felix Frankfurter to Robert H. Jackson, June 8, 1945, Box 19, Frankfurter Papers, Manuscript Division, Library of Congress.

[43] Mason, *Harlan Fiske Stone: Pillar of the Law* (New York: The Viking Press, 1956), pp. 640-45. See John P. Frank, "Disqualification of Judges," *Yale Law Journal*, v. 56 (April 1947), 605-39.

[44] Mason, *Stone*, pp. 765-69.

[45] As quoted by Sen. James Eastland, *Cong. Rec.*, v. 92, pt. 6, p. 7,065. *NYT*, June 11, 1946, p. 2:6.

[46] Stanley Reed to FM, April 18, 1945, No. 721, Box 134.

[47] Undated handwritten note, FM to Robert H. Jackson, Box 19, Frankfurter Papers, Manuscript Division, Library of Congress.

[48] Felix Frankfurter to FM, March 27, 1943, Box 28, Manuscript Division, Library of Congress. *NYT*, June 11, 1946, p. 2:3. Eugene C. Gerhart, *America's Advocate: Robert H. Jackson* (Indianapolis: Bobbs-Merrill, 1958), pp. 250-51.

[49] *Detroit Free Press*, June 12, 1946. *NYT*, June 13, 1946, p. 1:7. *St. Louis Post-Dispatch*, June 13, 1946. *Washington Star*, June 14, 1946.

50 *Detroit Free Press*, June 12, 1946. *Baltimore Sun*, June 12, 1946.

51 *Cong. Rec.*, June 18, 1946, pp. 7,065-66. Drew Pearson in *Washington Post*, June 21, 1946; Jonathan Daniels, in *St. Louis Post-Dispatch*, Aug. 23, 1946. *NYT*, July 4, 1946, p. 17:8. See Albert P. Blaustein and Andrew H. Field, " 'Overruling' Opinions in the Supreme Court," *Michigan Law Review*, v. 57 (Dec. 1958), 160-61.

52 *Houston Post*, June 3, 1944.

53 Mason, *Stone*, p. 608.

54 Henry M. Bates to FM, Sep. 7, 1943, Box 109.

55 FM to Elinor Greene, Feb. 10, 1944, Box 111.

56 Copy, FM to Roberts, July 6, 1945, Box 116.

57 Undated handwritten note, FM to Felix Frankfurter, Box 28, Frankfurter Papers, Manuscript Division, Library of Congress.

58 See Owen J. Roberts to Felix Frankfurter, July 28, 1945, Box 33, Frankfurter Papers, Manuscript Division, Library of Congress.

59 Felix Frankfurter to FM, March 9, 1946, Box 28, Frankfurter Papers, Manuscript Division, Library of Congress. 328 U.S. 152 (1946).

60 Felix Frankfurter to FM, March 25, 1948, Box 28, Frankfurter Papers, Library of Congress. *United States* v. *Felin & Co.*, 334 U.S. 624 (1948).

61 Memorandum, Oct. 16, 1945, Box 28, Frankfurter Papers, Manuscript Division, Library of Congress.

62 *Ibid.*, pp. 2-3.

63 *Ibid.*, pp. 4-5.

64 Felix Frankfurter to FM, June 10, 1946, Box 28, Frankfurter Papers, Manuscript Division, Library of Congress.

65 Felix Frankfurter to Hugo L. Black, Sep. 30, 1950, Box 4; Frankfurter to Robert H. Jackson, June 12, 1946, Box 19, Frankfurter Papers, Manuscript Division, Library of Congress.

66 FM to Robert H. Jackson, April 13, 1947; Jackson to FM, May 1, 1947, Box 122.

67 Felix Frankfurter to FM, Feb. 6, 1947, Box 28, Frankfurter Papers, Manuscript Division, Library of Congress.

68 Jackson address to American Law Institute, "Decisional Law and *Stare Decisis*," reprinted *A.B.A.J.*, v. 30 (June 1944), 334.

69 Mason, *Stone*, p. 610. Wiley Rutledge to FM, Dec. 1, 1943, No. 53, Box 132. *Commissioner of Internal Revenue* v. *Gooch Milling & Elevator Co.*, 320 U.S. 418 (1943).

70 Conference notes, No. 71, Box 133. *United States* v. *Laudani*, 320 U.S. 543 (1944), No. 173, Box 132. *U.S. ex rel. Marcus* v. *Hess*, 317 U.S. 537 (1943).

71 FM to Dorothy Kemp Roosevelt, April 7, 1944, Box 111.

72 FM to William G. Woolfolk, March 5, 1945, Box 115.

73 325 U.S. 821, 830-31 (1945).

74 FM to John J. Adams, Christmas, 1943, Box 110. FM to Grace Tully, June 28, 1943, Box 109. Cf. slip opinions, No. 474, Box 135. *United States* v. *Carbone*, 327 U.S. 633 (1947).

75 FM to Arthur B. Cuddihy, Jr., Feb. 12, 1947, Box 121.

76 *Ibid.*

77 FM to Osborn, June 13, 1944, No. 409, Box 133.

78 328 U.S. 680, 692 (1946).

79 *NYT*, Jan. 14, 1947, p. 4:3; Ray A. Brown, "Vested Rights and the Portal-to-Portal Act," *Michigan Law Review*, v. 46 (April 1948), 728. See Hearings before a Subcommittee of the Senate on the Judiciary, 80th Cong., 1st Sess. (Jan. 1947), pp. 49, 65, 92.

80 *Detroit Labor News*, Dec. 6, 1946. George E. Cotter, "Portal to Portal Pay," *Virginia Law Review*, v. 33 (Jan. 1947), 45.

81 *Cong. Rec.*, v. 93, pt. 2, p. 1,562. *NYT*, Jan. 17, 1947, p. 22:5; and Feb. 11, 1947, p. 20:2. *Walling* v. *Portland Terminal Co.*, 330 U.S. 148, 154 (1947).

82 William F. Stringer, in *Christian Science Monitor*, Dec. 26, 1946. Pusey, in *Washington Post*, Dec. 24, 1946.

83 *NYT*, Dec. 24, 1946, p. 16:1. 69 F. Supp. 710 (1947).

84 For CIO admissions that many claims were ill-founded, see Lee Pressman re-

marks, *Washington Post*, Jan. 19, 1947. Cf. Dillard Stokes, in *Washington Post*, Dec. 25, 1946. FM to George Murphy, Sep. 9, 1946, Box 120. FM to Arthur B. Cuddihy, Jr., Feb. 12, 1947, Box 121.

[85] *Louisville Courier-Journal*, Jan. 19, 1947.

[86] Brown, "Vested Rights," pp. 728-31. See Note, *University of Chicago Law Review*, v. 15 (Winter 1948), 352.

[87] FM to Henry M. Bates, Nov. 15, 1947, Box 123.

[88] FM to Arthur B. Cuddihy, Jr., Feb. 12, 1947, Box 121.

[89] FM to Henry M. Bates, June 26, 1947, Box 122.

[90] FM to Arthur B. Cuddihy, Jr., Feb. 12, 1947, Box 121.

[91] Jackson, J., in *Craig* v. *Harney*, 331 U.S. 367, 396 (1947).

[92] "Vinson's Dilemma," *Washington Post*, June 11, 1946.

[93] FM to Harry S. Truman, Nov. 6, 1945; FM to Harry S. Truman, Sep. 20, 1946, and reply, Sep. 23, 1946. Truman Library, Independence (Mo.): P.P.F.-2173. *NYT*, Aug. 23, 1946, p. 2:2; Aug. 20, 1946, p. 12:3. Franklin C. Gowen to FM, Aug. 24, 1946, Box 120.

[94] FM to John J. Adams, Sep. 24, 1946, Box 120.

[95] 327 U.S. 686 (1946); 329 U.S. 90 (1946).

[96] FM to Fred M. Vinson, Oct. 9, 1946, Nos. 4-5, Box 135.

[97] *Gibbons* v. *Ogden*, 9 Wheat. 1 (1824); 327 U.S. 686, 705; 329 U.S. 90, 103-104.

[98] *Ibid.*, p. 104.

[99] 336 U.S. 220, 224 (1949).

[100] *Nebbia* v. *New York*, 291 U.S. 502, 556 (1934).

[101] 329 U.S. 495 (1947).

[102] Docket book, Oct. 14, 1946, Box 138. Jackson memorandum opinion, Jan. 3, 1947, No. 47, Box 136. *Palmer* v. *Hoffman*, 318 U.S. 109 (1943).

[103] 329 U.S. 495, 514. Charles R. Taine, "Discovery of Trial Preparations in the Federal Courts," *Columbia Law Review*, v. 50 (Dec. 1950), 1,064.

[104] FM to George Murphy, Sep. 9, 1946, Box 120.

[105] FM to Fred M. Vinson, Oct. 9, 1946, Nos. 4-5, Box 136. FM to Vinson, Nov. 13, 1947, No. 14, Box 138. 332 U.S. 788 (1947). 334 U.S. 653 (1948).

[106] Wiley Rutledge to FM, Jan. 3, 1946, and comments on 1st circulation, No. 47, Box 136.

[107] *United States* v. *Yellow Cab Co.*, 332 U.S. 218 (1947). FM, memorandum to conference, June 19, 1947, No. 1,035, Box 138.

[108] Undated note to clerk, re rider 5, No. 962, Box 130. *Goldman* v. *United States*, 316 U.S. 129 (1942).

[109] FM to clerk on typed draft opinion, *SEC* v. *Engineers Public Service Co.*, 332 U.S. 788, Nos. 2-3, Box 135. FM to clerk, Nov. 14, 1947, No. 7, Box 138. *Morris* v. *McComb*, 332 U.S. 442 (1947).

[110] Harlan F. Stone to FM, Dec. 4, 1945, referring to *Chatwin* v. *United States*, 326 U.S. 455; and March 14, 1946, regarding *North American Co.* v. *SEC*, 327 U.S. 686. Stone Papers, Manuscript Division, Library of Congress.

[111] Comment on slip opinion, Nov. 15, 1946, Nos. 4-5, Box 136.

[112] Felix Frankfurter to FM, Feb. 26, 1947, No. 265, Box 137. *Cardillo* v. *Liberty Mutual Insurance Co.*, 330 U.S. 469 (1947). *United States National Bank* v. *Chase Manhattan Bank*, 331 U.S. 29 (1947). Frankfurter memorandum to conference, March 28, 1947, No. 371, Box 137.

[113] Felix Frankfurter to FM, May 14, 1947, No. 718, Box 137. *United States* v. *Walsh*, 331 U.S. 432 (1947).

[114] Frankfurter comment on first circulation, *American Power & Light Co.* v. *SEC*, 329 U.S. 90 (1946), Nos. 4-5, Box 136.

[115] 331 U.S. 432 (1947). Reed comment on slip opinion, May 13, 1947, No. 718, Box 137.

[116] Comments on slip opinions, Nos. 50-61, Box 134. *Dow Chemical Co.* v. *Halliburton Oil Well Cementing Co.*, 324 U.S. 320 (1945). Rutledge comment in *Cardillo* slip opinion, see note 112 above.

[117] FM to Felix Frankfurter, Nov. 13, 1946, Nos. 4-5, Box 136. See the *Kirschbaum* case, 316 U.S. 517, 520 (1942).

[118] 334 U.S. 653 (1948).

[119] 336 U.S. 725 (1949). Copy, letter to Justice Frankfurter, March 28, 1949, No. 355, Box 139.

[120] 330 U.S. 258 (1947); 332 U.S. 194 (1947).

[121] *Washington Times-Herald*, March 7, 1947.

[122] Docket notes, Nos. 759-60, Box 138.

[123] 330 U.S. 258, 305, 307, 341 (1947). See memo to conference, Feb. 24; circulated opinions of Feb. 28 and March 4, 1947, Nos. 759-60, Box 137.

[124] 330 U.S. 258, 336-38. Krug statement quoted in Watt, "The Divine Right of Government by Judiciary," *University of Chicago Law Review*, v. 14 (April 1947), 436.

[125] 330 U.S. 258, 338-42.

[126] *St. Louis Post-Dispatch and Washington Times-Herald*, March 7, 1947. See letters, Nos. 759-60, Box 137.

[127] Watt, "Divine Right," pp. 448, 454. John P. Frank, "Court and Constitution: The Passive Period," *Vanderbilt Law Review*, v. 4 (April 1951), 410. Charles O. Gregory, "Government by Injunction Again," *University of Chicago Law Review*, v. 14 (April 1947), 368-69.

[128] 332 U.S. 194 (1947).

[129] 318 U.S. 80 (1943).

[130] 18 S.E.C., 231 (1945).

[131] Lord George Gordon Hewart, *The New Despotism* (New York: Cosmopolitan Book Co., 1929).

[132] Jackson, pp. 334-35.

[133] Docket book, Nos. 81-82, Box 138.

[134] Slip opinion, June 17, 1947, Nos. 81-82, Box 137.

[135] Conference notes, Nos. 56-57, Box 138. *NLRB* v. *E. C. Atkins & Co.*, 331 U.S. 398 (1947).

[136] 332 U.S. 194, 202-203.

[137] Circulated draft and Frankfurter memorandum to conference, June 18, 1947, Nos. 81-82, Box 137.

[138] Memorandum to conference, June 18, 1947, Nos. 81-82, Box 137.

[139] Wiley Rutledge to Felix Frankfurter, and reply, June 18, 1947, Box 34, Frankfurter Papers, Manuscript Division, Library of Congress.

[140] 332 U.S. 194, 210, 214-16.

[141] See, *e.g.*, Kenneth Culp Davis, *Administrative Law Treatise* (St. Paul: West Publishing Co., 1958), pp. 536-41. Jaffe, "Mr. Justice Jackson," p. 986n 187; Note, *Harvard Law Review*, v. 62 (Jan. 1949), 478. See *American Ship Building Co.* v. *NLRB*, 380 U.S. 300, 327 (1965).

[142] FM to Mrs. James Roosevelt, June 21, 1947, Box 122.

[143] Frankfurter to Hugo L. Black, as quoted in Mason, *Stone*, p. 470n.

[144] Eugene Gressman, "The Controversial Image of Mr. Justice Murphy," *Georgetown Law Journal*, v. 47 (Summer 1959), 640.

[145] *Washington Post*, June 9, 1944.

CHAPTER 15

[1] See "The Supreme Court: 1947," *Fortune*, v. 35 (Jan. 1947), 73-79.

[2] G. Mennen Williams to FM, May 29, 1948, Box 124.

[3] FM to Stasia Buhl, Oct. 31, 1945, Box 117.

[4] Copy, FM to Henry M. Bates, Aug. 16, 1948, Box 125.

[5] FM to Warren, Jan. 27, 1942, Box 101.

[6] Note, Eleanor Bumgardner to FM, Jan. 12, 1947, Box 121.

[7] Rutledge to Joan Cuddihy, and FM comment, Nov. 19, 1947, Box 123.

[8] Rutledge to FM, July 3, 1947, Box 122.

[9] Comment on circulated opinion, June 11, 1947, No. 1,035, Box 138.

[10] FM to Rutledge, June 29, 1947, Box 122.

[11] Eugene Gressman, "The Controversial Image of Mr. Justice Murphy," *Georgetown Law Journal*, v. 47 (Summer 1959), 652n.

[12] Comment on circulated opinion, June 2, 1947, No. 970, Box 137. *Brotherhood of Railroad Trainmen* v. *B. & O. R.R. Co.*, 331 U.S. 519 (1947).

[13] FM to Rutledge, June 29, 1947; Rutledge to FM, July 3, 1947, Box 122.

[14] S. Sidney Ulmer, "Homeostatic Tendencies in the United States Supreme Court," in Ulmer, *Introductory Readings in Political Behavior* (Chicago: Rand Mc-

Nally, 1961), pp. 174-77. Figures for 1947-48 terms, undated Court memorandum, Box 125. FM to E. Blythe Stason, June 26, 1947, Box 122.

[15] See *Brown* v. *Mississippi*, 297 U.S. 278 (1936); *Chambers* v. *Florida*, 309 U.S. 227 (1940); *Norris* v. *Alabama*, 294 U.S. 587 (1935); and *Powell* v. *Alabama*, 287 U.S. 45 (1932).

[16] 316 U.S. 455 (1942).

[17] 302 U.S. 319 (1937).

[18] 287 U.S. 45 (1932).

[19] Conference notes, No. 837, Box 132. Quotes, *Joint Anti-Fascist Refugee Committee* v. *McGrath*, 341 U.S. 123, 174 (1951); *National Mutual Insurance Co.* v. *Tidewater Transfer Co.*, 337 U.S. 582, 646 (1949); *Adamson* v. *California*, 332 U.S. 46, 68 (1947); *Haley* v. *Ohio*, 332 U.S. 596, 604 (1948).

[20] Conference notes, No. 837, Box 132. Also, No. 25, Box 132. *McNabb* v. *United States*, 318 U.S. 332 (1943).

[21] Felix Frankfurter to Hugo L. Black, Nov. 13, 1943, Box 4, Frankfurter Papers, Manuscript Division, Library of Congress.

[22] *Adamson* v. *California*, 332 U.S. 46 (1947). See Charles Fairman, "Does the Fourteenth Amendment Incorporate the Bill of Rights: The Original Understanding," *Stanford Law Review*, v. 2 (Dec. 1949), 5-139.

[23] Conference notes, Nos. 25 and 31, Box 132. 318 U.S. 332 (1943); and *United States* v. *Rice*, 317 U.S. 61 (1942). See, *e.g., Ashcraft* v. *Tennessee*, 332 U.S. 143 (1944); *Lyons* v. *Oklahoma*, 322 U.S. 596 (1944); *Malinski* v. *New York*, 324 U.S. 401 (1945). Jackson, J., in *Irvine* v. *California*, 347 U.S. 128, 137-38 (1954).

[24] *Screws* v. *United States*, 325 U.S. 91 (1945).

[25] C. Herman Pritchett, *The American Constitution* (New York: McGraw-Hill, 1959), p. 552.

[26] 328 U.S. 217 (1946). *Fay* v. *New York*, 332 U.S. 261 (1947); *Moore* v. *New York*, 333 U.S. 565, 570 (1948).

[27] See, *e.g., Malinski* v. *New York*, 324 U.S. 401, 433 (1945); and *Parker* v. *Illinois*, 333 U.S. 571, 577 (1948).

[28] *Lyons* v. *Oklahoma*, 322 U.S. 596, 605 (1944).

[29] 332 U.S. 742 (1948). Cf. comments of Justices Black and Frankfurter, No. 91, Box 138.

[30] *Canizio* v. *New York*, 327 U.S. 82, 87-89 (1946). *Escobedo* v. *Illinois*, 378 U.S. 478 (1964). *Miranda* v. *Arizona*, 384 U.S. 436 (1966).

[31] 329 U.S. 173 (1946). Notes, clerk to FM and reply, undated, No. 36, Box 136.

[32] 329 U.S. 173, 183 (1946).

[33] *Taylor* v. *Alabama*, 335 U.S. 252, 275 (1948). See *Wade* v. *Mayo*, 334 U.S. 672, 681 (1948).

[34] Conference notes, No. 34, Box 136. *Harris* v. *United States*, 331 U.S. 145 (1947).

[35] *Zap* v. *United States*, 328 U.S. 624 (1946), and 330 U.S. 800 (1947); *Davis* v. *United States*, 328 U.S. 582 (1946). Justice Frankfurter, memorandum to conference, April 25, 1947, No. 34, Box 136. Also see conference note, No. 473, Box 135. *Pennekamp* v. *Florida*, 328 U.S. 331 (1946).

[36] 331 U.S. 145 (1947).

[37] Felix Frankfurter to FM, Feb. 15, 1947; conference notes; and FM to clerk, undated, No. 34, Box 136.

[38] *Ibid.* Note, Rutledge to FM, April 12, 1947; and comment on slip opinion, April 7, 1947, No. 34, Box 136.

[39] Frankfurter to FM, Feb. 15, 1947, No. 34, Box 136.

[40] *Goldstein* v. *United States*, 316 U.S. 114 (1942); *Goldman* v. *United States*, 316 U.S. 129 (1942).

[41] Frankfurter to FM, Feb. 15, 1947, No. 34, Box 136.

[42] 331 U.S. 145, 193-94. FM note to clerk, undated, No. 34, Box 136.

[43] Frankfurter comment on slip opinion, April 3, 1947; and Rutledge comment on slip opinion, April 11, 1947, No. 34, Box 136.

[44] Comment of *Washington Post, Washington Star,* and *St. Louis Post-Dispatch,* May 7, 1947.

[45] *Trupiano* v. *United States*, 334 U.S. 699 (1948).

[46] FM to Felix Frankfurter, April 10, 1948, No. 427, Box 139.

[47] 334 U.S. 699, 710. Cf. Jackson comment on copy of Vinson opinion, June 9, 1948, No. 427, Box 139.

[48] 334 U.S. 699, 716. Black, J., in *United States* v. *Rabinowitz*, 339 U.S. 56, 67 (1950).

[49] *Ibid.*, p. 86.

[50] 329 U.S. 459 (1947); and 332 U.S. 46 (1947).

[51] Docket book, No. 142, Box 138.

[52] 329 U.S. 459, 471 (1947). See Frankfurter, J., memorandum opinion, Jan. 2, 1947, No. 142, Box 137. Frankfurter to Fred M. Vinson, Jan. 4, 1946 [*sic*], Box 40, Frankfurter Papers, Manuscript Division, Library of Congress.

[53] *United States* v. *White*, 322 U.S. 694 (1944); *Hickman* v. *Taylor,* 329 U.S. 495 (1947).

[54] Rutledge circulation, Dec. 14, 1946; Murphy statement, undated, No. 142, Box 137.

[55] *Ibid.*, pp. 1-3.

[56] *Adamson* v. *California*, 332 U.S. 46 (1947).

[57] 211 U.S. 78 (1908).

[58] 332 U.S. 46, 75, 90.

[59] *Ibid.*, pp. 59-68. Conference note, Nos. 56-57, Box 138.

[60] 332 U.S. 46, 123-25.

[61] Frankfurter in *Malinski* v. *New York*, 324 U.S. 401, 415 (1945); *Adamson* v. *California*, 332 U.S. 46, 68. Murphy in *Carter* v. *Illinois*, 329 U.S. 173, 186 (1946). Undated note to clerk, No. 1,035, Box 138.

[62] See handwritten notes, June 19, 1947, No. 102, Box 137. Cf. 309 U.S. 227, 238 (1940).

[63] *Jackson* v. *Denno*, 378 U.S. 368, 407 (1965).

[64] *Gideon* v. *Wainwright*, 372 U.S. 335 (1963). *Malloy* v. *Hogan*, 378 U.S. 1 (1964); *Murphy* v. *New York Waterfront Commission*, 378 U.S. 52 (1964). *Griffin* v. *California*, 380 U.S. 609 (1965); *Robinson* v. *California*, 370 U.S. 660 (1962). *Pointer* v. *Texas*, 380 U.S. 400 (1965). *NAACP* v. *Alabama*, 357 U.S. 449 (1958). *Kent* v. *Dulles*, 357 U.S. 116 (1958); *Aptheker* v. *Secretary of State*, 378 U.S. 500 (1964). *Griswold* v. *Connecticut*, 381 U.S. 479 (1965).

[65] Cf. *Griffin* v. *California*, 380 U.S. 609 (1965); *Johnson* v. *New Jersey*, 384 U.S. 719 (1966). See John Raeburn Green, "The Bill of Rights, the Fourteenth Amendment, and the Supreme Court," *Michigan Law Review*, v. 46 (May 1948), 901-902. Thomas Reed Powell, "Authority and Freedom in a Democratic Society," *Columbia Law Review*, v. 44 (July 1944), 486.

[66] *Stein* v. *New York*, 346 U.S. 156 (1953); *Rochin* v. *California*, 342 U.S. 165 (1952); *Irvine* v. *California*, 347 U.S. 128 (1954); and John A. Gorfinkel, "The Fourteenth Amendment and State Criminal Proceedings—'Ordered Liberty' or 'Just Deserts,'" *California Law Review*, v. 41 (Winter, 1953-54), 672-91.

[67] *Miranda* v. *Arizona*, 384 U.S. 436 (1966).

[68] *Griswold* v. *Connecticut*, 381 U.S. 479, 508-10, 486-87 (1965). *Berger* v. *New York*, 388 U.S. 41 (1967); *Katz* v. *United States*, 36 L.W. 4080 (Dec. 19, 1967). See Douglas, J., in *Poe* v. *Ullman*, 367 U.S. 497, 516 (1961).

[69] *In re Yamashita*, 327 U.S. 1 (1946). *Jewell Ridge Coal Corp.* v. *Local No. 6167*, 325 U.S. 161 (1945).

[70] Cf. Harlan, J., in *Poe* v. *Ullman*, 367 U.S. 497 (1961), and Hugo L. Black, "The Bill of Rights," *New York University Law Review*, v. 35 (April 1960), 865-81. Quote, "Selected Addresses," p. 16.

[71] FM to Francis Cardinal Spellman, June 14, 1947; FM to Anthony Weitzel, June 29, 1947, Box 122. 322 U.S. 78 (1944), and 329 U.S. 187 (1946); 330 U.S. 1 (1947).

[72] Cf. *Reynolds* v. *United States*, 98 U.S. 145 (1879); *Pierce* v. *Society of Sisters*, 268 U.S. 510 (1925); and *Cochran* v. *Board of Education*, 281 U.S. 370 (1930).

[73] See FM, "Politics," *Christian Front* (Haverford, Pa.), March 1939.

[74] *Minersville School District* v. *Gobitis*, 310 U.S. 586 (1940); *McCollum* v. *Board of Education*, 333 U.S. 203 (1948).

[75] Martin Shapiro, "Stability and Change in Judicial Decision-Making: Incrementalism or Stare Decisis?" *Law in*

Transition Quarterly, v. 2 (Summer 1965), 134-57.

[76] 322 U.S. 78 (1944).

[77] Conference notes, Nos. 392 and 472, Box 133.

[78] 322 U.S. 78, 95.

[79] 329 U.S. 187 (1946).

[80] Conference notes, No. 37, Box 138.

[81] 329 U.S. 187, 193-94.

[82] Louis E. Goodman, "Federal Jury Selection as Affected by Thiel v. Southern Pacific Company," *Journal of the State Bar of California*, v. 21 (Sep.-Oct. 1946), 352-58.

[83] J.F.T. O'Connor to FM, Jan. 29, 1947, Box 121. See O'Connor to FM, Oct. 19, 1943, Box 110.

[84] FM to O'Connor, Feb. 25, 1947, Box 121.

[85] 330 U.S. 1 (1947).

[86] *McCollum* v. *Board of Education*, 333 U.S. 203, 213.

[87] Docket notes, No. 52, Box 138. Conference notes, No. 52, Box 138.

[88] *United States* v. *Classic*, 313 U.S. 299 (1941); *Screws* v. *United States*, 325 U.S. 91 (1945). Conference notes, No. 52, Box 138.

[89] See Philip B. Kurland, *Religion and the Law* (Chicago: Aldine Publishing Co., 1962), pp. 80-85.

[90] Frankfurter to Murphy, undated, Box 28, Frankfurter Papers, Manuscript Division, Library of Congress.

[91] 330 U.S. 1, 19.

[92] FM to O'Connor, Feb. 25, 1947, Box 121.

[93] 333 U.S. 203 (1948).

[94] FM to clerk, Jan. 19, 1948, No. 124, Box 137.

[95] FM to William Murphy, May 10, 1948, Box 124.

[96] 343 U.S. 306 (1952).

[97] *McGowan* v. *Maryland*, 366 U.S. 420 (1961); *Two Guys* v. *McGinley*, 366 U.S. 582 (1961). *Engel* v. *Vitale*, 370 U.S. 421 (1962). *Abingdon School District* v. *Schempp*, 374 U.S. 203 (1963).

[98] William W. Van Alstyne, "Constitutional Separation of Church and State: the Quest for a Coherent Position," *A.P.S.R.*, v. 42 (Dec. 1963), 865-82. See

Kurland, *Religion and the Law*, pp. 17-18.

[99] See, *e.g.*, Harold W. Chase *et al.*, "Catholics on the Court," *New Republic*, v. 143 (Sep. 26, 1960), 13-15.

[100] *Chaplinsky* v. *New Hampshire*, 315 U.S. 568 (1942). See Paul G. Kauper, "Church and State: Cooperative Separatism," *Michigan Law Review*, v. 60 (Nov. 1961), 35.

[101] 321 U.S. 158 (1944).

[102] "The Return of Religion," address at St. Joseph's College, Philadelphia, June 13, 1939, *MS*, partial text, *NYT*, June 14, 1939, p. 18:4.

[103] FM to Douglas A. MacArthur, May 31, 1946, Box 119. Jack Manning to FM, Jan. 17, 1943, Box 107.

[104] *Detroit News*, Sep. 11, 1945.

[105] "The Higher Duty," address before Carroll Club of New York, Jan. 14, 1940, *MS*. "Youth in the World of Tomorrow," address, World's Fair, June 6, 1939, *MS*. FM to FDR, May 14, 1940, RL:P.P.F.-1,662.

[106] *New Orleans Times-Picayune*, June 12, 1941. Keynote address, National Parole Conference, April 17, 1939, *MS*.

[107] "The Higher Duty," *loc.cit.*

[108] FM to FDR, May 14, 1940, RL: P.P.F.-1,662.

[109] Shannon, *The American Irish* (New York: Macmillan, 1963), p. 353.

[110] FM to Leland Stanford Wood, Oct. 24, 1947, Box 123.

[111] FM to Gomon, April 24, 1948, Box 124.

[112] FM to Fred M. Vinson, Sep. 30, 1948, Box 125.

[113] FM to George Murphy, Feb. 10, 1949, Box 126.

[114] Rutledge to FM, Sep. 27, 1948, Box 125. FM to Fred M. Vinson, Nov. 5, 1948, Box 125.

[115] FM to Frankfurter, Jan. 31, 1949; Feb. 4, 1949, Box 28, Frankfurter Papers, Manuscript Division, Library of Congress. See John P. Frank, "The United States Supreme Court: 1947-1948," *University of Chicago Law Review*, v. 16 (Autumn 1948), 52-53.

[116] 336 U.S. 725 (1949); 338 U.S. 189 (1949); and 336 U.S. 704 (1949).

[117] Clerk to FM, Nov. 20, 1948, Box 125. 335 U.S. 890 (1948); 336 U.S. 907 (1949).

[118] *Hirota* v. *MacArthur*, 338 U.S. 197 (1948); *AFL* v. *American Sash & Door Co.*, 335 U.S. 538 (1949). For propriety of participating after missing oral arguments, cf. Glendon Schubert, *Judicial Policy-Making* (Chicago: Scott, Foresman, 1965), p. 18.

[119] See note, Feb. 28, 1949, Box 126. Clerk to FM, Nov. 18, 1948, Box 125. 336 U.S. 77 (1949).

[120] Clerk to FM, May 21, 1949; typed copy of note, "June 4th, 1949 Conference," No. 671, Box 140. 337 U.S. 241, 252-53 (1949).

[121] See David J. Danelski, "A Supreme Court Justice Steps Down," *Yale Review*, v. 54 (Spring 1965), 411-25. Undated Court memorandum, Box 125.

[122] FM to E. Blythe Stason, April 25, 1949; FM to Fred M. Vinson, May 14, 1949, Box 127.

[123] 338 U.S. 25 (1949); 338 U.S. 74 (1949).

[124] *Weeks* v. *United States*, 232 U.S. 383 (1914).

[125] 338 U.S. 25, 27-33.

[126] Clerk to William O. Douglas, June 15, 1949; Rutledge slip opinion, June 27, 1949, Nos. 17 & 18, Box 139.

[127] 338 U.S. 25, 41.

[128] *Ibid.*, pp. 39-40. Cf. Black, J., in *Berger* v. *New York*, 388 U.S. 41, 76 (1967).

[129] 338 U.S. 25, 46. Comment on typed draft of Murphy opinion, Nos. 17 and 18, Box 139.

[130] 338 U.S. 74, 80.

[131] *Elkins* v. *United States*, 364 U.S. 206, 219, 213-14 (1960).

[132] 367 U.S. 643, 657, 652, 656 (1961). See Francis A. Allen, "Federalism and the Fourth Amendment: A Requiem for

Wolf," *Supreme Court Review* (1961), pp. 1-48.

[133] 367 U.S. 643, 666. See John P. Frank, "Review and Basic Liberties," Cahn, ed., *Supreme Court and Supreme Law*, pp. 134-35.

[134] *Adams* v. *United States ex rel. McCann*, 317 U.S. 269, 286 (1942).

[135] John P. Frank, "The United States Supreme Court: 1948-1949," *University of Chicago Law Review*, v. 17 (Autumn 1949), 34.

[136] 338 U.S. 84 (1949). Comment on slip opinion, June 15, 1949, No. 528, Box 140.

[137] *Eisler* v. *United States*, 338 U.S. 189 (1949).

[138] Conference notes, No. 255, Box 139.

[139] 338 U.S. 189, 193, 195. *Schneiderman* v. *United States,* 320 U.S. 118 (1943). Draft opinion, circulated June 3, 1949, No. 255, Box 139.

[140] *Ibid.* See 10-page memorandum by clerk, May 6, 1949, No. 255, Box 139.

[141] Draft opinion, circulated June 3, 1949, p. 11, No. 255, Box 139.

[142] *Thornhill* v. *Alabama*, 310 U.S. 88 (1940). See *Baggett* v. *Bullitt*, 377 U.S. 360, 372-73 (1964). *Aptheker* v. *Secretary of State*, 378 U.S. 500, 516-17 (1964). *Dombrowski* v. *Pfister*, 380 U.S. 479, 486-87 (1965).

[143] Draft opinion, June 3, 1949, pp. 13-14, No. 255, Box 139. (Italics added.)

[144] Memorandum opinion, "not filed," May 31, 1949, No. 255, Box 139.

[145] 338 U.S. 189, 196. Cf. *United States* v. *Bryan*, 339 U.S. 323 (1950).

[146] Printed opinion, June 7, 1949, No. 255, Box 139.

[147] FM to Fred M. Vinson, June 23, 1949, Box 127.

[148] 338 U.S. 189, 194.

[149] *Brinegar* v. *United States*, 338 U.S. 160 (1949).

CHAPTER 16

[1] *NYT*, July 20, 1949, pp. 1:2 and 26:3; *NYT*, July 21, 1949, p. 26:6; *Detroit Free Press*, July 20, 1949; and *Washington Post*, July 20, 1949, p. 1:1. *Cong. Rec.*, v. 95, pt. 7, pp. 9,733-34; 9,739-40; and v. 95, pt. 15,

pp. 4,673-74; 4,751; 4,930-31; 4,932-33.

[2] *Washington Post*, July 22, 1949, p. 2B:5; *NYT*, July 22, 1949, p. 20:2; and, quotes, *Detroit Times*, July 20-21, 1949.

[3] "The Supreme Court's Great Loss,"

New Republic, v. 121 (Aug. 1, 1949), 5-6. Eugene Gerhart, *America's Advocate: Robert H. Jackson* (Indianapolis: Bobbs-Merrill, 1958), p. 304.

[4] Frank W. Grinnell, "The New Guesspotism," *A.B.A.J.*, v. 30 (Sep. 1944), 507.

[5] John R. Schmidhauser, *The Supreme Court, Its Politics, Personalities and Procedures* (New York: Holt, Rinehart & Winston, 1960), pp. 66-70, 78-83.

[6] *San Francisco Examiner*, Feb. 10, 1944. *St. Louis Post-Dispatch*, Aug. 8, 1946.

[7] *Detroit Free Press*, June 12, 1946. *Washington Post*, July 25, 1944, and June 9, 1944.

[8] Schmidhauser, *Supreme Court*, pp. 14-27. Joel B. Grossman, *Lawyers and Judges* (New York: John Wiley & Sons, 1965).

[9] *Washington Star*, July 20, 1949. *NYT*, July 20, 1949, p. 24:3.

[10] *Detroit Free Press*, July 20, 1949. *Time*, v. 54 (Aug. 1, 1949), 12.

[11] *Detroit News*, undated; *Washington Daily News*, July 20, 1949.

[12] Doris Fleeson, *Washington Star*, July 21, 1949; "Supreme Court's Great Loss," p. 5. *America*, v. 81 (July 30, 1949), 472. *Washington Star*, July 20, 1949.

[13] *Washington Post*, July 20, 1949, p. 12:3.

[14] I. F. Stone, "A Final Tribute to Frank Murphy," *Daily Compass* (New York), July 22, 1949; letter to editor, Howard M. Schott, *Washington Post*, July 23, 1949, p. 4:4; and *Trainman's News*, Aug. 8, 1949, p. 3.

[15] See, *e.g.*, memorial issue, *Michigan Law Review*, v. 48 (April 1950), 737-810; Thurman Arnold, "Mr. Justice Murphy," *Harvard Law Review*, v. 63 (Dec. 1949), 289-93; John P. Frank, "Justice Murphy: The Goals Attempted," *Yale Law Journal*, v. 59 (Dec. 1949), 1-26; Charles Fahy, "The Judicial Philosophy of Mr. Justice Murphy," *Yale Law Journal*, v. 60 (May 1951), 812-20; Eugene Gressman, "Mr. Justice Murphy: A Preliminary Appraisal," *Columbia Law Review*, v. 50 (Jan. 1950), 29-47; Albon P. Man, Jr., "Mr. Justice Murphy and the Supreme Court," *Virginia Law Review*, v. 36 (Nov. 1950), 889-943; and Resolutions of the Supreme Court Bar, March 6, 1951, 340 U.S. v-xxv (1950).

[16] Roche, "The Utopian Pilgrimage of Mr. Justice Murphy," *Vanderbilt Law Review*, v. 10 (Feb. 1957), 394 and 369. See Wallace Mendelson, "The Neo-Behavioral Approach to the Judicial Process: A Critique," *A.P.S.R.*, v. 57 (Sep. 1963), 596.

[17] See, *e.g.*, F.M. Kiplinger, *Washington Is Like That* (New York: Harper & Bros., 1942), p. 250.

[18] Wesley McCune, *The Nine Young Men* (New York: Harper & Bros., 1947), p. 151. Schlesinger, "The Supreme Court: 1947," *Fortune*, v. 35 (Jan. 1947), 74-76. Pritchett, *The Roosevelt Court* (New York: Macmillan, 1948), p. 285.

[19] Kurland, Book Review, *University of Chicago Law Review*, v. 22 (Autumn 1954), 299.

[20] See Robert S. Allen and William V. Shannon, *The Truman Merry-Go-Round* (New York: Vanguard Press, 1950), p. 360. McCune, *Nine Young Men*, pp. 137-38.

[21] *Thornhill* v. *Alabama*, 310 U.S. 88 (1940); *Jewell Ridge Coal Corp.* v. *Local No. 6167*, 325 U.S. 161 (1945); *Christoffel* v. *United States*, 338 U.S. 84 (1949). See *NYT*, Feb. 12, 1950, p. 66:3; *Cong. Rec.*, v. 95, pt. 2, p. 1,562.

[22] Eugene Gressman, "The Controversial Image of Mr. Justice Murphy," *Georgetown Law Journal*, v. 47 (Summer 1959), 651n.

[23] FM to E. Blythe Stason, Jan. 26, 1948, Box 124.

[24] Alpheus T. Mason, *Harlan Fiske Stone: Pillar of the Law* (New York: The Viking Press, 1956), p. 513.

[25] See undated notes, Justice Rutledge to clerks, No. 83, Box 139. *Commissioner of Internal Revenue* v. *Phipps*, 336 U.S. 410 (1949). Cf. *Hirabayashi* opinion, 320 U.S. 81, 111 (1943), and "Selected Addresses," p. 78.

[26] Roche, "Utopian Pilgrimage," p. 393. *Korematsu* v. *United States*, 323 U.S. 214 (1944).

[27] Cox, "The Influence of Mr. Justice Murphy on Labor Law," *Michigan Law Review*, v. 48 (April 1950), 773. Also,

Arnold, p. 293; Frank, p. 3; Roche, p. 393, works cited, note 15 above.

[28] 325 U.S. 398, 407 (1945). Harlan F. Stone to Stanley Reed, May 25, 1946, Stone Papers, Manuscript Division, Library of Congress.

[29] David Fellman, "Recent Tendencies in Civil Liberties Decisions of the Supreme Court," *Cornell Law Quarterly*, v. 34 (Spring 1949), 337. *Oyama v. California*, 332 U.S. 633 (1948); *Takahashi v. Fish and Game Cmsn.*, 334 U.S. 410 (1948). *Washington Post*, July 20, 1949, p. 12:5.

[30] Slip opinions, Nos. 297 and 355, Box 139. 336 U.S. 220 (1949); 336 U.S. 725 (1949). Roche, "Utopian Pilgrimage," p. 393.

[31] Merlo Pusey, "The Roosevelt Supreme Court," *American Mercury*, v. 58 (May 1944), 600; Thomas Reed Powell, "Behind the Split in the Supreme Court," *NYT Magazine* (Oct. 9, 1949), p. 52; and "Our High Court Analyzed," *NYT Magazine* (June 18, 1944), p. 45. Frank, "Goals Attempted," p. 3.

[32] "The Labor Governors," *Fortune*, v. 15 (June 1937), 81.

[33] *The Secret Diary of Harold L. Ickes* (New York: Simon & Schuster, 1954), v. 3, p. 88.

[34] See J.F.T. O'Connor to FDR, Sep. 14, 1942, RL:P.P.F.—1,513.

[35] Frank, "Goals Attempted," pp. 1-2. FM to FDR, Dec. 22, 1941, RL:OF-400-PI.

[36] Henry F. Pringle, *The Life and Times of William Howard Taft* (New York: Farrar and Rinehart, 1939), v. 2, p. 967.

[37] Gressman, "Controversial Image," p. 654.

[38] Roscoe Pound, *The Introduction to the Philosophy of Law* (New Haven: Yale University Press, 1959), p. 54. See Paul A. Freund, "Rationality in Judicial Decision," *Nomos VII—Rational Decision* (New York: Atherton, 1964), pp. 109-25.

[39] *Burdeau v. McDowell*, 256 U.S. 465, 477 (1921). Roche, "Utopian Pilgrimage," p. 393.

[40] *Carter v. Illinois*, 329 U.S. 173, 182 (1946); *Falbo v. United States*, 320 U.S.

549, 561 (1944); *Eisler v. United States*, 338 U.S. 189, 195 (1949).

[41] "The Courts—A National Bulwark," *Vital Speeches*, v. 5 (May 1, 1939), 437. FM to Chase S. Osborn, Dec. 20, 1943, Box 110. "Selected Addresses," p. 57.

[42] Quoted in Gressman, "Controversial Image," p. 653.

[43] Henry M. Hart, Jr., "Holmes' Positivism—An Addendum," *Harvard Law Review*, v. 64 (April 1951), 930.

[44] Frankfurter and Landis, "The Business of the Supreme Court," *Harvard Law Review*, v. 40 (1927), 1,110, 1,121.

[45] William O. Douglas, "The Dissenting Opinion," *Lawyer's Guild Review*, v. 7 (Nov.-Dec. 1948), 468.

[46] *Southern Pacific Co. v. Jensen*, 244 U.S. 205, 221 (1917). Frankfurter in Mason, *Stone*, p. 470n.

[47] Benjamin N. Cardozo, *The Nature of the Judicial Process* (New Haven, Yale University Press, 1921), pp. 165-66. See Fred V. Cahill, Jr., *Judicial Legislation* (New York: Ronald Press, 1952). Cf. *Linkletter v. Walker*, 381 U.S. 618, 622-24 (1965).

[48] Hand, *The Bill of Rights* (Cambridge: Harvard University Press, 1958), p. 70.

[49] See Glendon Schubert, *The Judicial Mind* (Evanston: Northwestern University Press, 1965), p. 13. Cf. Henry M. Hart, Jr., "Foreword: The Time Chart of the Justices," *Harvard Law Review*, v. 73 (Nov. 1959), 84-125; and Thurman Arnold, "Professor Hart's Theology," *Harvard Law Review*, v. 73 (May 1960), 1,298-1,317.

[50] See Walter F. Murphy, *Elements of Judicial Strategy* (Chicago: University of Chicago Press, 1964). Also the author's "On the Fluidity of Judicial Choice," *A.P.S.R.*, v. 62 (March 1968), 43-56.

[51] 328 U.S. 549 (1946); 337 U.S. 1 (1949).

[52] Conference notes, No. 804, Box 136. Docket book, 1945 term, Box 92, Burton Papers, Manuscript Division, Library of Congress.

[53] Conference notes, No. 272, Box 140. Docket book, 1948 Term, Box 182; and

conference notes, Box 184, Burton Papers, Manuscript Division, Library of Congress.

[54] Quoted in Gressman, "Controversial Image," p. 654n.

[55] Cf. Cahill, *Judicial Legislation*, pp. 126-37.

[56] Charles P. Curtis, *Law as Large as Life* (New York: Simon & Schuster, 1959), p. 51. Arthur M. Schlesinger, "Extremism in American Politics," *Saturday Review*, v. 48 (Nov. 27, 1965), 24.

[57] Leo Weiss, "Justice Murphy and the Welfare Question," *Michigan Law Review*, v. 53 (Feb. 1955), 565-66. Cf. George D. Braden, "The Search for Objectivity in Constitutional Law," *Yale Law Journal*, v. 57 (Feb. 1948), 571-94.

[58] See memorandum of clerks, May 9, 1949, p. 7, No. 255, Box 139. *Eisler v. United States*, 338 U.S. 189 (1949).

[59] *Detroit News*, Sep. 24, 1938; *Manila Tribune*, May 13, 1936.

[60] Interview, Aug. 12, 1958.

[61] Cardozo, *Nature of Judicial Process*, p. 66.

[62] Samuel Hendel, "The Liberalism of Chief Justice Hughes," *Vanderbilt Law Review*, v. 10 (Feb. 1957), 261.

[63] Stone to Wiley Rutledge, March 31, 1944, Stone Papers, Manuscript Division, Library of Congress.

[64] *NYT*, April 6, 1937, p. 15:1.

[65] Cf. C. Herman Pritchett, "Libertarian Motivations on the Vinson Court," *A.P.S.R.*, v. 47 (June 1953), 321-36.

[66] See William M. Beaney and Edward N. Beiser, "Prayer and Politics: The Impact of *Engel* and *Schempp* on the Political Process," *Journal of Public Law*, v. 13 (1965), 475; Gordon Patric, "The Impact of a Court Decision: Aftermath of the McCollum Case," *Journal of Public Law*, v. 6 (1957), 455; Frank Sorauf, "*Zorach v. Clauson*: The Impact of a Supreme Court Decision," *A.P.S.R.*, v. 54 (1959), 777; Robert H. Birkby, "The Supreme Court and the Bible Belt," *Midwest Journal of Political Science*, v. 3 (1966), 304; and Michael Katz, "The Supreme Court and the States: An Inquiry into *Mapp v. Ohio* in North Carolina," *North Carolina Law Review*, v. 45 (1966), 119. Cf. Robert A. Dahl, "Decision-Making in a Democracy: The Role of the Supreme Court as a National Policy-Maker," *Journal of Public Law*, v. 6 (1957), 293-95; and Charles L. Black, Jr., *The People and the Court* (New York: Macmillan, 1960), pp. 34-86.

[67] 322 U.S. 694 (1944); 329 U.S. 495 (1947).

[68] See John R. Schmidhauser, "*Stare Decisis*, Dissent and the Background of the Justices of the Supreme Court of the United States," *University of Toronto Law Journal*, v. 14, No. 2 (1962), 194-212; Stuart S. Nagel, "Judicial Backgrounds and Criminal Cases," *Journal of Criminal Law, Criminology and Police Science*, v. 53 (Sep. 1962), 333-39; and "Political Party Affiliation and Judges' Decisions," *A.P.S.R.*, v. 55 (Dec. 1961), 843-50; and "Ethnic Affiliations and Judicial Propensities," *Journal of Politics*, v. 24 (Feb. 1962), 92-110.

[69] Cox, "Influence of Murphy," p. 810.

[70] Hand, *Bill of Rights*, p. 71.

[71] Alpheus T. Mason, "The Supreme Court: Temple and Forum," *Yale Review*, v. 48 (Summer 1959), 524-40. Alfred L. Scanlan, "The Passing of Justice Murphy —The Conscience of a Court," *Notre Dame Lawyer*, v. 25 (Fall 1949), 7-39.

[72] Address at Hunter College, April 12, 1946, *MS*.

[73] *Detroit News*, Sep. 24, 1938.

[74] *Manila Post*, July 31, 1946. FM to Francis Cardinal Spellman, Oct. 8, 1946, Box 120. Cf. Roosevelt in Clinton Rossiter, *The American Presidency*, rev. edn. (New York: Harcourt, Brace, 1960), pp. 147-48.

[75] Roche, "Utopian Pilgrimage," pp. 369-73.

[76] "Selected Addresses," p. 56; "The Challenge of Intolerance," *Cong. Rec.*, v. 86, pt. 13, pp. 81-82.

[77] "The Democratic Crisis in America," reprint, *Philadelphia Record*, April 14, 1939.

[78] *Ibid.* Quote, "All Men are Brothers," p. 14, pamphlet, published privately.

[79] "The World We're Coming To," *Commonweal*, v. 42 (Aug. 10, 1945), 398-401; *San Francisco Chronicle*, Sep. 12,

1944. "The American Way of Life—Can It Survive?" partial text, *NYT*, Sep. 11, 1944, p. 13:7.

⁸⁰ See "The Physician's Responsibilities," reprint, *Journal of the Philippine Islands Medical Association*, v. 14 (Jan. 1934); *Manila Tribune*, Sep. 3, 1935. Quote, "Selected Addresses," p. 12.

⁸¹ "Youth in the World of Tomorrow," address at World's Fair, June 6, 1939, *MS*.

⁸² *Los Angeles Daily News*, Aug. 19, 1937.

⁸³ *In re Yamashita*, 327 U.S. 1 (1946).

⁸⁴ Quoted in Paul A. Freund, *The Supreme Court of the United States* (Cleveland: Meridian Books, 1961), p. 114.

⁸⁵ Francis Biddle, *In Brief Authority* (New York: Doubleday, 1962), pp. 92-94.

⁸⁶ FM to FDR, June 10, 1940, RL:OF -41A–Supreme Court.

⁸⁷ FM to Jerome Barry, Aug. 7, 1935, Box 27.

⁸⁸ "Goals Attempted," p. 1.

⁸⁹ "Selected Addresses," p. 67.

INDEX